CONTRACTS OF CARRIAGE BY LAND AND AIR

SHIPPING MONOGRAPH SERIES

Bills of Lading: Law and Contracts
Nicholas Gaskell
and
Regina Asariotis, Yvonne Baatz
(2000)

Modern Law of Marine Insurance, Volume 2
Edited by Professor D. Rhidian Thomas
(2002)

Maritime Fraud
Paul Todd
(2003)

Port State Control
2nd edition
Dr Z. Oya Özçayír
(2004)

War, Terror and Carriage by Sea
Keith Michel
(2004)

Freight Forwarding and Multimodal Transport Contracts
David A. Glass
(2004)

CONTRACTS OF CARRIAGE BY LAND AND AIR

BY

MALCOLM A. CLARKE

M.A., LL.B., Ph.D. (Cantab.)

Fellow of St John's College, Cambridge

Professor of Commercial Contract Law at the University of Cambridge

AND

DAVID YATES

M.A. (Oxon. et Cantab.)

Solicitor

Warden of Robinson College, Cambridge

|L|L|P|

LONDON SINGAPORE

2004

Informa Professional
(a trading division of Informa UK Ltd)
Informa House
30–32 Mortimer Street
London W1W 7RE

EAST ASIA
Informa Professional Asia
No. 1 Grange Road
08–02 Orchard Building
Singapore 239693

First published 2004

British Library Cataloguing-in-Publication Data
A catalogue record for
this book is available from the
British Library

ISBN 1–84311–330–9

Text set in 10 on 12 pt Plantin by
Interactive Sciences Ltd, Gloucester
Printed in Great Britain by
MPG Books
Bodmin, Cornwall

ACKNOWLEDGEMENTS

We gratefully acknowledge the assistance and in some cases the permission to reproduce from their copyright material, the following:

British Waterways and Roy Parker their Freight Marketing Manager
English Welsh & Scottish Railway Ltd., UK
Freightliner Ltd., UK
International Air Transport Association, Canada
Organisation for International Carriage by Rail (COTIF)
Road Haulage Association Ltd., UK
United Nations, New York

PREFACE

This book has grown out of the looseleaf work *Contracts for the Carriage of Goods*, (Yates, Ed., 1993) Part 2 of which was written by David Yates and Parts 3 and 4 by Malcolm Clarke. Part 5 on Carriage by Air was written by Nicholas Hughes and his team at Barlow, Lyde & Gilbert, Solicitors. Part 3 of this book is based on their work, for which we are grateful.

The aim of this book, as with its predecessor, is to provide a detailed commentary on the various "common form" clauses appearing in contracts used in the business of transporting goods by road, rail, air and inland water in the United Kingdom. It does not address in any detail issues of multimodal transport and freight forwarding. A companion volume in this series, adopting a similar pattern of commentary to that found in this book, is Glass, *Freight Forwarding and Multimodal Transport Contracts* (2004) where these two topics are considered. Nor does this book cover contracts for the carriage of goods by sea. One volume in this series dealing with bills of lading (Gaskell, Asariotis & Baatz, 2001) has already been published and a further volume covering charterparties will be published later. Contracts for the carriage of goods by road, rail and air are significantly impacted by international Conventions: the Convention on the International Carriage of Goods by Road (CMR), the Uniform Rules Concerning International Carriage of Goods by Rail (CIM) and the several international Conventions governing the carriage of goods by air, notably the Warsaw Convention as amended in 1955 by the Protocol and most recently the Montreal Convention of 1999 which came into force in the United Kingdom in 2004. These Conventions are set out in their entirety, in addition to the "common form" clauses found in individual carriers' documentation, and appropriate detailed comment is made on each Article.

The choice of clauses cited, quoted and discussed has been dictated by the range of significant variations in the particular type of clause to be found among the various standard forms in use in the relevant industry sector, the commercial importance of the various clauses themselves and the extent to which the authors have been able to secure copyright clearance for extensive quotation. Any selection will inevitably contain a certain element of subjectivity save in those industries (such as rail) where the narrow range of possible providers operates as a natural limit on the number of standard forms in use. Nevertheless, in making the selection the authors have borne constantly in mind the needs of those in industry, commerce and the legal profession engaged in drafting, negotiating and advising on contracts for the carriage of goods by land and air. In the comments on and annotations to the clauses every effort has been made to extrapolate points of practical guidance for use in the drafting and construing of carriage of goods contracts.

Many individuals, trade associations and professional bodies have assisted in the preparation of this book. A full list of acknowledgements is to be found on page v. The authors are grateful to those who have given permission to reproduce the whole or portions of their standard form documents. The clauses have been reproduced *verbatim* (including any typographical errors appearing in the originals). However, while several organisations have co-operated in the collection and reproduction of the standard clauses to be found in this book, readers will appreciate that most of them are subject to copyright and may not, therefore, be further reproduced without the permission of the relevant copyright holder.

The authors would like to thank the Publishers for compiling the Index and the Tables of Cases and Legislation and for their support and efficiency in turning our manuscript copy into book form in very short order.

The law stated in this book is as we believe it to be on 1 August 2004.

MALCOLM CLARKE
DAVID YATES

Cambridge, 1 October 2004

OUTLINE TABLE OF CONTENTS

DETAILED TABLE OF CONTENTS

II. CARRIAGE OF GOODS BY ROAD WITHIN THE UNITED KINGDOM

PART 2—CARRIAGE OF GOODS BY RAIL

BY MALCOLM CLARKE

I. INTERNATIONAL CARRIAGE OF GOODS BY RAIL: CIM (1980)

IV. CARRIAGE OF GOODS BY RAIL WITHIN THE UNITED KINGDOM: ENGLISH WELSH & SCOTTISH RAILWAY LIMITED GENERAL CONDITIONS OF CARRIAGE 2004 2.695

PART 3—CARRIAGE OF GOODS BY AIR

BY MALCOLM CLARKE

I. INTRODUCTION

II. THE 1955 AMENDED CONVENTION AS GIVEN FORCE OF LAW IN THE UK BY THE 1961 ACT, SCHEDULE 1

III. THE MP4 CONVENTION AS GIVEN FORCE OF LAW IN THE UK BY THE 1961 ACT, SCHEDULE 1A

PART 4—CARRIAGE OF GOODS BY INLAND WATER WITHIN THE UNITED KINGDOM

BY DAVID YATES

BIBLIOGRAPHICAL AND OTHER ABBREVIATIONS

1961 Act: Carriage by Air Act 1961 (c. 27)
1962 Act: Carriage by Air (Supplementary Provisions) Act 1962 (c. 43)
1967 Order: Carriage by Air (Application of Provisions) Order 1967 (1967/480)
1979 Act: Carriage by Air and Road Act 1979 (c. 28)
2002 Order: Carriage by Air Acts (Implementation of the Montreal Convention 1999) Order 2002 (2002/263)

ADR: The European Agreement concerning the International Carriage of Dangerous Goods by Road, 1957, Cmnd 3769
Air Waybill Handbook: *IATA Air Waybill Handbook* (26th ed., 2003)
Allégret: M. Allégret, *Transports Internationaux Ferroviaires* (Paris 1989, but updated annually in the relevant section of *Juris-Classeur Commercial*, Paris)
ASLR: *Aviation & Space Law Reports*
Avi. Cas.: C.C.H. *Aviation Law Reporter*
Avn Law: *Lloyd's Aviation Law* (Vols. 1–15, 1982–1996) and Lloyd's Aviation Insurance and Law (Vols. 16 *et seq.*)
Basedow: J. Basedow, *Munchener Kommentar zur Handelgesetzbuch*, Bd 7 (Munich 1997)
Benjamin: Benjamin, *Sale of Goods* (5th ed., London, 1997)
BGH: *DerBundesgerichthof*
BIFA Conditions: British International Freight Association Standard Conditions
BT: *Bulletin de Transports* (now BTL)
BTL: *Bulletin des Transports et de la Logistique*
Bull.OCTI: *Bulletin des Transports Internationaux Ferroviaires*
BW Freight: *British Waterways Carriage of Freight Conditions*, 2003
BW Vessel: *British Waterways Freight Vessel Conditions*, 2003
Central Office: *see* OCTI
Butterworths *Contract*: Butterworths *The Law of Contract* (2nd ed., London 2003)
CFF: Chemin de Fer Fédéral
CIM: Règles uniformes concernant le transport international ferroviaire des marchandises (Uniform Rules concerning the Contract for International Carriage of Goods by Rail)
CIT: Comité International des Transports Ferroviaires
CIV: Règles uniformes concernant le contrat de transport international ferroviaire des voyageurs et des bagages (Uniform Rules concerning the Contract for International Carriage of Passengers and Luggage by Rail)
Clarke, *Air*: Malcolm A. Clarke, *Contracts of Carriage by Air* (London: LLP, 2002)
Clarke, *CMR*: Malcolm A. Clarke, *International Carriage of Goods by Road: CMR* (4th ed., London: LLP, 2003)

Clarke, *Insurance*: Malcolm A. Clarke, *The Law of Insurance Contracts* (4th ed., London: LLP, 2002)

CMR: La Convention relative au Contrat de Transport International de Marchandises par Route (the Convention on the International Carriage of Goods by Road)

COTIF: Convention relative aux transports internationaux ferroviaires (Convention Concerning International Carriage by Rail)

DB: Deutsches Bundesbahn

DCU: *Les Dispositions Complémentaires Uniformes*

DOCIMEL: Document CIM Électronique

ETL: *European Transport Law*

EVO: Eisenbahn-Verkehrsordnung, an appendix to Article 460 of the HGB

EWS Conditions: English Welsh & Scottish Railway Limited General Conditions of Carriage, 2004

For. it: *Foro italiano*

Freightliner Conditions: Freightliner Standard Conditions of Carriage 2002

Giemulla: Giemulla, Schmid, Ehlers, Muller-Rostin, *Warsaw Convention* (Deventer, 1992)

Glass/Cashmore: D.A. Glass and C. Cashmore, *Introduction to the Law of Carriage of Goods* (London, 1989)

Goldhirsch: Lawrence V. Goldhirsch, *The Warsaw Convention Annotated* (Dordrecht, 1988)

Greiter: I. Greiter, *CMR-Gerichtsurteile* (Eisenstadt, 1986)

Haak: K.F. Haak, *The Liability of the Carrier under the CMR* (The Hague, 1986)

Haenni: *International Encyclopedia of Comparative Law*, vol. XII, *Law of Transport*, Chap. 2 Carriage by Rail, by J. Haenni (Tubingen, 1973)

Helm: HGB, *Grosskommentar*, vol. V/2 (Berlin, 1982, Ed. J.G. Helm)

HGB: *Handelgesetzbuch*

HM: Hill and Messent: *Contracts for the International Carriage of Goods by Road* (3rd ed. by A. Messent with D.A. Glass, London, LLP, 2000)

HP: The 1955 amended Warsaw Convention as given force of law in the UK by the 1961 Act, Schedule 1

IATA: International Air Transport Association

ICAO: International Civil Aviation Organisation

Kahn-Freund: O. Kahn-Freund, *The Law of Carriage by Inland Transport* (London, 1965)

Koller: Ingo Koller, *Transportrecht* (5th ed., Munich 2004)

Loewe: Roland Loewe, "Commentary on the Convention of 19 May 1956 on the Contract for the Carriage of Goods by Road (CMR)" (1976) 11 ETL 311

L.S.G.: *Law Society Gazette*

Mankiewicz: Rene H. Mankiewicz, *The Liability Regime of the International Air Carrier* (London, 1981)

MC: The Montreal Convention 1999

MP4: The MP4 Convention as given force of law in the UK by the 1961 Act, Schedule 1A

Nanassy: B. de Nanassy, *Le Droit International des Transports par Chemins de Fer* (Basel, 1946)

NJW: *Neue Juristische Wochenschrift*

OCTI: Office central des transports internationaux ferroviaires (Central Office for International Carriage by Rail)

OTIF: l'Organisation intergouvernementale pour les transports internationaux ferroviaires (The Intergovernmental Organisation for International Carriage by Rail)

O.J.: Official Journal of the European Communities

Palmer: Norman E. Palmer, *Bailment* (2nd ed., London, 1991)

Peyrefitte: L. Peyrefitte, *Juris-Classeur de Droit International*, Fasc. 565–B–1, *Transports Internationaux Ferroviaires* (Paris, 1988)

RHA Conditions: Road Haulage Association Ltd. Conditions of Carriage 1998

RIEx: Regulations Concerning the International Carriage of Express Parcels by Rail

Rodière: R. Rodière, *Droit des Transports* (2nd ed., Paris, 1977)

SDR: Special Drawing Right of the International Monetary Fund

Shawcross & Beaumont: Shawcross & Beaumont, *Air Law* (4th ed., London, 2000)

SNCF: Société Nationale des Chemins de Fer Français

Spera: K. Spera, *Internationales Eisenbahnfrachtrecht* (Vienna)

S & S: *Schip en Schade*

Theunis: *International Carriage of Goods by Road* (J. Theunis (Ed.), London, 1987)

TIEx, Standard Regulations Concerning the International Carriage of Express Parcels Traffic by Rail

TranspR: *Transportrecht*

Treitel: G.H. Treitel, *The Law of Contract* (11th ed., London, 2003)

UIC: Union Internationale des Chemins de Fer

ULC: *Uniform Law Cases*

Unif. L. Rev.: *Uniform Law Review*

VersR: *Versicherungsrecht*

WC: The Warsaw Convention 1929 as implemented by the 1967 Order, Schedule 2

Wick: J. Wick, *Le Droit International des Transports par Chemins de Fer* (Neuchatel, 1976)

ZLW: *Zeitschrift fur Luft und Weltraumrecht*

TABLE OF CASES

All references are to paragraph numbers.

TABLE OF INTERNATIONAL CONVENTIONS

*All references are to paragraph numbers. References in **bold** type indicate where the text of the material is set out.*

TABLE OF LEGISLATION

All references are to paragraph numbers.

TABLE OF STATUTORY INSTRUMENTS

TABLE OF TRADE CONDITIONS

*All references are to paragraph numbers. References in **bold** type indicate where the text of the material is set out*

PART 1

CARRIAGE OF GOODS BY ROAD

INTERNATIONAL CARRIAGE OF GOODS BY ROAD: CMR

A. INTRODUCTION

1. The scope of the CMR

1.1 The CMR was signed at Geneva on 19 May 1956. The United Kingdom acceded to the CMR on 21 July 1967.

1.2 As regards the accession of the UK, by a reservation in the Protocol of Signature, CMR does not apply to traffic between the United Kingdom of Great Britain and Northern Ireland and the Republic of Ireland. However, as regards "(a) the Isle of Man; (b) any of the Channel Islands; (c) any colony; (d) any State or territory which is for the time being a protectorate or protected State for the purposes of the British Nationality Act 1948", section 9 of the Carriage of Goods by Road Act 1965 provides that CMR may be extended to these places by Order in Council, subject to such exceptions, adaptations and modifications as may be specified in the Order. The Act came into operation in the United Kingdom on 5 June 1967. The United Kingdom extended CMR to Gibraltar,[1] the Isle of Man[2] and Guernsey.[3] An associated supposition is that movements by road vehicle between these territories or between these territories and the United Kingdom mainland are not international and not subject to CMR. A possible corollary, that the movement of goods between the mainland of the United Kingdom and Jersey in respect of which no S.I. has been made, was a carriage of goods to which CMR applied, because the mainland United Kingdom was party to CMR and Jersey was another "country", has been rejected[4]: as a "contracting country" under Article 1, the United Kingdom includes Gibraltar, the Isle of Man, Guernsey and the remainder of the Channel Isles including Jersey.

1.3 The CMR was enacted as a Schedule to the Carriage of Goods by Road Act 1965 and came into force in the United Kingdom on 19 October 1967. The Act was

1. S.I. 1967/820, as amended by S.I. 1981/604.
2. S.I. 1981/1543.
3. S.I. 1986/1882.
4. *Chloride Industrial Batteries Ltd.* v. *F. & W. Freight Ltd.* [1989] 3 All E.R. 86 (C.A.).

amended by the Carriage by Road and Air Act 1979. The English and the French texts of the CMR are of equal authority. English courts refer but cautiously to the French text.[5] The CMR contains a scheme of liability which was modelled on that of CIM: see below, paras. 2.1 *et seq.*

1.4 The CMR applies to certain contracts for the international carriage of goods by road (Article 1), and the provisions of the CMR become terms of those contracts.[6] The contract provides a significant frame of reference for matters on which the CMR itself is silent or unclear. When the contract does not fall within the scope of the CMR, the parties may nonetheless adopt the provisions of the CMR as contract terms. When the CMR applies to a contract *proprio vigore*, the parties may not contract out of its provisions (Article 41)—except as regards certain exceptional matters specified by the CMR (for example, Article 40).

2. The liability of the carrier under CMR

1.5 Under the CMR, the carrier is liable for loss of or damage to the goods occurring between the time when they were taken over by the carrier and the time of delivery, as well as for delay in delivery (Article 17.1). To be excused liability, the carrier may plead one of two kinds of defence. The first is that the loss or damage was caused by fault on the part of the claimant, by inherent vice or by unavoidable circumstances (Article 17.2). The second is the existence of special circumstances which raise a presumption that the carrier is not liable for the loss or damage, unless in reply the claimant proves that it can be attributed not to the special circumstances but to the carrier (Article 18). The special circumstances, such as the fact that loading was carried out by the sender, are listed (Article 17.4). If the carrier fails to establish one of these two kinds of defence, the carrier may fall back on the further defences that the claim is out of time (Article 32) or that, while there is liability in principle, the amount of the liability is limited (Articles 23–25). These further defences will fail, however, if the claimant can establish wilful misconduct on the part of the carrier: this removes the limits on the amount of liability (Article 29) and extends the period of limitation (Article 32).

1.6 Behind these provisions of CMR is, first, by inference from the CMR itself, a residual duty of care. This inference arises from many of the cases in which the claimant is able to prove (under Article 18) that the loss or damage is attributable not to the special circumstance pleaded by the carrier but to an act or neglect by the carrier: it is breach of the residual duty that justifies the attribution. The residual duty of care appears also as the corollary of the defence of unavoidable circumstances (Article 17.2): only if a certain level of care has been shown by the carrier, can it be said that the circumstances leading to loss or damage were unavoidable. The level of care required, described as "utmost care", is high.[7]

5. See *Buchanan & Co.* v. *Babco Forwarding & Shipping (UK)* [1978] A.C. 141, 152, and 161.
6. *Buchanan* (above) at p. 152.
7. See Art. 17, Comment 7, paras. 1.98 *et seq.*, below, and Clarke, *CMR*, para. 79.

3. Subjacent common law

Behind the provisions of CMR is, secondly, the liability of the carrier at common law: *1.7*

(a) The central obligation of CMR itself (Article 17.1) is the corollary of the contractual obligation, if not express then usually implied by common law, to carry the goods to the agreed destination on time and deliver them there in the same good order and condition in which they were taken over.
(b) CMR is silent on certain matters, such as the person obliged to load the goods or the meaning of "inherent vice", and the English court must resolve these matters by reference to common law.
(c) The scope of CMR is limited to the fate of goods after they have been taken over by the carrier: the carrier who does not perform his promise to take them is liable not under the CMR but under common law. German courts have adopted the same view of goods taken over by the carrier and later abandoned,[8] but this view is difficult to support.
(d) The carrier can be sued in tort. However, if he is so sued, he can defend the action with CMR defences (Article 28).

B. THE TEXT OF THE CMR

Chapter I, Scope of application: Article 1 *1.8*

1. This Convention shall apply to every contract for the carriage of goods by road in vehicles for reward, when the place of taking over[1] of the goods and the place designated for delivery, as specified in the contract, are situated in two different countries,[2] of which at least one is a contracting country, irrespective of the place of residence and the nationality of the parties.

2. For the purpose of this Convention "vehicles" means motor vehicles, articulated vehicles, trailers and semi trailers as defined in article 4 of the Convention on Road Traffic dated 19th September 1949.[3]

3. This Convention shall also apply where carriage coming within its scope is carried out by States or by government institutions or organizations.

4. This Convention shall not apply:
   (a) to carriage performed under the terms of any postal convention;
   (b) to funeral consignments;
   (c) to furniture removal.

5. The Contracting Parties agree not to vary the provisions of this Convention by special agreements between two or more of them, except to make it inapplicable to their frontier traffic or to authorize the use in transport operations entirely confined to their territory of consignment notes representing a title to the goods.

Comments

Article 1 defines the contracts to which CMR applies. It is a rule of the conflict of *1.9*
laws in the sense that, if the court has characterised the contract before it as one

8. E.g. *BGH 9.2.79* (1980) 15 ETL 84.

1. See Art. 17, Comment 3.

2. What counts is the journey contracted for and hence, if one is made out, indicated by the consignment note: *Paris 2.7.1992*, BTL 1992.639.

3. Held to include Swap-Bodies: *OLG Hamburg 13.3.1993*, TranspR 1994.193.

falling within the scope of CMR as stated in Article 1, the other provisions of CMR as enacted by the *lex fori* must be applied to that contract.

1. Contracts of carriage

1.10 CMR applies to contracts of carriage and not to associated contracts such as forwarding contracts, whereby a company contracts to arrange carriage, usually, by another company.[4] To distinguish forwarding contracts, courts look at the substance of the promise rather than the description used and, in particular, they are influenced by the way in which the charges are calculated.[5] One company may be a carrier for one stage of the journey and a forwarder for the next.

1.11 Umbrella contracts for carriage may be subject to the CMR. *Gefco* v. *Mason*[6] concerned an umbrella contract between carrier M and sub-carrier G which provided for the carriage of goods from time to time from a place in Coventry to a place near Paris. M argued that this was no more than a contractual framework for contracts for specified goods as and when required; and that the CMR applied to the latter but not to the former. The reason was that there were many details required by Article 6 to be included in a consignment note which were not known when the umbrella contract was made or at any time before the contract for the individual delivery was concluded, such as the identity of the goods. However, the Court of Appeal rejected that argument because "Article 4 makes it plain that the absence of a note, for whatever reason, does not affect the validity of the contract or the application of the Convention".[7] The Court underlined that a purposive construction was one that promoted harmonisation across national boundaries, and held that the CMR applied to the umbrella contract.

1.12 If the contract is a contract for the carriage of goods by road, under certain circumstances stated in Article 2 CMR may apply to a phase of carriage by another mode, such as carriage by sea. Moreover, if the contract is a contract for the carriage of goods by road in the sense of Article 2, it does not cease to be a contract for the carriage of goods by road governed by the CMR because the carriage had been preceded by (a much longer) movement by air undertaken by the same carrier and evidenced by that carrier's air waybill.[8]

2. Goods

1.13 Goods are all things carried by road, except those specified in Article 1.4. Goods include their packing (Article 23.4) and thus, in the view of most commentators,

4. *Ulster-Swift* v. *Taunton Meat Haulage* [1977] 1 Lloyd's Rep. 346 (C.A.); and *Tetroc* v. *Cross-Con (International)* [1981] 1 Lloyd's Rep. 192, 195.

5. *Elektronska* v. *Transped* [1986] 1 Lloyd's Rep. 49, 52; and *Lacey's Footwear (Wholesale) Ltd.* v. *Bowler Int. Freight Ltd.* [1997] 2 Lloyd's Rep. 369 (C.A.); *OGH 14.7.1993*, TranspR 1994. 189, *OGH 17.3.98*, TranspR 1998. 361. Cf. *Aqualon (U.K.) Ltd.* v. *Nilsson Int. B.V.* [1994] 1 Lloyd's Rep. 669.

6. [1998] 2 Lloyd's Rep. 584 (C.A.).

7. *Ibid.* p. 590.

8. *Quantum Ltd.* v. *Plane Trucking Ltd.* [2002] 2 Lloyd's Rep. 24 (C.A.).

containers.[9] The goods to be carried do not have to be specified or ascertained when the contract of carriage is concluded.[10]

Among the exceptions, furniture (removal) was excluded in the expectation that, like postal material and funeral consignments, furniture would be the subject of a special Convention, however, for furniture no such Convention has been concluded. Unfortunately, courts in different countries do not agree on the distinction between removal (of furniture) and carriage (of goods). One view, found in France, looks to the range of tasks contracted for: if the company is obliged to extract, prepare and pack the goods, as well as move them, it is removal rather than carriage.[11] Another view, found in Germany, looks to the context or purpose of the movement: a movement of goods from A to B is carriage unless it is also associated with a change of establishment.[12] *1.14*

Article 2 *1.15*

1. Where the vehicle containing the goods is carried over part of the journey by sea, rail, inland waterways or air, and, except where the provisions of article 14 are applicable, the goods are not unloaded from the vehicle, this Convention shall nevertheless apply to the whole of the carriage. Provided that to the extent that it is proved[1] that any loss, damage or delay in delivery of the goods which occurs during the carriage by the other means of transport[2] was not caused by an act or omission of the carrier by road,[3] but by some event which could only have occurred in the course of and by reason of the carriage by that other means of transport,[4] the liability of the carrier shall be determined not by this Convention but in the manner in which the liability of the carrier by the other means of transport would have been determined if a contract for the carriage of the goods alone had been made by the sender with the carrier by the other means of transport in accordance with the conditions prescribed by law for the carriage of goods by that means of transport. If, however, there are no such prescribed conditions, the liability of the carrier by road shall be determined by this Convention.

2. If the carrier by road is also himself the carrier by the other means of transport, his liability shall also be determined in accordance with the provisions of paragraph 1 of this article, but as if, in his capacities as carrier by road and as carrier by the other means of transport, he were two separate persons.

Comments

1. The purpose of Article 2

This cumbersome provision has been described in Belgium as "the English nightmare". It was introduced at the request of the United Kingdom for multimodal through traffic, in particular, traffic across the English Channel and the North Sea. *1.16*

9. See Clarke, *CMR*, para. 11, and references cited.

10. *Gefco* (above).

11. *Cass. France 19.6.1957,* D.1958.113. The rule was maintained, but applied in a way that reduces the role of CMR in *Cass. 3.4.2001,* BTL 2001.285.

12. *OLG Hamburg 28.2.1985,* NJW 1986.670.

1. The person who alleges this bears the burden of proof, i.e. in practice, the person claiming against the carrier: *Paris 13.10.1986,* BT 1986.689.

2. See *Thermo Engineers* v. *Ferrymasters* [1981] 1 All E.R. 1142.

3. I.e., the act or omission of his sub-contractor, the carrier by sea (e.g. *Thermo Engineers* (above)) or by rail.

4. See *Thermo Engineers* (above). Cf. *Cass. France 30.11.1982,* BT 1983.129.

Article 2 was intended to align the legal regime of the main contract between sender and road carrier with that between the road carrier and the sea carrier, who is usually a sub-contractor of the road carrier. At the same time, it sought to respect the sphere of application of the legal regime appropriate to the sea stage: the Hague or Hague-Visby Rules.[5]

1.17 One aspect of the "nightmare" stems from the view of some courts that this is limited (in accordance with the end of the second sentence of Article 2.1) to when the Rules (conditions) are "prescribed by law", and therefore to the case in which the alternative regime (found in the Rules) applies *proprio vigore* and not when it is adopted voluntarily by a choice.[6] Even if in the latter case Article 2 does apply after all, there seems to be a legal vacuum for the cases of unauthorised deck carriage and, especially, the common case of carriage by sea waybill, to which the Rules do not purport to apply.[7] One solution to this problem is to ignore the exclusionary scope provisions of the Rules and apply the Rules to all cases of carriage by sea coming within the second sentence of Article 2.1 in the version (Hague or Hague-Visby) found in the *lex fori*.[8] Another solution, based on strict interpretation of the second sentence as providing an exception to the otherwise general application of CMR, is that the "legal vacuum" is not a vacuum at all but a case to which the exception does not apply and which, therefore, is governed by CMR.[9]

2. *Multimodal carriage*

1.18 The scope of Article 2 is determined mainly by the fact that, when a new stage of the overall carriage starts, the goods are not unloaded from the road vehicle used on the previous stage. Thus CMR applies when the entire vehicle (with the goods) or the goods and trailer (without the tractor) are sent on by the other mode. Distinguish the cases of multimodal through carriage, to which CMR does not apply, as when goods are loaded from both vehicle and the trailer and put on a ship or a train—a series of movements by different modes, which may or may not be governed by separate contracts.

1.19 Unloading means unloading for the purpose of transfer to another vehicle or another means of transport as contemplated by the contract of carriage. Hence, the case is not taken out of CMR by unloading to achieve some purpose (usually of the carrier's) not contemplated by the contract of carriage or to safeguard the goods or better to perform the contract, for example, transfer from a defective vehicle to another road vehicle[10] or even to an alternative mode such as the railway[11]—CMR applies.

5. See Clarke, *CMR*, para. 15; Glass [2000] J.B.L. 562.
6. E.g. *Cass. France 5.7.1988*, (1989) 24 ETL 49.
7. *Browner International Transport Ltd.* v. *Monarch SS. Co. Ltd.* [1989] 2 Lloyd's Rep. 185; *Hoge Raad, Netherlands 29.6.1990* (1990) 25 ETL 589.
8. *Hoge Raad* (above).
9. Clarke, *CMR*, para. 15(a)(iii).
10. *Moto Vespa* v. *MAT (Britannia Express)* [1979] 1 Lloyd's Rep. 175.
11. *Cass. France 30.11.1982*, BT 1983.129.

3. The dominant stage of carriage

In *Quantum* v. *Plane Trucking,*[12] Air France had contracted to carry goods from Singapore to Dublin: by air from Singapore to Paris, and from there to Dublin on a lorry operated by AF. The goods were stolen from the lorry between AF's Manchester depot and Dublin. Tomlinson J. held that, as the contract was not "predominantly" one for carriage by road, the CMR did not apply and the liability for loss was limited by the terms (not of the Warsaw Convention for carriage by air but) of AF's contract. The decision was reversed.[13] According to Mance L.J., to require a court to characterise the contract overall "would open up a prospect of metaphysical arguments about the essence of a multimodal contract", arguments best avoided.[14] In any event, it might be said, the carriage was "predominantly" one for carriage by air in one important regard but in one only: the distance by air between Singapore and Paris, and associated cost. However, that was not the only factor in point. As regards duration and, more importantly perhaps risk, i.e. where loss or damage was most likely to occur, of greater significance were the land and sea stages between Paris and Dublin. 1.20

Chapter II, Persons for whom the carrier is responsible: Article 3 1.21

For the purposes of this Convention the carrier shall be responsible for the acts and omissions of his agents and servants and of any other persons of whose services he makes use for the performance of the carriage, when such agents, servants or other persons are acting within the scope of their employment, as if such acts or omissions were his own.

Comment

The purpose of Article 3 is to forestall a defence available in the law of some countries that a contractor is not liable for the acts or omissions of the servants or agents appointed to perform the contract. The defence is available if the action is in tort and the servant or agent is outside the scope of his employment as understood in English law. As far as English law is concerned, however, if the action is based on the contract of carriage, the fact that the appointed servant or agent is outside the scope of his appointment, while relevant to the punitive provision of Article 29 concerning wilful misconduct attributable to the carrier,[1] is irrelevant to whether the carrier is liable for less serious breaches of the contract of carriage.[2] It particular, it is irrelevant if the loss, damage or delay is covered by Article 17.1.[3] 1.22

12. *Quantum Corp. Ltd.* v. *Plane Trucking Ltd.* [2001] 2 Lloyd's Rep. 133.
13. [2002] 2 Lloyd's Rep. 24 (C.A.).
14. At [62].
1. See Art. 29, Comment 5, paras. 1.174 *et seq.*, below.
2. Generally, see *Armagas* v. *Mundogas S.A.* [1986] A.C. 717.
3. Clarke, *CMR*, paras. 234 *et seq.*; HM, paras. 3.1 *et seq.*

1.23 **Chapter III, Conclusion and performance of the contract of carriage: Article 4**

The contract shall be confirmed by the making out of a consignment note. The absence, irregularity or loss of the consignment note shall not affect the . . . existence or the validity of the contract of carriage which shall remain subject to the provisions of this Convention.

Comment

1.24 Although Article 4 requires a transport document in the form of a consignment note, CMR is like the air regime (WC, HP, MP4 or MC) but unlike CIM or the uniform regime for carriage by sea (Hague or Hague-Visby) in that the existence of the document is not a precondition of the application of the regime as a whole, although its absence means that certain provisions cannot be applied: see, for example, Articles 8.2, 9, 12 and perhaps 34. When issued, the consignment note functions as a receipt for the goods and as evidence of the contract of carriage, but has no role as a document of title.

1.25 **Article 5**

1. The consignment note shall be made out in three original copies signed by the sender and by the carrier. These signatures may be printed or replaced by the stamps of the sender and the carrier if the law of the country in which the consignment note has been made out so permits.[1] The first copy shall be handed to the sender, the second shall accompany the goods and the third shall be retained by the carrier.

2. When the goods which are to be carried have to be loaded in different vehicles, or are of different kinds or are divided into different lots, the sender or the carrier shall have the right to require a separate consignment note to be made out for each vehicle used, or for each kind or lot of goods.

Comment

1.26 Article 5 contains the only guidance found in CMR concerning the form of the consignment note. The inference is that it must be a paper document. Moves are under way to provide for electronic consignment notes. The requirement of three original parts, like that of WC and HP for air waybills for the international carriage of goods by air, reflects maritime practice in respect of bills of lading in the 1950s when CMR was being drafted.

1.27 In practice it is usually the sender who makes out the three copies. The first copy is for the sender's file, and facilitates disposal of the goods under Article 12. The second part goes with the goods *inter alia* to check the import and authenticity of any instructions issued under Article 12, and the identity of the person claiming the goods under Article 13 at destination. The purpose of requiring the sender's signature is to establish the responsibility of the sender under Article 7. The carrier's signature, of course, is to acknowledge receipt of the cargo as described in the note under Article 9.

1. This is permitted by English law: *Goodman* v. *Eban* [1954] 1 Q.B. 550.

Article 6 *1.28*

1. The consignment note shall contain the following particulars:
   (a) the date of the consignment note and the place at which it is made out;
   (b) the name and address of the sender;
   (c) the name and address of the carrier;
   (d) the place and the date of taking over of the goods and the place designated for delivery;
   (e) the name and address of the consignee;
   (f) the description in common use of the nature of the goods[1] and the method of packing, and, in the case of dangerous goods,[2] their generally recognised description;
   (g) the number of packages and their special marks and numbers[3];
   (h) the gross weight of the goods or their quantity otherwise expressed[4];
   (i) charges relating to the carriage (carriage charges, supplementary charges, Customs duties, and other charges incurred from making of the contract to the time of delivery);
   (j) the requisite instructions for Customs and other formalities[5];
   (k) a statement that the carriage is subject, notwithstanding any clause to the contrary, to the provisions of this Convention.
2. Where applicable, the consignment note shall also contain the following particulars:
   (a) a statement that transhipment is not allowed;
   (b) the charges which the sender undertakes to pay;
   (c) the amount of "cash on delivery" charges[6];
   (d) a declaration of the value of the goods and the amount representing special interest in delivery[7];
   (e) the sender's instructions to the carrier regarding insurance of the goods;
   (f) the agreed time-limit within which the carriage is to be carried out;
   (g) a list of the documents handed to the carrier.[8]
3. The parties may enter in the consignment note any other particulars which they may deem useful.

Comment

Whereas Article 5 concerns the form of the consignment note, Article 6 is concerned with the contents of a conforming consignment note and states them in three categories. Article 6.1 states matters that must be included in all cases. Article 6.2 states matters that must be included in relevant cases. Article 6.3 states that other matters may be included if the parties think fit; examples from the practice of carriers are arbitration clauses and jurisdiction clauses.[9] *1.29*

The purpose of stating the matters, which according to Article 6.1 must be included in all cases, is mostly self-evident. However, it should be noted that the carrier named in accordance with Article 6.1(c) is not necessarily the person liable as carrier under CMR; see Article 34.[10] Moreover, the statement required by Article 6.1(k), known as the Paramount clause, has a double purpose. One is to promote *1.30*

1. See Art. 8 and Art. 9.
2. See Art. 22.
3. See Art. 8.1.
4. See Art. 8.3 and Art. 23.3.
5. See Art. 11.
6. See Art. 13.2 and Art. 21.
7. See Art. 23.6, Art. 24 and Art. 26.
8. For example, Customs documents; see Art. 11.1.
9. See Art. 31, para. 1.184, below.
10. See also *Tetroc* v. *Cross-Con (International)* [1981] 1 Lloyd's Rep. 192, 196, 198.

CMR as a central part of the proper law of the contract. The other is to alert sub-contractors, such as carriers for a purely national stage of an international journey, that they may be liable as a successive carrier under CMR: see Article 34 and Article 39.

1.31 Such is the importance of the requirement that it is sanctioned as provided for by Article 7.3. For example, if a consignee's action against the carrier for loss, damage or delay comes before a non-contracting State and, as a result of the omission of the Paramount clause required by Article 6.1(k) and the application of law other than CMR, the consignee recovers an amount of compensation less than that fixed under CMR, Article 7.3 entitles the consignee to the difference from the carrier—in an action brought before a court that will apply CMR.

1.32 Heading the list of the matters, which according to Article 6.2 must be included in relevant cases, is transhipment. In general, transhipment is allowed. In particular, transhipment to another road vehicle as a matter of operational convenience, whether that of the carrier or of a sub-contractor, is implicitly permitted. Transhipment to another mode altogether may be permitted if it is a matter of unexpected operational necessity.[11] However, short of necessity, transhipment is not allowed if prohibited by a statement of the kind contemplated by Article 6.2(a) or even, it has been held,[12] by the very conclusion of a contract for carriage by road. In such cases transhipment is breach of the underlying contract subject to the usual remedies. It has been contended,[13] however, that prohibited transhipment is a "deviation" at common law which thus deprives the carrier of CMR defences but, as CMR is a text of uniform commercial law applicable in civil law countries, this is doubtful.[14]

1.33 The content of many of the matters specified can be supplied only by the sender. If his failure to do so or to do so accurately causes loss to the carrier, the sender will be liable under Article 7. However, although the omission of one of the particulars is an "irregularity" in the consignment note and, although it may be a breach of contract by the party responsible, CMR nonetheless applies to the contract: Article 4.

1.34

Article 7

1. The sender shall be responsible for all expenses, loss and damage sustained by the carrier by reason of the inaccuracy or inadequacy of:
   (a) the particulars specified in article 6, paragraph 1, (b), (d), (e), (f), (g), (h) and (j);
   (b) the particulars specified in article 6, paragraph 2;
   (c) any other particulars or instructions given by him to enable the consignment note to be made out or for the purpose of their being entered therein.

2. If, at the request of the sender, the carrier enters in the consignment note the particulars referred to in paragraph 1 of this article, he shall be deemed, unless the contrary is proved, to have done so on behalf of the sender.

11. E.g. road to sea: *OGH 10.2.1981*, Greiter, p. 88.
12. *Cass. France 30.11.1982*, BT 1983.129.
13. HM, para. 2.16.
14. Clarke, *CMR*, para. 31a. In this sense as regards the Hague-Visby Rules: *The Antares* [1986] 2 Lloyd's Rep. 633, 637, decision affirmed: [1987] 1 Lloyd's Rep. 424 (C.A.).

3. If the consignment note does not contain the statement specified in article 6, paragraph 1(k), the carrier shall be liable for all expenses, loss and damage sustained through such omission by the person entitled to dispose of the goods.

Comment

The content of many of the matters, which are specified as information required to be stated in the consignment note, can be supplied only by the sender. This is one reason why, in practice, it is the sender who usually obtains and completes the three copies required by Article 5. If his failure to do so or to do so accurately causes loss to the carrier, the sender will be liable under Article 7 and in full: the limits on liability found in Article 23 *et seq.* refer only to the liability of the carrier. A somewhat controversial illustration of the extent of the sender's liability under Article 7 is that of the sender who, having overloaded the vehicle, was obliged to pay the carrier the amount of the fine imposed on the latter.[1] *1.35*

Article 8 *1.36*

1. On taking over the goods, the carrier shall check:
   (a) the accuracy of the statements in the consignment note as to the number of packages and their marks and numbers, and
   (b) the apparent condition of the goods and their packaging.

2. Where the carrier has no reasonable means of checking the accuracy of the statements referred to in paragraph 1(a) of this article, he shall enter his reservations in the consignment note together with the grounds on which they are based. He shall likewise specify the grounds for any reservations which he makes with regard to the apparent condition of the goods and their packaging. Such reservations shall not bind the sender unless he has expressly agreed to be bound by them in the consignment note.

3. The sender shall be entitled to require the carrier to check the gross weight of the goods or their quantity otherwise expressed. He may also require the contents of the packages to be checked. The carrier shall be entitled to claim the cost of such checking. The result of the checks shall be entered in the consignment note.

Comments

1. Checking: the effect

The carrier's obligation under Article 8 to check the goods must be read with Article 9, which assumes that the duty has been performed and, on that basis, establishes a presumption that the goods have been received by the carrier in the quantity and condition stated in the consignment note. The presumption in Article 9 refers only to the matters specified in Article 8.1 and is silent on the matters mentioned in Article 8.3. In the view of commentators,[1] however, the effect of the latter is no less strong than the presumption arising out of Article 9 for the former. *1.37*

If the carrier fails to make the checks required by Article 8, that is not *per se* a breach of the contract of carriage for which he is liable to the sender. Nonetheless, there may be consequences adverse to the carrier in the form of lost opportunities. *1.38*

1. *Colmar 16.6.1972*, BT 1972.320.
1. E.g. Loewe, paras. 95 and 105.

First, the presumption established by Article 9 operates whether the carrier has made the checks or not. Thus he may have lost an opportunity to safeguard his position, for example by noting defects in the apparent condition of the goods (Article 8.1(b)) or entering reservations (Article 8.2). Secondly, if a consequence of his failure to check is a failure to discover deterioration in the goods, which might have been averted, he may be liable for that deterioration.[2]

2. Scope of the obligation

1.39 As regards those matters that the carrier is required to check when he takes over the goods,[3] Article 8.2 offers the carrier an excuse for not checking when he "has no reasonable means" of doing so. Moreover, the French courts have made it clear that, if the goods are of such a nature that to open them and examine them would involve the carrier in unacceptable delay, then even when the state of the packing suggests that something *might* be wrong with them any damage that becomes apparent later is not treated as being apparent earlier in such a way that raises the presumption against the carrier under Article 9.[4]

1.40 Effective reservations are conditional on their being recorded on the consignment note stating the reasons, however, they do not bind the sender unless the sender agrees: Article 8.2 *in fine*. Such agreement is unlikely. Signature by the sender of the kind required by Article 5.1 probably does not amount to agreement. Nonetheless, although commentators are divided, the better view is that valid reservations defeat the presumption stated in Article 9.[5]

1.41 Although the carrier is only required by Article 8 to *check* the matters stated, the inference of Article 9 is that he is expected to *mention* his findings in the consignment note—at the very least in the first copy which is handed to the sender and, preferably, also in the second copy which accompanies the goods: it is to the note that reference will be made if a dispute over the quantity or condition of the goods arises later.

3. Apparent condition

1.42 The meaning of the "apparent condition of the goods", which is not explained or defined by CMR, is a matter governed by national law. Common law is clear: apparent condition refers only to what is discernible externally on a reasonable examination—"so far as meets the eye".[6] Thus the carrier is not obliged to investigate the core temperature of refrigerated meat, for example.[7] However, apparent condition, both at common law[8] and under CMR,[9] is understood to refer

2. See Art. 17, Comment 6, para. 1.96, and Art. 18, Comment 1, para. 1.119, below.
3. Concerning the time of take-over, see Art. 17, Comment 3, para. 1.88, below.
4. *Bordeaux 28.4.1997*, BTL 1998.417.
5. See Clarke, *CMR*, para. 25(b)(ii); Haak, pp. 88 *et seq.*; HM, para. 4.29.
6. Clarke, *CMR*, para. 25a. Cf. Holland: the carrier must open packing unless it is sealed (*Amsterdam 2.11.1989*, 1990 S & S No. 298).
7. *Ulster-Swift* v. *Taunton Meat Haulage* [1975] 2 Lloyd's Rep. 502, affirmed [1977] 1 Lloyd's Rep. 346 (C.A.).
8. *Silver & Layton* v. *Ocean SS. Co.* [1930] 1 K.B. 416 (C.A.).
9. E.g. *Cass. France 15.2.1982*, BT 1982.182.

not only to condition at the time that the goods are taken over but also to whether the goods and their packaging appear at that time to be fit to withstand the rigours of the intended journey and also to be in the condition expected for a reasonable time thereafter. Moreover, if it is apparent to the carrier that something is actually wrong with the goods, it may not be enough simply to record this in the consignment note; he may be obliged to take steps to deal with the problem as an aspect of his residual duty of care.[10]

If the carrier mentions matters affecting the condition of goods outside those specified in Article 8, for example, the non-apparent condition of goods, such as their internal temperature, a similar presumption to that raised by Article 9 might arise not, however, from CMR but from common law.[11] *1.43*

Article 9 *1.44*

1. The consignment note shall be prima facie evidence of the making of the contract of carriage, the conditions of the contract and the receipt of the goods by the carrier.

2. If the consignment note contains no specific reservations by the carrier, it shall be presumed, unless the contrary is proved, that the goods and their packaging appeared to be in good condition when the carrier took them over and that the number of packages, their marks and numbers corresponded with the statements in the consignment note.

Comment

Article 9 must be read with Article 8. Together these provisions establish a presumption about the "goods" that the carrier has received: their identity, quantity and apparent condition. The presumption only arises if a consignment note has been issued and as regards matters mentioned in the note; if there is no note, or if the note has not been signed by the carrier, or in any case as regards features of the goods not mentioned in the note made out, the onus is on the claimant to prove the allegation by whatever other means available. The note may nonetheless have some probative effect according to the *lex fori*.[1] *1.45*

Article 10 *1.46*

The sender shall be liable to the carrier for damage to persons, equipment or other goods, and for any expenses due to defective packing of the goods, unless the defect was apparent or known to the carrier[1] at the time when he took over[2] the goods and he made no reservations concerning it.

10. See Art. 17, Comment 1, paras. 1.78 *et seq.*, below, and Comment 7, paras. 1.98 *et seq.*, below.
11. *C.N. Vascongada* v. *Churchill & Sim* [1906] 1 K.B. 237.
1. *BGH 9.12.1979* (1980) 15 ETL 215; *BGH 17.4.1997*, TranspR 1998.21; ULR 1998.206.
1. See Art. 17, Comment 11, paras. 1.110 *et seq.*, below.
2. See Art. 17, Comment 3, paras. 1.88 *et seq.*, below.

Comments

1. Liability

1.47 The liability of the sender to the carrier is strict and potentially extensive, being for not only persons and equipment but also the goods of other customers of the carrier (see Comment 2), as well as any expenses incurred due to defective packing of the sender's goods. These include the cost to the carrier of averting or limiting the consequences of defective packing not only to the sender's goods but to those of others; the carrier may well be obliged to incur the former costs in order to comply with the carrier's residual duty of care.[3] However, although the sender is liable to the carrier for damage to "equipment", it has been held that the sender is not liable under CMR for replacing parts of the vehicle damaged by (leaking) goods.[4]

1.48 Under Article 8 "apparent condition of . . . packing" refers only to what is discernible externally on a reasonable examination—"so far as meets the eye"[5] of a professional carrier. In practice, this means what is apparent to the driver. Some courts have made allowance for a lack of experience on the part of a driver who, for example, had not carried goods of the kind in question before.[6]

2. Third parties

1.49 The liability of the sender to the carrier is based on Article 10 as a term in the contract of carriage, hence Article 10 does not appear to assist a sub-carrier with whom the sender has no contract. Equally, it does not assist another sender, B, whose goods are damaged by those of sender A: sender B must proceed against the carrier and, if liable, the carrier must seek to recover the amount of that liability from sender A as an "expense" under Article 10. Such problems might be solved by contract terms drafted with an eye to the Contracts (Rights of Third Parties) Act 1999 whereby third parties to the carrier's contract with the sender, such as sub-carriers, are entitled to benefit from Article 10. More specifically, section 1(1) of the Act confers a right of enforcement on "a person who is not a party to a contract", a "third party", and by section 1(3), to be a "third party", a person must be "expressly identified in the contract by name, as a member of a class or as answering to a particular description". According to the Law Commission in the Report[7] that led up to the Act examples of description sufficient to identify the third party include "sub-contractors". Thus, it will now be a simple matter to extend the benefit of that cover to sub-carriers yet to be engaged but who are later contracted to perform the particular carriage, if the parties to the contract of carriage so choose.

3. See Art. 17, Comment 1 (paras. 1.78 *et seq.*, below and Comment 7, paras. 1.98 *et seq.*, below.
4. *OGH 2.4.1982*, TranspR 1984.151. Cf. national law.
5. Clarke, *CMR*, para. 25a. See Art. 8, Comment 3, paras. 1.42 to 1.43, above.
6. *Lyon 21.2.1991*, BTL 1992.166.
7. Law Com. No. 242, July 1996, Part VIII. See also Merkin (Ed), *Privity of Contract* (2000), paras. 5.33 *et seq.*

Article 11 *1.50*

1. For the purposes of the Customs or other formalities which have to be completed before delivery of the goods, the sender shall attach the necessary documents to the consignment note or place them at the disposal of the carrier and shall furnish him with all the information which he requires.

2. The carrier shall not be under any duty to enquire into either the accuracy or the adequacy of such documents and information. The sender shall be liable to the carrier for any damage caused by the absence, inadequacy or irregularity of such documents and information, except in the case of some wrongful act or neglect on the part of the carrier.

3. The liability of the carrier for the consequences arising from the loss or incorrect use of the documents specified in and accompanying the consignment note or deposited with the carrier shall be that of an agent, provided that the compensation payable by the carrier shall not exceed that payable in the event of loss of the goods.

Comment

The sender is the person best placed to obtain the relevant information and paperwork and thus, if it is incorrect or insufficient, bears the responsibility under Article 11, which thus has the same roles for example as Article 16 of HP.[1] The sender's liability is such that if, for example, loss or destruction of documents is entirely accidental or the incorrect information or documents came from another apparently reliable person other than the sender, the sender is liable nonetheless for "any damage caused"[2]: liability is strict. Moreover, it is not limited in amount by Article 23 but such questions of the measure of damage are governed by national law. *1.51*

If the inaccuracy or insufficiency arises from advice provided by the carrier and (reasonably) relied on by the consignor, the consignor is excused by the second sentence of Article 11(2). Unlike that of the sender, however, any liability of the carrier under this provision is limited by Article 11(3) *in fine* to that under Article 23(1). The role of the carrier is not passive. The carrier is obliged by Article 6.2(g) to list the documents handed to him by or on behalf of the sender in the consignment note and, although Article 9, which concerns the status of the consignment note, does not state any presumption on this point, it is not unlikely that, in the absence of protest or reservation on the part of the carrier, common law would presume that the carrier had received the documents listed. *1.52*

Article 12 *1.53*

1. The sender has the right to dispose of the goods, in particular by asking the carrier to stop the goods in transit, to change the place at which delivery is to take place or to deliver the goods to a consignee other than the consignee indicated in the consignment note.

2. This right shall cease to exist when the second copy of the consignment note is handed to the consignee or when the consignee exercises his right under article 13, paragraph 1; from that time onwards the carrier shall obey the orders of the consignee.

3. The consignee shall, however, have the right of disposal from the time when the consignment note is drawn up, if the sender makes an entry to that effect in the consignment note.

1. Part 3, para. 3.96, below.
2. This includes expense, for example, the cost of delay: *Paris 2.12.1981*, BT 1982.73.

4. If in exercising his right of disposal the consignee has ordered the delivery of the goods to another person, that other person shall not be entitled to name other consignees.

5. The exercise of the right of disposal shall be subject to the following conditions:

(a) that the sender or, in the case referred to in paragraph 3 of this article, the consignee who wishes to exercise the right produces the first copy of the consignment note on which the new instructions to the carrier have been entered and indemnifies the carrier against all expenses, loss and damage involved in carrying out such instructions;

(b) that the carrying out of such instructions is possible at the time when the instructions reach the person who is to carry them out and does not either interfere with the normal working of the carrier's undertaking or prejudice the senders or consignees of other consignments;

(c) that the instructions do not result in a division of the consignment.

6. When, by reason of the provisions of paragraph 5(b) of this article, the carrier cannot carry out the instructions which he receives, he shall immediately notify the person who gave him such instructions.

7. A carrier who has not carried out the instructions given under the conditions provided for in this article, or who has carried them out without requiring the first copy of the consignment note to be produced, shall be liable to the person entitled to make a claim for any loss or damage caused thereby.

Comments

1. The existence and duration of the right of disposal

1.54 Article 12 confers on the sender the right to dispose of the goods while they are in the charge of the carrier. If, however, the consignment note confers the right to dispose of the goods on the consignee, the consignee alone has that right. Otherwise the sender has the right to dispose of the goods until the second copy of the consignment note has been handed (by the carrier) to the consignee,[1] or the goods have arrived at destination and the consignee has required delivery of the goods in accordance with Article 13. Until then Article 12(1) and the right of disposal empowers the sender to designate a new consignee or a new destination, including return to sender.[2]

1.55 The right of disposal of the goods is linked to possession of the consignment note. If the sender has no consignment note, for example when goods are grouped to be sent, *prima facie* the sender has no right of disposal. The BGH has held that, nonetheless, the carrier is obliged to obey the instructions of the sender.[3] The purpose of requiring production of a note is to protect the rights of the person truly entitled to dispose of the goods, and also to protect the carrier from liability to that person by following disposal instructions from someone else. When there is no consignment note the carrier knows that there is nobody other than the sender with the right of disposal and therefore the need for protection does not arise. In these circumstances the BGH considered that the sender's instructions should be obeyed.

1. Note that, this being so, the consignee does not lose the right because he later refuses to take delivery of the goods: *BGH 15.10.1998*, TranspR 1999.102.

2. *Brussels 6.4.77* (1977) 12 ETL 881.

3. *BGH 27.1.82*, (1985) 20 ETL 349. See also *BGH 4.7.02*, TranspR 2002.399.

2. The nature of the right

Exercise of the right of disposal by the sender does not discharge the original contract of carriage but alters its terms.[4] Moreover, the sender, who has exercised the right of disposal or lost it to the consignee, retains any rights that have accrued under the contract of carriage in respect of rights of suit against the carrier.[5] The right of disposal is a right unilaterally to change the terms of the contract. Distinguish a variation of the terms of the contract, which is agreed by both parties and to which the rules of Article 12 do not apply.[6] Unilateral alteration of the terms of the contract in this way poses obvious practical problems for the carrier (see Comment 3) but poses no difficulties in legal theory. The note is an instrument of entitlement and not a negotiable instrument or a document of title: the right to dispose of the goods is distinguished from ownership of the goods.[7] In English law questions of ownership are regulated by the contract of sale and, when applicable, the Sale of Goods Act 1979. *1.56*

3. Conditions of exercise

Exercise of the right of disposal poses practical problems especially for the carrier and for that reason Article 12.5 puts conditions on its exercise, conditions aimed mainly at protecting the position of the other persons concerned. It is for the person, sender or consignee as the case may be, who seeks to exercise the right, to prove that the conditions are satisfied.[8] *1.57*

(a) To carry out the new instructions must be "possible at the time when the instructions reach the person who is to carry them out".

(b) The sender (or consignee) must produce "the first copy of the consignment note", i.e. the one originally handed to the sender,[9] "on which the new instructions to the carrier have been entered", unless the parties concerned have agreed that that shall not be required.[10]

(c) The sender (or consignee) must give the carrier an indemnity of some kind (unspecified) against all expenses, loss or damage involved in carrying out the new instructions. Arguably this includes lost operating profits as consequential loss or damage.[11]

(d) If the sender seeks to exercise the right, the sender has not lost the right because the carrier has delivered the second copy of the consignment note to the consignee.[12]

4. *Brussels 6.4.77* (above).
5. *BGH 10.4.1974* (1975) 10 ETL 83.
6. In this sense: *OLG Hamburg 7.4.1994*, TranspR 1994.444.
7. Loewe, para. 119; Maccarone, Theunis, p. 62.
8. E.g. the feasibility of carrying out the instructions: *BGH 27.1.82* (1985) 20 ETL 349, 353.
9. See Art. 5(1), para. 1.25, above.
10. *BGH 7.7.02*, (2002) ETL 817; TranspR 2002.399.
11. Maccarone, Theunis, p. 74.
12. Art. 12.2 by reference to Art. 13.1. See *OLG Munich 23.4.93*, TranspR 1993.348.

(e) A sender loses the right of disposal, if the consignee has required delivery of the goods[13] or if the consignee, knowing that the goods have been lost or delayed, has taken steps to establish a claim against the carrier.

(f) The right of disposal cannot be exercised, if the fulfilment of the new instructions prejudices the senders or consignees of other consignments, for example, by causing undue delay in their delivery; or interferes with "the normal working of the carrier's undertaking". However, arguably, in many such cases of interference the carrier can recover indemnity from the sender and thus cannot then refuse on that ground to carry out the instructions.[14]

(g) The instructions must not result in a division of the consignment.[15]

1.58

Article 13

1. After arrival of the goods at the place designated for delivery,[1] the consignee shall be entitled to require the carrier to deliver to him, against a receipt, the second copy of the consignment note and the goods. If the loss of the goods[2] is established or if the goods have not arrived after the expiry of the period provided for in article 19, the consignee shall be entitled to enforce in his own name against the carrier any rights arising from the contract of carriage.

2. The consignee who avails himself of the rights granted to him under paragraph 1 of this article shall pay the charges shown to be due on the consignment note,[3] but in the event of dispute on this matter the carrier shall not be required to deliver the goods unless security has been furnished by the consignee.

Comment

1.59 Article 13 states, what is usually evident from the contract of carriage itself, that the designated consignee is entitled to demand the goods from the carrier, when they have arrived at the designated place of delivery. The designated consignee, even when the name is that of a bank or of a person to be notified[4] and perhaps has suffered no loss,[5] and the designated place of delivery are those stated in the consignment note.[6]

1.60 More significant is the interaction between Article 13 and Article 12, whereby it is in the circumstances set out in Article 13 that the consignee acquires (and the sender loses) the right to dispose of the goods under Article 12.[7] See Article 12, Comment 1. Also significant is the second sentence of Article 13.1: from that moment the consignee is entitled to enforce the contract of carriage against the

13. Art. 12.2 by reference to Art. 13.1.
14. See Clarke, *CMR*, para. 32a.
15. There is some controversy about what this means. Cf. Clarke, *CMR*, para. 32a *in fine*; HM, para. 5.6; and Loewe, para. 123.
1. See Art. 17, Comment 3.
2. Also damage to the goods: *BGH 24.9.87*, 1988 ULR II. 713.
3. See Art. 6.1(i) and Art. 21.
4. *OLG Karlsruhe 25.2.1999*, TranspR 1999.349.
5. *Cass. Belgium 13.6.1980* (1980) 15 ETL 851; but cf. *BGH 6.5.1981* (1982) 17 ETL 313.
6. Art. 6.1(d) and Art. 12.5(a).
7. See Art. 12, Comment 1, paras. 1.54 to 1.55, above.

carrier. The second sentence is independent of the first sentence: events mentioned in the first, such as delivery of the second copy of the note which accompanies the goods, are not preconditions of the consignee's entitlement to sue under the second in respect of an action based on CMR.[8] The consignee may also have a right of action against the carrier under national law.[9]

Unless and to the extent that the sender contracts with the carrier as the agent of the consignee, the rights of the consignee are not affected by any terms agreed between sender and carrier of which the consignee is unaware. Decisions to this effect can be found under the common law of carriage[10] as well as CMR.[11] However, English courts are inclined to see the sender as the agent of the consignee.[12] *1.61*

Article 14 *1.62*

1. If for any reason it is or becomes impossible to carry out the contract in accordance with the terms laid down in the consignment note before the goods reach the place designated for delivery, the carrier shall ask for instructions from the person entitled to dispose of the goods in accordance with the provisions of article 12.

2. Nevertheless, if circumstances are such as to allow the carriage to be carried out under conditions differing from those laid down in the consignment note and if the carrier has been unable to obtain instructions in reasonable time from the person entitled to dispose of the goods in accordance with the provisions of article 12, he shall take such steps as seem to him to be in the best interests of the person entitled to dispose of the goods.

Comments

1. Impossibility

Article 14 is concerned with obstacles to performance en route and Article 15 is concerned with obstacles to delivery at destination. Both are concerned, together with Article 16, with what the carrier is to do next, if an obstacle arises. These provisions are not centrally concerned with the liability of the carrier, if any, for failure to perform the contract of carriage in accordance with its terms: that is the concern of Article 17.[1] *1.63*

The particular obstacle dealt with by Article 14 is that it has become impossible to carry out the contract in accordance with the terms stated in the consignment note, for example, terms as to the route or the time of delivery. Impossibility is unlikely to be construed literally as an absolute impossibility. Arguably it means that the degree of effort and initiative required of the carrier is in line with that which can *1.64*

8. *Cass. Belgium 13.6.1980* (1980) 15 ETL 851.

9. *Brandt* v. *Liverpool, Brazil & River Plate SN Co.* [1924] 1 K.B. 575 (C.A.); Clarke [1991] L.M.C.L.Q. 5. Clarke, *CMR*, para. 41; Haak, p. 257.

10. By sea: *Leduc* v. *Ward* (1888) 20 Q.B.D. 475 (C.A.).

11. *Cass. France 5.7.1988*, (1989) 24 ETL 49.

12. *Texas Instruments Ltd.* v. *Nasan (Europe) Ltd.* [1991] 1 Lloyd's Rep. 146, 148–149; Clarke, *CMR*, para. 42; Palmer, pp. 959 *et seq.*

1. But see Comment 2, below.

be expected of the carrier under Article 12.5(b) by way of altered performance and under Article 17.1 as regards steps to avoid loss or damage to the goods.[2]

2. Instructions

1.65 A feature of Articles 14–16 is that, if an obstacle to performance occurs, the carrier may be obliged to seek and obey instructions from the person entitled to dispose of the goods in accordance with Article 12. The carrier must ask for instructions within a reasonable time and also provide the sender with as much information as possible to enable the sender to make an appropriate decision. Pending receipt of instructions the carrier is entitled to unload the goods in accordance with Article 16.2. If suitable instructions have been received, in particular, instructions that satisfy Article 12.5(b), the situation is governed by Article 12 and the carrier must obey the instructions accordingly. The cost of requesting instructions and any expenses entailed in carrying them out are recoverable under Article 16(1), unless such expenses were caused by the wrongful act or neglect of the carrier.

1.66 If the carrier is in breach of this obligation, it is assumed that the carrier is liable but the basis of that liability is not clear.[3] It appears that, if the breach causes loss, damage or delay to the goods prior to delivery at destination, the carrier's liability is governed by Article 17.[4] If, however, the loss or damage does not arise until after delivery at destination, the matter is governed not by CMR but by national law.[5]

3. Lack of instructions

1.67 If the carrier has been unable to obtain instructions in a reasonable time from the person entitled to dispose of the goods and if the carriage can be performed, albeit on terms such as to route or timing that differ from those required by the consignment note, the carrier must take such steps "as seem to him to be in the best interests" of the person entitled. Such steps may include finding an alternative and more appropriate means of transport, such as transport by sea rather than by road,[6] or transfer to a lorry small enough to reach the designated place of delivery.[7] However, in such a case, it appears that the original carrier remains liable under CMR,[8] although it has also been argued that he may assume the role and responsibility of a forwarder.[9] Such steps may also include unloading the goods and storing them pending an alternative manner of performance. Indeed, this may also be the right action to take when it is apparent that the original contract of carriage cannot be performed at all: Article 16.2.

2. Clarke, *CMR*, para. 33a(i). See, in particular, Art. 17, Comment 7, paras. 1.98 *et seq.*, below.
3. Clarke, *CMR*, para. 33d.
4. In this sense: *Amiens 28.10.1992*, BTL 1992.766.
5. *OLG Hamm 11.3.1976*, NJW 1976.2077.
6. *OGH 10.2.1981*, Greiter, p. 88.
7. E.g. *OGH 16.5.02*, (2003) 38 ETL 512.
8. Clarke, *CMR*, para. 33c(i); Glass/Cashmore, para. 3.34.
9. HM, para. 5.28.

Article 15 1.68

1. Where circumstances prevent delivery of the goods after their arrival at the place designated for delivery, the carrier shall ask the sender for his instructions. If the consignee refuses the goods[1] the sender shall be entitled to dispose of them without being obliged to produce the first copy of the consignment note.

2. Even if he has refused the goods, the consignee may nevertheless require delivery so long as the carrier has not received instructions to the contrary from the sender.

3. When circumstances preventing delivery of the goods arise after the consignee, in exercise of his rights under article 12, paragraph 3, has given an order for the goods to be delivered to another person, paragraphs 1 and 2 of this article shall apply as if the consignee were the sender and that other person were the consignee.

Comment

Article 15 is concerned with the obligations of carriers when, after arrival at the place designated for delivery, they are prevented from delivering the goods. Prevention is unlikely to be construed literally as an absolute bar to delivery. As with the impossibility referred to in Article 14.1, prevention will probably be construed as requiring of the carrier utmost endeavour (to deliver) of the kind required to avoid loss or damage to goods under Article 17.1.[2] However, the first step required of the carrier under Article 15 is to seek instructions which, as with those to be sought under Article 14, must be sought within a reasonable time after the sender has been provided with as much information as possible to enable the sender to make an appropriate decision. 1.69

The cost of requesting instructions and any expenses entailed in carrying them out are recoverable under Article 16(1) unless such expenses were caused by the wrongful act or neglect of the carrier. If the carrier is too slow in seeking instructions, he will be liable for the consequences.[3] If the sender fails to give instructions, unlike Article 14, Article 15 offers no guidance and it appears that the carrier must fall back on Article 16. 1.70

Article 16 1.71

1. The carrier shall be entitled to recover the cost of his request for instructions and any expenses entailed in carrying out such instructions, unless such expenses were caused by the wrongful act or neglect of the carrier.

2. In the cases referred to in article 14, paragraph 1, and in article 15, the carrier may immediately unload the goods for account of the person entitled to dispose of them and thereupon the carriage shall be deemed to be at an end. The carrier shall then hold the goods on behalf of the person so entitled. He may however entrust them to a third party, and in that case he shall not be under any liability except for the exercise of reasonable care in the choice of such third party. The charges due under the consignment note and all other expenses shall remain chargeable against the goods.

3. The carrier may sell the goods, without awaiting instructions from the person entitled to dispose of them, if the goods are perishable or their condition warrants such a course, or

1. See, for example, *Moto Vespa* v. *MAT (Britannia Express)* [1979] 1 Lloyd's Rep. 175.
2. See Art. 17, Comment 7, paras. 1.98 *et seq.*, below.
3. E.g. for deterioration in the goods: *Cass. France 23.5.1977*, BT 1977.388.

when the storage expenses would be out of proportion to the value of the goods. He may also proceed to the sale of the goods in other cases if after the expiry of a reasonable period he has not received from the person entitled to dispose of the goods instructions to the contrary which he may reasonably be required to carry out.

4. If the goods have been sold pursuant to this article, the proceeds of sale, after deduction of the expenses chargeable against the goods, shall be placed at the disposal of the person entitled to dispose of the goods. If these charges exceed the proceeds of sale, the carrier shall be entitled to the difference.

5. The procedure in the case of sale shall be determined by the law or custom of the place where the goods are situated.

Comments

1.72 Article 16 wraps up certain issues that might arise as a result of the operation of Articles 14 and 15. These are payment of costs incurred by the carrier seeking instructions under those provisions (Article 16(1)), unloading the goods either during transit or at the place designated for delivery (Article 16(2)), and selling the goods there on behalf of the person entitled thereto, i.e., the person entitled to dispose of the goods under Article 12 (Article 16(3) and (4)).

1. Unloading the goods

1.73 Article 16.2 provides that, in certain cases, the carrier may unload the goods for account of the person entitled thereto, and without necessarily waiting for instructions.[1] If the unloading is undertaken on the initiative of the carrier, the cost of unloading is expressed by Article 16.2 to be for account of the person entitled to the goods, but the cost of subsequent storage is not mentioned. If storage is confirmed by instructions from the person entitled thereto, that person bears the cost but, if not, the carrier may have to exercise the power of sale in Article 16(3) to recover the cost of storage.[2]

1.74 Unless unloading is from one vehicle to another in order to continue the carriage,[3] unloading has the effect of delivery under Article 17.[4] However, the carrier "shall then hold the goods on behalf of" the person entitled thereto (Article 16(2)) and the carrier is liable for loss of or damage to the goods not under CMR but under national law[5] such as the law of bailment in England. Moreover, Article 16.2 states that the carrier may entrust the goods to a third party, such as a warehouseman, and that "in that case he shall not be under any liability except for the exercise of reasonable care in the choice of such third party". The CMR does not require the carrier to inform the person entitled to the goods that the goods have been unloaded but it is difficult to see how the carrier can properly seek instructions,

1. See Clarke, *CMR*, para. 33(c)(ii); cf. HM, para. 5.29.
2. *Paris 21.12.82*, BT 1983.233.
3. E.g. *OGH 16.5.02*, (2003) 38 ETL 512.
4. Loewe, para. 139.
5. *Cass.civ 8.10.97*, BTL 1997.799; but cf. *OGH 16.5.02*, TranspR 2002.403.

as required by Articles 14 and 15, without stating what has happened to the goods.

2. Selling the goods

Article 16(3) gives the carrier a power of sale limited to the circumstance there stated but also, in view of the context, to the case of impossibility (Article 14) or prevention (Article 15). Sale must be according to a procedure determined by the law or custom of the place where the goods are situated: Article 16(5). Local law may require notice of the sale to the sender or consignee, but the CMR does not. *1.75*

In each case Article 16(4) provides, on the one hand, that "the proceeds of sale, after deduction of the expenses chargeable against the goods" including, according to Article 16(2), the charges due under the consignment note and the cost of requesting and carrying out instructions under Article 16(1) and (2) shall be placed at the disposal of the person entitled to the goods. If, on the other hand, "these charges exceed the proceeds of sale", Article 16(4) provides that "the carrier shall be entitled to the difference". *1.76*

Chapter IV, Liability of the carrier: Article 17 *1.77*

1. The carrier shall be liable for the total or partial loss of the goods and for damage thereto occurring between the time when he takes over the goods and the time of delivery, as well as for any delay in delivery.

2. The carrier shall however be relieved of liability if the loss, damage or delay was caused by the wrongful act or neglect of the claimant, by the instructions of the claimant given otherwise than as the result of a wrongful act or neglect on the part of the carrier, by inherent vice of the goods or through circumstances which the carrier could not avoid and the consequences of which he was unable to prevent.

3. The carrier shall not be relieved of liability by reason of the defective condition of the vehicle used by him in order to perform the carriage, or by reason of the wrongful act or neglect of the person from whom he may have hired the vehicle or of the agents or servants of the latter.

4. Subject to article 18, paragraphs 2 to 5, the carrier shall be relieved of liability when the loss or damage arises from the special risks inherent in one or more of the following circumstances:

(a) Use of open unsheeted vehicles, when their use has been expressly agreed and specified in the consignment note;
(b) the lack of, or defective condition of packing in the case of goods which, by their nature, are liable to wastage or to be damaged when not packed or when not properly packed;
(c) handling, loading, stowage or unloading of the goods by the sender, the consignee or persons acting on behalf of the sender or the consignee;
(d) the nature of certain kinds of goods which particularly exposes them to total or partial loss or to damage, especially through breakage, rust, decay, desiccation, leakage, normal wastage, or the action of moth or vermin;
(e) insufficiency or inadequacy of marks or numbers on the packages;
(f) the carriage of livestock.

5. Where under this article the carrier is not under any liability in respect of some of the factors causing the loss, damage or delay, he shall only be liable to the extent that those factors for which he is liable under this article have contributed to the loss, damage or delay.

Comments

(a) Liability

1. The liability of the carrier

1.78 Article 17 is the central provision of the liability regime of the CMR. Article 17 was modelled on Article 36 of CIM.[1] If there is delay or if there is loss or damage to the goods occurring during carriage, the carrier is liable under Article 17.1 unless the carrier can establish a defence. If the case against the carrier is that he failed to take the goods over at all, liability is not governed by Chapter IV of CMR[2] but by common law.[3]

1.79 If the allegation against the carrier is delay, the claimant must prove that the goods arrived later than promised or, if it is loss or damage, that the loss or damage occurred to the goods between the time that they were taken over by the carrier and the time of delivery. Loss or damage is proved by contrasting evidence of the state or quantity of the goods on arrival or, if they have not arrived, by reliance on Article 20.1, and evidence of the quantity and/or condition of the goods when taken over by the carrier, in particular, by reference to the consignment note as recognised by Articles 8 and 9.

1.80 In the case of some goods, however, the claimant will derive little assistance from the consignment note. In the case of frozen goods, for example, the claimant must prove that the goods were kept at a suitable temperature prior to consignment, so that they were taken over in good condition for the transport in question.[4] However, if the carrier has undertaken to test the temperature of goods on take over but fails to do so, it will be presumed that the goods were in good condition in that respect.[5]

1.81 If the claimant has made a case against the carrier, Article 18.1 states that it is for the carrier to seek exoneration by proving (on the balance of probabilities) that the loss, damage or delay was due to one of the causes specified in Article 17.2 or, in respect of dangerous goods, Article 22. Where the carrier is excused in respect of some of the factors causing the loss etc. but not others, the carrier is only liable to the extent that it is the former factors which have contributed to the loss, damage or delay: Article 17.5. However, unlike the rule of common law, it is not for the carrier who is seeking exoneration to prove the extent to which the loss etc. is due to the exonerating causes but for the court to make an apportionment as best it can.[6]

1.82 Alternatively, if the carrier can establish (a) the existence of one of the special risks set out in Article 17.4, and (b) not that the risk did cause the loss etc. but that it *could* have caused it, it is presumed to have been the cause (Article 18.2). In that case the carrier is excused unless the claimant can prove (on the balance of

1. See Part 2, paras. 2.271 *et seq.*, below.
2. *Obiter, Shell Chemicals UK Ltd.* v. *P. & O. Roadtanks Ltd.* [1993] 1 Lloyd's Rep. 114; affirmed [1995] 2 Lloyd's Rep. 297 (C.A.); Clarke, *CMR*, para. 65.
3. See Clarke, *CMR*, ch. 12.
4. *Brandenburgische OLG 29.3.2000*, TranspR 2000.358.
5. *OLG Hamm 2.11.98*, TranspR 2000.361.
6. *OLG Saarbrücken 21.11.74* (1976) 11 ETL 261; *OGH 13.2.2003*, TranspR 2003.311.

probabilities) that the loss etc. was not attributable to one of those special risks after all, but to some other cause which may or may not indicate fault on the part of the carrier. In theory, the claimant does not have to prove the real cause: it is enough to establish alternative hypotheses that weaken the carrier's case that the loss etc. could have been caused by the special risk; but in practice the claimant's case is best made by proof of what did actually occur.

One way of defeating the presumption raised by the special risks pleaded by the carrier is for the claimant to establish that the loss etc. was attributable to the carrier.[7] If so, the carrier is liable. From this it becomes apparent that the carrier owes a general or residual duty of care in respect of the goods.[8] With the exception of certain matters particularly within the sphere of risk of the sender or consignee, the level of care required is high: the carrier must exercise "utmost care". This is also the corollary of Article 17.2 which, certain specific defences apart, excuses the carrier only if the circumstances giving rise to loss etc. were "unavoidable".[9] *1.83*

If the carrier's defence is unsuccessful, the carrier is liable to pay compensation for the financial loss caused by the "the total or partial loss of the goods and for damage thereto", according to Article 17.1. Liability "for any delay" indicates that the carrier is liable not only for consequent deterioration in perishable goods but also for the (purely) economic consequences of delay such as lost market. However, the actual amount of compensation payable is limited in accordance with Articles 23 *et seq.* *1.84*

2. *Entitlement to sue the carrier*

Although Article 13.1 entitles the consignee to sue the carrier, it is widely assumed[10] that the CMR contains no general or definitive rule governing who is entitled to sue the carrier. Subject to Article 13,[11] courts tend to apply the *lex fori.* In English common law, it is clear that action lies at the suit of the person who has contracted for the carriage.[12] Many other countries recognise actions by one or other of those who are parties to the contract, in particular, the sender.[13] Moreover, in England (but not other countries) there appears to be a presumption that it is the owner of the goods who has contracted with the carrier.[14] *1.85*

Unfortunately, the theoretical position is indeed different in different countries. In Germany, for example, the rule is that the person entitled to sue is the person entitled to dispose of the goods.[15] As there can be only one such person at any one time, double exposure of the carrier is avoided. However, in many other CMR states *1.86*

7. See Art. 18, Comment 1, paras. 1.119 *et seq.*, below.

8. *OLG Saarbrücken 21.11.74*, (1976) 11 ETL 261, 264; *Metz 28.10.87*, BT 1988.168. Clarke, *CMR*, para. 79. See also Comment 7, below.

9. See Comment 7, below, and Clarke, *CMR*, para. 79.

10. E.g. Haak, p. 257, Koller, Art. 13, 8.

11. See the Comment on Art. 13.

12. Cashmore [1990] J.B.L. 377.

13. E.g. Belgium: *Brussels 30.10.75* (1976) 11 ETL 238, 243. France: *Cass. 27.10.75*, BT 1975.526; *Cass.com. 25.6.91*, BTL 1992.4. Germany: *BGH 20.4.89*, 1989 ULR II 806. Haak, p. 253.

14. See Clarke, *CMR*, Chap. 11.

15. *BGH 6.7.79* (1980) 15 ETL 863, 869–870. Basedow, Art. 13, 24.

such as Austria,[16] Belgium[17] and France,[18] concurrent rights of action against the carrier have been recognised. A uniform basis for entitlement to sue might have been that the claimant has suffered loss caused by the carrier's breach of contract; but this solution sits uncomfortably with CMR itself, which clearly countenances actions by the consignee under Article 13 regardless of whether the consignee has suffered loss.[19] Still, although it is not the general ground of entitlement to sue, loss is relevant when a court must choose between two claimants, each with a distinct right of action: a claimant recovers only if and to the extent that that claimant has suffered loss.[20] Loss does not determine title to sue, but it does determine how much can be recovered.

1.87 Whoever is the person entitled to sue the carrier, in order to sustain a claim against the carrier, that person must commence proceedings in the usual way and then establish that the goods suffered loss, damage or delay during the carrier's period of responsibility.

3. *The period of responsibility*

1.88 The carrier is responsible for what happens to the goods, according to Article 17.1, "between the time when he takes over the goods and the time of delivery".

1.89 The carrier takes over the goods when they come into his custody and control for the purpose of carriage, although the goods not yet have begun to move physically towards the agreed place of delivery.[21] Thus when, having received the goods, the carrier loads the goods, loading is an operation for which the carrier is responsible. Indeed, if with a view to carriage the carrier first stores the goods prior to loading, the carrier is responsible for the goods during the period of storage under CMR.[22] If, however, loading is carried out by the sender, the operation of loading may commence or even be complete before the carrier takes over the goods.

1.90 The carrier delivers the goods when custody and control of the goods passes from the carrier to the right person, the designated consignee, in the right place.[23] Distinguish unloading which, if the carrier retains the goods pending collection by the consignee, occurs before delivery or which, if carried out by the consignee, occurs after delivery. On the other hand, if unloading is carried out by the consignee with the assistance of the driver, the driver acts as agent not of the carrier but the consignee; and the goods have been delivered to the consignee at the commencement of unloading.[24] If the carrier is prevented from delivery, the position is affected by Article 15 and Article 16. Moreover, if through no fault of his own the carrier is unable to find the consignee, after a reasonable time a notional delivery occurs in

16. *OGH 12.4.84*, Greiter 215, 220. Cf. *OGH 22.3.2002*, (2004) 39 ETL 79.
17. *Brussels 16.11.77* (1980) 15 ETL 319.
18. *Paris 10.2.84*, BT 1984.558.
19. In this sense, e.g., *Cass. Belge 13.6.80* (1980) 15 ETL 851, 861.
20. *BGH 10.4.74*, (1975) 10 ETL 83; *Brussels 16.11.77* (1980) 15 ETL 319, 329. Haak, p. 270.
21. Clarke, *CMR*, para. 27; Haak, p. 180; HM, para. 6.8. Cf. *Lyon 5.5.1995*, BTL 1995.451.
22. *Hoge Raad 6.4.90*, SS 1990, No. 78.
23. *OGH 6.7.1989*, VersR 1990.1180; Clarke, *CMR*, para. 37; Haak, p. 181; Loewe, para. 149. Cf. *OLG Munich 23.4.1993*, TranspR 1993.348.
24. *OGH 28.3.2000*, (2003) 38 ETL 231.

the sense that the carrier ceases to hold the goods as carrier and ceases to be liable under CMR but assumes the role and liability of a bailee at common law.[25]

4. Loss, damage and delay

1.91 Goods are lost when, although it is known where they are, they are not where they should be, for example because they have been delivered to the wrong person.[26] Goods are lost, too, when they have been destroyed or their physical condition is such that they are commercially useless to the consignee.[27] Moreover, in certain circumstances delay may be treated as total loss in accordance with Article 20.1. However, note that loss does not include constructive total loss of the kind known to English law.[28]

1.92 Damage to goods means any change in the physical condition of the goods which reduces their value.[29] This is also the meaning of damage in English law.[30]

1.93 Delay in delivery means delivery later than the time agreed (and usually but not necessarily recorded in the consignment note) or beyond a reasonable time: Article 19. The carrier is not liable for dawdling en route unless that results in delay in delivery in that sense.

(b) Defences

5. Wrongful act or neglect of the claimant; instructions of the claimant

1.94 Both the sense (meaning) and the significance of these defences, which have counterparts in other transport Conventions,[31] are less obvious than it might appear. "Neglect" implies fault but, in the mind of the drafter, so too does "wrongful".[32] In practice most relevant instances of fault on the part of the sender, notably defective packing or loading, are likely to be raised as special risks under Article 17.4. Remaining instances that might arise under Article 17.2 include sending contraband goods and understating the weight of goods.[33] However, the "claimant" might be the consignee and, in any event, "claimant" is not read literally: the carrier may plead the conduct of the sender or consignee, whether he be the claimant or not unless, it has been held,[34] the wrongful act or neglect in question is not attributable to the actual claimant.

1.95 "Instructions" can amount to a defence distinct from "wrongful act etc." only if, as suggested above, "wrongful" connotes fault. If so, "instructions" embrace

25. See Art. 16, Comment 1, paras. 1.73 to 1.74, above.
26. *BGH 27.10.1978*, NJW 1979.2473; *BGB 18.5.1945*, TranspR 1995.383.
27. *BGH 3.7.1974*, 1974 ULR II.216.
28. *ICI plc* v. *MAT Transport* [1987] 1 Lloyd's Rep. 354, 359.
29. *OGH 31.3.1982*, TranspR 1984.196; *Paris 2.10.2003*, BTL 2003.814.
30. See *Promet Engineering (Singapore) Pte Ltd.* v. *Sturge* [1997] 2 Lloyd's Rep. 146 at 151, *per* Hobhouse L.J.
31. See e.g. Art. 21.1 of MP4 and Art. 20 of MC as regards carriage by air; and, in particular, Art. 36.2 of CIM on which Art. 17 of CMR was modelled.
32. Loewe, para. 151.
33. Clarke, *CMR*, para. 70.
34. *OLG Hamburg 31.3.1994*, TranspR 1995.245.

conduct which is not blameworthy, such as erroneous instructions about the care of the goods in transit. In any event the instructions must cause loss. For example, it has been held that the instruction to take the afternoon ferry to Corsica, which meant that the goods could not be delivered until the next day, was not the cause of their theft there overnight.[35] Moreover, even where the instructions are a significant cause of loss, not surprisingly, the provision indicates that they are not the relevant, effective or proximate cause of loss where they were issued by the claimant in response to an emergency that arises from a breach of contract by the carrier.

6. *Inherent vice*

1.96 Inherent vice in the goods is a defence found in other transport Conventions, not only in Article 36 of CIM, on which CMR was modelled, but also the air Conventions such as MP4 (Article 18.3) and MC (Article 18.2). In each case the meaning of "inherent vice" is taken to be the same as that of inherent vice at common law: some defect in the goods which by its development through ordinary processes going on in those goods tends to the injury or destruction of the goods. Common examples are the effect of too much moisture[36] or too little refrigeration[37] on goods so that the goods do not survive the normal rigours of the journey in question or remain fit for their normal commercial purpose for a reasonable time after delivery.

1.97 Note, however, that, although "inherent vice" is not the same as "latent defect", a defence found in the Carriage of Goods by Sea Act 1971 (Hague-Visby Rules),[38] the carrier's general and residual duty of care under CMR is such that a defect will not avail him as a defence unless it is also a latent defect, i.e., one that he could not be expected to have noticed. If he had noticed it he would be expected to do something to put it right or minimise its effects. Compare also sensitive goods which are the subject of Article 17.4(d).

7. *Unavoidable circumstances*

1.98 This defence is the key to CMR in that the corollary of the defence is the benchmark of the general degree of care and skill required of the carrier under the CMR regime. With one exception mentioned below, circumstances, through which loss etc. occurs to the goods, are unavoidable and their consequences unpreventable only if the carrier has exercised the "utmost care" with regard to the goods in those circumstances. Utmost care is "a standard which is somewhere between, on the one hand, a requirement to take every conceivable precaution, however extreme, within the limits of the law and, on the other hand, a duty to do no more than act

35. *BGH 8.10.1998*, TranspR 1999.59. See further Clarke, *CMR*, para. 71; Glass/Cashmore, para. 3.45.

36. *Noten* v. *Harding* [1990] 2 Lloyd's Rep. 283 (C.A.).

37. *Ulster-Swift* v. *Taunton Meat Haulage* [1975] 2 Lloyd's Rep. 502, 505, affirmed [1977] 1 Lloyd's Rep. 346 (C.A.).

38. Clarke, *CMR*, para. 89a.

reasonably in accordance with current practice".[39] The carrier's duty extends not only to avoiding the incidents which are the initial cause of the loss etc. but also to mitigating the effect of loss etc. once it has been caused.[40]

The exception referred to above concerns circumstances particularly within the claimant's area of risk. A less rigorous standard, one of reasonable care in the light of current haulage practice, is expected of the carrier in such circumstances, viz. when he is responding to a threat to the goods arising from the wrongful act or neglect of the claimant himself or from certain special risks, viz., the manner of packing or loading by the sender or of unloading by the consignee.[41] *1.99*

Although the legal onus of proof is on the carrier to establish the defence, Mustill J. has suggested[42] that the claimant should propose what the carrier could and should have done to avoid the loss etc., and that it is then for the carrier to show that that was too much to expect of him in the particular circumstances. Alternatively, his defence will succeed if, although he did not exercise utmost care, the loss would have occurred anyway.[43] *1.100*

In reaching a decision the trial court considers a number of factors such as the knowledge available to the carrier (or driver) at the time (e.g. of safety measures available), the likelihood of the loss etc. (certain goods are more likely to be stolen than others), and the legal regulations governing the carriage of goods (notably permitted driving hours). Thus sometimes the expense of a second driver is justified.[44] However, whereas that is a measure that may be effective against robbery by stealth, it is not effective against robbers with guns and in such cases the carrier, who did not employ a second driver, has successfully raised the defence.[45] *1.101*

8. *Defects in the vehicle*

A vehicle is defective not only if it is unroadworthy but also if it is unfit to receive and contain goods of the kind in question in some respect for which the carrier rather than the sender is responsible.[46] This will clearly be the case if the vehicle used is not equipped in the way required by the contract.[47] In this regard a defective vehicle is like the common law concept of the unseaworthy ship.[48] The CMR *1.102*

39. *Silber* v. *Islander Trucking* [1985] 2 Lloyd's Rep. 243, 247, *per* Mustill J. See also *Cicatiello* v. *Anglo-European Ltd.* [1994] 1 Lloyd's Rep. 678. The judge in *Silber* referred *inter alia* to a decision in Austria: *OGH 29.6.1983* (1984) 19 ETL 526; Austrian courts have continued to take this line: *OGH 19.1.1994*, TranspR 1994.282. See also in this sense in Germany: *BGH 5.6.1981* (1982) 17 ETL 301; *BGH 10.4.2003*, TranspR.2003.303, (2003) 38 ETL 782. See further Clarke, *CMR*, paras. 75 *et seq.*; HM, para 6.28.

40. E.g. *Cass. France 9.10.1974*, BT 1974.491.

41. Clarke, *CMR*, para. 69b.

42. *Silber*, *loc. cit.* above.

43. *Ciciatello*, above; *OGH 19.1.1994* (above).

44. See *Silber* [1985] 2 Lloyd's Rep. 243 at 250.

45. E.g. *OLG Köln 3.12.1998*, TranspR 2000.462; *Karlsruhe 21.12.2000*, TranspR 2003.347.

46. See for example, the case of works of art being transported to an exhibition: Cass. *22.2.1994*, BTL 1994.263.

47. *OGH 13.2.2003*, TranspR 2003.311 (2004) 39 ETL 244.

48. *Stanton* v. *Richardson* (1875) 45 L.J.K.B. 78 (H.L.).

concept does not apply to the special equipment referred to in Article 18.4: if it did, the carrier's duty stated in Article 18.4 would be otiose.[49]

1.103 A defence under Article 17.2, which is advanced on the basis that the loss etc. could not be avoided on account of the defective condition of the vehicle, is thus ruled out by Article 17.3,[50] unless the defect was caused between taking over and delivery through some unavoidable circumstance *external* to the vehicle.[51] The same rule operates in a recourse action between carrier and sub-carrier.[52] Thus, in the paradigm borderline case of a bursting tyre, unless the carrier can prove that this was caused by some external agency such as vandalism and thus eliminate the more likely explanation of a defect in manufacture or mounting, the carrier is liable.[53]

1.104 As it is an exception to a defence, in principle the burden of proving the defect is on the claimant. In practice, however, it is so difficult for the carrier in a case of this kind to prove that the loss etc. was unavoidable that in practice the carrier will have to eliminate a defect in the vehicle as a cause in any case in which such a defect might have been the cause.[54]

(c) Special risks

9. Risk and proof

1.105 It is in the nature of transportation that goods are subject to risk, however, in some cases, not extraordinary cases, goods are subjected to "special" risks and thus CMR contains special rules, mainly regarding the onus of proof. Special rules for special risks are a feature of the CIM,[55] the precursor of CMR, but not of the Conventions for other modes of carriage.

1.106 A special risk is either that a greater risk of damage is an attribute of the goods in question, such as the sensitive goods dealt with in Article 17.4(d), or a risk that is normally in the carrier's risk sphere but in the particular case is in that of the sender, such as when loading and stowage are carried out not by the carrier but by the sender, the case dealt with by Article 17.4(c).

1.107 In this last case, for example, the carrier does not have to prove that one or more of the operations (of handling, loading, stowage or unloading) were carried out defectively. What the carrier must establish is that the loss etc. could have been attributed to the operation in question: Article 18.2. On this see Comment 12, below. Nonetheless if the carrier does have evidence that the operation was carried out defectively, to bring forward the evidence would be to settle the matter.

10. Open unsheeted vehicles

1.108 An open unsheeted vehicle is not only one that is open at the top but also one open at the sides, as the essence of the risk is exposure to weather and the likelihood of

49. For the meaning of special equipment, see Art. 18, Comment 2, paras. 1.122 *et seq.*, below.
50. Art. 17.3 does not affect a defence based on Article 17.4: *OLG Hamburg 27.10.1988*, VersR 1989.719.
51. *OLG Düsseldorf 18.11.1971* (1973) 8 ETL 510.
52. Cf. *Walek* v. *Chapman & Ball* [1980] 2 Lloyd's Rep. 279; Glass [1981] L.M.C.L.Q. 384.
53. *OGH 10.7.1991*, TranspR 1991.422; *Paris 29.2.2000*, BTL 2000.211.
54. See Clarke, *CMR*, paras. 75 *et seq.*; HM, paras. 6.53 *et seq.*
55. Art. 36.3.

wastage. If there is an "abnormal" wastage (shortage), however, the finger of suspicion turns back to the carrier and the possibility of theft or of a defect in the vehicle and, in particular, its fitness for the goods in question.[56]

The preconditions of relief on this ground have been applied literally. As regards party agreement, although specification in the consignment note is just one way of recording party agreement, courts have insisted on it[57]; and although there is an established trade custom of carrying motor vehicles on open transporters, evidence of such a custom is no substitute for express agreement.[58] *1.109*

11. Packing

Packing is lacking only if it is the usual trade practice to pack goods of that kind for a journey of that kind. Given the established trade custom of carrying motor vehicles on open transporters, for example, it cannot be said that vehicles thus transported lack packing.[59] *1.110*

Packing is defective if it is not such as should enable the goods in question to withstand the journey contracted for in a vehicle of the kind required by the contract.[60] Goods should not be packed on the assumption that they will be handled with kid gloves: some degree of abuse by the carrier must be expected.[61] However, the carrier does have a duty to check the packing provided by the sender for defects that might affect the safety of the public; and if it is obvious, that the sender's packing is defective in any significant sense, the carrier must bring this to the attention of the sender.[62] *1.111*

The packing in question is that which was or should have been provided for the goods of the claimant. If the claimant's goods are damaged as a result of the lack of or defective condition of packing of the goods of another sender, the latter are within the sphere of risk not of the claimant but of the carrier. Unless the carrier can establish some other defence, such as unavoidable circumstances, the carrier will be liable to the claimant and must seek recourse against the third party under Article 10. *1.112*

12. Loading and unloading

The special risk is simply that one or more of the listed operations was carried out by the sender. The CMR does not indicate whether it is the sender or the carrier who is responsible for loading: that is a matter of contract for party agreement, although what counts for the special risk, it has been held, is not who is obliged by *1.113*

56. See Comment 8, above. See also CIM, Art. 36, Comment 10, paras. 2.301 *et seq.*, below.
57. Loewe, para. 159.
58. *OLG Düsseldorf 8.5.1969* (1970) 5 ETL 446.
59. *OLG Düsseldorf 8.5.1969* (above); *Orléans 18.1.95*, BTL 1995.129. See also CIM, Art. 36, Comment 11, paras. 2.304 *et seq.*, below.
60. *Tetroc* v. *Cross-Con (International)* [1981] 1 Lloyd's Rep. 192, 199; *OGH 18.12.1984*, Greiter, p. 270. See also CIM, Art. 36, Comment 11, paras. 2.304 *et seq.*, below.
61. *Decca Radar* v. *Caserite* [1961] 2 Lloyd's Rep. 301, 308.
62. See Art. 18, Comment 1, paras. 1.119 *et seq.*, below.

contract to load but who actually does load.[63] When the operation is carried out by personnel of both sender and carrier jointly, loading is the responsibility of whichever party is in general charge and oversight of the operation.[64]

1.114 The risk is a defence for the carrier when the particular loss etc. could be attributed to that fact: Article 18.2. The implication is that the operation might have been carried out defectively and that that led to the loss etc. in question. Loading and stowage, for example, is defective if it is not such as should enable the goods in question to withstand the journey in question in a vehicle of the kind in question.[65] Often the carrier invites the court to infer, that loading or stowage was defective, from subsequent events. Courts do not do so readily. Evidence that the vehicle overturned is not likely to be enough unless there is also evidence of speed and road conditions that is not inconsistent with that possibility, so that defective loading or stowage could have been the cause.

1.115 Note that the legal effect of the inference is qualified by the duty of the carrier to check the sender's loading. If the loading is carried out by the sender, the carrier will be at least partly liable for defects in the loading that affect the safety of the vehicle and of which the carrier (in practice the driver) was or should have been aware. That apart, the carrier has no general duty to check the work.[66]

13. Sensitive goods; livestock

1.116 Sensitive goods, which have been well described as "difficult travellers",[67] are goods which are sensitive to loss or damage having regard to the journey in prospect, including the kind of vehicle contracted for and the time of year. If goods are indeed "particularly" exposed to the hazards listed, they are regarded as sensitive goods in the sense of Article 17.4(d) and do not cease to be so because it is possible to guard against these hazards. Examples include metal prone to rust,[68] perishable goods such as meat,[69] fragile goods such as glassware and even alcohol free beer, which quickly freezes in cold weather.[70]

1.117 Livestock is also a case in point but is the subject of a separate category: Article 17.4(f). One reason for separate treatment is that livestock is a special case of such long standing. However, more to the point is that it is also differentiated from the sensitive goods under Article 17.4(d) in that a defence based on the latter is conditional on performance of the carrier's duty with respect to special equipment under Article 18.4. A further distinction of a more general kind, which courts sometimes fail to make, is between goods that are sensitive in the sense of

63. *OLG Düsseldorf 25.3.1993*, TranspR 1994.439; *OGH 13.2.2003*, TranspR 2003.311.

64. *OGH 13.2.2003* (above).

65. *BGH 28.3.1985* (1986) 21 ETL 174.

66. But cf. France where such a duty has been imposed by the courts, e.g., *Cass.com. 28.3.2000*, BTL 2000.276.

67. Glass (1979) 14 ETL 687, 709.

68. *Tetroc* v. *Cross-Con (International)* [1981] 1 Lloyd's Rep. 192, 199–200.

69. *Ulster-Swift* v. *Taunton Meat Haulage* [1977] 1 Lloyd's Rep. 346 (C.A.); *Donald & Son Ltd.* v. *Continental Freeze*, 1984 S.L.T. 182.

70. *OLG Frankfurt am Main 3.12.2003*, TranspR 2004.125.

Article 17.4(d) and goods suffering from inherent vice, a ground of exoneration under Article 17.2.[71]

Article 18 *1.118*

1. The burden of proving that loss, damage or delay was due to one of the causes specified in article 17, paragraph 2, shall rest upon the carrier.

2. When the carrier establishes that in the circumstances of the case, the loss or damage could be attributed to one or more of the special risks referred to in article 17, paragraph 4, it shall be presumed that it was so caused. The claimant shall however be entitled to prove that the loss or damage was not, in fact, attributable either wholly or partly to one of these risks.

3. This presumption shall not apply in the circumstances set out in article 17, paragraph 4(a), if there has been an abnormal shortage, or a loss of any package.

4. If the carriage is performed in vehicles specially equipped to protect the goods from the effects of heat, cold, variations in temperature or the humidity of the air, the carrier shall not be entitled to claim the benefit of article 17, paragraph 4(d), unless he proves that all steps incumbent on him in the circumstances with respect to the choice, maintenance and use of such equipment were taken and that he complied with any special instructions issued to him.

5. The carrier shall not be entitled to claim the benefit of article 17, paragraph 4(f), unless he proves that all steps normally incumbent on him in the circumstances were taken and that he complied with any special instructions issued to him.

Comments

1. The burden of proof

Article 18 is concerned mainly with the burden of proof relating to defences stated in Article 17. Article 18.1 confirms the application of the usual rule, whereby "he who alleges must prove"; thus it is the carrier who must prove the standard defences specified by Article 17.2. However, Article 17.4 sets out the pattern of responsibility in the case of "special risks" and Article 18.2 states the unusual burden of proof for such cases: not that on the balance of probabilities (the usual rule) the loss etc. *is* attributable to the risk but that it *could be*. The carrier is required to establish no more than a plausible hypothesis.[1] *1.119*

If the carrier succeeds in establishing a plausible hypothesis, that will amount to a successful defence unless the claimant can rule out the hypothesis by showing that the loss etc. was not in fact attributable to the risk in question: Article 18.2 *in fine*. That he might achieve by proving (on the balance of probabilities) that it was caused by something entirely different for which the carrier was responsible. However, in many cases, the claimant will seek to show that the loss etc. or part of it was attributable to a breach of the carrier's residual duty of care[2] as regards the way in which the carrier did or not respond to the incidence of the special risk. *1.120*

Defective packing, for example, is a special risk: Article 17.4(b). The carrier is not obliged to check the sender's packing unless the nature of the packing or of the *1.121*

71. See CIM, Art. 36, Comment 6, paras. 2.288 *et seq.*, below; Clarke, *CMR*, para. 89; and HM, paras. 6.95 *et seq.*

1. *Ulster-Swift* v. *Taunton Meat Haulage* [1975] 2 Lloyd's Rep. 502, 506; affirmed [1977] 1 Lloyd's Rep. 346 (C.A.); Clarke, *CMR*, para. 77; Glass/Cashmore, para. 3.48.

2. See Art. 17, Comment 1, paras. 1.78 *et seq.*, above, and Comment 7, paras. 1.98 *et seq.*, above.

goods is such as to endanger other goods or the public at large. If it is or should be evident to the carrier that the sender's packing is defective, the carrier must bring this to the attention of the sender if possible. If that is not possible, the carrier must either refuse to take the goods or take any viable steps to cure the defect, except in the unlikely event that it is clear anyway that the sender wishes to take the risk of having the goods transported as they are. The carrier must also do what he reasonably can to cure defects that become apparent en route.[3] Broadly speaking, the same is also true of the special risks stated in Article 17.4(c).[4] In France the Court of Cassation has decided simply that the carrier who is or should be aware of defective stowage on the part of the sender cannot plead Article 17.4(c).[5] An English court, however, is likely to see failure by the carrier as the operation of the second sentence of Article 18.2 to be categorised as breach of the carrier's residual duty of care.

2. *Special equipment*

1.122 If the carrier pleads the sensitive nature of the goods, a special risk under Article 17.4(d), indeed it is for the carrier to prove that, if the vehicle was fitted with special equipment to protect the goods, it was in accordance with Article 18.4. Special equipment means not supplementary equipment but equipment "to protect the goods from the effects of heat, cold, variations in temperature or the humidity of the air", including, it has been held in France, mere tarpaulins. Such things, however, are squarely in the carrier's sphere of risk as haulier and, it is submitted, the view taken by the English court in *Walek* v. *Chapman & Ball*,[6] that a tilt cover is not special equipment but part of the vehicle in the sense of Article 17.3, for which the carrier is strictly liable, is to be preferred. Tarpaulins are not "special" enough, and the drafter seems to have had his mind fixed on equipment such as refrigeration.[7]

1.123 The level of duty imposed on the carrier is not clear. Some statements suggest a rather strict duty,[8] whereas others suggest something less strict[9] for special equipment—which is also the inference of the strict terms of Article 17.3 concerning defects in the vehicle: otherwise it is not obvious why CMR contains both provisions. The general context suggests a duty in line with if not part of the residual duty of "utmost care".[10] This, however, may be thought too onerous for the carrier and there are some grounds for the argument that the level in Article 18.5 is no

3. Clarke, *CMR*, para. 84.
4. *OGH 6.3.1991*, TranspR 1991.424; Clarke, *CMR*, paras. 86–87.
5. *Cass. 1.12.92* (1993) 28 ETL 618.
6. [1980] 2 Lloyd's Rep. 279, 283.
7. See further, Glass [1981] L.M.C.L.Q. 384; Chao, Theunis, pp. 114–115.
8. E.g. *Ulster-Swift* v. *Taunton Meat Haulage* [1975] 2 Lloyd's Rep. 502, 507, affirmed [1977] 1 Lloyd's Rep. 346 (C.A.).
9. E.g. *Centrocoop Export-Import S.A.* v. *Brit European Transport* [1984] 2 Lloyd's Rep. 618, 626.
10. In this sense *OGH 22.11.1984*, Greiter, pp. 253, 260. As to the residual duty, see Clarke, *CMR*, para. 79 and Comment 1, above. For discussion of cases on this, see Chao, Theunis, pp. 113 *et seq.*; Clarke, *CMR*, para. 89b(ii); Haak, pp. 168 *et seq.*

more than one of reasonable care in the light of current haulage practice.[11] Doubt persists.

Article 19 *1.124*

Delay in delivery shall be said to occur when the goods have not been delivered within the agreed time-limit or when, failing an agreed time-limit, the actual duration of the carriage having regard to the circumstances of the case, and in particular, in the case of partial loads, the time required for making up a complete load in the normal way, exceeds the time it would be reasonable to allow a diligent carrier.

Comments

Article 19 defines delay in delivery. Where a claimant against the carrier seeks to establish delay as a breach of contract by the carrier, the claimant must prove either that the time taken by the carrier exceeded the agreed time limit or, if there was no such agreement, that the time actually taken was unreasonably long. *1.125*

As regards an agreed limit, evidence of the agreement is required by Article 6.2(f) to be recorded in the consignment note. However, if it is not entered in the note, according to Article 4 the agreement is valid nonetheless and may be proved by any means.[1] In one case, for example, where a service was advertised as "express" but the carriage in question took several weeks, the court found that the case against the carrier had been made.[2] Where the time limit is more precise, the claimant can resort to Article 20 and the 30-day period to establish breach of the agreement. Once that is the case, the carrier's breach of contract is presumed and, moreover, the goods are treated as lost rather than merely delayed and the potential liability of the carrier is higher. It is then for the carrier to defend, for example under Article 17.2, by pointing to delays on the road as "unavoidable circumstances"—a more difficult burden of proof, as it is not enough that the carrier has acted reasonably.[3] *1.126*

As regards a reasonable time to perform the contract, that is a question of fact and a fact of life in the haulage industry is that carriers may have to load at more than one place to complete the load. This factor is mentioned in Article 19 to avoid doubt. Other circumstances, to which an English court is likely to have regard, include the nature of the goods, the type of vehicle, the permitted driving hours, the road conditions and any proper instructions given to the carrier by the sender. Road conditions may include not only severe weather problems but also difficulties posed by social and political instability in the areas through which the transport had to be undertaken.[4] *1.127*

11. Clarke, *CMR*, para. 91.
1. Hardingham [1979] L.M.C.L.Q. 193.
2. *Paris 25.3.1994*, BTL 1994.389.
3. See Art. 17, Comment 7, paras. 1.98 *et seq.*, above.
4. *CA Trento 21.5.98* (1999) 32 ETL 380

1.128 **Article 20**

1. The fact that goods have not been delivered within thirty days following the expiry of the agreed time-limit, or, if there is no agreed time-limit, within sixty days from the time when the carrier took over the goods, shall be conclusive evidence of the loss of the goods, and the person entitled to make a claim may thereupon treat them as lost.

2. The person so entitled may, on receipt of compensation for the missing goods, request in writing that he shall be notified immediately should the goods be recovered in the course of the year following the payment of compensation. He shall be given a written acknowledgment of such request.

3. Within the thirty days following receipt of such notification, the person entitled as aforesaid may require the goods to be delivered to him against payment of the charges shown to be due on the consignment note and also against refund of the compensation he received less any charges included therein but without prejudice to any claims to compensation for delay in delivery under article 23 and, where applicable, article 26.

4. In the absence of the request mentioned in paragraph 2 or of any instructions given within the period of thirty days specified in paragraph 3, or if the goods are not recovered until more than one year after the payment of compensation, the carrier shall be entitled to deal with them in accordance with the law of the place where the goods are situated.

Comment

1.129 The purpose of Article 20 is that the parties, especially the consignee, know where they stand although they may not know what has happened to the goods or when they will be delivered. In this situation the goods are treated as lost rather than merely delayed. For this purpose lost means lost to the consignee and includes the case of goods which have been neither mislaid or destroyed but, for example, delivered to the wrong person.[1] Further, if goods damaged en route are not delivered to the consignee, but are sent back to the sender and it is uncertain whether they can or will be repaired, they can be treated as lost under Article 20, even if the action in respect of total loss is brought against the carrier not by the consignee but by the sender.[2]

1.130 The effect is that a breach of contract by the carrier has been established or at least presumed[3]; and that, as the goods are treated as lost rather than merely delayed the upper limit of recoverable compensation is the value of the goods subject to a unit limit (Article 23.3) rather than the amount of the carriage charges (Article 23.5). Moreover, the date of commencement for the limitation period is different (Article 32.1). The effect is also to allow the claimant to elect later to refund compensation and take possession of the goods[4]: Article 20.3.

1.131 **Article 21**

Should the goods have been delivered to the consignee without collection of the "cash on delivery" charge which should have been collected by the carrier under the terms of the contract of carriage, the carrier shall be liable to the sender for compensation not exceeding the amount of such charge without prejudice to his right of action against the consignee.

1. *BGH 27.10.1978*, NJW 1979.2473.
2. Cf. *BGH 3.7.1974*, 1974 ULR II.216.
3. Whether the fact is rebuttable has been debated: Haak, p. 202.
4. Goods only; not the proceeds of their sale: *OLG Düsseldorf 26.3.1997*, TranspR 1998.32.

Comments

Article 21 states the liability of the carrier for having delivered the goods to the consignee without collection of a COD charge, which he contracted to collect. *1.132*

Charges include not only charges incidental to the movement of the goods but also a debt (such as the purchase price of the goods) owed by the consignee (as buyer) to the sender (as seller).[1] Cash is not defined and reference is made to national law.[2] It might appear to be a clear enough concept in commercial practice but courts in Germany have held that cash does not include commercial paper[3] whereas the more general view is that it refers to any form of payment.[4] *1.133*

Contractual obligations such as collection are required to be mentioned in the consignment note: Article 6.2. Failure to mention such matters does not in general invalidate the contract: Article 4. However, in so far as the consignee's duty to pay a charge is based on CMR, it has been held in Germany to be a duty (apparently limited by Article 13.2) to pay only charges "shown to be due on the consignment note".[5] This interpretation might suggest the unfortunate conclusion that the carrier may be liable to the sender for failing to extract from the consignee a charge, which the consignee is not obliged by CMR to pay; however, that has been denied by a court in Belgium.[6] *1.134*

If the carrier fails to collect the charge, the carrier is liable to the sender for compensation assessed not under Article 23 but under Article 21 as "not exceeding the amount of such charge". However, being nonetheless part of Chapter IV of CMR, liability under Article 21 is affected by other provisions of Chapter IV and it as been held, on the one hand, that a carrier in breach is liable to pay interest under Article 27 but, on the other hand, that the claimant cannot resort to national law to recover compensation not recoverable under CMR.[7] If the carrier endeavours to perform his contract and collect the charge but the consignee does not pay, performance of the contract of carriage has been prevented and the situation is governed by Article 15. *1.135*

Article 22 *1.136*

1. Where the sender hands goods of a dangerous nature to the carrier, he shall inform the carrier of the exact nature of the danger and indicate, if necessary, the precautions to be taken. If this information has not been entered in the consignment note, the burden of proving, by some other means, that the carrier knew the exact nature of the danger constituted by the carriage of the said goods shall rest upon the sender or the consignee.

2. Goods of a dangerous nature which, in the circumstances referred to in paragraph 1 of this article, the carrier did not know were dangerous, may, at any time or place, be unloaded, destroyed or rendered harmless by the carrier without compensation; further, the sender

1. *Eastern Kayam Carpets* v. *Eastern United Freight*, 6 December 1983, unreported.
2. See e.g. Benjamin, Chap. 9–026 *et seq.*
3. E.g. *OLG Hamburg 18.4.1991*, TranspR 1991.297.
4. Clarke, *CMR*, para. 39a; HM, paras. 7.32 *et seq.*; in this sense in France: *Cass. 6.6.1995*, BTL 1995.474.
5. *OLG Hamm 12.11.1973*, 1974 ULR II.212.
6. *Ghent 13.9.1995* (1997) 32 ETL 602.
7. *BGH 10.10.1991* (1992) 27 ETL 260.

shall be liable for all expenses, loss or damage arising out of their handing over for carriage or of their carriage.

Comments

1. Dangerous goods

1.137 Article 22 contains for the carrier what amounts to a defence of necessity in respect of dangerous goods. Some dangerous goods may also be classified as sensitive goods under Article 17.4(d), but obviously some are not; the defence provided for by Article 22 is in addition to the defences provided for by Article 17.

1.138 Goods are "of a dangerous nature" if, in the context of *normal* carriage by road, they are a source of immediate physical danger to people or to property.[1] Thus they are goods which are inherently dangerous rather than goods which become dangerous, as could be the case of most goods that are insecurely loaded for example.[2] Moreover, the danger must be to property other than the vehicle and its load.[3] The ADR offers a convenient but non-exhaustive list of dangerous goods.[4] ADR also sets standards for the way in which such goods are carried.[5]

1.139 Article 22 was modelled on Article IV, Rule 6, of the Hague Rules[6] and the scheme is not to rule out dangerous goods so that they will be subject to a special regime, but that the usual CMR regime applies as long at the carrier knows what he has taken on. Information is critical; nonetheless, it may well be enough that the dangerous nature of the goods is apparent from the information that the sender enters when completing the consignment note: Article 6.1(f) and Article 6.3. Further, a degree of knowledge both of the potential for danger of certain goods,[7] as well as the significance of marks and abbreviations,[8] can be expected of a professional carrier. However, the carrier is not obliged to make any special inspection of the goods when taking them over, in the absence of a trade custom to the contrary or of patent evidence that all is not well.[9]

2. Responding to danger

1.140 When the carrier was not initially aware of the danger posed by the goods but becomes aware of the danger while in charge of the goods, Article 22.2 entitles the carrier to unload or destroy the goods or render them harmless without compensating anyone with an interest in the goods, *semble* whether or not that person is the sender: if it is the consignee, the consignee must look to the sender for compensation.

1. Loewe, para. 186; see also *The Giannis NK* [1998] A.C. 605.
2. HM, para. 8.1.
3. *OLG Düsseldorf 23.1.1992*, TranspR 1992.218.
4. *Ibid.*
5. See the Carriage of Dangerous Goods and Use of Transportable Pressure Equipment Regulations 2004 (S.I. 2004/568), which came into force on 10 May 2004.
6. Carriage of Goods by Sea Act 1971, Sched.
7. E.g. cigarette lighters: *Cass. France 20.6.1978*, BT 1978.468.
8. *BGH 16.10.1986*, VersR 1987.304.
9. See Art. 18, Comment 1, paras. 1.119 *et seq.*, above.

The carrier does not have an entirely free hand. The measures should be taken in the light of an overriding concern with the public safety but without ignoring altogether the contractual duty to the goods' interest. In less serious cases the carrier may be obliged to seek instructions under Article 14. The sender is liable for the cost of whatever measures are taken by the carrier in response to the danger. If those measures are totally unreasonable, it is likely that a tribunal would relieve the sender of liability by resort to basic ideas of causation. *1.141*

In addition to liability for costs, the sender is liable to the carrier for "damage", which apparently means damage of any kind, including damage to the vehicle.[10] Moreover, although under Article 22.2 the sender is liable to the carrier but not, it seems, to other senders whose goods have been affected, they may have a direct action in tort; otherwise they are likely to be able to recover from the carrier who will then have recourse against the sender responsible. Finally, the sender's liability is without the unit limit on the amount of liability under Article 23. Article 23 does not apply as it is concerned only with the liability of the carrier. *1.142*

Article 23 *1.143*

1. When, under the provisions of this Convention, a carrier is liable for compensation in respect of total or partial loss of goods, such compensation shall be calculated by reference to the value of the goods at the place and time at which they were accepted for carriage.

2. The value of the goods shall be fixed according to the commodity exchange price or, if there is no such price, according to the current market price, or, if there is no commodity exchange price or current market price, by reference to the normal value of goods of the same kind and quality.

3. Compensation shall not, however, exceed 8.33 units of account per kilogram of gross weight short.

4. In addition, the carriage charges, Customs duties and other charges incurred in respect of the carriage of the goods shall be refunded in full in case of total loss and in proportion to the loss sustained in case of partial loss, but no further damages shall be payable.

5. In the case of delay, if the claimant proves that damage has resulted therefrom the carrier shall pay compensation for such damage not exceeding the carriage charges.

6. Higher compensation may only be claimed where the value of the goods or a special interest in delivery has been declared in accordance with articles 24 and 26.

7. The unit of account mentioned in this Convention is the Special Drawing Right as defined by the International Monetary Fund. The amount mentioned in paragraph 3 of this Article shall be converted into national currency of the state of the court seised of the case on the basis of the value of that currency on the date of the judgment or the date agreed by the parties.

Comments

1. Compensation: the scope of Article 23

Article 23.1 and Article 23.2 establish methods of calculating the amount of the carrier's liability in the case of total or partial loss of goods. These provisions must be read with Article 25, which does the same for the case of damage to goods, and with Article 27, concerning the payment of interest. The loss in question is "loss of *1.144*

10. *BGH 16.10.1986*, VersR 1987.304; however, decisions in Belgium have denied recovery in such a case: see Clarke, *CMR*, para. 73a.

goods". From this it has been inferred that the carrier is only liable for consequential loss, such as loss of commercial profit, in certain cases: when there is (a) a declaration of special interest under Article 27; (b) wilful misconduct on the part of the carrier in accordance with Article 29; (c) a claim to recover charges under Article 23.4; or (d) a claim based on delay under Article 23.5

1.145 Article 23.5 deals with "damage" resulting from delay, which has been distinguished from the physical damage governed by Article 25 and has been interpreted as (purely) financial damage, such as lost profit[1] or the sender's liability to the consignee under their contract of sale.[2] If delay causes physical deterioration in the goods, that has been regarded not as a case of delay under Article 23.5 but as a case of damage governed by Article 25.[3]

2. *The value of goods*

1.146 Under Article 23.1 compensation is calculated by reference to the value of the goods at the place and time at which they were accepted for carriage, i.e., when they were taken over.[4] *Ceteris paribus* the court will accept as the value of the goods the amount stated in the sender's invoice to the consignee,[5] unless it is clear that the figure is insufficiently related to the value of the goods.[6] If the invoice price contains an element for carriage charges, which may be the subject of a distinct claim under Article 23.4, it will be accepted only with an appropriate deduction for that element.[7] In other cases reference will be made to the market, if any, at the place of acceptance.[8]

3. *Limitation of liability*

1.147 Article 23.3 establishes a general ceiling on the amount of compensation payable. It must be read with Article 28, which reinforces the ceiling as regards non-CMR actions, as well as Articles 24 and 26 which remove the ceiling by agreement of the parties and Article 29 which removes it in case of wilful misconduct on the part of the carrier. In all cases the carrier is liable only to the extent that the claimant has proved actual loss of the amount claimed. CMR does not envisage punitive damages. Moreover, CMR contains a provision designed to prevent double recovery: Article 31.2; see also section 3 of the Carriage of Goods by Road Act 1965.

1.148 Article 23.3, as it now reads with reference to the units of account defined in Article 23.7, was substituted for the original text of the CMR, which referred to

1. *OGH 31.3.1982*, TranspR 1984.137 and *OGH 22.3.1994*, TranspR 1994.439; but cf. *BGH 30.9.1993*, TranspR 1994.16.
2. *Cass. France 26.6.1984*, BT 1984.610.
3. *OGH 31.3.1982*, TranspR 1984.196; *Cass. France 5.12.1989*, BT 1990.310; *BGH 15.10.92*, TranspR 2 1993.137; Clarke, *CMR*, para. 59b; HM, para. 9.44.
4. See Art. 17, Comment 3.
5. *Cass. France 7.12.1983*, BT 1984.538.
6. *BGH 15.10.1992*, TranspR 1993, 137; *OGH 13.7.1994*, TranspR 1995.285. Cf. transfer pricing between associated companies: *Cass. France 10.1.1983* (1983) 18 ETL 43.
7. *Buchanan & Co.* v. *Babco Forwarding & Shipping (UK)* [1978] A.C. 141, 151.
8. *Ibid., loc. cit.*

gold francs. The change was the result of a protocol agreed by the Inland Transport Committee of the ECE and enacted in England by section 4(2)(a) of the Carriage by Air and Road Act 1979. The limit by reference to weight includes packing and applies whether the goods are potatoes to Munich or paintings by Magritte.[9] Arbitrary as it might seem, the intention is to give the carrier a rough and ready idea of the potential liability for any one load without having to open it up or break the seals.[10]

4. Charges

The "carriage charges", are those for the journey contracted for and not, for example, the cost of returning or reforwarding damaged goods.[11] "Customs duties" are usually well understood; for example they do not include excise duty.[12] So much is clear but there is controversy about the "other charges". In some CMR countries,[13] the UK included, both return costs and excise duties chargeable because goods do not reach destination may be recovered as "other charges". *1.149*

"Other charges" have been interpreted in two ways, narrowly and broadly. The narrow interpretation, adopted by the minority of the House of Lords in *Buchanan*,[14] is that they mean charges, such as the cost of packing and insurance, incurred *for the purpose* of carriage. The broad view, preferred by the majority of the House of Lords in *Buchanan*, is that they include expenses *consequential* on the way in which the carriage was actually carried out; and hence that they include the expenses consequential on breach of the contract of carriage, such as the cost of surveying damaged goods,[15] the amount of extra duty[16] or VAT[17] payable because the goods did not reach their designated destination, and return carriage charges.[18] *1.150*

The point was revisited by the Court of Appeal in The "*Seagram*" case, *Sandeman S.A.* v. *Transitos y Transportes Integrales*.[19] The defendants agreed with the claimants, whisky manufacturers, to carry from Spain to the UK tax seals which, once affixed to the claimants' whisky bottles, indicated that the requisite Spanish excise duty had been paid. The seals were delivered to a cargo terminal in the UK where they were lost. Consequently the claimants were obliged to pay a large sum of money to the Spanish tax authorities under a guarantee of which the defendant carriers had no specific knowledge. The court held that the amount of the guarantee could not be *1.151*

9. As in *Paris 24.10.1991*, BTL 1991.783.
10. *BGH 30.1.1981* (1981) 16 ETL 455, 458.
11. *OLG Celle 29.10.98*, TranspR 1999.106.
12. *Buchanan & Co.* v. *Babco Forwarding & Shipping (UK)* [1978] A.C. 141.
13. E.g. Belgium: *Gent 10.5.2000*, (2000) 35 ETL 428; and Germany: *OLG Celle 29.10.98*, TranspR 1999.106; and *BGH 26.4.2003*, TranspR 2003.453. The latter concerned the corresonding provision (Art. 40.3) of CIM, however, the court made it clear that it took the same view of Art. 23.4 of CMR.
14. Above.
15. *ICI plc* v. *MAT Transport* [1987] 1 Lloyd's Rep. 354.
16. *Buchanan* (above).
17. *Cass. France 28.1.1975*, BT 1975.442.
18. *Thermo Engineers* v. *Ferrymasters* [1981] 1 All E.R. 1142, 1150.
19. [2003] EWCA Civ 113, [2003] Q.B. 1270.

recovered as a "charge". It distinguished *Buchanan* because, said the court,[20] the duty payable in *Buchanan* "was, as a matter of English law, an automatic consequence of the loss of the goods within the jurisdiction . . . The liability under the guarantee in this case is not a duty payable in respect of the goods carried. It is a liability arising under a guarantee that arose as a result of the inability of [the claimants] to account for the seals." The liability, said the court,[21] is "a more remote consequence of the loss of the seals than is excise duty payable on whisky that is stolen".[22]

1.152

Article 24

The sender may, against payment of a surcharge to be agreed upon, declare in the consignment note a value for the goods exceeding the limit laid down in article 23, paragraph 3, and in that case the amount of the declared value shall be substituted for that limit.

Comment

1.153 Together with Article 26, Article 24 is a provision of CMR that enables the claimant to recover loss not recoverable under the general rules of compensation in Article 23. The carrier is free to refuse to carry the goods on this basis,[1] however, if the carrier agrees to do so, it is expected but not required[2] that the carrier will make an extra charge for the extra liability. If the carrier wants to make a surcharge, it is arguable that the contract of carriage has not been finally concluded until agreement on the amount has been reached—unless perhaps performance of the contract has been commenced. In any event, in practice not much use is made of Article 24.

1.154

Article 25

1. In case of damage, the carrier shall be liable for the amount by which the goods have diminished in value, calculated by reference to the value of the goods fixed in accordance with article 23, paragraphs 1, 2 and 4.

2. The compensation may not, however, exceed:

20. At [39], *per* Lord Phillips M.R. who handed down the judgment of the court.

21. *Ibid.*

22. One must wonder why. In *Buchanan* as a direct result of the loss (by theft) of the goods the claimants were obliged (by law) to pay money (duty) to a third party (the UK tax authority). In the *Seagram* case as a direct result of the loss (cause uncertain) of the goods the claimants were obliged (by contract) to pay (guarantee) money to a third party (Spanish tax authority). As long as the goods were not recovered, the precise cause of the loss made no difference. Was the UK tax authority more likely to enforce the claimants' obligation than the Spanish tax authority? Surely not. Was the UK tax authority better placed to enforce the claimants' obligation than the Spanish tax authority? In theory, yes, but in practice not as the claimants would not wish to prejudice their future exports to Spain. So, was the *Seagram* loss really more remote? See further Clarke [2004] J.B.L. 378. See also on this and other issues raised by the case Glass 4(2) S. & T.L.I. 34 (2003).

1. Clarke, *CMR*, para. 100; Theunis, p. 105; Haak, p. 233.

2. *Paris 28.2.2001*, BTL 2001.210; Clarke, *CMR*, para. 100.

(a) if the whole consignment has been damaged the amount payable in the case of total loss[1];
(b) if part only of the consignment has been damaged, the amount payable in the case of loss of the part affected.[2]

Comment

Article 25 establishes methods of calculating the amount of the carrier's liability in the case of damage to goods. It must be read with Article 23, which does the same for the case of total or partial loss of goods, and with Article 27, which provides for the payment of interest. Damage to goods means any change in the physical condition of the goods which reduces their value.[3] It includes the case of deterioration caused by delay, which is treated not as delay governed by Article 23.5 but as damage governed by Article 25.[4] *1.155*

The liability of the carrier is measured by loss of market value rather than by the "cost of cure", i.e., repair. However, the claimant may recover "charges incurred in respect of the carriage of goods" under Article 23.4; these charges may include the cost of mitigating loss and thus to a degree the cost of salvage and repair.[5] Further, although the general rule is that a sensible commercial assessment is made of the overall loss in market value, for which the carrier is liable, an exception may be made when a damaged part can be repaired in a reasonable time; in that case the carrier is liable for the cost of the repair.[6] If, however, damage to part renders the whole less valuable, it is treated as a case of total loss.[7] If all discernible parts of a single consignment are damaged, that is also treated as a case of total loss,[8] unless it is a case of groupage and, although there is a single consignment note and just one (nominal) consignee, each part of the groupage is treated as a separate consignment.[9] *1.156*

Article 26 *1.157*

1. The sender may, against payment of a surcharge to be agreed upon, fix the amount of a special interest in delivery in the case of loss or damage or of the agreed time-limit being exceeded, by entering such amount in the consignment note.

2. If a declaration of a special interest in delivery has been made, compensation for the additional loss or damage proved may be claimed, up to the total amount of the interest declared, independently of the compensation provided for in articles 23, 24 and 25.

1. See Arts. 23.1 and 23.3.
2. *Ibid.*
3. See Art. 17, Comment 4, paras. 1.91 *et seq.*, above.
4. See Art. 23, Comment 1, paras. 1.144 to 1.145, above.
5. *OGH 21.2.1985*, Greiter, p. 285.
6. *OLG Hamburg 15.1.98*, TranspR 1998.290, 292.
7. *BGH 3.7.1974*, 1974 ULR II.216; Haak, p. 217; Loewe, para. 201. Cf. *BGH 6.2.1997*, ULR 1997, 834.
8. *BGH 30.1.1981* (1981) 16 ETL 455; *OLG Stuttgart 15.9.93*, TranspR 1994.156 Loewe, para. 202.
9. *Cass. Belgium 3.7.1976*, 1977 ULR II.220, 224; Haak, p. 216.

Comment

1.158 Together with Article 24, Article 26 is a provision of CMR that enables the claimant to recover consequential loss, notably lost profit in a market at the designated destination, which would not be recoverable under the general rules of compensation in Article 23.[1] The carrier is free to refuse to carry the goods on this basis,[2] however, if the carrier agrees to do so, it is expected but not required[3] that the carrier will make an extra charge for the extra liability. If the carrier wants to make a surcharge, it is arguable that the contract of carriage has not been finally concluded until agreement on the amount has been reached—unless perhaps performance of the contract has been commenced. Article 26 is not much used.[4]

1.159

Article 27

1. The claimant shall be entitled to claim interest on compensation payable. Such interest, calculated at five per centum per annum, shall accrue from the date on which the claim was sent in writing to the carrier or, if no such claim has been made, from the date on which legal proceedings were instituted.

2. When the amounts on which the calculation of the compensation is based are not expressed in the currency of the country in which payment is claimed, conversion shall be at the rate of exchange applicable on the day and at the place of payment of compensation.[1]

Comment

1.160 A provision such as Article 27, which provides for the claimant to recover interest on the compensation that is due, is also found, for example, in Article 47.2 of CIM (Article 37.2 of CIM 1999). In this case the right to interest runs from when the claim is sent to the carrier. A claim is a general intimation that the claimant considers the carrier to be liable, without necessarily any quantification of the complaint.[2] In the absence of a claim of this kind, the right runs from the date on which legal proceedings were instituted, in accordance with the procedural law of the forum.[3] Article 27 has been interpreted *a contrario* to mean that that is the only interest that can be awarded not only under CMR but also under national law; and, in particular, that no interest can be awarded for the period prior to the making of a claim or the institution of proceedings.[4]

1.161

Article 28

1. In cases where, under the law applicable, loss, damage or delay arising out of carriage under this Convention gives rise to an extra-contractual claim, the carrier may avail himself

1. See, however, Art. 23 Comment 4, paras. 1.149 *et seq.*, above.
2. Clarke, *CMR*, para. 100; Glockner, Theunis, p. 105; Haak, p. 233.
3. Clarke, *CMR*, para. 100; Glass/Cashmore, para. 3.66; HM, p. 200.
4. See also the Comment on Art. 23, paras. 1.144 *et seq.*, above.

1. Cf. Art. 23.7, para. 1.143, above.
2. *William Tatton & Co.* v. *Ferrymasters* [1974] 1 Lloyd's Rep. 203, 207; see also Art. 32.2, para. 1.196, below.
3. Loewe, para. 206.
4. But cf. HM, p. 204, who see this as a gap in CMR to be filled by national law.

of the provisions of this Convention which exclude his liability or which fix or limit the compensation due.

2. In cases where the extra-contractual liability for loss, damage or delay of one of the persons for whom the carrier is responsible under the terms of article 3 is in issue, such person may also avail himself of the provisions of this Convention which exclude the liability of the carrier or which fix or limit the compensation due.

Comment

The purpose of Article 28 is to preserve the CMR regime, i.e., the allocation of risk and responsibility intended under CMR.[1] A claimant should not be better served by bringing an action in tort or delict according to the *lex fori* than under CMR.[2] *1.162*

As regards the scope of Article 18, on the one hand, it extends to "loss, damage or delay arising out of carriage under this Convention". If these words were read literally, Article 28 would apply to tortious actions arising out of incidents before the goods had been taken over or after delivery and thus outside the scope of CMR, provided that there was a contract which, if performed, would have been subject as to the journey itself to CMR. This does not appear to have been the intention of the drafters, so the words quoted must be read as "loss . . . for which the carrier is liable under this Convention".[3] On the other hand, although they are not strictly speaking provisions "which exclude his liability or which fix or limit the compensation", the purpose of Article 28 suggests that the special risk provisions in Article 17.4 should be treated in the same way.[4] *1.163*

Article 29 *1.164*

1. The carrier shall not be entitled to avail himself of the provisions of this chapter which exclude or limit his liability or which shift the burden of proof if the damage was caused by his wilful misconduct or by such default on his part as, in accordance with the law of the court or tribunal seised of the case, is considered as equivalent to wilful misconduct.

2. The same provision shall apply if the wilful misconduct or default is committed by the agents or servants of the carrier or by any other persons of whose services he makes use for the performance of the carriage, when such agents, servants or other persons are acting within the scope of their employment. Furthermore, in such a case such agents, servants or other persons shall not be entitled to avail themselves, with regard to their personal liability, of the provisions of this chapter referred to in paragraph 1.

Comments

1. The significance of Article 29

This provision is of a kind found in other transport Conventions, whereby the carrier is deprived of defences under the Convention in question when in sufficiently serious breach of the contract of carriage, i.e., in the case of CMR, guilty of "wilful misconduct or . . . such default on his part as, in accordance with the law of *1.165*

1. Haak, p. 237.
2. *OGH 14.11.1984*, Greiter, p. 245.
3. *OGH 14.11.1984*, Greiter, p. 245; Clarke, *CMR*, para. 68; HM, p. 207; but cf. Loewe, para. 212.
4. Clarke, *CMR*, para. 68 but cf. HM, p. 207.

the court or tribunal seised of the case, is considered as equivalent to wilful misconduct". In English law, unlike that for example of France and Germany, there is no concept of default equivalent to wilful misconduct.[1] What counts in England is wilful misconduct, which under Article 29 has the same role but without having the same meaning as the doctrine of deviation at common law; and its inclusion in CMR is one of the arguments against the application of the common law doctrine of deviation to CMR carriage.

2. *The burden of proof*

1.166 To benefit from Article 29 the claimant must prove that the damage sustained by the claimant was caused by wilful misconduct on the part of the carrier (Article 29.1) or that of an agent or servant of the carrier (Article 29.2). "Damage" does not mean damage in the narrow sense of physical damage to the goods but includes loss and, probably, delay. Certainly, the notion of wilful misconduct has been applied to cases of loss such as theft.[2] In any event proof that the wilful misconduct caused the damage is essential.[3]

1.167 The burden of proof is the usual burden in such cases under the *lex fori* and, in England, first thoughts have been that wilful misconduct must be proved on the balance of probabilities by the claimant. In some countries, however, the usual burden of proof has been tempered. In Austria, when the sender has alleged equivalent default in respect of missing goods, because the evidence was very much in the carrier's sphere of activity, the Supreme Court has held that the underlying duty of good faith in Austrian law indicated that the carrier owed a duty of explanation, *in casu* an obligation to explain his security measures both in general and in the particular case.[4] Similar reasoning leading to a similar result can be found in Germany once the claimant has made a plausible case for the application of Article 29.[5] These decisions may well remind the English lawyer of the common law response to an allegation that a bailee is guilty of fundamental breach: "because it is quite likely that the goods were stolen by one of his servants; or delivered by a servant to the wrong address; or damaged by his reckless or wilful misconduct", if in these circumstances he "leaves the cause of damage undiscovered and unexplained", he is liable.[6] All this suggests a similar onus for a case under Article 29, however, the point has yet to come before an English court.

3. *Exclusions and limits*

1.168 According to Article 29.1, the carrier guilty of wilful misconduct loses the benefit of "provisions of this chapter which exclude or limit his liability". According to Article

1. For German law, for example, see *BGH 16.7.98*, TranspR 1999.19.
2. E.g. in England in *Texas Instruments Ltd.* v. *Nasan (Europe) Ltd.* [1991] 1 Lloyd's Rep. 146; in France in *Cass. 13.1.1981* (1981) 16 ETL 686; *Cass. 14.2.1981* (1983) 18 ETL 51; and in Germany in *BGH 14.7.1983*, 1986 ULR II.596.
3. *Longwill Corp.* v. *Merzario Ltd.*, unreported, 1995: *BGH 16.7.98*, TranspR 1999.19.
4. *OGH 14.7.1993*, TranspR 1994.189.
5. See *OLG Stuttgart 11.6.2003*, TranspR 2003.308.
6. *Levison* v. *Patent Steam Carpet Cleaning Co.* [1978] Q.B. 69, 82, *per* Lord Denning M.R. (C.A.); *The Sansei Maru* [1979] 1 Lloyd's Rep. 11 (P.C.); Palmer, pp. 1552 *et seq.*

29.2 *in fine*, agents or servants of the carrier guilty of wilful misconduct also lose the benefit of provisions of this chapter which exclude or limit their liability. Dispute has arise about the provisions affected.

1.169 In so far as Article 23.1 establishes a basis of valuation that rules out the recovery of consequential loss,[7] Article 23.1 appears to be such a provision. However, in England the Court of Appeal has taken the view[8] that, in the interests of the greatest possible uniformity and thus the least operation of purely domestic law, the effect of Article 29 should be limited strictly to the exclusion of Chapter IV provisions "excluding or limiting" the liability of the carrier, such as Article 23.4.

1.170 Consequently, it should not exclude the operation of provisions of CMR fixing the basis of liability of the carrier, such as Article 23.1 and Article 23.2 (value of goods where consigned) and Article 27 (rate of interest and rate of exchange). A similar decision has been handed down in France as regards Article 23.1[9] but a contrary decision has been given as regards Article 27 by the Supreme Court in Holland.[10] However, it is clear from the reference to provisions "which shift the burden of proof" in the first sentence of Article 29.1 that Article 29 applies to Article 17.4[11]; and in Germany the Supreme Court has held that Article 29 applies to Article 17.5 (apportionment).[12]

4. *Wilful misconduct*

1.171 Wilful misconduct is a rough translation of *dol* in the authentic French text of CMR.[13] Regrettably, perhaps, wilful misconduct has been construed in the same way as not only the equivalent provision of WC (the original version of the Warsaw Convention on carriage by air[14]) but also the identical words found in contracts of carriage by rail subject to common law. As such it means "misconduct to which the will is a party, something opposed to accident or negligence; the *mis*conduct, not the conduct, must be wilful". It includes not only a deliberate intent to inflict mischief but also recklessness whereby the actor neither knows nor cares whether mischief will result.[15]

1.172 The classic illustration is that of the driver who approaches traffic lights knowing that he cannot cross them "before the red" but does so nonetheless because he tells himself that there is unlikely to be traffic in his path at the time and place. He does not believe that a collision is likely but is aware nonetheless that he is taking a risk. That is wilful misconduct, something regarded as worse than negligence or even

7. See Art. 23, Comment 1 (paras. 1.144 to 1.145, above) and Comment 4 (paras. 1.149 *et seq.*, above).
8. *Lacey's Footwear (Wholesale) Ltd.* v. *Bowler International Freight Ltd.* [1997] 2 Lloyd's Rep. 369 (C.A.).
9. *Paris 22.4.1992*, BTL 1992.362; but this decision is wrong in the view of most French writers.
10. *HR 20.11.1998* (1999) 34 ETL 254.
11. See also the Comment on Art. 28 *in fine*, paras. 1.162 to 1.163, above.
12. *BGH 27.6.1985* (1986) 21 ETL 102.
13. McGilchrist [1977] L.M.C.L.Q. 539, 542.
14. See WC, Art. 25, below, Part 3, para. 3.350.
15. *Jones* v. *Bencher* [1986] 1 Lloyd's Rep. 54, 59; see also *Texas Instruments Ltd.* v. *Nasan (Europe) Ltd.* [1991] 1 Lloyd's Rep. 146, 154 and *Lacey's Footwear (Wholesale) Ltd.* v. *Bowler International Freight Ltd.* [1997] 2 Lloyd's Rep. 369 (C.A.) concerning the theft of goods.

gross negligence, and in such circumstances Article 29 applies. That driver is distinguished from the driver who crosses the same red light but does so because he is not paying enough attention, and does so without thinking about it; that is not wilful misconduct but negligence. In the English interpretation of wilful misconduct, the emphasis is less on the objective probability of mischief than on the state of mind of the actor. What is required is that the person concerned took a risk (a) deliberately, whether that decision made mischief objectively probable or not, and (b) wrongfully, thus excluding the case of a person who has to make a decision, perhaps a quick decision, as to the lesser of two evils.[16]

1.173 To conform to current industry practice, e.g. as regards precautions against robbery, is not a ground of exoneration under Article 17.2; however, in such a case it is most unlikely that the carrier would be found guilty of gross negligence still less of wilful misconduct.[17] On the other hand, deliberate overloading that makes the vehicle unsafe is wilful misconduct,[18] as is the deliberate use of an unsuitable vehicle to carry goods that needed to be kept cool.[19] Moreover, "a persistent failure by the owners to maintain a lorry over a period of time would clearly be wilful misconduct because everyone engaged in the transport business must know that a persistent lack of maintenance may cause the vehicle to be in a dangerous condition".[20]

5. *Agents and servants*

1.174 According to Article 29.2 the rule about wilful misconduct, stated in Article 29.1, also applies if the wilful misconduct "is committed by the agents or servants of the carrier or by any other persons of whose services he makes use for the performance of the carriage, when such agents, servants or other persons are acting within the scope of their employment". The carrier is liable for breach of the contract of carriage, whether the person instrumental in that breach is acting within the scope of that person's employment or not.[21] However, the carrier is affected by Article 29 only if it is so. Moreover, according to the last sentence of Article 29.2, the servant or agent is also liable personally in the same way as the carrier.

1.175 Examples include that of the driver who, in spite of an express prohibition from his employer, smuggles prohibited goods such as alcoholic liquor,[22] as well as the driver who drives having drunk too much alcohol.[23] Again, in areas where there is a high risk of theft the driver must stop only in a guarded parking place; if that is not possible the carrier must provide a co-driver. Failure to do so has been regarded as

16. See *Jones* v. *Bencher* [1986] 1 Lloyd's Rep. 54, 59–60; *National Semiconductors (UK) Ltd.* v. *UPS Ltd.* [1996] 2 Lloyd's Rep. 212.

17. *OLG Düsseldorf 5.7.97*, TranspR 1999, 23. For further discussion and illustration, see Clarke, *CMR*, paras. 101 *et seq.*; Haak, pp. 241 *et seq.*; and HM, pp. 208 *et seq.* Dutch decisions have been summarised (in English) by Smeele (2000) 35 ETL 329. See in particular, *HR 5.1.2001*, (2001) 36 ETL 97, 111 (in English).

18. *Brussels 21.1.1987* (1987) 22 ETL 741.

19. *OLG Hamburg 23.6.1999*, TranspR 2000.175.

20. *Alena* v. *Harlequin Transport Services* [2002] EWHC (Comm) 2461, (2003) 38 ETL 218 at [29], *per* Morison J.

21. See the Comment on Art. 3, para. 1.22, above.

22. E.g. Saudi Arabia: *BGH 27.6.1985* (1986) 21 ETL 102.

23. *OGH 10.10.1974*, Greiter, p. 37.

wilful misconduct.[24] Examples also include the driver who delivers the goods at destination without checking the identity or entitlement of the person to whom they are delivered,[25] and the driver who, on the instructions of the carrier, dumps the goods in an exposed place in order to make the vehicle available to a more favoured customer.[26]

Chapter V, Claims and actions: Article 30 *1.176*

1. If the consignee takes delivery of the goods without duly checking their condition with the carrier or without sending him reservations giving a general indication of the loss or damage, not later than the time of delivery in the case of apparent loss or damage and within seven days of delivery, Sundays and public holidays excepted, in the case of loss or damage which is not apparent, the fact of his taking delivery shall be prima facie evidence that he has received the goods in the condition described in the consignment note. In the case of loss or damage which is not apparent the reservations referred to shall be made in writing.

2. When the condition of the goods has been duly checked by the consignee and the carrier, evidence contradicting the result of this checking shall only be admissible in the case of loss or damage which is not apparent and provided that the consignee has duly sent reservations in writing to the carrier within seven days, Sundays and public holidays excepted, from the date of checking.

3. No compensation shall be payable for delay in delivery unless a reservation has been sent in writing to the carrier, within twenty-one days from the time that the goods were placed at the disposal of the consignee.

4. In calculating the time-limits provided for in this article the date of delivery, or the date of checking, or the date when the goods were placed at the disposal of the consignee, as the case may be, shall not be included.

5. The carrier and the consignee shall give each other every reasonable facility for making the requisite investigations and checks.

Comments

1. The presumption of due delivery

The claimant must prove his case against the carrier. To do this the claimant must overcome the presumption stated in Article 30.1, that the goods were delivered at destination in the same order and condition in which they were sent. That depends on how the consignee (who of course may well be the claimant) responds to any loss or damage at destination, as indicated in Article 30. An appropriate response by the consignee will assist the claimant to establish that the carrier is liable by showing the difference between the quantity or condition of the goods on take over, the focus of Articles 8 and 9, and their quantity or condition on delivery, the focus of Article 30.[1] The best response is a joint survey by consignee and carrier, as the findings are conclusive: Article 30.2. The other possibility dealt with in Article 30.1 is to send reservations to the carrier. *1.177*

24. E.g. *OLG Nuremberg 24.2.1999*, TranspR 2000.81; *OLG Köln 10.12.2002*, TranspR 2003.459; *Versaillles 30.11.2003*, BTL 2003.834.

25. *Cass. France 12.12.1989* (1991) 26 ETL 359.

26. *Versailles 14.11.96*, BTL 1997, 198; see also *OGH 17.3.1998*, TranspR 1998.361.

1. *City Vintages* v. *SCAC Transport International*, unreported 1 December 1987; Clarke, *CMR*, paras. 60 *et seq.*; HM, paras. 10.1 *et seq.*

2. Checking with the carrier

1.178 A procedure of this kind comes easily to the mind of many lawyers in civil law countries such as France because a formal confrontation to agree evidence is a feature of their procedural law. It is found in CMR because CMR was originally based on CIM,[2] which was drafted by civil lawyers, where it was included also because it was felt that railways were state institutions that could be trusted to carry out the procedure fairly. Nonetheless, Article 30.5, which has no direct forebear in CIM, requires the parties to give each other every reasonable facility for making the requisite investigations and checks. Although intended to be an application of a general duty of good faith of the kind found in the law of Germany and France, this provision has been dismissed in Belgium as "a dead letter for lack of sanctions".[3] In any case, the checking must occur soon after arrival to defeat any subsequent suggestion that the loss or damage could have occurred in the time between delivery and checking.

3. Reservations

1.179 As stated in Article 30.1, the reservations must give a general indication of the loss or damage. The degree of generality that is acceptable is a matter of disagreement. Perhaps "goods received in poor condition" is sufficient,[4] even it seems in a case of delay,[5] in so far as it alerts the carrier to the need to investigate before the evidence is lost or obscured. According to Article 30.1, in the case of non-apparent loss or damage, the reservations must be in writing and the inference is that, in the case of apparent loss or damage, they may be oral.[6] Note that, as regards delay in delivery,[7] Article 31.3 differs from Article 31.1, in that the claimant is not required to give any general indications about loss or damage: there may be none and, in any event, he may be poorly placed to supply the information.

1.180 The reservations must be in writing; writing is not defined in CMR and left to national law. In France it has been held that the reservations may be scribbled on the carrier's copy of the consignment note.[8] An English court is unlikely to disagree. In England, according to the Interpretation Act 1978, Sched. 1, writing is not required to be contained in any special document. A printed telex or fax message would also suffice. Indeed, in the opinion of the Law Commission, an e-mail message would suffice because it can be displayed on screen or printed out.[9]

1.181 As stated in Article 30.1, the reservations must be sent not later than the stated times. In the case of apparent loss or damage[10] the time is the time of delivery. In this context, the time is less a point in time than a period of time: at any time during

2. See CIM, Art. 52, Part 2, para. 2.399, below.
3. Buyl, Theunis, p. 284. Cf. *OGH 6.12.2000*, (2003) 38 ETL 236.
4. *Cass. France 29.4.1975*, 1977 ULR I.334; OGH *19.2.2002* (2004) 39 ETL 400.
5. See *OGH 19.1.2002*, TranspR 2003.243.
6. Loewe, Theunis, p. 146.
7. As regards delay, see Art. 17, Comment 4, para. 1.91, above.
8. *Cass. France 29.4.1975*, 1977 ULR I.334.
9. *Electronic Commerce: Formal Requirements in Commercial Contracts* (2001). Treitel *Law of Contract* (11th ed., 2003), Chap. 5.2.4.
10. As to what is apparent see Art. 8, Comment 3, paras. 1.42 to 1.43, above.

the operation rather than the moment of completion.[11] As the requirement is that the reservations be sent (rather than actually received) it is probably enough to give them to the driver who is not the agent of the carrier to receive them but is the proper agent to communicate them to his employer, the carrier. In the case of loss or damage which is not apparent the time is within seven days of delivery, Sundays and public holidays at the place of delivery[12] excepted. In the case of delay, it is within 21 days from the time that the goods were (not delivered but) placed at the disposal of the consignee. Thus, if the consignee refuses delivery, the period runs from the time that the goods were tendered to the consignee.[13]

4. The effect of reservations

Failing (a joint survey or) reservations, the presumption discussed in Comment 1 arises in favour of the carrier. However, in English law the impact of unilateral reservations is slight anyway. If the claimant does not send reservations, as they are not exclusive evidence and the absence of reservations does not bar a claim, the claimant can bring other evidence of the state of the goods at the time of delivery.[14] If the claimant does send reservations, they do little to advance the claimant's case that the goods were short or damaged at destination: the allegation must still be proved, by whatever means available. However, as regards delay in delivery, as the language of Article 31.3 is stronger than that of Article 31.1, the conclusion has been drawn that, in the absence of reservations, the right of action has been lost.[15] *1.182*

Moreover, in all cases, as notice to the carrier that the customer is dissatisfied, the sending of reservations does serve the purpose of alerting the carrier to the possibility of a claim and the desirability of conducting an investigation before evidence disappears and the trail becomes "cold". *1.183*

Article 31 *1.184*

1. In legal proceedings arising out of carriage under this Convention, the plaintiff may bring an action in any court or tribunal of a contracting country designated by agreement between the parties and, in addition, in the courts or tribunals of a country within whose territory
   (a) the defendant is ordinarily resident, or has his principal place of business, or the branch or agency through which the contract of carriage was made, or
   (b) the place where the goods were taken over by the carrier or the place designated for delivery is situated and in no other courts or tribunals.

2. Where in respect of a claim referred to in paragraph 1 of this article an action is pending before a court or tribunal competent under that paragraph, or where in respect of such a claim a judgment has been entered by such a court or tribunal no new action shall be started between the same parties on the same grounds unless the judgment of the court or tribunal before which the first action was brought is not enforceable in the country in which the fresh proceedings are brought.

11. See Art. 17, Comment 3, paras. 1.88 *et seq.*, above.
12. Loewe, para. 225.
13. *OGH 19.1.2002*, TranspR 2003.243.
14. *Cass. France 19.6.1968*, BT 1968.315; *Cass. Belgium 7.6.1974* (1975) 10 ETL 68; *BGH 14.11.1991*, TranspR 1992.135, 138. Cf., however, the stronger language of Art. 30.3.
15. *BGH 14.11.1991*, TranspR 1992.135, 138. See also *OGH 19.1.2002*, TranspR 2003.243, 244.

3. When a judgment entered by a court or tribunal of a contracting country in any such action as is referred to in paragraph 1 of this article has become enforceable in that country, it shall also become enforceable in each of the other contracting States, as soon as the formalities required in the country concerned have been complied with. The formalities shall not permit the merits of the case to be re-opened.

4. The provisions of paragraph 3 of this article shall apply to judgments after trial, judgments by default and settlements confirmed by an order of the court, but shall not apply to interim judgments or to awards of damages, in addition to costs against a plaintiff who wholly or partly fails in his action.

5. Security for costs shall not be required in proceedings arising out of carriage under this Convention from nationals of contracting countries resident or having their place of business in one of those countries.

Comments

1. The scope of Article 31

1.185 Article 31 is the provision of CMR which, together with Article 39.2 for recourse actions between successive carriers, deals with jurisdiction. The domestic rules on jurisdiction take effect subject to any relevant statutory provisions and hence subject to those of CMR.[1] The Civil Jurisdiction and Judgments Act 1982, which gives effect to the Brussels Convention on Jurisdiction and the Enforcement of Judgments in Civil and Commercial Matters 1968, does not apply.[2] The same is true of E.C. Regulation No. 44/2001.[3] Jurisdiction in matters arising out of CMR carriage can be founded only on Article 31 or Article 39.2.[4] However, in theory the English court might still decline jurisdiction in such a case on the common law ground of *forum non conveniens*.[5]

1.186 If the carriage is one to which CMR applies, the balance of opinion is that Article 31 applies whether the precise dispute is governed by the substantive rules of CMR or not.[6] If the carriage is one to which CMR would have applied, if the goods had been taken over by the carrier, one view is that, as CMR does not apply as intended, CMR and hence Article 31 do not apply.[7] Moreover, on the one hand, Article 31.1 provides that, in legal proceedings arising out of carriage under CMR, the jurisdiction of the courts specified is exclusive. On the other hand, however, the proceedings must arise out of the substantive rules of CMR concerning the liability of the parties to the contract. The arguable corollary, is that exclusivity does not apply to disputes about jurisdiction and over whether Article 31 applies at all.[8]

1. *Arctic Electronics Co. (UK) v. McGregor Sea & Air Services* [1985] 2 Lloyd's Rep. 510.
2. *Supreme Court of Denmark 10.9.2003, 517/2001,* (2004) 39 ETL 74.
3. *OGH 13.12.2002,* (2003) 38 ETL 656; *OGH 7.1.2003,* (2003) 38 ETL 658.
4. *Harrison & Sons Ltd. v. R.T. Stewart Transport Ltd.* (1993) 28 ETL 747. See also *OGH 18.12.2000,* (2003) 38 ETL 354; *BGH 27.2.2003,* (2003) 38 ETL 652.
5. Cf. Glass [1984] L.M.C.L.Q. 30, 39.
6. Loewe, paras. 235 and 238; Thume, p. 708; but cf. Haak, pp. 278–279.
7. *OGH 12.6. 2001,* (2003) 38 ETL 357. In this sense: HM, para. 10.25; Loewe, Theunis, p. 148; but cf. Clarke, *CMR*, para. 46b; Haak, p. 281.
8. See *BGH 20.11.2003,* TranspR 2004.77.

2. The courts with jurisdiction

The courts (or tribunals) with jurisdiction are as set out below. Only courts in category (a) are required to be in a contracting country; however, even as regards courts in the other categories, the claimant may prefer a contracting country as only then are judgments enforceable in other contracting countries: Article 31.3. *1.187*

Category (a) is the court of a contracting country designated by agreement between the contracting parties; however, if they are the carrier and the sender, their agreement does not bind the consignee unless the sender was acting as the consignee's agent or the consignee had sufficient notice of the jurisdiction agreement. For the latter purpose, it may suffice that when taking delivery of the goods the consignee also takes a consignment note recording the agreement.[9] Moreover, the words "in addition" in line 4 of Article 31 rule out the possibility of an agreement that the designated jurisdiction is to be exclusive. *1.188*

Category (b) is the court of the country where the defendant is ordinarily resident. Only a natural person can have an ordinary residence.[10] Speaking of foreign corporations and the corresponding provisions (Article 28) of WC, Mustill J. once observed that sometimes the test of presence within the jurisdiction "has been expressed by asking whether the company 'resides' or 'carries on business' within the jurisdiction", and continued: "I think it unlikely that this is what was intended. International conventions of this kind tend to prescribe jurisdiction in narrow terms, on the assumption that the case where the defendant has insufficient assets to satisfy claims in any of the stipulated countries is catered for by the ready availability of enforcement in other countries which is available via the various conventions on mutual recognition of judgments."[11] *1.189*

Category (c) is the court of the country where the defendant has its principal place of business. Its principal place of business is "the centre from which instructions are given, and from which control is exercised, and the centre from which the company is managed *without any further control* except such control as every company or the directors of a company are liable to by the larger body which they represent, the share-holders of the company".[12] If the main depot is in one place but the company is managed mostly in another place, the principal place of business is the latter.[13] *1.190*

Category (d) is the court of the country in which is located the branch or agency through which the contract of carriage was made. On the one hand, some commentators have suggested that the reference to an agency rather than to an agent shows that in some sense the agency must belong to the carrier.[14] On the other hand, as in the case of airlines, times and practices have changed to accommodate contracts through agencies more distant in every sense than in the past, although more recently still on-line booking has changed the picture yet *1.191*

9. *Paris 14.11.1969*, 1970 ULC 133.

10. *Rothmans of Pall Mall (Overseas)* v. *Saudi Arabian Airlines* [1981] Q.B. 368 (C.A.).

11. *Rothmans* (above), p. 374, adding that on a wider interpretation of Art. 28 the concepts of residence and place of business are almost, if not exactly, the same.

12. *The Rewia* [1991] 2 Lloyd's Rep. 325, 334, *per* Leggatt L.J. (C.A.).

13. *Ibid.*

14. Clarke, *CMR*, para. 46b(iii); Loewe, para. 243; Thume, pp. 713–714.

further. All this suggests that today a purely literal interpretation of these words may not be satisfactory.

1.192 Categories (e) and (f) are the courts of the country where the goods were taken over by the carrier or where they were to be delivered.[15] If the action is brought against a sub-contractor effecting carriage on a stage other than the first stage, take over occurs nevertheless in the place where the goods were taken over for the first stage.[16] The designated place of delivery is that stated in the consignment note, in accordance with Article 6.1, even though the goods and the vehicle never arrive there, for example, because they have been destroyed by fire en route.[17] However, if in exercise of the right of disposal under Article 12 the place of delivery is changed, the designated place is the new place of delivery.[18]

3. *Lis pendens*

1.193 Article 31.2 concerns actions started when an action is already pending before a court or tribunal competent under Article 31.1, or where in respect of such a claim a judgment has been entered by such a court or tribunal. According to Rix L.J in *Andrea Merzario* v. *Leitner*,[19] for the purposes of Articles 21 and 22 of the Brussels Convention 1968, an action is "pending" in English law only from the date of service of a claim form. He concluded that, in order to do justice in an international context, the same rule should apply to Article 31.2 of CMR. This conclusion was reinforced, in his view, by the language of Article 31.2 which draws a distinction "between the concept of an action being pending . . . and the concept of an action being started"[20]; and by the continental understanding of *lis pendens* apparent from decisions such as *Zelger* v. *Salinitri*.[21]

1.194 In such a case Article 31.2 provides that no new action shall be started between the same parties on the same grounds. These words should be read in the light of the corresponding words in the French text, "pour la même cause".[22] In *Andrea Merzario* v. *Leitner*,[23] Chadwick L.J. and Sir Andrew Morritt, V.-C. (Rix L.J. dissenting) took the view that there was no good reason "for restricting the application of art. 31(2) to cases where the claims in both the pending action and the proposed new action are claims for substantive relief". Claims "for declarations of non-liability are common in continental jurisdictions [and] it must have been intended to include them".[24] It was unnecessary for the Court of Appeal to decide

15. For the meaning of take over and delivery, see Art. 17, Comment 3, paras. 1.88 *et seq.*, above. See also *Cummins Engine Co.* v. *Davis Freight Forwarding (Hull)* [1981] 2 Lloyd's Rep. 402, 409 (C.A.).
16. *OGH 1.4.99*, TranspR 2000.34.
17. *Paris 24.10.1991*, BTL 1991.779; *Cass. Civ. 20.12.2000*, BTL 2001.54; *BGH 18.12.2003*, TranspR 2004.169.
18. *OLG Hamburg 7.4.1994*, TranspR 1995.115.
19. [2001] 1 Lloyd's Rep. 490, 500 at [47] (C.A.) bearing in mind the decision in *Dresser UK Ltd.* v. *Falcongate Freight Management Ltd.* [1992] Q.B. 502 (C.A.).
20. At [48].
21. Case 129/83 [1984] E.C.R. 2397 (para. 50). On this point Chadwick L.J. and Sir Andrew Morritt, V.-C. agreed.
22. HM, para. 10.39; Loewe, Theunis, p. 152.
23. Above.
24. At [96], *per* Chadwick L.J.

the point but it is one of importance and had been fully argued in that case.[25] In contrast, it has been strongly argued in Germany that exclusivity does not apply to disputes about jurisdiction and over whether Article 31 applies at all.[26]

4. The enforcement of judgments

In England the enforcement of judgments entered and enforceable in another CMR State, the subject of Article 31.3, is governed by the Foreign Judgments (Reciprocal Enforcement) Act 1933: Carriage of Goods by Road Act 1965, s.4. Although arbitration awards are not enforceable as such, a judgment entered and enforceable abroad (in a contracting State) in respect of an arbitration award is enforceable like any other judgment, with the qualification set out in Article 31.4. In particular, the reference there to "awards of damages" is understood to be a reference to awards of damages that might be made against a claimant for vexatious litigation. *1.195*

Article 32 *1.196*

1. The period of limitation for an action arising out of carriage under this Convention shall be one year. Nevertheless, in the case of wilful misconduct, or such default as in accordance with the law of the court or tribunal seised of the case, is considered as equivalent to wilful misconduct, the period of limitation shall be three years. The period of limitation shall begin to run:

(a) in the case of partial loss, damage or delay in delivery, from the date of delivery;
(b) in the case of total loss, from the thirtieth day after the expiry of the agreed time-limit or where there is no agreed time-limit from the sixtieth day from the date on which the goods were taken over by the carrier;
(c) in all other cases, on the expiry of a period of three months after the making of the contract of carriage.

The day on which the period of limitation begins to run shall not be included in the period.

2. A written claim shall suspend the period of limitation until such date as the carrier rejects the claim by notification in writing and returns the documents attached thereto. If a part of the claim is admitted the period of limitation shall start to run again only in respect of that part of the claim still in dispute. The burden of proof of the receipt of the claim, or of the reply and of the return of the documents, shall rest with the party relying upon these facts. The running of the period of limitation shall not be suspended by further claims having the same object.

3. Subject to the provisions of paragraph 2 above, the extension of the period of limitation shall be governed by the law of the court or tribunal seised of the case. That law shall also govern the fresh accrual of rights of action.

4. A right of action which has become barred by lapse of time may not be exercised by way of counter-claim or set-off.

Comments

1. The scope of Article 32

Article 32 concerns the time within which a claim must be brought against a carrier under the contract of carriage. The claimant must be one entitled to bring an action *1.197*

25. At [80], *per* Chadwick L.J. On this point the decision in *Frans Maas Logistics (UK) Ltd.* v. *CDR Trucking B.V.* [1999] 2 Lloyd's Rep. 179 was considered but not followed.

26. *BGH 20.11.2003*, TranspR 2004.77.

against the carrier.[1] The action must be one "arising out of carriage" under CMR, whether the action is based in contract, tort[2] or restitution.[3] Although the liability of a carrier who has failed to take over the goods is not governed by CMR, the better view, it is submitted, is that Article 32 does apply to an action in such a case.[4]

1.198 The limitation period fixed by Article 32.1 is short—normally one year but three years in the case of wilful misconduct—in order to promote certainty in the haulage industry.[5] Read literally and in isolation, wilful misconduct leads to the three-year period whether such conduct by the carrier had caused the loss or damage in question or not. However, the words must be read in the context of CMR as a whole. The wilful misconduct is that envisaged by Article 29, from which it is clear that wilful misconduct counts only if the loss or damage in question was caused by the wilful misconduct.[6]

1.199 Article 32.1 refers also to "such default as in accordance with the law of the court or tribunal seised of the case, is considered as equivalent to wilful misconduct". However, whether the point arises under Article 29 or Article 32, in English law, unlike that for example of France and Germany, there is a concept of wilful misconduct but no concept of default "considered as equivalent to wilful misconduct".

2. The period

1.200 The commencement date is fixed by Article 32.2. For (a) a case of partial loss, damage[7] or delay[8] in delivery[9] it is the date of delivery. For (b) a case of total loss it is the thirtieth day after the expiry of the agreed time-limit[10] or, where there is no agreed time-limit, the sixtieth day from the date on which the goods were taken over[11] by the carrier. For (c), other cases not falling within (a) or (b), it is three months after the contract of carriage was concluded. Note that "total loss" refers to total loss of the goods the subject of a particular contract of carriage, although other goods grouped in the same vehicle may have been delivered.[12]

1.201 Other cases subject to rule (c) include (i) claims by the carrier for carriage charges[13] or for damages[14]; and (ii) any claims against the carrier which are not within rule (a) because there has been no delivery of the goods. It also includes cases

1. *OGH 10.11.1981*, Greiter, p. 108.
2. *Shell Chemicals UK Ltd.* v. *P & O Roadtanks Ltd.* [1993] 1 Lloyd's Rep. 114; [1995] 2 Lloyd's Rep. 297 (C.A.); *OGH 14.1.1976*, 1976 ULR II.366; *BGH 27.10.78*, NJW 1979.2473; *OGH 22.2.1990*, TranspR 1992.357; but cf. *BGH 18.2.1972*, 1973 ULC 264.
3. *OLG Düsseldorf 11.7.96*, ULR 1998.202; *OLG Munich 29.9.1999*, TranspR 2000.123. See Clarke, *CMR*, para. 43a.
4. Clarke, *loc cit*; cf. Loewe, Theunis, p. 153.
5. *ICI plc* v. *MAT Transport* [1987] 1 Lloyd's Rep. 354, 360.
6. See Art. 29, Comment 2.
7. For the meaning of damage, see Art. 17, Comment 1 (paras. 1.78 *et seq.*, above) and Comment 4 (para. 1.92, above).
8. For the meaning of delay, see Art. 17, Comment 4, para. 1.93, above.
9. For the meaning of delivery, see Art. 17, Comment 3, para. 1.90, above.
10. For the meaning of agreed time-limit, see the Comment on Art. 19, para. 1.126, above.
11. For the meaning of taken over, see Art. 17, Comment 3, paras. 1.88 *et seq.*, above.
12. For the meaning of loss, see Art. 17, Comment 4, para. 1.91, above.
13. *Muller Batavier* v. *Laurent Transport Co.* [1977] 1 Lloyd's Rep. 411.
14. *BGH 11.12.1981* (1983) 18 ETL 63.

not within rule (b) because there has been no total loss. On this basis, the common case of goods damaged and not delivered (but abandoned, sold en route or sent back) is in this category and thus under rule (c). Although most writers take this view,[15] English decisions differ: the case has been placed under rule (b)[16] or, if the goods are returned and delivered to the sender, under rule (a),[17] or even outside Article 32 altogether.[18]

In the case of an umbrella contract for a series of transports over a period of time, it has been suggested that that too is an "other case" but that the period under rule (c) should run not from the making of the contract but from the commencement of the particular transport.[19] *1.202*

3. *Claims*

The period of limitation is suspended, in accordance with Article 32.2, when a written claim has been made. The claim must come from a person who appears to have reason to claim against the carrier, which includes a goods insurer who has indemnified his insured; alternatively it may come from someone authorised to act on the claimant's behalf.[20] *1.203*

The claim, moreover must be a claim against the carrier: Article 32.2, unlike Article 32.1, does not apply to claims *by* carriers but only to claims *against* carriers.[21] Claims by carriers may have the period prescribed by Article 32.1 suspended nonetheless, not by Article 32.2 but by rules of the *lex fori*, which were intended to apply to all CMR claims as regards any matter not regulated by CMR.[22] Thus the *lex fori* applies, for example, to the question whether claimant A can suspend the period for claimant B as regards claims arising out of the same incident.[23] *1.204*

The content of the claim must amount to a general intimation of intention to hold the carrier liable and thus be something which, in the language of Article 32.2, the carrier may wish to "reject".[24] To request proper performance[25] or to enter reservations at the time of joint survey[26] is not enough. It is not necessary, however, to make a precisely formulated claim with full details, but only to give such information as will enable the carrier to prepare to meet the claim by obtaining the *1.205*

15. See Clarke, *CMR*, para. 44a.
16. *ICI plc* v. *MAT Transport* [1987] 1 Lloyd's Rep. 354.
17. *Worldwide Carriers* v. *Ardtran International* [1983] 1 Lloyd's Rep. 61, 65.
18. *Moto Vespa* v. *MAT (Britannia Express)* [1979] 1 Lloyd's Rep. 175.
19. Wetter [1979] L.M.C.L.Q. 504, 506.
20. *Jones* v. *Bencher* [1986] 1 Lloyd's Rep. 54, 61; *Moto Vespa* v. *MAT (Britannia Express)* [1979] 1 Lloyd's Rep. 175, 180; see also *Muller Batavier* v. *Laurent Transport Co.* [1977] 1 Lloyd's Rep. 411, 415.
21. *BGH 28.2.1975* (1975) 10 ETL 523; *OGH 22.5.1978*, Greiter, p. 66.
22. *BGH 28.2.1975* (1975) 10 ETL 523, 525.
23. *BGH 24.10.1991*, TranspR 1992.177.
24. *Moto Vespa* v. *MAT (Britannia Express)* [1979] 1 Lloyd's Rep. 175. French courts have become both more specific and more demanding: *Cass.com.15.5.2001*, BTL 2001.417.
25. *Muller Batavier* v. *Laurent Transport Co.* [1977] 1 Lloyd's Rep. 411, 416.
26. *BGH 9.2.1984* (1985) 20 ETL 274.

appropriate evidence.[27] The same reason has been given[28] for the view that it is not necessary to quantify the claim[29] but there is force in the view that the carrier should be given some idea of the amount involved in order to be able to decide on an appropriate response.[30]

3. Suspension of the period of limitation

1.206 If the claim satisfies the requirements discussed in Comment 2, the effect is to suspend the period of limitation once the claim has been received by the carrier or by the carrier's agent, such as his insurer.[31] If more than one carrier has taken part in the movement, the claims must have been received by the right carrier—the one against whom the claim is made.[32] However, it has been held that, if a claim is brought against one of the parties jointly liable, that is effective to suspend the period in respect of all of them.[33] In all cases the claim has been received when it arrives at the address, postal or electronic, held out by the recipient as the address to which such communications should be sent.[34] Receipt must be proved by the claimant.

1.207 Effective suspension continues until the carrier makes the response stated in Article 32.2, viz., until the carrier rejects the claim by notification in writing and returns the documents attached to the claim. To be a rejection, the carrier's response must be such as to leave the claimant in no doubt that the claimant will have to take legal steps to enforce the claim.[35] The documents to be attached to the rejection are not documents in support of the allegation but simply the paper document(s) comprising the written claim itself, although the claimant may find it appropriate to send documents in support. If the claimant does send documents in support of the substance of the claim, it has been assumed that such documents would be original documents.[36] If so, then indeed those documents must be returned but, if copies were sent, this requirement seems unnecessary.[37] Be that as it may, the burden of proving the rejection and the return of the documents in compliance with Article 32.2, as Article 32.2 itself provides, rests on the carrier.

27. *ICI plc* v. *MAT Transport* [1987] 1 Lloyd's Rep. 354, 360; *Muller Batavier* v. *Laurent Transport Co.* [1977] 1 Lloyd's Rep. 411, 416; *OLG Munich 24.4.1992*, TranspR 1992.360; Loewe, Theunis, p. 157.

28. *Moto Vespa* v. *MAT (Britannia Express)* [1979] 1 Lloyd's Rep. 175, 180.

29. In this sense: *OGH 29.8.1994*, TranspR 1995.111; *OLG Karlsruhe 28.9.2001*, TranspR 2004.33.

30. Glass/Cashmore, para. 3.72; Loewe, Theunis, p. 157. In this sense see *OLG Hamm 7.11.96*, TranspR 1998.459, *Cass.com.5.1. 1999*, BTL 1999.80. *Gefco (UK) Ltd.* v. *Mason* [2000] 2 Lloyd's Rep. 555.

31. *Poclain S.A.* v. *SCAC* [1986] 1 Lloyd's Rep. 404, 406 (C.A.).

32. *Worldwide Carriers* v. *Ardtran International* [1983] 1 Lloyd's Rep. 61, 66; but cf. Glass [1984] L.M.C.L.Q. 30, 45; and Haak, p. 303.

33. *Mons 14.5.2002*, (2004) 39 ETL 99.

34. Clarke, *CMR*, para. 45c.

35. *Zerowatt Spa* v. *International Express Co.*, 6 October 1989, unreported. See also *Microfine Minerals & Chemicals Ltd.* v. *Transferry Shipping Co. Ltd.* [1991] 2 Lloyd's Rep. 630.

36. *Muller Batavier* v. *Laurent Transport Co.* [1977] 1 Lloyd's Rep. 411, 416; but cf. *Basel 12.5.2000*, TranspR 2000.372. HM, p. 253 and Loewe, Theunis, p. 160.

37. But cf. *Microfine Minerals & Chemicals Ltd.* v. *Transferry Shipping Co. Ltd.* [1991] 2 Lloyd's Rep. 630; *Cass. Belgium 27.9.1984*, 1984 ULR 406; and *HB Antwerp 2.6.2004* (2004) 39 ETL 407.

Suspension of the period of limitation implies that the period has begun to run. *Prima facie*, therefore, suspension can occur only after the limitation period has commenced in accordance with Article 32.1. However, it has been suggested that a claim made prior to commencement is effective nonetheless to suspend the period, albeit not at once but later when the period has begun.[38] Similarly, the language of Article 32.2 suggests that rejection cannot take effect to start the limitation period again until the period has been effectively suspended.[39] *1.208*

If the carrier does not reject the claim but admits liability that is the end of the matter as regards the period of limitation. If, however, only part of the claim is admitted, as Article 32.2 provides, the period of limitation starts to run again in respect of that part of the claim that is not admitted but is still in dispute. If the carrier has made an effective response and the period has started to run again, the claimant cannot suspend it again simply by repeating the claim or, as it is expressed in Article 32.2, by making "further claims having the same object". Moreover, if action has not been commenced within the limitation period action is barred and cannot be admitted in the guise of a counterclaim or right of set-off: Article 32.4.[40] *1.209*

4. *Extension of the period of limitation*

Extension of the period of limitation is not regulated by CMR but referred by Article 32.3 to the "law of the court or tribunal seised of the case". Thus for the English court extension of the period is governed by the Limitation Act 1980. When, as it may, the English court interferes with arbitration, it has power to order that the period between the date on which the arbitration commenced and the date of interference shall be excluded in computing the limitation period: Limitation Act 1980, s.34(5). On other questions, the Act does not apply: section 39. This appears to rule out extension of time by agreement between the parties—under the Act, however, such agreements are valid at common law.[41] Moreover, the court is not obliged to take notice of the expiry of the limitation period, and the time bar may be waived.[42] *1.210*

Article 33 *1.211*

The contract of carriage may contain a clause conferring competence on an arbitration tribunal if the clause conferring competence on the tribunal provides that the tribunal shall apply this Convention.

38. *ICI plc* v. *MAT Transport* [1987] 1 Lloyd's Rep. 354, 361. The point did not have to be decided.

39. *OGH 1.7.1981*, Greiter, p. 168.

40. For what is meant by a counterclaim, see *Dole Dried Fruit & Nut Co.* v. *Trustin Kerwood* [1990] 2 Lloyd's Rep. 309, 311 (C.A.). Cf. a deduction or abatement which, in any event, is not effective in respect of a carriage claim: *Aries Tanker Corp.* v. *Total Transport* [1977] 1 All E.R. 398 (H.L.), applied to CMR in *R.H. & D. International* v. *IAS Animal Air Services* [1984] 2 All E.R. 203.

41. *Zerowatt Spa* v. *International Express Co.*, 6 October 1989, unreported.

42. Clarke, *CMR*, para. 45f(i).

Comment

1.212 An arbitration clause is construed in accordance with the proper law of the contract.[1] Nonetheless, if an arbitration clause in a contract subject to CMR comes before the English court, it must comply with Article 33. In particular, to "provide" that the tribunal shall apply the CMR requires an express contract term to that effect.[2] If, in spite of a contract term that complies with Article 33, a party to the contract ignores it and brings proceedings in one of the courts with jurisdiction under Article 31, the question whether the latter will be stayed is resolved by the *lex fori*. If the forum is in England, the proceedings will be stayed so that the arbitration may proceed.[3]

1.213 **Chapter VI, Provisions relating to carriage performed by successive carriers: Article 34**

If carriage governed by a single contract is performed by successive road carriers, each of them shall be responsible for the performance of the whole operation, the second carrier and each succeeding carrier becoming a party to the contract of carriage, under the terms of the consignment note, by reason of his acceptance of the goods and the consignment note.

Comments

1. Successive carriers

1.214 If carrier X employs sub-contractors for all or part of the journey and a separate consignment note is made out for each part, carrier X alone is liable in contract and under CMR to the sender. To the sub-contractors, however, carrier X is in the position of sender dealing with carriers for the relevant part and their relations with carrier X as sender are governed by their contract and by CMR on that basis, if the relevant part of the journey is international and within the scope of Article 1.

1.215 If carrier X employs sub-contractors for all or part of the journey and no separate consignment note is made out for each part but the original consignment note is passed on like a baton down the line of sub-contractors, with one reservation, they are all successive carriers under CMR. The reservation is that the "whole operation" referred to in Article 34 refers to carriage by road: hence the successive road carriers are not responsible for what might occur on a sea or rail stage.[1] Between such successive carriers certain features of the situation are regulated by Chapter VI—even as regards a part of the journey that does not satisfy Article 1 because it is entirely within one State,[2] provided that the carrier/sub-contractor on that part of the journey has been alerted to the applicability of CMR.[3]

1. *Bofors-UVA* v. *Skandia Transport* [1982] 1 Lloyd's Rep. 410.
2. *Ibid.*
3. *Ibid.* at p. 413.

1. *Antwerp 15.3.1989* (1989) 24 ETL 574.
2. Loewe, para. 275.
3. Clarke, *CMR*, para. 52b; Glass/Cashmore, para. 3.74.

2. Acceptance: assumption of responsibility

In a case of successive carriage within the meaning of Article 34, Article 36 entitles the claimant to sue either the first carrier, the last carrier or the carrier performing the part on which the loss etc. occurred. Each carrier is responsible for the performance of the whole operation provided that that carrier has accepted the goods and the consignment note.[4] Such acceptance, which occurs when the carrier takes them over,[5] indicates the carrier's assumption of responsibility for the goods to the sender and consignee; acceptance is a condition of a carrier's liability as a successive carrier.[6] If sub-contractor B in turn sub-contracts to C, so that it is not B who accepts the note and the goods but C, C also accepts it as agent for B.[7] Acceptance is subject to any reservations that the accepting carrier may wish to make about the accuracy of statements made in the note and the apparent condition of the goods: Article 35.1. *1.216*

In the event of defective performance the successive carrier sued is liable jointly and severally with the others,[8] and, it has been argued,[9] the wilful default of one carrier affects the others. Articles 37 to 40 deal with recourse between carriers. *1.217*

Article 35 *1.218*

1. A carrier accepting the goods from a previous carrier shall give the latter a dated and signed receipt. He shall enter his name and address on the second copy of the consignment note. Where applicable, he shall enter on the second copy of the consignment note and on the receipt reservations of the kind provided for in article 8, paragraph 2.

2. The provisions of article 9 shall apply to the relations between successive carriers.

Comment

Acceptance of the goods and the consignment note, when the carrier takes them over, indicates (the degree of) assumption of responsibility by a successive carrier for the goods to the sender and consignee,[10] and, in a recourse action, to the *1.219*

4. I.e. the original consignment note: *Harrison & Sons Ltd.* v. *R.T. Stewart Transport Ltd.*, 30 July 1992, unreported. Cf. the application of Art. 34 *et seq.* to a case in which there was no such consignment note in the "*Seagram*" case, *Sandeman Coprimar S.A.* v. *Transitos Y Transportes Integrales S.L.* [2003] EWCA Civ 113, [2003] Q.B. 1270, [2003] 2 Lloyd's Rep. 172. Noted critically by Glass 4 (2) S. & T.L. 34 (2003).

5. *SGS-ATES Componenti Elettronici Spa* v. *Grappo* [1978] 1 Lloyd's Rep. 281, 284. For the meaning of taking over see Art. 17, Comment 3, paras. 1.88 *et seq.*, above.

6. *Dresser UK Ltd.* v. *Falcongate Freight Management Ltd.* [1991] 2 Lloyd's Rep. 557 (C.A.); *Cass. Italy 19.12.1978*, Foro it. 1979 I.1512; *BGH 10.5.1990*, TranspR 1990.418.

7. *SGS-ATES loc. cit.*; *Coggins T/A PC Transport* v. *L.K.W. Walter Int. Transportorganisation A.G.* [1999] 1 Lloyd's Rep. 255. See also *OGH 29.1.2002*, (2002) 37 ETL 809. Anfray ULR 2003.733.

8. *ITT Schaub-Lorenz Vertriebgesellschaft mbH* v. *Birkart Johann Internationale Spedition GmbH* [1988] 1 Lloyd's Rep. 487, 493 (C.A.); Haak, p. 113; HM, para. 11.70.

9. HM, para. 11.54; but cf. Hardingham [1978] L.M.C.L.Q. 499, 504.

10. See Art. 34, Comment 2, paras. 1.216 to 1.217, above.

previous carrier. Thus acceptance is subject to any reservations that the accepting (successive) carrier may wish to make about the accuracy of statements made in the note and the apparent condition of the goods. This is the concern of Article 35 and, in particular, Article 35.2 confirms that, as regards matters such as the condition of the goods and the probative force of reservations entered, the accepting carrier is in the position of a carrier taking over goods from a sender.

1.220 Compliance with the specific requirements of Article 35.1, such as entering name and address, however, is not a condition precedent to acceptance of responsibility under Article 34.[11]

1.221

Article 36

Except in the case of a counter-claim or a set-off raised in an action concerning a claim based on the same contract of carriage, legal proceedings in respect of liability for loss, damage or delay may only be brought against the first carrier, the last carrier or the carrier who was performing that portion of the carriage during which the event causing the loss, damage or delay occurred; an action may be brought at the same time against several of these carriers.

Comment

1.222 The provision of such a range of targets for the dissatisfied customer and potential claimant has been described as "a bold concept for which there is no equivalent in any other convention on transport".[1] In fact, however, there is a similar provision in CIM (1980) Article 55.3. The claimant may sue whichever of the specified carriers is most convenient for the claimant to sue, however, not any other carrier involved.[2] The carrier sued is liable jointly and severally with the other CMR carriers and thus in full, being responsible for the performance of the entire operation on the basis of the CMR, as if the other carriers involved were that carrier's own servants or agents. The carrier sued cannot escape liability by showing that performance has been delegated or sub-contracted.[3]

1.223 If the claimant is the sender, the target may well be the first carrier. The first carrier is not necessarily the one that first loads the goods but is the one that contracts with the sender; if A contracts with the sender but sub-contracts the entire operation to B, the first carrier is A.[4] If the claimant is the consignee, the carrier sued is likely to be the last carrier. The consignee would be poorly placed if, as has been maintained by some courts in Belgium and Holland, the consignee's only right of action was against the first carrier, whose seizable assets might be no more than an office in another country.[5] The last carrier is not necessarily the last carrier due

11. *SGS-ATES Componenti Elettronici Spa* v. *Grappo* [1978] 1 Lloyd's Rep. 281. Loewe, para. 275; Muller (1988) 23 ETL 726, 729.

1. Rodière (1971) 6 ETL 574, 580.

2. *SGS-ATES* at 284. Also in this sense: *OGH 12.4.1984*, Greiter, p. 215.

3. *ITT Schaub-Lorenz Vertriebgesellschaft mbH* v. *Birkart Johann Internationale Spedition GmbH* [1988] 1 Lloyd's Rep. 487, 493 (C.A.).

4. *Ulster-Swift* v. *Taunton Meat Haulage* [1977] 1 Lloyd's Rep. 346, 359–360 (C.A.); *OGH 4.6.1987* (1988) 23 ETL 714; *Cass. France 3.3.1998*, BTL 1998.231.

5. See Clarke, *CMR*, para. 50.

to have carried the goods but the last one to have accepted them and the consignment note; thus, if the goods are destroyed en route the performing carrier is also the last carrier even though that carrier was due to hand the goods over to another carrier for the last stage.

Article 37 *1.224*

A carrier who has paid compensation in compliance with the provisions of this Convention, shall be entitled to recover such compensation, together with interest thereon and all costs and expenses incurred by reason of the claim, from the other carriers who have taken part in the carriage, subject to the following provisions:

(a) the carrier responsible for the loss or damage shall be solely liable for the compensation whether paid by himself or by another carrier;

(b) when the loss or damage has been caused by the action of two or more carriers, each of them shall pay an amount proportionate to his share of liability; should it be impossible to apportion the liability, each carrier shall be liable in proportion to the share of the payment for the carriage which is due to him;

(c) if it cannot be ascertained to which carriers liability is attributable for the loss or damage, the amount of the compensation shall be apportioned between all the carriers as laid down in (b) above.

Comment

The carrier sued in accordance with Article 36,[1] being liable jointly and severally with the other CMR carriers and thus in full, has a right of recovery or contribution under Article 37, which must be exercised in accordance with Article 39. However, it is a condition precedent of recovery or contribution that the carrier seeking recovery or contribution has actually paid the claim.[2] Such payment must also have been "in compliance with the provisions of this Convention", however, that condition is subject to contrary agreement between the carriers under Article 40. Subject to contribution, the right is to recover the amount of compensation paid to the claimant, together with interest which, it has been held,[3] is to be calculated in accordance with Article 27.1. *1.225*

The right of recourse is against those carriers who were successive carriers in respect of the same contract of carriage.[4] The primary target is identified in paragraph (a) as being the carrier responsible for "the loss or damage", whereas in other provisions, such as Article 36, the reference is to "loss, damage and delay"; however, there is no reason for thinking that the omission of "delay" here was intended to be significant. In any event *prima facie* the carrier responsible is the carrier on whose stage of the journey the loss, damage or cause of delay occurred.[5] Although the carriers are jointly and severally liable, if the carrier responsible can be identified, paragraph (a) is taken quite literally: that carrier alone is responsible *1.226*

1. And no other carrier: *BGH 25.10.1984* (1985) 20 ETL 268, 273.
2. *ITT Schaub-Lorenz Vertriebgesellschaft mbH* v. *Birkart Johann Internationale Spedition GmbH* [1988] 1 Lloyd's Rep. 487, 494 (C.A.).
3. *BGH 27.11.2003*, TranspR 2004.79.
4. *Cummins Engine Co.* v. *Davis Freight Forwarding (Hull)* [1981] 3 All E.R. 567, 575 (C.A.); cf. *Harrison & Sons Ltd.* v. *R.T. Stewart Transport Ltd.* (1993) 28 ETL 747.
5. *ITT* v. *Birkhart Johann* [1988] 1 Lloyd's Rep. 487 (C.A.).

under Article 37,[6] unless insolvent, in which event the position is regulated by Article 38.

1.227 If the loss or damage has been caused by two or more of the successive carriers, the position is governed by paragraph (b); and if part of the loss can be apportioned and part not, it is thought that both sentences of paragraph (b) apply accordingly.[7]

1.228

Article 38

If one of the carriers is insolvent, the share of the compensation due from him and unpaid by him shall be divided among the other carriers in proportion to the share of the payment for the carriage due to them.

Comment

1.229 If one of the carriers liable in a recourse action under Article 37 is insolvent, in the sense simply of unable to pay, the loss is spread proportionately in relation to their liability under Article 37 among the other carriers except, of course, the carrier seeking recovery.

1.230

Article 39

1. No carrier against whom a claim is made under articles 37 and 38 shall be entitled to dispute the validity of the payment made by the carrier making the claim if the amount of the compensation was determined by judicial authority after the first mentioned carrier had been given due notice of the proceedings and afforded an opportunity of entering an appearance.

2. A carrier wishing to take proceedings to enforce his right of recovery may make his claim before the competent court or tribunal of the country in which one of the carriers concerned is ordinarily resident, or has his principal place of business or the branch or agency through which the contract of carriage was made. All the carriers concerned may be made defendants in the same action.

3. The provisions of article 31, paragraphs 3 and 4, shall apply to judgments entered in the proceedings referred to in articles 37 and 38.

4. The provisions of article 32 shall apply to claims between carriers. The period of limitation shall, however, begin to run either on the date of the final judicial decision fixing the amount of compensation payable under the provisions of this Convention, or, if there is no such judicial decision, from the actual date of payment.

Comment

1.231 Carrier A, who has paid a goods claim and wishes to take proceedings to enforce the right of recovery against one or more of the other successive carriers identified in Article 37, must do so in one of the courts stated in Article 39.2. If A paid in performance of an out of court settlement with the claimant, carrier B defending the

6. *Cummins Engine Co.* v. *Davis Freight Forwarding (Hull)* [1981] 2 Lloyd's Rep. 402 (C.A.); *Cass. Belgium 30.5.1980* (1983) 18 ETL 79.

7. Rodière (1971) 6 ETL 574, 586.

recourse action can dispute the settlement but not if the compensation paid was determined by judicial authority,[1] as is made clear in Article 39.1.[2] Even in the case of determination by judicial authority, however, carrier B is nonetheless free to raise any defence which is available against carrier A but which was not open to A against the claimant including, of course, that B was not responsible for the loss, damage or delay in question. Broadly speaking, carrier A stands in the position of sender and carrier B in that of the carrier for the stage performed by him[3]; and the consignment note, as qualified in accordance with Article 35, has the usual evidentiary role for that stage.[4]

The limitation period for a recourse action is the same as for other CMR actions, *1.232* however, for obvious reasons it has the later starting date stated in Article 39.4. Although the heading to Chapter VI refers to successive carriers, it has been held that Article 39.4 applies also to claims between a carrier and a sub-carrier that is not a successive carrier.[5] If A brings a successful recourse action under Chapter VI, judgment can be enforced in other contracting States in the same way as any other CMR action: Article 39.3.

The recourse action must be brought before one of the courts or tribunals *1.233* identified in Article 39.2. Although Article 39.2 refers to the courts or tribunals where carrier A "may" make a claim, "may" has been interpreted as "must": A cannot bring a recourse action in any other court or tribunal.[6] The courts or tribunals listed in Article 39.2 are the same as those listed in Article 31.1(a) for actions brought by the goods interest,[7] i.e., those of the ordinary residence, or principal place of business or contracting branch or agency of the carrier but in a recourse action of "one of the carriers concerned". This, according to the narrow construction applied by the courts, refers to carriers who are defendants in the recourse action and were successive carriers in respect of the same contract of carriage[8]; and excludes the (court of the) carrier bringing the recourse action.[9]

Article 40 *1.234*

Carriers shall be free to agree among themselves on provisions other than those laid down in articles 37 and 38.

1. Not defined in CMR.
2. As to the required notice, see *Cummins Engine Co.* v. *Davis Freight Forwarding (Hull)* [1981] 3 All E.R. 567, 575 (C.A.).
3. Glass [1981] L.M.C.L.Q. 384, 385.
4. *Cass. France 5.7.1988*, BT 1988.546.
5. *Ulster-Swift* v. *Taunton Meat Haulage* [1977] 1 Lloyd's Rep. 346 (C.A.); *OGH 20.6.2000*, TranspR 2001.79. Cf. Loewe, Theunis, p. 158. The contrary view of *inter alia* Loewe was applied in *Mons 14.5.2002*, (2004) ETL 99, 109.
6. *Cummins* case, *loc. cit.*; but cf. *ibid.* p. 576 and *Arctic Electronics Co. (UK)* v. *McGregor Sea & Air Services* [1985] 2 Lloyd's Rep. 510, 514; *Harrison & Sons Ltd.* v. *R.T. Stewart Transport Ltd.* (1993) 28 ETL 747.
7. For discussion of their meaning, see Art. 31, Comment 2, paras. 1.187 *et seq.*, above.
8. *Cummins* case, *loc. cit.*; cf. *Harrison & Sons Ltd.* v. *R.T. Stewart Transport Ltd.* (above).
9. *Cummins* (above); and *Blue Water Shipping A/S* v. *Melship Eesti* (2000) 35 ETL 772 (Danish Supreme Court).

Comment

1.235 Evidently Article 40 must be read with Articles 37 and 38, to which it refers. See in particular the Comment on Article 37.

1.236 **Chapter VII, Nullity of stipulations contrary to the Convention: Article 41**

1. Subject to the provisions of Article 40, any stipulation which would directly or indirectly derogate from the provisions of this Convention shall be null and void. The nullity of such a stipulation shall not involve the nullity of the other provisions of the contract.

2. In particular, a benefit of insurance in favour of the carrier or any other similar clause, or any clause shifting the burden of proof shall be null and void.

Comments

1. Public policy

1.237 Article 41 reflects the underlying public policy that, in the interests of uniformity of commercial law, CMR provisions should apply to all contracts within the scope of CMR as laid down by Article 1, subject only to a few permitted modifications: Article 31.1 (choice of forum), Article 33 (arbitration) and Article 40 (recourse between carriers). A corollary is that Article 41 does not apply when there are gaps in CMR to invalidate provisions designed to fill those gaps,[1] for example, contract terms concerning security for performance[2]; and or containing precise instructions on mode of performance such as the temperature at which the goods should be transported.[3]

1.238 Unlike the corresponding provision in other carriage regimes, such as Article III, rule 8, of the Hague-Visby Rules for carriage by sea or Article 23 of HP for carriage by air, the CMR carrier's liability may not be increased, for example by a penalty clause for late delivery, except in so far as the sender has made a declaration of special interest under Article 26.

2. Benefit of insurance

1.239 A clause shifting the burden of proof is mentioned to avoid any doubt about the effect of such clauses. A clause giving the carrier the benefit of insurance is a device well tried by carriers to achieve a similar effect and its mention in the CMR reflects the lessons of maritime law. The insurance, invalidated by Article 41.2, is goods insurance taken out and paid for by the sender which enures to the benefit of the carrier. Article 41.2 does not invalidate, for example, liability insurance contracted by the carrier,[4] unless the premiums for that insurance were paid by the sender. Moreover, it has been held that clauses (not in the contract of carriage but) in the goods insurance contracted and paid for by the sender, whereby the insurer

1. *BGH 9.2.1979* (1980) 15 ETL 84.
2. *OGH 20.1.1981*, Greiter, p. 82.
3. *OGH 22.11.1984*, Greiter p. 253.
4. *OGH 15.12.1977*, Greiter, p. 62.

undertakes not to exercise rights in subrogation against the carrier, are probably also invalidated by Article 41.[5] Courts are more concerned here with the effect of the arrangement than with the form.[6] That accords with the spirit of Article 41.2 in so far as it refers also to "any other similar clause". An example is a clause whereby the sender himself promises indemnity *inter alia* against the carrier's liability to the consignee.[7]

[*Chapter VIII of the Convention is not reproduced here. It deals with the coming into force of the Convention, the settlement of disputes between the High Contracting Parties and related matters.*] 1.240

Protocol of signature 1.241

1. This Convention shall not apply to traffic between the United Kingdom of Great Britain and Northern Ireland and the Republic of Ireland.

[*The next paragraph is 1.251*]

5. Clarke, *CMR*, para. 92a.
6. *BGH 10.12.1998*, TranspR 1999.155, 159.
7. *Shell Chemicals UK Ltd.* v. *P & O Roadtanks Ltd.* [1993] 1 Lloyd's Rep. 114; [1995] 2 Lloyd's Rep. 297 (C.A.).

II. CARRIAGE OF GOODS BY ROAD WITHIN THE UNITED KINGDOM

A. INTRODUCTION

1.251 The movement of goods by road within the United Kingdom is governed by private conditions of carriage, notably those published for the use of its members by the Road Haulage Association Ltd. (RHA). Other conditions are in use. They have no statutory force.

1.252 Being private contract conditions, they do not bind the carrier's customer unless the customer signs them or has actual or constructive notice that the carrier intends to include conditions of carriage: see HP, Article 1, Comment 2, paragraph 3.40.

1.253 The RHA Conditions are subject to the Unfair Contract Terms Act 1977: whereas contracts for the carriage of goods by sea were largely saved from the Act, other contracts of carriage were not. As the Conditions concern the business liability of the carrier, they come within the scope of the Act: section 1. Being standard terms on which the customer is invited to contract, they will be enforced only to the extent that they are reasonable: section 3. Whether a term is reasonable or not is a matter for the carrier to prove: section 12. This depends on a number of factors.

1.254 On the one hand, the terms offered by a business such as a carrier in a stronger economic position than the other party are scrutinised with some severity. Moreover, factors tending against any carrier are that it is the best risk avoider and, usually, the party best placed to insure against loss of or damage to goods in transit. Carriers, like other bailees, have been favoured by insurance contract law for over a hundred years with a special rule that enables them to offer such insurance to customers.[1] Clauses limiting the amount of liability (such as Condition 11) are more favourably viewed than clauses (such as Condition 9(1)) that exclude liability altogether.[2] Moreover, if the carrier contracts on conditions such as these to carry certain goods but collects other goods by mistake and loses or damages them, the carrier cannot plead the conditions to exclude or limit liability.[3] This appears to be because the carrier has placed himself outside the four corners of the contract,[4] a case which has also been described as one of "fundamental breach" of contract. See Condition 9, Comment 4, paragraph 1.295.

1.255 On the other hand, in the case of terms in established and in widespread use in a particular trade context such as road carriage, a court will be hesitant to declare that a term is unreasonable and hence unenforceable.[5] This perception has been reinforced in the case of the RHA Conditions by a statement on the face of the Conditions that they have been registered with the Office of Fair Trading. Currently

1. Clarke, *Insurance*, Chap. 5–6.
2. Generally, see Clarke, *CMR*, para. 239a.
3. *Shell Chemicals UK Ltd.* v. *P & O Roadtanks Ltd.* [1993] 1 Lloyd's Rep. 114; [1995] 2 Lloyd's Rep. 297 (C.A.).
4. *Chanter* v. *Hopkins* (1838) 4 M. & W. 399; *Lilley* v. *Doubleday* (1881) L.R. 7 Q.B.D. 510; Palmer pp. 989 *et seq.*
5. *George Mitchell (Chesterhall)* v. *Finney Lock Seeds* [1983] 2 A.C. 803. See also *Schenkers Ltd.* v. *Overland Shoes Ltd.* [1998] 1 Lloyd's Rep 498 (C.A.); but cf. *Overseas Medical Supplies Ltd.* v. *Orient Transport Services Ltd.* [1999] 2 Lloyd's Rep. 273 (C.A.).

the courts are reluctant and unlikely to condemn conditions such as those in the RHA Conditions.

1.256 The current tone has been set by Tuckey L.J. in *Granville Oil*: "The 1977 Act obviously plays a very important role in protecting vulnerable consumers from the effects of draconian contract terms. But I am less enthusiastic about its intrusion into contracts between commercial parties of equal bargaining strength, who should generally be considered capable of being able to make contracts of their choosing and expect to be bound by their terms. Here the transaction includes carriage of goods by sea and insurance. These spheres of commercial activity standing on their own are excluded from the Act (see Schedule 1, para. 1a (insurance) and 2c and 3 (carriage of goods by ship)). In this case the element of road transport was sufficient to render the transaction subject to the Act, but the mixed nature of the contract of carriage emphasizes the interest of the freight forwarder in having a time limitation which is applicable across the spectrum of his obligations."[6]

B. THE TEXT OF THE ROAD HAULAGE ASSOCIATION LTD.'S CONDITIONS OF CARRIAGE 1998*

1.257 **Preamble**

[XXX Ltd]

(hereinafter referred to as "the Carrier") is not a common carrier and accepts goods for carriage only upon that condition and the Conditions set out below. No servant or agent of the Carrier is permitted to alter or vary these Conditions in any way unless expressly authorized in writing to do so by a Director, Principal, Partner or other authorised person. If any legislation is compulsorily applicable to the Contract and any part of these Conditions is incompatible with such legislation, such part shall, as regards the Contract, be overridden to that extent and no further.

* RHA Conditions of Carriage 1998 are copyright and may only be used by members of the Road Haulage Association.

Comment

1.258 The RHA Conditions 1998 replaced those of 1991 with effect from 1 September 1998. In explanatory notes attached to the Conditions the RHA states that the 1998 Conditions were designed to meet the changing needs of the industry. These Conditions have been submitted to the Office of Fair Trading and have been placed on the public register. The Conditions are private contract terms without force of law and apply only to the extent that they have been effectively incorporated in the contract.

1.259 In an attempt to ensure that they are applied in preference to the common law rules for common carriers, the Preamble asserts that the carrier is not a common carrier, however, although such statements are indeed evidence of the status of the

6. *Granville Oil & Chemicals Ltd.* v. *Davis & Turner Ltd.* [2003] EWCA Civ 570, [2003] 2 Lloyd's Rep. 356 at [31]. Hart J. and Potter L.J. agreed at [32]. The case concerned the BIFA Conditions (1989 edition).

carrier concerned, they are not conclusive of the question which is one of law.[1] In an attempt to ensure that they are applied when the carriage is multimodal, Condition 2(4) contains a "network" provision. In an attempt to ensure that they are interpreted in a way that the drafter intended, Condition 16 refers disputes to English law and the courts of the United Kingdom.

1.260 **Condition 1: Definitions**

In these Conditions:

"*Customer*" means the person or company who contracts for the services of the Carrier including any other carrier who gives a Consignment to the Carrier for carriage.

"*Contract*" means the contract of carriage between the Customer and the Carrier.

"*Consignee*" means the person or company to whom the Carrier contracts to deliver the Consignment.

"*Consignment*" means goods, whether a single item or in bulk or contained in one parcel, package or container, as the case may be, or any number of separate items, parcels, packages or containers sent at one time in one load by or for the Customer from one address to one address.

"*Dangerous Goods*" means goods named individually in the Approved Carriage List issued from time to time by the Health and Safety Commission, explosives, radioactive substances and any other substance presenting a similar hazard.

Comment

1.261 Condition 1 is of a type that is commonly found which defines major terms used in the Conditions. The "Customer", which replaces the reference to "Trader" in the 1982 Conditions, is defined as the person who contracts for the services of the carrier. That person may be the sender but more commonly is the consignee. "It is clear that where goods are despatched by a carrier, the contract for payment of carriage is between him and the consignee, even though the goods should have been booked by the consignor; and though the property in these goods turned out afterwards to be in the consignor".[1] This is the presumption as long as the carrier is entitled to assume, as is usually the case, that the goods are the property of the consignee.[2] Although the "Customer" is defined, there is no definition of "Carrier". The particular carrier is the person identified and described in the Preamble.

1.262 The meaning of "Consignment" came before the court in *Spectra*,[3] in which the appropriate limit of liability under Condition 11 depended on the meaning of the word. The defendants argued that, as the entirety of the goods on their vehicle had been stolen, that was a loss to the whole of the consignment. The plaintiffs argued that, as there were two vehicles which were the subject-matter of the bailment and one had not been stolen, the loss was to part of the consignment. In so far as that includes goods sent "by or for the Customer from one address to another address", Condition 1 supported the plaintiffs. However, the goods must also be "in one

1. *Eastman Chemical A.G.* v. *NMT Trading Ltd.* [1972] 2 Lloyd's Rep. 25, 30–31.

1. *Stephenson* v. *Hart* (1828) 4 Bing. 476, 487.

2. Clarke, *CMR*, para. 42; Palmer, pp. 959 *et seq.* and 1095; see also C. Cashmore, *Who Can Sue on a Contract of Carriage of Goods* (London, 1990), Chap. 3.

3. *Spectra International plc* v. *Hayesoak Ltd.* [1997] 1 Lloyd's Rep. 153.

load". A load is not defined by the conditions but Judge Hallgarten, Q.C., thought that "what is contemplated is the assembly of all parcels, packages or containers upon one vehicle"; otherwise the reference to load would be redundant.[4]

Condition 2: Parties and Sub-Contracting 1.263

(1) The Customer warrants that he is either the owner of the Consignment or is authorised by such owner to accept these Conditions on such owner's behalf.

(2) The Carrier and any other carrier employed by the Carrier may employ the services of any other carrier for the purpose of fulfilling the Contract in whole or in part and the name of every other such carrier shall be provided to the Customer upon request.

(3) The Carrier contracts for itself and as agent of and trustee for its servants and agents and all other carriers referred to in (2) above and such other carrier's servants and agents and every reference in these Conditions to "the Carrier" shall be deemed to include every other such carrier, servant and agent with the intention that they shall have the benefit of the Contract and collectively and together with the Carrier be under no greater liability to the Customer or any other party than is the Carrier hereunder.

(4) Notwithstanding Condition 2(3) the carriage of goods in any Consignment by rail, sea, inland waterway or air is arranged by the Carrier as agent of the Customer and shall be subject to the Conditions of the rail, shipping, inland waterway or air carrier contracted to carry the Consignment. The Carrier shall be under no liability whatever to whomsoever and however arising in respect of such carriage. Provided that where the Consignment is carried partly by road and partly by such other means of transport any loss, damage or delay shall be deemed to have occurred while the Consignment is being carried by road unless the contrary is proved by the Carrier.

Comments

1. Authority to contract and to sub-contract

One purpose of the warranty in Condition 2(1), that the customer is either the owner of the consignment or is authorised to contract on the basis of the Conditions, is to assure the carrier that the person most likely to suffer loss, if the goods are damaged in transit, is a party to the contract and bound by the Conditions, notably those that limit the amount of the carrier's liability. The drafting assumption, now doubtful as a matter of law,[1] was that, were it otherwise, the carrier might be liable in full in tort. 1.264

The purpose of Condition 2(2) is to negate common law cases that raise doubt about whether a carrier is entitled to sub-contract the carriage.[2] On the one hand, it has been held that to sub-contract without permission the carriage of goods particularly attractive to thieves was a "fundamental" breach of contract.[3] On the other hand, common law always accepted that vicarious performance with the consent of the creditor was permitted and could discharge the debtor.[3a] Condition 1.265

4. *Ibid.* at 157.

1. See the Contracts (Rights of Third Parties) Act 1999, s. 1, discussed in Condition 2, Comment 2, paras. 1.266 *et seq.*, below.

2. Glass/Cashmore, para. 1.77.

3. *Garnham, Harris & Elton Ltd.* v. *Alfred W. Ellis (Transport) Ltd.* [1967] 1 W.L.R. 940.

3a. Provided that the consent is clear: *MRS Distribution Ltd* v. *O.S. Smith (UK) Ltd.*, 2004 S.L.T. 631.

2(2) settles the matter in the latter sense for carriage subject to the RHA Conditions.

2. The rights of third parties

1.266 Condition 2(3) purports to confer the benefit of defences and limits on liability on others involved in the carriage such as sub-contractors. Its purpose was to overcome an obstacle posed by the common law rule of privity of contract, whereby third parties cannot benefit from defences in contracts to which they are not party.[4] Common law courts have developed a number of ways around the privity rule.

1.267 One way is to use rules of agency by inferring that the carrier has authority to contract with the customer not only as principal but also as agent on behalf of the sub-contractor.[5] The consequence of allowing the sub-contractor to plead a defence in the contract of carriage was that the claimant (customer), who had paid freight on the basis that he bore part of the risk himself, could not evade that burden by recovering in full in tort from the sub-contractor. The use of agency in this way in the past ensured that the claimant customer could not defeat the distribution of risk in the Hague Rules governing international carriage of goods by sea. It is not clear that the same decision would have been reached when no international regime, such as the Rules, was involved. Be that as it may, it was in any event common law orthodoxy going back to the nineteenth century, in the case of successive carriage by rail, that carrier A contracted not only on its own behalf but also as agent for carrier B.[6] The difficulty about the agency device is, first, that it is often artificial; and, secondly, it is workable only when the sub-contractor has been identified at the time of the contract of carriage. Agency law allows a person to contract as agent for an unnamed principal but not for an unknown principal. These objections can be dealt with, however, by recasting a condition such as Condition 2(3) as an offer by the customer to any sub-contractor as might later be appointed to carry out a carriage operation to accord that sub-contractor the benefit of the Conditions. When such a sub-contractor commences the operation in question, the sub-contractor accepts the offer and a contract is concluded directly between customer and sub-contractor on that basis.[7]

1.268 Another way around the privity rule lies in the law of bailment. If a bailor of goods bails goods to a bailee, such as a carrier, who has authority to sub-bail the goods (the inference of Condition 2(2)), the bailor is bound by the terms of the sub-bailment, unless those terms are unusual. The bailor "is bound by the conditions if he has expressly or impliedly consented to the bailee making a sub-bailment containing those conditions".[8] So, if the carrier contracts with a sub-contractor on the basis that the latter shall enjoy the benefit of the RHA Conditions, the customer too is bound by that arrangement. Such was the decision in respect of RHA Conditions in

4. *Midland Silicones Ltd.* v. *Scruttons Ltd.* [1962] A.C. 446.

5. *New Zealand Shipping Co.* v. *Satterthwaite* (*The Eurymedon*) [1975] A.C. 154 (P.C.).

6. *Hall* v. *N.E. Ry.* (1875) L.R. 10 Q.B. 437. Treitel Chap. 15.4.1.(1).

7. For a statement admitting this possibility, see *Burke* v. *Mersey Docks* [1986] 1 Lloyd's Rep. 155, 162; and *The Rigoletto* [2000] 2 Lloyd's Rep. 532, 543 (C.A.).

8. *Morris* v. *Martin & Sons* [1966] 1 Q.B. 716, 729 (C.A.); *The Pioneer Container* [1994] 2 A.C. 324; but cf. *The Mahkutai* [1996] 3 All E.R. 502 (P.C.); see Palmer, pp. 1631 *et seq.*

Spectra v. *Hayesoak*.[9] This rule was subsequently applied by the Court of Appeal to carriage by road in the "*Seagram*" case.[10]

When the sub-contractor is sued in tort (negligence), a third solution to the problem of privity lies in the law of tort and a restricted view of the duty of care. As the customer and the sub-contractor "have come together against a contractual structure [the RHA Conditions] which provides for compensation in the event of a failure of one of the parties involved, the court will be slow to superimpose an added duty of care beyond that which was in the contemplation of the parties at the time that they came together".[11] So, the RHA Conditions form the setting in which the law considers the scope of a duty of care owed by the sub-contractor to the customer, and an unambiguous condition limiting the liability of a sub-contractor will qualify the sub-contractor's duty of care. This approach has been applied by the Canadian Supreme Court to give the employees of a warehouse a defence to suit by the bailor of goods in the warehouse.[12] *1.269*

Although these rules remain law in force, in most cases they have lost their importance to the 1999 Act: the Contracts (Rights of Third Parties) Act 1999. Section 1(1) of the Act confers a right of enforcement on "a person who is not a party to a contract", referred in the Act as the "third party", who, according to section 1(3), must be "expressly identified in the contract by name, . . . or as answering to a particular description". Examples of description sufficient to identify the third party include "sub-contractors".[13] The right of enforcement can be conferred by contract on the third party in two ways, one of which, according to section 1(1)(b), is when a contract "term purports to confer a benefit on him". A "term" that confers a "benefit" includes an exemption or limitation clause. This is confirmed for contracts generally by section 1(6): as regards a term of the contract which "excludes or limits liability" enforcement shall be understood as the third party's "availing himself of the exclusion or limitation". The "purport", according to section 1(2), is no more than a presumption that the benefit is to be enforceable by the third party, which can be rebutted; however, the presumption is unlikely to be defeated in the case of sub-contracted carriage by road. Thus, it is should now be a simple matter to extend the benefit of contractual terms to sub-contractors even those yet to be appointed. *1.270*

Condition 3: Dangerous Goods *1.271*

Dangerous Goods must be disclosed by the Customer and if the Carrier agrees to accept them for carriage they must be classified, packed and labelled in accordance with the

9. *Spectra International plc* v. *Hayesoak Ltd.* [1997] 1 Lloyd's Rep. 153; Clarke [1997] J.B.L. 590; Glass [1997] L.M.C.L.Q. 478.

10. *Sandeman Coprimar S.A.* v. *Transitos y Transportes Integrales S.L.* [2003] EWCA Civ 113, [2003] Q.B. 1270, [2003] 2 Lloyd's Rep. 172. Noted critically by Glass 4 (2) S. & T.L. 34 (2003).

11. *Pacific Associates Inc.* v. *Baxter* [1989] 2 All E.R. 159, 170 (C.A.); *Mayfair Photographic Supplies (London)* v. *Baxter Hoare & Co.* [1972] 1 Lloyd's Rep. 410, 416; generally, see Clarke, *CMR*, para. 229a.

12. *London Drugs* v. *Kuehne & Nagel* (1993) 97 D.L.R. (4th) 261, noted by MacMillan in [1994] L.M.C.L.Q. 22.

13. Law Commission Report No. 242, para. 8.1.

statutory regulations for the carriage by road of the substance declared. Transport Emergency Cards (Tremcards) or information in writing in the manner required by the relevant statutory provisions must be provided by the Customer in respect of each substance and must accompany the Consignment.

Comment

1.272 Dangerous goods are defined in Conditions 1.[1] The liability of the customer for goods which are in a state that makes them unfit for carriage is based on a warranty by the senders at common law that the goods are fit for carriage.[2] It is a strict warranty, breach of which does not depend on the knowledge or negligence of the sender.[3] The customer is liable to the carrier not only for damage done by the goods to the property of the carrier but also faces the possibility of action by the carrier (as bailee) on behalf of other customers affected,[4] unless they have already been indemnified by the customer who sent the dangerous goods.[5] The Conditions contain an indemnity to this effect in Condition 12(2).

1.273 If, however, the customer delivers dangerous goods to the carrier in a state fit for carriage and in compliance with Condition 3, the carrier's liability for those goods is the same as that for any other class of goods. If special care or precautions must be taken during transit, the carrier must act accordingly and will be liable if he does not—unless he is neither aware nor should have been aware of the need for such: in that event, a claim in respect of consequent loss or damage may be defended under Condition 9, for example, paragraph 2(b)(iv).[6]

1.274 **Condition 4: Loading and Unloading**

(1) Unless the Carrier has agreed in writing to the contrary with the Customer:

(a) The Carrier shall not be under any obligation to provide any plant, power or labour, other than that carried by the vehicle, required for loading or unloading the Consignment.

(b) The Customer warrants that any special appliances required for loading or unloading the Consignment which are not carried by the vehicle will be provided by the Customer or on the Customer's behalf.

(c) The Carrier shall be under no liability whatever to the Customer for any damage whatever, however caused, if the Carrier is instructed to load or unload any Consignment requiring special appliances which, in breach of the warranty in (b) above, have not been provided by the Customer or on the Customer's behalf.

(d) The Carrier shall not be required to provide service beyond the usual place of collection or delivery but if any such service is given by the Carrier it shall be at the sole risk of the Customer.

(2) The Customer shall indemnify the Carrier against all claims and demands whatever which could not have been made if such instructions as are referred to in (1)(c) of this Condition and such service as is referred to in (1)(d) of this Condition had not been given.

1. But see also the Carriage of Dangerous Goods and Use of Transportable Pressure Equipment Regulations 2004 (S.I. 2004/568), which came into force on 10 May 2004.
2. See Palmer, pp. 999 *et seq.*
3. *Bamfield* v. *Goole and Sheffield Transport Co.* [1910] 2 K.B. 94 (C.A.).
4. *The Winkfield* [1902] P. 42; *G.N. Ry.* v. *L.E.P. Transport* [1922] 2 K.B. 742 (C.A.).
5. *O'Sullivan* v. *Williams* [1992] 3 All E.R. 385 (C.A.).
6. Cf. CMR, Art. 22, para. 1.136, above.

Comments

Condition 4 was revised for the 1998 version of the Conditions to facilitate the use of plant, power and labour carried on the carrier's vehicle for loading and unloading. At the same time Condition 4(1)(a) makes it clear that, in the absence of special agreement, the carrier has no duty to provide any other equipment. Condition 4(1)(b) states the corollary that it is for the customer to provide any special appliances required for (un)loading; and Condition 4(1)(c) provides that, if the customer is in breach of Condition 4(1)(b) and the carrier is nonetheless compelled to (un)load, it is entirely at the risk of the customer[1]: see also Condition 9, Comment 5. Such clauses are common in the haulage industry and this aspect of the clause is not open to serious challenge under the Unfair Contract Terms Act 1977.[2] *1.275*

Condition 5: Signed Receipts *1.276*

The Carrier shall, if so required, sign a document prepared by the sender acknowledging the receipt of the Consignment but no such document shall be evidence of the condition or of the correctness of the declared nature, quantity, or weight of the Consignment at the time it is received by the Carrier and the burden of proving the condition of the Consignment on receipt by the Carrier and that the Consignment was of the nature, quantity or weight declared in the relevant document shall rest with the Customer.

Comment

The inclusion of Condition 5 has puzzled some commentators,[1] however, the first line of the Condition suggests that it was included in view of Article III, rule 3, of the Hague Rules and was designed to negate the probatory effect that Article III, rule 3, and common law give to bills of lading, unless, as allowed by common law, the document was claused with stamped wording such as "weight, quantity and contents unknown". This impression was confirmed in the current 1998 edition of the RHA Conditions by the addition of the last three lines, in particular, of the words "and the burden . . . shall rest with the Customer". See the corresponding provision in Freightliner's Standard Conditions, Condition 6(b), paragraph 2.620, below. *1.277*

Condition 6: Transit *1.278*

(1) Transit shall commence when the Carrier takes possession of the Consignment whether at the point of collection or at the Carrier's premises.

(2) Transit shall (unless otherwise previously determined) end when the Consignment is tendered at the usual place of delivery at the Consignee's address within the customary cartage hours of the district.

Provided that:

(a) if no safe and adequate access or no adequate unloading facilities there exist then transit shall be deemed to end at the expiry of one clear day after notice in writing

1. *Smith* v. *South Wales Switchgear* [1978] 1 All E.R. 18, 25–26 (H.L.).
2. Palmer, p. 1099, citing *Thompson* v. *T. Lohan (Plant Hire) Ltd.* [1987] 2 All E.R. 631 (C.A.).
1. Palmer, p. 1099.

(or by telephone if so previously agreed in writing) of the arrival of the Consignment at the Carrier's premises has been sent to the Consignee; and

(b) when for any other reason whatever a Consignment cannot be delivered or when a Consignment is held by the Carrier "to await order" or "to be kept till called for" or upon any like instructions and such instructions are not given or the Consignment is not called for and removed, within a reasonable time, then transit shall be deemed to end.

Comment

1.279 Transit begins when possession, and hence custody and control, pass from the customer (or his agent) to the carrier; and ends when tender of the goods, and hence an offer of possession and control, is made by the carrier to the consignee. The period (and thus Condition 6) is important notably because, when transit ends, Condition 9(3) purports to excuse the carrier in respect of any loss of or damage to the goods occurring later. In the carriage of goods, whatever the mode of carriage, when possession and hence control change there is a significant change in the risk and usually therefore a change of legal regime.[1]

1.280 The key point being change of possession and control, the primary rule for the ending of transit is actual delivery of the consignment of goods to the consignee. However, provision has to be made for cases in which, through no fault of the carrier, that cannot be done. Hence Condition 6(2) reaffirms the common law rule[2] that tender of the goods at the right time and place amounts to delivery for the purpose of ending transit. Moreover, transit may end differently and/or earlier, i.e., sooner than in the cases envisaged in the proviso to Condition 6(2), if possession and control pass to the consignee short of the consignee's address or if the goods are sold or destroyed en route.

1.281 Proviso (b) to Condition 6(2) reflects the common law rule in such a case.[3] It is supplemented by Condition 7 which gives the carrier a right to sell undelivered goods. Proviso (a) to Condition 6(2), however, is different from common law where the general rule is that notice is not effective until it has been received.[4] On the other hand, it is likely that a court would apply common law to proviso (a) by concluding that notice is considered to have been sent when it has been put in the course of transmission so as to be out of the power of the sender to revoke.

1.282 **Condition 7: Undelivered or Unclaimed Goods**

Where the Carrier is unable for any reason to deliver a Consignment to the Consignee or as he may order, or where by virtue of the proviso to Condition 6(2) hereof transit is deemed to be at end, the Carrier may sell the Consignment and payment or tender of the proceeds after deduction of all proper charges and expenses in relation thereto and of all outstanding charges in relation to the carriage and storage of the Consignment shall (without prejudice to any claim or right which the Customer may have against the Carrier otherwise arising

1. Clarke, *Insurance*, Chap. 16–2A6.
2. Glass/Cashmore, para. 1.67. See *Startup* v. *Macdonald* (1843) 6 Man. & G. 593; *Heugh* v. *L.N.W. Ry.* (1870) L.R. 5 Ex. 51.
3. *Chapman* v. *G.W. Ry.* (1880) 5 Q.B.D. 278, 281–282; Palmer pp. 1003–1004.
4. *Holwell Securities Ltd.* v. *Hughes* [1974] 1 All E.R. 164 (C.A.).

under these Conditions) discharge the Carrier from all liability in respect of such Consignment, its carriage and storage.

Provided that:

(1) the Carrier shall do what is reasonable to obtain the value of the Consignment and

(2) the power of sale shall not be exercised where the name and address of the sender or of the Consignee is known unless the Carrier shall have done what is reasonable in the circumstances to give notice to the sender or, if the name and address of the sender is not known, to the Consignee that the Consignment will be sold unless within the time specified in such notice, being a reasonable time in the circumstances from the giving of such notice, the Consignment is taken away or instructions are given for its disposal.

Comment

As regards the ending of transit and of the carrier's role and responsibility as carrier, *1.283*
Condition 7 confirms the provisos to Condition 6(2), with the important addition of a power of sale not found in Condition 6 or at common law. The carrier is given the power whatever the reason for the carrier's inability to deliver. If the reason lies in circumstances which render the carrier in breach of the contract of carriage, Condition 7 has been seen as an exemption clause liable to challenge under the Unfair Contract Terms Act 1977.[1] In any event, proviso (2) of Condition 7 requires the carrier to do what is reasonable in the circumstance to give the customer or consignee, as appropriate, notice that the goods will be sold. It has been inferred that notice has the meaning it has in Condition 6.[2]

Condition 8: Carrier's Charges *1.284*

(1) The Carrier's charges shall be payable by the Customer without prejudice to the Carrier's rights against the Consignee or any other person. Provided that when any Consignment is consigned "carriage forward" the Customer shall not be required to pay such charges unless the consignee fails to pay after a reasonable demand has been made by the Carrier for payment thereof.

(2) Charges shall be payable on the expiry of any time limit previously stipulated and the Carrier shall be entitled to interest at 5 per cent above the Clearing Bank Base Rate current at this time, calculated on a daily basis on all amounts overdue to the Carrier.

Comments

1. Who pays ?

Condition 8(1) is consistent with common law rules.[1] Charges are payable by the *1.285*
customer. Usually the customer is the person who contracts with the carrier; but the saving reference to the consignee does not reflect the common law position, which is that the person who contracts with the carrier (and is thus the customer) is presumed to be the consignee.[2] Moreover, even when the charges in a particular

1. Palmer, p. 1101. But see the statement in *Granville Oil*, quoted in the Introduction to these Conditions, para. 1.256, above.
2. See the Comment on Condition 6, *in fine*, paras. 1.279 *et seq.*, above.

1. See Glass/Cashmore, para. 1.106; and Palmer, p. 1101.
2. See the Comment on Condition 1, paras. 1.261 *et seq.*, above.

case are payable by the sender, if the goods are delivered to the consignee, common law implies a contract whereby unpaid charges become payable by the consignee.[3] However, the provision for consignments "carriage forward" purports to change the common law rule.[4]

2. The time for payment

1.286 The time for payment and, in particular, the consequences of non-payment are the subject of Condition 8(2). In the absence of a contract term on the question, the common law rule is that freight charges are payable at the time of delivery: this is the rule for carriage by sea which is believed by commentators to apply also to carriage by land.[5] In any event, whether a time limit has been stipulated or not, the payment rule is subject to the proviso of common law that the goods have been delivered or tendered.[6] Freight is payable at common law, however, if the goods are delivered short in quantity or damaged[7]; this too is a rule for carriage by sea but one which has been applied to carriage by road with "unconcealed reluctance".[8] The rule is controversial[9] but the argument, that a "no set off" clause in BIFA standard conditions was unreasonable under the Unfair Contract Terms Act 1977 has been rejected by the Court of Appeal because such clauses were common and, in the view of the Court, that reflected a general view of what was reasonable in the trade.[10] Although the rule is controversial, Condition 8(2) seeks to maintain it, as do both the BIFA Conditions, Condition 7.6 of the EWS Conditions and Condition 13b of the Freightliner Conditions: paragraphs 2.728 and 2.641, below, respectively.

1.287 If the sender is obliged to pay charges and has not done so, the carrier can simply refuse to carry the goods until freight has been paid or sufficient security given. In the event of non-payment by the consignee, the carrier's primary remedy is a lien on the goods, which is provided for in Condition 14.

1.288

Condition 9: Liability for Loss and Damage

(1) The Customer shall be deemed to have elected to accept the terms set out in (2) of this Condition unless, before the transit commences, the Customer has agreed in writing that the Carrier shall not be liable for any loss or mis-delivery of or damage to or in connection with the Consignment however or whenever caused and whether or not caused or contributed to directly or indirectly by any act, omission, neglect, default or other wrongdoing on the part of the Carrier, its servants, agents or sub-contractors.

(2) Subject to these Conditions the Carrier shall be liable for:

(a) physical loss, mis-delivery of or damage to living creatures, bullion, money, securities, stamps, precious metals or precious stones comprising the Consignment only if:

(i) the Carrier has specifically agreed in writing to carry any such items and

3. *World Transport Co.* v. *Tealing & Co.* [1936] 2 All E.R. 573; Clarke [1991] L.M.C.L.Q. 5.
4. Palmer, p. 1016.
5. Glass/Cashmore, paras. 1.107 and 5.52; Palmer, p. 1015.
6. Palmer, p. 1102.
7. *Aries Tanker Corp.* v. *Total Transport* [1977] 1 W.L.R. 185 (H.L.).
8. *United Carriers Ltd.* v. *Heritage Food Group (UK) Ltd.* [1995] 4 All E.R. 95, 102.
9. See Clarke, *CMR*, para. 45g.
10. In *Overland Shoes Ltd.* v. *Schenkers Ltd.* [1998] 1 Lloyd's Rep. 498.

(ii) the Customer has agreed in writing to reimburse the Carrier in respect of all additional costs which result from the carriage of the said items; and
(iii) the loss, mis-delivery or damage is occasioned during transit and is proved to be due to the negligence of the Carrier, its servants, agents or sub-contractors;

(b) any loss or mis-delivery of or damage to any other goods comprising the Consignment unless the same has arisen from, and the Carrier has used reasonable care to minimise the effects of:
(i) Act of God;
(ii) any consequences of war, invasion, act of foreign enemy, hostilities (whether war or not), civil war, rebellion, insurrection, terrorist act, military or usurped power or confiscation, requisition, or destruction or damage by or under the order of any government or public or local authority;
(iii) seizure or forfeiture under legal process;
(iv) error, act, omission, mis-statement or mis-representation by the Customer or other owner of the Consignment or by servants or agents of either of them;
(v) inherent liability to wastage in bulk or weight, faulty design, latent defect or inherent defect, vice or natural deterioration of the Consignment;
(vi) insufficient or improper packing;
(vii) insufficient or improper labelling or addressing;
(viii) riot, civil commotion, strike, lockout, general or partial stoppage or restraint of labour from whatever cause;
(ix) Consignee not taking or accepting delivery within a reasonable time after the Consignment has been tendered.

(3) The Carrier shall not in any circumstances be liable for loss or damage arising after transit is deemed to have ended within the meaning of Condition 6(2) hereof, whether or not caused or contributed to directly or indirectly by any act, omission, neglect, default or other wrongdoing on the part of the Carrier, its servants, agents or sub-contractors.

Comments

1. Levels of liability

Condition 9 is the provision central to the carrier's liability under the RHA Conditions. Condition 9 provides for three levels of liability, all of which reduce the liability of the carrier from that of a carrier at common law, and which the customer can choose according to the carriage charge he is willing to pay. *1.289*

2. Carriage at customer's risk

The first and lowest level of liability is that of Condition 9(1) whereby, if it has been agreed in writing,[1] the goods are carried entirely at the customer's risk. This is no liability at all and *prima facie* it is difficult to see how the Condition can survive attack under the Unfair Contract Terms Act 1977, unless the rate charged by the carrier is very low indeed.[2] In recent cases, however, courts have shown great reluctance to strike out clauses in established and widespread use in the trade.[3] If, nonetheless, this condition were to be struck out as unreasonable under the Unfair *1.290*

1. For the meaning of writing see, CMR, Art. 30, Comment 3, para. 1.180, above.
2. In this sense: Glass/Cashmore, para. 1.55; and Palmer, p. 1103.
3. *Sonicare Int. Ltd.* v. *East Anglia Freight Terminal Ltd.* [1997] 2 Lloyd's Rep. 48; *Monarch Airlines Ltd.* v. *London Luton Airport Ltd.* [1998] 1 Lloyd's Rep. 403; *Overland Shoes Ltd.* v. *Schenkers Ltd.* [1998] 1 Lloyd's Rep. 498; but cf. *Overseas Medical Supplies Ltd.* v. *Orient Transport Services Ltd.* [1999] 2 Lloyd's Rep. 273 (C.A.).

Contract Terms Act 1977, the carrier's liability would be that of a bailee for reward at common law.

1.291 A further doubt about the efficacy of Condition 9(1) in the past concerned the attempt to extend the benefit of the exclusion to servants, agents or sub-contractors.[4] However, under the Contracts (Rights of Third Parties) Act 1999, s. 1(1), a "person who is not a party to a contract (a 'third party') may in his own right enforce a term of the contract if . . . the term purports to confer a benefit on him". Benefit may be conferred on groups such as sub-contractors; and section 1(6) states: "Where a term of a contract excludes or limits liability in relation to any matter references in this Act to the third party enforcing the term shall be construed as references to his availing himself of the exclusion or limitation."

3. *Liability for valuable goods*

1.292 The second level of liability provided for in Condition 9(2)(i) is a liability in respect of the carriage of special items, the presence of which the carrier has consented in writing[5] to carry: living creatures, bullion, money, securities, stamps, precious metals and precious stones. In the 1998 edition "living creatures" replaced "livestock", thus increasing the scope of the category to include exotic species, many of which are relatively valuable.

1.293 The carrier is liable if loss, misdelivery of or damage to these items is due to the negligence of the carrier, its servants, agents or sub-contractors. In so far as consent in writing appears to be a condition of the carrier's liability, it has been suggested that this requirement must be open to challenge under the Unfair Contract Terms Act 1977,[6] however, whether such a challenge would be successful is far from clear; see the Introduction to these Conditions, paragraphs 1.253 *et seq.*, above.

1.294 Subject to the operation of the 1977 Act, the carrier is liable, according to Condition 9(2)(a)(iii) only if the loss, mis-delivery or damage is occasioned during transit and is proved to have been due to the negligence of the carrier or of those engaged by the carrier to perform the contract of carriage. *Prima facie* this is a difficult burden of proof for a customer to meet. Consequently, at common law, evidence at destination of loss of or damage to goods carried has led to a presumption of liability unless the carrier disproves negligence.[7] In Condition 9(2)(a), however, negligence appears to be a condition of the carrier's liability and expressly a matter to be proved by the customer.

4. *Liability for other goods*

1.295 Condition 9(2)(b) is residual; it applies to cases not governed by Condition 9(1) or Condition 9(2)(a) and in practice it seems to most cases. Like the second level of

4. See Condition 2, Comment 2, paras. 1.266 *et seq.*, above.
5. For the meaning of writing see, CMR Art. 30, Comment 3, para. 1.180, above.
6. Palmer, p. 1105.
7. *Travers, Joseph & Sons Ltd.* v. *Cooper* [1915] 1 K.B. 73. See also *Levison* v. *Patent Steam Carpet Cleaning Co. Ltd.* [1978] Q.B. 69 (C.A.); applied in *Euro Cellular Ltd.* v. *Danzas Ltd.* [2004] 1 Lloyd's Rep. 521 at [65]. Palmer, p. 1104.

liability under Condition 9(2)(a) (above) the third and highest level of liability, provided for in Condition 9(2)(b), is ultimately a liability for some degree of negligence. However, it is framed differently. Condition 9(2)(b) starts from the strict liability of the carrier at common law but then reduces it by a string of specific exceptions, which excuse the carrier only if the carrier has used reasonable care, care not to prevent or avoid the excepted causes as would be required under Condition 9(2)(a), but reasonable care to minimise their effects.

The liability of the carrier under Condition 9(2)(b) differs, by way of contrast, from that of the carrier in the common law of carriage by sea and, subject to qualifications, in CMR, according to which, if the carrier proves a liability exception, it is then left to the claimant to defeat that defence by proving that the carrier had been negligent. Under Condition 9(2)(b), if the excepted event has "arisen", which it appears must be proved by the carrier in the usual way, the carrier is still not excused unless he "has used reasonable care to minimise its effects" and, presumably, he must prove that too. *1.296*

The Carrier is liable for any loss or mis-delivery of or damage to any goods comprising the Consignment. "Consignment" is defined in Condition 1. *1.297*

"Loss" is expressed as "physical" loss to eliminate doubt that had arisen under earlier conditions that referred simply to "loss"[8]; and thus distinguishes "loss" in Condition 9(2)(b) from "loss" in Condition 9(3), which is pecuniary loss. "Damage" to goods means any change in the physical condition of the goods which reduces their value.[9] It includes deterioration in goods as the result of delay.[10] Condition 9(2)(b) does not mention delay, which suggests that the carrier is not liable for consequent pecuniary loss to the customer, unless it results in physical damage to goods, and not therefore for loss of market at destination. *1.298*

"Misdelivery" is delivery other than to the right person or to a person who is reasonably believed to be the right person, and to the right place or what is reasonably believed to be the right place.[11] If misdelivery occurs, the carrier will be liable to the customer, only if misdelivery has caused loss of, or damage or delay to, the goods. Misdelivery of goods, however, is not only a breach of the contract of carriage but may well also amount to the tort of conversion. Conversion is a tort of strict liability and, in addition to whatever sum be the value of the converted goods, the claimant is *prima facie* entitled to recover all financial losses "flowing naturally and directly from the defendant's act of conversion, provided that they are not too remote". This was the view of Brooke L.J. in the Court of Appeal in the *Kuwait Airways* case.[12] An appeal against the decision of the court was dismissed,[13] however, on the question of causation the House held that each party in a series of conversions wrongfully excluded the owner from possession of his goods and was liable for loss which the owner would not have sustained if he had retained the *1.299*

8. *Young & Son (Wholesale Fish Merchants) Ltd.* v. *British Transport Commission* [1955] 2 Q.B. 177. Kahn-Freund, p. 263.
9. See in *Promet Engineering (Singapore) Pte Ltd.* v. *Sturge* [1997] 2 Lloyd's Rep. 146 at 151.
10. *Hartstoke Fruiterers Ltd.* v. *L.M.S. Ry. Co.* [1943] K.B. 362 (C.A.).
11. *M'Kean* v. *M'Ivor* (1870) L.R. 6 Ex. 36.
12. *Kuwait Airways* v. *Iraq Airways* [2001] 1 Lloyd's Rep. 161, 248, *per* Brooke L.J. delivering the judgment of the court (C.A.).
13. [2002] UKHL 19, [2002] 2 A.C. 883.

goods. Some of their Lordships, more than others, were clear that usual rules of causation did not necessarily apply. Thus Lord Nicholls, for example, observed of the simple "but for" test in cases of conversion that, "if the test is to be applied at all, the answer lies in keeping in mind, as I have said, that each person in a series of conversions wrongfully excludes the owner from possession of his goods. The exclusionary threshold test is to be applied on this footing. Thus the test calls for consideration of whether the plaintiff would have suffered the loss in question had he retained his goods and not been unlawfully deprived of them by the defendant."[14]

1.300 The tortious action, if brought by the customer, will be affected by the terms of the contract of carriage, unless the carrier has deliberately delivered to the wrong person or the wrong place. In that case, the contract exceptions do not apply either as a matter of construction *contra proferentem*[15] or because the breach of contract is a "fundamental breach" or deviation and exceptions are therefore disapplied,[16] also as a matter of construction.[17]

5. *Exceptions to strict liability*

1.301 If the customer has made a case against the carrier, that there has been loss or misdelivery of or damage to the goods, it is for the carrier to prove[18] that the loss, misdelivery or damage complained of is excused by one of the exceptions listed in Condition 9.2(b)(i) *et seq.* The carrier must prove that the loss etc. has "arisen from" one of the listed events, i.e., that it was caused by one of them.[19] If so, unless there has been deviation from the contract route amounting to "fundamental breach" and the carrier is thus disentitled from pleading any contractual exceptions,[20] the carrier will be excused.

1.302 *Prima facie*, like all contractual exceptions, the listed exceptions will be construed *contra proferentem*, strictly against the carrier. It has been argued that, as the carrier assumes an initial liability stricter than that of a common carrier, the exceptions should not be construed *contra proferentem*.[21] However, this has not been the attitude of the courts to other kinds of carrier, notably the carrier by sea, and it is not obvious that the RHA carrier should be in a better position in this respect.[22] Much depends on the interpretation of the exceptions in question, most of which have an established meaning.

1.303 (i) *An Act of God* is some elemental force of nature, which was the direct cause of the loss or damage and which could not have been foreseen or, if foreseen, could not have been guarded against by any ordinary or reasonable precaution.[23] Such events

14. At [83]. See Cane (2002) 118 L.Q.R. 544, 548.
15. *Alexander* v. *Railway Executive* [1951] 2 K.B. 882.
16. *Sze Hai Tong Bank* v. *Rambler Cycle Co.* [1959] A.C. 576 (P.C.).
17. *Photo Production Ltd.* v. *Securicor Transport Ltd.* [1980] A.C. 827.
18. Glass/Cashmore, para. 1.57; Palmer, p. 1106.
19. *Motor Union Ins. Co.* v. *Boggan* (1924) 130 L.T. 588, 590 (H.L.). See Comment 2 on Condition 16 of the Freightliner Conditions, para. 2.654, below.
20. See the Introduction to these Conditions, paras. 1.251 *et seq.*, above.
21. Glass/Cashmore, paras. 1.57 and 1.63.
22. Also in this sense: Kahn-Freund, p. 294.
23. Kahn-Freund, p. 243; *Nugent* v. *Smith* (1876) 1 C.P.D. 423, 437 concerning carriage by sea.

are rare. Kahn-Freund suggested a consignment struck by lightning.[24] Past cases suggest livestock injured by cold weather, when snow blocked the road,[25] and damage caused when a driver, apparently in good health, suffered a sudden heart attack at the wheel.[26]

(ii) *War* connotes aggression on the part of a government which exists at least *de facto*. A formal declaration of war is not necessary and anyway, if there has been no declaration, the case is probably a case of "hostilities". Hostilities are situations in which, whether or not a state of war exists within the increasingly obscure sense of international law, there is "armed conflict between competing nations".[27] The acts of terrorists do not fall into this category, unless the terrorists are sponsored by a government.[28] 1.304

A civil war "is a war which has the special characteristic of being civil—i.e. internal rather than external".[29] Having said this, Mustill J. declined to define "civil war" but observed that "a decision on whether such a war exists will generally involve a consideration of three questions: (1) Can it be said that the conflict was between opposing 'sides'? (2) What were the objectives of the 'sides', and how did they set about pursuing them? (3) What was the scale of the conflict, and of its effect on public order and on the life of the inhabitants?"[30] 1.305

Insurrection, like rebellion, connotes an organised attempt to overthrow a government,[31] whether or not the attempt is supported or inspired by another government.[32] The various causes mentioned in exception (ii) overlap. 1.306

(iii) *Seizure or forfeiture under legal process* is detention or interference by the courts as a result of legal proceedings and in this respect has been distinguished from the orders of government, referred to at the end of exception (ii). 1.307

(iv) *Error etc.* is a catchall exception by reference to the conduct of the customer. On the one hand, it is not clear what "mis-statement" and "misrepresentation" add to "error".[33] On the other hand, it is clear that exception (iv) overlaps with other excepted causes, such as insufficient or improper labelling, the subject of exception (vii). A prime example of exception (iv) is something done or omitted by the customer during loading or unloading, as to which, see also Condition 4. It seems that the carrier is excused under exception (iv) regardless of fault on the part of the customer.[34] Fraud by the customer is the subject of a specific provision, Condition 10. 1.308

(v) *Inherent defect*, it seems, is the same as the well-known concept of "inherent vice". Inherent vice, both in contract conditions and international carriage regimes, 1.309

24. Kahn-Freund, p. 244.
25. *Briddon* v. *Great Northern Ry.* (1858) 28 L.J.Ex. 51.
26. *Ryan* v. *Youngs* [1938] 1 All E.R. 522, 524 (C.A.).
27. *Kawasaki Kisen Kabushiki Kaisha* v. *Bantham S.S. Co. (No. 2)* (1938) 61 Ll.L.Rep. 131, 138, affirmed [1939] 2 K.B. 544 (C.A.).
28. *Pan American World Airways Inc.* v. *Aetna Casualty & Surety Co.* [1975] 1 Lloyd's Rep. 77 (U.S.C.A. 2 Cir., 1974).
29. *Spinney's (1948) Ltd.* v. *Royal Ins. Co. Ltd.* [1980] 1 Lloyd's Rep. 406, 429.
30. *Ibid.* at 429–430.
31. E.g. *ibid.*
32. *National Oil Co. of Zimbabwe (Pte)* v. *Sturge* [1991] 2 Lloyd's Rep. 281.
33. Palmer, p. 1106.
34. Cf. CMR, Art. 17.2 which refers to the "wrongful" act of the sender or consignee.

is taken to mean what it means at common law[35]: some defect in the goods which by its development through ordinary processes going on in those goods tends to the injury or destruction of the goods.[36]

1.310 Inherent defect is the central feature of exception (v) and characterises what is another catch-all exception. It embraces "inherent liability to wastage in bulk or weight" and "natural deterioration".[37] It overlaps "latent defect", which is a defect of any kind at all which could not be expected to be discovered by any inspection or test which the carrier could reasonably be expected to make.[38] Between them, inherent defect and latent defect cover "faulty design", which was included in 1998 nonetheless to avoid doubt.

1.311 (vi) *Insufficient or improper packing* is also a kind of inherent defect (exception (v)) and in most cases an instance of "act or omission . . . by the Customer" (exception (iv)). Packing is insufficient if it does not enable the particular goods to withstand the normal dangers of the kind contemplated by the particular transit. These include the handling to be expected by the carrier, and this must be considered in the light of what the person concerned can be taken to know about the contents of the package, bearing in mind that he has neither a right nor a duty to open a package to investigate its contents, unless stipulated in the contract.[39]

1.312 (vii) *Insufficient or improper labelling or addressing* is often a particular kind of act or omission of the customer (exception (iv)) or possibly of insufficient or improper packing (exception (vi)).

1.313 Exception (viii) is another catch-all exception taking in forms of public disorder of a lesser magnitude than those falling within exception (ii). For a riot there must be 12 or more persons with a common purpose, which must have been at least incepted and in a manner which involves the use or threat of unlawful violence and was "such as would cause a person of reasonable firmness present at the scene to fear for his personal safety".[40] There is a presumption that contracts use terms such as "riot", which have a technical sense in criminal law, in that same sense.[41]

1.314 Civil commotion, which may overlap with riot,[42] is "something considerably more serious than a leaderless mob"[43] and "is used to indicate a stage between riot and civil war".[44] It is a "rising of the people . . . for purposes of general mischief".[45]

1.315 A strike at common law is "a general concerted refusal by workmen to work in consequence of an alleged grievance".[46] For the purposes of labour law and

35. For a relatively recent decision see *Noten* v. *Harding* [1990] 2 Lloyd's Rep. 283 (C.A.).
36. See further CMR, Art. 17, Comment 6, paras. 1.96 *et seq.*, above.
37. Cf., however, *Donald & Son (Wholesale Meat Contractors) Ltd.* v. *Continental Freeze*, 1984 S.L.T. 182.
38. *The Amstelslot* [1963] 2 Lloyd's Rep. 223 (H.L.). On the distinction with "inherent vice", see further Clarke, *CMR*, para. 89a.
39. See further CMR, Art. 17, Comment 11, paras. 1.110 *et seq.*, above.
40. Public Order Act 1986, s.1. See Clarke, *Insurance*, Chap. 19–3E.
41. *London & Lancashire Fire Ins. Co.* v. *Bolands Ltd.* [1924] A.C. 836.
42. *Kuwait Airways* v. *Kuwait Ins. Co.* [1999] 1 Lloyd's Rep. 803 (H.L.).
43. *Spinney's (1948) Ltd.* v. *Royal Ins. Co. Ltd.* [1980] 1 Lloyd's Rep. 406, 437.
44. *Levy* v. *Assicurazioni Generali* [1940] A.C. 791, 800 (P.C.).
45. *Spinney's* case [1980] 1 Lloyd's Rep. 406, 438.
46. *William* v. *Naamlooze* (1915) 21 Com. Cas. 253, 257. See also *Tramp Shipping Corp.* v. *Greenwich Marine Inc.* [1975] 2 All E.R. 989, 992 (C.A.)

industrial relations it now has a statutory definition.[47] A restraint of labour does not seem to have been defined but certainly includes a threat by employees not to move or handle certain goods.[48]

(ix) *Failure by the Consignee to collect the goods* appears to be covered by exception (iv). In such circumstances the liability of the carrier would be that of an involuntary bailee.[49] See also Condition 6(2), proviso (b). 1.316

Condition 10: Fraud 1.317

The Carrier shall not in any circumstances be liable in respect of a Consignment where there has been fraud on the part of the Customer or the owner or the servants or agents of either in respect of that Consignment, unless the fraud has been contributed by the complicity of the Carrier or of any servant of the Carrier acting in the course of his employment.

Comment

At common law a statement is fraudulent if it is "made (1) knowingly, or (2) without belief in its truth, or (3) recklessly, careless whether it be true or false".[1] More recently in *Twinsectra*[2] Lord Hutton observed[3] that 1.318

"the courts often draw a distinction between subjective dishonesty and objective dishonesty, there are three possible standards which can be applied to determine whether a person has acted dishonestly. There is a purely subjective standard, whereby a person is only regarded as dishonest if he transgresses his own standard of honesty, even if that standard is contrary to that of reasonable and honest people. This has been termed the 'Robin Hood test' and has been rejected by the courts . . . Secondly, there is a purely objective standard whereby a person acts dishonestly if his conduct is dishonest by the ordinary standards of reasonable and honest people, even if he does not realise this. Thirdly, there is a standard which combines an objective test and a subjective test, and which requires that before there can be a finding of dishonesty it must be established that the defendant's conduct was dishonest by the ordinary standards of reasonable and honest people and that he himself realised that by those standards his conduct was dishonest. I will term this 'the combined test'."

The "combined test" was the decision of the majority of the House of Lords.

In practice, this is hard to prove. The main instance in the present context would be a fraudulent declaration about the nature or value of the goods consigned. Thus, if a carrier negligently damaged goods and split packing revealed that the goods, although declared to be of type A, were actually of type B for which the carrier normally made higher carriage charges, the carrier would be absolved, although at 1.319

47. See Deakin & Morris, *Labour Law* (3rd ed., London, 2001), Chap. 11.12.
48. *Young & Son (Wholesale Fish Merchants) Ltd.* v. *British Transport Commission* [1955] 2 Q.B. 177; Kahn-Freund, p. 249.
49. See Palmer, Chap. 15.
1. *Derry* v. *Peek* (1889) 14 App. Cas. 337, 374.
2. *Twinsectra Ltd.* v. *Yardley* [2002] UKHL 12, [2002] 2 A.C. 164.
3. *Ibid.* at [27]. Lord Slynn (at [6]), Lord Steyn (at [7]) Lord Hoffmann (at [20]) agreed. Lord Millett dissented (at [146]).

fault and although there was no causal connection between the fraud and the damage.

1.320

Condition 11: Limitation of Liability

(1) Except as otherwise provided in these Conditions, the liability of the Carrier in respect of claims for physical loss, mis-delivery of or damage to goods comprising the Consignment, howsoever arising shall in all circumstances be limited to the lesser of:

(a) the value of the goods actually lost, mis-delivered or damaged; or
(b) the cost of repairing any damage or of reconditioning the goods; or
(c) a sum calculated at the rate of £1,300 Sterling per tonne on the gross weight of the goods actually lost, mis-delivered or damaged; and the value of the goods actually lost, mis-delivered or damaged shall be taken to be their invoice value if they have been sold and shall otherwise be taken to be the replacement cost thereof to the owner at the commencement of transit, and in all cases shall be taken to include any Customs and Excise duties or taxes payable in respect of those goods:

Provided that:

(i) in the case of loss, mis-delivery of or damage to part of the Consignment the weight to be taken into consideration in determining the amount to which the Carrier's liability is limited shall be only the gross weight of that part regardless of whether the loss, mis-delivery or damage affects the value of other parts of the Consignment;
(ii) nothing in this Condition shall limit the liability of the Carrier to less than the sum of £10;
(iii) the Carrier shall be entitled to proof of the weight and value of the whole of the Consignment and of any part thereof lost, mis-delivered or damaged;
(iv) the Customer shall be entitled to give to the Carrier written notice to be delivered at least 7 days prior to commencement of transit requiring that the £1,300 per tonne limit in 11(1)(c) above be increased, but not so as to exceed the value of the Consignment, and in the event of such notice being given the Customer shall be required to agree with the Carrier an increase in the carriage charges in consideration of the increased limit, but if no such agreement can be reached the aforementioned £1,300 per tonne limit shall continue to apply.

(2) The liability of the Carrier in respect of claims for any other loss whatsoever (including indirect or consequential loss or damage and loss of market), and howsoever arising in connection with the Consignment, shall not exceed the amount of the carriage charges in respect of the Consignment or the amount of the claimant's proved loss, whichever is the lesser, unless:

(a) at the time of entering into the Contract with the Carrier the Customer declares to the Carrier a special interest in delivery in the event of physical loss mis-delivery or damage or of an agreed time limit being exceeded and agrees to pay a surcharge calculated on the amount of that interest, and
(b) at least 7 days prior to the commencement of transit the Customer has delivered to the Carrier written confirmation of the special interest, agreed time limit and amount of the interest.

Comment

1.321 Condition 11, which limits the amount of the carrier's liability, was completely revised in the 1998 edition of the Conditions. The terms of Condition 11(1)(a) and (b) bring the Condition as a whole more into line with other standard trading conditions and with general principles of law.[1]

1.322 Condition 11(1) limits the liability of the carrier in respect of claims for physical loss, mis-delivery of or damage to goods comprising the Consignment, howsoever

1. Also to avoid disputes such as that arising in *Spectra International plc* v. *Hayesoak Ltd.* [1997] 1 Lloyd's Rep. 153.

arising, thus for any breach[2] of contractual duty assumed under Condition 9. The Carrier is liable under Condition 9 not strictly but only for one degree or another of negligence. Hence, when an earlier version of this phrase ("however sustained") was considered by the Commercial Court,[3] it held that, in spite of the well known rules of construction *contra proferentem* stated in the *Canada Steamship* case,[4] the limit in Condition 11 applied when the loss or damage had been caused by the carrier's negligence.

Condition 11(2) limits the liability of the carrier in respect of claims for any other loss whatsoever to the amount of the carriage charges. The statement that "any other loss whatsoever" includes "indirect or consequential loss" is evidently an attempt to broaden the scope of the Condition. However, a restrictive view of such wording in an earlier version of the RHA Conditions was taken by Saville J. in *Shell* v. *P & O*.[5] *1.323*

Broadly speaking, courts have been slow to condemn standard conditions in widespread use as unreasonable under the Unfair Contract Terms Act 1977.[6] Moreover, quite apart from that, courts are less hostile to limitation clauses such as Condition 11 than to exclusion clauses.[7] However, a condition not unlike Condition 11 was struck out in *Overseas Medical Supplies* v. *Orient Transport Services*.[8] The "carrier" in that case was a firm that specialised in the carriage of goods and associated services, including notably the provision of a specialist service importing and exporting exhibition equipment, a service which frequently involved a "round trip" for the goods or equipment exhibited. The Condition was struck out because it was a case *1.324*

"of a trading organization which, under a single contract had agreed to combine at least two activities or functions in respect of which the nature of the work undertaken, the incidence of risk as between the parties, and the effect of a breach of duty by the ['carrier'] were all of different character, yet were treated without distinction as subject to a single [and relatively low] limitation of liability. . . . Whereas it may be that, in relation to certain 'package' services, a broad brush approach to limitation of liability will be reasonable, and indeed may largely be dictated by the type of insurance cover available in the market to the supplier, the Judge held that, in this case, such an approach was unjust and inappropriate for reasons which he clearly and comprehensively stated."[9]

Condition 12: Indemnity to the Carrier *1.325*

The Customer shall indemnify the Carrier against:

(1) all liabilities and costs incurred by the Carrier (including but not limited to claims, demands, proceedings, fines, penalties, damages, expenses and loss of or damage

2. See, in particular, Condition 9, Comment 4, paras. 1.295 *et seq.*, above.
3. *Cert plc* v. *George Hammond plc* [1999] 2 All E.R. (Comm.) 976.
4. *Canada Steamships Line Ltd.* v. *R.* [1952] A.C. 192 (P.C.). See also *Alderslade* v. *Hendon Laundry Ltd.* [1945] K.B. 189 (C.A.).
5. Shell *Chemicals UK Ltd.* v. *P & O Roadtanks Ltd.* [1993] 1 Lloyd's Rep. 114, 118, with reference to *Croudace Construction Ltd.* v. *Cawoods Concrete Products Ltd.* [1978] 2 Lloyd's Rep. 55 (C.A.).
6. See the Introduction to the RHA Conditions, paras. 1.251 *et seq.*, above.
7. *Ailsa Craig Fishing Co. Ltd.* v. *Malvern Fishing Co. Ltd.* [1983] 1 W.L.R. 964 (H.L.).
8. [1999] 2 Lloyd's Rep. 273 (C.A.). But cf. *Frans Maas (UK) Ltd.* v. *Samsung Electronics (UK) Ltd.* [2004] 2 Lloyd's Rep. 251.
9. *Ibid.*, *per* Potter L.J. at [21].

to the carrying vehicle and to other goods carried) by reason of any error, omission, mis-statement or misrepresentation by the Customer or other owner of the Consignment or by any servant or agent of either of them, insufficient or improper packing, labelling or addressing of the Consignment or fraud as in Condition 10;

(2) all claims and demands whatsoever (including for the avoidance of doubt claims alleging negligence), by whosoever made and howsoever arising (including but not limited to claims raised by or arising out of the carriage of Dangerous Goods and claims made upon the Carrier by HM Customs and Excise in respect of dutiable goods consigned in bond) in excess of the liability of the Carrier under these Conditions in respect of any loss or damage whatsoever to, or in connection with, the Consignment whether or not caused or contributed to directly or indirectly by any act, omission, neglect, default or other wrongdoing on the part of the Carrier, its servants, agents or sub-contractors.

Comment

1.326 Condition 13, which was substantially revised in 1998,[1] requires the customer to indemnify the carrier in respect of (1) liability and cost incurred by the carrier as a result of errors or mis-statements, or insufficient packing or labelling of the consignment by the customer; and (2) "all claims or demands whatsoever" arising out of the carriage of Dangerous Goods (see Condition 3) or claims by HM Customs and Excise. The Court of Appeal held[2] that the words "all claims or demands whatsoever" in an earlier version of this Condition applied to negligence; and words such as "howsoever caused" have also been held to cover negligence.[3] However, later in the House of Lords one judge, Lord Fraser, held that the word "whatsoever" in a contractual indemnity did not have that effect, but was no more than a word of emphasis.[4]

1.327 It should be noted, in respect of breach of the criminal law, that, if a breach is no more than a possibility at the time that the contract of carriage is concluded, an indemnity of this kind will be enforced. If, however, the commission of an offence is likely and, in particular, if it occurs with the encouragement or connivance of the customer—for example excessive loading—the indemnity is contrary to public policy and unenforceable.[5] Indeed, the contract of carriage as a whole may be unenforceable in such circumstances on that ground.[6]

1.328

Condition 13: Time Limits for Claims

(1) The Carrier shall not be liable for:

(a) damage to the whole or any part of the Consignment, or physical loss, mis-delivery or non-delivery of part of the Consignment unless advised thereof in writing within seven days, and the claim is made in writing within fourteen days, after the termination of transit;

1. Cf. a decision on an earlier version of the Condition: *Chas. Davis (Metal Brokers) Ltd.* v. *Gilyott & Scott Ltd.* [1975] 2 Lloyd's Rep. 422.
2. *Gillespie Bros. Ltd.* v. *Roy Bowles Transport Ltd.* [1973] Q.B. 400 (C.A.).
3. See Treitel, Chap. 7.1.2(2).
4. *Smith* v. *South Wales Switchgear Ltd.* [1978] 1 All E.R. 18, 26 (H.L.). See further *Shell Chemicals UK Ltd.* v. *P & O Roadtanks Ltd.* [1995] 2 Lloyd's Rep. 297 (C.A.) and Palmer, p. 1111.
5. *Askey* v. *Golden Wine Co. Ltd.* (1948) 64 T.L.R. 379, 380.
6. *Ashmore, Benson, Pease & Co.* v. *A.V. Dawson* [1973] 1 W.L.R. 828 (C.A.); Clarke, *CMR*, para. 243a.

(b) any other loss unless advised thereof in writing within twenty-eight days, and the claim is made in writing within forty-two days, after the commencement of transit.

Provided that if the Customer proves that,

(i) it was not reasonably possible for the Customer to advise the Carrier or make a claim in writing within the time limit applicable, and

(ii) such advice or claim was given or made within a reasonable time, the Carrier shall not have the benefit of the exclusion of liability afforded by this Condition.

(2) The Carrier shall in any event be discharged from all liability whatsoever and howsoever arising in respect of the Consignment unless suit is brought within one year of the date when transit commenced.

(3) In the computation of time where any period provided by these Conditions is seven days or less, Saturdays, Sundays and all statutory public holidays shall be excluded.

Comments

1. Notice of claims

Condition 13, which was substantially revised in 1998, first requires the customer to give notice of claims to the carrier. If action is brought late in the limitation period the carrier will be badly placed to find evidence to mount a defence. Hence, it is generally regarded as reasonable for carriers to require notice of some kind within a short time after the events that may give rise to a claim, followed, if the matter is to be taken further, by a more detailed claim within a certain time after that. Thus Condition 13(1)(b) requires the customer to "advise" the carrier in writing[1] within seven days of damage, physical loss, mis-delivery or non-delivery of part, and within 28 days of any other loss. "Advice" means notification,[2] and notification means that the communication must have been received to be effective.[3] The content of the "advice" is not that the customer intends to claim but the allegation of damage etc. so that the carrier can investigate the allegation before the facts become obscure or evidence hard to obtain. Computation of time is in accordance with Condition 13(3). *1.329*

2. Claims

The periods for claims are respectively 14 days after the end of transit and 42 days after the commencement of transit.[4] Condition 13(2) superimposes a contractual limit of one year on the time within which action may be brought by the customer against the carrier. Computation of time is in accordance with Condition 13(3). Condition 13(2) amounts to a considerable restriction on the time allowed by statute. Claims against a carrier, whether based in contract, tort or bailment are subject to sections 2 and 5 of the Limitation Act 1980, and must be brought within six years of the date on which the cause of action accrued, subject to extension in certain cases. Such conditions are found in other transport documents, however, notably international Conventions. In practice, it is likely to be difficult for a carrier *1.330*

1. For the meaning of writing see, CMR Art. 30, Comment 3, para. 1.180, above.
2. Kahn-Freund, p. 393.
3. *Holwell Securities Ltd.* v. *Hughes* [1974] 1 All E.R. 164 (C.A.).
4. See Condition 6, para. 1.278, above.

to gather evidence to resist a claim unless given prompt notice that a claim will be brought or is likely.

1.331 The provision of the BIFA Conditions corresponding to Condition 13(2), which requires notice of claims within 14 days and proceedings within nine months, was held to be unreasonable under the Unfair Contract Terms Act 1977 at first instance in *Granville Oil*. On appeal, however, the provision was upheld.[5] See the Introduction to these Conditions, paragraph 1.256, above.

1.332

Condition 14: Lien

(1) The Carrier shall have a general lien against the Customer, where the Customer is the owner of the Consignment, for any monies whatever due from the Customer to the Carrier. If such a lien is not satisfied within a reasonable time, the Carrier may, at his absolute discretion sell the Consignment, or part thereof, as agent for the Customer and apply the proceeds towards the monies due and the expenses of the retention, insurance and sale of the Consignment and shall, upon accounting to the Customer for any balance remaining, be discharged from all liability whatever in respect of the Consignment.

(2) Where the Customer is not the owner of the Consignment, the Carrier shall have a particular lien against said owner, allowing him to retain possession, but not dispose of, the Consignment against monies due from the Customer in respect of the Consignment.

Comment

1.333 At common law every carrier or at least every common carrier,[1] which however according to the Preamble the RHA carrier is not, has a "particular" lien on goods in his possession for freight and charges in relation to goods which he is ready and able to deliver. This lien is distinguished from a "general lien" in respect of debts due under previous contracts of carriage between the same parties. A general lien does not arise as a matter of law but is often granted by a condition of the contract of carriage. Condition 14 is such a condition. As is usual in such conditions, Condition 14 gives the carrier a right to sell the goods if the debt is not paid within a reasonable time. In so far as the carrier is empowered to sell the goods without giving notice to the owner of the goods, Glass/Cashmore[2] suggested that this part of the clause is likely to fail under the Unfair Contract Terms Act 1977.

1.334

Condition 15: Unreasonable Detention

The Customer shall be liable to pay demurrage for unreasonable detention of any vehicle, trailer, container or other equipment but the rights of the Carrier against any other person in respect thereof shall remain unaffected.

Comment

1.335 Demurrage is a charge made for delay caused to valuable property, a penalty because the delay prevents the property being used to its full commercial potential

5. *Granville Oil & Chemicals Ltd.* v. *Davis & Turner Ltd.* [2003] EWCA Civ 570, [2003] 2 Lloyd's Rep. 356.

1. Cf. Glass/Cashmore, para. 1.110.

2. Para. 1.113. Generally, see Palmer, p. 577 and pp. 1112–1113.

by its owner. It has its origin in maritime law as far back as the seventeenth century as regards delay caused to a ship by the charterer of the ship. The concept is found in the nineteenth century in respect of the detention of railway wagons and has been used since the early twentieth century in the way it is used in Condition 15.

Condition 16: Law and Jurisdiction *1.336*

The Contract shall be governed by English law and the United Kingdom courts alone shall have jurisdiction in any dispute between the Carrier and the Customer.

PART 2

CARRIAGE OF GOODS BY RAIL

I. INTERNATIONAL CARRIAGE OF GOODS BY RAIL: CIM

A. CIM 1980: INTRODUCTION

1. CIM: history and sources

COTIF was signed at Berne in 1980 and given effect in the United Kingdom by section 1(1) of the International Transport Conventions Act 1983 with effect from 1 May 1985.[1] As regards passengers and luggage, the uniform system of law is CIV, set out in Appendix A to COTIF and, as regards goods, the uniform system of law is CIM, set out in Appendix B to COTIF. CIV and CIM are sometimes referred to as the Berne Conventions. Whereas originally CIM (and/or CIV) was the Convention, to which states became party, since 1980 the treaty, to which states may become party, is COTIF. COTIF consolidates earlier Conventions, and also provides a constitution for OTIF, the principal aim of which is "to establish a uniform system of law applicable to the carriage of passengers, luggage and goods in international through traffic by rail between Member States, and to facilitate the application and development of this system": COTIF, Article 2.1. *2.1*

The original version of CIM dates from 1890, the most recent versions before 1980 being those of 1970, 1961 and 1952, the last being the first to which the United Kingdom was party.[2] The 1980 version appended to COTIF was subjected to minor amendments at the second session of the Revision Committee[3] of OTIF held at the end of May 1990, and which came into force on 1 June 1991.[4] It is also the subject of a Protocol, which modifies Articles 1, 3, 4, 7 and 11 of COTIF, and Articles 1, 18, 40, 43, 44, 47 and 58 of CIM. The Protocol was ratified by the United Kingdom on 6 October 1994.[5] It became part of United Kingdom legislation by S.I. 1994/1907 to come into force on 1 November 1996.[6] The English *2.2*

1. S.I. 1985/612. The text of COTIF was published as Cmnd. 8535 and republished as Cm. 41.
2. For an outline of the history of CIM, see Kahn-Freund, pp. 408 *et seq.*; Anglade, Bull.OCTI 1967.199; Rodière, No. 252 and Allégret, Bull.OCTI 1994.3.
3. Established by Arts. 5 and 8 of COTIF.
4. BT 1991.106.
5. Bull.OCTI 1994.113.
6. Bull.OCTI 1995.177. For the English and French texts see Cm. 2232 of 1993.

text of the revised RID, which concerns the carriage of dangerous goods by rail, has also been published.[7]

2.3 The working languages of OTIF are French and German.[8] There are official translations of CIM and of other documents emanating from OTIF in English and other languages too, such as Arabic, Italian and Dutch.[9] However, in case of doubt or ambiguity in the interpretation of the text, since 1924 the official language of CIM has been French.[10] The acronym CIM is a shortened version of the acronym RUCIM used in France for the full title of the Convention: "Regles uniformes concernant le transport international ferroviaire des marchandises".[11] In many States party to COTIF, although not the United Kingdom, the national law governing purely national movements of goods by rail is aligned to CIM.[12] In the tradition of European uniform law, this commentary refers not only to decided cases but also to the opinion of jurists and commentators on CIM, notably Allégret (France), Helm (Germany) and Spera (Austria).

2. The liability regime

2.4 CIM contains compulsory uniform contract terms for the international carriage of goods by rail,[13] as defined by CIM, Articles 1 and 2. Like the Hague Rules on carriage by sea, but unlike CMR, CIM applies only if the appropriate transport document, in the case of CIM a consignment note (Articles 11, 12, 13 and 18), is issued. CIM governs the performance of the contract of carriage: whether and on what terms a railway is obliged to accept goods for carriage (Articles 3, 4, 5 and 8), acceptance for carriage (Article 11), carriage and other charges (Articles 6, 14, 15, 17 and 29), including surcharges (Article 24), the route (Article 14) and time period for transit (Article 27), the condition, packing and marking of goods (Article 19), loading (Articles 20 and 23), checking goods (Articles 21 and 22), documentation (Article 25), completion and modification of transit (Articles 30, 31 and 32), response to circumstances preventing carriage (Article 33), delivery (Article 28), and response to circumstances preventing delivery (Article 34).

2.5 CIM regulates the liability of the carrier. If a person entitled to claim (Article 53) can prove that the goods have suffered loss, damage or delay between the time of acceptance for carriage and the time of delivery (Article 28), a cause of action arises on the basis of Article 36.1 and action can be brought against one or more of the railways involved in the transit (Articles 35 and 55) in the appropriate court (Article 56). With some important qualifications,[14] the burden of proving that the railway has not performed the contract is on the claimant. Apart from Article 11 regarding the significance of the consignment note and Article 52 regarding ascertainment of

7. Bull.OCTI 2000.290. See the Carriage of Dangerous Goods and Use of Transportable Pressure Equipment Regulations 2004 (S.I. 2004/568), which came into force on 10 May 2004.
8. COTIF, Art. 1.3.
9. COTIF, Art. 28.
10. *Ibid.*
11. Peyrefitte, No. 26.
12. Haenni, pp.14–15. For example, the EVO in Germany.
13. *Cass. 12.12.11*, S 1912.1.284; *Cass. It. 12.2.73* (1976) 11 ETL 137.
14. See Art. 21 (verification) and Art. 28 (delivery).

loss or damage at the time of delivery, the nature of the proof required of the claimant is largely left to the *lex fori*. The railway responds to the case against it either by proof that the loss or damage did not in fact occur while it was responsible for the goods or, while admitting that it did, by pleading a ground of exoneration, as a defence. The railway may plead a defence under Article 36.2 or, as regards normal wastage, Article 41, or a special risk under Article 36.3, but in the latter case the plea will be defeated if, nonetheless, the claimant can prove that the loss or damage was not attributable to the risk: Article 37.2. Arguably, the railway has a general or residual duty of care in relation to goods carried.[15] If these defences fail, the railway is liable to pay compensation (Article 40), unless the action has been extinguished (Article 57) or the limitation period has run (Article 58). If compensation is payable, the amount is limited by Articles 42 and 43; however, that limit will be lifted to the extent of a declaration of special interest in delivery (Articles 16 and 46) or if the claimant can prove that the loss, damage or delay was caused by wilful misconduct or gross negligence on the part of the railway (Article 44).

3. The revision of CIM

The Revision Committee of OTIF is empowered to amend secondary provisions of CIM,[16] such as those concerning the maximum liability of the railway.[17] Any such amendments come into force automatically "for all Member States on the first day of the twelfth month following the month in which the Central Office notifies them to the Member States, unless one-third of the Member States have objected within four months from the date of such notification",[18] and hence without positive approval by Parliament. Such changes are published in the United Kingdom by command paper. Changes in primary provisions of CIM must be agreed by the General Assembly of OTIF, recorded in a Protocol subject to signature and ratification by Member States, in the usual way.[19] A revised version of the entire text of CIM was agreed in 1999 and is set out at paragraphs 2.482 *et seq.*, below. *2.6*

B. THE TEXT OF THE CIM 1980[1]

(As amended by the Protocol of 20 December 1990)

Title I, General provisions: Article 1, Scope *2.7*

1. Subject to the exceptions provided for in Article 2, the Uniform Rules shall apply to all consignments of goods for carriage under a through consignment note made out for a route over the territories of at least two States and exclusively over lines or services included in the list provided for in Articles 3 and 10 of the Convention, as well as, where appropriate, to

15. See Art. 20, Comment 3.
16. COTIF, Art. 19.3. Note also Art. 9 (supplementary provisions).
17. CIM, Art. 40.
18. COTIF, Art. 21.2.
19. COTIF, Art. 20.1.
1. Appendix B to the Convention concerning International Carriage by Rail (COTIF) of 9 May 1980, Uniform Rules Concerning the Contract for International Carriage of Goods by Rail (CIM).

carriage treated as carriage over a line in accordance with Article 2.2, second sub-paragraph of the Convention.

2. In the Uniform Rules the expression "station" covers: railway stations, ports used by shipping services and all other establishments of transport undertakings, open to the public for the execution of the contract of carriage.

Comments

1. Contracts for the international carriage of goods by rail

2.8 Article 1, as qualified by Article 2, concerns the scope of CIM. CIM applies to the contractual relations between consignor, consignee and railway, however, not those between consignor and forwarder. The contract is for the consignment of goods for carriage under a through consignment note made out for a route over the territories of at least two contracting States and exclusively over listed lines or for listed services.

2.9 The reference to goods in the context of COTIF means anything capable of carriage, except passengers and luggage (regulated by CIV), and includes such things as corpses and wagons on wheels.[2]

2. The consignment note

2.10 CIM applies only if a through consignment note is made out for transport (exclusively) over the listed lines of (at least two) contracting states. Thus carriage cut into national segments, whereby goods are passed on at the border and without a through consignment note, is not governed by CIM.[3] To this extent and subject to this inconvenience, parties to a contract of carriage may choose not to be regulated in that regard by CIM.[4] Even if the parties want their contract to be subject to CIM and prepare a consignment note, in the absence of a consignment note duly stamped, as required by Article 11.5, it has been maintained that CIM does not apply.[5] In this regard CIM differs radically from CMR, in respect of which it was not considered practicable to expect strict compliance, so "absence, irregularity or loss of the consignment note shall not affect the existence or validity of the contract".[6] However, some courts[7] have held that the railway may refuse a consignment note that does not satisfy the requirements of CIM, Articles 12 and 13, but if it accepts a note that does not conform in some respect, CIM may still apply.[8]

3. Listed routes

2.11 The route must be over the territories of at least two States and exclusively over listed lines or for listed services. This condition is strictly applied. If the note

2. Allégret, Fasc. 683, 2; Spera, Art. 1 Anm. 5.
3. Helm, Art. 1, Anm 8.
4. Rodière, No. 254.
5. *Brussels 27.1.72*, ULR 73 (II) 450; Rodière, No 334–337.
6. See CMR, Art. 4, para. 1.23, above.
7. Cited by Rodière, No. 254.
8. Also in this sense: Helm, Art. 6, Anm 6. *Contra*: Wick, p. 23.

provides for carriage from France to the Ruritanian border via the Czech Republic, on-carriage from the border into Ruritania being the subject of a further transport document, carriage to the border is subject to CIM. If, however, the note purports to cover the entire journey, CIM does not apply, as Ruritania is not a contracting party and its lines are not listed.[9] It is disputed whether CIM may be adopted voluntarily by the contracting parties in such a case. However, the better view is that it may.[10]

The list referred to in Article 1.1 is of States which have given effect to CIM: Albania, Algeria, Austria, Belgium, Bulgaria, Croatia (from 1 December 1992), Czech Republic, Denmark, Finland, France, Germany, Greece, Hungary, Iran, Iraq, Ireland, Italy, Georgia, Latvia, Lebanon, Liechtenstein, Lithuania (from 1 November 1995), Luxembourg, Macedonia (from 1 November 1995), Morocco, Norway, Netherlands, Poland, Portugal, Rumania, Slovakia (from 1 June 1994), Slovenia (from 1 November 1995), Sweden, Switzerland, Syria, Spain, Tunisia, Turkey, Ukraine, the United Kingdom and Yugoslavia. The list is drawn up and kept up to date by OCTI. The lines include not only railway lines between stations, but sidings and marshalling yards and, in a few instances, also routes by road and sea.[11] *2.12*

For example, the maritime stage across the Channel to France is a listed line, so that, in theory at least, there can be a movement by rail, for example, from Lille to Birmingham "exclusively over lines" listed, without resort to a tunnel. The Channel Tunnel was added to the list with effect from 14 March 1994.[12] This line is on the French list, as well as maritime lines from France to Ireland, Morocco, Algeria and Tunisia.[13] In consequence, Article 1.2 provides that a reference in CIM to a station covers a port (*gare-maritime*) or any place or depot used by the railway in connection with the movement of goods by rail.[14] However, CIM will apply to a listed sea stage only if the consignment note is made out for a route that also embraces a rail stage: a movement from the port of Dieppe to the port of Newhaven without contemplating movement by rail is not governed by CIM.[15] If these conditions are met, CIM will apply to the sea stage. However, Article 48 allows the railway in question to include a note in its listing adopting certain exemptions appropriate to carriage by sea. These exemptions are mostly derived from the Hague Rules, in addition to those provided by Article 36.[16] *2.13*

If a conforming consignment note has been issued for carriage on a route over the territories of at least two states, the international element takes the case out of national law and into the domain of CIM[17] and CIM regulates the rights and liabilities arising under the contract of carriage regardless of where the damage *2.14*

9. *Rheims 23.6.75*, ULR 1977 (I) 360, confirmed: *Cass 16.5.77*, JCP 78, II.18881.
10. Allégret, Fasc. 683, 8.
11. Allégret, Fasc. 683, 12; Spera, Art. 1, Anm 9.
12. Bull.OCTI 1994.1.
13. Allégret, Fasc. 683, 13.
14. Spera, Art. 1, Anm 11.
15. Allégret, Fasc. 683, 19.
16. Glass/Cashmore, para. 4.04. As regards combined carriage by road and rail see Allégret, Bull.OCTI 1995.56, and Compère, *ibid.*, p. 69.
17. Cf. *Paris 18.5.76*, Bull.OCTI 1977.112.

occurs,[18] or whether the actual route taken differs from that initially intended,[19] or whether the goods get any further than the first State.[20]

2.15 **Article 2, Exceptions from scope**

1. Consignments between sending and destination stations situated in the territory of the same State, which pass through the territory of another State only in transit, shall not be subject to the Uniform Rules;

(a) if the lines or services over which the transit occurs are exclusively operated by a railway of the State of departure; or

(b) if the States or the railways concerned have agreed not to regard such consignments as international.

2. Consignments between stations in two adjacent States and between stations in two States in transit through the territory of a third State shall, if the lines over which the consignments are carried are exclusively operated by a railway of one of those three States, be subject to the internal traffic regulations applicable to that railway if the sender, by using the appropriate consignment note, so elects and where there is nothing to the contrary in the laws and regulations of any of the States concerned.

Comment

2.16 Article 2 concerns the scope of CIM and qualifies the effect of Article 1. In particular, as regards territorial connecting factors significant in Article 1, transit movements are disregarded; for example, a movement between stations in France that passes through Monaco. In case (a) referred to in Article 2.1, the law governing this movement is indicated by rules of private international law and is likely to be the *lex loci contractus*.[1] In case (b), which was designed to accommodate existing bilateral arrangements,[2] the agreement is likely to indicate the governing law.[3]

2.17 An example of a consignment between stations in two adjacent States where the lines are exclusively operated by a railway of one of those States, is carriage from any French station to certain stations in Basle and Geneva or to Ventimiglia. Ventimiglia is the French frontier station situated in Italy, however, a movement from Paris to Ventimiglia would be treated as one internal to France.[4] As an example of a consignment between stations in two States but with transit through the territory of a third State where the lines are exclusively operated by a railway of one of those three States, Spera gives a movement between Switzerland and Austria via Liechtenstein.[5]

18. *Cass 12.12.11*, S 1912.1.284; *Cass. It. 12.2.73*, Giur. It. 1973.1681, (1976) 11 ETL 137.
19. Spera, Art. 1, Anm 7.
20. *OGH 28.2.2001*, TranspR 2002.346; Bull.OCTI 2003.10; see also Allégret, Fasc. 683, 7 and cases cited.
1. Allégret, Fasc. 683, 23.
2. Spera, Art. 2, Anm 4.
3. Allégret, Fasc. 683, 24.
4. Allégret, Fasc. 683, 29.
5. Spera, Art. 2, Anm 8.

Article 3, Obligation to carry *2.18*

1. The railway shall be bound to undertake all carriage of any goods in complete wagon-loads, subject to the terms of the Uniform Rules, provided that:
   (a) the sender complies with the Uniform Rules, the supplementary provisions and the tariffs;
   (b) carriage can be undertaken by the normal staff and transport resources which suffice to meet usual traffic requirements;
   (c) carriage is not prevented by circumstances which the railway cannot avoid and which it is not in a position to remedy.

2. The railway shall not be obliged to accept goods of which the loading, transhipment or unloading requires the use of special facilities unless the stations concerned have such facilities at their disposal.

3. The railway shall only be obliged to accept goods the carriage of which can take place without delay; the provisions in force at the forwarding station shall determine the circumstances in which goods not complying with that condition must be temporarily stored.

4. When the competent authority decides that:
   (a) a service shall be discontinued or suspended totally or partially,
   (b) certain consignments shall be refused or accepted only subject to conditions,
   (c) certain goods shall be accepted for transport in priority,

these measures shall, without delay, be brought to the notice of the public and the railways; the latter shall inform the railways of the other States with a view to their publication.

5. The railways may, by joint agreement, concentrate goods traffic between certain places on specified frontier points and transit countries.

These measures shall be notified to the Central Office. They shall be entered by the railways in special lists, published in the manner laid down for international tariffs, and shall come into force one month after the date of notification to the Central Office.

6. Any contravention of this Article by the railway may constitute a cause of action for compensation for loss or damage caused.

Comments

1. The Obligation

Article 3 reflects the public service role of the railway and the fact that national railways have usually enjoyed a monopoly within the state.[1] For practical commercial reasons the carrier's obligation, stated in Article 3.1, is now confined to complete wagon-loads, whereas under previous versions of CIM it extended to smaller consignments. The change was introduced to reflect changes in national practice.[2] Of course, smaller consignments may be grouped into wagon-loads, which the railway would be obliged to take. However, express parcels are governed by RIEx, which contains special provisions for parcels.[3] *2.19*

The obligation stated in Article 3.1 is sanctioned by the provision contained in Article 3.6. As with the position of a common carrier at common law, failure to carry when required by the law gives rise to liability for consequential loss or damage. However, as this stems from a public service element in CIM, this is true only when CIM applies *proprio vigore*, and not when it applies purely as part of a contract of carriage or as part of foreign law subject to which the contract has been made.[4] Evidently, refusal to contract cannot be a breach of the contract which, *ex* *2.20*

1. Allégret, Fasc. 683, 34.
2. Allégret, Fasc. 683, 35.
3. See Part II.
4. Kahn-Freund, p. 413.

hypothesi, has not come into existence[5]; the action is statutory and hence free of the limits of liability in Article 40 which are designed to be part of a contract.[6] Anyway, commentators have suggested that there is a cause of action under Article 3.6 only when there has been fault on the part of the railway.[7]

2. Qualifications

2.21 The obligation stated in the first sentence of Article 3.1 is qualified in self-evidently sensible ways by Article 3.1(a) to (c), Article 3.2 , Article 3.3 and Article 4. Thus it is a condition of the obligation that carriage can be undertaken by the normal transport resources (Article 3.1(b)), which include motive power, rolling-stock, depots, and storage space, etc.; however, it is controversial whether personnel are included.[8] Again, the carrier cannot be expected to take goods, such as swapbodies, for which handling requires the use of special facilities unless the stations concerned have such facilities at their disposal. Less obviously, the carrier is not obliged to accept goods which cannot be moved "without delay"[9] because the sender cannot use the railway as a convenient warehouse pending transportation. But if the railway does accept the goods in such a case, it is obliged to transport them and, if it does not, it will be liable unless excused by the terms of the contract, for example, the defences in Article 33 and Article 36.[10] If acceptance of such goods involves storage pending carriage, the railway holds them as warehouseman rather than carrier under CIM.[11]

2.22 The obligation stated in the first sentence of Article 3.1 is also qualified by Article 3.4, which contemplates overriding interests of State or *ordre public*, such as measures to safeguard persons or property or to protect the environment. The competent authority is the department of government concerned such as the Department of Trade and Industry in the UK. Similar considerations of economic efficiency explain Article 3.5, the idea of which is to rationalise the movement of goods in the light of the facilities available. The corollary is that the consignor may not be able to choose the route. The agreement in question is that of the railways concerned. If another railway objects, for example on the ground of unfair competition, it must object by means of the procedures envisaged by COTIF, Article 9.

2.23

Article 4, Articles not acceptable for carriage

The following shall not be accepted for carriage:

(a) articles the carriage of which is prohibited in any one of the territories in which the articles would be carried;

5. Allégret, Fasc. 683, 53.
6. Spera, Art. 3, Anm 38.
7. Spera, Art. 3, Anm 37.
8. Spera, Art. 3, Anm 9.
9. I.e. within normal time limits: Spera, Art. 3, Anm 18.
10. Spera, Art. 3, Anm 12.
11. Allégret, Fasc. 683, 42.

(b) articles the carriage of which is a monopoly of the postal authorities in any one of the territories in which the articles would be carried;
(c) articles which, by reason of their dimensions, their mass, or their packaging, are not suitable for the carriage proposed, having regard to the installations or rolling stock of any one of the railways which would be used;
(d) substances and articles which are not acceptable for carriage under the Regulations concerning the international carriage of dangerous goods by rail (RID), Annex 1 to the Uniform Rules, subject to the exceptions provided for in Article 5.2.

Additional Uniform Regulations (DCU) *2.24*

DCU 1 *If it is discovered during transit that goods which are not acceptable for carriage have been accepted, even under their prescribed descriptions, carriage must be stopped. If necessary, instructions shall be requested from the sender; these must conform to the national laws of the State in which the consignment has been stopped. The sender shall be required to pay the carriage and other charges which have been incurred up to the point where the consignment has been stopped, and also any surcharges raised in accordance with Article 24, even if the consignee has modified the contract of carriage in accordance with Article 31.*

If, however, it is a question of articles the carriage of which is reserved to the postal authorities in one of the States concerned, they may be handed over to the postal authorities against payment of the charges due by cash on delivery.

Comment

The obligation to carry stated in the first sentence of Article 3.1 is qualified not only by Article 3.1(a) to (c), Article 3.2 and Article 3.3 but also by Article 4 as regards articles which be their very nature (cases (c) and (d)) or for some extraneous reason (cases (a) and (b)) are not acceptable for carriage under CIM. Case (a) covers, for example, local public opinion demanding the exclusion of certain toxic substances or, in a Muslim state, alcoholic drinks. *2.25*

Whereas some of the exceptions regulated by Article 3 may be ignored by the carrier, Article 4 is mandatory: the railway has not just a right of refusal but a duty to refuse the goods, at least, as regards international carriage: purely national carriage is still possible, if permitted by national law.[1] If the railway finds that it has accepted goods for carriage in breach of Article 4 because, for example, the sender misled the railway about the nature of the goods, the opinion of writers is that the contract is not void lest the railway lose CIM defences.[2] This conclusion is supported by DCU 1 to Article 4. *2.26*

Article 5, Articles acceptable for carriage subject to conditions *2.27*

1. The following shall be acceptable for carriage subject to conditions:
(a) substances and articles acceptable for carriage subject to the conditions laid down in the RID or in the agreements and tariff clauses provided for in paragraph 2;
(b) funeral consignments, railway rolling stock running on its own wheels, live animals and consignments the carriage of which presents special difficulties by reason of their dimensions, their mass or their packaging: subject to the conditions laid down in the supplementary provisions, these may derogate from the Uniform Rules. Live

1. Spera, Art. 4, Anm 3.
2. Allégret, Fasc. 683, 55; Spera, Art. 4, Anm 3.

animals must be accompanied by an attendant provided by the consignor. Nevertheless an attendant shall not be required when the international tariffs permit or when the railways participating in the carriage so permit at the consignor's request; in such cases, unless there is an agreement to the contrary, the railway shall not be liable for any loss or damage resulting from any risk which the attendant was intended to avert.

2. Two or more States, by agreement, or two or more railways, by tariff clauses, may jointly determine the conditions with which certain substances or articles not acceptable for carriage under the RID must comply if they are nevertheless to be accepted.

States or railways may, in the same manner, make the conditions for acceptance laid down in the RID less rigorous.

Such agreements and tariff clauses must be published and notified to the Central Office which will bring them to the notice of the States.

2.28 Additional Uniform Regulations (DCU)

DCU 1, to §1(b) *Funeral consignments shall be accepted subject to the following conditions:*

1. *the charges shall be paid by the sender;*
2. *cash-on-delivery and disbursements shall not be permitted;*
3. *the consignment note shall not be marked "to await order";*
4. *the carriage shall be subject to the laws and regulations of each State, except in so far as such carriage is governed by a special convention between States; an attendant is not necessary if the sender undertakes by indicating on the consignment note to have the body collected within the time limit laid down in the destination State.*

2.29 **DCU 2b, to §1(b)** *Railway rolling stock running on its own wheels shall be accepted under the following conditions;*

1. *a railway must have verified that such rolling stock is in running order and have certified this by an inscription on the vehicle or by a special certificate;*
2. *locomotives, tenders, rail motor-coach units and railcars must be accompanied by an attendant, who is provided by the sender and is competent to maintain the vehicle in running order. Other railway vehicles may be accompanied by an attendant.*

2.30 **DCU, 3 to §1(b)** *In addition, the following conditions shall be applicable to the acceptance of livestock for carriage:*

1. *the sender shall comply with the veterinary regulations of the departure, destination and transit States;*
2. *the consignment note shall not be marked "to await order".*

Small animals consigned in a package need not be accompanied.

2.31 **DCU 4, to §1(b)** *The conditions of acceptance of consignments the carriage of which presents special difficulties shall be determined in each case by the railway, after consultation with the sender.*

Comment

2.32 The obligation to carry stated in the first sentence of Article 3.1 is qualified not only by Article 3.1(a) to (c), Article 3.2, Article 3.3 and Article 4 but also by Article 5. Whereas Article 4 is concerned with goods that the carrier is not allowed to carry under CIM, Article 5 is concerned with goods that the carrier is obliged to carry but under special rules. These rules may be rules drafted by carriers for the transportation of human remains, for example, which must be moved speedily in view of the possibility of decomposition[1] (case (b)); or rules agreed at diplomatic level between

1. Spera, Art. 5, Anm 4.

states such as RID (case (a)). RID, containing rules for the carriage of dangerous goods, is to be found in Annex 1 to CIM.[2] As regards liability to third parties, note also the Convention on Civil Liability for Damage caused during the Carriage of Dangerous Goods by Road, Rail and Inland Navigation Vessels 1989 (CRTD), which became open for signature on 1 February 1990.[3]

Article 6, Tariffs, private agreements 2.33

1. Carriage charges, whether or not calculated separately for different sections of the route, and supplementary charges shall be calculated in accordance with the tariffs which are legally in force and duly published in each State and which are applicable at the time when the contract of carriage is made.

2. The tariffs must indicate all the special conditions applicable to the carriage, in particular the information necessary for calculating carriage and supplementary charges and, where appropriate, the conditions governing the conversion of currencies.

The conditions of the tariffs may not derogate from the Uniform Rules unless the latter expressly so provide.

3. The tariffs must be applied to all users on the same conditions.

4. Railways may enter into private agreements for reduced charges or other concessions, provided that comparable conditions are granted to users in comparable circumstances.

Reductions in charges or other concessions may be granted for the purpose of railway or public services, or for charitable purposes.

Publication of the measures taken under the first and second subparagraphs shall not be compulsory.

5. International tariffs may be declared compulsorily applicable in international traffic to the exclusion of the internal tariffs.

The application of an international tariff may be made conditional on there being an express request for it in the consignment note.

6. The tariffs and amendments to the tariffs shall be regarded as duly published from the time when the railway makes all the details thereof available to the users.

The publication of international tariffs shall be compulsory only in those States whose railways are parties to such tariffs as railways of departure or destination.

7. Increases in international tariff charges and any other provisions which would have the effect of making the conditions of carriage laid down by such tariffs more rigorous shall not come into force until at least fifteen days after their publication, except in the following cases:

(a) if an international tariff makes provision for the extension of an internal tariff to cover the whole route, the periods for publication of such internal tariff shall be applicable;

(b) if increases in the charges contained in an international tariff follow a general increase in the charges contained in the internal tariffs of a participating railway, they shall come into force on the day after their publication, on condition that the adjustment of the international tariff charges caused by such general increase has been announced at least fifteen days in advance; nevertheless, such announcement may not be made prior to the publication of the increase in the internal tariff charges in question;

(c) if the carriage and supplementary charges provided for in the international tariffs have to be modified to take account of fluctuations in rates of exchange or if obvious errors have to be corrected, such adjustments and corrections shall come into force on the day after their publication.

8. In States where there is no obligation to publish certain tariffs or to apply them to all users under the same conditions, the provisions of this Article, to the extent that they contain such an obligation, shall not be binding.

2. See the Carriage of Dangerous Goods and Use of Transportable Pressure Equipment Regulations 2004 (S.I. 2004/568), which came into force on 10 May 2004.

3. See Visser, Bull.OCTI 1993.51 and Kafka, Bull.OCTI 1993.57.

9. The railways may not charge any amount over and above the carriage and supplementary charges laid down in the tariffs other than the amounts disbursed by them. Such amounts shall be duly noted and entered separately in the consignment note, together with any relevant supporting information. When this information is provided in documents attached to the consignment note and if the corresponding amounts are to be paid by the consignor, the documents shall not be delivered to the consignee with the consignment note, but shall be forwarded to the consignor with the account of charges referred to in Article 15.7.

Additional Uniform Regulation (DCU)

2.34 **DCU 1, to § 9** *The sums disbursed by the railways shall consist mainly of Customs duties, local dues, or other administrative charges, of cartage costs from one station to another, which are not shown in the tariff, cost of repairing the external or internal packing of goods, necessary for ensuring that they are kept in good condition, cost of transhipment and adjustment of the load, cost of re-icing and other similar expenses.*

Comments

1. Uniform terms and conditions

2.35 The object of Article 6 is that the same terms and conditions, especially charges, should apply to all customers, and with sufficient publicity. However, provision for special agreements for certain kinds of transport is made by Article 6.4. and Article 8. The person responsible for the payment of charges is indicated by Article 15.

2.36 Although the primary meaning of tariff is a list of charges, in CIM tariff has a special meaning. It has been variously defined as the administrative regulations specifying the terms of the contract of carriage which are to be established and published in advance[1]; or as any statement of the conditions of carriage laid down in advance.[2] Nonetheless the main terms or conditions are those concerning charges dealt with in Article 6.1. These are first, carriage charges which are calculated according to distance and hence according to route: see Article 14; and secondly, supplementary charges such as charges for warehousing goods or for weighing goods.

2.37 Fairness requires equal treatment of customers: Article 6.3. Originally this meant the same terms and the same scale of charges for all customers. However, Article 6.4, which allows special rates to be agreed for certain categories of goods[3] but in all such cases, was introduced in 1961 to enable railways to compete with other forms of transport, notably road transport[4]; an example is that of express delivery of frozen meat overnight at special rates.[5] Fairness also requires openness. Hence the charges must be "duly published". This does not mean that the charges must be published in some kind of official journal; it suffices that copies of the tariffs can be obtained from the railway and that a new tariff has been publicly announced so that users know that they may need to get a new copy.[6]

1. *Liège 12.1.78*, ULR 1979 (II) 242, 244.
2. Spera, Art. 6, Anm 2.
3. Concerning the legal status of these agreements, see *T. Vienna 31.10.96*, Bull.OCTI 1996.202.
4. *BGH 14.4.76* (1976) 11 ETL 787, 794.
5. *BGH 14.4.76*.
6. Allégret, Fasc. 683, 67. See Art. 6.6.

2. Application in the United Kingdom

English law, however, does not require railway companies to publish tariffs at all or to apply them uniformly to users, as envisaged by CIM. In the past the British Railways Board used standard conditions. The same is true of railway companies today such as Freightliner (paras. 2.603 *et seq.*, below) and EWS (paras. 2.695 *et seq.*, below). To accommodate the situation in the United Kingdom, an Additional Protocol to CIM was signed in 1961, to the effect that provisions of CIM such as Article 6 do not apply in the United Kingdom but that the carriage charges and supplementary charges which the railway companies are authorised to make in the United Kingdom shall be applicable there to international traffic governed by CIM.[7] The British position is accommodated by Article 6.8. *2.38*

Article 7, Unit of Account. Rate of exchange or of acceptance of foreign currency *2.39*

1. The unit of account referred to in the Uniform Rules shall be the Special Drawing Right as defined by the International Monetary Fund.

The value in Special Drawing Right of the national currency of a State which is a Member of the International Monetary Fund shall be calculated in accordance with the method of valuation applied by the International Monetary Fund for its own operations and transactions.

2. The value in Special Drawing Right of the national currency of a State which is not a member of the International Monetary Fund shall be calculated by the method determined by that State.

The calculation must express in the national currency a real value approximating as closely [*sic*] to that which would result from the application of paragraph 1.

3. In the case of a State which is not a member of the International Monetary Fund and whose legislation does not permit the application of paras. 1 or 2 above, the unit of account referred to in the Uniform Rules shall be deemed to be equal to three gold francs.

The gold franc is defined as 10/31 of a gramme of gold of millesimal fineness 900.

The conversion of the gold franc must express in the national currency a real value approximating as closely [*sic*] to that which would result from the application of paragraph 1.

4. Within three months after the entry into force of the Convention and each time that a change occurs in their method of calculation or in the value of their national currency in relation to the unit of account. States shall notify the Central Office of their method of calculation in accordance with paragraph 2, or of the results of the conversion in accordance with paragraph 3.

The Central Office shall notify the States of this information.

5. The railway shall publish the rates at which:

(a) it converts sums expressed in foreign currencies but payable in domestic currency (rates of conversion);

(b) it accepts payment in foreign currencies (rates of acceptance).

Comment

Article 7 is important mainly for the payment in convertible currency of the compensation according to Article 40 *et seq*. Like other carriage conventions such as CMR, WC or MC, the Special Drawing Right (SDR) is the unit for converting currency values, one which was developed by the International Monetary Fund (IMF) and which is based on a basket of the currencies of certain members of the *2.40*

7. Kahn-Freund, p. 431.

IMF. Conversion of SDRs into sterling is regulated by the International Transport Conventions Act 1983, s. 5. The rate of "exchange" between any local currency such the pound and SDRs is published in the daily financial press in contracting States, such as the *Financial Times*.

2.41 **Article 8, Special provisions for certain types of transport**

1. In the case of the haulage of privately owned wagons, special provisions are laid down in the Regulations concerning the international haulage of private owners' wagons by rail (RIP), Annex II to the Uniform Rules.

2. In the case of the carriage of containers, special provisions are laid down in the Regulations concerning the international carriage of containers by rail (RICo), Annex III to the Uniform Rules.

3. In the case of express parcels traffic, railways may, by tariff clauses, agree on special provisions in accordance with the Regulations concerning the international carriage of express parcels by rail (RIEx), Annex IV to the Uniform Rules.

4. Two or more States, by special agreement, or two or more railways by supplementary provisions or by tariff clauses, may agree on terms derogating from the Uniform Rules for the following types of consignments:

(a) consignments under cover of a negotiable document;
(b) consignments to be delivered only against return of the duplicate of the consignment note;
(c) consignments of newspapers;
(d) consignments intended for fairs or exhibitions;
(e) consignments of loading tackle and of equipment for protection of goods in transit against heat or cold;
(f) consignment over all or part of the route under cover of consignment notes which are not used for charging and billing;
(g) consignments sent under cover of an instrument suitable for automatic data transmission.

Comment

2.42 Article 8 provides for special agreements for certain kinds of transport and thus derogates from Article 6, which established the general rule that the same terms and conditions, especially charges, should apply to all customers. The reason for allowing special agreements for the categories listed in Article 8 is self-evident. For example, the carriage of newspapers (category (c)) is specially regulated in view of the need for speed.[1] However, as regards categories (a) and (b), the CIM consignment note is not a negotiable document; the movements envisaged do not appear to occur often.

2.43 **Article 9, Supplementary provisions**

1. Two or more States or two or more railways may make supplementary provisions for the execution of the Uniform Rules. They may not derogate from the Uniform Rules unless the latter expressly so provide.

1. Spera, Art. 8, Anm 15.

2. The supplementary provisions shall be put into force and published in the manner required by the laws and regulations of each State. The Central Office shall be notified of the supplementary provisions and of their coming into force.

Comments

1. The nature and source of supplementary provisions

The purpose of supplementary provisions, also referred to as additional regulations, is to complete or fill out the CIM rules. Supplementary provisions must be supplementary in that they add to CIM or fill a gap. Any attempt to pass a supplementary provision in order to adopt a particular interpretation of CIM on a matter which is capable of resolution solely by interpretation of CIM is a derogation that is not permitted.[1] *2.44*

It was envisaged that they might be drafted by States or by railways and, in practice, model supplementary provisions (DCU) have been elaborated and published by the railways under the auspices of the *Comité International des Transports Ferroviaires* (CIT), a non-governmental international organisation, the secretariat of which was established at the headquarters of Swiss Railways (CFF) in Berne.[2] The provisions, which are model contract terms and lack any statutory force,[3] are agreed by representatives of the railways of contracting states. *2.45*

2. Derogation

Derogation is provided for: *2.46*

(a) by Article 5.1(b) in relation to the carriage of funeral consignments, railway rolling stock running on its own wheels, live animals and consignments the carriage of which presents special difficulties by reason of their dimensions, their mass or their packaging;
(b) by Article 8.4 in relation to consignments under cover of a negotiable document, consignments to be delivered only against return of the duplicate of the consignment note, consignments of newspapers, consignments intended for fairs or exhibitions, consignments of loading tackle and of equipment for protection of goods in transit against heat or cold, consignments over all or part of the route under cover of consignment notes which are not used for charging and billing, and consignments sent under cover of an instrument suitable for automatic data transmission;
(c) by Article 12 in relation to the form and contents of the consignment note;
(d) by Article 19.6 in relation to the manner of carriage of goods which are fragile or may become scattered in wagons and goods which may taint or damage other goods; and

1. *Cass. 17.4.1980*, BT 1981.284; Allégret, Fasc. 683, 103. Cf. Rodière No. 255.
2. See Leimgruber Bull.OCTI 1981.128.
3. Cf Bull.OCTI 1995.1.

(e) by Article 30 in relation to the subsequent orders, i.e. orders modifying the contract initially agreed, that the consignor is entitled to give to the railway.

2.47 **Article 10, National law**

1. In the absence of provisions in the Uniform Rules, supplementary provisions or international tariffs, national law shall apply.

2. "National law" means the law of the State in which the person entitled asserts his rights, including the rules relating to conflict of laws.

Comments

1. The law governing the international carriage of goods by rail

2.48 CIM, the most detailed of the international Conventions regulating the carriage of goods, is intended to provide a self-sufficient regime, and thus, in principle, national law is irrelevant. Certain points of detail are left to supplementary provisions: Article 9. Such other points as might arise are specifically left to national law by Article 10. This is a reference not only to national law relating specifically to carriage by rail but to all relevant substantive law, as well as private international law.[1] The object is to prevent the automatic application of the substantive law of the forum.[2]

2.49 Although a reference to national law does not suggest a reference to national tariffs, not least because the CIM versions of 1961 and 1970 contained an express reference to tariffs which is absent from the version of 1980, it has been argued that purposive interpretation suggests the contrary.[3] In any event, as regards the United Kingdom, the relevant national law does not contain tariffs: see Article 6, Comment 2, and Article 14

2. The domain of national law

2.50 The points left to national law are as follows:

(i) The law of the place of the forwarding station governs (a) whether the railway is obliged to offer temporary storage at the forwarding station: Article 3.3; (b) prepayment of charges: Article 11.2; (c) the handing of goods to the railway, the duty of loading and, absent relevant international tariffs, the type of wagons used: Article 20.1, 2 and 4; and (d) disbursements in connection with COD payments: Article 17.5.

(ii) The law of the place of the destination station governs certain aspects of delivery: Article 28.3 and 6; and, as will in most cases be the same, the law

1. Allégret, Fasc. 683, 108; Haenni, p. 14; Helm, Art. 54, Anm 3(b).
2. Helm, Art. 54, Anm 3(a).
3. Helm, Art. 54, Anm 3(b).

"in force at the place of delivery" governs certain aspects of the railway's responsibility when circumstances prevent delivery as originally contracted for: Article 34.5; and again, as will in most cases be the same, the procedure for the ascertainment of partial loss or damage is governed by the law of "the State in which such ascertainment takes place": Article 52.2. The law will be different in cases in which carriage to (Article 33) or delivery at (Article 34) the destination station has been prevented and so delivery has to made at a station other than the destination station.

(iii) The *lex fori* is the "national law" mentioned in Article 58.5 that governs the suspension and interruption of periods of limitation.[4]

(iv) In other cases, the law to be applied is resolved by the conflicts rules of the forum. For example, Article 22.1 concerning the duty of the railway to "ascertain the mass of the goods or the number of packages and the actual tare of the wagons" refers to the "provisions in force in each State" and this will usually result in a reference to the law of the place of loading.

Title II, Making and execution of the contract of carriage: Article 11, Making the contract of carriage *2.51*

1. The contract of carriage shall come into existence as soon as the forwarding railway has accepted the goods for carriage together with the consignment note. Acceptance is established by the application to the consignment note and, where appropriate, to each additional sheet, of the stamp of the forwarding station, or accounting machine entry, showing the date of acceptance.

2. The procedure laid down in paragraph 1 must be carried out immediately after all the goods to which the consignment note relates have been handed over for carriage and—where the provisions in force at the forwarding station so require—such charges as the consignor has undertaken to pay have been paid or a security deposited in accordance with Article 15.7.

3. When the stamp has been affixed or the accounting machine entry has been made, the consignment note shall be evidence of the making and content of the contract.

4. Nevertheless, when the loading of the goods is the duty of the consignor in accordance with tariffs or agreements existing between him and the railway, and provided that such agreements are authorised at the forwarding station, the particulars in the consignment note relating to the mass of the goods or to the number of packages shall only be evidence against the railway when that weight or number of packages has been verified by the railway and certified in the consignment note. If necessary these particulars may be proved by other means.

If it is obvious that there is no actual deficiency corresponding to the discrepancy between the mass or number of packages and the particulars in the consignment note, the latter shall not be evidence against the railway. This shall apply in particular when the wagon is handed over to the consignee with the original seals intact.

5. The railway shall certify receipt of the goods and the date of acceptance for carriage by affixing the date stamp to or making the accounting machine entry on the duplicate of the consignment note before returning the duplicate to the consignor.

The duplicate shall not have effect as the consignment note accompanying the goods, nor as a bill of lading.

4. *Cass. 18.12.84*, BT 1985.331.

Comments

1. Conclusion of the contract

2.52 Article 11 concerns the conclusion of the contract of carriage, and the evidence of that contract in the consignment note The tacit assumption behind Article 11 is that the contract is a contract between the consignor and the railway; and that the consignee is not a party to the contract, unless the consignor concludes it as agent for the consignee or the consignee has accepted the consignment note: Article 28.[1] These assumptions reflect French and German domestic law [2] and differ from those of English common law, whereby *prima facie* the consignor contracts with the railway as agent for the consignee. In the French view, however, the eventual consignee can enforce the contract but as the beneficiary of a *stipulation pour autrui* [3]; and in the German tradition, it is a *Vertrag zugunsten eines Dritten* with similar effect.[4] That was not the case in England, at least not until the Contracts (Rights of Third Parties) Act 1999, came into force. Concerning the effect of the Act on contracts of carriage, see the Freightliner Conditions, Condition 4, Comment 2, paragraphs 2.616 *et seq.*, below.

2.53 The contract is concluded not (like other contacts) by any unequivocal indication of consent on the part of the railway, such as a fax, but by a particular and substantial act: acceptance of the goods by the railway together with a conforming consignment note. This reference to acceptance by the railway replaces reference (in versions up to 1952) to acceptance at the forwarding station, to make it clear that a contract may be formed not only when the consignor brings goods to the station but also when the railway collects goods from the consignor.[5] One effect is that, unlike contracts to carry goods by other modes of transport, the contract of international carriage by rail is never entirely executory, thus reflecting the limits on the discretion of the railway to refuse goods: Article 3. In France this feature has given rise to debate about the nature of the contract—whether it is based entirely on consent (*contrat consensuel*) or whether some act of performance is a prerequisite of contracting (*contrat réel*).[6]

2. The consignment note

2.54 A conforming consignment note is essential. Without a stamped consignment note of the kind required by Article 11, there is no contract of carriage,[7] although where the note is lost or destroyed, alternatives, for example as to proof, are acceptable.[8] Once the goods have been accepted by the railway by this stamping procedure, the railway becomes responsible for the goods and liable for theft of the

1. *Reims 9.6.88*, BT 1989.481.
2. Kahn-Freund, p. 424 .
3. Allégret, Fasc. 684, 8.
4. Spera, Art. 11, Anm 2.
5. Haenni, p. 69; Spera, Art. 11, Anm 3.
6. Allégret, Fasc. 684, 4.
7. Haenni, p. 57. Cf. Spera, Art. 11, Anm 13.
8. Spera, *loc. cit.*

goods, even if they are still in a wagon in the consignor's siding.[9] However, if a consignment consists of several parcels or units, acceptance does not occur until all of the consignment in question has been accepted by stamping of the consignment note.[10]

Whether or not stamping itself is essential, assuming that a consignment note has been issued, is controversial. A Belgian court has held that, in the absence of a stamp, no acceptance of the goods has been established[11]; but most commentators consider that stamping is just one means of proving the existence of a contract, which may therefore be proved by other means.[12] Payment of charges, however, is clearly not a precondition of the conclusion of the contract of carriage[13] In modern practice payment may or may not take place where the goods are accepted. *2.55*

When the loading of the entire wagon of goods is the duty of the consignor, a special rule found in Article 11.4 is necessary. This, of course, is because, unless the railway exercises its right of verification, the railway may have no knowledge of the contents of the wagon. Moreover, in some countries, such as France, local regulations allow the railway to refuse the consignor's request for verification.[14] In this situation Article 11.4 provides that particulars such as number of packages and weight may be "proved by other means".[15] This sentence was introduced in CIM 1961 because before that some courts, in particular the French courts,[16] would not permit the matter to be proved by other means. *2.56*

French courts, it appears, are still reluctant to accept other means of proof. For example, when the verification was inadmissible because, by mistake, the railway had stamped the note in the wrong place and that stamp had later been stamped over at the destination station, the claimant sought to rely on an invoice of contents accompanying the goods. That too was rejected by the court, as it had been drawn up by the consignor and not been agreed by the railway.[17] In the same vein a forwarder (*transitaire*) had the goods officially weighed before being placed in sealed railway wagons, but did not get verification by the railway. The forwarder was held liable to his client for having failed to get sufficient proof of weight to enable the client to bring a successful action against the railway for shortage.[18] The French courts are not alone in this stance. In a case decided in Hungary, the railway refused the consignor's request to have the number of parcels stated in the consignment note but did not object to a loading list, stating the number of parcels, which accompanied the note. While accepting that evidence of the number apart from the *2.57*

9. *Cass 21.1.24*, BT 1924.33.
10. Spera, Art. 11, Anm 4.
11. *Brussels 27.1.72*, ULR 1973 (II) 450.
12. Allégret, Fasc. 684, 7; Spera, Art. 11, Anm 5.
13. Spera, Art. 11, Anm 10.
14. Allégret, Fasc. 684, 15.
15. *T. Budapest, No. 56 Pf. 27 202/1971*, Bull.OCTI 1973.87, ULR 1974 (I) 350; *Lyon 24.11.70*, Bull.OCTI 1973.186; *OLG Hamburg 21.6.79*, Bull.OCTI 1980.13; *Athens 28.2.2003*, Bull. OCTI 2004.21.
16. E.g. *Cass. 9.5.49*, G.P. 1949.2.162.
17. *Rouen 29.4.82*, BT 1982.474.
18. *Aix 24.1.80*, BT 1980.173; Bull.OCTI 1980.112.

note was admissible, however, the court held this was not sufficient to establish the number of parcels sent.[19]

3. *The evidential role of the consignment note*

2.58 The evidential value of what is said in the consignment note is not a matter comprehensively dealt with by CIM and thus depends in part, at least, on the *lex fori*.[20] The issue is still one that is the subject of debate,[21] as follows. As regards damage, if the railway enters no reservation about damage which, if the damage had been present on consignment, would have been apparent, that is, generally, evidence that it was not there on consignment and must have been sustained later.[22] As regards the weight of goods received, although the weight of the goods is entered in the note by the consignor, it has been held in France that that figure may be sufficient evidence to make a case of weight loss (by reference to a discrepancy at destination) even if the railway has not checked.[23] The decision, however, turned in part on French law: the court pointed out that by Article 29 French law determined "the circumstances in which the railway must ascertain the mass of the goods" and that, by the French tariff rules, the railway is bound by a declaration of weight that it does not verify.

2.59 If the claimant does have enough evidence against the railway to establish *prima facie* that loss or damage occurred while the railway was responsible for the goods, that presumption may be rebutted by the railway. For example, in one case[24] the SNCF was able to show that the weight was stated in error by an inexperienced person (who had not deducted the weight of the wagon from the total weight in order to ascertain the weight of contents!) and this was sufficient to rebut the case although that person was an employee of SNCF. Moreover, according to Article 11.4, para. 2, where it is obvious that there is an error in the particulars in the consignment note, the latter shall not be evidence against the railway. A particular instance is where the wagon is handed over to the consignee with the original seals intact. Seals intact are not alone conclusive evidence that there has been no deficiency,[25] however, *ceteris paribus*, the fact that they are intact is enough to allow the judge to reach that conclusion.[26]

4. *The duplicate consignment note*

2.60 The duplicate of the consignment note in the hands of the consignor lacks the effect of the consignment note accompanying the goods (Article 11.5), however, the duplicate is not without importance:

19. *T. Budapest, No. 56 Pf. 27 202/1971*, Bull.OCTI 1973.87, ULR 1974 (I) 350.
20. See note by OCTI to *OLG Düsseldorf 13.7.67*, Bull.OCTI 1969.88.
21. Allégret, Fasc. 684, 14.
22. *Ibid.*
23. *Paris 14.10.68*, Bull.OCTI 1969.153.
24. *Lyon 24.11.70*, Bull.OCTI 1973.186
25. *OLG Hamburg 21.6.79*, Bull.OCTI 1980.13.
26. Allégret, Fasc. 684, 19. E.g. *Amiens 28.9.92*, BTL 1994.130.

(a) As the top copy accompanies the goods, it is the duplicate that the consignor retains as proof of what the railway has received from the consignor and of what the railway has promised to do. "With a bill of lading it shares the feature of being a receipt and evidence of the terms of the contract, but unlike a bill of lading it is not a document of title."[27]
(b) Production of the duplicate is required if the consignor is to modify the contract, for example by delivery to a different consignee (Article 30.2). Hence, although it is expressly provided that the duplicate does not have the role of a bill of lading (Article 11.5), control of the duplicate gives effective control of the goods.[28]
(c) It is the duplicate copy which is put into the hands of the consignee to enable the consignee to obtain delivery.[29]
(d) The duplicate is evidence that the consignor has paid the charges referred to in Article 11.[30]
(e) The duplicate must be produced by the consignor or the consignee, as the case may be (see Article 53) to show entitlement to bring a claim against the railway.[31]

Article 12, Consignment note *2.61*

1. The consignor shall present a consignment note duly completed.
A separate consignment note shall be made out for each consignment. One and the same consignment note may not relate to more than a single wagon load. The supplementary provisions may derogate from these rules.
2. The railways shall prescribe a standard form of consignment note, which must include a duplicate for the consignor.
In the case of certain traffic, notably between adjacent countries, the railways may prescribe, in the tariffs, the use of a simplified form of consignment note.
In the case of certain traffic with countries which have not acceded to this Convention, tariffs may provide for recourse to a special procedure.
3. The consignment note must be printed in two or where necessary three languages, at least one of which shall be one of the working languages of the Organisation.
International tariffs may determine the language in which the particulars to be filled in by the consignor in the consignment note shall be entered. In the absence of such provisions, they must be entered in one of the official languages of the State of departure and a translation in one of the working languages of the Organisation must be added unless the particulars have been entered in one of those languages.
The particulars entered by the consignor in the consignment note shall be in Roman lettering, save where the supplementary provisions of international tariffs otherwise provide.

Additional Uniform Regulations (DCU)

DCU 1, to § 1, sub-para. 1 *The railways shall publish the instructions relating to the completion of those parts of the consignment note which directly affect the sender.* *2.62*

27. Kahn-Freund, p. 415. *Idem*: Spera, Art. 11, Anm 13 and Anm 22.
28. Allégret, Fasc. 684, 22.
29. Kahn-Freund, *loc. cit.*
30. Allégret, Fasc. 684, 20.
31. Spera, Art. 11, Anm 23.

2.63 **DCU 2, to § 1, sub-para. 2** *The following can be tendered for carriage with a single consignment note:*

(a) indivisible articles and articles of exceptional dimensions requiring the use of more than one wagon;

(b) consignments loaded in several wagons, when special arrangements for the traffic in question, international tariffs or agreements between the railways concerned so permit over the entire route. In this case, each wagon shall constitute a separate consignment. However, the subsequent orders referred to in Articles 30 and 31 must not have the effect of separating wagons tendered for transport with a single consignment note.

The following must not be tendered for carriage under cover of a single consignment note:

(a) goods which, by reason of their nature, cannot be loaded together without detriment;

(b) goods which are to be loaded partly by the railway and partly by the sender;

(c) goods which cannot be loaded together without infringing the regulations of the Customs or other administrative authorities;

(d) goods accepted for carriage subject to certain conditions, when loading them together or with other goods is prohibited by virtue of the RID or agreements and tariff clauses mentioned in Article 5, § 2.

2.64 **DCU 3, to § 1, sub-para. 2** *In the case of traffic conveyed over lines of different gauges, the number of consignment notes to be used for the throughout journey is determined by the number of wagons loaded on the forwarding railway.*

In the case of traffic originating at a station situated on a narrow gauge line (less than 1.435 metre gauge), the number of consignment notes to be used for the throughout journey is determined by the number of wagons loaded on the line of wider gauge connecting with the railway line of narrow gauge. The regulations of the forwarding railway operating lines of narrow gauge may, however, provide that the number of consignment notes to be used for the throughout journey is determined by the number of wagons loaded at the forwarding station.

2.65 **DCU 4, to § 2, sub-para. 1** *The railways shall publish the model of the consignment note, which must be capable of being completed by carbon copying. The form shall be printed on substantial non-transparent white writing-paper; when relating to Grande Vitesse each sheet shall bear two red borders, one on the top edge and the other on the bottom edge, both back and front. The sheet to be handed to the consignee shall be described as the "original of the consignment note", and the one retained by the sender as the "duplicate consignment note".*

2.66 **DCU 5, to § 2, sub-para. 1** *With regard to the publication of the model consignment note, the railways shall comply with the procedure laid down by their national law.*

2.67 **DCU 6, to § 2, sub-para. 1** *The competent railway organisations shall contact the principal international rail users associations, also the international organisations with responsibility in Customs matters, before introducing amendments to those parts of the consignment note which directly concern the sender or the Customs authorities.*

2.68 **DCU 7, § 2, sub-para. 1** *Consignment notes must be certified that they conform with the prescribed document by the impression of a railway stamp, where applicable at the cost of the requesting party.*

2.69 **DCU 8, to § 2, sub-para. 1** *The model shall indicate which parts of the form are to be completed by the sender and which are usually to be completed by the railway. The details entered on the consignment note must be clearly legible on all sheets of the form.*

Should the consignment note not provide a special space for any particular details to be given by the sender, the sender shall enter these in the space provided for his declarations, unless the international tariff applicable prescribes the use of a different space.

2.70 **DCU 9, § 2, sub-para. 1** *The particulars entered in the consignment note shall be written or printed in indelible characters. Consignment notes in which entries have been written over or erased or those on which pieces of paper have been pasted shall not be accepted. Entries* *may be struck out on condition that the sender authenticates the deletion by his signature and that, where the number or the mass of the packages is concerned, he inserts the corrected quantities in words.*

DCU 10, to § 2, sub-para. 1 *On delivery, the person entitled may require the railway to transfer the details relating to extensions of the transit period from the back of the sheet which is retained by the consignee railway to the back of the original of the consignment note. As an alternative to transfer of these details, the railway may provide the authorised party with a photocopy.* *2.71*

Within a period of three months after arrival of the goods, the person entitled may, in justified cases, ask to see that sheet of the consignment note which is retained by the destination railway and which contains the transit stamps. The railway may either allow such authorised party to examine this document on its own premises, send it to him on loan, or supply a photocopy.

DCU 11, to § 3, sub-para. 3 *The entries made on the consignment note by the sender can be in other than Latin characters, provided they are in one of the official languages of the departure State and are translated into one of the working languages of the Organisation (French or German).* *2.72*

Comment

Article 12 contains basic rules about the consignment note, the number of notes (Article 12.1) and the form of the consignment note (Article 12.2 and Article 12.3 but with most of the detail stated in the DCUs). *2.73*

As regards Article 12.1, it makes self-evident sense to have a basic rule on one separate consignment note for each consignment unless the consignment was so large that it stretched over more than one wagon. Even if it is intended that a single consignment for a single destination shall be spread over more than one wagon the wagons may have to be separated. There may, for example, be a mechanical problem with one of the wagons and the railway cannot be sure that all wagons will travel together in the same movement for the entire transit.[1] *2.74*

The working languages of the Organisation (COTIF), referred to in Article 12.3, are French and German: Article 1.3. As regards other aspects of content, see Article 13. *2.75*

Article 13, Wording of the consignment note *2.76*

1. The consignment note must contain:
   (a) the name of the destination station;
   (b) the name and address of the consignee; only one individual or legal person shall be shown as consignee;
   (c) the description of the goods;
   (d) the mass, or failing that, comparable information in accordance with the provisions in force at the forwarding station;
   (e) the number of packages and a description of the packing in the case of consignments in less than wagon loads, and in the case of complete wagon loads comprising one or more packages, forwarded by rail-sea and requiring to be trans-shipped;
   (f) the number of the wagon and also, for privately-owned wagons, the tare, in the case of goods where the loading is the duty of the consignor;

1. Spera, Art. 12, Anm 5.

(g) a detailed list of the documents which are required by Customs or other administrative authorities and are attached to the consignment note or shown as held at the disposal of the railway at a named station or at an office of the Customs or of any other authority;

(h) the name and address of the consignor; only one individual or legal person shall be shown as the consignor; if the provisions in force at the forwarding station so require, the consignor shall add to his name and address his written, printed or stamped signature.

The provisions in force at the forwarding station shall determine the meanings of the terms "wagon load" and "less than wagon load" for the whole of the route.

2. The consignment note must, where appropriate, contain all the other particulars provided for in the Uniform Rules. It shall not contain other particulars unless they are required or allowed by the laws and regulations of a State, the supplementary provisions or the tariffs, and are not contrary to the Uniform Rules.

3. Nevertheless, the consignor may insert in the consignment note in the space set apart for the purpose, but as information for the consignee, remarks relating to the consignment, without involving the railway in any obligation or liability.

4. The consignment note shall not be replaced by other documents or supplemented by documents other than those prescribed or allowed by the Uniform Rules, the supplementary provisions or the tariffs.

Additional Uniform Regulations (DCU)

2.77 **DCU 1, to § 1(a)** *The name of the destination station must include the necessary information to avoid any confusion between stations serving the same locality or localities of the same or similar names.*

When the forwarding station finds that details relating to the description of the destination station are incorrect or incompatible or, for consignments destined for places served by several stations, the destination station is not indicated sufficiently clearly for it to be exactly determined, it must draw the attention of the sender to the irregularity. If the sender does not correct or complete the consignment note or if he can no longer be contacted, the consignment note shall nevertheless be accepted and the railway shall decide to which station the consignment is to be forwarded.

2.78 **DCU 2, to § 1(b)** *An entry showing the station or an official of the destination station as consignee shall only be accepted if the tariff applicable or other regulations make specific provision for this, or if the sender presents to the forwarding station a written authorisation from the destination railway. Addresses not indicating the name of the consignee, such as "to the order of . . ." or "to the holder of the duplicate of the consignment note" are not allowed.*

If possible, the sender shall indicate on the consignment note, with the name and address of the consignee, the telephone, telex or telefax number or telegraphic address of the consignee. He shall also indicate if possible, in the space on the consignment note reserved for this purpose, the customer code of the consignee and, in the cases allowed in centralised charging conforming to art. 8 para 4(f) where the consignee is not at the same time the payer of non pre-paid charges, the customer code of the person paying charges.

2.79 **DCU 3, to § 1(c)** *The sender shall describe by the name prescribed for them goods which are accepted for carriage subject to conditions in accordance with Article 5, § 1(a) and § 2; in the case of other goods, for which the sender requests the application of a particular tariff, by the name given to them in that tariff; and in all other cases by the ordinary commercial description, according to their nature, given to the goods in the State of departure. The sender shall also indicate, if possible, in the space on the consignment note reserved for this purpose, the customs tariff number.*

2.80 **DCU 4, to § 1(c)** *When goods are handed in for carriage in packing which bears an international stamp, certifying that it is of suitable quality or has been approved, and this stamp has been affixed under railway supervision, the sender must, if he wishes to obtain the benefit of the concessions granted by the railway when such packing is used, indicate in the consignment note, in the space provided for the description of the goods, that the packing* *bears a stamp showing that it is of suitable quality or that it has been approved. The wording to be used is as follows: "UIC, certified packing".*

DCU 5, to § 1(d) *When the laws or regulations of the State of departure authorise the sender to tender his consignments without entering the mass or details in place of it, this mass or these details must be entered by the forwarding railway.* 2.81

DCU 6, to § 1(f) *The sender must enter the number of the wagon, in the space provided for this purpose on the consignment note, in the following manner: 0185 137 0315 9.* 2.82

DCU 7, to § 1(h) *Should he consider it desirable, the sender may complete his address with his telephone, telex or telefax number or telegraphic address. He shall also indicate if possible, in the space on the consignment note reserved for this purpose, his customer code and, in the cases allowed in centralised charging conforming to art. 8 para 4(f) where the consignee is not at the same time the payer of non pre-paid charges, the customer code of the person paying charges.* 2.83

DCU 8, to § 2 *The sender shall enter, in the space on the consignment note reserved for this purpose, the transport regime governing the consignment (CIM or TIEx parcel express).* 2.84

When it appears to the station of departure that this entry is lacking or that the entry is not compatible with other entries in the consignment note, it shall draw this irregularity to the attention of the sender. If the sender does not make the required entry or correct the consignment note or if he cannot be contacted, the railway shall nonetheless accept the consignment note and select the transport regime which appears to the railway to be in the best interest of the sender.

DCU 9, to § 2 *If necessary, other entries shall be made on the consignment note, in particular the following:* 2.85

- *(a) the tariffs to be applied, and in particular the special or exceptional tariffs provided for in Article 27, § 4(c), and in Article 45;*
- *(b) the amount in figures representing the interest in delivery declared in accordance with Article 16;*
- *(c) the charges which the sender undertakes to pay in accordance with Article 15;*
- *(d) the amount of "cash on delivery" and disbursements in accordance with Article 17, in figures;*
- *(e) the route prescribed in accordance with Article 14, § 1, the names of the stations at which the formalities required by Customs or other administrative authorities are to take place and, in addition, in traffic with the United Kingdom and Ireland, the shipping route or routes by which the traffic is to be forwarded;*
- *(f) the particulars relating to the formalities required by Customs or other administrative authorities in accordance with Article 26, § 3, it being understood that when the indication of the place at which clearance through the Customs is to be effected is shown only on the Customs documents or is entered in a space on the consignment note other than that reserved for sender's declarations, such indication will not be binding on the railway and that the designation of a station shown in the space on the consignment note provided for the entry of the route and of the tariffs, also cannot be accepted as the designation of the station where the Customs formalities are to be carried out;*
- *(g) the statement that the consignee is not entitled to modify the contract of carriage, worded as follows: "Consignee not authorised to give further instructions", in the space on the consignment note provided for sender's declarations;*
- *(h) in the case of every accompanied consignment, in the space on the consignment note provided for sender's declarations, the number of attendants or, where applicable, when one attendant for several consignments is accepted by the railway, the remark, entered on each consignment note ". . . common attendant(s) for . . . wagons" or the remark "unattended" when, in accordance with Article 5, § 1(b), sub-para. 2, attendance is not required or has been dispensed with;*

(i) *the number and description of the seals affixed by the sender on the wagons in accordance with Article 20, §5, in the space on the consignment note reserved for the description of the goods.*

2.86 **DCU 10, to §§ 1 and 2** *In addition to the information prescribed in §§ 1 and 2 and in the RIP and in the RICo, the sender must indicate, on the consignment note, where appropriate:*

(a) *for loading tackle belonging to the railway, for example: sheets, chains, ropes, etc.*
- *in the space provided for this purpose: their category, owner's mark and number (for loading tackle which is not numbered, details of the category must be preceded by their quantity);*
- *in the space provided for details of the number of packages, the nature of the packing and the description of the goods: their quantity and description (separately, according to the category):*
- *in the space provided for details of the mass: their tare;*

(b) *for privately-owned loading tackle, materials used to protect the goods against heat or cold and other privately-owned equipment specified in the tariffs*
- *in the space provided for details of the number of packages, the nature of the packing and the description of the goods: their quantity, their description (separately, according to category) and, where applicable, their numbers or marks;*
- *in the space reserved for details of the mass; their tare;*

(c) *for exchangeable pallets, marked "EUR", to be exchanged within the framework of the European Flat Pallet Pool or the European Box Pallet Pool*
- *in the space provided for details of exchangeable pallets:*
  - *the quantity of "EUR" flat pallets—against the symbol* (as appropriate)
  - *the quantity of "EUR" Y box pallets—against the symbol* (as appropriate)
- *in the space provided for details of the number of packages, the nature of the packing and the description of the goods: their quantity and description (separately, according to category);*
- *in the space provided for details of the mass; their tare;*

(d) *for exchangeable pallets, marked "EUR", which are not for exchange within the framework of the European Flat Pallet Pool or the European Box Pallet Pool*
- *in the space provided for details of exchangeable pallets: a diagonal cross instead of the quantity of pallets—against the relevant symbol;*
- *in the space provided for details of the number of packages, the nature of the packing and the description of the goods; their quantity and description (separately, according to category), also the remark "not to be exchanged";*
- *in the space provided for details of the mass; their tare;*

(e) *for non-exchangeable flat pallets or box pallets, railway-owned and designed for international traffic*
- *in the space provided for details of the number of packages, the nature of the packing and the description of the goods; their quantity, their description, their numbers and the marks of the owning railway;*
- *in the space provided for details for the mass; their tare;*

(f) *for flat pallets or box pallets, privately-owned and approved by the railway, bearing the sign* kP
- *in the space provided for details of the number of packages, the nature of the packing and the description of the goods; their quantity, their description (separately, according to category), the mark of the approving railway, the* kP *sign and, where applicable, their numbers;*
- *in the space provided for details of the mass; their tare;*

(g) *for special privately-owned pallets, not bearing the sign* kP *and accepted subject to an agreement between the railways participating in wagon-load traffic*
- *in the space provided for details of the number of packages, the nature of the packing and description of the goods; their quantity, their description (separately, according to category) and the reference to the agreement concluded between the participating railways, for example: ". . . special privately-owned flat pallets—by agreement under reference number . . . between the railways . . . and . . . ";*

— in the space provided for details of the mass; their tare.
The tares are to be entered below the details of the mass, as per § 1(d), which includes the mass of the goods, also, where applicable, the mass of the packing and that of privately-owned pallets not approved by the railway.

DCU 11, to §§ 1 and 2 *When the space provided in the consignment note for the particulars to be entered by the sender is insufficient, additional sheets must be used and these shall then become integral parts of the consignment note. These additional sheets shall be of the same format as the consignment note and shall be made out by means of carbon copying in the same number of copies as the consignment note. The consignment note shall mention the existence of such additional sheets. If the total mass of the consignment is indicated, this indication shall be entered on the consignment note itself.* *2.87*

Comment

The practical significance of the information required by Article 13 is evident. Article 12.1 states that the consignor must "present the consignment note duly completed" and Article 13 indicates what that means. The consignor's responsibility for errors is the subject of Article 18. Moreover, inaccurate information may render the consignor liable to pay surcharges under Article 24. The corollary is that, if the note is not "duly completed", that does not vitiate the contract of carriage except, of course, that it will be ineffective if essential points have not been agreed, such as the destination station and the goods to be carried.[1] As regards ambiguity in the designation of the destination, see DCU 1. *2.88*

Apart from the features indicated by Article 12 and Article 13, no particular form of consignment note is required by CIM, but a standard form has been prepared by the CIT for voluntary adoption; cf. Article 12.2 *in fine*. It is curious that there is no general requirement that information be stated about goods that might be dangerous, except in so far as this follows from the application of RID. See Annex I of RID. *2.89*

The long list of obligatory entries contained in Article 13.1 is not all. Article 13.2. requires "where appropriate" mention of all the other particulars provided for in the Uniform Rules. These are route instructions (Article 14.1), applicable tariffs (Article 14.5), charges prepaid (Article 15.8), any declaration of special interest in delivery (Article 16.1), amounts of cash on delivery and of disbursements (Article 17.6), and any prohibition of modification by the consignee (Article 31.1). Article 13.2 then "draws a line" by ruling out other particulars unless they are required or allowed by the laws and regulations of a State, the supplementary provisions or the tariffs, and are not contrary to the Uniform Rules. One such, for example, allowed in Switzerland, is "*cargo domizil*". *2.90*

Moreover, Article 13.3 allows the consignor to insert in the space set apart for the purpose, as information for the consignee, useful remarks relating to the consignment (without involving the railway in any obligation or liability) such as the person (for example a bank) at the disposal of which the goods are held by the named consignee.[2] If the consignor renders (other) particulars illegible as a result of the *2.91*

1. Spera, Art. 13, Anm 3.
2. *Paris 31.10.74* (1976) 11 ETL 120, 130–131.

manner or quantity inserted for this kind of purpose, the consignor bears the consequences.[3]

2.92

Article 14, Route and tariff applicable

1. The consignor may stipulate in the consignment note the route to be followed, indicating it by reference to frontier points or frontier stations and where appropriate, to transit stations between railways. He may only stipulate frontier points and frontier stations which are open to traffic between the forwarding and destination places concerned.

2. The following shall be regarded as routeing instructions:

(a) designation of stations where formalities required by Customs or other administrative authorities are to be carried out, and of stations where special care is to be given to the goods (attention to animals, re-icing etc.);

(b) designation of the tariffs to be applied, if this is sufficient to determine the stations between which the tariffs requested are to be applied;

(c) instructions as to the payment of the whole or a part of the charges up to X (X indicating by name the point at which the tariffs of adjacent countries are applied).

3. Except in the cases specified in Article 3.4 and 5 and Article 33.1 the railway may not carry the goods by a route other than that stipulated by the consignor unless both:

(a) the formalities required by Customs or other administrative authorities, as well as the special care to be given to the goods, will in any event be carried out at the stations indicated by the consignor; and

(b) the charges and the transit periods will not be greater than the charges and transit periods calculated according to the route stipulated by the consignor.

Subparagraph (a) shall not apply to consignments in less than wagon loads if one of the participating railways is unable to adhere to the route chosen by the consignor by virtue of the routeing instructions arising from its arrangements for the international carriage of consignments in less than wagon loads.

4. Subject to the provisions of paragraph 3, the charges and transit periods shall be calculated according to the route stipulated by the consignor or, in the absence of any such indication, according to the route chosen by the railway.

5. The consignor may stipulate in the consignment note which tariffs are to be applied. The railway must apply such tariffs if the conditions laid down for their application have been fulfilled.

6. If the instructions given by the consignor are not sufficient to indicate the route or tariffs to be applied, or if any of those instructions are inconsistent with one another, the railway shall choose the route or tariffs which appear to it to be the most advantageous to the consignor.

7. The railway shall not be liable for any loss or damage suffered as a result of the choice made in accordance with paragraph 6, except in the case of wilful misconduct or gross negligence.

Additional Uniform Regulations (DCU)

2.93 **DCU 1, to §§ 1 and 5** *Vague instructions such as "the shortest route", "the lowest tariff" shall not be binding upon the railway.*

2.94 **DCU 2, to § 2** *In accordance with the Uniform Regulations and the following conditions, the sender has the right to request re-icing during transit, on the consignment note.*

It may only be requested that re-icing shall be carried out at stations specially designated by the railways for that purpose; information regarding such stations will be given to the sender on request by the forwarding station.

The sender must indicate in the consignment note the party who is to carry out the re-icing operations. The railways may require that such party be approved by them. The sender shall

3. Spera, Art. 13, Anm 21.

make the request for re-icing by entering in the space on the consignment note provided for his declarations the remark "Re-icing at . . . (station) by . . . (designated agent, i.e. a private company or the railway if the latter undertakes to effect re-icing)."

The railway will, where appropriate, indicate in their tariffs if and under what conditions orders for re-icing are accepted from the sender, the authorised consignee or agent of one of them, in cases where re-icing has not been requested in the consignment note.

DCU 3, to § 2 *The sender has the right to indicate on the consignment note, in the space provided for his declarations, those stations where attention must be given to livestock. This attention, such as foddering and watering, may only be requested for provision at stations specially designated for this purpose by the railways, information regarding such stations shall be given to the sender on request by the forwarding station.* *2.95*

DCU 4, to §§ 6 and 7 *For the calculation of a difference in the freight charges to be refunded in conformity with §§ 6 and 7, the exchange rate to be applied is that which would be used under the provision of DCU 1, Article 29.* *2.96*

DCU 5, to § 8 *For calculation of the amount to be refunded in conformity with § 8, the exchange rate to be applied shall be that which was originally used for calculation of the carriage charge, or which would have been used if either an international tariff or a combination of tariffs had not been applied. The amount to be refunded is equal to the sum thus calculated.* *2.97*

Comments

1. Choice of route

Article 14 governs two connected matters: the choice of route and the tariff charges. *2.98* Indeed, in some cases the choice of a route dictates the tariff applicable. The principle set out in Article 14.1, that it is the consignor who chooses the route and the tariff, reflects the network of the nineteenth century. Not only is the network now less extensive and the choice correspondingly more limited, but railways have been allowed to "rationalise" movements and thus to restrict the consignor's options still further under Article 3.5 and Article 6.5. This apart, however, the railway can depart from clear route instructions only in the two cases indicated in Article 14.3. If the railway does so in other cases, it will be liable for the consequences.[1]

As regards Article 14.3(b), a literal interpretation suggests that the railway is not *2.99* permitted to carry by an alternative route unless the charges and the transit periods will not be greater than those on the route stipulated by the consignor. However, the opinion of most writers[2] is that the railway may do so, but may not charge more than would have been chargeable or take longer than permitted on the consignor's choice of route. See also in this connection Article 33.1.

If the consignor does not give clear instructions sufficient to indicate a (lawful and *2.100* viable) route or tariff, Article 14.6 provides that the railway must choose the route or tariffs which appear to it to be the most advantageous to the consignor; however, as the risk has been triggered by the consignor, the railway is not liable for any consequential loss or damage to the consignor unless it is guilty of wilful misconduct or gross negligence: Article 14.7. For the meaning of wilful misconduct

1. Spera, Art. 14, Anm 11.
2. See Spera, Art. 14, Anm 13 and Anm 15(b).

and gross negligence, see Article 44. This rule is quite unlike the common law rule that the railway must take the ordinary or usual route,[3] subject to the strict doctrine of deviation in the event of non-compliance.[4] However, the existence of Article 14.7 suggests that any notions like common law deviation are inappropriate to CIM.[5]

2. Stations

2.101 As regards the consignor's choice of stations, the reference in Article 14.1 to frontier stations and, where appropriate, to transit stations between railways is a reference to stations where the goods are handed over by one railway to another, either the railway of one state to that of another state or perhaps (there is controversy) from one railway to another within one state.[6] The latter may well occur e.g. in Switzerland.

2.102 The reference, in Article 14.3(a), to the special care to be given to the goods at the stations indicated by the consignor, reflects concern that the station chosen by the consignor might not be equipped to provide the special care required by the consignor. In that case it is the duty of the forwarding station to warn the consignor and to decline the goods if the consignor insists on the chosen station.[7]

2.103 **Article 15, Payment of charges**

1. The charges (carriage charges, supplementary charges, Customs duties and other charges incurred from the time of acceptance for carriage to the time of delivery) shall be paid by the consignor or the consignee in accordance with the following provisions.

In applying these provisions, charges which, according to the applicable tariff, must be added to the standard rates or special rates when calculating the carriage charges, shall be deemed to be carriage charges.

2. A consignor who undertakes to pay a part or all of the charges shall indicate this on the consignment note by using one of the following phrases:

(a) (i) "carriage charges paid", if he undertakes to pay carriage charges only;

(ii) "carriage charges paid including . . . ", if he undertakes to pay charges additional to those for carriage; he shall give an exact description of those charges; additional indications, which may relate only to the supplementary charges or other charges incurred from the time of acceptance for carriage until the time of delivery as well as to sums collected either by Customs or other administrative authorities shall not result in any division of the total amount of any one category of charges (for example, the total amount of Customs duties and of other amounts payable to Customs, value added tax being regarded as a separate category);

(iii) "carriage charges paid to X" (X indicating by name the point at which the tariffs of adjacent countries are applied), if he undertakes to pay carriage charges to X;

(iv) "carriage charges paid to X including . . . " (X indicating by name the point at which the tariffs of adjacent countries are applied), if he undertakes to pay charges additional to those for carriage to X, but excluding all charges relating to the subsequent country or railway; the provisions of (ii) shall apply analogously;

3. Kahn-Freund, p. 284; Palmer, pp. 992 *et seq.*
4. *Taylor* v. *G.N.R. Co.* (1866) L.R. 1 C.P. 385, 388; *L.N.W.R.* v. *Neilson* [1922] A.C. 263.
5. Kahn-Freund, p. 418.
6. Spera, Art. 14, Anm 4.
7. Spera, Art. 14, Anm 12.

(b) "all charges paid", if he undertakes to pay all charges (carriage charges, supplementary charges, Customs duties and other charges);
(c) "charges paid not exceeding . . . ", if he undertakes to pay a fixed sum: save where the tariffs otherwise provide, this sum shall be expressed in the currency of the country of departure.

Supplementary and other charges which, according to the provisions in force at the forwarding station, are to be calculated for the whole of the route concerned, and the charge for interest in delivery laid down in Article 16.2, shall always be paid in full by the consignor in the case of payment of the charges in accordance with (a) (iv).

3. The international tariffs may, as regards payment of charges, prescribe the exclusive use of certain phrases set out in paragraph 2 of this Article or the use of other phrases.

4. The charges which the consignor has not undertaken to pay shall be deemed to be payable by the consignee. Nevertheless, such charges shall be payable by the consignor if the consignee has not taken possession of the consignment note nor asserted his rights under Article 28.4, nor modified the contract of carriage in accordance with Article 31.

5. Supplementary charges, such as charges for demurrage and standage, warehousing and weighing, which arise from an act attributable to the consignee or from a request which he has made, shall always be paid by him.

6. The forwarding railway may require the consignor to prepay the charges in the case of goods which in its opinion are liable to undergo rapid deterioration or which, by reason of their low value or their nature, do not provide sufficient cover for such charges.

7. If the amount of the charges which the consignor undertakes to pay cannot be ascertained exactly at the time the goods are handed over for carriage, such charges shall be entered in a charges note and a settlement of accounts shall be made with the consignor not later than thirty days after the expiry of the transit period. The railway may require as security a deposit approximating to the amount of such charges, for which a receipt shall be given. A detailed account of charges drawn up from the particulars in the charges note shall be delivered to the consignor in return for the receipt.

8. The forwarding station shall specify, in the consignment note and in the duplicate, the charges which have been prepaid, unless the provisions in force at the forwarding station provide that those charges are only to be specified in the duplicate. In the case provided for in paragraph 7 of this Article these charges are not to be specified either in the consignment note or in the duplicate.

Additional Uniform Regulations (DCU)

DCU 1, to § 1 *The charges for re-icing requested in accordance with DCU 2 to Article 14 shall be brought to account in full on the consignment note and paid by the sender or by the consignee in accordance with the pre-payment instructions, unless the person entitled stipulates, at the time he gives the order for re-icing, that he will pay such charges directly to the undertaking responsible for carrying out the re-icing.* 2.104

DCU 2, to § 2 *The sender must enter the pre-payment instructions in the space on the consignment note reserved for this purpose, whether or not he undertakes to pay the charges himself. A combination of the instructions provided for in § 2(a), (b) and (c) must not be used.* 2.105

If the forwarding station finds that the pre-payment instructions are inadequate, are not compatible with other entries on the consignment note or do not state clearly the sender's wishes, it must draw the sender's attention to the matter (see also DCU 9 to art. 12). If the sender does not put the matter right or cannot be found, all such charges shall be deemed to be payable by the consignee.

DCU 3, to § 2 *If the sender has chosen the indication provided for in § 2(a), by inserting a cross in the appropriate space on the consignment note without having made any other entries in the printed prepayment instructions, it will be assumed that he only accepts responsibility for the carriage charges up to the destination station.* 2.106

DCU 4, to § 2 *In regard to the use of the indications "carriage charges paid including . . ." (para 2 of § 2(a)) and "carriage charges paid including . . . up to X" (para 4 of § 2(a)), the following rules shall apply:* 2.107

(a) In accordance with § 1, the charges include, in addition to carriage charges
— supplementary charges,
— Customs duties,
— other charges incurred from the time of acceptance for carriage until delivery (see Article 6 § 9).

(b) If the sender wishes to pay the Customs duties, he must indicate this clearly in the prepayment instructions. The Customs duties shall include the total amount of the Customs duties and other amounts to be paid to Customs, with the exception of value added tax (VAT), which is considered to be a separate category of charge.

(c) If the sender restricts prepayment to one section only of the route (indication "carriage charges paid including . . . up to X"), this restriction shall apply both to the carriage charges and to the other charges included in the prepayment instructions.

(d) Where additional charges are involved for a particular journey, which may be defined by the words "up to X", then the total amount of any one category of such charges must not be divided.

(e) With reference to the list of uniform codes covering supplementary charges, Customs duties and other charges, published by the railway, the sender may, in the case of payment of charges in accordance with § 2(a), 2 or 4, show additions, in the space on the consignment note reserved for pre-payment instructions charges against the appropriate instruction, in codes, letters, or in codes and letters, as appropriate, separating the different categories of charges by the sign "+". When designating the categories of charges by letters and codes, the sender must always show the corresponding code in front of the letters.
To designate the supplementary charges, Customs duties and other charges in the fiscal section of the consignment note, the railway shall utilise only the codes.

2.108 **DCU 5, to § 7** *An appropriate entry on the consignment note may serve instead of a receipt for any prepayment made to cover charges.*

Comments

1. Charges

2.109 Article 15 is concerned with charges, i.e., all sums required by Article 6.9 to be entered in the consignment note[1] except surcharges, the payment of which is dealt with by Article 24.3. Apart from carriage charges, other charges include the expense of weighing the goods, of completing Customs formalities, of providing covers for the goods, payment of VAT on the carriage charges, and expenses not foreseen and for which the railway is not responsible but which prove necessary to carry out the particular carriage, such as customs charges[2] and salvage. Moreover, the charges include not only those to which the claimant railway is entitled but also those of other railways participating in the transport in question and for which the claimant railway is acting. Thus in one case the railway (SNCFB) at destination was entitled to claim charges incurred by the railway (SNCF) on the first stage of carriage—a Customs penalty imposed because the documents supplied by the consignor were not in order.[3]

2.110 Charges also include the "supplementary charges", the subject of Article 15.5. As indicated by Article 15.5, supplementary charges include demurrage and standage. "Demurrage" refers to agreed damages for delay: for unreasonable detention of

1. Spera, Art. 15, Anm 2.
2. *Cass. Belge 16.2.67* (1967) 2 ETL 1023.
3. *Ibid.*

wagons, containers and ancillary equipment during and after transit. "Standage" means a charge for permission to stand (*Oxford English Dictionary*). Demurrage and standage together are a rough translation of "stationnement" in the French version and "Standgeld" in the German.

2. Liability to pay charges

Article 15.1 provides that, in principle, charges are payable by the consignor, with whom the railway contracts: Article 11.4. Although debatable, it seems that the provisions of Article 15 are not obligatory.[4] Consequently, unless otherwise agreed, it is against the consignor rather than the consignee that the railway has enforceable rights to recover charges; in any case, to the railway the consignee's creditworthiness may be uncertain. Yet, not all charges can be ascertained and demanded from the consignor at the time of contract. In these circumstances, the "compromise solution"[5] is that the consignor pays the charges payment of which is promised in the consignment note, and the rest must be paid by the consignee unless the consignee declines to get involved (Article 28.4), in which case, with the exception of charges mentioned in Article 15.5, the consignor must pay them. This might leave the carrier in a weak position. However, the compromise assumes that by national law the carrier has a lien on the goods; and, in case the goods appear to be worth less than the charges, Article 15.6 provides for prepayment by the consignor or, if the amount cannot be ascertained, Article 15.7 provides for security.[6] As regards the lien in English law, see the Comment on Condition 14 of the Freightliner Conditions, paragraph 2.648, below. *2.111*

3. The position of the consignee

The consignee is the person designated as consignee, whatever that person's actual role in the movement of the goods.[7] According to Article 15.4 the consignee is liable to pay the charges which the consignor has not undertaken to pay,[8] provided that the consignee has "adhered" to the contract by requiring the railway to hand over the consignment note and deliver the goods (Article 28.4) or by modifying the contract of carriage (Article 31). Such acts by the consignee are seen as evidence of "adherence" to the contract on the part of the consignee by which, in the traditions of French and German law, the consignee becomes a party to the contract and acquires rights and duties under the contract.[9] *2.112*

Moreover, as it has been underlined that adherence to the contract is a right and not a duty,[10] it appears that supplementary charges referred to in Article 15.5 as being payable by the consignee, do not "arise out of an act for which the consignee *2.113*

4. See Art. 15.3 and Helm, Art. 17, Anm 2.
5. Kahn-Freund, p. 426.
6. See Allégret, Fasc. 684, 45; Kahn-Freund, p. 427.
7. *Brussels 6.1.77*, ULR 1978 (II) 310, Bull.OCTI 1978.167.
8. And none other: Spera, Art. 15, Anm 5 and 20.
9. Allégret, Fasc. 684, 42; Spera, Art. 15, Anm 21 and Anm 24. Examples include *Rheims 8.6.88*, BT 1989.481; and *Paris 6.2.90*, BT 1990.759.
10. *Rheims 8.6.88* (above).

is responsible", still less "out of a request which he has made". True, the goods would not have arrived but for the consignee's dealings with the consignor, but these are not the concern of the railway and the railway cannot rely on such dealings to impose liability on the consignee. However, in one case,[11] goods were sent from Rheims to Prato and the consignee led the consignor to believe that he would accept the goods, but did not do so or demand the consignment note. Seven months later, the uncollected goods were sold but as the proceeds were insufficient to cover charges, the railway brought an action against the consignor for the balance. The court held that the railway was entitled to this sum under Article 17 (now Article 15), but that the action was barred under Article 47 (now Article 58). The court also observed[12] that the charges were the responsibility not of the consignor but of the consignee under Article 17.5 (now Article 15.5), but on this point the court may well have been influenced by the fact that the consignee, far from remaining passive, had telexed the consignor (but not the railway) that he would pay storage costs at destination.

2.114 **Article 16, Interest in delivery**

1. Any consignment may be the subject of a declaration of interest in delivery. The amount declared shall be shown in figures in the consignment note in the currency of the country of departure, in another currency determined by the tariffs or in units of account.

2. The charge for interest in delivery shall be calculated for the whole of the route concerned, in accordance with the tariffs of the forwarding railway.

Comment

2.115 The purpose of the declaration provided for in Article 16 is to increase the amount recoverable from the railway in the event of loss or damage to take in the actual loss of the claimant consignor: Article 46. Hence the interest is declared in terms of an amount of money, which the consignor estimates as the actual monetary loss if the goods are lost or damaged, or such part of that amount as he does not choose to insure himself. The unit of account referred to there is the SDR, which is the subject of Article 7.The loss may include consequential loss, for example, loss of production while a factory stands idle because an essential machine has been damaged in transit.

2.116 As the railway bears an additional risk of liability, it makes an additional charge on the basis of a tariff agreed *inter se* by the railways: "insurance money".[1] However, it should not be forgotten that, unlike certain kinds of insurance, Article 16 envisages that the railway will pay for the lost interest only when (a) the loss occurs *and* (b) the railway is liable under the contract of carriage and hence, in some significant sense, responsible for the loss. Moreover, whether a special interest can be enforced without meticulous observance of the formal requirements set out in

11. *Ibid.*
12. *Ibid.* at 482.
1. Kahn-Freund, p. 440.

the second sentence is disputed.[2] Hence it is scarcely surprising that studies suggest that consignors rarely take advantage of this kind of provision.

Article 17, Cash on delivery and disbursements *2.117*

1. The consignor may make the goods subject to a cash on delivery payment not exceeding their value at the time of acceptance at the forwarding station. The amount of such cash on delivery payment shall be expressed in the currency of the country of departure; the tariffs may provide for exceptions.

2. The railway shall not be obliged to pay over any amount representing a cash on delivery payment unless the amount in question has been paid by the consignee. That amount shall be placed at the consignor's disposal within thirty days of payment by the consignee; interest at five per cent per annum shall be payable from the date of the expiry of that period.

3. If the goods have been delivered, wholly or in part, to the consignee without prior collection of the amount of the cash on delivery payment, the railway shall pay the consignor the amount of any loss or damage sustained up to the total amount of the cash on delivery payment without prejudice to any right of recovery from the consignee.

4. Cash on delivery consignments shall be subject to a collection fee laid down in the tariffs; such fee shall be payable notwithstanding cancellation or reduction of the amount of the cash on delivery payment by modification of the contract of carriage in accordance with Article 30.1.

5. Disbursements shall only be allowed if made in accordance with the provisions in force at the forwarding station.

6. The amounts of the cash on delivery payment and of disbursements shall be entered in figures on the consignment note.

Additional Uniform Regulation (DCU)

DCU 1, to § 1 *The original of the consignment note or the duplicate of the consignment note, showing a "C.O.D." and bearing a date stamp or references of the accounting machine, shall be accepted as proof that this "C.O.D." has been charged against the goods. The making out of "C.O.D." certificates is governed by the regulations in force at the forwarding station.* *2.118*

Comment

Article 17 gives the consignor the option of making the goods subject to a cash on delivery payment, subject to suspension of the right in difficult times: Article 65.1(c). This is a useful option found also in CMR.[1] The amount of the payment may not exceed the value of the goods at the time of acceptance at the forwarding station even though that may be less than their value at destination and hence less than the purchase price paid or to be paid by the consignee.[2] This limitation is strictly observed.[3] Moreover, the amount must be expressed in the currency of the country of departure so that the railway officials understand the obligation that the railway is taking on, although the tariffs may provide for exceptions to the currency requirement.[4] *2.119*

Assuming that any reference in any paragraph of Article 17 to a COD payment is the same, i.e. to a payment the amount of which has been thus entered on the *2.120*

2. See Spera, Art. 16, Anm 4.
1. See CMR Art. 13, para. 1.58, above.
2. See Spera, Art. 17, Anm 4.
3. *Ghent 17.2.70* (1977) 12 ETL 892.
4. See Spera, Art. 17, Anm 6.

consignment note, CIM avoids an impasse found under the parallel provision of CMR, Article 13. Under Article 13 the carrier is obliged to collect the charges agreed to be collected "under the contract of carriage", whereas the consignee is only obliged to hand over the charges "shown to be due under the consignment note".[5]

2.121 States differ on how literally they apply the reference to "cash". For an English court, this question is determined by the applicable law.[6] In Germany, for example, a cheque will not suffice[7] or, at least, the railway must assume the risk that the cheque will not be honoured.[8] However, a cheque will suffice if payment by cheque is the general commercial practice in context, as it is in England; and analogous CMR cases indicate that the same is true in France[9] and in Holland.[10]

2.122 According to Article 17.2 the railway is not obliged to pay over any amount representing a cash on delivery payment unless the amount in question has been paid by the consignee. If the consignee has paid, the amount paid must be placed at the consignor's disposal within 30 days at the forwarding station, although local law may allow payment to be made to the consignor by post.[11]

2.123 If the railway delivers goods to the consignee without prior collection of the required amount of cash, Article 17.3 obliges the railway to pay the consignor the amount of any proven loss[12] not exceeding the amount of the required cash payment and without prejudice to any right of recovery from the consignee. Some commentators doubt whether an independent right of action can be based on the wording of Article 17.3 (*any right*), and look to national law for a remedy; for example, an action in restitution, for money paid to the use of the defendant consignee.[13] The railway's right to recover an amount undercharged is not barred by delivery of the goods to the consignee.[14]

2.124 **Article 18, Responsibility for particulars furnished in the consignment note**

The consignor shall be responsible for the correctness of the particulars inserted by, or for, him, in the consignment note. He shall bear all the consequences in the event of those particulars being irregular, incorrect, incomplete, or entered elsewhere than in the allotted space.

Comment

2.125 Under Article 18 the consignor's liability for the consequences of incorrect particulars in the consignment note is strict.[1] If an employee of the railway enters

5. *OLG Hamm 12.11.73*, NJW 1974.1056.
6. Dicey & Morris, *The Conflict of Laws* (13th ed., 2000), Chap. 32.
7. *BGH 10.2.82* (1983) 18 ETL 32, 40.
8. Helm, Art. 72, EVO, Anm 5.
9. *Paris 31.1.83*, BT 1983.183.
10. *Rb Breda 16.12.69*, 1970 ULC 298.
11. Spera, Art. 17, Anm 8.
12. Loss is not to be presumed: Spera, Art. 17, Anm 11.
13. See Kahn-Freund, p. 421; and Konow, Bull.OCTI 1987.61.
14. *Ghent 17.2.70* (1977) 12 ETL 892.
1. Helm, Art. 7, Anm 1 and Spera, Art. 18, Anm 3—although not all commentators agree.

the particulars at the behest of the consignor, the responsibility for their correctness remains that of the consignor.[2] *Quaere* whether the consignor can raise contributory fault by the railway.[3]

If the particulars are incorrect, in many instances it will be the consignor (directly or through the consignee) and not the railway that bears resulting loss, for example, when goods are mislaid; that follows in the nature of things and is confirmed by the railway's defence in such circumstances, found in Article 36.2.[4] Article 18 is concerned with loss suffered by the railway as a result of incorrect particulars and with compensation for the railway in respect of that loss.[5] It is an instance of a liability which the consignor has for particulars in general under Article 13.[6] Moreover and regardless of such compensation, the railway is entitled to impose a surcharge in certain cases: Article 24. *2.126*

Article 19, Condition, packing and marking of goods *2.127*

1. When the railway accepts for carriage goods showing obvious signs of damage, it may require the condition of such goods to be indicated in the consignment note.

2. When the nature of the goods is such as to require packing, the consignor shall pack them in such a way as to protect them from total or partial loss and from damage in transit and to avoid risk of injury or damage to persons, equipment or other goods.

Moreover the packing shall comply with the provisions in force at the forwarding station.

3. If the consignor has not complied with the provisions of paragraph 2, the railway may either refuse the goods or require the sender to acknowledge in the consignment note the absence of packing or the defective condition of the packing, with an exact description thereof.

4. The consignor shall be liable for all the consequences of the absence of packing or defective condition of packing and shall in particular make good any loss or damage suffered by the railway from this cause. In the absence of any particulars in the consignment note, the burden of proof of such absence of packing or defective condition of the packing shall rest upon the railway.

5. The supplementary provisions of the tariffs shall regulate the marking of packages by the consignor.

Additional Uniform Regulations (DCU)

DCU 1 *The railway may require that small packages of sundries consignments of the same kind (small articles of iron, etc.), the acceptance and handling of which give rise to considerable loss of time, shall be tied or packed in such a way that they constitute more bulky units.* *2.128*

DCU 2 *Packages containing plates, films and paper covered with an emulsion which is sensitive to light, radioactive, or other, radiations (e.g. photographic plates or paper, cinematograph or photographic films, X-ray films, etc.) must be provided by the sender with labels measuring 10.5 × 14.8 cm (A6 horizontal); these labels must bear the inscription "FOTO" in letters at least 4 cm high, and display a reproduction of a strip of cinematographic film, at least 8 cm in width, perforated on each side. The packages may also be marked by means of a stencil with the above characteristics.* *2.129*

2. Spera, Art. 18, Anm 4.
3. Helm, *loc. cit.*
4. Kahn-Freund, p. 416.
5. But cf. Allégret, Fasc. 684, 55.
6. Spera, Art. 18, Anm 3.

2.130 **DCU 3** *Apart from exceptions dealt with in the tariffs, goods which are fragile or have a tendency to spread themselves in the wagons, as well as those which might sully or damage other goods, shall only be carried in complete wagon loads, unless packed or gathered together in such a way that they will not break, spread or sully or damage other goods.*

2.131 **DCU 4, to § 3** *When a sender habitually despatches from the same station goods of the same nature requiring packing, and habitually hands them over either without packing or with similar defective packing, he need not comply with the provisions of § 3 of this Article in respect of each consignment, if he deposits at that station a general declaration in the form laid down by the railways and published by them. In such cases, the sender shall make reference on the consignment note to the general declaration deposited at the forwarding station.*

In publishing the model general declaration form regarding the absence or defective condition of the packing, the railways shall have regard to the procedure laid down in the national law.

2.132 **DCU 5, to § 5** *Apart from exceptions dealt with in the tariffs, the sender of small packages of sundries consignments must label each package in a manner acceptable to the railway. The label shall indicate in legible, indelible Roman letters the station and country of destination, as well as the name and address of the sender and of the consignee, exactly as indicated on the consignment note. The label must be affixed to the package itself or, if the latter is such that this is not possible, it must be a durable label tied firmly to the package.*

In the case of complete wagon loads being sent by rail and by sea and having to be transhipped, there must be a label for each part of the load.

Comments

1. Evidence of condition of the goods and their packing

2.133 Article 19 concerns the fitness and condition of goods for transport by rail and, in particular, their packing. Article 19 also has a bearing on the evidential role of the consignment note. Thus, according to Article 19.1, if the goods accepted for carriage show "obvious" signs of damage, the railway may require the condition of such goods to be indicated in the consignment note. As the railway is entitled to "require" the indications, rather than simply enter them itself as occurs in the carriage of goods by road or sea, for reasons of proof the indications must be made by the consignor; and if the consignor fails to do so, the railway may refuse to carry the goods: Article 19.3.[1] If the consignment note does not indicate that packing is defective, the inference of the second sentence of Article 19.4 is that there is a rebuttable presumption that the goods were suitably packed for the journey. However, the absence of any provision corresponding to the second sentence of Article 19.4 in Article 19.1 in respect of the condition of goods has led to the suggestion that no such rebuttable presumption arises in respect of the condition of the goods, apart from packing.[2] In any event, any presumption about the state of packing is limited to what is obvious to the railway, i.e., what is "apparent" to the carrier by sea or by road—something external that meets the eye.[3] The railway is not obliged to check or test the packing.[4]

1. Spera, Art. 19, Anm 6.
2. Glass/Cashmore para. 4.09; but cf. Spera, Art. 19, Anm 2.
3. Spera, Art. 19, Anm 5.
4. Spera, Art. 19, Anm 14.

2. Packing

As regards packing, the first question is whether the goods require packing at all: only then does any question of liability arise. Most goods are better protected packed than unpacked; it appears that whether the goods "require packing", depends on current trade practice. Thus motor cars can be sent unpacked on transporters by road[5] and the same is true today of motor cars sent by rail. It is for the railway to prove that unpacked goods should have been packed.[6] 2.134

If the goods do require packing,[7] the next question is whether it has been done and done properly. This is determined *in concreto* with reference to the particular goods and the particular transit in prospect.[8] On this question, the judgment in one case[9] suggests that the consignor should be entitled to seek the advice of the railway; to a degree this kind of information is obtained by reference to "the provisions in force at the forwarding station". Together with reference to current trade practice, that should indicate the degree to which the goods should be protected from the vicissitudes of travel by the consignor's packing and the degree to which protection can be expected from the railway's wagon. To take a simple example, if the consignor is entitled to expect the railway to provide a covered wagon (see Article 20.4), the packing does not have to be as weather resistant as if the wagon were uncovered. It is for the railway to prove that the packing of the goods was inadequate.[10] 2.135

3. Defective packing: the position of the railway

If packing is indeed defective, Article 19.3 provides that the railway may either refuse the goods or require the sender to acknowledge in the consignment note the absence of packing or of the defective condition of the packing, with an exact description thereof. From this it might be inferred that, if the railway does take the goods with the consignor's acknowledgement, the railway is not liable for the consequences. Arguably this was the early position at common law.[11] However, this was qualified later by Lord Atkinson in *L.N.W. Ry. Co.* v. *Hudson*: "if the defect in the packing from which damage is likely to occur be discovered on the journey, the carrier should take reasonable means to arrest the loss or deterioration therefrom. And if the defect be discovered in time to prevent the forwarding of the goods, they should not be forwarded till the defect has been remedied."[12] Whether the latter is true of CIM, depends on whether the railway has a residual duty of care. This is arguably so,[13] however, in one case,[14] it was held that, if the railway accepted 2.136

5. *OLG Düsseldorf 8.5.69* (1970) 5 ETL 446.
6. Allégret, Fasc. 684, 58.
7. On what is meant by packing, see Spera, Art. 19, Anm 3.
8. *Paris 7.7.82*, BT 1982.430, 432.
9. *Ibid.*
10. Allégret, Fasc. 684, 58. *Quaere* whether packing should take account of the likelihood of pilfering and theft: Spera, Art. 19, Anm 9.
11. *Barbour* v. *S.E. Ry. Co.* (1876) 34 L.T. 67.
12. [1920] A.C. 324, 330.
13. See Article 20, Comment 3. Cf. Spera, Art. 19, Anm 10 and Anm 14.
14. *OLG Hamm 13.2.89*, TranspR 1989.432; ULR 1989 II.840.

goods that were obviously defectively packed, the railway was not liable for the consequences; and, in particular, that the consequent damage was not attributable to any cause other than the defective packing in terms of Article 36.3(b) and Article 37.2. In any event, if the consignor has not packed and sheeted goods in accordance with the requirements of Customs, the railway is entitled to do so and to charge the cost to the goods: Article 25.4.

2.137 To the extent that the railway is not in breach of its residual duty of care, defective packing is likely to be "a fault on the part of the person entitled" under Article 36.2 and hence, if loss of or damage to the goods is the result, the state of the packing will provide a defence to an action in respect of damage brought against the railway.[15] Or, more simply, it may amount to a case of special risk, "absence or inadequacy of packing", under Article 36.3(b).

4. Defective packing: the liability of the consignor

2.138 According to Article 19.4, the consignor is liable to the railway for all the consequences of the absence of packing or defective condition of packing. This is probably regardless of fault, it being a matter of risk allocation,[16] and the liability is for the consequences to the railway[17] and, as some argue, to others such as the consignee. However, liability can be based on Article 19.4 only as regards loss or damage originating in the course of transit. In a case in which goods caught fire at the destination station after delivery the Swedish Supreme Court held that CIM did not apply.[18]

2.139 In particular, if there is loss or damage to third parties which the railway must compensate, the railway may have a right of recovery against the consignor under Article 19.[19] For example, in a French case,[20] goods, which were, in the opinion of the court, falsely described in the consignment note, exploded. The SNCF indemnified a third party, whose wagons had been damaged in the explosion and to which the SNCF was liable, and recovered the amount of the indemnity from the consignor. However, whereas the corresponding provision of CMR (Article 10) states only that the consignor shall be liable to the carrier, the implication of this sentence of CIM, Article 19, is that the consignor may be liable not only to the carrier but also directly to other persons, for example, other persons whose goods are damaged as a result of the defective packing. The difficulty about that implication is that, whereas Article 19 is a term of the contract between the defendant consignor and the railway, no such legal relationship exists between one consignor and another, so in the latter case a ground of liability may have to be found apart from Article 19.

15. Kahn-Freund, p. 434.
16. Helm, Art. 12, Anm 4.
17. Spera, Art. 19, Anm 16.
18. *Court of Justice, Sweden, 4.10.67*, Bull.OCTI 1972.47, ULR 1973 (I) 290.
19. E.g. *TC Seine 26.12.60*, Bull.OCTI 64.123.
20. *Ibid.*

Article 20, Handing over of goods for carriage and loading of goods *2.140*

1. The handing over of goods for carriage shall be governed by the provisions in force at the forwarding station.

2. Loading shall be the duty of the railway or the consignor according to the provisions in force at the forwarding station, unless otherwise provided in the Uniform Rules or unless the consignment note includes a reference to a special agreement between the consignor and the railway.

When the loading is the responsibility of the consignor, he shall comply with the load limit. If different load limits are in force on the lines traversed, the lowest load limit shall be applicable to the whole route. The provisions laying down load limits shall be published in the same manner as tariffs. If the consignor so requests, the railway shall inform him of the permitted load limit.

3. The consignor shall be liable for all the consequences of defective loading carried out by him and shall, in particular, make good any loss or damage suffered by the railway through this cause. Nevertheless Article 15 shall apply to the payment of costs arising from the reloading of goods in the event of defective loading. The burden of proof of defective loading shall rest upon the railway.

4. Unless otherwise provided in the Uniform Rules, goods shall be carried in covered wagons, open wagons, sheeted open wagons or specially equipped wagons according to the international tariffs. If there are no international tariffs, or if they do not contain any provisions on the subject, the provisions in force at the forwarding station shall apply throughout the whole of the route.

5. The affixing of seals to wagons shall be governed by the provisions in force at the forwarding station.

The consignor shall indicate in the consignment note the number and description of the seals affixed to the wagons by him.

Comments

1. Handing over the goods

"Handing over" the goods, the subject of Article 20.1, should be distinguished, first, from the "acceptance of goods" whereby the contract of carriage comes into existence (Article 11) and the railway becomes responsible for what befalls them (Article 35.1 and Article 36.1); and, secondly, from the "very act of taking over the goods" (Article 35.2), whereby a succeeding railway becomes a party to the contract of carriage and assumes obligations arising therefrom. "Handing over" and "taking over", but not "acceptance",[1] point to a definitive act whereby the railway assumes (custody and) control of the goods or, at least, of the wagon in which they have been loaded. *2.141*

2. Loading: the responsibility of the consignor

Article 20 mainly concerns responsibility for loading. Subject to what might be said in "the provisions in force at the forwarding station", loading includes not only loading on but also stowage and dunnage.[2] In the event of overloading, the consignor may be required to pay a surcharge: Article 24.1(b). Responsibility for loading, however, does not necessarily include responsibility for the fitness or suitability of wagons, even if there is a local regulation to that effect[3]; but, in the case *2.142*

1. See Art. 36, Comment 3, paras. 2.279 *et seq.*, below.
2. Allégret, Fasc. 684, 62; Spera, Art. 20, Anm 3.
3. *Brussels 5.4.73* (1973) 8 ETL 528; *Brussels 28.5.76* (1976) 11 ETL 780; Helm, Art. 14, Anm 3.

of special wagons such as refrigerated wagons, that responsibility is allocated to the consignor by the special regulations of RIP in CIM, Annex II.[4]

2.143 The central provision of Article 20 is that, having assumed responsibility for loading, the consignor is liable for the consequences of defective loading—liable to the railway and, as some argue, to others such as the consignee. Certainly, if there is loss or damage to third parties which the railway must compensate, the railway may have a right of recovery against the consignor under Article 20.[5] Commentators do not agree on the consignor's level of duty— on whether, for example, there is liability only if there is fault.[6] If loading is the responsibility of the railway, the level of duty required of the railway is that of the railway's general duty under Article 36.1.[7]

2.144 In a French case,[8] for example, DB recovered the cost of the decontamination of the track necessitated by a leak of arsenic. As with the corresponding provision of CIM concerning packing (Article 19.4), the implication of this sentence of Article 20 is that the consignor may be liable not only to the carrier but also to other persons, for example, other consignors whose goods are damaged as a result of the defective packing. The difficulty about that is that, whereas Article 20 is a term of the contract between the defendant consignor and the railway, no such legal relationship exists between one consignor and another, so in the latter case a ground of liability may have to be found apart from Article 20.

2.145 Article 20 is not primarily concerned with who bears the loss of or damage to the goods caused by defective loading, except when it is the work of the consignor: Article 20.3. However, in addition, defective loading may amount to "a fault on the part of the person entitled" under Article 36.2 and hence provide a defence to an action in respect of damage brought against the railway or, more simply, it may amount to a case of special risk, "loading operations carried out by the consignor" under Article 36.3(c) or of "defective loading" under Article 36.3(d).

3. Loading: the railway's residual duty of care

2.146 Although Article 20.3 places the responsibility for defective loading by the consignor solely on the consignor, without mention of the railway, the railway may retain some responsibility by virtue of a residual duty of care in relation to goods in its charge. A duty of this kind is found in analogous regimes, notably CMR.[9] A duty of this kind is also found in national law relating to the carriage of goods by rail. For example, under French domestic law, the railway must check the apparent state of the consignor's loading with a view not only to public safety but also to the preservation of the goods.[10] Again, in English common law relating to carriage by rail, there is a residual duty of care.[11] This alone does not support a residual duty

4. *Montpellier 16.1.86*, BT 1987.125.
5. See, for example, cases cited by Allégret, Fasc. 684, 63.
6. Helm, Art. 14, Anm 4.
7. Helm, Art. 14, Anm 4.
8. *TC Seine 4.12.62* Bull.OCTI 1965.176; see also *T. Budapest, No. 25. P.21 289/1968/29.*
9. Clarke, *CMR*, para. 85.
10. Rodière, No. 399.
11. See Article 19, Comment 3, paras. 2.136 *et seq.*, above.

of care in CIM in view of the limited role of national law: Article 10. Nonetheless a residual duty of care can be inferred from CIM, for the following reasons:

(a) it is the implication of cases in which the claimant proves that loss or damage was not attributable to one of the special risks (Article 37.2) but to the conduct of the railway, from the standard of conduct expected of the railway;
(b) the existence of an implied duty explains occasional references in judgments to a general duty of care[12]; and
(c) a duty of care is the corollary of a successful defence of unavoidable circumstances (Article 36.2) that the railway has come up to a certain standard of conduct. That standard is met by the performance of a residual duty of care; the existence of the duty is the corollary of the defence.

However, Article 25.4, provides that the railway is entitled but not, apparently, obliged to pack and sheet the goods as they should have been. The implications of this provision do not help, it is submitted, because the underlying purpose is less to safeguard the goods in the interests of the consignor or consignee than to ensure that the goods comply with Customs and administrative regulations and that defects in packing and sheeting do not delay the train.[13] *2.147*

If the defective nature of the loading is apparent to the railway at the outset, it has been suggested that liability to a third party who suffers loss or damage may be apportioned between the consignor and the railway.[14] *2.148*

Article 21, Verification *2.149*

1. The railway shall always have the right to verify that the consignment corresponds with the particulars furnished in the consignment note by the consignor and that the provisions relating to the carriage of goods accepted subject to conditions have been complied with.

2. If the contents of the consignment are examined for this purpose, the consignor or the consignee, according to whether the verification takes place at the forwarding station or the destination station, shall be invited to be present. Should the interested party not attend, or should the verification take place in transit, it shall be carried out in the presence of two witnesses not connected with the railway, unless the laws or regulations of the State where the verification takes place provide otherwise. The railway may not however carry out the verification in transit unless compelled to do so by operational necessities or by the requirements of the Customs or of other administrative authorities.

3. The result of the verification of the particulars in the consignment note shall be entered therein. If verification takes place at the forwarding station, the result shall also be recorded in the duplicate of the consignment note if it is held by the railway.

If the consignment does not correspond with the particulars in the consignment note or if the provisions relating to the carriage of goods accepted subject to conditions have not been complied with, the costs of the verification shall be charged against the goods, unless paid at the time.

12. For example, *Paris 1.3.51*, G.P. 1951.1.409; and quite clearly in *OLG Düsseldorf 18.1.1996*, Bull. OCTI 2000.179, 182.
13. Spera, Art. 25, Anm 18.
14. In this sense Allégret, Fasc. 684, 62.

Comments

1. Verification

2.150 The right of verification entitles the railway to check the truth of what the consignor has stated in the consignment note.[1] Although the obvious time to do so is when the goods are taken over, the railway is entitled to verify these matters at any time that the goods are in the railway's custody, subject to Article 21.2: the railway is not encouraged to carry out verification in a tunnel en route.[2] Thus the third sentence of Article 21.2 states that the railway is not permitted to carry out the verification in transit unless compelled to do so by operational necessities or by the requirements of the Customs or of other administrative authorities. An "operational necessity" might arise, for example, if the railway becomes suspicious that the goods are dangerous or it is necessary in order to prevent or to arrest deterioration in the condition of the goods.[3]

2.151 The purpose is to enable the railway to check, in particular but not only, what has been stated about "accepted subject to conditions" (Article 5) and that the regulations relating to special goods, notably dangerous goods, have been observed. Only if verification reveals a discrepancy ("differences from the particulars shown in the consignment note"), does the railway get extra time in which to carry the goods: Article 27.7(a). The railway is not obliged to conduct a verification; in the case of dangerous goods, the railway may be ill-equipped to try to verify the goods.

2.152 Verification also has a role in relation to the evidential value of the consignment note and this is important when the consignor or the consignee seek to establish a claim against the railway. Thus Article 21.2 requires that the consignor or the consignee, as appropriate, must be invited to be present. Ideally the appropriate party is the one, the consignor or consignee, who bears the risk—the evidential force of the verification depends on those present having an interest in the findings.[4] However, convenience may dictate that it be the person who can be persuaded to come, whether for reasons of interest or, simply, physical proximity. Thus, if the verification is at the forwarding station, it should be the consignor and, if at the destination station, the consignee: *semble* the stipulation of Article 21.2 must be observed; and, if the appropriate party does not attend (or verification takes place in transit) it shall be carried out, unless local law provides otherwise, "in the presence of two witnesses not connected with the railway".

2. Proof of loss or damage

2.153 In the event of loss of or damage to the goods, the onus is on the claimant to prove the liability of the railway and thus that there was "total or partial loss of, or damage

1. I.e. the particulars, for which see Art. 13, para. 2.76, above.
2. Spera, Art. 21, Anm 4.
3. Spera, Art. 21, Anm 12.
4. Helm, KVO, Art. 16, Anm 5.

to, the goods between the time of acceptance for carriage and the time of delivery" (Article 36.1).

Sometimes, a claimant may be able to prove a particular incident during the transit, such as a fire or derailment and thus establish that the loss or damage occurred while the railway was responsible for the goods. In most cases, however, there is less drama, less smoke and less evidence. More often, therefore, a claimant makes a *prima facie* case against the railway by contrasting the position at destination with that when the goods were accepted at the forwarding station.[5] *2.154*

As regards evidence of the position at destination, see Article 52. As regards evidence of the position at the forwarding station, in the case of carriage by sea or carriage by road the corresponding evidence is based on the statements made in the bill of lading (or waybill) or CMR consignment note, as the case may be: the bill of lading is conclusive evidence in the hands of a claimant consignee (Hague-Visby Rules, Article III.4), whereas the consignment note is at least *prima facie* evidence in favour of the claimant under the CMR (Article 9). Moreover, under the Rules and the CMR the document is evidence not only of the quantity of goods received but also of their order and condition. If this is true also of CIM, however, it is not obvious from the text of the Convention.[6] *2.155*

3. *The quantity of goods*

As regards the mass of the goods or the number of packages CIM, Article 11.4, provides that "the particulars in the consignment note relating to the mass of the goods or to the number of packages shall only be evidence against the railway when that weight or number of packages has been verified by the railway and certified in the consignment note. If necessary these particulars may be proved by other means." This is a limit ("only"), which assumes a rule, but a rule found outside CIM: the status of the consignment note as evidence of the mass or number of packages depends on local law: Article 22.1. Local law usually does provide that the acknowledgment of mass, etc., is evidence against the railway: for example, this would be the effect at common law. And so, together with verification of other matters, the note is often evidence enough for the claimant's *prima facie* case against the railway under CIM.[7] *2.156*

Whereas the ascertainment of mass and the number of packages has clear implications for the liability of the railway to the consignor or consignee, most commentators believe that it does not make the railway liable to third parties, such as a buyer from the consignee who relies on the statements in the consignment note. However, a minority anticipate extra-contractual liability.[8] *Quaere* whether under English law the railway might be liable to that buyer in tort; the decision in *Caparo Industries plc* v. *Dickman* suggests not.[9] *2.157*

5. *OLG Hamburg 21.6.79*, Bull.OCTI 1980.13; Brunat, BT 1982.462.
6. Brunat, BT 1982.462.
7. Rodière, No. 349.
8. See Spera, Art. 22, Anm 3.
9. [1990] 2 A.C. 605, but cf. statements in *The Zephyr* [1985] 2 Lloyd's Rep. 529, 538 (C.A.).

4. The condition of the goods

2.158 As regards the condition of the goods, although the railway "may require the condition of . . . goods to be indicated in the consignment note" (Article 19.1), it seems that no inference, that the goods were in apparent good order and condition, can be drawn from the failure of the railway to enter reservations about condition.[10] Article 21 provides for verification, but as a power and not a duty.[11] Article 21 does not assist the claimant's case unless information about condition is stated in the note *and* the railway exercises its "right" to verify under Article 21.1 and finds that the statements are true. Even then, when the result of the verification has been entered in the consignment note as required by Article 21.3, CIM is silent on the evidential effect.

5. Contents

2.159 As regards contents, if the railway acknowledges receipt of a carton, that is no evidence about the contents of the carton.[12] Moreover, if the railway accepts a wagon fully loaded by the consignor there is little that the consignor or a person in his position, such as an agent, can do to ensure that the note contains evidence of contents against the railway. However, that is true of any kind of sealed container and of any mode of carriage.[13]

2.160 **Article 22, Ascertainment of weight and number of packages**

1. The provisions in force in each State shall determine the circumstances in which the railway must ascertain the mass of the goods or the number of packages and the actual tare of the wagons.

The railway shall enter in the consignment note the results ascertained.

2. If weighing by the railway, after the contract of carriage has been made, reveals a difference, the mass ascertained by the forwarding station or, failing that, the mass declared by the consignor, shall still be the basis for calculating the carriage charges:

(a) if the difference is manifestly due to the nature of the goods or to atmospheric conditions; or

(b) the weighing takes place on a weighbridge and does not reveal a difference exceeding two per cent of the mass ascertained by the forwarding station or, failing that, of that declared by the consignor.

Additional Uniform Regulation (DCU)

2.161 **DCU 1, to § 1** *In the case of weighing on a weighbridge, the mass shall be determined by deducting the tare indicated on the wagon from the total mass of the loaded wagon, unless a different tare results from a special weighing of the empty wagon.*

Masses ascertained on a privately-owned weighbridge shall be treated as if they were the masses ascertained on a railway-owned weighbridge, so long as the relevant conditions laid down by the railway concerned have been fulfilled.

10. Glass/Cashmore, para. 4.09.

11. Brunat *loc. cit.*; cf. Spera, Art. 21, Anm 3.

12. *Supreme Court, Hungary No. GF III 31 237/1973/5*, ULR 1976 (I) 262.

13. See *International Carriage of Goods: Some Legal Problems and Possible Solutions* (Schmitthoff and Goode ed., London, 1988), Chap. 4.

Comment

Article 22 develops certain matters dealt with in Article 21. See, in particular, Article 21, Comment 2. When Article 22.1. states that the circumstances in which the railway must ascertain these matters shall be determined by the provisions in force in each State, that is a reference to the law in force where the goods are accepted for carriage. Most states require the railway to ascertain these matters at that point, except when the goods have been loaded by the consignor.[1] The reference to mass is in practice a reference to the kilogram, which in this context is regarded as a unit of mass rather than a unit of weight. This is important *inter alia* because it determines the maximum liability of the railway under Article 40.2. *2.162*

Article 23, Overloading *2.163*

1. When overloading of a wagon is established by the forwarding station or by an intermediate station, the excess load may be removed from the wagon even if no surcharge is payable. Where necessary the consignor or, if the contract of carriage has been modified in accordance with Article 31, the consignee shall be asked without delay to give instructions concerning the excess load.

2. Without prejudice to the payment of surcharges under Article 24, the excess load shall be charged for the distance covered in accordance with the carriage charges applicable to the main load. If the excess load is unloaded, the charge for unloading shall be determined by the tariffs of the railway which carries out the unloading.

If the person entitled directs that the excess load be forwarded to the same destination station as the main load or to another destination station, or directs that it be returned to the forwarding station, the excess load shall be treated as a separate consignment.

Additional Uniform Regulation (DCU)

DCU 1, to § 1 *The station at which the excess load has been established and the frontier stations of entry into subsequent States shall decide whether the consignment may be carried without any adjustment over the lines of the State in which they are situated.* *2.164*

If a station is of the opinion that the load must be adjusted, it shall proceed as follows:

(a) *if the whole consignment can be transhipped without special risk on to a suitable wagon, the latter must be forwarded to the destination of the consignment, instructions being obtained from the person entitled where applicable;*

(b) *if transhipment cannot be effected on to a single wagon, the station shall decide in the best interests of the person entitled, whether it is necessary to obtain instructions from him in regard to the manner in which to proceed or whether the excess load shall automatically be forwarded to destination.*

When the sender is asked for his decisions in regard to the consignment, he may give his instructions to the station which has established the excess load, either direct or through the forwarding station.

In the event of modification of the contract of carriage in accordance with Article 31, the consignee shall give his instructions direct to the station which has established the excess load.

Comment

In view of the overriding importance of safety, if overloading of a wagon is established by the forwarding station or by an intermediate station, the railway is *2.165*

1. Spera, Art. 22, Anm 3.

entitled to remove the excess at its sole discretion, without prior consultation with the consignor or consignee and whatever the origin or cause of the overloading.[1] The railway is entitled to do this, even though the nature of the goods is such that, to remove the excess, a part of the goods may have to be removed such that the remaining load is less than the maximum permitted.[2]

2.166 Under the circumstances stated the railway must seek instructions from the consignor about what to do with the excess load. If no instructions are forthcoming within a reasonable time, it is a matter for local law; the goods are likely to be treated in the same way as uncollected goods.

2.167

Article 24, Surcharges

1. Without prejudice to the railway's entitlement to the difference in carriage charges and to compensation for any possible loss or damage, the railway may impose:
   (a) a surcharge equal to one unit of account per kilogramme of gross mass of the whole package;
      (i) in the case of irregular, incorrect or incomplete description of substances and articles not acceptable for carriage under the RID;
      (ii) in the case of irregular, incorrect or incomplete description of substances and articles which under the RID are acceptable for carriage subject to conditions, or in the case of failure to observe such conditions;
   The supplementary provisions may provide for other methods of calculating the surcharge, in particular a fixed surcharge for empty private owners' wagons.
   (b) a surcharge equal to five units of account per 100 kilogrammes of mass in excess of the load limit, where the wagon has been loaded by the consignor.

3. The surcharges shall be charged against the goods irrespective of the place where the facts giving rise to the surcharges were established.

4. The amount of the surcharges and the reason for imposing them must be entered in the consignment note.

5. The supplementary provisions shall specify the case in which no surcharge is due.

Additional Uniform Regulation (DCU)

2.168 **DCU 1, to § 1(a)** *The surcharge provided for in* § 1*(a) may also be collected for goods which, by reason of an agreement concluded between two or more States or tariff clauses applied between two or more railways, in virtue of Article* 5, § 2, *are acceptable for carriage although excluded by the RID or subject to less severe conditions than those which are laid down in these Regulations.*

Comment

2.169 Surcharges, which are the subject of Article 24, are penalties or agreed fines.[1] In the past, some writers have seen a surcharge as *obligatio ex lege*.[2] The typical case is that in which the railway has charged too low a rate for the goods because of misstatements by the consignor in the note. It presupposes a mistake although not necessarily fault on the part of the consignor, by whom, therefore, surcharges are

1. Spera, Art. 23, Anm 4 and Anm 6.
2. Spera, Art. 23, Anm 5.

1. *Une amende conventionelle* or *eine Vertragsstrafe*: Allégret, Fasc. 684, 73; Haenni, No. 123; Spera, Art. 24, Anm 3.
2. Spera, *loc. cit.*

payable.[3] However, as the amounts are charged against goods (Article 24.2), this has given rise to the suggestion that they may be payable by the consignee.[4]

The railway may impose surcharges for an excess of the load limit, where the wagon has been loaded by the consignor, and for irregular, incorrect or incomplete description of certain substances. What is meant by "irregular, incorrect or incomplete" is not defined by CIM and is determined largely by reference to trade practice.[5] The surcharges are to be charged against the goods, i.e., the railway has a lien or right of retention.[6] *2.170*

Article 25, Documents for completion of administrative formalities. Customs seals *2.171*

1. The consignor must attach to the consignment note the documents necessary for the completion of formalities required by Customs or other administrative authorities before delivery of the goods. Such documents shall relate only to goods which are the subject of one and the same consignment note, unless otherwise provided by the requirements of Customs or of other administrative authorities or by the tariffs.

However, when these documents are not attached to the consignment note or if they are to be provided by the consignee, the consignor shall indicate in the consignment note the station, the Customs office or the office of any other authority where the respective documents will be made available to the railway and where the formalities must be completed. If the consignor will himself be present or be represented by an agent when the formalities required by Customs or other administrative authorities are carried out, it will suffice for the documents to be produced at the time when those formalities are carried out.

2. The railway shall not be obliged to check whether the documents furnished are sufficient and correct.

3. The consignor shall be liable to the railway for any loss or damage resulting from the absence or insufficiency of or any irregularity in such documents, save in the case of fault by the railway.

The railway shall, where it is at fault, be liable for any consequences arising from the loss, non-use or misuse of the documents referred to in the consignment note and accompanying it or deposited with the railway; nevertheless any compensation shall not exceed that payable in the event of loss of the goods.

4. The consignor must comply with the requirements of Customs or of other administrative authorities with respect to the packing and sheeting of the goods. If the consignor has not packed or sheeted the goods in accordance with those requirements the railway shall be entitled to do so; the resulting costs shall be charged against the goods.

5. The railway may refuse consignments when the seals affixed by Customs or other administrative authorities are damaged or defective.

Comments

1. Documents required for Customs or other administrative authorities

Article 25 concerns mainly the consignor's obligation to attach to the consignment note the documents necessary for the completion of formalities required by Customs or other administrative authorities. Although the language of the first sub-paragraph of Article 25.1 (which is stronger than that used in the previous version *2.172*

3. Spera, *loc. cit.* Allégret, Fasc. 684, 74.
4. Allégret *loc. cit.*; Spera, Art. 24, Anm 19.
5. Spera, Art. 24, Anm 6.
6. Helm, Art. 7, Anm 7.

of CIM) might suggest that attachment is (absolutely) obligatory, the alternative procedure contemplated by the second sub-paragraph of Article 25.1 suggests otherwise and, it is believed that the latter is precisely for cases in which the consignor is unable to attach the documents to the note: this is the inference of the earlier versions of CIM. Indeed, courts have sometimes spoken of an option, whereby the consignor can choose whether to send the documents with the goods or to send them separately to the appropriate authority.[1]

2.173 In this connection, attention should be paid to the second sub-paragraph of Article 25.1, whereby it is contemplated that documents may not in fact be attached to the consignment note or that it may be agreed that they are to be provided by the consignee at some other station or office, where the documents will be made available to the railway and where the formalities must be completed. This provision enables the consignor to route documents as seems best, for example, directly to the office of the relevant official. If the consignor is late in getting the documents to the place indicated, the consignor will be liable.[2]

2.174 Except as just mentioned, the consignor's obligation must be performed "before delivery of the goods" (Article 25.1) because it is the railway that is obliged to complete the formalities in transit (Article 26) and is likely to need the documents at an early stage to do this. The documents to be attached are required (by Article 13.1(g)) to be listed in the consignment note. This does not oblige the railway (Article 25.2) to check that the documents attached are as required by the authorities but it does entitle the railway to do so. If the railway finds that the documents are not as required, the railway is entitled (by Article 3.1(a)) to refuse to carry the goods.

2. *The liability of the consignor*

2.175 The consignor's liability under Article 25.3 for any loss or damage resulting from the absence or insufficiency of or any irregularity in the documents is a liability regardless of fault,[3] "eine reine Erfolgshaftung des Absenders, ohne Rücksicht auf sein allfälliges Verschulden".[4] The consignor is excused only in the case of fault by the railway. On the one hand, failure to check the documents is not necessarily blameworthy because railway officials may not be qualified or competent to check them.[5] On the other hand, cases under the equivalent provision of CMR (Article 11, para. 1.50, above) suggest that, if the consignor attaches documents which are patently insufficient or irregular and the railway does not demur, consequent loss to the railway will be assumed in part at least by the railway.[6]

1. *Vienna 22.10.71*, ULR 1975 (II) 380, Bull.OCTI 1975.69.
2. *Ibid.*
3. Helm, Art. 13, Anm 1.
4. *Vienna 22.10.71* (above).
5. Spera Art. 25, Anm 9.
6. *OLG Düsseldorf 12.2.81*, VersR 1982.302. *Idem* as regards CIM, Art. 25.3: Spera, Art. 25, Anm 11. As concerns the case in which the railway gives the consignor wrong advice about the documentation required, see Spera, *loc. cit.*

3. The liability of the railway

Where it is at fault, the railway is liable for any consequences arising from the loss,[7] non-use or misuse of the relevant documents, as indicated in the second sub-paragraph of Article 25.3. Misuse includes delay in use.[8] Compensation is regulated by Article 25.3 in that it shall not exceed that payable in the event of loss of the goods.[9] Nevertheless some courts have based the liability of the railway in these circumstances, such as liability for delay to the goods, not on (the earlier provisions equivalent to) Article 25.3 but on Article 36. An instance is *Lg Hannover 24.11.66.*[10] The decision was doubted by the Central Office in a note to the report of the case[11]: the ceiling on the amount of damages expressly mentioned in the last sub-paragraph of Article 25.3 (the ceiling for loss of goods) appears to apply to delay within the scope of Article 25 and is thus, in a case of delay, a higher ceiling than the normal ceiling on damages for delay based on Article 36. *2.176*

4. Packing and sheeting

Article 25.4 provides that the consignor must comply with the requirements, if any, e.g. of Customs or of other administrative authorities with respect to the packing and sheeting of the goods set out in Article 19.2. If the consignor has not packed or sheeted the goods in accordance with those requirements, the railway is entitled to do so; the resulting costs are to be charged against the goods.[12] When and whether the railway is obliged take such remedial action is a more complex point.[13] *2.177*

Article 26, Completion of administrative formalities *2.178*

1. In transit, the formalities required by Customs or other administrative authorities shall be completed by the railway. The railway may, however, delegate that duty to an agent.

2. In completing such formalities, the railway shall be liable for any fault committed by itself or by its agent; nevertheless, any compensation shall not exceed that payable in the event of loss of the goods.

3. The consignor, by so indicating in the consignment note, or the consignee by giving orders as provided for in Article 31, may ask:

(a) to be present himself or to be represented by an agent when such formalities are carried out, for the purpose of furnishing any information or explanations required;

(b) to complete such formalities himself or to have them completed by an agent, in so far as the laws and regulations of the State in which they are to be carried out so permit;

(c) to pay Customs duties and other charges, when he or his agent is present at or completes such formalities, in so far as the laws and regulations of the State in which they are carried out permit such payment.

Neither the consignor, nor the consignee who has the right of disposal, nor the agent of either may take possession of the goods.

7. E.g. *Supreme Court Hungary, Gf III, 30.194/1988*, Bull.OCTI 1990.21.
8. Note by the Central Office to *Lg Hannover 24.11.66*, Bull.OCTI 1968.59, 63.
9. See Arts. 40 and 44–46, para. 2.341 and paras. 2.365 *et seq.*, below.
10. Bull.OCTI 1968.59, 62.
11. Above. Also against the decision: Helm, Art. 13, Anm 1.
12. Cf. Art. 19.4, para. 2.127, above.
13. See Art. 19, Comment 3, paras. 2.136 *et seq.*, above.

4. If, for the completion of the formalities, the consignor designated a station where the provisions in force do not permit of their completion, or if he has stipulated for the purpose any other procedure which cannot be followed, the railway shall act in the manner which appears to it to be the most favourable to the interests of the person entitled and shall inform the consignor of the measures taken.

If the consignor, by an entry in the consignment note, has undertaken to pay charges including Customs duty, the railway shall have the choice of completing Customs formalities either in transit or at the destination station.

5. Subject to the exception provided for in the second sub-paragraph of paragraph 4, the consignee may complete Customs formalities at the destination station if that station has a Customs office and the consignment note requests Customs clearance on arrival, or, in the absence of such request, if the goods arrive under Customs control. The consignee may also complete these formalities at a destination station that has no Customs office if the national laws and regulations so permit or if the prior authority of the railway and the Customs authorities has been obtained. If the consignee exercises any of these rights, he shall pay in advance the amounts chargeable against the goods.

Nevertheless, the railway may proceed in accordance with paragraph 4 if the consignee has not taken possession of the consignment note within the period fixed by the provisions in force at the destination station.

Additional Uniform Regulations (DCU)

2.179 **DCU 1, to § 3** *When the Customs office is situated at some distance from the intermediate station at which sender has specified Customs clearance must be effected, the railway shall decide, in compliance with the Customs regulations applicable in the State to which it belongs, whether the traffic must be transferred to the Customs warehouse or whether Customs clearance shall be effected at the station. The expenses shall be treated as a charge against the goods.*

2.180 **DCU 2, to § 3** *Senders who wish to avail themselves of one of the rights laid down in* § 3*(a) to (c), must so prescribe on the consignment note, in the space provided for their declarations, by indicating the station at which the Customs formalities must be completed; consignees who wish to avail themselves of one of these rights must so prescribe in their instructions, indicating the station at which Customs formalities must be completed.*

Comment

2.181 Article 26 concerns the obligation of the railway, the railway itself or its agent, to complete the formalities required by Customs or other administrative authorities while the goods are in transit. Transit does not necessarily connote movement. Goods are in transit between the time of their acceptance for carriage by the railway and, if it occurs, their delivery to the consignee.[1] In other words, goods are in transit while they are in the custody of the railway as carrier.[2] However, the obligation imposed on the railway by Article 26 is limited to the completion of formalities. If, as national tariffs sometimes provide, the Customs or other administrative authority requires payment of charges which, of course, is the responsibility of the consignor or consignee in accordance with Article 15, the railway is entitled to reimbursement as soon as possible.[3] Moreover, the charges in question are to be understood in the context of Article 26 and thus to mean only charges levied by the Customs and administrative authorities.[4]

1. Spera, Art. 26, Anm 3.
2. Clarke (1988) 23 ETL 645.
3. *TC Valenciennes 17.5.83*, BT 1984.327.
4. Spera, Art. 26, Anm 13.

As to the role of agents acting for the railway, earlier versions of CIM stated that both the railway and any delegate had the duties of an agent (*Kommissionär*). There was some disagreement about what this meant and the matter was resolved by finding a gap in CIM and resorting therefore (under provisions equivalent to Article 10.1) to national law, usually that of the place where the formalities in question had to be completed.[5] *2.182*

Article 27, Transit periods *2.183*

1. The transit periods shall be specified either by agreement between the railways participating in the carriage, or by the international tariffs applicable from the forwarding station to the destination station. For certain special types of traffic and on certain routes these periods may also be established on the basis of transport plans applicable between the railways concerned; in that case they must be included in international tariffs or special agreements which, where appropriate, may provide for derogations from paragraphs 3 to 9 below.

Such periods shall not in any case exceed those which would result from the application of the following paragraphs.

2. In the absence of any indication in regard to the transit periods as provided for in paragraph 1, and subject to the following paragraphs, the transit periods shall be as follows:

(a) for wagon-load consignments:
period for despatch .... 12 hours
period for carriage, for each 400 km or fraction thereof .... 24 hours

(b) for less than wagon-load consignments:
period for despatch .... 24 hours
period for carriage, for each 200 km or fraction thereof .... 24 hours

All these distances shall relate to the kilometric distances contained in the tariffs.

3. The period for despatch shall be counted only once, irrespective of the number of systems traversed. The period for carriage shall be calculated on the total distance between the forwarding station and the destination station.

4. The railway may fix additional transit periods of specified duration in the following cases:

(a) consignments handed in for carriage, or to be delivered, at places other than stations;
(b) consignments to be carried:
  (i) by lines of different gauge;
  (ii) by sea or inland navigable waterway;
  (iii) by road if there is no rail link;
(c) consignments charged at reduced rates in accordance with special or exceptional internal tariffs;
(d) exceptional circumstances causing an exceptional increase in traffic or exceptional operating difficulties.

5. The additional transit period provided for in paragraphs 4 (a) to (c) shall be shown in the tariffs or in the provisions duly published in each State.

Those provided for in paragraph 4 (d) must be published and may not come into force before their publication.

6. The transit period shall run from midnight next following acceptance of the goods for carriage.

7. Except in the case of any fault by the railway, the transit period shall be extended by the duration of the period necessitated by:

5. Helm, Art. 15, Anm 3.

(a) verification or ascertainment in accordance with Article 21 and Article 22.1, which reveals differences from the particulars shown in the consignment note;
(b) completion of the formalities required by Customs or other administrative authorities;
(c) modification of the contract of carriage under Article 30 or 31;
(d) special care to be given to the goods;
(e) the trans-shipment or reloading of any goods loaded defectively by the consignor;
(f) any interruption of traffic temporarily preventing the commencement or continuation of carriage.

The reason for and the duration of such extensions shall be entered in the consignment note. If necessary proof may be furnished by other means.

8. The transit period shall be suspended on Sundays and statutory holidays. It shall be suspended on Saturdays when the provisions in force in any State provide for the suspension of domestic railway transit periods on those days.

9. When the transit period ends after the time at which the destination station closes, the period shall be extended until two hours after the time at which the station next opens.

10. The transit period is observed if, before its expiry:
(a) in cases where consignments are to be delivered at a station and notice of arrival must be given, such notice is given and the goods are held at the disposal of the consignee;
(b) in cases where consignments are to be delivered at a station and notice of arrival need not be given, the goods are held at the disposal of the consignee;
(c) in the case of consignments which are to be delivered at places other than stations, the goods are placed at the disposal of the consignee.

Comments

1. The transit period

2.184 Article 27 is concerned with transit periods for full or partial wagon-load consignments of goods. The period and the regime is different for express parcels, which are regulated by the CIM Annexe (RIEx). These have been published in the United Kingdom as TIEx.

2.185 Transit periods are conceived in three parts: despatch, carriage (distinguished by Article 27.2(a) and (b)) and arrival (see Article 27.10), which may include the time taken for the railway to run a feeder service by other means of transport to the consignee's address (Article 27.10(c)). The obligation of the railway is to deliver within the relevant transit period for the entire transport operation. There is no obligation, for example, to complete despatch during the time allocated for despatch[1] or to reach a certain point on the journey by a certain point in the period[2]: time lost in one part of transit may be made up later.[3] Nor is there any supporting obligation of reasonable despatch which might oblige the railway to deliver sooner than the total period allowed.

2.186 The primary rule, to be found in Article 27.2, allows X hours per Y kilometres. The implication of the second paragraph of Article 27.1 is that the periods may be freely shortened but not increased, except as provided in Article 27.4 and Article 27.7; see Comment 2. According to Article 27.6 the period begins at midnight following acceptance of the goods which, if the railway has stored the goods prior to carriage, means the point in time at which the railway's role changes from

1. Spera, Art. 27, Anm 12.
2. *Lg Hannover 24.11.66*, Bull.OCTI 1968.59; *Paris 16.6.71*, 1971 ULC 311.
3. Allégret, Fasc. 684, 89; Spera, *loc. cit.*

warehouseman to carrier.[4] A longer period is allowed for less than full wagon-loads, as determined by provisions in force at the forwarding station.[5] The period ends when the relevant period ends, however, what counts is observance of the period by the railway, i.e. delivery within the period.[6] In that connection see Article 27.10 and Article 28.2.

2. Extension of the transit period

The transit periods may be extended by the railway concerned for carriage in general under Article 27.4, if particular circumstances are anticipated to require more time for transit, as well as the catch-all "exceptional circumstances" stated in Article 27.4(d). As an example of the latter Spera gives the case of a line blocked by snow or made dangerous by flooding,[7] however, the requirement of prior publication in the second sentence of Article 27.5 suggests that this will be so only in truly exceptional circumstances. Article 27.4(d) contemplates something more general than circumstances preventing the carriage of the (particular) goods, which is itself a ground of exoneration under Article 33.1.[8] *2.187*

The transit period may also be extended under Article 27.7 for a particular movement of goods to take account of special factors which may delay unexpectedly the movement of those goods, such as Customs formalities and transhipment. The normal period is extended by the extra period "necessitated" by the factors in question. In each case the period is extended not only by the time necessitated by the particular cause of delay, for example (c) the time taken to complete the formalities required by Customs, but also the time lost in consequence, for example time waiting for the next appropriate train, before the goods can continue their journey.[9] *2.188*

In any event, delay beyond the relevant period does not necessarily constitute a breach of contract by the railway. If circumstances prevent delivery of the goods, whether temporarily or permanently, the railway may be excused under Article 36.2. Distinguish extra time necessitated by the fault of the railway: in that case the extra time must be taken but it is not permitted to extend the contract transit period and the railway is liable for loss caused by the excess time, i.e. the delay. If the railway delivers outside the permitted transit period, it is liable for compensation not exceeding three times the carriage charges: Article 43.1. If, however, the carrier has not delivered the goods or held them at the disposal of the consignee 30 days after the expiry of the permitted transit period, the case is treated as one of total loss: Article 39.1. In that case the level of compensation is higher: Article 40. *2.189*

4. Spera, Art. 27, Anm 27.
5. Spera, Art. 27, Anm 10. On the practical significance of the distinction see Spera, Art. 27, Anm 14.
6. See Art. 28, Comment 3, paras. 2.194 *et seq.*, below.
7. Art. 27, Anm 23.
8. Spera, Art. 27, Anm 37.
9. Spera, Art. 27, Anm 31.

2.190 **Article 28, Delivery**

1. The railway shall hand over the consignment note and deliver the goods to the consignee at the destination station against a receipt and payment of the amounts chargeable to the consignee by the railway.

Acceptance of the consignment note obliges the consignee to pay to the railway the amounts chargeable to him.

2. It shall be equivalent to delivery to the consignee if, in accordance with the provisions in force at the destination station:

(a) the goods have been handed over to Customs or *Octroi* authorities at their premises or warehouses, when these are not subject to railway supervision;

(b) the goods have been deposited for storage with the railway, with a forwarding agent or in a public warehouse.

3. The provisions in force at the destination station or the terms of any agreements with the consignee shall determine whether the railway is entitled or obliged to hand over the goods to the consignee elsewhere than at any railway depot. If the railway hands over, or arranges for them to be handed over in a private siding, at his domicile or in a depot, delivery shall be deemed to have been effected at the time when they are so handed over. Save where the railway and the user of a private siding have agreed otherwise, operations carried out by the railway on behalf of and under the instructions of that user shall not be covered by the contract of carriage.

4. After the arrival of the goods at the destination station, the consignee may require the railway to hand over the consignment note and deliver the goods to him.

If the loss of the goods is established or if the goods have not arrived after the expiry of the period provided for in Article 39.1 the consignee may assert in his own name, any rights against the railway which he may have acquired by reason of the contract of carriage.

5. The person entitled may refuse to accept the goods, even when he has received the consignment note and paid the charges, so long as an examination for which he has asked in order to establish alleged loss or damage has not been made.

6. In all other respects, delivery of the goods shall be carried out in accordance with the provisions in force at the destination station.

Additional Uniform Regulation (DCU)

2.191 **DCU 1, to §§ 1 and 4** *If a proportion of the articles declared in the consignment note is missing on delivery, the total amount due, as shown in the consignment note, shall nevertheless be paid. The right of the consignee to claim refund of the carriage charges for articles which have not been delivered shall be reserved.*

Comments

1. Introduction

2.192 Article 28 concerns not only delivery and the duty of the consignee to pay charges (Article 28.1) but also the right of the consignee (Article 28.4), once the goods have been claimed or delivery of the goods taken by the consignee, to assert rights against the railway under the contract of carriage. So, Article 28 must be read with Article 54, which concerns actions which might be brought against the railway. Underlying these provisions is the idea to rule out the possibility that the sender and consignee might have concurrent rights of action.[1]

2. The significance of delivery

2.193 Delivery is the time at which control of and responsibility for the goods on the part of the railway come to an end. Delivery being when the goods are taken over by the

1. Rodière No. 573; Durand, Bull.OCTI 1964.257, 266; von Tegelen, Bull.OCTI 1966.178.

consignee, that is usually also when the goods are accepted by the consignee. Under CIM acceptance of the goods is the moment in time by reference to which, in the absence of "ascertainment" of loss or damage (Article 52), rights of action against the railway are extinguished: Article 57.1. Moreover, if there has been ascertainment, in certain cases the limitation period runs from the time of delivery: Article 58. In spite of its importance, delivery is not defined by CIM (except to the extent of Article 28.2) and the inquirer must follow the path marked by Article 10 to national law.[2] Nonetheless, a broadly common notion of delivery can be found in national law.

3. Delivery

From Article 28.1 it appears that, for the purposes of Article 18, there is no delivery until the note has been handed to the consignee *and* the goods have been delivered to him. So, according to commentators,[3] if the consignee takes delivery of the goods but does not have handed to him the consignment note, he is not, for example, liable to pay charges. However, one of them also contends that nonetheless the consignee becomes party to the contract of carriage, if he accepts the goods.[4] *2.194*

In general, however, delivery of the goods is a bilateral operation that involves co-operation between railway and consignee.[5] Consequently, the railway cannot deliver by dumping the goods outside the premises of the consignee. Delivery occurs when control of the goods passes from carrier to (a willing) consignee.[6] The particular case mentioned in Article 28.2(b) is consistent with the general rule, as the warehouseman is likely to be seen as the agent of the consignee. Control implies exclusive possession. Nonetheless, as argued below in Comment 4, delivery may sometimes be partial or symbolic in terms of the physical movement of the goods themselves. Thus, in the case of a private siding, delivery occurs at the point of entry.[7] These are principles widely accepted not only for carriage by rail but also for carriage by other modes. For the operational detail at what may be large and busy stations, such as notification of arrival to the consignee, mode of acceptance of the consignment note, storage of the goods and so on, reference is made to national law in accordance with Article 28.6.[8] Common law too takes account of "any established practice on the part of the railway company in dealing with goods, addressed to, and to be delivered at the railway station".[9] *2.195*

2. Spera, Art. 28, Anm 2.

3. Allégret, Fasc. 684, 92; Spera, Art. 28, Anm 11 and 12.

4. Spera Art. 28, Anm 4. Also in this sense: *Court of Justice, Sweden, 4.10.67*, Bull.OCTI 1972.47, ULR 1973 (I) 290 re CIM 1952 (Art. 16).

5. *BGH 14.2.63*, Bull.OCTI 1964.173; *Cass. It. 18.12.68*, Bull.OCTI 1970.80. Allégret, Fasc. 684, 90; Helm, EVO, Art. 75, Anm 5; Spera, Art. 28, Anm 2.

6. In this sense in Austria: Spera, Art. 28, Anm 2; in France: *Douai 18.1.43*, GP 1943.184; in Italy: *Cass. It. 18.12.68*, Bull.OCTI 1970.80, 83; and in Germany: *BGH 14.2.63*, Bull.OCTI 1964.173.

7. Rodière, No. 440, citing *Cass 29.11.71*, Bull.OCTI 1973.139, a decision on French domestic law. See also in this sense in regard to an international movement: *T.C. Valenciennes 17.5.83*, BT 1984.326.

8. *Court of Justice, Sweden, 4.10.67*, Bull.OCTI 1972.47, ULR 1973 (I) 290.

9. *Chapman* v. *G.W. Ry. Co.* (1880) 5 Q.B.D. 278, 280–281.

2.196 Similarly, acceptance of the goods occurs when control passes to a willing consignee,[10] who is also the right consignee.[11] If, however, the consignee "accepts" the goods but under protest because he thinks that they might be damaged and wants ascertainment of the goods under Article 52, there is neither acceptance nor delivery for the purposes of Article 57 (extinction of the right of action). Until the examination referred to in Article 28.5 has been made and the state of the goods ascertained, the cost of storage and the risk remain with the railway. The position after that depends on the consignee's response to what has been ascertained.

2.197 Commentators disagree about whether and to what extent delivery can be equated with or amount to acceptance of the goods by the consignee.[12] One view is that the operation is one and the same operation viewed from two sides, delivery being the viewpoint of the railway and acceptance that of the consignee. Others see two distinct and successive operations, with delivery being immediately prior to acceptance. The essential idea seems to be that of the transfer of control with the consent of each party, and on this basis, the former view seems preferable—with one reservation: handing over to the Customs authorities, which is stated (Article 28.2(a)) to be equivalent to delivery, may not amount to acceptance by the consignee. However, specific provision for this case suggests that otherwise the former view is indeed the better view.

4. Acts equivalent to delivery

2.198 Article 28.2 provides that, if the goods are (a) handed over to Customs or *Octroi* authorities or (b) deposited for storage in certain places, for the purposes of Article 28 these acts are to be regarded as equivalent to delivery

2.199 In case (a), subject to the payment of duty and relevant charges, the authority holds the goods for the consignee.[13] In a case in the Italian Court of Cassation,[14] the railway's argument, that delivery occurred symbolically when the wagon was placed in the Customs area and in the control of the Customs authorities, failed. If the consignment had been a complete wagon-load, however, the argument might have succeeded, but the case was one of groupage and it remained the responsibility of the railway to unload the wagon and separate the various individual consignments. Only when that occurred did delivery take place.[15] But, according to a note to the case by the Central Office, the more general view is that it is enough in such a case for the railway to open the wagon and thus place the contents at the disposal of the consignee (through the agency of the Customs authority): it is not necessary for the railway to unload and separate the individual consignments before delivery can occur.[16]

2.200 In case (b), the role of the railway, which together with a forwarding agent and a warehouse open to the public is one of the specified depositaries, has changed. As

10. Spera, Art. 57, Anm 3.
11. *Paris 23.3.29,* GP 1929.II.129. See Comment 6, below.
12. Allégret, Fasc. 686, 88; Spera, Art. 57, Anm 3.
13. *Marten* v. *Nippon Sea & Land Ins. Co. Ltd.* (1898) 3 Com. Cas. 164, 168.
14. *Cass. It. 18.12.68,* Bull.OCTI 1970.80.
15. *Ibid.* at 85.
16. *Idem* in Germany: *BGH 14.2.63,* Bull.OCTI 1964.173.

far as the railway is concerned, the carriage has ended and the railway's responsibility for the goods is governed not by CIM but by local law.[17] In England the matter would be governed by the law of bailment: the railway as bailee/warehouseman holds to the order of the consignee.[18] Difficulty arises if the railway then re-assumes the role of carrier in order to transport the goods to another destination. See Article 38, Comment 2, paragraphs 2.332 *et seq.*, below.

5. *Non-delivery*

If the cause of non-delivery is breach of contract on the part of the carrier, that is a matter for Chapter IV. If the cause of non-delivery is that the consignee declines to take delivery, the position appears to be governed by national law because Article 28.6 indicates a reference to national law for matters concerning delivery not regulated by Article 28. According to English common law, a tender of delivery to the consignee may be treated as delivery if failure to achieve actual delivery cannot be attributed to the carrier,[19] however, probably not tender to the correct address if the consignee cannot be found.[20] *2.201*

In any event, a solution both legal and practical is to be found in Article 28.2(b): it is equivalent to delivery if the goods have been put into storage in a proper place. The common law rule is similar.[21] However, if it has been agreed that the goods shall be "kept till called for", the common law rule is that the carrier holds as carrier (hence subject to CIM) rather than as warehouseman[22]; and that the carrier is obliged to give notice of arrival to the consignee and holds as carrier for a reasonable time thereafter.[23] The common law rules may be modified by the contract of carriage.[24] *2.202*

6. *The consignee's rights and duties on delivery*

The consignee with rights and duties under Article 28 is the person designated as consignee in the consignment note. If the carrier delivers the goods to anyone else, such as the person to notify, that is a breach of the contract of carriage.[25] However, the person designated may be altered by the exercise of rights under Article 30 and Article 31. In particular, if goods are damaged in transit, they may be ordered back to the consignor for salvage or repair: in a case like that delivery occurs when they are returned to the consignor.[26] *2.203*

If the consignee has taken possession of the consignment note, in accordance with Article 28.1, the consignee acquires a right of action against the railway under *2.204*

17. *Court of Justice, Sweden, 4.10.67,* Bull.OCTI 1972.47, ULR 1973 (I) 290.
18. See Condition 12 of the Freightliner Conditions, para. 2.638, below.
19. Glass/Cashmore, No. 1.67 and Palmer, pp. 1007 *et seq.*
20. Spera, Art. 28, Anm 22.
21. *Heugh* v. *L.N.W. Ry.* (1870) L.R. 5 Ex. 51.
22. *Chapman* v. *G.W. Ry. Co.* (1880) 5 Q.B.D. 278, 281.
23. *Mitchell* v. *Lancashire & Yorkshire Ry. Co.* (1875) L.R. 10 Q.B. 256, 260.
24. See, for example, Condition 6 of the RHA Conditions, para. 1.278, above.
25. *Cass. com. 12.5.92,* BTL 1992.396.
26. *OLG Celle 13.11.68,* Bull.OCTI 1970.45.

Article 54.3(b). Taking possession of the note is also important because that extinguishes the consignee's right to modify the contract of carriage: Article 31.3(a). However, whereas the railway is obliged by Article 28.1 to hand over the note on request in accordance with Article 28.4, the inference of Article 28.4 is that the consignee is not obliged to take it: not least because the consignee might thus incur obligations.

2.205 Acceptance of the note obliges the consignee, in accordance with Article 28.1, to pay all outstanding charges except those the payment of which has been promised by the consignor: Article 15.4. The railway is not entitled to demand from the consignee charges which the consignor should have paid but has not.[27] However, as stated above, the obligation to pay is contingent on acceptance of the note. Although the consignee who refuses to accept the goods may thus be in breach of contract with the consignor, as regards the railway, the consignee has a right to accept the goods and the note but is under no duty to do so.[28] If the consignee does refuse the note, the charges, which would otherwise have been payable by the consignee, must be paid by the consignor: Article 15.4.

2.206 **Article 29, Correction of charges**

1. In case of incorrect application of a tariff or of error in the calculation or collection of charges, undercharges shall be paid or overcharges repaid.

Undercharges shall be paid and overcharges shall be repaid only if they exceed eight units of account per consignment note. The repayment shall be made as a matter of course.

2. If the consignee has not taken possession of the consignment note the consignor shall be obliged to pay to the railway any amounts undercharged. When the consignment note has been accepted by the consignee or the contract of carriage modified in accordance with Article 31, the consignor shall be obliged to pay any undercharge only to the extent that it relates to the costs which he has undertaken to pay by an entry in the consignment note. Any balance of the undercharge shall be paid by the consignee.

3. Sums due under this Article shall bear interest at five per cent per annum from the day of receipt of the demand for payment or from the day of the claim referred to in Article 53 or, if there has been no such demand or claim, from the day on which legal proceedings are instituted.

If, within a reasonable period allotted to him, the person entitled does not submit to the railway the supporting documents required for the amount of the claim to be finally settled, no interest shall accrue between the expiry of the period laid down and the actual submission of such documents.

Additional Uniform Regulation (DCU)

2.207 **DCU 1, to § 1** *For the purpose of calculating sums due, the rate of exchange to be applied is that which was originally used to calculate the charges or which would have been used if no error had arisen. The amount of the payment to be made is equal to the sum calculated in this manner.*

27. Spera, Art. 28, Anm 7.
28. *Rheims 8.6.88*, BT 1989.481.

Comments

Article 29 concerns correction of errors in the charges[1] paid, errors of all kinds—not only of arithmetic but also, for example, in the basis of a charge, such as the weight of goods consigned. As regards undercharges, the railway's right to recover the amount due is not barred by delivery of the goods to the consignee,[2] or by any kind of estoppel based on what it has represented to a customer in communications made after the end of the carriage in question.[3] However, whether recovery is possible, when the error was caused by erroneous information supplied by the claimant, is a question on which opinion has been divided.[4] *2.208*

The railway's right of recovery is from the consignor or the consignee, as appropriate and indicated by Article 29.4. *Prima facie* the consignee liable to pay is the person mentioned as consignee in the consignment note. If the contract has been modified under Article 30 or Article 31, the new consignee is not obliged to pay the undercharge unless he has been identified as consignee in the consignment note.[5] See also Article 28, Comment 6, paragraphs 2.203 *et seq.*, above. *2.209*

The juridical basis of the right of recovery provided for in Article 29 is that of *paiement de l'indu* and *enrichissement sans cause*, i.e., in general terms, unjust enrichment.[6] However, it has been contended that, if the claimant has lost the right under Article 29, for example because action is time barred under Article 58.1, the claimant cannot fall back on more favourable rules of national law.[7] Nonetheless, the provision in Article 29.3 for interest has been seen as *lex specialis* which does not rule out claims for interest on other more general grounds.[8] *2.210*

Title III, Modification of the contract of carriage: Article 30, Modification by the consignor *2.211*

1. The consignor may modify the contract of carriage by giving subsequent orders:
   (a) for the goods to be withdrawn at the forwarding station;
   (b) for the goods to be stopped in transit;
   (c) for delivery of the goods to be delayed;
   (d) for the goods to be delivered to a person other than the consignee shown in the consignment note;
   (e) for the goods to be delivered at a station other than the destination station shown in the consignment note;
   (f) for the goods to be returned to the forwarding station;
   (g) for the consignment to be made subject to a cash on delivery payment;
   (h) for a cash on delivery payment to be increased, reduced or cancelled;
   (i) for charges relating to a consignment which has not been prepaid to be debited to him, or for charges which he has undertaken to pay in accordance with Article 15.2 to be increased.

1. Concerning the charges, see Art. 6.9 (para. 2.33, above) and Art. 15 (para. 2.103, above); and COD payments, see Art. 17.3 (para. 2.117, above).
2. *Ghent 17.2.70* (1977) 12 ETL 892.
3. *Liège 12.1.78*, ULR 1979 (II) 242.
4. Spera, Art. 29, Anm 7.
5. Spera, Art. 29, Anm 11.
6. *Liège 12.1.78*, ULR 1979 (II). 242. See Zweigert & Kötz, *Introduction to Comparative Law*, vol. II, pp. 230 *et seq.*
7. Spera, Art. 29, Anm 7.
8. Helm, Art. 18, Anm 4.

The tariffs of the forwarding railway may provide that orders specified in (g) to (i) are not acceptable.

The supplementary provisions or the international tariffs in force between the railways participating in the carriage may provide for the acceptance of orders other than those listed above.

Orders must not in any event have the effect of splitting the consignment.

2. Such orders shall be given by means of a written declaration, in the form laid down by the railway.

The declaration shall be reproduced and signed by the consignor in the duplicate of the consignment note which shall be presented to the railway. The signature may be printed or replaced by the despatch stamp.

Any order given in a form other than that laid down shall be null and void.

3. If the railway complies with the consignor's orders without requiring the production of the duplicate, where this has been sent to the consignee, the railway shall be liable to the consignee for any loss or damage caused thereby. Nevertheless, any compensation shall not exceed that payable in the event of loss of the goods.

4. The consignor's right to modify the contract of carriage shall, notwithstanding that he is in possession of the duplicate of the consignment note, be extinguished in cases where the consignee:

(a) has taken possession of the consignment note;
(b) has accepted the goods;
(c) has asserted his rights in accordance with Article 28.4;
(d) is entitled, in accordance with Article 31, to give orders as soon as the consignment has entered the Customs territory of the country of destination.

From that time onwards, the railway shall comply with the orders and instructions of the consignee.

Additional Uniform Regulations (DCU)

2.212 **DCU 1, to § 1(e) and (f)** *The sender may prescribe the tariff to apply and the route to follow. If he has undertaken to pay the charges up to the point at which the tariffs applied by adjacent countries take effect in accordance with article 15, § 2, and if, as a result of modification of the contract of carriage, the consignment is no longer routed through this point, the sender must also give new prepayment instructions. The new prepayment instructions may not, however, involve any changes in the original instructions relating to countries already crossed except in the case of the modification permitted in § 1(i).*

2.213 **DCU 2, to § 1** *In addition, the sender may modify the contract of carriage by giving instructions*

(a) that the consignee shall not be entitled to give subsequent orders,
(b) for delivery of the goods at a specified place of delivery or for a change in the place of delivery entered in the space on the consignment note reserved for stating the place of delivery.

2.214 **DCU 3, to § 2** *The declaration shall be in writing in the form laid down and published by the railway. It must be drawn up in accordance with the second sub-paragraph of article 12 § 3, and made at the forwarding station.*

In publishing the form of declaration, the railway shall observe the procedure laid down by national law.

2.215 **DCU 4, to § 2** *The forwarding station which receives a subsequent order shall certify receipt of that order by stamping the date on the duplicate consignment note, below the written declaration of the sender, to whom the duplicate shall then be handed back.*

2.216 **DCU 5, to § 2** *When the sender orders a cash on delivery payment to be increased, reduced or cancelled, he shall produce the document which was delivered to him. When the cash on delivery payment is to be increased or reduced, the document shall be returned to the sender after it has been amended; when it has been cancelled it shall not be returned.*

Comments

1. The nature and effect of modification

Article 30 regulates the right of the consignor to modify the contract in such matters as the timing and place of delivery, a right which is lost when a similar right of modification is acquired by the consignee, whose rights in this respect are the subject of Article 30.4 and Article 31. In CMR, Article 12 (para. 1.53, above), a similar but simpler scheme of modification, based on CIM, can be found. Unlike CMR, however, the central rule of CIM is that, unless the consignor has written "Consignee not authorised to give subsequent orders" in the consignment note and has agreed to pay charges relating to carriage in the country of destination (Article 31.1), the right passes to the consignee in accordance with Article 30.4. *2.217*

Evidently, ownership of the goods is distinct from possession or control. The consignee may have acquired ownership of the goods before acquiring any right under Article 31 to control their movement. Articles 30 and 31 are not concerned with the rights and duties of consignor and consignee *inter se* or with any sale that might have occurred, but with the contractual and commercial position of the carrier.[1] The carrier's obligation as carrier corresponds to a right enjoyed by the consignor or consignee as such, a right which other texts such as CMR call the right of disposal, but which CIM calls modification, perhaps to indicate that it is based not in property law but in the law of obligations.[2] *2.218*

2. The mode of modification

Modification of the contract of carriage occurs when certain orders are given by the consignor relating to the goods which are different from what had been originally agreed in the contract of carriage. The orders that are permitted are listed in Article 30.1; they are not mutually exclusive, an obvious example being that order (d), changing the person to whom the goods are to be consigned, and order (e), changing the station of delivery, may well be given together. The station, as well as the station for stoppage in transit, order (b), must indeed be what is recognised as a station and not at a point between stations, and on the actual route.[3] If the new station of destination is in the same state as the forwarding station, the contract of carriage remains subject to CIM.[4] Delivery of the goods, referred to in orders (c), (d) and (e) and implied in order (f), is regulated by Article 28. In any event, in the case of order (f), return to the forwarding station, the person, who may well be the sender, who takes delivery of the goods at the forwarding station, has the role, the rights and the duties of a consignee.[5] *2.219*

The orders must be given in writing in a form laid down by the railway in accordance with Article 30.2.[6] If the required procedure is not observed, for *2.220*

1. Rodière, No. 424.
2. Helm, Art. 433, HGB, Anm 2.
3. Spera, Art. 30, Anm 8.
4. Spera, Art. 30, Anm 11.
5. Spera, Art. 30, Anm 12.
6. On questions of form, see Spera, Art. 30, Anm 22.

example when changing the identity of the consignee, the consignor and the railway may be liable to the original consignee.[7] Liability is strict.[8]

2.221 The required procedure reflects times past when, for example, a telephone call to the railway was not sufficient. Nor, presumably, would a fax have been sufficient because, although it may duplicate the consignment note, it is not *the* duplicate to which Article 12.2 and hence Article 30.2 refer. The procedure has been defended on the ground that the uniqueness of the duplicate note assures the consignee, who has obtained possession of it from the consignor, that the contract cannot be modified by the consignor.[9] However, on the one hand, the person in possession of the duplicate has no rights against the railway unless that person is also the consignor or the named consignee.[10] On the other hand, some writers have entertained the possibility that, although the consignor has lost the duplicate, he may nonetheless give orders.[11]

3. *The effect of modification*

2.222 The effect of modification is not discharge of the original contract and the conclusion of a new contract, but modification of the original contract which, subject to the modification, remains in effect.[12] Although for all practical purposes the meaning of modification has always been well enough understood, the conception of a contract that might be altered unilaterally by one of the parties has caused discomfort among theorists in some countries, such as France.[13] However, English common law has long recognised that a party, such as a buyer or a charterer, might have options concerning the performance exigeable of the other party and so, the CIM scheme in Articles 30 to 32 will surprise, if at all, only by its scope and its complexity. The scope is perhaps a consequence of the view of the railway as a public service and the complexity is a consequence of the scope. A right to modify a contract of carriage by rail was recognised by common law at an early stage.[14]

2.223 The consignor loses the right to modify the contract, in accordance with Article 30.4, if the consignee has taken possession of the duplicate consignment note or, whether the consignor is still in possession of the note or not, the consignee has accepted the goods, or has required delivery in accordance with Article 28.4. Moreover, the consignor also loses the right to modify the contract, when the consignee has acquired the right to modify the contract because the goods have entered the Customs territory of the country of destination as contemplated by Article 31.1 *in fine*. The latter is a rule entirely particular to CIM and one not found, notably, in CMR or CIM (1999). If the consignor has lost the right to modify the contract and to dispose of the goods, but the consignee has acquired these rights but

7. *Cass 19.7.76*, BT 1976.364.
8. Helm, Art. 21, Anm 6.
9. Helm, *loc. cit.*
10. *Paris 31.10.74* (1976) 11 ETL 120.
11. Spera, Art. 30, Anm 21.
12. Spera, Art. 30, Anm 5.
13. Rodière, No. 425.
14. *Scothorn* v. *South Staffordshire Ry. Co.* (1853) 8 Exch. 341, 345; Palmer, pp. 1011 *et seq.*

is not interested in exercising them, what then? According to a leading commentator the vacuum is filled by resort to national law.[15]

Article 31, Modification by the consignee *2.224*

1. When the consignor has not undertaken to pay the charges relating to carriage in the country of destination, and has not inserted in the consignment note the words "Consignee not authorised to give subsequent orders", the consignee may modify the contract of carriage by giving subsequent orders:

(a) for the goods to be stopped in transit;
(b) for delivery of the goods to be delayed;
(c) for the goods to be delivered in the country of destination to a person other than the consignee shown in the consignment note;
(d) for the goods to be delivered in the country of destination at a station other than the destination station shown in the consignment note, subject to contrary provisions in international tariffs;
(e) for formalities required by Customs or other administrative authorities to be carried out in accordance with Article 26.3.

The supplementary provisions or the international tariffs in force between the railways participating in the carriage may provide for the acceptance of orders other than those listed above.

Orders must not in any case have the effect of splitting the consignment.

The consignee's orders shall only be effective after the consignment has entered the Customs territory of the country of destination.

2. Such orders shall be given by means of a written declaration, in the form laid down and published by the railway.

Any order given in a form other than that laid down shall be null and void.

3. The consignee's right to modify the contract of carriage shall be extinguished in cases where he has:

(a) taken possession of the consignment note;
(b) accepted the goods;
(c) asserted his rights in accordance with Article 28.4;
(d) designated a person in accordance with paragraph 1(c) and that person has taken possession of the consignment note, [accepted the goods] or asserted his rights in accordance with Article 28.4.

4. If the consignee has given instructions for delivery of the goods to another person, that person shall not be entitled to modify the contract of carriage.

Additional Uniform Regulations (DCU)

DCU 1, to § 1(d) *The consignee may stipulate that a consignment forwarded initially by* petite vitesse *shall be reforwarded by* grande vitesse *or* vice versa, *if the station where the consignment has been stopped provides both kinds of service; he may also indicate the tariff to be applied and the route to be followed.* *2.225*

DCU 2, to § 2, sub-para. 1 *In publishing the model written declaration, the railways shall observe the procedure laid down in their national law.* *2.226*

Comment

Article 31, together with Article 30.4, regulates the right of the consignee to modify the contract in such matters as the timing and place of delivery. Concerning the legal nature of the right see Article 30, Comment 1. The right is acquired by the *2.227*

15. Helm Art. 21, Anm 8.

consignee only when it has been lost by the consignor: see Article 30.4. Further, it is a basic feature of the consignee's right of modification that it can be exercised only when, in the words of the last sentence of Article 31.1, "the consignment has entered the Customs territory of the country of destination". Note, however, that the consignee is entitled to give orders and the railway is obliged to take note of them before the consignment has entered the territory.[1]

2.228 According to Article 31.1, it is a condition of the consignee's right to modify the contract of carriage that it is not the consignor (but the consignee) who has agreed to pay charges, the subject of Article 15. The underlying idea is that, if it is the consignor who is obliged to pay carriage charges at destination, the consignee should not be in a position to increase those charges by ordering the goods to a different destination.[2] The orders, which the consignee is entitled to give in exercise of the right of modification are set out in Article 1 and most are similar to those which the consignor is entitled to give under Article 30.1: see Article 30, Comment 2.

2.229 If the consignee has exercised the right to modify the contract of carriage by ordering the carrier to deliver the goods to another person, that person does not thereby acquire any right to modify the contract. The possibility of permitting such a right was rejected on the ground that most movements by rail were too short to make any other solution practical.[3] However, a similar outcome can be achieved with the co-operation of the original consignee: having ordered the railway to deliver the goods to person X (Article 31.1(c)), he is entitled (at the request of X) to give a further order to the railway to deliver to person Y, and so on. The consignee's right to modify the contract is extinguished altogether by the events listed in Article 31.3, most of which are the same as those which extinguish the right of modification of the consignor; see Article 30, Comment 3. These events extinguish not only the right to modify but also the obligation of the railway to carry out any orders previously given but as yet unexecuted.[4]

2.230 **Article 32, Execution of subsequent orders**

1. The railway may not refuse to execute orders given under Articles 30 or 31 or delay doing so save where:
   (a) it is no longer possible to execute the orders by the time they reach the station responsible for doing so;
   (b) compliance with the orders would interfere with normal railway operations;
   (c) a change of destination station would contravene the laws and regulations of a State, and in particular the requirements of the Customs or of other administrative authorities;
   (d) in the case of a change of destination station, the value of the goods will not, in the railway's view, cover all the charges which would be payable on the goods on arrival at the new destination, unless the amount of such charges is paid or guaranteed immediately.

1. Spera, Art. 31, Anm 17.
2. Spera, Art. 31, Anm 4.
3. Spera, Art. 31, Anm 27.
4. Spera, Art. 31, Anm 23.

The person who has given the orders shall be informed as soon as possible of any circumstances which prevent their execution.

If the railway is not in a position to foresee such circumstances, the person who has given the orders shall be liable for all the consequences of starting to execute them.

2. The charges arising from the execution of an order, except those arising from any fault by the railway, shall be paid in accordance with Article 15.

3. Subject to paragraph 1, the railway shall, in the case of any fault on its part, be liable for the consequences of failure to execute an order or failure to execute it properly. Nevertheless, any compensation shall not exceed that payable in the event of loss of the goods.

Additional Uniform Regulations (DCU)

DCU 1 *If it is laid down in the subsequent instructions that the goods are to be delivered to an intermediate station, carriage shall be charged from the forwarding station to such intermediate station. If, however, the goods have already been carried beyond that intermediate station, carriage shall be charged from the forwarding station to the station at which the goods are stopped and from that station back to the intermediate station.* 2.231

If it is laid down in the subsequent orders that the goods are to be carried to a different destination station or returned to the forwarding station, carriage shall be charged from the forwarding station to the station at which the goods are stopped and from that station to the new destination station or back to the forwarding station as the case may be.

The tariffs applicable shall be those in force for each section of the route on the day on which the contract of carriage is made.

The foregoing provisions shall apply in the same way to supplementary charges and other charges, also to the rates of exchange when the sender is responsible for payment of the charges.

DCU 2, to § 2 *The raising of any charge at the time of issue of subsequent instructions shall be determined in accordance with the tariff applied to the consignment:* 2.232

— *by the forwarding railway, when the subsequent instruction is given by the sender;*

— *by the destination railway, when the subsequent instruction is given by the consignee.*

Comment

Whereas the railway has no power, apart from Article 32, to *stop doing* what it is doing, i.e. performing the contract of carriage according to contract, Article 32.1 allows the railway to refuse to obey new instructions (modification of the contract), to refuse to do something different, in four situations. If the railway has not been in a position to make a decision to refuse, because the railway was not in a position to foresee the situation, the person who gave the order is liable for all the consequences of the railway's having started to execute the order: Article 32.1 *in fine*. The inference is that once the railway is in a position to foresee the consequences, it may refuse further execution of the order. The standard of foresight and anticipation expected of the railway is that of a reasonable professional.[1] 2.233

As regards case (a), impossibility, the view has been expressed in relation to the parallel provision of CMR, Article 12.5(b) (para. 1.53, above), that "possible" should not be construed literally but that it means "reasonable and possible". The context of Article 32.1(a), more clearly than that of Article 12.5(b), suggests that it is for the railway which refuses to execute orders to prove that compliance was impossible. 2.234

1. Spera, Art. 32, Anm 10: *die Sorgfalt eines ordentlichen Frachtführers.*

2.235 As regards case (b), interference with normal railway operations, not surprisingly commentators have been unable to agree on the meaning of "interference".[2] A similar provision is found in CMR, Article 12.5(b) (para. 1.53, above), and in that context commentators agree that the interference must be "serious" if it is to be a ground of refusal.

2.236 As regards case (c), illegality, *prima facie* illegality is an excuse only when the order concerns a change of destination. However, it should be recalled that illegality is also an excuse of a more general kind under Article 65.1(d).

2.237 Case (d), in which there is a possibility that the railway may lose money if it obeys the order is like case (b) in supporting the premise that the railway should not be required to undertake or continue an operation that would be commercially unreasonable.

2.238

Article 33, Circumstances preventing carriage

1. When circumstances prevent the carriage of goods, the railway shall decide whether it is preferable to carry the goods as a matter of course by modifying the route or whether it is advisable in the consignor's interest to ask him for instructions and at the same time give him any relevant information available to the railway.

Save fault on its part, the railway may recover the carriage charges applicable to the route followed and shall be allowed the transit periods applicable to such route.

2. If it is impossible to continue carrying the goods, the railway shall ask the consignor for instructions. It shall not be obliged to do so in the event of carriage being temporarily prevented as a result of measures taken in accordance with Article 3.4.

3. The consignor may enter in the consignment note instructions to cover the event of circumstances preventing carriage.

If the railway considers that such instructions cannot be executed, it shall ask for fresh instructions.

4. The consignor, on being notified of circumstances preventing carriage, may give his instructions either to the forwarding station or to the station where the goods are being held. If the instructions of the consignor change the consignee or the destination station or are given at the station where the goods are being held, the consignor must enter them in the duplicate of the consignment note and present this to the railway.

5. If the railway complies with the consignor's instructions without requiring the production of the duplicate, when this has been sent to the consignee, the railway shall be liable to the consignee for any loss or damage caused thereby. Nevertheless, any compensation shall not exceed that payable in the event of loss of the goods.

6. If the consignor, on being notified of a circumstance preventing carriage, fails to give within a reasonable time instructions which can be executed, the railway shall take action in accordance with the provisions relating to circumstances preventing delivery, in force at the place where the goods have been held up.

If the goods have been sold, the proceeds of sale, less any amounts chargeable against the goods, shall be held at the disposal of the consignor. If the proceeds are less than those costs, the consignor shall pay the difference.

7. When the circumstances preventing carriage cease to obtain before the arrival of instructions from the consignor, the goods shall be forwarded to their destination without waiting for such instructions; the consignor shall be notified to that effect as soon as possible.

8. When the circumstances preventing carriage arise after the consignee has modified the contract of carriage in accordance with Article 31, the railway shall notify the consignee. Paragraphs 1, 2, 6, 7 and 9 shall apply analogously.

9. Save fault on its part, the railway may raise demurrage or standage charges if circumstances prevent carriage.

10. Article 32 shall apply to carriage undertaken in accordance with Article 33.

2. Spera, Art. 32, Anm 6.

Additional Uniform Regulations (DCU)

DCU 1, to §§ 1, 2 and 3, sub-para. 2 *Advices addressed to the sender shall be worded in one of the official languages of the country of departure or in one of the official languages of the Organisation (French or German).* *2.239*

When the language used is not that of the country in which the forwarding station is situated, the sender shall be responsible for translating the advice.

DCU 2, to § 3, sub-para. 1, § 4 and § 8 *The raising of any charge at the time of receipt of instructions shall be determined in accordance with the tariff applied to the consignment:* *2.240*

— by the forwarding railway, when the instructions are given by the sender;
— by the destination railway, when they are given by the consignee.

When, however, the sender addresses his instructions direct to the station at which the goods are on hand and if a charge is laid down on the basis of which the consignment has been charged up to that station, such amount shall be charged against the goods. The position shall be the same when the Railway carries out instructions which the sender has given in the consignment note in conformity with § 3, sub-para. 1.

DCU 3, to § 8 *The consignee shall give his instructions direct to the station of stoppage.* *2.241*

Comments

1. Introduction

Articles 33 and Article 34 are "prevention of performance" provisions of a kind found also in an appropriately simpler form in CMR (Articles 14 and 15, paras. 1.62 and 1.68, above, respectively) but, in the nature of things, not found (as such) in Conventions for carriage by air or sea: the consignor of a single package has no say in the matter when the "vehicle" is a large ship, or a large aircraft, which may be carrying passengers too, on a scheduled flight. *2.242*

A typical problem might be that faced by the carrier of goods by rail from London through France to Italy routed, as would be normal, through Modane in the central French Alps and a closure of the frontier just beyond Modane. The carrier must take the initiative (Article 33.1) either by modifying the route or by seeking instructions from the consignor. If the carrier elects to modify the route, it might move the goods via the south of France and Ventimiglia: an increase of distance within France from 291 km to 523 km, with a corresponding increase in charges payable. The railway must have regard to that but also to the effect on the goods. If the goods are perishable, it is arguable that they should be routed forthwith and expensively via Ventimiglia. If not, they should await the reopening of the frontier beyond Modane or the railway should seek instructions.[1] Indeed, if contact with the consignor is easy, because the latter is a regular customer with whom the railway can communicate easily, perhaps instructions should be sought in most cases. *2.243*

2. Prevention

As to the "circumstances" that "prevent the carriage of goods" (Article 33.1), an impediment relating to route (such as that posed in Comment 1) is clearly the *2.244*

1. See Spera, Art. 33, Anm 3.

typical example, but it can also be inferred from Article 33.1 that it is the only instance of prevention to which Article 33 applies: the extra cost of an alternative route is provided for, but not for example the cost of obtaining alternative wagons or locomotive power to replace units that break down or the cost of repacking the goods, if that proves necessary for their safety. The replacement of wagons or locomotives provided by the railway is surely the responsibility of the railway. In most legal systems, performance of a contract is not prevented or excused simply because the performance as promised becomes more difficult or more expensive. With the exception of the ship that leaks in spite of having been maintained with "due diligence",[2] in carriage Conventions breakdown in the "vehicle" is not in general an excuse but a ground of carrier liability. Still, some writers see interference by government as an instance of Article 33.1.[3]

2.245 Another kindred possibility is a change in the law, but that problem might be solved by reference to Article 32.1(c) and Article 65.1(d), as appropriate. Yet another possibility is that the goods cannot be carried further because they have been physically destroyed or confiscated. Clearly, these are not cases of prevention under Article 33 but of loss.[4] Moreover, the argument that Article 33 applies to partial loss of the goods has been rejected by the Supreme Court of Hungary.[5] Nonetheless, the line will sometimes be fine between loss and prevention, so it is desirable that the level of duty required of the railway should be the same in each case.

2.246 As to the level of impediment that prevents carriage, it is submitted as a matter of both sense and symmetry that carriage has not been prevented (Article 33.1) nor delivery prevented (Article 34.1) if the impediment could have been overcome by the railway by the degree of effort and care expected of the railway under the general CIM liability regime of Article 36. The impediment may cause delay and thus deterioration in the goods and only if the impediment and its effect is an unavoidable circumstance (Article 36.2), is it also a circumstance which prevents carriage (Article 33.1) or delivery (Article 34.1). See also Article 20, Comment 3 (paragraphs 2.146 *et seq.*, above), Article 33, Comment 5 (below) and Article 36, Comment 1 (paragraphs 2.274 *et seq.*, below) and 7 (paragraphs 2.291 *et seq.*, below).

3. *Instructions*

2.247 If to seek instructions is the appropriate railway response to the circumstances preventing carriage (see Comment 2), the instructions must be sought within a reasonable time.[6] Moreover, Article 31 requires the railway to give the consignor "relevant information", which means all information that the railway has or should have that might help the consignor to formulate instructions. It includes, therefore,

2. See Clarke in Rose (Ed.), *Lex Mercatoria* (London 2000) Chap. 6.
3. E.g. Allégret, Fasc. 684, 114.
4. Spera, Art. 33, Anm 2.
5. *No. Gf III.30 385.1990*, Bull.OCTI 1992.30.
6. *Montpellier 8.1.87* BT 1987.589: a decision under the corresponding provision of CMR.

not only information about the circumstances preventing carriage but also information about available options.[7]

Unlike the disposal instructions that the consignor may give under Article 30 and the consignee under Article 31, there are no apparent limits to the kind of instructions that may be given to the railway under Article 33.2, within the bounds of what is feasible, and they include therefore, for example, sale or even destruction of the goods.[8] *2.248*

4. The response of the railway

If the railway receives proper instructions, of course, it must carry out the instructions. If, however, the railway obtains instructions, which it is possible to carry out, it must follow a procedure in Article 33.4 and Article 33.5, a procedure which reflects that for modifications initiated by the consignor under Article 30. Moreover, if the railway contacts the consignor, but the consignor "fails to give within a reasonable time instructions which can be executed", Article 33.6 provides that the situation is treated as a case of prevention of delivery, governed by Article 34. For example, in one case, the consignor, having been advised of the impediment, arrived two days later to collect the goods and, it was held, had thus given "instructions" within a reasonable time. *2.249*

If, however, the situation cannot be saved by modifying the route and the consignor cannot be found, what then? As the consignor has not been notified, it appears that Article 33.6 does not apply. But the discretion of the railway appears to be limited to either modifying the route or notifying the consignor; it has no discretion, for example, to send the goods on by road. This situation appears to disclose a gap in CIM, to be filled by national law and, perhaps, the exercise by the railway of a power of sale as agent of necessity. *2.250*

5. Liability of the railway

If the railway fails properly to perform its obligations under Article 33, the implication is that the railway is liable, but on what basis? The particular case mentioned in Article 33.5, which shadows Article 30.3, suggests that the basis is the same in both instances and thus a strict liability: See Article 30, Comment 2 (paragraphs 2.219 *et seq.*, above). However, the railway that fails to exercise its discretion under Article 33.1 loses the right to carriage charges, if there is "fault on its part" and this, perhaps, has led to the suggestion that any other liability attaching to Article 33.1 is based on fault.[9] There are, of course, different degrees of fault and perhaps the safest view is that any liability of the railway must be an instance of (or at least be in line with) the general duty (and liability) of the railway under Article 36.[10] This suggests a rather high level of duty. See Article 20, Comment 3 (paras. *2.251*

7. Spera, Art. 33, Anm 4.

8. *Nîmes 31.3.71* Bull.OCTI 1972.164. Spera, Art. 33, Anm 7.

9. Allégret, Fasc. 684, 122; Helm, Art. 24, Anm 3. Allégret, Fasc. 684, 122; Helm, Art. 24, Anm 3.

10. Spera (Art. 33, Anm 3) speaks of *die Sorgfalt eines ordentlichen Frachtführers.*

2.146 *et seq.*, above) and Article 36, Comment 1 (paras. 2.274 *et seq.*, below) and Comment 7 (paras. 2.291 *et seq.*, below).

2.252 For similar reasons, as well as the perspective of principle, the railway must justify its decision taken under Article 33.1. *Ex hypothesi*, the railway has not carried out its contract according to its original terms and is potentially liable for breach of that contract, and must therefore prove that it was justified in what it did or did not do. First of all, that implies that it is for the railway to prove that circumstances prevented carriage and that Article 33 applied. If, as it is here submitted, Article 33 contemplates a particular case of unavoidable circumstances, a more general defence under Article 36.2, then the burden of proof is explicitly placed on the railway by Article 37.1.

2.253 **Article 34, Circumstances preventing delivery**

1. When circumstances prevent delivery of the goods, the railway shall without delay notify the consignor to ask for his instructions.
2. When the circumstances preventing delivery cease to obtain before arrival at the destination station of instructions from the consignor the goods shall be delivered to the consignee. The consignee shall be notified without delay.
3. If the consignee refuses the goods, the consignor shall be entitled to give instructions even if he is unable to produce the duplicate of the consignment note.
4. The consignor may also request, by an entry in the consignment note, that the goods be returned to him as a matter of course in the event of circumstances preventing delivery. Unless such request is made, his express consent is required.
5. Except as otherwise provided for above, the railway responsible for delivery shall proceed in accordance with the provisions in force at the place of delivery.

If the goods have been sold, the proceeds of sale, less any costs chargeable against the goods, shall be held at the disposal of the consignor. If such proceeds are less than those costs, the consignor shall pay the difference.

6. When the circumstances preventing delivery arise after the consignee has modified the contract of carriage in accordance with Article 31, the railway shall notify the consignee. Paragraphs 1, 2 and 6 shall apply analogously.
7. Article 32 shall apply to carriage undertaken in accordance with Article 34.

Additional Uniform Regulations (DCU)

2.254 **DCU 1, to § 1** *The goods interest shall bear the cost of sending this advice.*

2.255 **DCU 2, to §§ 1 and 2** *Advices addressed to the sender shall be worded in one of the official languages of the country of departure or in one of the official languages of the Organisation (French or German). When the language used is not that of the country in which the forwarding station is situated, the sender shall be responsible for translating the advice.*

2.256 **DCU 3, to §§ 1 and 5** *The sender who, in conformity with § 1, has made a request in the consignment note to be advised directly of any circumstances preventing delivery, either in writing, by telegram or by telex, may forward his instructions to the destination station direct. The sender must attach the duplicate of the consignment note, on which the instructions must be repeated and signed by him. If the goods have been refused by the consignee, it shall suffice for the sender to return the advice, issued by the destination station, of the circumstances preventing delivery, after having entered his instructions thereon.*

If the instructions contain one of the orders provided for in Article 30, § 1(g), (h) or (i), or an order specifying the cancellation or reduction of disbursements, they may only be given through the intermediary of the forwarding station. Instructions requesting the establishment or increase of disbursements are not allowed.

DCU 4, to § 7 *Instructions requesting the cancellation or reduction of a "cash on delivery" charge or a disbursement, the acceptance of charges on a "to pay" consignment or the acceptance of further charges under Article 15, § 2, may be issued by a consignee who has modified the contract of carriage under Article 31, only on production of the sender's written authority.* 2.257

DCU 5, to §§ 4, 5 and 7 *The raising of any charge at the time of receipt of instructions shall be determined in accordance with the tariff applied to the consignment:* 2.258

— by the forwarding railway, when instructions are given by the sender;

— by the destination railway, when they are given by the consignee.

When, however, in accordance with DCU 2, the sender addresses his instructions to the destination station direct, and if a charge is laid down in the tariff on the basis of which the consignment has been charged up to that station, such amount shall be charged against the goods. The position is the same when the sender, in conformity with § 4, has made a request in the consignment note that the goods are automatically to be returned to him.

Comments

1. The domain of Article 34

Article 33 and Article 34 are "prevention of performance" provisions of a kind found also in an appropriately simpler form in CMR (Articles 14 and 15, paras. 1.62 and 1.68, above, respectively). Whereas Article 33 concerns problems arising during transit, Article 34 provides for problems arising at the point of delivery and originating outside and beyond the contract route.[1] Typically Article 34 applies when delivery by the carrier has been prevented by circumstances originating with the consignee, however, not in all cases. The goods may, for example, have been confiscated by officials there, or the goods may have been sold off to cover unpaid charges.[2] 2.259

In any event, Article 34 is not concerned with liability and must be distinguished from the railway's defence based on unavoidable circumstances: Article 36.2. Article 34 operates whether or not the railway is at fault.[3] 2.260

2. Prevention

As to the "circumstances" which "prevent delivery", "prevent" has not been taken absolutely literally. A leading commentator has suggested that, if delivery would involve the railway in unreasonable delay or if the delay is such that the goods would become unmerchantable, delivery in accordance with contract has been prevented.[4] The same must be true of unreasonable expense. Thus, if delivery has been prevented because, for example, the consignee has moved from the address given in the consignment note, the railway is not obliged to employ investigators to find him.[5] 2.261

As has been contended in Article 33, Comment 2 (paragraphs 2.244 *et seq.*, above), both sense and symmetry suggest that neither carriage (Article 33.1) nor delivery (Article 34.1) have been prevented, if the impediment could have been 2.262

1. Allégret, Fasc. 684, 123; Spera, Art. 34, Anm 2.
2. *OLG Saarland 26.11.96*, TranspR 1998.119, Bull.OCTI 1998.279.
3. Spera, Art. 34, Anm 2. Cf., however, *OLG Saarland 26.11.96* (above).
4. Helm, Art. 25, Anm 1, by reference to analogous rules of the BGB.
5. Spera, Art. 34, Anm 2.

overcome by the railway by the degree of effort and care expected of the railway under the general CIM liability regime of Article 36. Article 34, like Article 33, does not operate unless the impediment, in the present cases inability to deliver the goods, is for all practical purposes unavoidable: see Article 36, Comment 7.

3. The response of the railway

2.263 The initial response required of the railway is to notify the consignor and seek instructions: Article 34.2. Notice must be in the correct form, i.e., in this case in accordance with the DCU.[6] Instructions must be sought "without delay", i.e., within a reasonable time.[7] The instructions may simply contain information enabling the railway to deliver the goods, such as the correct address of the consignee. Unlike the instructions in modification of the contract that the consignor may give under Article 30 and the consignee under Article 31, there are no apparent limits to the kind of instructions that may be given under Article 34.1, within the bounds of what is feasible; and they include therefore sale or even destruction of the goods.[8]

2.264 If the carrier obtains instructions within a reasonable time, the inference, for example, of Article 34.8, is that the railway must obey those instructions. However, the inference *a contrario* of Article 34.3 is that, if the cause of prevention is something other than refusal of the consignee, the consignor who gives instructions must also produce the duplicate of the consignment note. If that is a correct interpretation of Article 34.3, and the note is not with the consignor but with the consignee, there may be a hiatus, unless the consignor is seen as the agent of the consignee or "the provisions in force at the place of delivery" untie the knot and, for example, allow the carrier to sell the goods. A further hiatus, to which perhaps the solution is the same, occurs if the consignor, having perhaps lost interest in the goods, simply fails to give any instructions. It is a curious feature of CIM (and also CMR), that in case the consignor fails to respond with instructions to deal with a prevention of carriage, there is a default provision (Article 33.6), but if he fails to respond with instructions to deal with a prevention of delivery, there is no default provision.

2.265 **Title IV, Liability, Article 35, Collective responsibility of railways**

1. The railway which has accepted goods for carriage with the consignment note shall be responsible for the carriage over the entire route up to delivery.

2. Each succeeding railway, by the very act of taking over the goods with the consignment note, shall become a party to the contract of carriage in accordance with the terms of that document and shall assume the obligations arising therefrom, without prejudice to the provisions of Article 55.3, relating to the railway of destination.

6. *OLG Saarland 26.11.96* (above).
7. *Montpellier 8.1.87*, BT 1987.589: a decision under the corresponding provision of CMR.
8. Spera, Art. 34, Anm 5.

Comments

1. Collective responsibility

Article 35.1 concerns what German commentators call *eine Haftunggemeinschaft* and *eine Solidarverpflichtung*,[1] whereas French commentators speak of *une collectivité juridique* and *la solidarité passive*.[2] This might have been more meaningfully translated into English as joint liability, however, the essence of the idea is that each railway is responsible for the entire movement of goods and liable for loss or damage occurring during transit according to Article 36. *2.266*

Nonetheless the claimant does not have an entirely free choice of railway to sue. In this connection Article 35 should be read with Article 55, concerning railways against which an action may be brought. If the action concerns loss of or damage to goods, Article 55 provides that the action may be brought not only against the forwarding railway, which is usually also the railway which accepted the goods and to which Article 35.1 refers, but also the railway of destination and the railway on which the event giving rise to loss or damage occurred. If the goods reach destination damaged or short, the obvious target for the consignee is the railway of destination. *2.267*

2. Assumption of responsibility

Commonly the railway, notably the railway to destination, will face action based on events occurring before it took over the goods, so Article 35.2 provides the legal basis for its responsibility, as does the equivalent provision of CMR (Article 34, para. 1.213, above), subject to the reference to Article 55.3, which provides that action may be brought against the railway of destination whether it has taken over the goods and the consignment note or not. Hence Article 35.2 has effect mainly on the other railways involved. *2.268*

Article 35.2 ensures liability has a basis in the contract of carriage, which provides the framework for the obligations of each railway detailed in Article 36. Article 35.2 provides for the mechanism whereby each succeeding railway becomes a party to the contract of carriage. Consent or adherence to the contract of carriage, as it might be described by a French jurist, is signified by the double act of taking over the goods and the consignment note; each must be taken over although it is not necessary that they be taken over at the same time.[3] *2.269*

The importance of the note lies also in that the succeeding railway is liable in accordance with the terms of the consignment note alone and is unaffected by any collateral terms agreed by the accepting railway, which do not appear on the note. Thus, the succeeding railway can plead the inadequacy of the consignor's packing, a defence under Article 37.3(b)), even though the type of packing was chosen on the *2.270*

1. Spera, Art. 35, Anm 2.
2. Allégret, Fasc. 685, 9.
3. Spera, Art. 35, Anm 5.

advice of the accepting railway.[4] However, modifications made under Article 30 and Article 31 and recorded on the note are regarded as terms of the consignment note, by which the succeeding railway is bound.

2.271

Article 36, Extent of liability

1. The railway shall be liable for loss or damage resulting from the total or partial loss of, or damage to, the goods between the time of acceptance for carriage and the time of delivery and for the loss or damage resulting from the transit period being exceeded.

2. The railway shall be relieved of such liability if the loss or damage or the exceeding of the transit period was caused by a fault on the part of the person entitled, by an order given by the person entitled other than as a result of a fault on the part of the railway, by inherent vice of the goods (decay, wastage, etc.) or by circumstances which the railway could not avoid and the consequences of which it was unable to prevent.

3. The railway shall be relieved of such liability when the loss or damage arises from the special risks inherent in one or more of the following circumstances:

(a) carriage in open wagons under the conditions applicable thereto or under an agreement made between the consignor and the railway and referred to in the consignment note;
(b) absence or inadequacy of packing in the case of goods which by their nature are liable to loss or damage when not packed or when not properly packed;
(c) loading operations carried out by the consignor or unloading operations carried out by the consignee under the provisions applicable thereto or under an agreement made between the consignor and the railway and referred to in the consignment note, or under an agreement between the consignee and the railway;
(d) defective loading, when loading has been carried out by the consignor under the provisions applicable thereto or under an agreement made between the consignor and the railway and referred to in the consignment note;
(e) completion by the consignor, the consignee or an agent of either, of the formalities required by Customs or other administrative authorities;
(f) the nature of certain goods which renders them inherently liable to total or partial loss or damage, especially through breakage, rust, interior and spontaneous decay, desiccation or wastage;
(g) irregular, incorrect or incomplete description of articles not acceptable for carriage or acceptable subject to conditions, or failure on the part of the consignor to observe the prescribed precautions in respect of articles acceptable subject to conditions;
(h) carriage of live animals;
(i) carriage which, under the provisions applicable or under an agreement made between the consignor and the railway and referred to in the consignment note, must be accompanied by an attendant, if the loss or damage results from any risk which the attendant was intended to avert.

Additional Uniform Regulations (DCU)

2.272 **DCU 1, to § 3(**a**)** *If the sender uses sheets in conjunction with the carriage of goods in open wagons, the railway shall assume the same liability as that which rests upon it for transport in unsheeted open wagons, even if, according to the instructions contained in the tariff, the goods are of a kind which should not be conveyed in open wagons.*

2.273 **DCU 2, to § 3(**c**)** *Apart from damage resulting from air and moisture, goods carried in large containers, swap bodies, semi-trailers or in other unit loads, which are closed, for the purpose of combined transport, or in closed vehicles by means of rolling motorway shall not be regarded as being carried in open wagons.*

4. *Ag. Frankfurt 25.8.89*, TranspR 1990.196.

Comments

(a) Liability

1. The liability of the carrier

Article 36 is central to the liability of the railway for what happens to the goods during transit. If there is evidence that there was, in the terms of Article 36.1, "total or partial loss of, or damage to, the goods between the time of acceptance for carriage and the time of delivery" or that the transit period (see Article 27) has been exceeded, the railway is presumed liable[1] for any consequential financial loss suffered by the claimant. The railway may then seek to rebut that presumption by establishing one of the defences in Article 36.2[2] or Article 36.3. Underlying the defences the carrier has a residual duty of care, for example, to take remedial measures when it is apparent that goods have suffered damage for which the carrier is not liable. Thus, a claimant may be able to destroy or weaken a defence by showing breach of that residual duty, for example in the way that the carrier responded to inherent vice or defective packing. Such a duty is found in CMR[3] and a similar duty has been recognized under CIM.[4] *2.274*

Courts in France and Belgium see the liability regime of CIM as essentially contractual[5] and describe it as *une obligation de résultat*, giving rise in cases of loss, damage or delay to *une présomption de responsabilité*.[6] To the German lawyer, CIM like CMR is seen as an instance of *Gefährdungshaftung*, a liability based on risk.[7] However, to the English lawyer the striking feature is that the railway's liability is based in contract rather than tort.[8] It premises breach of the railway's contractual duty to deliver the right goods to the right person in the quantity and condition in which they were taken over. Although an action framed in tort is not excluded, it can be sustained only subject to the essentially contractual regime established by CIM, whether the action is brought against the railway or against the servants or other persons employed by the railway to perform the carriage: Article 51. It is a regime of strict liability moderated by exceptions and limitations.[9] Indeed, the "legal nature of the liability provided by CIM . . . depends on the scope given to the grounds of relief".[10] Of these, the most important is unavoidable circumstances, with the corollary that the carrier has a "residual" duty of care (above), because the interpretation of this concept determines whether CIM imposes an absolute liability or liability based on wrongful act or neglect. *2.275*

1. Rodière, Nos. 501 *et seq.*
2. *Paris 14.4.47*, S 1947.2.111.
3. See CMR Art. 17, Comment 1 (paras. 1.78 *et seq.*, above) and Comment 7 (paras. 1.98 *et seq.*, above).
4. *OLG Düsseldorf 18.1.1996*, TranspR 1997.284, 285.
5. E.g. *Cass. 16.3.14*, D. 1916.1.145.
6. Allégret, Fasc. 685, 10.
7. Haenni, No. 243; Spera, Art. 36, Anm 2.
8. Kahn-Freund, p. 431.
9. Ramberg (1974) 9 ETL 3, 11.
10. Haenni No. 243.

2.276 The defences, which fundamentally shape the liability profile of the carrier, are in two groups, first, in Article 36.2 and, secondly, in Article 36.3. They are distinguished by and because of a difference in the burden of proof: see Article 37. Whereas the railway that defends under Article 36.2 is required to prove on the balance of probabilities that the exonerating event caused the loss or damage, the railway that defends by reference to the "special risks" grouped in Article 36.3 has a lighter burden of proof. First, it must prove on the balance of probabilities that the special risk occurred, for example, that the carriage was in open wagons (risk (a)). Secondly, however, as to causation, it does not have to prove that carriage in open wagons did cause the loss or damage, but only that it *could* have caused it: Article 37.2. Instead of the (normal) burden of proof, that the exonerating factor was the probable cause of the loss etc., it suffices to show that that was a mere possibility.[11] In a leading French case,[12] for example, the loss could have occurred during (and as a result of) unloading by the consignee but could equally have occurred at some other time. On this evidence, there would have been no defence under Article 36.2 but it was enough for a defence under Article 36.3(c).

2.277 Reasons for this difference are, first, the risks concern events about which the railway would find it difficult to establish a "normal" defence under Article 36.2. Secondly, the risks concern matters more within the sphere of the consignor or consignee than of the railway. They should bear loss or damage associated with these matters, unless they can prove, as envisaged by Article 37.2, that in reality the loss or damage was in fact attributable to the railway. These provisions served as a model for a similar regime for CMR (Article 18, para. 1.118, above), on which argument is often based by way of analogy, as the concept is the same.[13]

2. *Entitlement to sue*

2.278 The persons entitled to bring a claim against the railway on the basis of Article 36 are the designated consignor or the designated consignee and no other person; see Article 54, Comment 3 (paragraphs 2.425 *et seq.*, below). This view is widely held. The only reason to doubt it lies in the way that courts have interpreted the CMR. As regards CMR the assumption has been that CMR contains no provision corresponding to Article 54 and no general or definitive rule governing who is entitled to sue the carrier, and that courts are justified in applying the *lex fori*. In England action lies at the suit of the person who has contracted for the carriage, and in England (but not other countries) there appears to be a presumption that it is the owner of the goods who has contracted with the carrier; see CMR Article 17, Comment 2 (paragraphs 1.85 *et seq.*, above). However, although Article 54 does not expressly rule out actions by persons other than the designated consignor or the designated consignee, it is likely that the English court would reach that conclusion by implication.

11. Spera, Art. 37, Anm 4.
12. *Cass. 10.2.69*, J.C.P. 1979.15916.
13. Allégret, Fasc. 685, 71; Rodière, No. 543.

3. Period of responsibility

The railway is liable for the financial loss to the claimant resulting from events affecting the goods, as well as delay, during transit, i.e. between the time of acceptance of the goods for carriage and the time of their delivery. *2.279*

In this CIM differs from other transport Conventions such as CMR where the period of carrier responsibility begins when the carrier takes over the goods. That is generally interpreted to connote a change of possession or control. Under CIM, however, acceptance of the goods for carriage is established by the ritual set out in Article 11.1: the application to the consignment note and, where appropriate, to each additional sheet, of the stamp of the forwarding station, or accounting machine entry, showing the date of acceptance. This has to be distinguished, moreover, from "handing over" the goods (Article 20.1) and "very act of taking over the goods" (Article 35.2), whereby a succeeding railway becomes a party to the contract of carriage and assumes obligations arising therefrom. These expressions, unlike "acceptance of the goods", point to a definitive act whereby the railway assumes (custody and) control of the goods or, at least, of the wagon in which they have been loaded. *2.280*

Delivery, however, is an act whereby the goods pass to third parties specified in Article 28.2 or to the consignee under Article 28.1. Delivery is not defined by CIM and *prima facie* a meaning must be sought according to Article 10 in national law. The widespread understanding of delivery is that the custody and control of the goods pass from the railway to the appropriate person; see Article 28, Comment 3 (paragraphs 2.194 *et seq.*, above). *2.281*

4. The result of loss, damage and delay

Loss of the goods means shortage in the goods received by the carrier. A partial loss is any loss which is less than a total loss. Total loss is not defined by CIM and courts resort to national law; see Article 40, Comment 1. Loss of goods is distinguished from damage to the goods, which means any physical change in the goods received by the carrier which lowers their commercial value; see the Comment on Article 42. The carrier is not liable for delay in delivery of the goods as such but for exceeding the transit period. For most practical purposes there is little difference, however, transit periods are prescribed by Article 27. *2.282*

The carrier is liable for loss or damage, i.e. pecuniary loss to the claimant, resulting from, i.e., caused by, loss, damage or delay to the goods. In principle, the relevant rule of causation, which is not stated in CIM, is a matter for the *lex fori*. However, the nature of the link often depends to a degree on what is being linked; thus the relevant rule in CIM depends to a degree on the defence in question. *2.283*

For example, if the carrier can point to a cause, such as a strike, but for which the loss, damage or delay would not have occurred, and if the effect of that strike (loss, damage or delay) could not have been avoided (by the railway), the railway is excused. However, if an unavoidable circumstance intervenes when the railway has already exceeded the transit period (in breach of contract), *prima facie* the consequences are the result of the railway's breach of contract, and the railway is *2.284* liable.[14] If the cause is partly something for which the railway is excused and partly something for which it is not, Article 36 makes no mention, i.e., contains no power, of apportionment.[15] In many countries this power goes without saying because it is found in the *lex fori*, however, not in common law countries.[16]

(b) The defences

5. Fault on the part of or order given by the person entitled

2.285 These defences correspond to those of "wrongful act or neglect of the claimant" and "instructions of the claimant" in Article 17.2 of CMR (paras. 1.94 *et seq.*, above). Use in CIM Article 36.2 of the words "Person entitled", however, is an attempt to translate more accurately than "claimant", the previous translation in CIM, the French words "l'ayant droit". In any event, what is intended in CIM is a reference to the consignor or the consignee, whichever person has the right to sue the carrier under Article 54.[17] However, it is arguable in a case of orders rather than fault that the reference is to the person entitled to give the order in question. Nonetheless, it appears that the carrier may defend an action brought by the consignee by pleading the fault or order of the consignor.[18]

2.286 The most obvious instances of fault are in the mode of packing or loading by the consignor. However, as these are special risks under Article 36.3 for which the carrier bears an easier burden of proof, such cases are likely to be argued under Article 36.3 rather than Article 36.2. If the fault arises out of an order given by the person entitled, that is a distinct defence under Article 36.2, discussed below in this Comment. Remaining instances from the reports include delay when a consignment was minutely examined by customs officials after it was found to include contraband,[19] and delay caused by the failure of the consignor to provide documents or correct documents or to do so on time.[20]

2.287 Instances of orders given to the carrier include (but are not limited to) instructions about care of the goods during transit, information contained in the consignment note, such as the address of the consignee (with the implicit order to perform the contract on the basis of that information), as well as instructions about the disposal of the goods given under Articles 30, 31, 33 and 34.[21] This defence can be distinguished from that of fault in that the relevant order may be one to which no fault can be attached. Regardless of whether fault can be attached to the order, however, the qualification with reference to the railway's fault was made in view of a scenario in which the need for orders arises out of events during transit for which the carrier is liable: the carrier remains liable in full.

14. Allégret, Fasc. 685, 33.
15. *Paris 18.5.76.* Bull.OCTI 1977.112; cf. CMR, Art. 17.5, para. 1.71, above.
16. *Caledonian Ry.* v. *Hunter* (1858) 20 Sess. Cas. 2nd Ser. 1097; *Lambert* v. *Lewis* [1982] A.C. 225.
17. Allégret, Fasc. 685, 14; Helm, Art. 27, Anm 9; Spera, Art. 36, Anm 11.
18. Rodière, Nos. 538 and 542: any other outcome would be ridiculous.
19. *Cass. 14.2.1894,* D. 1894.1.163.
20. *Cass. 15.5.57,* BT 1957.255.
21 Spera, Art. 36, Anm 11.

6. Inherent vice

Inherent vice in Article 36.2 of CIM is thought to have the same meaning as inherent vice in other branches of the law of carriage,[22] including CMR (Article 17.2, paras. 1.96 *et seq.*, above), and as inherent vice at common law.[23] *2.288*

A vice is a defect; and goods are defective in the present sense less in absolute terms than in relative terms, i.e., if they are not fit for the transit contracted for and for use or consumption, as appropriate, for a reasonable time after delivery.[24] Moreover, goods sound in themselves but packed in such a way that they cannot survive the journey in question suffer from inherent vice.[25] A vice is inherent when it is in the goods themselves, a defect which "by its development tends to the injury or destruction of the thing carried".[26] Few defects develop without assistance from external agencies such as moisture or temperature, however, it is inherent vice if the main cause lies within the goods themsleves.[27] *2.289*

Some instances of inherent vice are likely to be treated under CIM as cases of sensitivity under Article 36.3(f). The main difference between the two notions is that, whereas sensitivity is a feature of all goods of that type, inherent vice is found in the goods in question but not in all goods of that type: see Comment 13, below.[28] *2.290*

7. Unavoidable circumstances

"Circumstances which the railway could not avoid and the consequences of which it was unable to prevent" constitute the defence that is the key to the level of the railway's liability under CIM: see Comment 1, above. Unfortunately, therefore, the interpretation of this defence has been a matter of some controversy.[29] However, a close analogy with the equivalent provision of CMR (Article 17.2, paras. 1.98 *et seq.*, above), on which reported case law is copious and a clear interpretation has emerged, is accepted by leading commentators on CIM.[30] In England that interpretation has been reached by a process of elimination, i.e., distinction, as follows. *2.291*

Unavoidable circumstances have been distinguished, first, from *force majeure*, because if "it had been the intention to restrict the carriers' defence to events of this kind, the words '*force majeure*' would have been used".[31] Indeed these words were used in early versions of CIM but discarded in 1952. The inference has been drawn *2.292*

22. Rodière, No. 542.

23. Kahn-Freund, p. 434.

24. *Kendall* v. *L.S.W. Ry.* (1872) L.R. 7 Ex. 373, 377; *Baldwin* v. *L.C. & D. Ry.* (1882) 9 Q.B.D. 582; *L.N.W. Ry. Co.* v. *Hudson* [1920] A.C. 324; *Albacora SRL* v. *Westcott & Laurance Line* [1966] 2 Lloyd's Rep. 53, 59, 62 (H.L.).

25. Allégret, Fasc. 685, 20.

26. *Blower* v. *G.W. Ry.* (1872) L.R. 7 C.P. 655, 662.

27. *Lister* v. *Lancashire & Yorkshire Ry.* [1903] 1 K.B. 878; *Noten BV* v. *Harding* [1990] 2 Lloyd's Rep. 283 (C.A.).

28. But cf. Spera, Art. 36, Anm 12.

29. Helm, Art. 27, Anm 5, with reference to Mutz, Bull.OCTI 1975.79, and Matyassy, Bull.OCTI 1978.12.

30. E.g. Allégret, Fasc. 685, 27.

31. Kahn-Freund, p. 433.

that the defence is different and less strict than *force majeure*. Secondly, for similar reasons the concept has been distinguished from other established notions such as "due diligence" and "reasonable care": under CIM more is expected of the railway than, for example, of the carrier by sea who has a "due diligence" obligation under Article III, r.3, of the Hague-Visby Rules. Thirdly, although a literal reading of the words "unavoidable" and "could not prevent" in Article 36.2 of CIM supports such a view, it is generally agreed that the liability of the carrier is not strict or absolute.

2.293 The result is that, according to continental commentators on CIM,[32] the level of the carrier's obligation is a level below that prescribed by *force majeure* but above that of normal or ordinary care in the light of general commercial practice. This is in line with the English view of the equivalent provision in CMR, Article 17.2, that the level of the carrier's obligation to avoid loss, damage or delay is "a standard which is somewhere between, on the one hand, a requirement to take every conceivable precaution, however extreme, within the limits of the law, and on the other hand a duty to do no more than act reasonably in accordance with prudent current practice".[33] The words "could not avoid" mean "could not avoid even with the utmost care", care that is "practical" and falls "short of the absurd".[34] This is substantially the same as the German view of CIM, that the railway must show *die äusserste wirtschaftlich zumutbare Sorgfalt.*[35]

8. Force majeure distinguished: defects in the vehicle

2.294 Given the importance of *force majeure* or its equivalent in civil law countries, it is noteworthy that this defence is distinguishable from *force majeure* on two further points, in particular, defects in the vehicle.

2.295 First, although "forewarned is forearmed" and what can be foreseen affects what can be avoided, unforeseeability as such is a requirement of *force majeure* but not of unavoidable circumstances,[36] which, in the view of a leading French commentator, is "notre force majeure, moins la condition d'imprévisibilité".[37] It must be unavoidable nonetheless.[38] According to commentators examples of the defence include, in general, natural phenomena such as earthquakes, landslides, flooding, lightning, torrential rain, hurricanes, exceptional cold or heat, as well as the unavoidable interference of third persons, official intervention such as confiscation or attachment, riots, acts of war or of terrorism. Circumstances that would not normally give rise to the defence include bad weather and theft.[39]

32. Haenni, No. 243; Mutz, Bull.OCTI 1975.79, 88; Ramberg (1974) 9 ETL 3, 14 reporting the opinion of Nanassy-Wick; Spera, Art. 36, Anm 2 and 15.

33. *Silber* v. *Islander Trucking* [1985] 2 Lloyd's Rep. 243, 247. See CMR, Art. 17, Comment 7, paras. 1.98 *et seq.*, above.

34. *Silber, loc. cit.*

35. Helm, *loc. cit.*

36. *Cass. 15.5.57,* GP 1957.2.106; Allégret, Fasc. 685, 27.

37. Rodière, No. 542.

38. *Douai 18.1.43,* GP 1943.1.184; *Cass. France 6.5.1997,* Bull.OCTI 1997.235.

39. Allegret, Fasc, 685, 28; Spera, Art. 36, Anm 15.

Secondly, it is not necessary that the circumstances should arise outside the carrier's sphere of operations.[40] For example, a wildcat strike by personnel employed by the railway is not a case of *force majeure* but is a defence under CIM if there is no practicable alternative way of moving the goods.[41] *2.296*

A more controversial example concerns railway equipment. Whereas the equivalent defence in Article 17.2 of CMR (para. 1.77, above) is clearly qualified by Article 17.3 (*ibid.*), which imposes strict liability for the defective condition of the vehicle, there is no such qualification in CIM regarding rolling stock, signals and items of equipment employed by the railway. It might be said that, being within the railway's sphere of operation, a provision corresponding to CMR, Article 17.2, was unnecessary because defects in such things cannot be regarded as unavoidable. However, a qualification along these lines was expressly rejected by a revision conference[42] and thus it seems that these defects in their condition may be pleaded as an unavoidable circumstance.[43] *2.297*

(c) Special risks

9. Risk and proof

Article 36.3, concerns loss or damage arising from a list of special risks, and does not apply to cases of delay as such, although serious cases of delay have been treated as cases of loss to which Article 36.3, therefore, applies.[44] *2.298*

It is in the nature of transportation that goods are subject to risk, however, certain risks were conceived as special by the original drafters of CIM. They remain a feature of CIM, and its progeny CMR, but not of the Conventions for other modes of carriage. In CIM and CMR a special risk is either a circumstance posing a greater than usual risk of damage to the goods in question, such as the sensitivity of the goods dealt with in Article 36.3(f), or a risk that is normally in the carrier's risk sphere but in the particular case is in that of the sender, such as when loading and stowage are carried out not by the carrier but by the sender, the case dealt with by Article 36.3(c). It should be noted, however, that the risks are not mutually exclusive. For example, a consignment may be a case of goods inadequately packed (risk (b)) as well as a case of goods inherently liable to damage (risk (f)). *2.299*

The importance of special risks lies in the effect of Article 37.1. To take special risk (c) as an example, the effect is that the carrier does not have to prove that one or more of the operations (of handling, loading, stowage or unloading) were carried out defectively. What the carrier must establish is that the loss etc. could be attributed to the operation in question. On this see Comment 12 below. Nonetheless, if the carrier does have evidence that the operation was carried out defectively, he will seek to reinforce his case by bringing forward the evidence. *2.300*

40. Mutz, Bull.OCTI 1975.79, 82 *et seq.*

41. *Paris 16.6.71*, 1971 ULC 311; Bull.OCTI 1971.216; *Caen 6.1.94*, Bull.OCTI 1994, 96; *Cass. France 6.5.97*, BTL 1997.404.

42. Mutz, Bull.OCTI 1975.79, 86.

43. But cf. Allégret, Fasc. 685, 31.

44. *Cass 17.4.80*, BT 1981.284.

10. *Risk (a) open wagons*

2.301 A last century case of risk (a) is that of goods, being hauled by a steam locomotive, which are ignited by sparks.[45] A more modern instance is the vulnerability of goods in open wagons to danger from escaping chemicals[46] or accidental fire[47] in adjacent wagons, or the impact of hail stones[48] or other kinds of bad weather,[49] or even objects that might fall on goods from bridges over the track.[50] However, the essence of the risk in most cases is the exposure of the goods to wastage and to the elements: not only the weather but anything in the air. Hence a wagon is an open wagon not only when it is open from the top but also when it is open from the side or when it is (merely) covered by a tarpaulin. There are court decisions to this effect[51] and it has been confirmed by Article 36, DCU 1.

2.302 The risk operates as such only in the circumstances stated in Article 36.3(a). The carriage must be "under conditions applicable thereto", which are those referred to in Article 20.4 or relevant provisions of RID 17; or by agreement between the consignor and the railway "referred to" in the consignment note. Reference of that kind, it has been held,[52] may simply be mention of the application of a tariff used for carriage in open wagons; but reference to industry practice is not enough.

2.303 As regards risk (a) as well as the other risks, the second sentence of Article 37.2 allows the claimant to defeat the railway's defence by counterproof that the loss or damage was not attributable to the risk but was attributable, for example, to the railway's fault. In the case of risk (a) such fault might lie, for example, in putting an open wagon of steel products immediately behind a wagon with corrosive chemicals.[53] Alternatively, the claimant may defeat the defence by showing that the damage would have occurred anyway and was thus not attributable to the risk.[54] Further, by Article 37.2 *in fine* the railway is not permitted to plead risk (a) "if an abnormally large quantity has been lost or if a package has been lost". In consequence theft and vandalism are not part of special risk (a)[55] and the railway must defend such cases under Article 36.2 as unavoidable loss or damage, a defence that will be difficult to make in such a case.

11. *Packing*

2.304 Most goods are better protected packed than unpacked so, to prove special risk (b), the railway must prove that the nature of the goods required better than it got, usually by reference to current practice and any regulations in force at the

45. *Cass. 19.1.70*, D.1970.241; *Rouen 14.3.72*, 1974 ULR (I) 27.
46. *Paris 19.3.82*, BT 1982.322.
47. *Pau 19.11.86*, BT 1988.104.
48. *LG Hannover 23.7.98*, TranspR 1998.405.
49. *OLG Düsseldorf 18.1.1996*, TranspR 1997.284.
50. *OLG Hamburg 8.2.96*, TranspR 1996.389.
51. *Cass. 19.1.70*, D.1970.241; *T.C. Brussels 1.2.73* (1974) 9 ETL 786; *The Hague 24.6.87*, S & S 1988, No. 73. See also Allégret, Fasc. 685, 42; and Spera, Art. 20, Anm 16.
52. *OLG Hamburg 8.2.1996*, Bull.OCTI 1997.76. See also cases mentioned by Allégret, Fasc. 685, 40.
53. *Paris 19.3.82*, above.
54. *OLG Hamburg 8.2.1996*, Bull.OCTI 1997.76.
55. Allégret, Fasc. 685, 43; Spera, Art. 37, Anm 7; but cf. Spera, Art. 36, Anm 18.

forwarding station. For example, whereas motor cars may be sent unpacked, it has been held that a motor cycle should have been packed.[56] Again, obviously perhaps, liquids carried in tankers need no further "packing".[57] In such cases, the container may be seen not as packing but as part of the goods.[58] Less obviously, when the consignor is entitled to expect the railway to provide a closed wagon in good condition, a consignment such as one of unwrapped cotton is not defectively packed.[59]

RICo, Article 1.2, treats standard containers as part of the transport operation, wagons without wheels. However, containers are also things carried rather than a means of transport and, it has been suggested,[60] should be treated as such unless they have been provided by the railway. In the latter case, it has been argued that the railway provides the container not as carrier under the contract of transport but under a distinct contract for the supply of goods.[61] *2.305*

Packing is inadequate if it is such that the particular goods cannot withstand the dangers of normal transit of the kind contemplated by the particular contract of carriage.[62] When assessing the adequacy of packing, courts take account of any regulations in force at the forwarding station[63] and any evidence of current practice for goods of the kind in question.[64] In the case of fragile goods, for example, the consignor cannot expect kid gloves: in view of the role of the railway, to move large volumes of goods at speed, allowance must be made for rough handling.[65] In the case of goods sensitive to heat, if a refrigerated wagon has not been used by the consignor or required of the railway, the goods themselves must be sufficiently insulated.[66] *2.306*

At common law, if the carrier finds that the consignor has brought forward goods that are defectively packed, early cases suggested that that is a matter for the consignor, who bears the risk, and that the carrier is not required to remedy the situation.[67] However, the later view was that if "the imperfect nature of the packing be obvious to the carrier when the goods are tendered for his acceptance, and he receives them without objection, he will not be excused for any damage which may subsequently result from the imperfect packing. . . . And if [a defect in the packing] should be discovered in time to prevent the forwarding of the goods, they should not be forwarded till the defect has been remedied".[68] But in CIM, unlike CMR, there is a provision (Article 19.2) which indicates that the risk in respect of packing remains with the consignor when the goods are accepted by the railway.[69] Moreover, *2.307*

56. *OLG Hamm 13.2.89*, TranspR 1989.432; ULR 1989 (II) 840; *Ag Karlsruhe 24.11.89*, Bull.OCTI 1990.117.
57. *BGH 4.2.55*, BGHZ 16,217, 230 *et seq.*
58. Spera, Art. 36, Anm 23.
59. *Rb Brussels 18.2.74* (1974) 9 ETL 622.
60. Tilche, BTL.1991.496.
61. *Ibid. sed quaere.*
62. *Paris 7.7.82*, BT 1982. 430; Spera, Art. 36, Anm 24.
63. Spera, Art. 36, Anm 25.
64. E.g. *Ag Karlsruhe 14.11.89*, TranspR 1990.197.
65. *Lg Kassel 11.1.90*, TranspR 1990.195: an antique table inadequately packed.
66. *OLG Celle 13.11.68*, Bull.OCTI 1970.45.
67. *Barbour* v. *S.E. Ry.* (1876) 34 L.T. 67.
68. *L.N.W. Ry. Co.* v. *Hudson* [1920] A.C. 324, 340.
69. *Lg Kassel 11.1.90*, TranspR 1990.195.

it has been held that the railway is not even obliged to warn the consignor that the packing is defective[70]; but that, the railway will be liable if it impedes the consignor's attempts to protect the goods.[71]

2.308 Less clear is the rule governing packing that becomes defective after the goods have been accepted by the railway, or in which a defect is discovered during transit. At common law, if "the defect in the packing from which damage is likely to occur be discovered on the journey, the carrier should take reasonable means to arrest the loss or deterioration therefrom".[72] But there may be no room here for common law, no gap in CIM to fill.

2.309 In one case[73] meat was delayed at the Spanish frontier because the documents (relating to other goods sent by the same consignor) were not in order. In these circumstances, the consignor's argument, that the railway was obliged to repack the goods to allow for the extra period of transit, was rejected; however, there is a suggestion in the judgment that the court was influenced by the fact that the delay was the fault of the consignor. It might be different, if the delay were caused by events (such as a strike or rough handling by customs officials) for which neither railway nor consignor was responsible. In any case, if the state of packing is such as to prevent carriage or prevent delivery, the railway may be obliged to seek and follow instructions from the consignor, in accordance with Articles 33 and 34, and the instructions may include repacking.[74] Further, in a note to the report of the meat case the Central Office adopts the view of Nanassy that, in failing to remedy patent defects in packing, the railway may be in breach of its implied or residual duty of care.[75] If so, there is some reason to believe that the true position under CIM is like that at common law and under CMR:

(a) The railway is not obliged to check the consignor's packing.
(b) If railway personnel observe a defect at the time of acceptance of the goods, the attention of the consignor should be drawn to the defect.
(c) If, after acceptance, it becomes clear that there is a defect in packing that will cause damage to the goods, the railway must take reasonable steps "to arrest the loss or deterioration".[76]

12. *Loading and unloading*

2.310 To establish risk (c), the railway must simply prove that loading was carried out by the consignor or that unloading was carried out by the consignee.[77] Although the claimant may be the consignee, the railway is entitled to plead loading by the consignor.[78] Unlike risk (d), which is specified as *defective* loading, to plead risk (c), the railway does not have to prove that the operation was carried out defectively, or

70. *Ag Karlsruhe 8.3.91*, TranspR 1993.299.
71. *LG Mainz 18.4.89*, Bull.OCTI 1994.60.
72. *L.N.W. Ry. Co.* v. *Hudson* [1920] A.C. 324, 340.
73. *OLG Celle 13.11.68*, Bull.OCTI 1970.45, 48.
74. In that sense: *ibid.* p. 50.
75. See Comment 1, above.
76. See Spera, Art. 36, Anm 21.
77. *Rb Antwerp 16.6.72* (1972) 7 ETL 1062.
78. Cf. *Paris 18.5.76*, Bull.OCTI 1977.112.

that loss or damage occurred during the operation or, of course, that the loss or damage was caused by the manner of the operation: see Comment 9, above. However, as the railway must also establish that the operation could have caused the loss or damage, it may be well advised to bring what evidence it can that the loading or unloading was in fact defective. In response to a successful plea by the carrier, in accordance with Article 37.2, the claimant may rebut the presumption raised by these risks and, to do so, commonly seeks to prove defects in the wagon (see below) or bad handling by the railway.[79]

As regards risk (c) the operation of loading includes that of covering the goods with tarpaulins or whatever material is appropriate.[80] It also includes stowage, in one case stowage such that heavy goods broke loose and the wagon was derailed.[81] Loading does not cease to be loading carried out by the consignor because the latter seeks the advice of a railway official on the best way of doing it.[82] In one case[83] the consignor sought and obtained reassurance from a railway official that the load was not too high, but this was untrue and the goods were damaged. In these circumstances, the railway was liable not, presumably, because loading ceased to be loading by the consignor but because, in the terms of Article 37.2, the damage was attributable not to the special risk (loading by the consignor) but to the wrong advice given by the railway. However, the provision of locks or other security devices on the wagons is not part of the loading operation and remains the responsibility of the railway.[84] Broken seals may be evidence that rebuts a *prima facie* case of special risk (d).[85] Similar considerations apply to unloading. *2.311*

As regards risk (d) whether loading is defective is a question of fact that can sometimes be determined by reference to tariffs or local regulations.[86] However, to load goods on a defective wagon is not defective loading for the purpose of Article 36.3, a point on which CIM 1980 differs from the 1970 version. In similar vein, it has been held that local regulations, whereby the consignor is required to check the state of the wagon, cannot displace the railway's duty under CIM to put at the disposal of the consignor a wagon that is in good condition and fit for the carriage concerned.[87] Moreover, the consignor is not obliged to inspect the wagon before loading.[88] However, it does not follow that the railway alone should bear the consequences of loading not by the railway but by the consignor of a wagon that is patently defective. It has been suggested that, if, in such a case, the consignor does not demand of the railway a wagon in good condition, that is fault on his part and thus a defence for the carrier under Article 36.2 and that liability will be *2.312*

79. E.g. *Antwerp 12.10.77* (1978) 13 ETL 636.
80. *Cass. 16.3.14*, D. 1916.1.145.
81. *Budapest No. 25. P., 21289/1968/29*, ULR 1973 (I) 286; Spera, Art. 36, Anm 26.
82. *Cass 13.11.90* (unreported); Spera, Art. 36, Anm 27.
83. *OLG Stuttgart 22.2.67*, Bull.OCTI 1968.75.
84. *Athens 28.2.2003*, Bull.OCTI 2004.21. Helm, Art. 27.3c, Anm 15.
85. *Athens 26.2.2003*, Bull.OCTI 2004.20.
86. Spera, Art. 36, Anm 33; but they are not decisive *Supreme Court, Hungary No. Gf. III. 31 542/1990*, Bull.OCTI 1993.80.
87. *Brussels 5.4.73* (1973) 8 ETL 528; *Brussels 28.5.76* (1976) 11 ETL 780.
88. *Rb Antwerp 6.2.79* (1980) 15 ETL 92.

apportioned.[89] See also the discussion of the response expected of the carrier faced with defective packing, Comment 11, above.

2.313 Neither risk (c) or risk (d) arises unless the operation was carried out "under the provisions applicable thereto", i.e. when the operation is required to be carried out by the consignor or consignee by local regulations *or* by agreement with the railway referred to in the consignment note. As local regulations apply to the carriage automatically by Article 20.2, they have this effect under Article 36.3, whether or not they are referred to in the consignment note, a reference of this kind being superfluous.[90]

13. Formalities undertaken by the consignor or consignee

2.314 Risk (e), completion by the consignor or consignee of the formalities required by Customs or other administrative authorities, together with the relevant part of Article 36.2, is the counterpart in the liability regime in Article 36 of the liberty accorded to the consignor and consignee by Article 26.3.[91] Risk (e), introduced to CIM for the first time in 1961, has given rise to little reported litigation, but a great deal of dispute at revision conferences.

14. Sensitive goods

2.315 Disagreement exists over the exact meaning of risk (f), here referred to as the case of sensitive goods, and its relationship with other concepts, notably inherent vice. All goods are liable sooner or later to decay but not all goods are sensitive. Their nature must be such that they are "inherently liable" to the listed kinds of damage, although the list is not exhaustive. Goods sensitive in one situation may not be sensitive in another. Risk (f) concerns sensitivity in context, i.e. when carried by rail at the particular time of year on the particular route. If goods are sensitive in that situation, they constitute risk (f), even though they may no longer be "inherently liable" to damage if carried with special care but such care has not been contracted for.[92] The idea is that the consignor knows his goods and that, if he chooses to expose them to carriage by rail, the risk is his, except to the extent that he can expect the railway to take care or that he transfers that risk to the railway by stipulating for special precautions; in each case, however, the goods remain sensitive in law and subject to Article 36.3(f).

2.316 As CIM also allows the railway to plead inherent vice in the goods as a distinct defence (Article 36.2) and imposes a different onus of proof (Article 37.1), this implies that sensitivity in goods under risk (f) is something different. Some confusion has arisen out of the use in Article 36.3(f) of the phrase "spontaneous decay". Whereas the French text uses the phrase *détérioration intérieure* and this appears to be the wording from which the English translation is taken, the German

89. Allégret, Fasc. 685, 57. In this sense: *Rb Antwerp 25.1.72*, ULR 74 (II) 33; Bull.OCTI 1974.57. Cf. Allégret, Fasc. 685, 56 and Spera, Art. 36, Anm 33.

90. *T.C. Brussels 27.12.76*, ULR 1980 (I) 288.

91. Spera, Art. 36, Anm 36.

92. *BGH 14.4.76* (1976) 11 ETL 789, 796; Helm, EVO, Art. 83, Anm 18.

text speaks of *innerer Verderb*, which elsewhere in CIM (notably Article 36.2) is translated as inherent vice. If there appears to be a conflict between the French and the German, the French prevails: COTIF, Article 28. The better view is that the concepts are indeed different They are not mutually exclusive, however, and precise demarcation is a matter of disagreement among commentators. Arguably,[93] the differences are as follows.

(a) As regards the journey in question, sensitivity is a feature of all goods of that type.[94] For example, all soft fruit is susceptible to bruising. Inherent vice, however, applies to some goods of that type but not to all goods of that type. For example, a particular consignment of coal may be in such a condition that it is liable to spontaneous combustion but that is not a feature of coal in general.

(b) For inherent vice, the vice must indeed be inherent in the sense that it arises mainly from characteristics of the goods themselves, as distinguished from external factors associated with carriage by rail, such as bruising and breakage. In contrast, most of the hazards to which sensitive goods are vulnerable, such as bruising and breakage, involve predominately external factors. Climate, however, plays a part in both concepts.

(c) Inherent vice relates to the particular journey.[95] Particular goods, which are fit for immediate use or consumption at the time of acceptance by the railway, suffer from inherent vice, if, assuming the required amount of care from the railway, they cannot withstand the normal incidents of the particular journey, including, in particular, the time that it is expected to take. To a large degree that is also true of sensitive goods. However, given the context, loss or damage in goods suffering from inherent vice is a *fait accompli* from the start. Whereas an inherent vice is present as a less than perfect state of the goods at the time of acceptance, damage to which goods are "inherently liable" (Article 36.3(f)) is the realisation of something, which was no more than *possible* when the (sensitive) goods were accepted for carriage, later during the journey.

(d) Most goods are liable to deterioration and most goods, sooner or later, suffer from inherent vice. But goods are sensitive only if at effectively all stages of their life their nature makes them "inherently liable" to damage during carriage by rail. In a sense, most goods are inherently liable to damage by, for example, "interior and spontaneous decay" and this has led some commentators[96] to suggest that any goods which will be adversely affected by delay are sensitive goods; *sed quaere*. The sense of case (f) appears more clearly from the corresponding provision of the CMR which speaks not of goods "inherently liable" to damage but of goods, the nature of which "particularly" exposes them to damage.[97]

93. Cf., for example, Rodière, No. 544(e).
94. *BGH 14.4.76* (1976) 11 ETL 789, 796.
95. Allégret, Fasc. 685, 20.
96. Helm, EVO, Art. 83, Anm 19.
97. See CMR, Art. 17, Comment 13, paras. 1.116 *et seq.*, above.

(e) Both sensitivity and inherent vice should be distinguished from the notion of latent defect. A latent defect is any kind of defect, whether arising from the sensitivity of the goods or from the inherent nature of the goods or from something else, if that defect cannot be discovered by the exercise of due diligence at a particular point in time, a time usually stated in the contract or the legislation in question. See, for example, Article III, Rule 1, of the Hague Rules: "before and at the beginning of the voyage". Latency has no bearing on whether there is sensitivity damage or inherent vice under CIM (or CMR), although it may affect the response to the situation expected of the carrier.

2.317 Examples of goods held by courts to be sensitive include meat[98] and fruit.[99] In addition, a leading commentator has suggested explosive goods, combustible goods, and goods liable to evaporation.[100]

2.318 Goods held not to be sensitive include packaged sewing-machines, cast-iron piping, and barrels of wine. Another is that of live animals but that is dealt with specifically in Article 36.3(h).

15. Errors in the description of certain goods

2.319 As regards the description of certain goods, risk (g) reinforces Article 18 whereby the consignor "bears the consequences" of errors in any of the particulars mentioned in the consignment note, as well as Article 36.2, whereby the railway is relieved from liability for loss, etc., resulting from the fault of the consignor. Thus the consequences of other errors, such as the consignor's entering an incomplete address for the consignee, are matters for Article 18 and Article 36.2, but not Article 18.3(g).

2.320 The relevant goods, goods not acceptable for carriage at all or acceptable subject to conditions, are those dealt with in Article 3.4, Article 4 and Article 5.[101] An important case is that of dangerous goods for which there are special regulations prescribed under Annex I: Regulations concerning the International Carriage of Dangerous Goods by Rail (RID).[102]

16. Live animals

2.321 Risk (h) was regarded as a particular case of sensitive goods, risk (f).[103] This risk was given separate treatment because, at least at the time of earlier versions of CIM, the

98. E.g. *BGH 14.4.76* (1976) 11 ETL 789.
99. *Supreme Court, Hungary No. GF III. 32 989/1974*, Bull.OCTI 1976.28; ULR 1976 (II) 391 (grapes).
100. Spera, Art. 36, Anm 39.
101. Helm, CIM, Art. 27, Anm 18.
102. See further Spera, Art. 36, Anm 49.
103. Rodière, No. 544(h).

law of some States did not regard live animals as goods. In any event, the view is still that the nature of live animals is such that they require special treatment and this is confirmed by Article 5.1(b).[104] For the purpose of risk (h), animals include birds,[105] as well as bees and fish.[106]

17. Accompanied goods

As a matter of the allocation of risk between railway and consignor, the intent behind this provision is obvious. Its relevance in practice has been doubted,[107] although one commentator considers that it reinforces the allocation of risk (h) in respect of live animals.[108] There is no corresponding provision in the CMR but it has been retained as a special risk by CIM (1999), Article 23(g). Indeed, another commentator reckons that it may apply to the carriage of corpses, railway rolling stock and objects of unusually great worth.[109] *2.322*

Article 37, Burden of proof *2.323*

1. The burden of proving that the loss, the damage or the exceeding of the transit period was due to one of the causes specified in Article 36.2 shall rest upon the railway.

2. When the railway establishes that, having regard to the circumstances of a particular case, the loss or damage could have arisen from one or more of the special risks referred to in Article 36.3, it shall be presumed that it did so arise. The person entitled shall, however, have the right to prove that the loss or damage was not attributable either wholly or partly to one of those risks.

This presumption shall not apply in the case referred to in Article 36.3 (a) if an abnormally large quantity has been lost or if a package has been lost.

Comments

1. The burden of proof under Article 36

Article 37.1 prescribes the "normal" burden of proof for the "normal" defences in Article 36.2. Contrast, however, Article 37.2. which prescribes the unusual burden of proof for the defences arising out of special risks listed in Article 36.3. See Article 36, Comment 1. *2.324*

2. Special risks: what could have been

The general effect of Article 37.2 is that, if the loss or damage could have arisen from the risk, it is presumed that it did arise from the risk and the carrier is exonerated unless the claimant can bring "counterproof": see Comment 3, below. *2.325*

104. For more detailed discussion, see *BG Switzerland 21.2.61* (1968) 3 ETL 426. Spera, Art. 36, Anm 50.

105. *Cass. 25.5.14*, D. 1916.1.145 (pheasants).

106. Spera, *loc. cit.*

107. Rodière, No. 544(i).

108. Helm, EVO, Art. 83, Anm 24.

109. Spera, Art. 36, Anm 51.

People differ, however, about what "could have" been, and this kind of provision has generated considerable litigation; see the corresponding provision of CMR, Article 18 (paragraph 1.118, above). Cases suggest that the carrier is required to establish no more than a plausible hypothesis: that the loss or damage is consistent with what might be expected of the risk in question and that that risk was (merely) a possible cause.[1] One leading commentator has contended that it is enough to merely *allege* the possibility,[2] however, the more general interpretation of Article 37.2 is that there must at least be sufficient evidence to suggest that the possibility is indeed there. It may be enough for the railway to show that there were no other plausible causes,[3] although, if there are other possible causes, the railway is not required to rule them out. English courts, which have yet to be called upon to apply Article 36.2, are likely to turn to a leading case on the parallel provision in the CMR: see Article 18, Comment 1 (paragraphs 1.119 *et seq.*, above). Here are two leading foreign decisions on CIM.

2.326 In a case before the French Court of Cassation,[4] a wagon of goods, including two bundles of cloth, was sent from Prato (Italy) to Paris and unloading was to be carried out by the consignee (a special risk under Article 36.3(c)). After arrival in Paris the bundles disappeared. The lower court decided for the claimant because, although the bundles might have disappeared while being unloaded by the consignee, they might well have disappeared later: as the cause was unknown, the carrier was liable. However, the Court of Cassation annulled this decision: it was enough that the carrier had shown that the loss might have arisen out of the unloading. It did not have to rule out other possibilities.

2.327 In a case before the Supreme Court of Hungary,[5] grapes had lost weight in excess of normal wastage but, given that the seals of the wagon were intact and that there was no sign that the loading was defective or that the goods had been disturbed en route, the court concluded that the loss of weight could have been the consequence of desiccation of the (particularly juicy) grapes and was thus within Article 27.3(e) of CIM 1961 (now Article 36.3(f)).

3. *Counterproof*

2.328 Counterproof, i.e., proof that the loss or damage was not attributable either wholly or partly to the special risk in question, is likely to be of some kind of alleged fault on the part of the railway. See, for example, Article 36, Comment 10 and Comment 11. To be "attributable" to the fault of the railway, its fault must at least have been a *causa sine qua non* of the loss or damage.[6] Alternatively, the claimant may be unable to prove the actual cause but, in order to defeat the railway's reliance on the special risk, the claimant may be able to convince the court that the railway's explanation, that the loss etc. could have been caused by the special risk,

1. *BG Switzerland 21.2.61* (1968) 3 ETL 426, 428; *OLG Hamburg 8.2.96.* TranspR 1996.389; Spera, Art. 37, Anm. 4.
2. Helm, EVO, Art. 83, Anm 25.
3. *Cass 13.11.90* (unreported).
4. *Cass. 10.2.69*, JCP 1979.15916.
5. *No. Gf. III. 32 989/1974*, Bull.OCTI 1976.28; ULR 1976 (II) 391.
6. *OLG Celle 13.11.68*, Bull.OCTI 1970.45, 51.

is not plausible. For example, according to one commentataor,[7] if the carrier proves that the goods were wet and that they were carried in open wagons, a case has been made under Article 36.3(a), which the claimant may refute by proof that there was no rain during transit.

Article 38, Presumption in case of reconsignment *2.329*

1. When a consignment despatched in accordance with the Uniform Rules has been reconsigned subject to the same Rules and partial loss or damage has been ascertained after the reconsignment, it shall be presumed that it occurred during the latest contract of carriage if the consignment remained in the care of the railway and was reconsigned in the same condition as it arrived at the station from which it was reconsigned.

2. This presumption shall also apply when the contract of carriage prior to the reconsignment was not subject to the Uniform Rules, if the Rules would have applied in the case of a through consignment from the original forwarding station to the final destination station.

This presumption shall moreover apply when the contract of carriage prior to the reconsignment was subject to a comparable international convention on international through rail transport, and when this contains the same presumption of law in favour of consignments sent in accordance with the Uniform Rules.

Comments

1. Reconsignment

Reconsignment occurs when the goods have arrived at the destination contracted for but, without having been taken from the custody of the railway,[1] are sent on by the consignee to a further destination.[2] The first contract has been performed by means of a symbolic delivery, whereby the goods are made available to the consignee but, instead of taking physical possession of the goods, the consignee arranges with the railway to have them sent on—to a new destination under a new consignment note.[3] Reconsignment should be distinguished from modification of the first contract of carriage of the kind envisaged by Article 30.1(e). *2.330*

Under early versions of CIM, between the time of the symbolic delivery ending the first transit and acceptance of the goods for the second transit, the railway holding the goods was not liable as a railway but only as a warehouseman. As such the railway could escape liability for what happened to the goods in this intervening period on the basis of exemption clauses in the storage contract. After much debate, the "gap" between transits was filled by a presumption that, if the consignment remains in the care of the railway in the intervening period, it was in the same condition at the end of that period (and the beginning of the second transit) as it was at the beginning of that period (and the end of the first transit), with the consequence that there is also a presumption that any "new" loss or damage occurred during the second transit and that the railway concerned is liable as railway under CIM. In effect, the beginning of the second transit (and the operation of *2.331*

7. Spera, Art. 37, Anm 6.
1. Spera, Art. 38, Anm 9 and 10.
2. Chimenti, Bull.OCTI 1958.120.
3. Spera, Art. 38, Anm 4.

CIM) are brought forward to the end of the first transit and cover the intervening period of custody.

2. The scope and consequences of Article 38

2.332 The assumption behind Article 38 is that the second transit is within the scope of Article 1 and thus itself subject to CIM. If not, Article 38 does not apply. Moreover, if the second transit is within the scope of Article 1 and subject to CIM, but the first transit was not subject to CIM because the original forwarding station was in another non-contracting state, the implication is that Article 38 does not apply. However, if the second transit is subject to CIM, but the first transit was not because it was a local feeder service within a CIM state, Article 38 applies.

2.333 Consequently the railway that undertakes a feeder service, i.e. a purely national first movement of goods to the station where the second international transit begins, must keep in mind that the goods may be reconsigned to another country and that, if so, its liability will be measured by CIM rather than by national law; and that liability on that basis will be presumed, unless it can show that the loss etc. occurred earlier.[4] This is reflected in the first paragraph of Article 38.2, whereas the second paragraph of Article 38.2 envisages SMGS,[5] which is in force in the states of eastern Europe.[6]

2.334 Further, if more than one railway is concerned, Article 38 is of importance as regards the liability of the last railway. For a train operating company in the UK, for example, it means that the company "will generally be liable for imported goods which arrive at a station in this country in a damaged condition not previously discovered and which have been re-consigned . . . ; but that it will not be so liable if under similar conditions goods exported from this country arrive in a damaged condition abroad".[7]

2.335 **Article 39, Presumption of loss of goods**

1. The person entitled may, without being required to furnish further proof, consider the goods lost when they have not been delivered to the consignee or are not being held at his disposal within thirty days after the expiry of the transit periods.

2. The person entitled may, on receipt of compensation for the lost goods, make a written request to be notified without delay should the goods be recovered within one year after the payment of compensation. The railway shall give a written acknowledgement of such request.

3. Within thirty days after receipt of such notification, the person entitled may require the goods to be delivered to him at any station on the route. In that case he shall pay the charges in respect of carriage from the forwarding station to the station where delivery is effected and shall refund the compensation received, less any costs which may have been included therein. Nevertheless he shall retain his rights to claim compensation for exceeding the transit period provided for in Articles 43 and 46.

4. Chimenti, p. 124.

5. Mutz TranspR 1992.126, 129.

6. On SMGS see Haenni, No. 14.

7. Kahn-Freund, pp. 436–437. See also Bras, Bull.OCTI 1962.128; and *Lg Lübeck 9.10.79*, Bull.OCTI 1981.76 (Bari-Chiasso-Lubeck, with interval at Chiasso: FS liable throughout under CIM).

In the absence of the request mentioned in paragraph 2 or of any instructions given within the period specified in paragraph 3, or if the goods are recovered more than one year after the payment of compensation, the railway shall dispose of them in accordance with the laws and regulations of the State having jurisdiction over the railway.

Comments

1. Compensation for missing goods

The main purpose of Article 39, whereby loss is presumed after 30 days if the goods have not been delivered, is to avoid uncertainty over the rights of the consignee and the amount of compensation recoverable from the railway in such a case, while retaining the possibility that the consignee may elect to have goods in lieu of compensation if, unexpectedly, the goods turn up later. If only part of the goods have been delivered within the period, nonetheless "the goods . . . have not been delivered . . . within thirty days" and Article 39 applies. It applies to both total and partial loss.[1] A similar provision is found in CMR (Article 20, para. 1.128, above) and has been included in Article 29 of CIM (1999) to deal with that kind of problem and it is necessary, according to Rodière,[2] as the absence of such a provision has given rise to difficulties in connection with carriage by air. *2.336*

A major consequence of Article 39 is that, when delay is treated as total loss in this way, the ceiling on compensation is not the ceiling for delay, a figure three times that of the carriage charges (Article 43.1), but a (higher) figure based on the value of the goods (Article 40.1). Further, the period of limitation begins to run, not from the day of delivery (Article 58.2(b)) but from a later point in time, the thirtieth day after the expiry of the transit period (Article 58.2(a)), i.e. from the day on which the case is to be treated as one of total loss rather than of delay. *2.337*

2. Recovered goods

The consignee's right to elect to have the goods in lieu of compensation arises only if the goods are recovered within one year after the payment of compensation. This means recovery by the railway in the sense that the goods are at the disposal of the railway which is, therefore, in a position to deliver the goods, if so required, to the person entitled. If, for example, goods are being held by Customs subject to payment of duty, they have not been recovered.[3] Moreover, the railway that becomes aware that the goods are being held like this is not obliged by Article 39.2 to notify the person entitled. However, if there is recovery of just a part of the goods, or of the whole or part in a damaged state, the better view is that the case does fall within Article 38.2 and that the railway must notify the person entitled.[4] *2.338*

If the consignee elects to take delivery of the goods, the consignee must refund compensation received, in accordance with Article 39.3, while retaining any rights to claim compensation for the railway's exceeding the transit period. If damage has *2.339*

1. Spera, Art. 39, Anm 2.
2. Rodière, No. 501.
3. Spera, Art. 39, Anm 11.
4. Spera, *loc. cit.*

been caused by the delay, compensation is governed by Article 43.1. But *quaere* the effect of Article 57.2(c) whereby rights of action in respect of delay may be extinguished by the passage of time.

2.340 Goods, the delivery of which the consignee neither wants nor is permitted to demand, the subject of the second paragraph of Article 39.3, are to be disposed of by the railway in accordance with the laws and regulations of the State having jurisdiction over the railway. In the case of English law, the goods would be treated as abandoned or uncollected goods.[5]

2.341 **Article 40, Compensation for loss**

1. In the event of total or partial loss of the goods the railway must pay, to the exclusion of all other damages, compensation calculated according to the commodity exchange quotation or, if there is no such quotation, according to the current market price, or if there is neither such quotation nor such price, according to the normal value of goods of the same kind and quality at the time and place at which the goods were accepted for carriage.

2. Compensation shall not exceed 17 units of account per kilogramme of gross mass short.

3. The railway shall in addition refund carriage charges, Customs duties and other amounts incurred in connection with carriage of the lost goods.

Comments

1. The measure of loss

2.342 Whereas Article 42 regulates compensation for damage to goods and Article 43 regulates compensation for damage to goods, Article 40 concerns compensation for partial or total loss of goods. Calculation or measure of the amount of such loss is regulated by Article 40.1. The default measure by reference to the exchange price at the place (or nearest place of exchange[1]) and time of acceptance of the goods, also the rule in Article 23.1 of CMR (para. 1.143, above), is quite unlike the rule of common law which, like that of the Hague-Visby Rules, refers to market value at destination. The idea behind the CIM rule is that the potential liability of the railway, like that of the carrier by road, should be relatively limited and the cost of transport relatively low[2]; and that, as the loss of a consignment might raise the price of such goods at destination, it was not right that that effect should inflate the damages recoverable.

2.343 Note the practice in some countries of taking the invoice price instead,[3] a practice apparently countenanced by Article 53, DCU 3. In so far as this will normally include the value added to the goods by performance of the contract of carriage, this is contrary to the principle underlying Article 40. However, if, perhaps to avoid the cost of argument, the parties accept the invoice value as the appropriate value, the court is unlikely to object and conduct its own investigation.

5. See Palmer, pp. 705 *et seq.*

1. Allégret, Fasc. 685, 90; Spera, Art. 40, Anm 4 and Art. 40, Anm 5. Re "exchange" or "market", see Benjamin, Chap. 16–052.

2. Koller, VersR 1989.2, 6.

3. Allégret, Fasc. 685, 93 and 94; Haenni, No. 250.

The measure is that of the monetary compensation recoverable from the railway by the claimant in the event of "total or partial loss of the goods". In this context, loss, which is distinguished from damage, means shortage in the goods. A partial loss is any loss which is less than a total loss subject, however, to the possible application of Article 41. Total loss is not defined by CIM and courts apply national law. At common law, goods are totally lost if they have been destroyed or if the owner has been irretrievably deprived of them, for example, when they have been confiscated.[4] So too in a case decided in France where the railway delivered not to the designated consignee, a bank interested by way of security, but the party to notify, the person wanting the goods. This was loss.[5] A commentator has suggested that the reason was that under CIM, as under French domestic law, delivery of all of the goods to the wrong person is treated as total loss.[6] However, the common law concept of constructive total loss is not appropriate in a regime of this kind.[7] Moreover, the common law rule that a thing is totally lost, if it is so damaged as to cease to be a thing of that kind in a commercial sense, is also inapplicable to Article 23 (para. 1.143, above) and Article 32 of CMR (para. 1.196, above),[8] and this too is probably also true of CIM. *2.344*

2. Consequential loss

Recovery under Article 40.1 is expressed to be "to the exclusion of all other damages". The inference is clear that, in principle, compensation for consequential loss is not recoverable under CIM.[9] The principle of indemnity in Article 40 is said to be objective (*damnum emergens*) rather than subjective (*lucrum cessans*).[10] However, the effect of reference in Article 40.1 to various commercial indices of value is that it is not the intrinsic value of the goods that is taken but a value that includes an element of profit. Moreover, the general principle established by Article 40 is qualified by other provisions of CIM, with the result that, although consequential loss is not recoverable in general under CIM, there are the following qualifications or exceptions: *2.345*

(a) The value of goods at the place of acceptance may be affected by their intended destination.[11]
(b) Loss representing lost carriage charges *from* the place of acceptance may be recovered under Article 40.3.
(c) A declaration of interest in delivery under Article 16 may enable the recovery of loss of profit.
(d) In the case of delay, a limited amount of consequential loss is recoverable under Article 43.1.

4. *ICI* v. *MAT Transport* [1987] 1 Lloyd's Rep. 354, concerning the parallel question under CMR.
5. *Cass. com 12.5.92*, BTL 1992.396.
6. Tilche, BTL 1992.391.
7. *ICI* v. *MAT*, above.
8. Respectively, *William Tatton & Co. Ltd.* v. *Ferrymasters* [1974] 1 Lloyd's Rep. 203 and *Worldwide Carriers* v. *Ardtran International* [1983] 1 Lloyd's Rep. 61.
9. *Cass. France 12.5.92.* BTL 1992. 396.
10. By Allégret, Fasc. 685, 89 and Spera, Art. 40, Anm 2.
11. Spera, Art. 40, Anm 5. *Idem* for the parallel provision of CMR: *Buchanan & Co.* v. *Babco Forwarding & Shipping Co (UK)* [1978] A.C. 141, 150–151.

(e) Under national law, consequential loss may be recovered if it can be established that the loss resulted from loss or damage to the goods occurring outside the time frame of Article 36.1, i.e., outside the transit period.

(f) Possibly, such loss may be recovered in a case of wilful misconduct or gross negligence under Article 44.

3. Compensation

2.346 The amount of compensation recoverable is based on the actual financial loss proved to have been suffered by the claimant,[12] up to the limit specified in Article 40.2. As is now usual in international Conventions, the limit is expressed in terms of so many units of account (see Article 7.1) per kilogramme of weight. One reason for liability by reference to weight is to enable the railway to estimate its potential liability without having to open the packaging of goods.[13] Thus the reference to weight probably includes the packaging of goods and, as CIM operates as part of the contract of carriage by rail, the reference is to those goods which are the object of the contract in question.

2.347 Hence, for example, it has been correctly decided that photographic goods consigned under separate contracts but consolidated by a forwarder and sent under a single consignment note, indicating neither the nature nor value of the goods, or the individual consignors and consignees, are to be treated separately as regards the limit on liability in this provision: there is not one limit for the total weight (mentioned in the note) but a limit for each parcel within the consolidation.[14] Such decisions would have been different perhaps, if the railway had not been aware of the situation.

4. Refunds

2.348 In addition to the compensation for loss, which is regulated by Article 40.1 and Article 40.2, the railway is required to refund monies of three kinds in accordance with Article 40.3. The first is carriage charges, which means the charges for the carriage in issue and not, for example, carriage charges to the place of acceptance by the railway; the cost of the latter is likely to be reflected in the value of the goods at that place recoverable under Article 40.1. The second is Customs duties. These do not include excise charges which, to be recovered at all, must be recovered under Article 40.3 as "other amounts".[15] The third is "other amounts incurred in connection with carriage of the lost goods". The meaning of these words has not been before the English court, however, the equivalent provision of CMR (Article

12. *Cass. Belge 3.6.76*, ULR 1977 (II) 220.

13. *BGH 30.1.81* (1981) 16 ETL 455, 458 the parallel provision of CMR.

14. *Cass. Belge 3.6.76*, ULR 1977 (II) 220. For more decisions in this sense in Belgium and France, see Allégret, Fasc. 685, 102.

15. *Buchanan & Co.* v. *Babco Forwarding & Shipping Co. (UK)* [1978] A.C. 141 in relation to CMR.

23.4, para. 1.143, above), which refers to "other charges incurred in respect of the carriage of the goods", has given rise to two quite different interpretations.

The first and narrower view, as it might apply to Article 40.3 of CIM, is that "amounts incurred in connection with carriage" means amounts incurred with a view to the carriage contracted for, disregarding consequential amounts incurred as a result of the way it was actually carried out (in breach of contract). This view, which allows the recovery of items such as the cost of packing, insurance and of obtaining certificates of quality, was taken by the dissenting minority in relation to CMR in the *Buchanan* case.[16] *2.349*

The second and broader view, taken by the majority in *Buchanan*, is that the amounts include all amounts which were actually incurred *in consequence of* the way in which the carriage was actually carried out, as long as they are not too remote. In addition to the amounts recoverable on the narrow view, the broad view would allow, for example, the cost of a survey to assess damage, the cost of returning damaged goods to the consignor, salvage costs, lost excise duty and legal costs. *2.350*

As a matter of interpretation of Article 40.3, the first view of "in connection with" is closer to the corresponding French words "á l'occasion de". Moreover, in view of the clear intention behind CIM to limit the liability of the railway to moderate and predictable levels and, therefore, to rule out the recovery of most items of consequential loss (see Comment 2, above), it is the view that is to be preferred. On the one hand, however, French decisions on the point have been inconsistent. In one case claims for the cost of getting containers to the place of consignment and the amount of (lost) hire paid to the container owner were ruled out.[17] However, in a later case incidental taxes were held to be recoverable.[18] On the other hand, the most recently reported decision of the German Supreme Court on the point prefers, correctly it is submitted, the first and narrower view.[19] *2.351*

In any case, the railway's obligation is to refund charges etc. "in connection with carriage of the lost goods", and the question arises whether, in the case of partial loss, the railway is obliged to refund all the charges etc. or only a part in proportion to the loss. The latter solution, explicit in the corresponding provision of CMR (Article 23.4, para. 1.143, above) but not in CIM, appears the better solution because the sums to be refunded are those incurred in connection with carriage of the *lost* goods. *2.352*

Article 41, Liability for wastage in transit *2.353*

1. In respect of goods which, by reason of their nature, are generally subject to wastage in transit by the sole fact of carriage, the railway shall only be liable to the extent that the wastage exceeds the following allowances, whatever the length of the route:

(a) two per cent of the mass for liquid goods or goods consigned in a moist condition;

(b) one per cent of the mass for dry goods.

16. Above.
17. *Paris 27.4.1993*, BTL 1993.455.
18. *Paris 13.9.2000*, BTL 2000.715; Unif.L.Rev. 2002.936.
19. *BGH 26.6.2003*, TranspR 2003. 453; Bull.OCTI 2004.16.

2. The limitation of liability provided for in paragraph 1 may not be invoked if, having regard to the circumstances of a particular case, it is proved that the loss was not due to causes which would justify an allowance.

3. Where several packages are carried under a single consignment note, the wastage in transit shall be calculated separately for each package if its mass on despatch is shown separately in the consignment note or can otherwise be ascertained.

4. In the event of total loss of the goods or in the case of loss of a package, no deduction for wastage in transit shall be made in calculating the compensation payable.

5. This Article shall not derogate from Articles 36 and 37.

Comment

2.354 As the railway's liability for short delivery is based on discrepancy in mass (Article 40.2) and hence weight, justice requires that it should not have to pay for differences attributable to the natural propensity of certain goods to lose weight and thus mass in normal transit. This is the purpose of Article 41, as well as one of the purposes behind Article 37.3(f). The difference between these two provisions lies, first, in the range of goods affected and, secondly, in the onus of proof. In the case of goods covered by Article 41, a claimant has no case at all against the railway unless he proves that the loss exceeds the percentages stated; or, if it does not, that the wastage was not due to causes which would justify a defence, for example, proof that the wastage was caused by rough handling during transit. In the case of sensitive goods within the scope of Article 37.3(f), sensitivity is a defence to be proved by the railway.

2.355

Article 42, Compensation for damage

1. In case of damage to goods, the railway must pay compensation equivalent to the loss in value of the goods, to the exclusion of all other damages. The amount shall be calculated by applying to the value of the goods as defined in Article 40 the percentage of loss in value noted at the place of destination.

2. The compensation may not exceed:

(a) if the whole consignment has lost value through damage, the amount which would have been payable in case of total loss;

(b) if only part of the consignment has lost value through damage, the amount which would have been payable had that part been lost.

3. The railway shall in addition refund the amounts provided for in Article 40.3, in the proportion set out in paragraph 1.

Comment

2.356 Whereas Article 40 regulates compensation for loss of goods, Article 42 regulates compensation for damage to goods. Whereas loss of goods refers to a reduction in quantity, it is said, damage to goods refers to a reduction in quality.[1] Damage means any change in the goods as a result of which the value of the goods has been diminished.[2] By reference to Article 40.1, Article 42.1 prescribes compensation by reference to loss of market value measured by reference to the exchange price at the place and time of acceptance of the goods. Although the damage is "noted" by an assessment made at destination, it is not the value at destination which is compared

1. Allégret, Fasc. 685, 111.
2. Spera, Art. 36, Anm 6.

with value on acceptance: the court is to seek the percentage difference in value by estimating what the value of the goods would have been on acceptance as goods in their actual condition (as it was at destination) and comparing that with their value on acceptance undamaged. Thus the rule is based on the difference in market value on acceptance rather than by reference to the cost of repair at destination.[3]

Like Article 40.1, Article 42.1 underlines that the compensation payable is "to the exclusion of all other damages". Thus, in a case in which parts of the consignment had been stolen, whereas the claimant could recover in respect of the parts stolen, a claim in respect of the consequential loss in the value of the remainder failed.[4] However, although the general principle established by Article 40 for loss and by Article 42 for damage is that consequential or profit loss is not recoverable under CIM, that is qualified by other provisions of CIM, and the result is that there are exceptions in certain cases: see Article 40, Comment 2. *2.357*

Article 43, Compensation for exceeding the transit period *2.358*

1. If loss or damage has resulted from the transit period being exceeded, the railway shall pay compensation not exceeding four times the carriage charges.
2. In case of total loss of the goods, the compensation provided for in paragraph 1 shall not be payable in addition to that provided for in Article 40.
3. In case of partial loss of the goods, the compensation provided for in paragraph 1 shall not exceed three times the carriage charges in respect of that part of the consignment which has not been lost.
4. In case of damage to the goods, not resulting from the transit period being exceeded, the compensation provided for in paragraph 1 shall, where appropriate, be payable in addition to that provided for in Article 42.
5. In no case shall the total of compensation payable under paragraph 1 together with that payable under Articles 40 and 42 exceed the compensation which would be payable in the event of total loss of the goods.
6. The railway may provide, in international tariffs or in special agreements, for other forms of compensation than those provided for in paragraph 1 when, in accordance with Article 27.1, the transit period has been established on the basis of transport plans.

If, in this case, the transit periods provided for in Article 27.2 are exceeded, the person entitled may demand either the compensation provided for in paragraph 1 above or that determined by the international tariff or the special agreement applied.

Additional Uniform Regulations (DCU)

DCU 1, to § 1 *No right to compensation exists unless the total transit period has been exceeded.* *2.359*

DCU 2, to § 1 *If a currency conversion has to be made, in order to arrive at the amount of compensation payable, the rate of exchange shall be as provided in Article* 40, § 4. *2.360*

Comments

1. The scope of Article 43

Whereas Article 40 regulates compensation for partial or total loss of goods and Article 42 regulates compensation for damage to goods, Article 43 deals with *2.361*

3. Allégret, Fasc. 685, 114; Spera, Art. 42, Anm 5.
4. *Paris 30.9.70*, Bull.OCTI 1972.69

compensation for exceeding the transit period, i.e., delay in the delivery of goods. Article 40 and Article 42 state rules "to the exclusion of all other damages". No such wording is found in Article 43, however, nonetheless, by reference to the *travaux préparatoires* of the 1961 version of CIM, courts have determined that Article 43 contains an exhaustive set of rules governing the determination of compensation due for damage sustained by the goods as a result of the transit period being exceeded.[1] Delay includes *prima facie* the case of goods which are never brought to destination,[2] however, once the delay exceeds stated periods, the case is treated as one of loss in accordance with Article 39.

2.362 If delay leads to damage, the intention was to treat that too as a case of delay.[3] However, in the past some courts have treated this case as one of damage and compensation has been assessed under Article 42,[4] partly as an inference from the general language of Article 42 and partly on the basis that, if there is a quantifiable result such as damage, that is the appropriate basis of assessment. This is still the position under equivalent provisions of CMR.[5] However, the conference that produced the 1980 revision of CIM sought to avoid this conclusion and settle the dispute between the courts of different countries. Unlike the corresponding provision of CMR and earlier versions of CIM, the scope of Article 43 is determined by the reference in Article 43.1 to "loss *or damage*". So, damage caused by delay is a matter for Article 43 and not Article 42.[6]

2. Compensation for delay

2.363 Article 43.1 makes it clear that the claimant can recover only in respect of loss or damage that has been caused by the delay. This is hardly surprising but the rule is different from that in previous versions of CIM, in which a specified "penalty" was recoverable, whether loss or damage had been caused by the delay or not.[7] Nonetheless in the current rule the ceiling on what is recoverable is assessed arbitrarily by reference to carriage charges. This is a reference to carriage charges in the strict sense and does not comprise ancillary charges of the kind referred to in Article 40.3.[8]

2.364 Underlying Article 40, Article 42 and Article 43 is the principle of indemnity which is respected expressly in Article 43. Thus whereas compensation for delay is recoverable in addition to compensation for loss in the case of partial loss, in accordance with Article 43.3, it is not recoverable in the case of total loss: Article 43.2. Moreover, although damage caused by delay is a matter for Article 43 and not Article 42 (see Comment 1, above), the claimant may recover under Article 42 in

1. *Amsterdam 21.11.74*, Bull.OCTI 1975.178; ULR 1976 (I) 265.
2. *Supreme Court, Hungary, No. Gf. III.31 095/1990*, Bull.OCTI 1993.78.
3. *Amsterdam 21.11.74* (above); Rodière, No. 567.
4. E.g. *Paris 31.5.78*, ULR 1979 (I) 332; *Cass 17.4.80*, BT 1981.284. Also in this general sense: *Cass. It. 24.11.71*, ULR 1973 (II) 442; *BGH 14.4.76* (1976) 11 ETL 787, 797, rejecting doctrine to the contrary.
5. See CMR Art. 23, Comment 1, para. 1.144, above.
6. Allégret, Fasc. 685, 125; Helm, Art. 34, Anm 4.
7. Allégret, Fasc. 685, 121; Spera, Art. 43, Anm 2.
8. Allégret, Fasc. 685, 123.

respect of damage suffered by the goods caused other than by delay. The damage in question is physical damage, such as impact damage in a derailment, although the derailment may have been the cause of the delay. At the same time, Article 43.5 reinforces the general limit on the liability of the railway and, in particular, the rule against recovery of consequential loss: see Article 40, Comment 2.

Article 44, Loss of the right to invoke the limits of liability *2.365*

The liability limits provided for in articles 25, 26, 30, 32, 33, 40, 42, 43, 45 and 46 shall not apply if it is proved that the loss or damage resulted from an act or omission, on the part of the railway, done with intent to cause such loss or damage, or recklessly and with knowledge that such loss will probably result.

Comment

Like the Hague Rules, CMR, HP and MC, CIM in Article 44 retains the principle that, if the carrier breaches the contract badly enough, it should be penalised by the loss of the relevant limit on the amount of its liability. In addition and for the same reason, a right of action against the railway, which would otherwise have been extinguished under Article 57.1, is kept alive by Article 57.2(d). In CMR still and in CIM until 1996, "bad enough" breach was expressed as breach amounting to gross negligence, which is irrelevant in English law because the concept is not recognised, and "wilful misconduct". *2.366*

"Wilful misconduct" is an expression that derives from contracts of carriage by rail in the UK in the nineteenth century. As far as the coverage of this book is concerned it survives only in WC, Article 25 (para. 3.350, below), and in one of the Freightliner conditions.[1] Since 1996 "wilful misconduct" has been replaced in other texts by "act or omission . . . done with intent to cause such loss or damage, or recklessly and with knowledge that such loss will probably result". This formula was first proposed but rejected at the 8th session of the Revision Committee. It is the wording found in the corresponding provision of the Hague-Visby Rules for carriage by sea (Article IV, rule 4—a rule that dates from 1968) of HP, Article 25 (para. 3.147, below), MC, Article 22.5 (para. 3.594, below), and, in particular, of CIM (1999), Article 36. For the meaning of "wilful misconduct" see CMR, Article 29, Comment 4 (paragraphs 1.171 *et seq.*, above). *2.367*

Full compensation means the full amount of the claimant's loss: he must be put in the position he would have occupied, if the contract of carriage had been performed according to its terms—subject, however, to national rules of law relating to causation and remoteness. Thus it includes not only *damnum emergens* but also *lucrum cessans*.[2] Not surprisingly, it has been held that the onus of proving that Article 44 applies is on the claimant.[3] Nonetheless, there is some doubt about this: see CMR Article 29, Comment 2 (paragraphs 1.166 to 1.167, above). *2.368*

1. See Condition 9, para. 2.627, below.
2. Allégret, Fasc. 685, 133.
3. *Cass. It. 24.11.71*, ULR 1973 (II) 442.

2.369 **Article 45, Limitation of compensation under certain tariffs**

When the railway agrees to special conditions of carriage through special or exceptional tariffs, involving a reduction in the carriage charge calculated on the basis of the general tariffs, it may limit the amount of compensation payable to the person entitled in the case of exceeding of the transit period, provided that such limit is indicated in the tariff.

When the special conditions of carriage apply only to part of the route, the limit may only be invoked if the event giving rise to the compensation occurred on that part of the route.

Comment

2.370 Article 45 allows the railway to limit liability yet further when it is carrying goods for a lower charge. An obvious example is carriage for charitable purposes of the kind envisaged by Article 6.4.

2.371 **Article 46, Compensation in case of interest in delivery**

In case of a declaration of interest in delivery, further compensation for loss or damage proved may be claimed, in addition to the compensation provided for in Articles 40, 42, 43 and 45, up to the amount declared.

Comment

2.372 In general, consequential loss is not recoverable under CIM: see Article 40, Comment 2. However, Article 46 enables the customer to obtain indemnity for consequential loss, such as loss of the profit that would have been made by selling or using the goods at destination, if the appropriate declaration is made. The declaration is to be made in the consignment note in accordance with Article 16.

2.373 Although Article 46, whereby the liability of the railway may be increased at the instance of the goods interest, is the natural complement of Article 45, whereby the liability of the railway may be lowered at the instance of the railway, and the latter envisages a lower carriage charge, no mention is made in Article 46 of an increased carriage charge to match the increased liability of the railway. However, it is normal for such a charge to be made and this is the clear inference of Article 16.2; such a charge does not appear to be a condition of a declaration. The declaration is an option, which the consignor may choose to exercise or not: Article 16.1. If the option is exercised it is to be expected but neither inevitable or required by CIM that the railway levy an extra charge.

2.374 **Article 47, Conversion of, and interest on compensation**

1. When the calculation of compensation requires the conversion of amounts expressed in foreign currencies, conversion shall be at the rate of exchange applicable on the day and at the place of payment of compensation.

2. The person entitled may claim interest on compensation payable, calculated at five per cent per annum, from the date of the claim referred to in Article 53 or, if no such claim has been made, from the day on which legal proceedings are instituted.

3. Interest shall only be payable if the compensation exceeds [eight] units of account per consignment note.

4. If, within a reasonable period allotted to him, the person entitled does not submit to the railway the supporting documents required for the amount of the claim to be finally settled, no interest shall accrue between the expiry of the period laid down and the actual submission of such documents.

Comment

The provision in Article 47.1 for conversion of currencies, most of which has been retained in CIM (1999), is not found in the other transport Conventions in which compensation is assessed entirely in terms of units of account. Article 47.2, providing for interest, is more commonplace but when it says that the person entitled "may" claim 5 per cent, that is all: 5 per cent is the maximum recoverable.[1] However, in other cases in which CIM provides for interest, such as Article 17.2, it specifies a different starting date.[2] When interest runs from the day on which legal proceedings are instituted, that day is determined by the *lex fori*.[3] The identical issue has come before the English court under CMR.[4] 2.375

Article 48, Liability in respect of rail-sea traffic 2.376

1. In rail-sea transport by the services referred to in Article 2.2 of the Convention each State may, by requesting that a suitable note be included in the list of lines or services to which the Uniform Rules apply, indicate that the following grounds for exemption from liability will apply in their entirety in addition to those provided for in Article 36.

The carrier may only avail himself of these grounds for exemption if he proves that the loss, damage or exceeding of the transit period occurred in the course of the sea journey between the time when the goods were loaded on board the ship and the time when they were discharged from the ship.

The grounds for exemption are as follows:

(a) act, neglect or default on the part of the master, mariner, pilot or the carrier's servants in the navigation or management of the ship;
(b) unseaworthiness of the ship, if the carrier proves that the unseaworthiness is not attributable to lack of due diligence on his part to make the ship seaworthy, to ensure that it is properly manned, equipped and supplied or to make all parts of the ship in which the goods are loaded fit and safe for their reception, carriage and protection;
(c) fire, if the carrier proves that it was not caused by his act or fault, or that of the master, a mariner, pilot or the carrier's servants;
(d) perils, dangers and accidents of the sea or other navigable waters;
(e) saving or attempting to save life or property at sea;
(f) the loading of goods on the deck of the ship, if they are so loaded with the consent of the consignor given in the consignment note and are not in wagons.

The above grounds for exemption in no way affect the general obligations of the carrier and, in particular, his obligation to exercise due diligence to make the ship seaworthy, to ensure that it is properly manned, equipped and supplied and to make all parts of the ship in which the goods are loaded fit and safe for their reception, carriage and protection.

Even when the carrier can rely on the foregoing grounds for exemption, he shall nevertheless remain liable if the person entitled proves that the loss, damage or exceeding

1. *Cass. 3.11.88*, BT 1989.164.
2. Spera, Art. 47, Anm 3.
3. Spera, Art. 47, Anm 6.
4. See *Impex Transport* v. *Thames Holdings* [1981] 2 Lloyd's Rep. 566.

of the transit period is due to a fault of the carrier, the master, a mariner, pilot or the carrier's servants, fault other than provided for under (a).

2. Where one and the same sea route is served by several undertakings included in the list referred to in Articles 3 and 10 of the Convention, the regime of liability applicable to that route shall be the same for all those undertakings.

In addition, where such undertakings have been included in the list at the request of several States, the adoption of this regime shall be the subject of prior agreement between those States.

3. The measures taken under this Article shall be notified to the Central Office. They shall come into force at the earliest at the expiry of a period of thirty days from the date of the letter by which the Central Office notifies them to the other States.

Consignments already in transit shall not be affected by such measures.

Comments

1. The purpose of Article 48

2.377 Article 48 was inserted in the 1952 version of CIM at the request of the United Kingdom, evidently in view of cross-Channel traffic, because according to Article 2.2 of COTIF (the "Convention" referred to in Article 48.1), CIM may be applied to "international through traffic using in addition to services on railway lines, land and sea services and inland waterways". The purpose of Article 48 is that, when goods are carried by sea under a contract of carriage within the scope of CIM, the liability of the railway as sea carrier should be based not on CIM but to a large degree on the appropriate liability regime, i.e. for the English Channel and the North Sea the maritime regime known then as the Hague Rules and, in its most current version, as the Hague-Visby Rules.

2.378 The effect of Article 48 is that, although the monetary limits on the railway's liability remain those of CIM, Articles 40 *et seq.*, the defences, the "grounds for exemption" set out in the third sub-paragraph of Article 48.1 are taken from (although not altogether identical to) those found in Article IV of the Hague-Visby Rules.

2.379 The Revision Committee was empowered to reconsider Article 48, when the Hamburg Rules came into force—which they did on 1 November 1992, however, Article 48 has remained as it was.[1] One reason may be that Article 48 has not given rise to the same level of controversy as the equivalent provision (Article 2, para. 1.15, above) of CMR, and its significance has diminished to the extent that goods are now moved through the Channel Tunnel. A second is that few European states have ratified the Hamburg Rules. A third is that, according to Article 48.1, it does not operate automatically: the request must be made. Any such request must extend to the entire list of grounds of exemption, selection is not permitted,[2] and certain Scandinavian countries, for example, have been reluctant to make a request.

2. The grounds for exemption

2.380 The grounds of exemption were based on grounds found in Article IV of the Hague Rules and repeated in Article IV of the Hague-Visby Rules:

1. On the possibility of revision, see Spera, Art. 48, Anm 2.
2. See Helm, Art. 2, Anm 6.

(a) Act, neglect or default in the navigation or management of the ship, which is found in Article IV, rule 2(a), of the Hague-Visby Rules, refers to a wrongful act or omission short of conduct of the kind called "wilful misconduct", referred to in Article 44 of CIM and in the past in Article IV, rule 5(e), of the Hague-Visby Rules. Dangerous or foolish acts of navigation affecting the ship also affect cargo but for exemption the conduct must primarily affect the ship rather than cargo.[3] A collision is an obvious example.

(b) The defence based on the unseaworthiness of the ship, as qualified, is a condensed and revised version of Article IV, rule 1, of the Hague (Visby) Rules; and the penultimate paragraph of Article 48.1 sets out the substance of the associated Article III, rule 1. Unseaworthiness of the ship is a relative concept. A ship is unseaworthy if the state of the ship's structure, equipment and cargo space or the (in)competence of its crew is such that a prudent shipowner would not send it to sea in that condition on the particular voyage and with the particular cargo. If the claimant can prove that the loss, damage or delay in question was caused by such unseaworthiness, the Rules make the carrier liable unless the carrier can show that the loss etc. occurred in spite of the exercise of due diligence by the carrier and those employed to attend to the seaworthiness of the ship, including independent contractors.[4] The requirement of due diligence as a condition of exoneration is the subject of Article III, rule 1 of the Hague-Visby Rules.[5]

The mention of unseaworthiness as a ground for exemption without the rest of Article IV, rule 1 reflects an erroneous view held in certain quarters in civil law countries[6] of that Rule.[7] Moreover, ground (b) has been interpreted[8] as confined to unseaworthiness arising after the voyage has begun, however, insofar as the unseaworthiness affected the integrity of the hull, such a case would be covered by ground (d).

(c) The ground of exemption in the case of fire is based on Article IV, rule 2(c), of the Rules. Fire at sea is a special hazard which has traditionally been the subject of special rules.[9]

(d) Perils of the sea are perils peculiar to ships at sea, such as stranding, collision, and storms at sea but not sources of damage experienced at both land and sea, such as heavy rain.[10]

(e) Saving or attempting to save life or property at sea, as a ground of exemption, seeks to ensure appropriate priorities in the navigation of the

3. See *Gosse Millerd* v. *Canadian Govt. Merchant Marine* [1929] A.C. 223. Generally, see Treitel and Reynolds, *Carver on Bills of Lading* (2001), para. 9–188.

4. See *Riverstone Meat Co.* v. *Lancashire Shipping Co.* [1961] A.C. 807; and *The Amstelslot* [1963] 2 Lloyd's Rep. 223 (HL).

5. See Carver (above) Chap 9–120 *et seq.*

6. E.g. Rodière, *Droit Maritime* (Paris 1967), No. 618.

7. View rejected in England in *Leesh River Tea Co.* v. *B.I.S.N.* [1967] 2 Q.B. 250 (C.A.).

8. Spera, Art. 48, Anm 10.

9. See Carver (above) para. 9–187.

10. *Canada Rice Mills* v. *Union Marine Ins. Co.* [1941] A.C. 55; The *Popi M* [1985] 2 Lloyd's Rep. 1 (H.L.); The *Bunga Seroja* [1999] 1 Lloyd's Rep. 512 (H.C.A.). Carver (above), para. 9–188.

ship. Ground (d) reflects Article IV, rule 4 of the Hague-Visby Rules, which provides that any "deviation in saving life or property at sea . . . shall not be deemed an infringement of these Rules or of the contract of carriage, and the carrier shall not be liable for any loss or damage resulting therefrom".[11] Such conduct by the ship often requires delay, which but for the ground of exemption would be a breach of contract, as well as deviation from the usual commercial route, at common law a serious breach of contract which automatically deprives the carrier of exemptions.[12]

(f) Loading of goods on the deck of the ship with the consent of the consignor is not a ground of exemption under Article IV of the Rules. However, the effect of Article I(c) of the Rules is that, if the goods are carried on deck and stated (with the implied consent of the consignor) to be so carried in the contract of carriage, the Rules do not apply and the carrier is permitted therefore to exempt or limit his liability contractually.

Grounds (a) and (b) have been deleted from the corresponding provision of CIM (1999), Article 38. They were considered by many to be archaic and ground (b) was found by many, especially civil lawyers, to be confusing in its wording as well as controversial in content.

3. Overriding Obligations

2.381 The last two paragraphs of Article 48.1 reflect two overriding obligations at common law, the breach of any one of which prevents the sea carrier from being excused by the grounds of exoneration.

2.382 One such overriding obligation, reflected in the penultimate paragraph of Article 48.1, concerns the seaworthiness of the ship. As modified in the Rules, a defence established by the carrier under Article IV, rule 2, may be defeated (overridden) if (i) the claimant can prove in accordance with Article IV, rule 1, that the loss or damage was caused by the unseaworthiness of the ship and (ii), in response to that proof, the carrier is unable to prove the exercise due diligence in the matters mentioned by Article 48.1 as "general obligations", in accordance with Article III, rule 1, of the Rules.

2.383 The final paragraph of Article 48.1 reflects the other overriding obligation at common law, the breach of which prevents the sea carrier from being excused by the grounds of exoneration. This one concerns negligence. If the claimant can prove that, for example, the goods were damaged by an unexpected incursion of sea water (ground (d)), the defence fails if the claimant can prove that this occurred because the crew had negligently failed to close a valve.

2.384 **Article 49, Liability in case of nuclear incidents**

The railway shall be relieved of liability under the Uniform Rules for loss or damage caused by a nuclear incident when the operator of a nuclear installation or another person who is

11. Carver (above), paras. 9–212 *et seq.*

12. *Thorley (Joseph) Ltd.* v. *Orchis SS. Co.* [1907] 1 K.B. 660 (C.A.). Carver (above), paras. 9–036 *et seq.*

substituted for him is liable for the loss or damage pursuant to a State's laws and regulations governing liability in the field of nuclear energy.

Comment

The object of Article 49 is to ensure that CIM does not trespass into the field of various other international Conventions dealing with loss or damage arising out of nuclear incidents. 2.385

Article 50, Liability of the railway for its servants 2.386

The railway shall be liable for its servants and for any other persons whom it employs to perform the carriage.

If however such servants and other persons, at the request of an interested party, make out consignment notes, make translations or render other services which the railway itself is under no obligation to render, they shall be deemed to be acting on behalf of the person to whom the services are rendered.

Additional Uniform Regulation (DCU)

DCU 1 *If the person entitled has omitted to submit, in accordance with the regulations in force, a translation into one of the languages provided for in the Uniform Regulations, the railway staff who make such a translation are nevertheless considered as acting on behalf of the person entitled.* 2.387

Comments

1. Vicarious liability

If a railway has contracted to do something, it is liable for failure to achieve that task, whether the failure is that of the managing director or *alter ego* of the railway at company headquarters or, as is more likely, it is that of one or more of the servants or agents employed for the purpose by the railway at "track level". This is the rule in most national systems of law, including English law, and it is the rule for CIM, set out in Article 50 for the avoidance of doubt, especially in some countries which do not have quite the same rule. 2.388

Doubt persists, however, over whether railwaymen on strike are "performing the carriage" and thus over whether the railway is responsible for their acts or omissions under Article 50.[1] There is also some doubt whether Article 50 applies to the additional services referred to in Article 44.[2] There is little doubt, however, that the railway is not liable under CIM for false or misleading information given to potential customers prior to conclusion of any contract of carriage; liability must be based on national law. Note also the second paragraph of Article 50. 2.389

If the action against the railway were based not on the contract of carriage but in tort, it would be open to the railway in some cases to argue that its servant had acted 2.390

1. Spera, Art. 50, Anm 5. For English law, see Markesinis & Deakin, *Tort Law* (5th ed., 2003), para. 6.4.3.
2. Spera, *loc. cit.*

outside the scope of his employment or that, being an agent, the railway was not vicariously responsible for his acts at all. If an action against the railway were based in tort, where it might also have been brought under the contract of carriage, it appears that the effect of Article 51 would be that these arguments would not succeed: the action would be subject to the "condition" in Article 50 that the railway remained responsible for these people. It would be otherwise if at the time the servants or agents were not "performing the carriage". For example, if the consignor is obliged to load the goods and the servants of the railway help him, they are not performing the carriage—they are the temporary servants of the consignor and Article 50 does not apply.[3]

2.391 It has been stressed[4] that, in view of the collective responsibility of railways for carriage under Article 35, a railway, the railway on the last stage, for example, is responsible not only for the acts or omissions of its own servants and agents but also those of railways performing earlier stages of carriage.

2. *Transferred agency*

2.392 The purpose of the second paragraph of Article 50 is to ensure that, if, for example, a helpful railway employee, who is confronted with a confused customer, assists him to fill out the forms drawn up by the railway, any statements or mistakes shall not be attributable to the railway: the employee is deemed to be acting on behalf of the customer or consignor under what is sometimes called transferred agency.[5] Modern critics consider that this kind of provision is archaic, as it enables the railway, which benefits from goodwill and business generated by people that the railway has put there to deal with customers and which is responsible for many of the documents the meaning and use of which gives rise to these "services", to evade its proper social, moral and commercial responsibilities. In England such a rule is out of step with the modern law of agency. In other contexts, when a person has placed reasonable reliance on the advice of an agent, common law courts have been ready to disregard contract terms like that found in Article 50.[6] Nonetheless, the letter of CIM has been applied strictly, for example in Germany.[7]

2.393 A further consequence of this paragraph is that "the person to whom the services are rendered", for example the consignee who has sought information, is vicariously liable for the negligence of the servant in question. However, whether the consignor owes any duty of care in that connection, for example, to the consignee, is a matter for national law.[8]

3. Allégret, Fasc. 685, 170.
4. See Spera, Art. 50, Anm 3.
5. Such a rule can be found in England in the controversial case of *Newsholme Bros.* v. *Road Transport & General Ins. Co.* [1929] 2 K.B. 365 (C.A.).
6. E.g. in relation to insurance agents and proposal forms, see *Stone* v. *Reliance Mutual Ins. Sy. Ltd.* [1972] 1 Lloyd's Rep. 469 (C.A.).
7. *Ag Karlsruhe 11.8.89*, TranspR 1989.436; ULR 1990 (I) 470.
8. Spera, Art. 50, Anm 9.

Article 51, Other actions *2.394*

In all cases to which the Uniform Rules apply, any action in respect of liability on any grounds whatsoever may be brought against the railway only subject to the conditions and limitations laid down in the Rules.

The same shall apply to any action brought against those servants and other persons for whom the railway is liable under Article 50.

Comments

1. Exclusivity of CIM

Article 51 was introduced to CIM in the 1961 version (Article 40) to settle disputes *2.395* and divergence between courts concerning concurrent liability.[1] Moreover, it was designed to ensure that the railway had a clear, uniform and limited level of liability. In this respect CIM follows the trend to make carriage Conventions exclusive of rights and duties within their particular domain; see, for example, HP, Article 1, Comment 1 (paras. 3.37 *et seq.*, below). In this respect Article 51 has been likened to Article 41 of CMR (para. 1.236, above).[2] The domain of CIM stated largely in Article 1 is ring-fenced in this regard by Article 51. In particular, it should be noted that the reference in the opening words of Article 51 to the case in question is a reference not to the carriage in question but to the legal dispute in question.[3] Were it otherwise, a literal reading of Article 51 would have the unintended result that a dispute outside the scope of CIM, for example concerning events before acceptance of the goods by the railway, would be affected by Article 51 and thus by CIM simply because CIM applied to other aspects of the carriage.

To achieve its purpose Article 51 states that action may only be brought "subject *2.396* to the conditions and limitations laid down" in CIM. Whereas a "limitation" is clearly a reference to ceilings on monetary liability, such as that in Article 40.2, and to time bars, such as that in Article 58, it is less clear what is meant by "conditions". A condition, it is submitted, refers to any provision of CIM such, that if it is applied, the railway would not be liable or liable less extensively in an action brought on the rest of the contract of carriage. In addition, one of the "conditions" limiting "*any* action in respect of liability on any grounds *whatsoever*" (emphasis added) appears to be that the claimant must be entitled to sue under Article 54, i.e., must be the consignor or the consignee. It also appears therefore that the owner of goods, for example the "real" consignee who is not, however, the nominal consignee, has no *locus standi* to bring an action in tort against the railway—subject to the following point.

2. Third parties

It might be argued that extra-contractual claimants, who are not parties to the *2.397* contract of carriage,[4] are unaffected by Article 51 which, like other provisions of

1. Von Tegelen, Bull.OCTI 1966.178.
2. *OGH 28.2.2001*, TranspR 2002.346, 347.
3. Including additional services. See Allégret, Fasc. 685, 173; Spera, Art. 51, Anm 3.
4. Helm, Art. 40.

CIM, functions as a term of the contract of carriage. That is unlikely to have been the intention of the drafters of Article 51. As regards an English court seised with this question, however, it is submitted that Article 51 contains a rule of a kind known to English common law, whereby a contracting party claimant will not be allowed to succeed in a claim against the other party by reframing the claim in tort in circumstances in which the claim would not have succeeded in contract. In terms of the tort of negligence, to take the most important example, the duty of care is set in its contractual context and limited accordingly.[5] Thus, if it is found that the consignor who contracted with the railway is a forwarder, the owner of goods damaged may wish to sue in tort, but being taken to be aware of the basis (CIM) on which railways accept goods for international carriage, any duty of care owed by the railway to the claimant owner is in effect subject to CIM.

2.398 As regards claims against servants and others employed to carry out the contract of carriage, the second paragraph of Article 51 was important in England because it provided a statutory exception to the application at common law of the privity rule, whereby such a person cannot plead a defence based on a contract to which he is not a party.[6] Arguably there has always been a common law exception to the privity rule here in that, when a claimant contracted with railway A, which performed the first stage of transit itself but then contracted the second stage to railway B, the claimant was bound by the terms agreed between the two railways. One explanation was that railway A contracted with railway B as agent of the claimant, but another was that the claimant was bound by the terms because "he must be taken to have assented" to them.[7] Be that as it may, it now seems that, if the contract of carriage is appropriately drafted, such persons can rely on section 1 of the Contracts (Rights of Third Parties) Act 1999. Although according to section 6(5)(b) of the Act, section 1 confers no rights on a third party in a case subject to CIM, an exception is made for third party reliance on an exclusion or limitation in the contract of carriage. Such persons do not need to rely on section 1 as long as they can point to CIM but at least English law is now in harmony with the second paragraph of Article 51.

2.399 **Title V, Assertion of Rights: Article 52, Ascertainment of partial loss or damage**

1. When partial loss of, or damage to, goods is discovered or presumed by the railway or alleged by the person entitled, the railway must without delay, and if possible in the presence of the person entitled, draw up a report stating, according to the nature of the loss or damage, the condition of the goods, their mass and, as far as possible, the extent of the loss or damage, its cause and the time of its occurrence.

A copy of the report must be supplied free of charge to the person entitled.

2. Should the person entitled not accept the findings in the report, he may request that the condition and mass of the goods and the cause and amount of the loss or damage be ascertained by an expert appointed either by the parties or by a court. The procedure to be followed shall be governed by the laws and regulations of the State in which such ascertainment takes place.

5. See *The Nicholas H* [1996] 1 A.C. 211, 239–240 as regards the Hague-Visby Rules.
6. *Scruttons* v. *Midland Silicones* [1962] A.C. 446.
7. *Hall* v. *North Eastern Ry. Co.* (1875) L.R. 10 Q.B. 437, 442.

Comments

1. Proof

To make a claim in the case of partial loss of or damage to goods, it is not enough that the claimant has satisfied the formal requirements of Article 53. The claimant has still to prove the truth of the allegations made in the written claim, that the loss or damage occurred between acceptance and delivery and that therefore the railway is liable under Article 36.1. In practice, if the claimant cannot prove a relevant accident or catastrophic event in that period, there must be proof that there was a difference between the quantity or condition of the goods accepted and the quantity or condition of the goods actually delivered, which invites the inference that the difference in the goods was caused between those two points in time. Evidence about the goods at the time of acceptance rests mainly on statements in the consignment note; see Article 11, Comment 3 (paragraphs 2.58 to 2.59, above). Evidence about the goods at the end of transit, when the allegation is one of partial loss or damage, is the concern of Article 52. *2.400*

When, however, the allegation is one of total loss (and non-delivery), an investigation of the kind prescribed by Article 52 is inappropriate. In the case of carriage by sea, the consignee who alleges non-delivery must prove that allegation, and usually does so by producing a bill of lading for the goods, the implication being that, if the carrier had delivered the goods in question, the consignee would not have been in possession of the bill. In the case of carriage by rail (and road), the consignee has no such document and in many cases might find it very difficult to prove non-delivery. To meet this difficulty, although the claimant must prove that there is a contract of carriage and that he is the person designated as consignee, as regards the allegation of non-delivery, under CIM (and CMR) the onus of proof is alleviated. The claimant is said to benefit from a presumption of loss (Article 39): if the goods have not been delivered within 30 days of the expiry of the transit period (Article 27), total loss is presumed. But if the carrier asserts that delivery has occurred, although consignee denies it, what then? In some states the carrier is required to prove delivery.[1] Otherwise the presumption of loss would carry little benefit, and the consignee's right of action would be fragile indeed. *2.401*

2. The requirement and role of ascertainment

Article 52 obliges the railway to ascertain the state of the goods, an obligation of a kind not found in the Conventions for other modes of carriage, and one which reflects the tradition of a railway as an organisation of the state. Thus, according to Article 52 the railway must ascertain the state of the goods (a) when "partial loss of, or damage to, goods is discovered or presumed by the railway". The railway must act without waiting for a complaint, although, as one might expect, the railway must also ascertain the state of the goods (b) when one of these matters is "alleged by the person entitled", i.e., by the consignor or consignee, as the case may be. To put the railway in this position, the claimant has only to establish *locus standi* as claimant *2.402*

1. *Supreme Court, Hungary, 1990*, Bull.OCTI 1991.109.

under Article 54. Still, the evidential weight to be attached to ascertainment under Article 52 is a matter for the *lex fori*.[2]

2.403 Apart from the role of ascertainment in proof of loss or damage, ascertainment has other consequences. If, in the case of apparent loss or damage, loss or damage is ascertained prior to acceptance of the goods by the consignee, the right of action against the railway is kept alive: Article 57.2. Otherwise it is extinguished. In the case of non-apparent loss or damage, the right of action is also kept alive, provided that the claimant asks for ascertainment within a certain period of time: *ibid.* However, in the latter case, in view of the passage of time, ascertainment is less effective to establish that the loss or damage occurred prior to delivery. On the one hand, the railway is not entitled to charge for the time taken[3] but, on the other hand, there appears to be no sanction in CIM to compel the railway to act expeditiously.[4]

2.404 Consequences of non-ascertainment by the railway, in breach of Article 52, are as follows: (a) The claimant does not have to prove the partial loss etc. alleged—the truth of his allegation will be presumed.[5] The same follows when the report is vague or incomplete but could and should have been clear and complete.[6] (b) A right of action against the railway, which might otherwise have been extinguished, is not extinguished in accordance with Article 57.2(a)(ii), provided that the allegation was made within a reasonable time.[7] (c) The claimant, in spite of having accepted the consignment note and paid charges, is not obliged to accept the goods: Article 28.5.

3. *Reports*

2.405 The railway is required to draw up a report stating the matters set out in Article 52.1. Although the railway is obliged to seek the presence of the claimant during this process, the claimant if present (usually through an agent) is not obliged to sign or accept the report. If the claimant does sign it, it has been held that that does not stop the claimant disputing the contents of the report later.[8] As stated in the second paragraph of Article 52.1, the claimant is entitled to a copy of the report but that does not entitle the claimant to inspect the documents or records on which the report is based.[9] The probative force of the report is a matter for the *lex fori*,[10] however, Article 52.2 prescribes the course open to a dissatisfied claimant not only when the claimant does not accept the (positive) findings of the report but also when he considers that it is incomplete.

2. Haenni, No. 268; *Paris 17.3.52*, GP 1952.I.386; *Paris 21.12.94*, Bull.OCTI 1995.228.
3. *Supreme Court, Hungary, Gf III 31.335.1987*, Bull.OCTI 1990.76.
4. *Cass 9.5.90* (reported by Lexis).
5. Allégret, Fasc. 686, 5; Matyassy, Bull.OCTI 1971.44, 51; Rodière, No. 523. See also Helm, Art. 45, Anm 1.
6. Spera, Art. 52, Anm 9.
7. *Paris 15.5.63*, Bull.OCTI 1965.196.
8. So held in *Paris 14.10.68*, Bull.OCTI 1969.153.
9. Helm, Art. 45, Anm 2.
10. Allégret, Fasc. 686, 6; Haenni, No. 268.

The main option available to a dissatisfied claimant under Article 52.2 is to seek the appointment of an expert. In France it has been held that the cost of ascertainment by an expert is to be paid by the person, if any, who is at fault.[11] The option is not available to the railway under Article 52 but there is no prohibition on such an initiative by the railway outside the framework of Article 52. As for the claimant, he is not obliged to exercise the option,[12] and, if he does not, he is not estopped from questioning the findings of the railway's report in other ways.[13] *2.406*

Article 53, Claims *2.407*

1. Claims relating to the contract of carriage shall be made in writing to the railway specified in Article 55.

2. A claim may be made by persons who have the right to bring an action against the railway under Article 54.

3. To make the claim, the consignor must produce the duplicate of the consignment note. Failing this, he must produce an authorisation from the consignee or furnish proof that the consignee has refused to accept the consignment.

To make the claim, the consignee must produce the consignment note if it has been handed over to him.

4. The consignment note, the duplicate and any other documents which the person entitled thinks fit to submit with the claim shall be produced either in the original or as copies, the copies to be duly authenticated if the railway so requires.

On settlement of the claim, the railway may require the production, in the original form, of the consignment note, the duplicate or the cash on delivery voucher so that they may be endorsed to the effect that settlement has been made.

Additional Uniform Regulations (DCU)

DCU 1, to §1 *Reasons must be given for all claims.* *2.408*

DCU 2, to §§ 1 and 4 *The person entitled shall attach to his application for refund all the relevant supporting documents and, in particular, the account of charges drawn up under Article 15, § 7.* *2.409*

DCU 3, to §§ 1 and 4 *The person entitled shall attach to his application for compensation for loss or damage all those documents which can be used to justify the claim and prove the value of the goods, in particular the purchase invoice.* *2.410*

DCU 4, to § 2 *Claims submitted by persons other than those entitled under Article 54, shall not be entertained unless they are accompanied by a declaration, on a separate sheet, in which the entitled person consents to the amount due being paid to the person submitting the claim. This declaration, the signature on which must be legally witnessed if so required by the railway, shall be drawn up in conformity with the legal requirements of the State in which the railway responsible for settlement is situated.* *2.411*

Comments

1. Claims

Article 53 is concerned with the form and content of a claim against the railway. *2.412*
Except in so far as the matter is regulated by CIM, notably in Article 53, the

11. See Allégret, Fasc. 686, 14.
12. Rodière, No. 524.
13. *Paris 14.10.68*, Bull.OCTI 1969.153, 157; *Paris 7.7.82*, BT 1982.430; Rodière, No. 523; but cf. *Paris 14.4.47*, S 1947.2.111; *Rb Antwerp 16.10.67* (1971) 6 ETL 689.

meaning of a claim is a matter for the *lex fori.*[1] Most courts are likely to agree with the German court which insisted that a claim must be express rather than implied and that a claim for interest could not be implied from a claim in respect of damage.[2] To express reservations is probably not enough. The gist of the communication must be not simply that loss or damage has occurred but that the writer holds the railway responsible.[3]

2.413 As the purpose is to put the railway on its guard, to alert the railway that an issue has arisen and should be taken seriously, the claim must contain enough information to have this effect.[4] By requiring reasons, DCU 1 settled what had been a point of past controversy. However, a related point remains unsettled. The "other documents", which appear to be an option for the claimant in Article 53.4,[5] appear to be made compulsory by DCU 2 and 3; no clear solution to this apparent contradiction is to be found in the decided cases.[6] Moreover, the address or office of the railway, to which the claim and documents should be sent, is not stated in CIM and this too remains the subject of some debate.[7]

2.414 An outstanding problem for claimants is that they may not be in a position supply the supporting evidence required before receiving the railway's report under Article 52. Merely to require ascertainment of the railway does not suspend the period of prescription and there appears to be no sanction in CIM to compel the railway to act expeditiously.[8] A problem for the railway in some instances is that it will not be in a position to gauge its response, unless the claim contains some indication of quantum. This too may well depend on ascertainment.

2. *Form*

2.415 A claim in the sense of Article 53 does not require any formal procedural steps, although the claimant may decide to move to a formal stage at once—apart from its significance in the procedural law of the forum, the issue of an appropriate writ would amount to a claim in the sense of Article 53. However, it does not have to take that form for the purpose of Article 53; what is primarily contemplated by Article 53 is an informal claim, which is a cheaper and more accommodating way of proceeding and which, as the effect of the (informal) claim is to suspend the limitation period, does not prejudice the possibility of formal action.[9] Further, conversely, to make an informal claim in the sense of Article 53 is not, as has been

1. *Rouen 13.1.87,* BT 1987.183, *sur renvoi* from *Cass. 18.12.84,* BT 1985.331. For the history of the notion of claim under CIM, see Matyassy, Bull.OCTI 1971.44.

2. *Lg Frankfurt 1.2.89,* TranspR 1989.363. For English law, generally, see *West Wake Price & Co.* v. *Ching* [1957] 1 W.L.R. 45; and, as regards a claim against a carrier, see: *Muller Batavier* v. *Laurent Transport Co.* [1977] 1 Lloyd's Rep. 411.

3. *Muller* (above).

4. Generally in this sense: *A/S Rendall* v. *Arcos* (1937) 58 Ll.L.Rep. 287, 292 (H.L.).

5. In this sense: Helm, Art. 41, Anm 4.

6. Helm (*loc. cit.*) cites *Paris 30.9.70,* Bull.OCTI 1972.69; *OLG Munich 22.9.77* VersR 1978.853; *OLG Cologne* Bull.OCTI 1977.106; *BGH 16.3.79* (1981) 16 ETL 718, 725; VersR 1979.765; *Lg Cologne 4 8.81,* Bull.OCTI 1982.32.

7. Spera, Art. 53, Anm 5.

8. *Cass 9.5.90* (reported on Lexis).

9. Helm, Art. 41, Anm 1.

held in some countries in the past, a condition precedent to the right to bring a (formal) action against the railway.[10] A proposal to include a rule to this effect in CIM was rejected in 1924 and again in 1970.[11] However, a claimant who does not make an informal claim before issuing a writ, may find that he must pay costs.[12]

The claim must be in writing: Article 53.1. Writing is not defined but its meaning is left to national law which, according to one leading commentator,[13] is the law of the place where the claim is made. English law on the point is to be found in Schedule 1 to the Interpretation Act 1978: writing includes "typing, printing, lithography, photography, and other modes of representing or reproducing words in visible form". The language of the claim is another point which must be determined by national law. This too is said to be the language of the place where the claim is made.[14] *2.416*

3. Effects

One of the concerns behind Article 53 is to safeguard the position of the railway. It is to ensure that on settlement sleeping dogs lie; and before that it is to ensure that, as between consignor and consignee, the railway is squaring up to the right one, the one truly entitled to claim under Article 54: hence the documentary requirements of article 53.3, which should be read with Article 54.3 and Article 31. One commentator speaks of the blocking effect (*Sperrwirkung*) of the duplicate consignment note.[15] This requirement has been strictly applied by the Belgian Court of Cassation on the ground that formalities must be observed to the letter in the interests of uniformity of interpretation of CIM. The court rejected the argument that other documents, containing all the information to be found in the consignment note, would do instead of the consignment note.[16] *2.417*

Another concern behind Article 53 is to safeguard the position of the claimant: a claim presented in accordance with Article 53 suspends the period of limitation: see Article 58.3 and also Article 57.2(c). Moreover interest runs for the claimant from the date of the claim: Article 27.3 and Article 47. *2.418*

A final and more general concern lies in the purpose of the second paragraph of Article 53.4 concerning documentary evidence of the settlement of a claim. This is to create a document which is conclusive that the claim has been settled.[17] Is it essential? In a case before the Hungarian Supreme Court,[18] the railway admitted liability for the theft of the goods but contended that it was not obliged to pay unless the original consignment note was produced. Finding no resolution of this argument in CIM, the court turned to national law. It found no answer in the law of carriage, and resorted to more general principles of proof. As there were other *2.419*

10. Allégret, Fasc. 686, 21; Spera, Art. 53, Anm 2.
11. Matyassy, Bull.OCTI 1971.44, 47–48.
12. Spera, *loc. cit.*
13. Spera, Art. 53, Anm 4.
14. Spera (*loc. cit.*).
15. Helm, Art. 41, Anm 3.
16. *Cass. Belg. 8.4.88*, ULR 1989 (II) 830.
17. See Spera, Art. 53, Anm 17.
18. *Supreme Court, Hungary, No. III. 31 077.1989*, Bull.OCTI 1991.112.

documents which satisfied the purpose of the second paragraph of Article 53.4, the railway's contention was rejected.

2.420 **Article 54, Persons who may bring an action against the railway**

1. An action for the recovery of a sum paid under the contract of carriage may only be brought by the person who made the payment.

2. An action in respect of the cash-on-delivery payments provided for in Article 17 may only be brought by the consignor.

3. Other actions arising from the contract of carriage may be brought:

(a) by the consignor, until such time as the consignee has:
  (i) taken possession of the consignment note,
  (ii) accepted the goods, or
  (iii) asserted his rights under Article 28.4 or Article 31;

(b) by the consignee, from the time when he has:
  (i) taken possession of the consignment note,
  (ii) accepted the goods,
  (iii) asserted his rights under Article 28.4, or
  (iv) asserted his rights under Article 31 provided that the right of action shall be extinguished from the time when the person designated by the consignee in accordance with Article 31.1(c) has taken possession of the consignment note, accepted the goods, or asserted his rights under Article 28.4.

4. In order to bring an action, the consignor must produce the duplicate of the consignment note. Failing this, in order to bring an action under paragraph 3(a) he must produce an authorisation from the consignee or furnish proof that the consignee has refused to accept the consignment.

In order to bring an action, the consignee shall produce the consignment note if it has been handed over to him.

Comments

1. Persons entitled to sue

2.421 Article 54 identifies the persons with the right to claim against a railway in respect of loss of or damage or delay to goods. Those persons are the consignor and consignee, the one or the other, not both, and nobody else. Thus, COD payments under Article 17 can be sought, as stated in Article 54.2, only by the consignor. Less obvious is the effect of Article 54.1, however, in practice only the consignor or the consignee can be persons who pay sums "under the contract of carriage".[1]

2.422 Actions other than those covered by Article 54.1 and Article 54.2, the actions referred to in Article 54.3, are principally actions for loss of, damage or delay to the goods, as well as actions such as those for loss of documents (Article 25.3), and for fault in the completion of Customs or administrative formalities (Article 26.2)—unless the claimant seeks recovery of a sum paid and it is a case of Article 54.1. Note that the consignee also has rights of action under Article 30.3 and Article 33.5, distinct of rights under Article 54.[2] Presumably, an action for refusal to carry goods (Article 3.6) does not arise from the contract of carriage.[3] But Article 54.3 does embrace actions for breach of the contract of carriage, although the breach is not

1. Spera, Art. 54, Anm 5.
2. Allégret, Fasc. 686, 48.
3. Spera, Art. 54, Anm 8.

concerned with carriage itself and is thus outside Article 36, such as damage to the environment.[4]

As regards "other actions" an obvious question is who, consignor or consignee, is entitled to sue? The answer is found in paragraphs (a) and (b). As soon as the consignee performs one of the acts listed in Article 54.3(b), thus asserting rights under the contract of carriage, the right of action passes to the consignee from the consignor,[5] unless, of course, the consignee assigns the rights (back) to the consignor.[6] In general terms the right of action passes with the right of modification under Article 30.[7] Moreover, when the consignee modifies the contract to require delivery to a third person, the right of action passes from the consignee to that person: Article 54.3(b)(iv). The underlying idea is that the person entitled to sue should be the person who has suffered the relevant loss.[8] However, this principle is compromised in the interests of certainty in order, in particular, to leave the railway in little doubt about who is entitled to bring claims. *2.423*

2. *The designated consignee*

If the claimant is the person entitled under Article 54, the clear implication is that it is irrelevant whether that person has paid carriage charges owed to the railway or refused to accept the goods: conditions (i) to (iv) of Article 54.3(b) are alternative conditions. More importantly perhaps, it is irrelevant, for example when the claimant is a designated consignee acting as the agent of somebody else, that the claimant has suffered no loss.[9] The consignee, who is entitled to sue under Article 54, is the person designated as consignee in the consignment note. Thus there is no right of action for the "real consignee", i.e. the person to whom the apparent or designated consignee, who may also be the consignor, has sold the goods.[10] This is the position even though the railway was aware of the situation[11] or the real consignee was mentioned in the note, although not as consignee but as the person to notify or who paid outstanding charges on behalf of the nominal consignee.[12] Also excluded is the person such as a bank at the disposal of which the goods are held by the nominal consignee.[13] The reason given for this strict and literal interpretation of Article 54 is that, in general, it is hard for the railway to know and, sometimes, for people to agree on who is the real consignee; certainty and practicality require simplicity, so it is the nominal consignee who is entitled to sue.[14] *2.424*

4. *BGH 14.11.1991* Bull.OCTI 1992.157; (1993) 28 ETL 621.
5. *Lyon 12.2.71*, Bull.OCTI 1973.209; *Cass. 15.5.74*, ULR 1975 (II) 384; Bull.OCTI 1976.13; *Paris 21.11.85*, BT 1986.645; *Cass. 13.6.89* (1990) 25 ETL 87, BT 1989.527; Allégret, Fasc. 686, 46. Cf. CMR: Rodière, No. 573.
6. *Lyon 3.4.98*, BTL 1998.739.
7. *BGH 6.7.79* (1980) 15 ETL 863, 869; Helm, Art. 42, Anm 5; Rodière, No. 573.
8. Spera, Art. 54, Anm 2.
9. *Cass. 13.6.89* (1990) 25 ETL 87; Matyassy, Bull.OCTI 1971.44, 52, 57.
10. *Lyon 24.11.70*, Bull.OCTI 1973.186. See also *Paris 10.4.62*, Bull.OCTI 1964.257.
11. *TC Paris 29.9.71*, ULR 1973 (II) 452.
12. *Cass. 19.4.82*, BT 1982.308; see also *Cass. 28.10.63*, JCP 1964–13496.
13. *Paris 31.10.74* (1976) 11 ETL 120, 130–131.
14. Durand, notes to *Paris 10.4.62* and again to *Cass. 28.10.63* (above); also in this sense: Matyassy, Bull.OCTI 1971.44, 57.

3. Persons excluded

2.425 Under Article 54 the entitlement of consignor or consignee is exclusive; other persons, not least the "real consignee" (see Comment 2, above), are not entitled to sue.[15] Exclusivity is reinforced by Article 51: if, as appears, Article 54 contains one of the "conditions and limitations" of CIM, no other persons can bring an action, contractual or extra-contractual, in respect of loss, damage or delay within the scope of CIM, not even the common law owner: although the owner's right action survives the less exclusive provisions of CMR,[16] it appears that his action would not be admitted under CIM.[17] If the person who has suffered the relevant loss, such as the owner of the goods, wants to claim but is not the person entitled, that person must obtain an assignment of the right of action from the consignor or the designated consignee.[18]

2.426 Assignees and subrogees have been allowed to sue under CIM, their entitlement being a matter on which CIM is silent and thus governed by the *lex fori* in accordance with Article 10.[19] In France[20] as well as England,[21] the insurer can sue once subrogated to the rights of the insured by payment of the insurance money. The rights of these persons, however, are derivative from the consignor or consignee, the persons primarily and exclusively entitled to sue.

2.427

Article 55, Railways against which an action may be brought

1. An action for the recovery of a sum paid under the contract of carriage may be brought against the railway which has collected that sum or against the railway on whose behalf it was collected.

2. An action in respect of the cash on delivery payments provided for in Article 17 may only be brought against the forwarding railway.

3. Other actions arising from the contract of carriage may be brought against the forwarding railway, the railway of destination or the railway on which the event giving rise to the proceedings occurred.

Such actions may be brought against the railway of destination even if it has received neither the goods nor the consignment note.

4. If the plaintiff can choose between several railways, his right to choose shall be extinguished as soon as he brings an action against any one of them.

5. An action may be brought against a railway other than those specified in paragraphs 1, 2 and 3 when instituted by way of counterclaim or by way of exception to the principal claim based on the same contract of carriage.

15. Haenni, No. 281.

16. See Cashmore in [1991] J.B.L. 362 on *Texas Instruments Ltd.* v. *Nasan (Europe) Ltd* [1991] 1 Lloyd's Rep. 146.

17. Allégret, Fasc. 686, 59; Haenni, No. 281; Matyassy, Bull.OCTI 1971.44, 51, 53.

18. Also the accepted solution in France: *Cass. com. 13.6.89*, BT 1989.527.

19. *Brussels 3.5.76*, Bull.OCTI 1978.167; ULR 1978 (II) 314; *BGH 16.3.79* (1981) 16 ETL 718, 724; *Paris 21.11.85*, BT 1986.645; *OLG Düsseldorf 18.1.1996*, Bull.OCTI 2000.179; Haenni, No. 281; Rodière, No. 573. The validity of assignment or subrogation are matters for national law: Spera, Art. 54, Anm 3.

20. *Paris 7.7.82*, BT 1982. 430; *Cass. com. 13.6.89*, BT 1989.527; Allégret, Fasc. 686, 61.

21. *Page* v. *Scottish Ins.* (1929) 33 Ll.L.Rep. 138 (C.A.).

Comments

1. Choice

Article 55 identifies the railways against which actions under CIM may be brought. The identified targets are lined up for claimants entitled to sue in the corresponding paragraphs (1 to 3) of Article 54. This symmetry reflects the legal thinking of "central Europe",[1] whereby the *Activlegitimation* of Article 54 is balanced by the *Passivlegitimation* of Article 55. Article 55 covers only actions (by consignor or consignee) *against* the railway, however, it should not be inferred that actions cannot be brought *by* the railway against the consignor or consignee; on the contrary actions can be brought by the railway under Article 19.4 (defective packing), Article 20.3 (defective loading), Article 25.3 (defective documents) and actions in respect of charges.[2] In these actions *Legitimation* is a matter for national law.[3] *2.428*

As regards actions for loss of, damage or delay to goods, the *2.429*

"principle governing the liability of successive carriers by rail participating in the transport of a through consignment under the Convention is quite similar to that which used to apply in [England] before the nationalisation of the railways. The contract is made by the railway which accepts the goods for carriage; and this railway is responsible for the entire journey, including delivery. At the same time, however, each succeeding railway is also liable, but unless it is the first or the last of the railways participating in the transport, it is only liable for what happens while it is responsible for the goods . . . The last carrier, however, the 'railway of destination' is in a special position, and this is the feature of the Convention which distinguishes its principles from those which used to apply in [England]. The policy which the Convention seeks to implement is clear: claims against railways for loss, damage or delay will normally be made by the consignor or the consignee. The Convention seeks to ensure that both of them are able to make their claims against the railway authorities of their own countries . . . The consignor is more likely to wish to claim from the first railway, and the consignee from the last, but both are free to do either."[4]

The right of choice is absolute: if the consignee chooses to sue the last railway, so be it, however clear it is that the damage was done while the goods were in the hands of a different railway,[5] so action against the intermediate railway is relatively rare. The second sentence of Article 55.3, which spells this out, was intended to remove doubt on the matter,[6] doubt which still dogs carriers by road as regards the corresponding provision of CMR, Article 36 (para. 1.221, above). Article 55.3 is a corollary of Article 54(3)(b)(iii).[7] *2.430*

2. The consequences of choice

Once the claimant has selected the target and brought an action in the appropriate court (see Article 56), the claimant's right of action against the other railways *2.431*

1. Allégret, Fasc. 686, 65.
2. Spera, Art. 55, Anm 2.
3. Spera, *loc. cit.*
4. Kahn-Freund, pp. 441–442.
5. Matyassy, Bull.OCTI 1971.44, 55.
6. Matyassy, *loc. cit.*
7. Spera, Art. 55, Anm 13.

involved is extinguished: Article 55.4. Moreover, if action is instituted as described in Article 55.5, the claimant is said to lose the right of action against the other railways identified in Article 55.1–3.[8] A right is extinguished under Article 55.4, it has been said,[9] even if the railway chosen is insolvent and unable to pay the compensation awarded. However, if an action is brought against an intermediate railway in the mistaken belief that it was on that railway that the event occurred, a later action will be allowed against one of the other railways.[10] An action is "brought" when proceedings are commenced according to the law of the court in question. If an action is brought against more than one railway, the court will entertain the action against the railway subject to the jurisdiction of the court and dismiss the other actions.[11] The railways are liable collectively (Article 35), and, if an action has been brought successfully against one railway and that railway has compensated the claimant, that railway may have a right of recourse against one or more of the other railways under Article 60.

2.432

Article 56, Competence

Actions brought under the Uniform Rules may only be instituted in the competent court of the State having jurisdiction over the defendant railway, unless otherwise provided in agreements between States or in acts of concession.

When a railway operates independent railway systems in different States, each system shall be regarded as a separate railway for the purposes of this Article.

Comments

1. The effect of Article 56

2.433 Article 56 regulates jurisdiction in respect of actions against the railway, but not in respect of actions by the railway against, for example, the consignor.[1] Moreover, if the action is a recourse action by one railway against another, jurisdiction is regulated not by Article 56 but by Article 63. Under Article 56, in principle, action may be brought only in the courts of the "State having jurisdiction over the defendant railway", i.e., the state in which the railway is established and thus domiciled. For this purpose, an overseas agency, it has been said, does not count.[2] Thus, *prima facie*, the High Court does not have jurisdiction over SNCF because SNCF has an office in Piccadilly. However, if, as discussed below, the Brussels Convention of 1968 applies, the High Court may have jurisdiction in such a case under Article 5(3) of the Brussels Convention, whereby a "person domiciled in a

8. Spera, Art. 55, Anm 18.
9. Spera, Art. 55, Anm 15.
10. Spera, *loc cit.*
11. Allégret, Fasc. 686, 71.
1. *Budapest No. 25. P21 289/1968/29*, Bull.OCTI 1972.215; ULR 1973 (I) 286; *TGI Laon 22.6.1999*, BTL 1999.895.
2. Matyassy, Bull.OCTI 1971.44, 56.

Contracting State", such as France, "may be sued in another Contracting State, as regards a dispute arising out of the operations of a branch, agency or other establishment, in the courts for the place in which the branch, agency or other establishment is situated".[3] An agency connotes "an organ or business presence which is in itself an extension or emanation of the defendant's own business and subject to its general control".[4]

Prima facie the Convention on Jurisdiction and the Enforcement of Judgments in Civil and Commercial Matters, signed at Brussels in 1968 and enacted in the United Kingdom by the Civil Jurisdiction and Judgments Act 1982, does not apply. Article 57 of the Convention provides that it "shall not affect any conventions to which the Contracting States are or will be parties and which, in relation to particular matters, govern jurisdiction". Thus *prima facie* carriage is not within the scope of the 1968 Convention because, for the particular matter of CIM carriage, jurisdiction is governed by Article 56 of CIM. However, Rodière contended that Article 56 does not in any significant sense "govern" jurisdiction,[5] but merely says that the court with jurisdiction has jurisdiction. Indeed, Article 46, the corresponding provision in CIM (1999) is based on Article 31.1 of CMR (para. 1.184, above) and is significantly more prescriptive than Article 56. If Rodière is right, the courts of England must apply the 1968 Convention and its central rule of domicile when CIM (1980) applies. 2.434

2. *The competent court*

In England the competent court is the High Court. That is clear, but the possibility of instituting an action in Paris against the SNCF or in Bonn against the DB poses a problem not found in the UK. When a dispute arises for settlement—a dispute arising out of carriage governed by CIM—jurisdiction is determined first at international level by Article 56 or, in the case of a recourse action, by Article 63 or perhaps by the Brussels Convention; see Comment 1, above. If the action is brought in England, it is brought in the High Court in London, which has competence in such cases throughout the State, and that is the end of the matter. If, however, action is to be brought in countries such as France or Germany, there remains the further problem of determining the court with territorial competence within France or Germany.[6] Whereas this problem has proved difficult under CMR, as some courts have considered that competence at the national level is also regulated by the CMR, if Rodière is right that Article 56 is almost no rule at all, the problem at national level will be governed by the *lex fori*. 2.435

3. Cf. Allégret, Fasc. 686, 80.

4. *New Hampshire Ins. Co.* v. *Strabag Bau AG* [1990] 2 Lloyd's Rep. 61, 69, affd. [1992] 1 Lloyd's Rep. 361 (C.A.). *De Bloos Sprl* v. *Bouyer SCA* [1976] E.C.R. 1497.

5. Rodière, No. 616 ; see also in this sense Spera, Art. 56, Anm 2, but cf. Allégret, Fasc. 686, 75 and 82.

6. Generally on this question, see Miller, *Liability in International Air Transport* (1977), pp. 285 *et seq.*; and, as regards French law, Allégret, Fasc. 686, 83 *et seq.*

2.436 **Article 57, Extinction of right of action against the railway**

1. Acceptance of the goods by the person entitled shall extinguish all rights of action against the railway arising from the contract of carriage in case of partial loss, damage or exceeding of the transit period.

2. Nevertheless, the right of action shall not be extinguished:

(a) in the case of partial loss or of damage, if:

(i) the loss or damage was ascertained before the acceptance of the goods in accordance with Article 52 by the person entitled;

(ii) the ascertainment which should have been carried out under Article 52 was omitted solely through the fault of the railway;

(b) in the case of loss or damage which is not apparent and is not ascertained until after acceptance of the goods by the person entitled, provided that he:

(i) asks for ascertainment in accordance with Article 52 immediately after discovery of the loss or damage and not later than seven days after the acceptance of the goods;

(ii) and, in addition, proves that the loss or damage occurred between the time of acceptance for carriage and the time of delivery;

(c) in cases where the transit period has been exceeded, if the person entitled has, within sixty days, asserted his rights against one of the railways referred to in Article 55.3;

(d) if the person entitled proves that the loss or damage results from an act or omission, done with intent to cause such loss or damage, or recklessly and with knowledge that such loss or damage would probably result.

3. If the goods have been reconsigned in accordance with Article 38.1 rights of action in case of partial loss or of damage, arising from one of the previous contracts of carriage, shall be extinguished as if there had been only one contract of carriage.

Comments

1. Extinction of rights of action

2.437 Article 57, which provides for the "extinction" of rights of action against a railway, follows closely the lines of the German EVO, Article 93. The central idea of Article 57, which is found in a number of legal systems, is that once the goods have been delivered to the consignee and been accepted and, it should be added, become vulnerable to loss or damage in the hands of the consignee, the right of action against the railway is and should be extinguished.

2.438 Evidently, a rule of extinction geared to the point of delivery and acceptance cannot be applied if the goods have been lost en route. For this situation, a different rule is found in Article 57.2(c). Equally, the rule is inappropriate for actions, for example, in respect of total loss, and is limited by Article 57.1 to actions for "partial loss, damage or exceeding the transit period". Other actions may be subject to limitation under Article 58 but not extinction under Article 57. Moreover, a different rule was also required for cases of reconsignment, as no actual delivery and acceptance and no opportunity for the consignee to see the goods and ask for ascertainment occurs between the ultimate and penultimate consignments in order to trigger the extinction rules in Article 57.1 and Article 57.2. In such a case Article 57.3 applies.

2.439 In addition, a punitive exception to the main rules of extinction, whereby the rules for extinction are disapplied, is made by Article 57.2(d) where the railway has been guilty of the conduct described. See the Comment on Article 44.

2. Exception: loss or damage ascertained before acceptance

When the goods are tendered by the railway to the consignee, the consignee must look at the goods before accepting them and taking delivery. In most if not all cases acceptance and delivery are concurrent and co-extensive: see Article 28, Comment 3 (paragraphs 2.194 *et seq.*, above). If there is any suspicion of loss or damage, the consignee must demand ascertainment under Article 52. If loss etc. has been ascertained, the right of action is not extinguished: Article 57.2(a).[1] When this procedure does not work, either because the railway is at fault in not having ascertained the state of the goods, or because the loss etc. is not apparent on delivery and acceptance, a different rule is provided in Article 57.2; see Comment 3, below. Fault means negligence or worse, i.e., that the railway should have discovered or presumed loss etc. but failed to do so, or did so but failed negligently to draw up a report, as required by Article 52.1.[2] If the procedure for ascertainment under Article 52.1 is followed by the railway, but its report concludes that no loss or damage has occurred, one view is that the right of action is extinguished. However, this view is controversial and the better view is that this does not follow until the claimant has had an opportunity to decide whether to seek the ascertainment of an expert under Article 52.2.[3] *2.440*

3. Exception: loss or damage not ascertained before acceptance

If the damage is not apparent at the time of acceptance, the consignee has seven days to discover it and demand ascertainment under Article 52. The driving considerations behind this provision are speed, certainty and economy[4] A leading commentator has pointed out that, if the loss etc. is not apparent, Article 57.2(b) applies even though the consignee *is* aware from other information acquired at an earlier time that loss etc. has occurred.[5] *2.441*

The meaning of apparent loss or damage is not explained by CIM. What is apparent depends in many cases on the point in time at which it is assessed. Here, the relevant time is the time at which delivery is tendered by the railway. In general, damage is not apparent when it falls within the well established notion of latent defect: a defect that could not have been discovered on a reasonable examination. Whether examination is reasonable depends not only on the manner in which the examination was carried out but also on whether it was reasonable to conduct an examination of that kind at all in the particular circumstances.[6] A latent defect is a defect which could not be discovered on such an examination as a reasonably careful skilled man would make. A similar notion of non-apparent damage is found in other carriage Conventions; see CMR Article 8, Comment 3 (paras. 1.42 *et seq.*, above) and HP Article 11, Comment 2 (paras. 3.75 *et seq.*, below). *2.442*

1. E.g. *Paris 21.12.94*, BTL 1995.163.
2. *Paris 15.5.63*, Bull.OCTI 1965.196. Spera, Art. 57, Anm 11.
3. Helm, EVO, Art. 93, Anm 5.
4. Spera, Art. 57, Anm 2.
5. Spera, Art. 57, Anm 12.
6. *The Amstelslot* [1963] 2 Lloyd's Rep. 223 (H.L.).

2.443 Approaching the issue in this way, it seems that loss or damage is apparent only when suspicion should have been aroused by what the consignee should have observed in the course of taking delivery of the goods.[7] Similarly, in relation to the provisions of German law (EVO) on which Article 57 was based, damage is apparent when there is clear external evidence suggesting that the goods might be damaged; the consignee cannot turn a blind eye and must open the package or container to see what has happened to the goods, otherwise he will be deemed to have accepted the goods and will lose his right of action against the railway.[8] In particular, if the obligation of the railway is to deliver an entire wagon load, a wagon which is covered and sealed, the state of the contents is not apparent at the relevant time. If, however, the goods form part of a load and have to be extracted from the wagon for delivery, it has been held that the same damage may be such that their actual condition is apparent.[9] Whether damage to the wagon or to packing necessarily suggests damage to the contents depends on the nature of the damage and the nature of the contents, for example their fragility.[10]

2.444 If the loss or damage is not apparent, the claimant is required by Article 57.2(b) to ask for ascertainment in accordance with Article 52 not later than seven days after the acceptance of the goods. If the person makes a claim[11] against the railway, that is regarded as "asking for ascertainment". However, although the claimant has seven days in which to ask for it, that means seven days to actually get the request to the railway; and, if the loss or damage is discovered much sooner, the request must be sent "immediately".[12] The additional requirement, to prove that the loss or damage occurred between the time of acceptance for carriage and the time of delivery, may be very difficult.[13] See Article 11, Comment 3.

2.445

Article 58, Limitation of actions

1. The period of limitation for an action arising from the contract of carriage shall be one year.

Nevertheless, the period of limitation shall be two years in the case of an action:

(a) to recover a cash on delivery payment collected by the railway from the consignee;
(b) to recover the proceeds of a sale effected by the railway;
(c) for loss or damage resulting from an act or omission done with intent to cause such loss or damage, or recklessly and with knowledge that such loss will probably result;
(d) arising from one of the contracts of carriage prior to the reconsignment in the case provided for in Article 38.1.

2. The period of limitation shall run:

(a) in actions for compensation for total loss, from the thirtieth day after the expiry of the transit period;

7. See Spera, Art. 57, Anm 12.
8. *Lg Aurich 5.11.75*, Bull.OCTI 1976.145; *Ag Frankfurt 8.8.90*, TranspR 1991.104; *OLG Düsseldorf 11.3.1993* Bull.OCTI 1994.20.
9. *Paris 30.3.73*, Bull.OCTI 1974.217; ULR 1975 (I) 278.
10. *Paris 30.9.70*, Bull.OCTI 1972.69, 75.
11. See Art. 53, Comment 1.
12. Spera, Art. 57, Anm 14 and 15.
13. See e.g. *Lyon 12.2.71*, Bull.OCTI 1973.209.

(b) in actions for compensation for partial loss, or damage or for exceeding the transit period, from the day when delivery took place;
(c) in actions for payment or refund of carriage charges, supplementary charges, other charges or surcharges, or for correction of charges in case of a tariff being wrongly applied or of an error in calculation or collection:
  (i) if payment has been made, from the day of payment;
  (ii) if payment has not been made, from the day when the goods were accepted for carriage if payment is due from the consignor, or from the day when the consignee took possession of the consignment note if payment is due from him;
  (iii) in the case of sums to be paid under a charges note, from the day on which the railway submits to the consignor the account of charges provided for in Article 15.7; if no such account has been submitted, the period in respect of sums due to the railway shall run from the thirtieth day following the expiry of the transit period;
(d) in an action by the railway for recovery of a sum which has been paid by the consignee instead of by the consignor or vice versa and which the railway is required to refund to the person entitled, from the day of the claim for a refund;
(e) in actions relating to cash on delivery as provided for in Article 17, from the thirtieth day following the expiry of the transit period;
(f) in actions to recover the proceeds of a sale, from the day of the sale;
(g) in actions to recover additional duty demanded by Customs or other administrative authorities, from the day of the demand made by such authorities;
(h) in all other cases, from the day when the right of action arises.

The day indicated for the commencement of the period of limitation shall not be included in the period.

3. When a claim18 is presented to a railway in accordance with Article 53 together with the necessary supporting documents, the period of limitation shall be suspended until the day that the railway rejects the claim by notification in writing and returns the documents. If part of the claim is admitted, the period of limitation shall recommence in respect of that part of the claim still in dispute. The burden of proof of receipt of the claim or of the reply and of the return of the documents shall rest on the party who relies on those facts.

The period of limitation shall not be suspended by further claims having the same object.

4. A right of action which has become time-barred may not be exercised by way of counter claim or relied upon by way of exception.

5. Subject to the foregoing provisions, the suspension and interruption of periods of limitation shall be governed by national law.

Additional Uniform Regulation (DCU)

DCU 1, to § 2(b) and (c) *In calculating limitation periods, the day of acceptance of the goods by the person entitled shall not be included.* 2.446

When a limitation period ends on a Saturday, Sunday or legal holiday, it shall be extended to the next working day.

Comments

1. The nature and scope of Article 58

Article 58, a complex provision of which a significantly simplified version is now found in Article 48 of CIM (1999), regulates what common lawyers usually call limitation of actions. If the period has run, the effect as seen by continental lawyers, however, is not just to bar the action but to extinguish it.[1] Nonetheless, whereas 2.447

1. E.g. Rodière, No. 628. See Matyassy, Bull.OCTI 1971.44.

Article 57 is headed "Extinction of right of action . . . ", Article 58 is headed "Limitation of actions".

2.448 Unlike Article 57, Article 58 applies to all actions, regardless of the type of loss or damage in question or of whether the action is brought by the consignor, consignee or the railway, provided that it is one "arising from the contract of carriage".[2] Article 58 does not apply, however, to actions against the railway for having refused to contract. Nor does it apply to recourse actions by one railway against another; or to actions by a railway against the owner of a wagon, defects in which have caused loss to the railway.[3] In such cases limitation is a matter for the *lex fori*.

2. The limitation period

2.449 The period of limitation, one year in most cases but two years in particular cases there listed, is the subject of Article 58.1. Of the listed cases for which the period is two years, case (a) is that of action to recover COD payments collected under Article 17. A longer period in this case, is said to be justified in order to prevent unjustified enrichment on the part of the railway.[4] The same is said of case (b), action to recover the proceeds of selling the goods under Article 33. Case (c) is self-explanatorily unsympathetic to the railway guilty of such conduct.[5] In case (d), when there has been reconsignment, the longer period is thought to be justified because the facts may not come to the knowledge of the eventual claimant until later than if there had been no reconsignment.

3. Starting dates

2.450 Starting dates are the subject of Article 58.2. The relevant date differs according to whether, on the one hand, it is a case of total loss,[6] or, on the other, a case of partial loss, damage[7] or delay.[8] Clearly, the day of delivery,[9] appropriate for the latter cases, is not appropriate for a case of total loss. It should be noted that, in the case of an international transit governed by CIM followed by a local movement governed not by CIM but by national law, delivery, for the purpose of limitation of actions under CIM, may not occur until the time when the goods are handed over at the end of the national movement.[10]

2.451 In addition, Article 58.2(c) prescribes starting dates for the action to recover charges of various kinds, including "carriage charges"[11] and "other charges". "Other charges" must be read in context, and cannot be read literally in isolation to

2. *OLG Düsseldorf 18.1.1996*, TranspR 1997.284, 286.
3. Allégret, Fasc. 686, 118 and 121; Spera, Art. 58, Anm 2.
4. Spera, Art. 58, Anm 6.
5. As to which, see Art. 44, above.
6. See Art. 40, Comment 1, above.
7. *Ibid.*
8. See Art. 27, Comment 1, above.
9. See Art. 28, Comment 3, above.
10. *Paris 10.4.62*, Bull.OCTI 1964.257, note by Durand.
11. See Art. 15, above.

cover, for example, the costs of selling the goods.[12] An action for "correction" of charges, which is also mentioned, is either an action for a "payment" or an action for a "refund" and thus, it seems, the reference to corrections is superfluous.[13]

The starting dates for particular kinds of case are by reference to important points in the sequence of events, such as acceptance of the goods for carriage,[14] when the consignee got possession of the consignment note,[15] or a date referable to the end of the transit period.[16] Article 58.2(h) has a residual rule for "all other cases" which include the following: *2.452*

(i) An action by the railway to recover the costs of storage and sale of goods. In one such case,[17] goods were sent from Rheims to Prato. The consignee led the consignor to believe that he would accept the goods and pay certain charges, but did not do so; nor did he demand the consignment note. Seven months later, the uncollected goods were sold but, as the proceeds were insufficient to cover charges, the railway brought an action against the consignor for the balance. The court held that the railway was entitled to this sum under (what is now) Article 15, but that the action was barred under (what is now) Article 58. The court rejected the argument that time should run from the sale, as this would allow the railway to prolong the effective limitation period. The claim for the costs of storage and sale, not being a charge relating to carriage under Article 58.2(c), was a case for Article 58.2(h).

(ii) An action by the railway in respect of damage caused to the property of the railway by the property of the defendant consignor or consignee. In one such case,[18] wagons owned by the defendant were registered with SNCF for use on the French network and, while carrying iron ore belonging to the defendant, derailed and damaged the track. An action by the railway was defeated by (what is now) Article 58. Although the wagons were granted entry to the network by a contract of registration (*contrat d'immatriculation*), damage occurred during the performance of an international contract for the carriage of goods, which was subject to CIM, and the court held that the CIM limitation period applied. However, the contract might well have been a contract to carry the goods of a third party and, if so, what then? The obligation alleged to have been broken concerned the defective condition of the wagons and had its basis less in the contract of carriage than in the contract of registration.[19] The decision can be supported, however, if the obligation is seen as an obligation of the

12. *Rheims 8.6.88*, BT 1989.481.
13. Spera, Art. 58, Anm 14.
14. See Art. 12, Comment 1, above, and Art. 20, Comment 1, above.
15. See Art. 28, Comment 3, above.
16. See Art. 27, Comment 1, above.
17. *Rheims 8.6.88*, BT 1989.481.
18. *Cass 11.4.67*, D.1967.649, JCP 1967–15212, (1969) 4 ETL 817, Bull.OCTI 1970.119.
19. Rodière, D.1967.649, 650; *idem*, but less emphatically, Durand, JCP 1967– 15212.

defendant incurred not *qua* owner of the wagon but *qua* consignor of the wagon load, hence an obligation based in the contract of carriage.[20]

(iii) An action in respect of total loss at destination. In one such case,[21] the goods had arrived at destination, but the railway was unable to prove, as the court required, that the goods had been delivered to the consignee. The goods were missing and the case was treated as one of total loss, to which, however, Article 58.2(a) was inappropriate, as the goods had arrived. The court applied sub-paragraph (h).

4. Suspension of the period

2.453 Suspension of the period of limitation, which is regulated by Article 58.3, occurs when a claim is properly made in accordance with Article 53. To require ascertainment by the railway under Article 52, however, is not the making of a claim and does not suspend the period of prescription—even though the would-be claimant may need the ascertainment in order to found a claim; see Article 52, Comment 1. Like the corresponding Article 32.2 of CMR (para. 1.196, above), Article 58 provides only for suspension of claims *against* the railway and not for the suspension of claims *by* the railway. There appears to be no satisfactory reason for this distinction.

2.454 On a natural and ordinary interpretation of these words, "the period of limitation" can "be suspended" only after the period has commenced.[22] Prior to commencement, during what has been called the antecedent period, there can be no suspension. This may mean, as has been held of CMR,[23] that if a claim is made in the antecedent period, any time between claim and the normal commencement date is a "suspended" period of suspension, to be *added* to the limitation period after the limitation period has begun.

2.455 Suspension of the period continues until the claim has been rejected in writing.[24] Concerning the meaning of rejection, see CMR Article 32, Comment 3 (paragraphs 1.203 *et seq.*, above). The requirement, that the railway must return "the documents" is the subject of controversy. A strict and literal view is that the railway must return each and every document sent in to sustain the claim.[25] However, the balance of opinion favours a less strict view whereby the railway is obliged to return only documents which are "indispensable" to the claimant,[26] and not those which could be easily replaced or of which the claimant has kept copies.[27] A similar dispute has persisted over the similar requirement in Article 32 of CMR.[28]

20. Rodière, *loc. cit.*
21. *Supreme Court, Hungary 1990*, Bull.OCTI 1991.109.
22. Loewe (1976) 11 ETL 311, 393, concerning Art. 32 of CMR.
23. *ICI plc* v. *MAT Transport* [1987] 1 Lloyd's Rep. 354.
24. See Art. 53, Comment 2.
25. Spera, Art. 58, Anm 27.
26. Allégret, Fasc. 686, 144.
27. *OLG Stuttgart 22.2.67*, Bull.OCTI 1968.75, 78.
28. See CMR Art. 32, Comment 3, paras. 1.203 *et seq.*, above.

5. Extension of the period

Article 58.4 contains a rule, found also in CMR Article 32.4 (para. 1.196, above), to prevent a dead claim being revived by way of counterclaim or exception thus obtaining a *de facto* extension of the period of limitation. The meaning of counterclaim or exception is a matter for the *lex fori*. For there to be a relevant counterclaim in English law, "claim and crossclaim must arise out of the same contract or transaction, and must also be so inseparably connected that the one ought not to be enforced without taking account of the other".[29] "Exception" in the authentic French version of CIM is sometimes translated not as "exception", as it is here, but as "set-off".[30] If the common law doctrine of deduction or abatement applies to set-off, it will be affected by the decision of the House of Lords in a case concerning the carriage of goods by sea,[31] that an action by a carrier for carriage charges cannot be abated in respect of loss of or damage to the goods. This rule has been applied also to CMR,[32] so its application to CIM cannot be ruled out. This will matter, however, only in the rare cases in which, in view of the differing commencement dates in Article 58, the period has run for an action by goods against the railway (for example, under Article 58.2(b)) before it has run for that of the railway against goods (for example, under Article 58.2(c)(iii)). *2.456*

Extension of the period is permitted in accordance with Article 58.5 by reference to national law. In England, extension of the period by party agreement is not permitted by the Limitation Act 1980: sections 27 *et seq.* on extension by agreement are inapplicable to CIM by virtue of section 39; however, such agreements are valid at common law[33] and have been allowed in relation to CMR.[34] *2.457*

Title VI, Relations between Railways: Article 59, Settlement of accounts between railways *2.458*

1. Any railway which has collected, either at the time of forwarding or on arrival, charges or other sums due under the contract of carriage must pay to the railways concerned their respective shares.

The methods of payment shall be settled by agreements between railways.

2. The forwarding railway shall be liable for carriage and other charges which it has failed to collect when the consignor has undertaken to pay them in accordance with Article 15.1

3. Should the railway of destination deliver the goods without collecting charges or other sums due under the contract of carriage, it shall be liable for these amounts.

4. Should one railway default in payment and such default be confirmed by the Central Office at the request of one of the creditor railways, the consequences thereof shall be borne by all the other railways which have taken part in the carriage in proportion to their shares of the carriage charges.

The right of recovery against the defaulting railway shall not be affected.

29. *Dole Dried Fruit & Nut Co.* v. *Trustin Kerwood Ltd* [1990] 2 Lloyd's Rep. 309, 311 (C.A.). For a German view, see *OLG Hamm 20.10.77*, Bull.OCTI 1979.73.

30. E.g. CIM 1961, Art. 47, and CMR, Art. 32, para. 1.96, above.

31. *The Aries* [1977] 1 All E.R. 398 (H.L.).

32. *R.H. & D. International* v. *IAS Animal Air Services* [1984] 2 All E.R. 203. See CMR Art. 32, Comment 3, paras. 1.203 *et seq.*, above.

33. *Lubovsky* v. *Snelling* [1944] K.B. 44 (C.A.).

34. *Zerowalt SpA* v. *International Express Co.*, 6 October 1989, unreported, but discussed by Clarke, *CMR*, para. 47e.

Comment

2.459 Article 59 and the whole of Title VI are concerned not with the contract of carriage but with relations between railways arising out of the contract of carrige. Although disputes arise between railways, they do not usually air their differences in the courts. Consequently, Title VI provoked little interest or comment until a scholarly analysis was published on successive carrige under CIM (1999).[1]

2.460

Article 60, Recourse in case of loss or damage

1. A railway which has paid compensation in accordance with the Uniform Rules, for total or partial loss or for damage, has a right of recourse against the other railways which have taken part in the carriage in accordance with the following provisions:

(a) the railway which has caused the loss or damage shall be solely liable for it;

(b) when the loss or damage has been caused by more than one railway, each shall be liable for the loss or damage it has caused; if such distinction cannot be made, the compensation shall be apportioned between those railways in accordance with (c);

(c) if it cannot be proved that the loss or damage has been caused by one or more railways in particular, the compensation shall be apportioned between all the railways which have taken part in the carriage, except those which can prove that the loss or damage was not caused on their lines; such apportionment shall be in proportion to the kilometric distances contained in the tariffs.

2. In the case of the insolvency of any one of the railways, the unpaid share due from it shall be apportioned among all the other railways which have taken part in the carriage, in proportion to the kilometric distances contained in the tariffs.

2.461

Article 61, Recourse in case of exceeding the transit period

1. Article 60 shall apply where compensation is paid for exceeding the transit period. If this has been caused by more than one railway, the compensation shall be apportioned between such railways in proportion to the length of the delay occurring on their respective lines.

2. The transit periods specified in Article 27 shall be apportioned in the following manner:

(a) where two railways have taken part in the carriage:

(i) the period for despatch shall be divided equally;

(ii) the period for transport shall be divided in proportion to the kilometric distances contained in the tariffs;

(b) where three or more railways have taken part in the carriage:

(i) the period for despatch shall be divided equally between the forwarding railway and the railway of destination;

(ii) the period for transport shall be divided between all the railways:

— one-third in equal shares

— the remaining two-thirds in proportion to the kilometric distances contained in the tariffs.

3. Any additional periods to which a railway may be entitled shall be allocated to that railway.

4. The interval between the time when the goods are handed over to the railway and commencement of the period for despatch shall be allocated exclusively to the forwarding railway.

5. Such apportionment shall only apply if the total transit period has been exceeded.

1. Glass [2003] BLI 72.

Article 62, Procedure for recourse *2.462*

1. The validity of the payment made by the railway exercising one of the rights of recourse under Articles 60 and 61 may not be disputed by the railway against which the right of recourse is exercised, when compensation has been determined by a court and when the latter railway duly served with notice, has been afforded an opportunity to intervene in the proceedings. The court seised of the main proceedings shall determine what time shall be allowed for such notification and for intervention in the proceedings.

2. A railway exercising its right of recourse must take proceedings by one and the same action against all the railways concerned with which it has not reached a settlement, failing which it shall lose its right of recourse in the case of those against which it has not taken proceedings.

3. The court shall give its decision in one and the same judgment on all recourse claims brought before it.

4. The railways against which such action has been brought shall have no further right of recourse.

5. Recourse proceedings may not be joined with proceedings for compensation taken by the person entitled on the basis of the contract of carriage.

Comment

According to a leading commentator,[1] Article 58, which concerns the limitation of actions, does not apply to recourse actions by one railway against another. Limitation of such actions is a matter for the *lex fori*. *2.463*

Article 63, Competence for recourse *2.464*

1. The courts of the country in which the railway against which the recourse claim has been made, has its headquarters shall have exclusive competence for all recourse claims.

2. When the action is to be brought against several railways, the plaintiff railway shall be entitled to choose the court in which it will bring the proceedings from among those having competence under paragraph 1.

Article 64, Agreements concerning recourse *2.465*

By agreement, railways may derogate from the provisions concerning reciprocal rights of recourse set out in Title VI, apart from that contained in Article 62.5.

Title VII, Exceptional provisions: Article 65, Temporary derogations *2.466*

1. If the economic and financial position of any State is such as to cause serious difficulty in applying Title VI, two or more States may, by agreements, derogate from Articles 15, 17 and 30 by determining, for traffic with the State in difficulty, that:

(a) consignments from each of them shall be forwarded charges paid by the consignor as far as the frontiers of the State in difficulty, but not beyond;

(b) consignments to destinations in each of them shall be forwarded charges paid by the consignor as far as the frontiers of the State in difficulty, but not beyond;

(c) consignments to or from the State in difficulty must not be made subject to any cash on delivery payment or disbursement, except up to specified amounts;

(d) the consignor may not modify the contract of carriage as far as concerns the country of destination, pre-payment of charges and cash on delivery payments.

1. Allégret, Fasc. 686, 118.

2. Under the conditions specified in paragraph 1 and with the authorisation of their Governments, the railways which have dealings with the railway of the State in difficulty may agree upon a derogation from Articles 15, 17 and 31 in the traffic exchanged between them and the railway of the State in difficulty.

Such a derogation shall be decided by a two thirds majority of the railways having dealings with the railway of the State in difficulty.

3. Measures taken in accordance with paragraph 1 and 2 shall be notified to Central Office.

The measures set out in paragraph 1 shall come into force at the earliest on the expiry of a period of eight days from the date of the letter by which the Central Office shall have notified such measures to the other States.

The measures set out in paragraph 2 shall come into force at the earliest on the expiry of a period of two days from the date of their publication in the States concerned.

4. Consignments already in transit shall not be affected by such measures.

5. Notwithstanding the provisions of this Article, each State may take unilateral measures in accordance with Article 3.4, letter (b).

[*The next paragraph is 2.477*]

II. INTERNATIONAL CARRIAGE OF GOODS BY RAIL: UNIFORM RULES CONCERNING THE CONTRACT OF INTERNATIONAL CARRIAGE OF GOODS BY RAIL: CIM (1999)[1]

A. CIM (1999): INTRODUCTION

A general revision of COTIF and also of CIV and CIM was adopted for signature on 3 June 1999 and called the Protocol of Vilnius.[2] The main features of the revised CIM, when compared with the current version are as follows. First, in view of the effective competition of alternative modes of transport, notably road transport and alternative train services, the railway's obligation to carry goods, which made sense only when there was a single railway with a dominant role in the movement of goods, has been abolished and, with it, the complex terms qualifying that obligation. *2.477*

Secondly, in these circumstances, the traditional and close regulation of carriage charges in Article 6 is no longer appropriate and has been abolished. *2.478*

Thirdly, the actual or potential separation of the entities responsible for the infrastructure from the train operators moving the goods lends itself to the CMR pattern of a single and simpler contract of carriage which (a) covers the entire movement, (b) drops the previous requirement of movement on specified lines and (c) focuses almost entirely on responsibility for the goods rather than anything other than the immediate environment (the wagon) in which they move. If, in the particular case of damage to goods, the cause lies in the infrastructure, that entity is regarded by the revised CIM as a service to which the train operator had recourse in order to carry out the contract of transport, and any action by the goods owner will be contractual (subject to CIM) against the train operator rather than delictual against the entity responsible. The purpose is to simplify CIM and at the same time to harmonise it as far as possible with the law governing other modes of transport. *2.479*

Although in many respects the new version of CIM is closer to the CMR than before, on some significant points it differs. For example, concerning scope, whereas it is enough for the CMR (Article 1) that either the place of taking over *or* the place of delivery be in a contracting state and that should also be enough now for carriage by rail, the revised CIM requires both. Moreover, feeder transport, notably by road, will be governed by CIM only if entirely within a single state—thus avoiding conflict with the CMR. *2.480*

According to a report by the Central Office,[3] one of the objectives of the 1999 text was to accommodate privatisation of the railways. *2.481*

1. Appendix B to the Convention concerning International Carriage by Rail (Cotif)
2. For the text see Bull.OCTI 1999.324. As regards its coming into force, see Bull.OCTI 1999.148. See also Burgmann [1995] Bull.OCTI 152. For an overview in English see Mutz, Unif. L. Rev. 1999.732. Concerning the unusually simple procedure for revising COTIF, see Mutz, Unif. L. Rev.2003.289, 292 *et seq*.
3. Bull.OCTI 1999.9, 15.

B. THE TEXT OF THE CIM (1999)

2.482 **Title I, General Provisions: Article 1, Scope**

§ 1 These Uniform Rules shall apply to every contract of carriage of goods by rail for reward when the place of taking over of the goods and the place designated for delivery are situated in two different Member States, irrespective of the place of business and the nationality of the parties to the contract of carriage.

§ 2 These Uniform Rules shall apply also to contracts of carriage of goods by rail for reward, when the place of taking over of the goods and the place designated for delivery are situated in two different States, of which at least one is a Member State and the parties to the contract agree that the contract is subject to these Uniform Rules.

§ 3 When international carriage being the subject of a single contract includes carriage by road or inland waterway in internal traffic of a Member State as a supplement to transfrontier carriage by rail, these Uniform Rules shall apply.

§ 4 When international carriage being the subject of a single contract of carriage includes carriage by sea or transfrontier carriage by inland waterway as a supplement to carriage by rail, these Uniform Rules shall apply if the carriage by sea or inland waterway is performed on services included in the list of services provided for in Article 24 § 1 of the Convention.

§ 5 These Uniform Rules shall not apply to carriage performed between stations situated on the territory of neighbouring States, when the infrastructure of these stations is managed by one or more infrastructure managers subject to only one of those States.

§ 6 Any State which is a party to a convention concerning international through carriage of goods by rail comparable with these Uniform Rules may, when it makes an application for accession to the Convention, declare that it will apply these Uniform Rules only to carriage performed on part of the railway infrastructure situated on its territory. This part of the railway infrastructure must be precisely defined and connected to the railway infrastructure of a Member State. When a State has made the above-mentioned declaration, these Uniform Rules shall apply only on the condition

(a) that the place of taking over of the goods or the place designated for delivery, as well as the route designated in the contract of carriage, is situated on the specified infrastructure or

(b) that the specified infrastructure connects the infrastructure of two Member States and that it has been designated in the contract of carriage as a route for transit carriage.

§ 7 A State which has made a reservation in accordance with § 6 may withdraw it at any time by notification to the Depositary. This withdrawal shall take effect one month after the day on which the Depositary notifies it to the Member States. The declaration shall cease to have effect when the convention referred to in § 6, first sentence, ceases to be in force for that State.

Comment

2.483 Article 1.1 is substantially the same as Article 1.1 of CMR (para. 1.8, above) except, of course, the reference is to rail rather than road but also, whereas CMR applies when one of the places concerned is situated in a Member State, CIM 1999 requires that both be situated in Member States. Voluntary adoption of CIM is possible but again CIM is more restrictive than CMR in that one of the States concerned must be situated in a Member State: Article 1.2.

2.484 Whereas CIM (1980) applies to a consignment of goods and the conclusion of the contract is a formal matter governed by Article 11 (para. 2.51, above), CIM (1999), like other modern carriage Conventions such as CMR and MC, applies to a contract of carriage concluded in the same manner as any other contract but subject to the evidentiary requirements of Article 6.

2.485 A feeder service (most likely to be by road) to the railway station is also regulated by CIM, provided that the service does not cross a State boundary, thus avoiding a clash with the compulsory scope of CMR: Article 1.3. Extended application to listed services such as ferries run by railways, a feature of CIM (1980), is preserved by Article 1.4

Article 2, Prescriptions of public law *2.486*

Carriage to which these Uniform Rules apply shall remain subject to the prescriptions of public law, in particular the prescriptions relating to the carriage of dangerous goods as well as the prescriptions of customs law and those relating to the protection of animals.

Comment

CIM (1999) eschews the complex provisions concerning dangerous and non-acceptable goods of the kind found in Article 4 and Article 5 of CIM (1980) (paras. 2.23 and 2.27, above); such matters are left to the relevant public law regulations of the *lex locus*. *2.487*

Article 3, Definitions *2.488*

For purposes of these Uniform Rules the term

(a) "carrier" means the contractual carrier with whom the consignor has concluded the contract of carriage pursuant to these Uniform Rules, or a subsequent carrier who is liable on the basis of this contract;

(b) "substitute carrier" means a carrier, who has not concluded the contract of carriage with the consignor, but to whom the carrier referred to in letter (a) has entrusted, in whole or in part, the performance of the carriage by rail;

(c) "General Conditions of Carriage" means the conditions of the carrier in the form of general conditions or tariffs legally in force in each Member State and which have become, by the conclusion of the contract of carriage, an integral part of it;

(d) "intermodal transport unit" means a container, swap body, semi-trailer or other comparable loading unit used in intermodal transport.

Comment

A definition provision such as Article 3 was not found in CIM (1980) but is commonly found in other transport Conventions or conditions. *2.489*

Article 4, Derogations *2.490*

§ 1 Member States may conclude agreements which provide for derogations from these Uniform Rules for carriage performed exclusively between two stations on either side of the frontier, when there is no other station between them.

§ 2 For carriage performed between two Member States, passing through a State which is not a Member State, the States concerned may conclude agreements which derogate from these Uniform Rules.

§ 3 Agreements referred to in §§ 1 and 2 as well as their coming into force shall be notified to the Intergovernmental Organisation for International Carriage by Rail. The Secretary General of the Organisation shall inform the Member States and interested undertakings of these notifications.

2.491 **Article 5, Mandatory law**

Unless provided otherwise in these Uniform Rules, any stipulation which, directly or indirectly, would derogate from these Uniform Rules shall be null and void. The nullity of such a stipulation shall not involve the nullity of the other provisions of the contract of carriage. Nevertheless, a carrier may assume a liability greater and obligations more burdensome than those provided for in these Uniform Rules.

Comment

2.492 Whereas CIM (1980) contains no "public policy" provision of this kind, CIM (1990) follows the model of other transport Conventions such as the Hague Rules (Article III, Rule 8) and CMR (Article 41, para. 1.236, above) except that unlike CMR, the rail carrier "may assume a liability greater and obligations more burdensome than those provided for" in the Uniform Rules. The perceived need to protect small businesses, in the case of road haulage, is not apparent in the case of carriage by rail.

2.493 **Title II, Conclusion and Performance of the Contract of Carriage: Article 6, Contract of carriage**

§ 1 By the contract of carriage, the carrier shall undertake to carry the goods for reward to the place of destination and to deliver them there to the consignee.

§ 2 The contract of carriage must be confirmed by a consignment note which accords with a uniform model. However, the absence, irregularity or loss of the consignment note shall not affect the existence or validity of the contract which shall remain subject to these Uniform Rules.

§ 3 The consignment note shall be signed by the consignor and the carrier. The signature can be replaced by a stamp, by an accounting machine entry or in any other appropriate manner.

§ 4 The carrier must certify the taking over of the goods on the duplicate of the consignment note in an appropriate manner and return the duplicate to the consignor.

§ 5 The consignment note shall not have effect as a bill of lading.

§ 6 A consignment note must be made out for each consignment. In the absence of a contrary agreement between the consignor and the carrier, a consignment note may not relate to more than one wagon load.

§ 7 In the case of carriage which enters the customs territory of the European Community or the territory on which the common transit procedure is applied, each consignment must be accompanied by a consignment note satisfying the requirements of Article 7.

§ 8 The international associations of carriers shall establish uniform model consignment notes in agreement with the customers' international associations and the bodies having competence for customs matters in the Member States as well as any intergovernmental regional economic integration organisation having competence to adopt its own customs legislation.

§ 9 The consignment note and its duplicate may be established in the form of electronic data registration which can be transformed into legible written symbols. The procedure used for the registration and treatment of data must be equivalent from the functional point of view, particularly so far as concerns the evidential value of the consignment note represented by those data.

Comment

2.494 Article 6.1 articulates the contractual undertaking in a way found, for example, in the EWS Conditions (Condition 3.1.1) but not in the transport Conventions where it is no more than implied from the central liability provision, such as Article 36.1 of CIM (1980) and Article 17.1 of CMR.

According to Article 6.2 the contract referred to in Article 6.1 must be evidenced by a consignment note, which may be "in the form of electronic data registration": Article 1.9. However, like CMR but unlike CIM (1980)[1] "the absence, irregularity or loss of the consignment note shall not affect the existence or validity of the contract which shall remain" subject to the Uniform Rules. Regularity requires that for evidential purposes the note be signed by carrier and consignor (Article 6.3) and that the carrier "certifies" the taking over of the goods by the carrier on the duplicate of the note which is then returned for obvious reasons to the consignor. Certification is to be "in an appropriate manner".[2] Thus the note, like other transport documents such as the CMR consignment note has a role as contract note and a receipt for the goods but not, as is the case of a maritime bill of lading, a document of title: to avoid all doubt the latter is confirmed by Article 6.5.[3] *2.495*

Article 1.6, like Article 12.1 of CIM (1980) (para. 2.61, above) provides that a consignment note must be made out for each consignment and that a consignment note may not relate to more than one wagon load, however, the latter only as a default provision, "in the absence of a contrary agreement between the consignor and the carrier", whereas under CIM (1980) the rule is obligatory.[4] *2.496*

Article 7, Wording of the consignment note *2.497*

§ 1 The consignment note must contain the following particulars:

(a) the place at which and the day on which it is made out;
(b) the name and address of the consignor;
(c) the name and address of the carrier who has concluded the contract of carriage;
(d) the name and address of the person to whom the goods have effectively been handed over if he is not the carrier referred to in letter (c);
(e) the place and the day of taking over of the goods;
(f) the place of delivery;
(g) the name and address of the consignee;
(h) the description of the nature of the goods and the method of packing, and, in case of dangerous goods, the description provided for in the Regulation concerning the International Carriage of Dangerous Goods by Rail (RID);
(i) the number of packages and the special marks and numbers necessary for the identification of consignments in less than full wagon loads;
(j) the number of the wagon in the case of carriage of full wagon loads;
(k) the number of the railway vehicle running on its own wheels, if it is handed over for carriage as goods;
(l) in addition, in the case of intermodal transport units, the category, the number or other characteristics necessary for their identification;
(m) the gross mass or the quantity of the goods expressed in other ways;
(n) a detailed list of the documents which are required by customs or other administrative authorities and are attached to the consignment note or held at the disposal of the carrier at the offices of a duly designated authority or a body designated in the contract;
(o) the costs relating to carriage (the carriage charge, incidental costs, customs duties and other costs incurred from the conclusion of the contract until delivery) in so far

1. *Semble* the view of most commentators but the point is disputed: see CIM (1980) Article 1, Comment 2, para. 2.10, above.
2. Cf. CIM (1980) Article 11.5, para. 2.51, above.
3. *Ibid.*
4. See the Comments on Article 12, paras. 2.73 *et seq.*, above.

as they must be paid by the consignee or any other statement that the costs are payable by the consignee;

(p) a statement that the carriage is subject, notwithstanding any clause to the contrary, to these Uniform Rules.

§ 2 Where applicable the consignment note must also contain the following particulars:

(a) in the case of carriage by successive carriers, the carrier who must deliver the goods when he has consented to this entry in the consignment note;
(b) the costs which the consignor undertakes to pay;
(c) the amount of the cash on delivery charge;
(d) the declaration of the value of the goods and the amount representing the special interest in delivery;
(e) the agreed transit period;
(f) the agreed route;
(g) a list of the documents not mentioned in § 1, letter (n) handed over to the carrier;
(h) the entries made by the consignor concerning the number and description of seals he has affixed to the wagon.

§ 3 The parties to the contract may enter on the consignment note any other particulars they consider useful.

Comment

2.498 Like Article 6 of CMR, Article 7 classifies the contents of the consignment note in three parts: particulars that the note must contain, particulars that the note must contain where applicable, and particulars that the note must contain if the parties consider it useful. The particulars required in all cases by Article 7.1 (j), (k) and (l) are not found in Article 6.1 of CMR but the rest are essentially the same as those required by CMR. Article 6 differs substantially from the its predecessor, Article 13 of CIM (1980) which, taken with its DCU, is more detailed.

2.499 The purpose of stating the matters, which according to Article 7.1 must be included in all cases, is mostly self-evident. However, it should be noted that the statement required by Article 7.1(p), sometimes known as the Paramount clause, is to ensure that CIM is applied as the law of the contract. Another is to alert sub-carriers for a purely national stage of an international journey that they may be liable as a successive carrier under CIM: see Article 26. Such is the importance of the requirement that it is sanctioned as provided for by Article 8.3. For example, if a consignee's action against the carrier for loss, damage or delay comes before a non-contracting State and, as a result of the omission of the clause required by Article 7.1(p) and the application of law other than CIM, the consignee recovers an amount of compensation less than that fixed under CIM, Article 8.3 entitles the consignee to the difference from the carrier—in an action brought before a court that will apply CIM.

2.500 **Article 8, Responsibility for particulars entered on the consignment note**

§ 1 The consignor shall be responsible for all costs, loss or damage sustained by the carrier by reason of

(a) the entries made by the consignor in the consignment note being irregular, incorrect, incomplete or made elsewhere than in the allotted space, or
(b) the consignor omitting to make the entries prescribed by RID.

§ 2 If, at the request of the consignor, the carrier makes entries on the consignment note, he shall be deemed, unless the contrary is proved, to have done so on behalf of the consignor.

§ 3 If the consignment note does not contain the statement provided for in Article 7 § 1, letter (p), the carrier shall be liable for all costs, loss or damage sustained through such omission by the person entitled.

Comment

Article 8 is similar to Article 7 of CMR (para. 1.34, above). The content of many of the matters, which are required to be stated in the consignment note in all cases, can be supplied only by the consignor. This is one reason why the consignor is responsible for the consequences: if any inaccuracy causes loss to the carrier, the consignor will be liable under Article 8 and in full: the limits on liability found in Article 30 *et seq*. refer only to the liability of the carrier. See CIM (1980), Article 18, paragraph 2.124, above. *2.501*

Article 9, Dangerous goods *2.502*

If the consignor has failed to make the entries prescribed by RID, the carrier may at any time unload or destroy the goods or render them innocuous, as the circumstances may require, without payment of compensation, save when he was aware of their dangerous nature on taking them over.

Comments

Compare CIM (1980) Article 4(d) (paragraph 2.23, above), as well as CMR Article 22 (paragraph 1.136, above). Under Article 22.2 of CMR the sender is liable for all kinds of loss arising out of their handing over for carriage or of their carriage, however the same result can be reached under CIM (1999) by means of Article 8. *2.503*

Article 10, Payment of costs *2.504*

§ 1 Unless otherwise agreed between the consignor and the carrier, the costs (the carriage charge, incidental costs, customs duties and other costs incurred from the time of the conclusion of the contract to the time of delivery) shall be paid by the consignor.

§ 2 When by virtue of an agreement between the consignor and the carrier, the costs are payable by the consignee and the consignee has not taken possession of the consignment note nor asserted his rights in accordance with Article 17 § 3, nor modified the contract of carriage in accordance with Article 18, the consignor shall remain liable to pay the costs.

Comments

Article 10 is a considerably shorter version of Article 15 of CIM (1980) and which retains the essence of Article 15.1 and Article 15.4. These provisions amount to a compromise, which assumes that the carrier has a lien on the goods under national law. As regards the lien in English law, see the Comments on Condition 14 of the Freightliner Conditions paragraph 2.647, below. *2.505*

Article 11, Examination *2.506*

§ 1 The carrier shall have the right to examine at any time whether the conditions of carriage have been complied with and whether the consignment corresponds with the entries in the consignment note made by the consignor. If the examination concerns the contents of the consignment, this shall be carried out as far as possible in the presence of the person entitled; where this is not possible, the carrier shall require the presence of two independent witnesses, unless the laws and prescriptions of the State where the examination takes place provide otherwise.

§ 2 If the consignment does not correspond with the entries in the consignment note or if the provisions relating to the carriage of goods accepted subject to conditions have not been complied with, the result of the examination must be entered in the copy of the consignment note which accompanies the goods, and also in the duplicate of the consignment note, if it is still held by the carrier. In this case the costs of the examination shall be charged against the goods, if they have not been paid immediately.

§ 3 When the consignor loads the goods, he shall be entitled to require the carrier to examine the condition of the goods and their packaging as well as the accuracy of statements on the consignment note as to the number of packages, their marks and numbers as well as the gross mass of the goods or their quantity otherwise expressed. The carrier shall be obliged to proceed with the examination only if he has appropriate means of carrying it out. The carrier may demand the payment of the costs of the examination. The result of the examination shall be entered on the consignment note.

Comment

2.507 Whereas under Article 8 of CMR the carrier is obliged to check the accuracy of the statements in the consignment note as to the number of packages and their marks and numbers, and the apparent condition of the goods and their packaging, Article 11 follows the model of Article 21 of CIM (1980) (para. 2.149, above) in so far as the carrier is entitled to check these matters but not obliged to. Moreover, checking has a role in relation to the evidential value of the consignment note and this is important when the consignor or the consignee seek to establish a claim against the carrier. Thus, like Article 21 of the earlier version, Article 11.1 seeks to ensure the presence of a person representing the goods interest. Article 11 goes further than Article 21 in that, like Article 8.3 of CMR, Article 11.3 entitles the consignor to require the carrier to examine "the condition of the goods and their packaging as well as the accuracy of statements on the consignment note as to the number of packages, their marks and numbers as well as the gross mass of the goods or their quantity otherwise expressed". The evidential effect of what is done is the subject of Article 12.

2.508

Article 12, Evidential value of the consignment note

§ 1 The consignment note shall be prima facie evidence of the conclusion and the conditions of the contract of carriage and the taking over of the goods by the carrier.

§ 2 If the carrier has loaded the goods, the consignment note shall be prima facie evidence of the condition of the goods and their packaging indicated on the consignment note or, in the absence of such indications, of their apparently good condition at the moment they were taken over by the carrier and of the accuracy of the statements in the consignment note concerning the number of packages, their marks and numbers as well as the gross mass of the goods or their quantity otherwise expressed.

§ 3 If the consignor has loaded the goods, the consignment note shall be prima facie evidence of the condition of the goods and of their packaging indicated in the consignment note or, in the absence of such indication, of their apparently good condition and of the accuracy of the statements referred to in § 2 solely in the case where the carrier has examined them and recorded on the consignment note a result of his examination which tallies.

§ 4 However, the consignment note will not be prima facie evidence in a case where it bears a reasoned reservation. A reason for a reservation could be that the carrier does not have the appropriate means to examine whether the consignment corresponds to the entries in the consignment note.

Comment

Article 12.1 and Article 12.2 are substantially the same as the two paragraphs of CMR, Article 9. The subsequent paragraphs of Article 12 develop the provision in the light of experience of carriage by other modes. Article 12.3 seeks to remove doubts about the matter when loading is undertaken not by the carrier but by the consignor. Article 12.4 is reminiscent of CMR, Article 8.2 (para. 1.36, above) and Article III, Rule 3, of the Hague Rules, as interpreted by the courts. *2.509*

Article 13, Loading and unloading of the goods *2.510*

§ 1 The consignor and the carrier shall agree who is responsible for the loading and unloading of the goods. In the absence of such an agreement, for packages the loading and unloading shall be the responsibility of the carrier whereas for full wagon loads loading shall be the responsibility of the consignor and unloading, after delivery, the responsibility of the consignee.

§ 2 The consignor shall be liable for all the consequences of defective loading carried out by him and must in particular compensate the carrier for the loss or damage sustained in consequence by him. The burden of proof of defective loading shall lie on the carrier.

Comment

The corresponding provision of CIM (1980) is Article 20. Unlike CMR, CIM (1999) resolves which party must load and unlike CIM (1980) the rule, which reflects the changing patterns of carriage by rail, leaves it to party agreement rather than regulations in force at the forwarding station. *2.511*

Article 14, Packing *2.512*

The consignor shall be liable to the carrier for any loss or damage and costs due to the absence of, or defects in, the packing of goods, unless the defectiveness was apparent or known to the carrier at the time when he took over the goods and he made no reservations concerning it.

Comment

Article 14, which concerns defective packing by the consignor, is the provision corresponding to Article 19.4 of CIM (1980) and Article 10 of CMR. See, in particular, Comment 4 on Article 19 of CIM (1980), paragraphs 2.138–2.139, above. *2.513*

The time when the consignor "took over" the goods, referred to in Article 14, like the "very act of taking over the goods" (Article 26), whereby a succeeding railway carrier becomes a party to the contract of carriage and assumes obligations arising therefrom., should be distinguished from "acceptance" of the goods by the person entitled, whereby rights of action are extinguished (Article 47). "Taking over", but *2.514* not "acceptance", usually points to a definitive act whereby the carrier assumes (custody and) control of the goods or, at least, of the wagon in which they have been loaded.

2.515

Article 15, Completion of administrative formalities

§ 1 With a view to the completion of the formalities required by customs and other administrative authorities, to be completed before delivery of the goods, the consignor must attach the necessary documents to the consignment note or make them available to the carrier and furnish him with all the requisite information.

§ 2 The carrier shall not be obliged to check whether these documents and this information are correct and sufficient. The consignor shall be liable to the carrier for any loss or damage resulting from the absence or insufficiency of, or any irregularity in, such documents and information, save in the case of fault of the carrier.

§ 3 The carrier shall be liable for any consequences arising from the loss or misuse of the documents referred to in the consignment note and accompanying it or deposited with the carrier, unless the loss of the documents or the loss or damage caused by the misuse of the documents has been caused by circumstances which the carrier could not avoid and the consequences of which he was unable to prevent. Nevertheless any compensation payable shall not exceed that provided for in the event of loss of the goods.

§ 4 The consignor, by so indicating in the consignment note, or the consignee by giving orders as provided for in Article 18 § 3 may ask

(a) to be present himself or to be represented by an agent when the customs or other administrative formalities are carried out, for the purpose of furnishing any information or explanation required;
(b) to complete the customs or other administrative formalities himself or to have them completed by an agent, in so far as the laws and prescriptions of the State in which they are to be carried out so permit;
(c) to pay customs duties and other charges, when he or his agent is present at or completes the customs or other administrative formalities, in so far as the laws and prescriptions of the State in which they are carried out permit such payment.

In such circumstances neither the consignor, nor the consignee who has the right of disposal, nor the agent of either may take possession of the goods.

§ 5 If, for the completion of the customs or other administrative formalities, the consignor has designated a place where the prescriptions in force do not permit their completion, or if he has stipulated for the purpose any other procedure which cannot be followed, the carrier shall act in the manner which appears to him to be the most favourable to the interests of the person entitled and shall inform the consignor of the measures taken.

§ 6 If the consignor has undertaken to pay customs duties, the carrier shall have the choice of completing customs formalities either in transit or at the destination place.

§ 7 However, the carrier may proceed in accordance with § 5 if the consignee has not taken possession of the consignment note within the period fixed by the prescriptions in force at the destination place.

§ 8 The consignor must comply with the prescriptions of customs or other administrative authorities with respect to the packing and sheeting of the goods. If the consignor has not packed or sheeted the goods in accordance with those prescriptions the carrier shall be entitled to do so; the resulting cost shall be charged against the goods.

Comment

2.516 Article 15, concerning the completion of administrative formalities, is the provision corresponding to Article 25 and Article 26 of CIM (1980) and the considerably less detailed Article 11 of CMR.

Article 16, Transit periods *2.517*

§ 1 The consignor and the carrier shall agree the transit period. In the absence of an agreement, the transit period must not exceed that which would result from the application of §§ 2 to 4.

§ 2 Subject to §§ 3 and 4, the maximum transit periods shall be as follows:

(a) for wagon-load consignments
- — period for consignment 12 hours,
- — period for carriage, for each 400 km or fraction thereof 24 hours;

(b) for less than wagon-load consignment
- — period for consignments 24 hours,
- — period for carriage, for each 200 km or fraction thereof 24 hours.

The distances shall relate to the agreed route or, in the absence thereof, to the shortest possible route.

§ 3 The carrier may fix additional transit periods of specified duration in the following cases:

(a) consignments to be carried
- — by lines of a different gauge,
- — by sea or inland waterway,
- — by road if there is no rail link;

(b) exceptional circumstances causing an exceptional increase in traffic or exceptional operating difficulties.

The duration of the additional transit periods must appear in the General Conditions of Carriage.

§ 4 The transit period shall start to run after the taking over of the goods; it shall be extended by the duration of a stay caused without any fault of the carrier. The transit period shall be suspended on Sundays and statutory holidays.

Comment

Article 16 is a simpler and shorter version of Article 27 of CIM (1980). It is concerned with how long the carriage should take once the carrier is in charge of the goods and is not concerned with whether the transit period begins or ends, an issue that determines the temporal scope of the carrier's liability under Article 23.1. Goods are "in transit" between the time of their acceptance for carriage by the railway and, if it occurs, their delivery to the consignee.[1] In other words, goods are in transit while they are in the custody of the railway as carrier.[2] *2.518*

Article 17, Delivery *2.519*

§ 1 The carrier must hand over the consignment note and deliver the goods to the consignee at the place designated for delivery against receipt and payment of the amounts due according to the contract of carriage.

§ 2 It shall be equivalent to delivery to the consignee if, in accordance with the prescriptions in force at the place of destination,

(a) the goods have been handed over to customs or octroi authorities at their premises or warehouses, when these are not subject to the carrier's supervision;

1. Spera, Art. 26, Anm 3.
2. Clarke (1988) 23 ETL 645.

(b) the goods have been deposited for storage with the carrier, with a forwarding agent or in a public warehouse.

§ 3 After the arrival of the goods at the place of destination, the consignee may ask the carrier to hand over the consignment note and deliver the goods to him. If the loss of the goods is established or if the goods have not arrived on the expiry of the period provided for in Article 29 § 1, the consignee may assert, in his own name, his rights against the carrier under the contract of carriage.

§ 4 The person entitled may refuse to accept the goods, even when he has received the consignment note and paid the charges resulting from the contract of carriage, so long as an examination which he has demanded in order to establish alleged loss or damage has not been carried out.

§ 5 In other respects, delivery of the goods shall be carried out in accordance with the prescriptions in force at the place of destination.

§ 6 If the goods have been delivered without prior collection of a cash on delivery charge, the carrier shall be obliged to compensate the consignor up to the amount of the cash on delivery charge without prejudice to his right of recourse against the consignee.

Comment

2.520 Article 17 concerns not only delivery but also the right of the consignee (Article 17.3), once the goods have been claimed or delivery of the goods taken by the consignee, to assert rights against the carrier under the contract of carriage. So, in that respect Article 17 must be read with Article 44, which concerns actions which might be brought against the railway. Underlying these provisions is the idea to rule out the possibility that the sender and consignee might have concurrent rights of action.

2.521 Delivery is the time at which control of and responsibility for the goods on the part of the railway come to an end. Delivery being when the goods are taken over by the consignee, that is usually also when the goods are accepted by the consignee. Under CIM acceptance of the goods is the moment in time by reference to which, in the absence of "ascertainment" of loss or damage (Article 42), rights of action against the railway are extinguished: Article 47. Moreover, if there has been ascertainment, in certain cases the limitation period runs from the time of delivery: Article 48.2(b). In spite of its importance, delivery is not defined by CIM (except to the extent of Article 28.2) and the inquirer must follow the path marked by Article 10 to national law. Nonetheless, a broadly common notion of delivery can be found in national law. See CIM (1980) Article 28, Comment 3, paragraphs 2.194 *et seq.*, above.

2.522 **Article 18, Right to dispose of the goods**

§ 1 The consignor shall be entitled to dispose of the goods and to modify the contract of carriage by giving subsequent orders. He may in particular ask the carrier

(a) to discontinue the carriage of the goods;
(b) to delay the delivery of the goods;
(c) to deliver the goods to a consignee different from the one entered on the consignment note;
(d) to deliver the goods at a place other than the place of destination entered on the consignment note.

§ 2 The consignor's right to modify the contract of carriage shall, notwithstanding that he is in possession of the duplicate of the consignment note, be extinguished in cases where the consignee

(a) has taken possession of the consignment note;
(b) has accepted the goods;
(c) has asserted his rights in accordance with Article 17 § 3;
(d) is entitled, in accordance with § 3, to give orders; from that time onwards, the carrier shall comply with the orders and instructions of the consignee.

§ 3 The consignee shall have the right to modify the contract of carriage from the time when the consignment note is drawn up, unless the consignor indicates to the contrary on the consignment note.

§ 4 The consignee's right to modify the contract of carriage shall be extinguished in cases where he has

(a) taken possession of the consignment note;
(b) accepted the goods;
(c) asserted his rights in accordance with Article 17 § 3;
(d) given instructions for delivery of the goods to another person in accordance with § 5 and when that person has asserted his rights in accordance with Article 17 § 3.

§ 5 If the consignee has given instructions for delivery of the goods to another person, that person shall not be entitled to modify the contract of carriage.

Comment

Article 18 regulates the rights of the consignor and consignee to modify the contract in such matters as the timing and place of delivery. The right of the consignor under Article 18.1 is lost when the right of modification is acquired by the consignee under Article 18.2. The mode of exercise of the right is the subject of Article 19. Delivery of the goods, referred to in Article 18.1 (b), (c) and (d) is regulated by Article 17. Article 18 replaces the more detailed provision of CIM (1980), Article 30. The corresponding provision of CMR is Article 12. *2.523*

Article 19, Exercise of the right to dispose of the goods *2.524*

§ 1 If the consignor or, in the case referred to in Article 18 § 3, the consignee wishes to modify the contract of carriage by giving subsequent orders, he must produce to the carrier the duplicate of the consignment note on which the modifications have to be entered.

§ 2 The consignor or, in the case referred to in Article 18 § 3, the consignee must compensate the carrier for the costs and the prejudice arising from the carrying out of subsequent modifications.

§ 3 The carrying out of the subsequent modifications must be possible, lawful and reasonable to require at the time when the orders reach the person who is to carry them out, and must in particular neither interfere with the normal working of the carrier's undertaking nor prejudice the consignors or consignees of other consignments.

§ 4 The subsequent modifications must not have the effect of splitting the consignment.

§ 5 When, by reason of the conditions provided for in § 3, the carrier cannot carry out the orders which he receives he shall immediately notify the person from whom the orders emanate.

§ 6 In the case of fault of the carrier he shall be liable for the consequences of failure to carry out an order or failure to carry it out properly. Nevertheless, any compensation payable shall not exceed that provided for in case of loss of the goods.

§ 7 If the carrier implements the consignor's subsequent modifications without requiring the production of the duplicate of the consignment note, the carrier shall be liable to the consignee for any loss or damage sustained by him if the duplicate has been passed on to the consignee. Nevertheless, any compensation payable shall not exceed that provided for in case of loss of the goods.

Comment

2.525 Article 19 is the descendant of Article 31 and Article 32 of CIM (1980), however, in certain features of form and content it is more akin to Article 12 of CMR (para. 1.53, above). Nonetheless, as regards Article 19.3, see the Comments on Article 32 of CIM (1980), paragraphs 2.233 *et seq.*, above.

2.526

Article 20, Circumstances preventing carriage

§ 1 When circumstances prevent the carriage of goods, the carrier shall decide whether it is preferable to carry the goods as a matter of course by modifying the route or whether it is advisable, in the interest of the person entitled, to ask him for instructions while giving him any relevant information available to the carrier.

§ 2 If it is impossible to continue carrying the goods, the carrier shall ask for instructions from the person who has the right to dispose of the goods. If the carrier is unable to obtain instructions within a reasonable time he must take such steps as seem to him to be in the best interests of the person entitled to dispose of the goods.

Comment

2.527 Articles 20 and Article 21 are "prevention of performance" provisions of a kind found with more complex content in Articles 33 and Article 34 of CIM (1980) and which in certain respects resemble Articles 14 and 15 of CMR. However, the rail carrier has more discretion under Article 20.1 to decide the appropriate response than the road carrier under Article 14.1 of CMR. In both cases one possibility is to seek instructions from the person entitled to dispose of the goods; as to this, see Article 33 of CIM (1980), Comment 3, paragraphs 2.247 *et seq.*, above. As to the meaning of "circumstances preventing carriage" see Article 33 of CIM (1980), Comment 2, paragraphs 2.244 *et seq.*, above.

2.528

Article 21, Circumstances preventing delivery

§ 1 When circumstances prevent delivery, the carrier must without delay inform the consignor and ask him for instructions, save where the consignor has requested, by an entry in the consignment note, that the goods be returned to him as a matter of course in the event of circumstances preventing delivery.

§ 2 When the circumstances preventing delivery cease to exist before arrival of instructions from the consignor to the carrier the goods shall be delivered to the consignee. The consignor must be notified without delay.

§ 3 If the consignee refuses the goods, the consignor shall be entitled to give instructions even if he is unable to produce the duplicate of the consignment note.

§ 4 When the circumstances preventing delivery arise after the consignee has modified the contract of carriage in accordance with Article 18 §§ 3 to 5 the carrier must notify the consignee.

Comment

2.529 Article 21 is similar in content to Article 15 of CMR and, disregarding Article 34.5 and the DCUs, Article 34 of CIM (1980). Whereas Article 20 concerns problems arising during transit, Article 21 provides for problems arising at the point of delivery and the consequences in each case are dealt with in Article 22. As to the meaning of "circumstances preventing delivery", see Article 34 of CIM (1980), Comment 2, paragraphs 2.261 to 2.262, above. As to the response required of the carrier, see Article 34 of CIM (1980), Comment 3, paragraphs 2.263 to 2.264, above.

Article 22, Consequences of circumstances preventing carriage and delivery *2.530*

§ 1 The carrier shall be entitled to recover the costs occasioned by
(a) his request for instructions,
(b) the carrying out of instructions received,
(c) the fact that instructions requested do not reach him or do not reach him in time,
(d) the fact that he has taken a decision in accordance with Article 20 § 1, without having asked for instructions,

unless such costs were caused by his fault. The carrier may in particular recover the carriage charge applicable to the route followed and shall be allowed the transit periods applicable to such route.

§ 2 In the cases referred to in Article 20 § 2 and Article 21 § 1 the carrier may immediately unload the goods at the cost of the person entitled. Thereupon the carriage shall be deemed to be at an end. The carrier shall then be in charge of the goods on behalf of the person entitled. He may, however, entrust them to a third party, and shall then be responsible only for the exercise of reasonable care in the choice of such third party. The charges due under the contract of carriage and all other costs shall remain chargeable against the goods.

§ 3 The carrier may proceed to the sale of the goods, without awaiting instructions from the person entitled, if this is justified by the perishable nature or the condition of the goods or if the costs of storage would be out of proportion to the value of the goods. In other cases he may also proceed to the sale of the goods if within a reasonable time he has not received from the person entitled instructions to the contrary which he may reasonably be required to carry out.

§ 4 If the goods have been sold, the proceeds of sale, after deduction of the costs chargeable against the goods, must be placed at the disposal of the person entitled. If the proceeds of sale are less than those costs, the consignor must pay the difference.

§ 5 The procedure in the case of sale shall be determined by the laws and prescriptions in force at, or by the custom of, the place where the goods are situated.

§ 6 If the consignor, in the case of circumstances preventing carriage or delivery, fails to give instructions within a reasonable time and if the circumstances preventing carriage or delivery cannot be eliminated in accordance with §§ 2 and 3, the carrier may return the goods to the consignor or, if it is justified, destroy them, at the cost of the consignor.

Comment

If circumstances prevent carriage (Article 20) or circumstances prevent delivery (Article 21) the consequences in each case are provided for in Article 22. However, in form and content Article 22 resembles Article 16 of CMR. Concerning the effect of unloading the goods under Article 22.2, see Article 16 of CMR, Comment 1 (paras. 1.73 to 1.74, above); and concerning sale of the goods, see Article 16 of CMR, Comment 2 (paras. 1.75 to 1.76, above). *2.531*

Title III, Liability: Article 23, Basis of liability *2.532*

§ 1 The carrier shall be liable for loss or damage resulting from the total or partial loss of, or damage to, the goods between the time of taking over of the goods and the time of delivery and for the loss or damage resulting from the transit period being exceeded, whatever the railway infrastructure used.

§ 2 The carrier shall be relieved of this liability to the extent that the loss or damage or the exceeding of the transit period was caused by the fault of the person entitled, by an order given by the person entitled other than as a result of the fault of the carrier, by an inherent defect in the goods (decay, wastage etc.) or by circumstances which the carrier could not avoid and the consequences of which he was unable to prevent.

§ 3 The carrier shall be relieved of this liability to the extent that the loss or damage arises from the special risks inherent in one or more of the following circumstances:

(a) carriage in open wagons pursuant to the General Conditions of Carriage or when it has been expressly agreed and entered in the consignment note; subject to damage sustained by the goods because of atmospheric influences, goods carried in intermodal transport units and in closed road vehicles carried on wagons shall not be considered as being carried in open wagons; if for the carriage of goods in open wagons, the consignor uses sheets, the carrier shall assume the same liability as falls to him for carriage in open wagons without sheeting, even in respect of goods which, according to the General Conditions of Carriage, are not carried in open wagons;
(b) absence or inadequacy of packaging in the case of goods which by their nature are liable to loss or damage when not packed or when not packed properly;
(c) loading of the goods by the consignor or unloading by the consignee;
(d) the nature of certain goods which particularly exposes them to total or partial loss or damage, especially through breakage, rust, interior and spontaneous decay, desiccation or wastage;
(e) irregular, incorrect or incomplete description or numbering of packages;
(f) carriage of live animals;
(g) carriage which, pursuant to applicable provisions or agreements made between the consignor and the carrier and entered on the consignment note, must be accompanied by an attendant, if the loss or damage results from a risk which the attendant was intended to avert.

Comments

1. The liabilty of the carrier

2.533 Article 23 is central to the liability of the carrier for what happens to the goods during transit, except railway vehicles running on their own wheels and consigned as goods, which are subject to a different regime found in Article 24. The persons entitled to bring a claim against the carrier on the basis of Article 23 (or Article 24) are the designated consignor or the designated consignee and no other person; see Article 44. If that person can prove loss of, or damage to the goods or that the transit period (see Article 33) has been exceeded, the carrier is presumed liable for any consequential financial loss suffered by the claimant. The carrier may then seek to rebut that presumption by establishing one of the defences.

2.534 Under CIM (1980) transit is the time between the "time of acceptance of the goods for carriage" and the time of their delivery. However, in Article 23 that phrase has been replaced by words found in other carriage Conventions (such as CMR, Article 17.1) "the time of taking over of the goods". These words, unlike "acceptance of the goods", point to a definitive act whereby the carrier assumes (custody and) control of the goods or, at least, of the wagon in which they have been loaded. Delivery, too, is not defined by CIM so a meaning must be sought in national law, means the act whereby custody and control of the goods pass from the railway to the appropriate person; it is a widely accepted definition. Note also, as regards the period of time, for which the carrier is presumed responsible for what befalls the goods, the presumption in case of reconsignment of the goods (CIM (1980) Article 38) has not been retained in CIM (1999).

2. Defences

The defences are in two groups, first, in Article 23.2 and, secondly, in Article 23.3. They are distinguished by and because of a difference in the burden of proof: see Article 25 and CIM (1980), Article 36, Comment 9 (paras. 2.298 *et seq.*, above). Underlying the liability scheme the carrier has a residual duty of care: see CIM (1980), Article 20, Comment 3 (paras. 2.146 *et seq.*, above), and CIM (1980), Article 36, Comment 1 (paras. 2.274 *et seq.*, above) and Comment 7 (paras. 2.291 *et seq.*, above). Generally, see Article 36, Comment 1. *2.535*

As regards "fault on the part of or order given by the person entitled", see the equivalent provision, Article 36 of CIM (1980), Comment 5 (paras. 2.285 *et seq.*, above). As regards "inherent defect", see Article 36 of CIM (1980), Comment 6 (paras. 2.288 *et seq.*, above) concerning "inherent vice". "Inherent defect" is thought to have the same meaning as "inherent vice". "Circumstances which the carrier could not avoid and the consequences of which he was unable to prevent" constitute the defence that is the key to the level of the railway's liability under CIM: see Article 36 of CIM (1980), Comment 1 (paras. 2.274 *et seq.*), Comment 7 (paras. 2.291 *et seq.*) and 8 (paras. 2.294 *et seq.*). It is also the key defence (found in Article 17.2) of CMR. *2.536*

As regards the nature of the special risks listed in Article 23.3, see CIM (1980), Article 36, Comment 9 (paras. 2.298 *et seq.*, above). As regards the special risk of "carriage in open wagons", see the equivalent provision of CIM (1980), Article 36, Comment 10 (paras. 2.301 *et seq.*). As regards "absence or inadequacy of packaging" see CIM (1980), Article 36, Comment 11 (paras. 2.304 *et seq.*). As regards "loading . . . and unloading" see CIM (1980), Article 36, Comment 12 (paras. 2.310 *et seq.*). As regards "sensitive goods" (risk (d)) see CIM (1980), Article 36, Comment 14 (paras. 2.315 *et seq.*). As regards incorrect description (risk (e)) see CIM (1980), Article 36, Comment 15 (paras. 2.319 *et seq.*). As regards "live animals", see CIM (1980), Article 36, Comment 16 (paras. 2.321 *et seq.*). As regards "accompanied goods" (risk (g)) see CIM (1980), Article 36, Comment 17 (paras. 2.322 *et seq.*). *2.537*

Article 24, Liability in case of carriage of railway vehicles as goods *2.538*

§ 1 In case of carriage of railway vehicles running on their own wheels and consigned as goods, the carrier shall be liable for the loss or damage resulting from the loss of, or damage to, the vehicle or to its removable parts arising between the time of taking over for carriage and the time of delivery and for loss or damage resulting from exceeding the transit period, unless he proves that the loss or damage was not caused by his fault.

§ 2 The carrier shall not be liable for loss or damage resulting from the loss of accessories which are not mentioned on both sides of the vehicle or in the inventory which accompanies it.

Comment

2.539 Article 24 contains a special regime for railway vehicles running on their own wheels and consigned as goods, different from that for other goods, which are dealt with in Article 23. This maintains the practice of treating railway vehicles differently; see CIM 1980, Article 5.1(b), paragraph 2.27, above.

2.540

Article 25, Burden of proof

§ 1 The burden of proving that the loss, damage or exceeding of the transit period was due to one of the causes specified in Article 23 § 2 shall lie on the carrier.

§ 2 When the carrier establishes that, having regard to the circumstances of a particular case, the loss or damage could have arisen from one or more of the special risks referred to in Article 23 § 3, it shall be presumed that it did so arise. The person entitled shall, however, have the right to prove that the loss or damage was not attributable either wholly or in part to one of those risks.

§ 3 The presumption according to § 2 shall not apply in the case provided for in Article 23 § 3, letter a) if an abnormally large quantity has been lost or if a package has been lost.

Comment

2.541 Article 25 is substantially the same as Article 37 of CIM (1980) and Article 18.1 to 3 of CMR.

2.542

Article 26, Successive carriers

If carriage governed by a single contract is performed by several successive carriers, each carrier, by the very act of taking over the goods with the consignment note, shall become a party to the contract of carriage in accordance with the terms of that document and shall assume the obligations arising therefrom. In such a case each carrier shall be responsible in respect of carriage over the entire route up to delivery.

Comment

2.543 Article 26 is substantially the same as Article 34 of CMR.

2.544

Article 27, Substitute carrier

§ 1 Where the carrier has entrusted the performance of the carriage, in whole or in part, to a substitute carrier, whether or not in pursuance of a right under the contract of carriage to do so, the carrier shall nevertheless remain liable in respect of the entire carriage.

§ 2 All the provisions of these Uniform Rules governing the liability of the carrier shall also apply to the liability of the substitute carrier for the carriage performed by him. Articles 36 and 41 shall apply if an action is brought against the servants and any other persons whose services the substitute carrier makes use of for the performance of the carriage.

§ 3 Any special agreement under which the carrier assumes obligations not imposed by these Uniform Rules or waives rights conferred by these Uniform Rules shall be of no effect in respect of the substitute carrier who has not accepted it expressly and in writing. Whether or not the substitute carrier has accepted it, the carrier shall nevertheless remain bound by the obligations or waivers resulting from such special agreement.

§ 4 Where and to the extent that both the carrier and the substitute carrier are liable, their liability shall be joint and several.

§ 5 The aggregate amount of compensation payable by the carrier, the substitute carrier and their servants and other persons whose services they make use of for the performance of the carriage shall not exceed the limits provided for in these Uniform Rules.

§ 6 This article shall not prejudice rights of recourse which may exist between the carrier and the substitute carrier.

Comment

Article 27 seeks to address modern practice whereby one rail carrier may sub- *2.545*
contract all or part of the carriage to another carrier, a situation not envisaged by the drafters of earlier versions of CIM. Article 27 seeks to ensure that the main-contractor cannot shed responsibility and that the sub-contractor assumes responsibilty to the goods interest on the basis of CIM while the goods are in the charge of that sub-contractor.

Article 28, Presumption of loss or damage in case of reconsignment *2.546*

§ 1 When a consignment consigned in accordance with these Uniform Rules has been reconsigned subject to these same Rules and partial loss or damage has been ascertained after that reconsignment, it shall be presumed that it occurred under the latest contract of carriage if the consignment remained in the charge of the carrier and was reconsigned in the same condition as when it arrived at the place from which it was reconsigned.

§ 2 This presumption shall also apply when the contract of carriage prior to the reconsignment was not subject to these Uniform Rules, if these Rules would have applied in the case of a through consignment from the first place of consignment to the final place of destination.

§ 3 This presumption shall also apply when the contract of carriage prior to the reconsignment was subject to a convention concerning international through carriage of goods by rail comparable with these Uniform Rules, and when this convention contains the same presumption of law in favour of consignments consigned in accordance with these Uniform Rules.

Comment

Reconsignment occurs when the goods have arrived at the destination contracted *2.547*
for but, without having been taken from the custody of the carrier, are sent on by the consignee to a further destination by a second rail carrier. Article 28 establishes a presumption about when any loss or damage might have occurred during this double transit. It is substantially the same as Article 38 of CIM (1980).

Article 29, Presumption of loss of the goods *2.548*

§ 1 The person entitled may, without being required to furnish further proof, consider the goods as lost when they have not been delivered to the consignee or placed at his disposal within thirty days after the expiry of the transit periods.

§ 2 The person entitled may, on receipt of the payment of compensation for the goods lost, make a written request to be notified without delay should the goods be recovered within one year after the payment of compensation. The carrier shall acknowledge such request in writing.

§ 3 Within thirty days after receipt of a notification referred to in § 2, the person entitled may require the goods to be delivered to him against payment of the costs resulting from the contract of carriage and against refund of the compensation received, less, where appropriate, costs which may have been included therein. Nevertheless he shall retain his rights to claim compensation for exceeding the transit period provided for in Articles 33 and 35.

§ 4 In the absence of the request referred to in § 2 or of instructions given within the period specified in § 3, or if the goods are recovered more than one year after the payment of compensation, the carrier shall dispose of them in accordance with the laws and prescriptions in force at the place where the goods are situated.

Comment

2.549 The main purpose of Article 29, whereby loss is presumed after thirty days if the goods have not been delivered, is to avoid uncertainty over the rights of the consignee and the amount of compensation recoverable from the carrier in such a case, while retaining the possibility that the consignee may elect to have goods in lieu of compensation if, unexpectedly, the goods turn up later. Article 29 is substantially the same as Article 39 of CIM (1980).

2.550

Article 30, Compensation for loss

§ 1 In case of total or partial loss of the goods, the carrier must pay, to the exclusion of all other damages, compensation calculated according to the commodity exchange quotation or, if there is no such quotation, according to the current market price, or if there is neither such quotation nor such price, according to the usual value of goods of the same kind and quality on the day and at the place where the goods were taken over.

§ 2 Compensation shall not exceed 17 units of account per kilogramme of gross mass short.

§ 3 In case of loss of a railway vehicle running on its own wheels and consigned as goods, or of an intermodal transport unit, or of their removable parts, the compensation shall be limited, to the exclusion of all other damages, to the usual value of the vehicle or the intermodal transport unit, or their removable parts, on the day and at the place of loss. If it is impossible to ascertain the day or the place of the loss, the compensation shall be limited to the usual value on the day and at the place where the vehicle has been taken over by the carrier.

§ 4 The carrier must, in addition, refund the carriage charge, customs duties already paid and other sums paid in relation to the carriage of the goods lost except excise duties for goods carried under a procedure suspending those duties.

Comment

2.551 In all of the most important matters Article 30 is substantially the same as Article 40 of CIM (1980). The differences are that Article 30.3 is new, as are the last words of Article 30.4: "except excise duties for goods carried under a procedure suspending those duties". Article 30.3 is consequential on the insertion in the 1999 version of Article 24.

2.552

Article 31, Liability for wastage in transit

§ 1 In respect of goods which, by reason of their nature, are generally subject to wastage in transit by the sole fact of carriage, the carrier shall only be liable to the extent that the wastage exceeds the following allowances, whatever the length of the route:

(a) two per cent of the mass for liquid goods or goods consigned in a moist condition;
(b) one per cent of the mass for dry goods.

§ 2 The limitation of liability provided for in § 1 may not be invoked if, having regard to the circumstances of a particular case, it is proved that the loss was not due to causes which would justify the allowance.

§ 3 Where several packages are carried under a single consignment note, the wastage in transit shall be calculated separately for each package if its mass on consignment is shown separately on the consignment note or can be ascertained otherwise.

§ 4 In case of total loss of goods or in case of loss of a package, no deduction for wastage in transit shall be made in calculating the compensation.

§ 5 This Article shall not derogate from Articles 23 and 25.

Comment

2.553 As the railway's liability for short delivery under Article 30.2 is based on discrepancy in mass and hence weight, justice requires that it should not have to pay for differences attributable to the natural propensity of certain goods to lose weight and thus mass in normal transit. This is the reason for Article 31, which is substantially the same as Article 41 of CIM (1980).

Article 32, Compensation for damage *2.554*

§ 1 In case of damage to goods, the carrier must pay compensation equivalent to the loss in value of the goods, to the exclusion of all other damages. The amount shall be calculated by applying to the value of the goods defined in accordance with Article 30 the percentage of loss in value noted at the place of destination.

§ 2 The compensation shall not exceed:
(a) if the whole consignment has lost value through damage, the amount which would have been payable in case of total loss;
(b) if only part of the consignment has lost value through damage, the amount which would have been payable had that part been lost.

§ 3 In case of damage to a railway vehicle running on its own wheels and consigned as goods, or of an intermodal transport unit, or of their removable parts, the compensation shall be limited, to the exclusion of all other damages, to the cost of repair. The compensation shall not exceed the amount payable in case of loss.

§ 4 The carrier must also refund the costs provided for in Article 30 § 4, in the proportion set out in § 1.

Comment

2.555 Article 32 is substantially the same as Article 42 of CIM (1980), except that Article 32.3 is new. Article 32.3 is consequential on the insertion in the 1999 version of Article 24.

Article 33, Compensation for exceeding the transit period *2.556*

§ 1 If loss or damage results from the transit period being exceeded, the carrier must pay compensation not exceeding four times the carriage charge.

§ 2 In case of total loss of the goods, the compensation provided for in § 1 shall not be payable in addition to that provided for in Article 30.

§ 3 In case of partial loss of the goods, the compensation provided for in § 1 shall not exceed four times the carriage charge in respect of that part of the consignment which has not been lost.

§ 4 In case of damage to the goods, not resulting from the transit period being exceeded, the compensation provided for in § 1 shall, where appropriate, be payable in addition to that provided for in Article 32.

§ 5 In no case shall the total of compensation provided for in § 1 together with that provided for in Articles 30 and 32 exceed the compensation which would be payable in case of total loss of the goods.

§ 6 If, in accordance with Article 16 § 1, the transit period has been established by agreement, other forms of compensation than those provided for in § 1 may be so agreed. If, in this case, the transit periods provided for in Article 16 §§ 2 to 4 are exceeded, the person entitled may claim either the compensation provided for in the agreement mentioned above or that provided for in §§ 1 to 5.

Comment

2.557 Article 33 is substantially the same as Article 43 of CIM (1980), except that Article 33.6 is drafted to reflect current conditions; and the maximum amount recoverable in Article 33.3 has been raised from three times the carriage charge (Article 43.3) to four.

2.558 **Article 34, Compensation in case of declaration of value**

The consignor and the carrier may agree that the consignor shall declare in the consignment note a value for the goods exceeding the limit provided for in Article 30 § 2. In such a case the amount declared shall be substituted for that limit.

2.559 **Article 35, Compensation in case of interest in delivery**

The consignor and the carrier may agree that the consignor may declare, by entering an amount in figures in the consignment note, a special interest in delivery, in case of loss, damage or exceeding of the transit period. In case of a declaration of interest in delivery further compensation for loss or damage proved may be claimed, in addition to the compensation provided for in Articles 30, 32 and 33, up to the amount declared.

Comment

2.560 Article 35 is essentially the same as the corresponding provision in CIM (1980), Article 46.

2.561 **Article 36, Loss of right to invoke the limits of liability**

The limits of liability provided for in Article 15 § 3, Article 19 §§ 6 and 7, Article 30 and Articles 32 to 35 shall not apply if it is proved that the loss or damage results from an act or omission, which the carrier has committed either with intent to cause such loss or damage, or recklessly and with knowledge that such loss or damage would probably result.

Comment

2.562 Like the other carriage Conventions Article 36 retains the principle that, if the carrier breaches the contract badly enough, it should be penalised by the loss of the relevant limit on the amount of its liability. In essence it is the same as Article 44 of CIM (1980) but some of the consequences are different and, in particular, the words "wilful misconduct" have been replaced by the formula now preferred in most other carriage Conventions "act or omission . . . committed either with intent to cause such loss or damage, or recklessly and with knowledge that such loss or damage would probably result". Thus the "bad enough" breach envisaged is now expressed in two parts.

The word "wilful" in the original formula "wilful misconduct" allowed courts to insist on evidence of actual awareness of wrongfulness and of the likely consequences. The deletion of "wilful" and the reference to awareness that loss or damage will "probably" result suggests an objective rule different from and perhaps narrower than the subjective rule previously applied in the United Kingdom as regards "wilful misconduct". Today guidance may be found in decisions of courts on the other carriage Conventions in which the current word formula is employed. See, in particular, HP, Article 25, Comments 2, 3 and 4 (paras. 3.150 to 3.160, below). There can be no doubting the intention of the drafters that the interpretation should be the same in both contexts. *2.563*

Article 37, Conversion and interest *2.564*

§ 1 Where the calculation of the compensation requires the conversion of sums expressed in foreign currency, conversion shall be at the exchange rate applicable on the day and at the place of payment of compensation.

§ 2 The person entitled may claim interest on compensation, calculated at five per cent per annum, from the day of the claim provided for in Article 43 or, if no such claim has been made, from the day on which legal proceedings were instituted.

§ 3 If the person entitled does not submit to the carrier, within a reasonable time allotted to him, the supporting documents required for the amount of the claim to be finally settled, no interest shall accrue between the expiry of the time allotted and the actual submission of such documents.

Comment

Article 37 is substantially the same as Article 47 of CIM (1980) except that Article 47.3 has been omitted. *2.565*

Article 38, Liability in respect of rail-sea traffic *2.566*

§ 1 In rail-sea carriage by the services referred to in Article 24 § 1 of the Convention any Member State may, by requesting that a suitable note be included in the list of services to which these Uniform Rules apply, add the following grounds for exemption from liability in their entirety to those provided for in Article 23:

(a) fire, if the carrier proves that it was not caused by his act or default, or that of the master, a mariner, the pilot or the carrier's servants;
(b) saving or attempting to save life or property at sea;
(c) loading of goods on the deck of the ship, if they are so loaded with the consent of the consignor given on the consignment note and are not in wagons;
(d) perils, dangers and accidents of the sea or other navigable waters.

§ 2 The carrier may only avail himself of the grounds for exemption referred to in § 1 if he proves that the loss, damage or exceeding the transit period occurred in the course of the journey by sea between the time when the goods were loaded on board the ship and the time when they were unloaded from the ship.

§ 3 When the carrier relies on the grounds for exemption referred to in § 1, he shall nevertheless remain liable if the person entitled proves that the loss, damage or exceeding the transit period is due to the fault of the carrier, the master, a mariner, the pilot or the carrier's servants.

§ 4 Where a sea route is served by several undertakings included in the list of services in accordance with Article 24 § 1 of the Convention, the liability regime applicable to that route must be the same for all those undertakings. In addition, where those undertakings have been included in the list at the request of several Member States, the adoption of this regime must be the subject of prior agreement between those States.

§ 5 The measures taken in accordance with §§ 1 and 4 shall be notified to the Secretary General. They shall come into force at the earliest at the expiry of a period of thirty days from the day on which the Secretary General notifies them to the other Member States. Consignments already in transit shall not be affected by such measures.

Comment

2.567 In most respects Article 38 is similar in substance to Article 48 of CIM (1980). The major differences lie in the deletion of two controversial grounds of exemption. The first is "act, neglect or default in the navigation and management of the ship", which many consider to be archaic in modern conditions. The second is the "unseaworthiness of the ship", of which the same could be said and which, in addition, was enacted in a way which many, especially civil lawyers, found confusing. These were deleted from the 1999 version.

2.568 **Article 39, Liability in case of nuclear incidents**

The carrier shall be relieved of liability pursuant to these Uniform Rules for loss or damage caused by a nuclear incident when the operator of a nuclear installation or another person who is substituted for him is liable for the loss or damage pursuant to the laws and prescriptions of a State governing liability in the field of nuclear energy.

Comment

2.569 Article 39 is substantially the same as Article 49 of CIM (1980).

2.570 **Article 40, Persons for whom the carrier is liable**

The carrier shall be liable for his servants and other persons whose services he makes use of for the performance of the carriage, when these servants and other persons are acting within the scope of their functions. The managers of the railway infrastructure on which the carriage is performed shall be considered as persons whose services the carrier makes use of for the performance of the carriage.

Comment

2.571 If a railway has contracted to do something, it is liable for failure to achieve that task, whether the failure is that of the managing director or *alter ego* of the railway at company headquarters or, as is more likely, it is that of one or more of the servants or agents employed for the purpose by the railway at "track level". The corresponding rule in CIM (1980), Article 50, is headed "Liability of the railway for its servants". Article 40 has been drafted to take account of changes in railway infrastructure as well as changes in the law of vicarious liability in general.

Article 41, Other actions *2.572*

§ 1 In all cases where these Uniform Rules shall apply, any action in respect of liability, on whatever grounds, may be brought against the carrier only subject to the conditions and limitations laid down in these Uniform Rules.

§ 2 The same shall apply to any action brought against the servants or other persons for whom the carrier is liable pursuant to Article 40.

Comment

Article 41 is substantially the same as Article 51 of CIM (1980). *2.573*

Title IV, Assertion of Rights: Article 42, Ascertainment of partial loss or damage *2.574*

§ 1 When partial loss or damage is discovered or presumed by the carrier or alleged by the person entitled, the carrier must without delay, and if possible in the presence of the person entitled, draw up a report stating, according to the nature of the loss or damage, the condition of the goods, their mass and, as far as possible, the extent of the loss or damage, its cause and the time of its occurrence.

§ 2 A copy of the report must be supplied free of charge to the person entitled.

§ 3 Should the person entitled not accept the findings in the report, he may request that the condition and mass of the goods and the cause and amount of the loss or damage be ascertained by an expert appointed either by the parties to the contract of carriage or by a court or tribunal. The procedure to be followed shall be governed by the laws and prescriptions of the State in which such ascertainment takes place.

Comment

Article 42 is substantially the same as Article 52 of CIM (1980). *2.575*

Article 43, Claims *2.576*

§ 1 Claims relating to the contract of carriage must be addressed in writing to the carrier against whom an action may be brought.

§ 2 A claim may be made by persons who have the right to bring an action against the carrier.

§ 3 To make the claim the consignor must produce the duplicate of the consignment note. Failing this he must produce an authorisation from the consignee or furnish proof that the consignee has refused to accept the goods.

§ 4 To make the claim the consignee must produce the consignment note if it has been handed over to him.

§ 5 The consignment note, the duplicate and any other documents which the person entitled thinks fit to submit with the claim must be produced either in the original or as copies, the copies, where appropriate, duly certified if the carrier so requests.

§ 6 On settlement of the claim the carrier may require the production, in the original form, of the consignment note, the duplicate or the cash on delivery voucher so that they may be endorsed to the effect that settlement has been made.

Comment

2.577 Article 43 is substantially the same as Article 53 of CIM (1980).

2.578

Article 44, Persons who may bring an action against the carrier

§ 1 Subject to §§ 3 and 4 actions based on the contract of carriage may be brought:
(a) by the consignor, until such time as the consignee has
1. taken possession of the consignment note,
2. accepted the goods, or
3. asserted his rights pursuant to Article 17 § 3 or Article 18 § 3.
(b) by the consignee, from the time when he has
1. taken possession of the consignment note,
2. accepted the goods, or
3. asserted his rights pursuant to Article 17 § 3 or Article 18 § 3.

§ 2 The right of the consignee to bring an action shall be extinguished from the time when the person designated by the consignee in accordance with Article 18 § 5 has taken possession of the consignment note, accepted the goods or asserted his rights pursuant to Article 17 § 3.

§ 3 An action for the recovery of a sum paid pursuant to the contract of carriage may only be brought by the person who made the payment.

§ 4 An action in respect of cash on delivery payments may only be brought by the consignor.

§ 5 In order to bring an action the consignor must produce the duplicate of the consignment note. Failing this he must produce an authorisation from the consignee or furnish proof that the consignee has refused to accept the goods. If necessary, the consignor must prove the absence or the loss of the consignment note.

§ 6 In order to bring an action the consignee must produce the consignment note if it has been handed over to him.

Comment

2.579 Article 44 identifies the persons with the right to claim against a railway in respect of loss of or damage or delay to goods. Those persons are the consignor and consignee, the one or the other, not both, and nobody else. Although the order in which the rules are stated has been changed, in substance Article 44 is the same as Article 54 of CIM (1980).

2.580

Article 45, Carriers against whom an action may be brought

§ 1 Subject to §§ 3 and 4 actions based on the contract of carriage may be brought only against the first carrier, the last carrier or the carrier having performed the part of the carriage on which the event giving rise to the proceedings occurred.

§ 2 When, in the case of carriage performed by successive carriers, the carrier who must deliver the goods is entered with his consent on the consignment note, an action may be brought against him in accordance with § 1 even if he has received neither the goods nor the consignment note.

§ 3 An action for the recovery of a sum paid pursuant to the contract of carriage may be brought against the carrier who has collected that sum or against the carrier on whose behalf it was collected.

§ 4 An action in respect of cash on delivery payments may be brought only against the carrier who has taken over the goods at the place of consignment.

§ 5 An action may be brought against a carrier other than those specified in §§ 1 to 4 when instituted by way of counter-claim or by way of exception in proceedings relating to a principal claim based on the same contract of carriage.

§ 6 To the extent that these Uniform Rules apply to the substitute carrier, an action may also be brought against him.

§ 7 If the plaintiff has a choice between several carriers, his right to choose shall be extinguished as soon as he brings an action against any one of them; this shall also apply if the plaintiff has a choice between one or more carriers and a substitute carrier.

Comment

Although the order in which the rules are stated has been changed, in substance Article 45 is the same as Article 55 of CIM (1980), except principally in the provision made in Article 45.6 for actions against substitute carriers, which is new. *2.581*

Article 46, Forum *2.582*

§ 1 Actions based on these Uniform Rules may be brought before the courts or tribunals of Member States designated by agreement between the parties or before the courts or tribunals of a State on whose territory

(a) the defendant has his domicile or habitual residence, his principal place of business or the branch or agency which concluded the contract of carriage, or

(b) the place where the goods were taken over by the carrier or the place designated for delivery is situated.

Other courts or tribunals may not be seized.

§ 2 Where an action based on these Uniform Rules is pending before a court or tribunal competent pursuant to § 1, or where in such litigation a judgment has been delivered by such a court or tribunal, no new action may be brought between the same parties on the same grounds unless the judgment of the court or tribunal before which the first action was brought is not enforceable in the State in which the new action is brought.

Comment

Article 46 regulates jurisdiction in respect of actions, whether actions brought by the railway or actions brought against the railway, when based on CIM. However, if the action is a recourse action by one railway against another, jurisdiction is regulated not by Article 46 but by Article 51.4. Article 46, which is significantly different from Article 56, the corresponding provision of CIM (1980), is based on Article 31.1 of CMR (para. 1.184, above). *2.583*

Article 47, Extinction of right of action *2.584*

§ 1 Acceptance of the goods by the person entitled shall extinguish all rights of action against the carrier arising from the contract of carriage in case of partial loss, damage or exceeding of the transit period.

§ 2 Nevertheless, the right of action shall not be extinguished:

(a) in case of partial loss or damage, if

1. the loss or damage was ascertained in accordance with Article 42 before the acceptance of the goods by the person entitled;
2. the ascertainment which should have been carried out in accordance with Article 42 was omitted solely through the fault of the carrier;

(b) in case of loss or damage which is not apparent whose existence is ascertained after acceptance of the goods by the person entitled, if he

1. asks for ascertainment in accordance with Article 42 immediately after discovery of the loss or damage and not later than seven days after the acceptance of the goods, and
2. in addition, proves that the loss or damage occurred between the time of taking over and the time of delivery;

(c) in cases where the transit period has been exceeded, if the person entitled has, within sixty days, asserted his rights against one of the carriers referred to in Article 45 § 1;

(d) if the person entitled proves that the loss or damage results from an act or omission, done with intent to cause such loss or damage, or recklessly and with knowledge that such loss or damage would probably result.

§ 3 If the goods have been reconsigned in accordance with Article 28 rights of action in case of partial loss or in case of damage, arising from one of the previous contracts of carriage, shall be extinguished as if there had been only a single contract of carriage.

Comment

2.585 With one significant exception, Article 47, which provides for the "extinction" of rights of action against a railway, is substantially the same as Article 57 of CIM (1980). The exception concerns the punitive exception to the main rules of extinction made by Article 47.2(d) where the word formula "act or omission, done with intent to cause such loss or damage, or recklessly and with knowledge that such loss or damage would probably result" replaces "wilful misconduct and gross negligence" found in Article 57. For the explanation, see the Comment on Article 36.

2.586

Article 48, Limitation of actions

§ 1 The period of limitation for an action arising from the contract of carriage shall be one year. Nevertheless, the period of limitation shall be two years in the case of an action

(a) to recover a cash on delivery payment collected by the carrier from the consignee;

(b) to recover the proceeds of a sale effected by the carrier;

(c) for loss or damage resulting from an act or omission done with intent to cause such loss or damage, or recklessly and with knowledge that such loss or damage would probably result;

(d) based on one of the contracts of carriage prior to the reconsignment in the case provided for in Article 28.

§ 2 The period of limitation shall run for actions

(a) for compensation for total loss, from the thirtieth day after expiry of the transit period;

(b) for compensation for partial loss, damage or exceeding of the transit period, from the day when delivery took place;

(c) in all other cases, from the day when the right of action may be exercised.

The day indicated for the commencement of the period of limitation shall not be included in the period.

§ 3 The period of limitation shall be suspended by a claim in writing in accordance with Article 43 until the day that the carrier rejects the claim by notification in writing and returns the documents submitted with it. If part of the claim is admitted, the period of limitation shall start to run again in respect of the part of the claim still in dispute. The burden of proof of receipt of the claim or of the reply and of the return of the documents shall lie on the party who relies on those facts. The period of limitation shall not be suspended by further claims having the same object.

§ 4 A right of action which has become time-barred may not be exercised further, even by way of counterclaim or relied upon by way of exception.

§ 5 Otherwise, the suspension and interruption of periods of limitation shall be governed by national law.

Comment

Article 48, a simplified version of Article 58 of CIM (1980), regulates what common lawyers usually call limitation of actions. If the period has run, the effect as seen by continental lawyers, however, is not just to bar the action but to extinguish it. Nonetheless, whereas Article 47 is headed "Extinction of right of action", Article 48 is headed "Limitation of actions". With one reservation, Article 48 is substantially the same as Article 58 of CIM (1980). The reservation concerns Article 48.2(d) which is a much shorter version of the corresponding part of the earlier text. For what "other actions" might mean, see Article 58 of CIM (1980), Comment 3, paragraphs 2.450 *et seq.*, above. *2.587*

Title V, Relations between Carriers: Article 49, Settlement of accounts *2.588*

§ 1 Any carrier who has collected or ought to have collected, either at departure or on arrival, charges or other costs arising out of the contract of carriage must pay to the carriers concerned their respective shares. The methods of payment shall be fixed by agreement between the carriers.

§ 2 Article 12 shall also apply to the relations between successive carriers.

Comment

Relations between carriers and questions of recourse provoked little interest or comment until a scholarly analysis was published on successive carriage under CIM (1999).[1] *2.589*

Article 50, Right of recourse *2.590*

§ 1 A carrier who has paid compensation pursuant to these Uniform Rules shall have a right of recourse against the carriers who have taken part in the carriage in accordance with the following provisions:

(a) the carrier who has caused the loss or damage shall be solely liable for it;

(b) when the loss or damage has been caused by several carriers, each shall be liable for the loss or damage he has caused; if such distinction is impossible, the compensation shall be apportioned between them in accordance with letter (c);

(c) if it cannot be proved which of the carriers has caused the loss or damage, the compensation shall be apportioned between all the carriers who have taken part in the carriage, except those who prove that the loss or damage was not caused by them; such apportionment shall be in proportion to their respective shares of the carriage charge.

§ 2 In the case of insolvency of any one of these carriers, the unpaid share due from him shall be apportioned among all the other carriers who have taken part in the carriage, in proportion to their respective shares of the carriage charge.

1. Glass [2003] BLI 72.

2.591 **Article 51, Procedure for recourse**

§ 1 The validity of the payment made by the carrier exercising a right of recourse pursuant to Article 50 may not be disputed by the carrier against whom the right of recourse is exercised, when compensation has been determined by a court or tribunal and when the latter carrier, duly served with notice of the proceedings, has been afforded an opportunity to intervene in the proceedings. The court or tribunal seized of the principal action shall determine what time shall be allowed for such notification of the proceedings and for intervention in the proceedings.

§ 2 A carrier exercising his right of recourse must make his claim in one and the same proceedings against all the carriers with whom he has not reached a settlement, failing which he shall lose his right of recourse in the case of those against whom he has not taken proceedings.

§ 3 The court or tribunal must give its decision in one and the same judgment on all recourse claims brought before it.

§ 4 The carrier wishing to enforce his right of recourse may bring his action in the courts or tribunals of the State on the territory of which one of the carriers participating in the carriage has his principal place of business, or the branch or agency which concluded the contract of carriage.

§ 5 When the action must be brought against several carriers, the plaintiff carrier shall be entitled to choose the court or tribunal in which he will bring the proceedings from among those having competence pursuant to § 4.

§ 6 Recourse proceedings may not be joined with proceedings for compensation taken by the person entitled under the contract of carriage.

2.592 **Article 52, Agreements concerning recourse**

The carriers may conclude agreements which derogate from Articles 49 and 50.

[*The next paragraph is 2.603*]

III. CARRIAGE OF GOODS BY RAIL WITHIN THE UNITED KINGDOM: FREIGHTLINER CONDITIONS 2002[1]

A. INTRODUCTION

The movement of goods by rail within the United Kingdom is governed by private conditions of carriage, notably those published by Freightliner. They have no statutory force. Being private contract conditions, they do not bind Freightliner's customer, referred to in the Conditions as the "Trader" or "Sender" according to context, unless the person concerned signs them or has actual or constructive notice that Freightliner intends to include standard conditions of carriage: see HP, Article 1, Comment 2 (para 3.40, below). *2.603*

The Conditions are subject to the Unfair Contract Terms Act 1977: whereas contracts for the carriage of goods by sea were largely saved from the Act, other contracts of carriage were not. As the Conditions concern the business liability of Freightliner, they come within the scope of the Act: section 1. Being standard terms on which the customer is invited to contract, the Conditions will be enforced only to the extent that they are reasonable: section 3. Whether a term is reasonable or not is a matter for Freightliner to prove: section 12. This depends on a number of factors discussed in this book in the Introduction to the RHA Conditions (paragraphs 1.251 *et seq.*, above). *2.604*

B. THE TEXT OF THE FREIGHTLINER CONDITIONS 2002

Standard Conditions of Carriage

1. Definitions *2.605*

"Carrier" (whether in regard to carriage or storage or otherwise) means Freightliner, its Subcontractor and their respective servants and agents and any of them.

"Consignment" means any Container and/or goods whether in a Container or not which are in the control of the Carriers for the purpose of carriage or storage or in respect of which Freightliner agrees to perform any services.

"Container" means the container (whether owned or provided by the Trader or by Freightliner) whether or not any contents including goods are contained therein.

"Contract" means the contract between Freightliner and the Sender for the carriage and/or storage of the Consignment.

"Dangerous Consignment" means a consignment comprising in whole or in part goods included in the "List of Dangerous Goods and Conditions of Acceptance by Rail" (BR 22426) or any superseding document published by Railtrack as amended from time to time or a Consignment which presents a comparable hazard.

"ERIC" means Enhanced Rail Intermodal Control.

"Freightliner" means Freightliner Limited.

"Private Siding" means a railway or siding under the control of the Trader.

"Sender" means any person who directly or indirectly through his agent or as an agent contracts for the services of Freightliner.

1. Freightliner Ltd., Third Floor, The Podium, 1 Eversholt Street, Euston, London NW1 2FL, October 2002, FL10.

"Subcontractor" means any person whose services Freightliner engages or makes use of to perform the whole or any part of the services which are the subject of this Contract.

"Trader" includes the Sender, and unless the context otherwise requires, the Owner/Receiver/Consignee of the Container and/or goods and the holder of the consignment note and their respective servants and agents.

Comment

2.606 Condition 1 is of a common type which defines major terms used in the Conditions. The "Sender" is defined as the person who contracts for the services of Freightliner. That person may be the actual sender but is commonly the consignee. "It is clear that where goods are despatched by a carrier, the contract for payment of carriage is between him and the consignee, even though the goods should have been booked by the consignor; and though the property in these goods turned out afterwards to be in the consignor."[1] This is still the inference drawn by English courts as long as the carrier, here Freightliner, is entitled to assume, as is likely to be the case, that the goods are the property of the consignee.[2]

2.607 "Consignment" came before the court for interpretation in *Spectra*,[3] in which the appropriate limit of liability under standard conditions of a contract of carriage of goods by road depended on the meaning of the word "consignment". See the Comments on Condition 1 of the RHA Conditions, paragraphs 1.261 to 1.262, above.

2.608 **2. The Basis for Providing Containers**

(a) When Freightliner agrees at the Sender's request to provide a Container, the same is provided on the basis that throughout the period from the initial providing receipt until final re-delivery after conclusion of the transit the Sender shall be responsible for the Container in all respects as if he were the owner Containers thereof.

(b) The Trader shall give Freightliner a receipt when taking the Container into his possession. Such receipt if unqualified shall be prima facie evidence of the good condition of the Container.

(c) Freightliner may refuse to permit the Trader to take possession of the Container if in its opinion the vehicle on which the Container is intended to be conveyed is unsuitable for such a purpose.

(d) The Trader shall not cause or permit the Container to be removed from any road vehicle by which it is being conveyed, whether before or after conveyance by the Carriers, without the consent of a duly authorised officer or servant of the Carriers.

(e) The Container is not to be loaded in excess of the loading capacity marked thereon.

(f) In the case of goods consigned to more than one Consignee, the Container is to be loaded in such a way as to facilitate delivery in the appropriate order.

(g) The Trader shall use the Container solely in connection with the services provided by Freightliner.

(h) The Trader shall without prejudice to Condition 16.1 redeliver the Container internally clean and in like good order and condition as upon initial receipt, fair wear and tear excepted. The Container shall be redelivered on the road vehicle of the Carriers on which it is conveyed.

1. *Stephenson* v. *Hart* (1828) 4 Bing. 476, 487.
2. Clarke, *CMR*, para. 42; Palmer, pp. 959 *et seq.* and 1095; see also C. Cashmore, *Who Can Sue on a Contract of Carriage of Goods* (London, 1990), Chap. 3.
3. *Spectra International plc* v. *Hayesoak Ltd.* [1997] 1 Lloyd's Rep. 153.

Comment

Condition 2 is of a kind not found in the other standard conditions discussed in this book. Condition 2 is necessary in view of the nature of the business of Freightliner which is to move goods by rail in unit loads. The nature of Condition 2 is that of a hiring agreement and it is subject to the Supply of Goods and Services Act 1982. In particular, there is an implied contract condition that the container is reasonably fit for the purpose of transporting the trader's goods.[1] *2.609*

3. Warranties *2.610*

The Sender warrants that he has and is exercising the authority of all persons owning or interested in the Consignment and each part thereof into the Contract and to bind them as well as himself by these Conditions.

Comment

The main purpose of the warranty in Condition 3 is to assure Freightliner, as carrier, that the person most likely to suffer loss, if the goods are lost or damaged in transit, is a party to the contract of carriage and bound by the Conditions, notably those that limit the amount of Freightliner's liability. The drafting assumption, now doubtful as a matter of law,[1] was that, were it otherwise, Freightliner might be liable in full in tort. *2.611*

4. Parties and Subcontracting *2.612*

(a) Freightliner enters into this Contract on behalf of itself and its servant and agents, to the intent [*sic*] that, in addition to Freightliner, Freightliner's servants subcontracting and agents concerned in the implementation of the Contract shall also be entitled to the benefit of these Conditions, and shall be under no liability greater than or in addition to that of Freightliner under the Contract.

(b) Freightliner is hereby authorised by the Sender to engage or make use of the services of Subcontractors to perform the whole or any part of the services which are the subject of the Contract on terms that the Subcontractors and each of their servants and agents shall have the benefit of these Conditions as against the Trader and anyone claiming through him and shall be under no liability to the Trader and anyone claiming through him in respect of any Consignment or part thereof greater than or in addition to that of Freightliner under the Contract. Further, in so far as any Subcontractor has without objecting to this clause, received notice of these Conditions the authority conferred hereby shall be taken to have been exercised in relation to each and every such engagement or use of the services of any such Subcontractor.

(c) The Sender agrees with Freightliner that neither the Trader nor anyone claiming through him in respect of the Consignment of any part thereof will seek to enforce by legal proceedings or otherwise any claim against the Carriers greater than or in addition to the liability of Freightliner under the Contract.

(d) Freightliner holds the benefit of clause (c) above and of Condition 14 hereof on trust for the Carriers.

1. S. 4(5).

1. See the Contracts (Rights of Third Parties) Act 1999, s. 1, discussed in Comment 2 on Condition 2 of the RHA Conditions of Carriage, paras. 1.266 *et seq.*, above.

(e) In the event of the Sender being a Carrier or bailee of the Consignment, he shall (without prejudice to Condition 3 hereof) hold to the benefit of Freightliner any like Conditions to those in clauses (a) to (d) above and in Condition 15 hereof which obtain in his own Contract with his own sender or bailor. Without prejudice to the foregoing in case of the Sender (being a Carrier or bailee as aforesaid) contracting on behalf of Freightliner for the benefit of like conditions for Freightliner, Freightliner hereby ratifies his act in making such Contract if Freightliner has not authorised such act.

Comments

1. Privity of contract and common law

2.613 Condition 4(a) purports to confer the benefit of contract defences and liability limits on the servants and agents of Freightliner. Its purpose is to overcome an obstacle posed by the common law rule of privity of contract, whereby third parties cannot benefit from defences in contracts to which they are not party.[1] Common law courts have developed a number of ways around the privity rule. One way is to use rules of agency by inferring that a carrier, such as Freightliner, has authority to contract with its customer not only as principal but also as agent on behalf of the sub-contractor.[2] The device may have been unnecessary because a number of nineteenth century decisions established that, in the case of successive carriage by railways A, B and C, carrier A contracted with the consignor or, more usually, the consignor as agent for the consignee, not only on its own behalf but also as agent for railways B and C.[3]

2.614 Another way around the privity rule lies in the law of bailment. If a bailor of goods bails goods to a bailee, such as a carrier, which has authority to sub-bail the goods, the bailor is bound by the terms of the sub-bailment, unless those terms are unusual. The bailor "is bound by the conditions if he has expressly or impliedly consented to the bailee making a sub-bailment containing those conditions".[4] This rule is reinforced here by Condition 4(e), so that if the bailor, such as the sender, is a carrier or other bailee, Freightliner as sub-contractor benefits from any of the specified terms of the sender's contract with its own customer.

2.615 Another way around the privity rule is to seek an indemnity and this device can be seen in Condition 15 as well as Condition 4(c), the effect of which is that, if Freightliner is threatened with liability to a third party, the sender will ensure that proceedings will not be brought; and, if nonetheless proceedings are brought, Freightliner will be indemnified by the sender to the extent that Freightliner is held liable in excess of the liability assumed by Freightliner under these Standard Conditions of Carriage.[5] Condition 4(c) is reinforced by Condition 4(d), which exemplifies yet another way around the privity rule. This is an express trust whereby other carriers, as beneficiaries of Condition 4(c) can compel Freightliner as trustee of the Sender's promise in Condition 4(c) to enforce it against the Sender. On the efficacy of the agency device, and other methods of evading the privity rule see

1. *Midland Silicones Ltd.* v. *Scruttons Ltd.* [1962] A.C. 446.
2. *New Zealand Shipping Co.* v. *Satterthwaite* (*The Eurymedon*) [1975] A.C. 154 (P.C.).
3. *Hall* v. *N.E. Ry.* (1875) L.R. 10 Q.B. 437. Treitel Chap. 15.4.1.(1).
4. *Morris* v. *Martin & Sons* [1966] 1 Q.B. 716, 729 (C.A.); *The Pioneer Container* [1994] 2 A.C. 324; but cf. *The Mahkutai* [1996] 3 All E.R. 502 (P.C.); see Palmer, pp. 1631 *et seq.*
5. See *Snelling* v. *John Snelling Ltd.* [1973] Q.B.87. Treitel, Chap. 15.2,5(1)(j).

Comment 2 on Condition 2 of the RHA Conditions, paragraphs 1.266 *et seq*, above.

2. Privity of contract and statute

Although these rules of common law remain law in force, in most cases they have lost their importance to the 1999 Act: the Contracts (Rights of Third Parties) Act 1999. Section 1(1) of the Act confers a right of enforcement on "a person who is not a party to a contract", referred in the Act as the "third party", who, according to section 1(3), must be "expressly identified in the contract by name, . . . or as answering to a particular description". Examples given by the Law Commission of description sufficient to identify the third party include "subcontractors",[6] who are defined in Condition 1 of these Conditions. *2.616*

The right of enforcement can be conferred by contract on the third party in two ways, one of which, according to section 1(1)(b), is when a contract "term purports to confer a benefit on him". A "term" that confers a "benefit" includes an exemption or limitation clause and this is confirmed for contracts generally by section 1(6): as regards a term of the contract which "excludes or limits liability" enforcement shall be understood as the third party's "availing himself of the exclusion or limitation". The "purport", according to section 1(2), is no more than a presumption that the benefit is to be enforceable by the third party, which can be rebutted; however, the presumption is unlikely to be defeated in the case of sub-contracted carriage by rail . Thus, it is should now be a simple matter to extend the benefit of contractual terms to servants, agents and sub-contractors of Freightliner. *2.617*

5. The Nature of Transport and Conditions for Rail, Road and Sea Carriage *2.618*

(a) A Consignment accepted by Freightliner for transit may be carried by such means of transport and by such route as Freightliner thinks fit and these Transport and Conditions shall apply to any such means and route.

(b) In the case of international carriage within the meaning of the International Convention concerning the Carriage of Goods by Rail (referred to as the Sea Carriage CIM Regulations) signed at Berne on 9th May 1980 together with provisions accepted by the UK, Freightliner will issue a CIM consignment note and the Consignment referred to therein will be carried in accordance with the said Regulations, provided that such Regulations are satisfied in all respects including as to the contracting parties and as to all parts of the route as well as the lines over which the Consignment is to travel.

(c) In the case of loss or mis-delivery or damage or delay occurring during carriage by sea, if Freightliner is not the owner or demise charterer of the vessel, the Trader shall have the same but no greater rights against Freightliner as Freightliner has in respect of the loss, mis-delivery, damage or delay under its contract of carriage pursuant to which the goods were shipped on the vessel.

(d) In so far as Articles 1 to 40 of the Convention on the Contract for the International Carriage of Goods by road (known as CMR) are compulsorily applicable to any carriage undertaken by the Carriers, such Articles shall apply and the provisions of these Conditions

6. Law Commission Report No. 242, para. 8.1.

shall be treated as modified to such extent (if any) as may be necessary to give effect to such Articles in relation to such carriage, but no further.

Comment

2.619 Condition 5(a) is a typical liberty clause and is self-explanatory. The rest of Condition 5 concerns intermodal transport. Condition 5(b) and Condition 5(d) seek to accommodate the application of CIM and CMR respectively when the transport falls within the (compulsory) scope of one of these regimes. Condition 5(c) echoes Article 2 of CMR (para. 1.15, above), which was intended to align the legal regime of the main contract between sender and road carrier with that between the road carrier and the sea carrier, usually a sub-contractor of the road carrier in a transport road-sea-road. At the same time the effect is to respect the sphere of application of the legal regime appropriate to the sea stage: the Hague or Hague-Visby Rules. Condition 5(c) seeks to put Freightliner in a position analogous to that of a CMR road carrier in that respect.

2.620

6. Marks and Consignment Notes

(a) Every consignment shall be clearly marked and except when otherwise agreed to be accompanied by a consignment note containing such particulars as Freightliner may reasonably require.

(b) Freightliner, shall, if so required, sign a document prepared by the Sender acknowledging receipt of the Consignment but no such document shall be evidence of the condition or correctness of the declared nature, quantity or weight of the Consignment at the time it is received by Freightliner, and the burden of proving the condition of the Consignment on receipt by Freightliner and that the Consignment was of the nature, quantity or weight declared in the relevant document shall rest with the Sender.

(c) In the case of goods consigned by Freightliner's ERIC procedure the Trader shall in particular communicate to Freightliner before the goods are accepted by Freightliner for conveyance a movement advice containing such particulars as Freightliner may reasonably require.

Comment

2.621 Condition 6 recognises the need that Freightliner may have for information about the contents of containers loaded by the sender, on the one hand, and the need of the sender for some kind of evidence that Freightliner has received the container, on the other hand. At the same time Condition 6(b) articulates the traditional practice (developed in carriage by sea) of clausing the transport document (bill of lading) with wording such as "weight, quantity and contents unknown" to ensure that the carrier, who may well be in no position to check these matter, is not bound or estopped in any way on these matters by the transport document, in the case of Freightliner, the consignment note. In principle, therefore, Freightliner acknowledges receipt of a container of "something" and, if Freightliner is to be liable under the contract and Condition 16, it remains to be proved by the sender (or whoever brings the action) that the contents of the container were lost, damaged or delayed in transit, as well as their nature and value. See the corresponding provision in the RHA Conditions, Condition 5, paragraph 1.276, above.

7. Compliance with Regulations *2.622*

The Trader shall comply with all regulations and requirements of Governments, and Customs, Port and other authorities.

Comment

See Condition 15. *2.623*

8. Conditions of Consignment *2.624*

(a) The Sender warrants the suitability of the following for transit or storage:
(i) Container (except where provided by Freightliner);
(ii) contents of the Container;
(iii) manner of packing within the Container.

(b) The Sender warrants that the Consignment is free from infestation by vermin, and insect pest of any description and from contamination from any cause what ever.

(c) The Carriers shall be entitled to open any Consignment and inspect any part thereof. If the Carriers are of the opinion that the Consignment or any part thereof cannot be safely or properly carried or stored the Carriers shall be empowered to take such remedial steps as they think fit provided that where practicable Freightliner will seek instructions regarding such steps from the Trader.

(d) Freightliner shall be entitled to recover from the Sender the cost of any remedial steps taken to enable safe and proper carriage or storage (including steps to remedy infestation or contamination).

Comment

Senders are liable for the state of the goods they send on the basis of a warranty by senders at common law that the goods are fit for carriage. See the Comments on Condition 9, below. *2.625*

As regards Condition 8(a)(i) see Condition 16.1(f) and Condition 2. As regards Condition 8(a)(ii) see Condition 16.1(e). As regards Condition 8(a)(iii) see Condition 16.1(f). As regards Condition 8(b) and Condition 8(d) see Condition 15. As regards Condition 8(c) see the power of sale in Condition 12(c)(ii) and Condition 14(b). Condition 8(c) is a common kind of provision, however, note that failure to mitigate loss or damage to the goods may make a carrier liable. See CMR, Article 17, Comment 1 (paras. 1.78 *et seq.*) and Comment 7 (paras. 1.98 *et seq*). *2.626*

9. Dangerous Consignments *2.627*

(a) The conditions of acceptance of dangerous consignments are subject to compliance with "The List of Dangerous Goods and Conditions of Acceptance Consignments by Rail"

(BR 22426) or any superseding document published by Railtrack as amended from time to time.

(b) The Sender shall notify Freightliner of the nature of any dangerous goods contained in a Consignment and the hazard presented by such goods prior to inviting Freightliner to quote for the carriage of such goods. Prior to the date of the Contract, the Sender shall agree with Freightliner any special conditions for the carriage and/or storage of such dangerous consignment, such arrangements to be at the cost of the Sender.

(c) Where Freightliner accepts a dangerous consignment for transit or storage it does so subject to these Conditions and to the following special provisions:

(i) The consignment note accompanying the dangerous consignment shall specify the technical and (where appropriate) popular names of the dangerous goods comprised therein, and the nature of the danger presented by such goods;

(ii) Dangerous consignments shall be labelled and packed and stowed in accordance with any applicable statutory regulations and, unless otherwise agreed in writing, with the regulations for packing, labelling, loading, and stowing of dangerous goods published by the British Railways Board;

(iii) Any additional conditions set out or referred to in the consignment note or otherwise agreed.

(d) In the event of any failure by the Sender to comply with any of the provision of clauses (a), (b) and (c) hereof, the Carriers shall be under no liability whatsoever in respect of the dangerous Consignment, save in the case of wilful misconduct by the Carriers in which event liability shall be determined in accordance with these conditions.

(e) Freightliner may at any time at the Sender's sole risk and expense return the whole or any part of the dangerous Consignment to the Trader (who shall receive it at once) or destroy or otherwise dispose of the whole or any part thereof if Freightliner is of the opinion that it is necessary or advisable to do so.

Comments

1. Dangerous consignments

2.628 Dangerous consignments are defined in Condition 1.[1] Underlying Condition 9 is the common law warranty that a sender is liable for goods which are in a state that makes them unfit for carriage.[2] It is a strict warranty, breach of which does not depend on the knowledge or negligence of the sender.[3] Moreover, the sender is liable to the carrier, not only for damage done by the goods to the property of the carrier but also faces the possibility of action by the carrier (as bailee) on behalf of others affected,[4] unless they have already been indemnified by the sender.[5] The Conditions contain an indemnity to this effect in Condition 15(a).

2.629 If, however, the sender delivers a dangerous consignment to Freightliner in a state fit for carriage (or storage) and in compliance with Condition 9(c), Freightliner's liability for those goods is the same as that for any other class of goods, subject to any special agreement of the kind referred in Condition 9(c)(iii). If special care or precautions must be taken during transit, Freightliner must act accordingly and it will be liable if it does not—unless it is neither aware nor should have been aware of the need for such. In that event, a claim in respect of consequent loss or damage may be defended under Condition 9(d).

1. But see also the Carriage of Dangerous Goods and Use of Transportable Pressure Equipment Regulations 2004 (S.I. 2004/568), which came into force on 10 May 2004.
2. See Palmer, pp. 999 *et seq.*
3. *Bamfield* v. *Goole and Sheffield Transport Co.* [1910] 2 K.B. 94 (C.A.).
4. *The Winkfield* [1902] P. 42; *G.N. Ry.* v. *L.E.P. Transport* [1922] 2 K.B. 742 (C.A.).
5. *O'Sullivan* v. *Williams* [1992] 3 All E.R. 385 (C.A.).

2. Wilful misconduct

At common law, a person is guilty of wilful misconduct if he intends to inflict loss or damage[6] or if he "acts with recklessness, not caring what the results of his carelessness may be".[7] The "*mis*conduct, not the conduct, must be wilful".[8] The wilfulness and the knowledge, which goes with it, must be on the part of the person whose conduct is in question: it cannot be imputed from the knowledge of another employee.[9] In *Horobin,*[10] Barry J. pointed out that the same act may amount on one occasion to mere negligence and on another to wilful misconduct, and continued: *2.630*

"Two men driving motor cars may both pass traffic lights after they have changed from yellow to red. In both cases there are the same act, the same traffic lights, the same cross-roads and the same motor cars. In the first case the man may have been driving a little too fast. He may not have been keeping a proper look-out, and he may not have seen the lights (although he ought to have seen them) until he was too close to them and was unable to stop, and therefore, crossed the roads when the lights were against him. He was not intending to do anything wrong . . . but he was careless . . . and, as a result, without intending to do anything wrong, he committed an act of misconduct. The second driver is in a hurry. He knows all about the lights, and he sees in plenty of time that they are changing from yellow to red, but he says to himself: 'Hardly any traffic comes out of this side road which I am about to cross. I will go on. I am not going to bother to stop.' He does not expect an accident to happen, but he knows that he is doing something wrong . . . [In] that frame of mind no jury would have very much difficulty in coming to the conclusion that he had committed an act of wilful misconduct."

Thus there will be wilful misconduct if Freightliner handles the goods in a way which it knows to be risky, whether the risk is one of damage[11] or the risk is one of theft[12]; or if, knowingly, it handles goods in breach of safety regulations[13]; or if its employees steal or vandalise goods entrusted to them[14]; or if the container of goods is delivered to the wrong person without any attempt to check the identity of the recipient.[15] For more cases, see CMR Article 29, Comment 4, paragraphs 1.171 *et seq.*, above. To summarise, there would be wilful misconduct if: *2.631*

(a) Freightliner (through its employees) intended to inflict the loss or damage in question; a person is considered to have intended the inevitable consequences of an intentional act or omission; or
(b) there was misconduct which increased the risk to the goods and Freightliner was aware of this.

6. *Lewis* v. *G.W. Ry.* (1877) 3 Q.B.D. 195, 206.
7. *Forder* v. *G.W. Ry.* [1905] 2 K.B. 532, 535; see also *Glenister* v. *G.W.R.* (1873) 29 L.T. 423; Kahn-Freund, p. 257.
8. *Lewis* (above), *loc. cit.*
9. *Forder* (above).
10. *Horobin* v. *BOAC* [1952] 2 All E.R. 1016, 1020.
11. *Lewis* (above).
12. *Texas Instruments Ltd.* v. *Nasan (Europe) Ltd.* [1991] 1 Lloyd's Rep. 146, 154.
13. *Bastable* v. *N. British Ry.*, 1912 S.C. 555.
14. *Rustenberg* v. *S. African Airways* [1979] 1 Lloyd's Rep. 19.
15. *Hoare* v. *G.W. Ry. Co.* (1877) 37 L.T. 186.

2.632 By way of corollary:

(i) Although relevant to (a), as regards (b) the objective probability of loss or damage is not decisive, so that, in an emergency which threatened the goods, if Freightliner was on the horns of a dilemma, in which it was probable that, whatever course of action was taken in response to the situation goods would be damaged, it would not be guilty of wilful misconduct.

(ii) Negligence or even gross negligence do not amount to wilful misconduct.

2.633

10. Loading and Unloading

(a) On collection or delivery the Carriers shall be under no obligation to provide any plant, power or labour for loading or unloading.

Unloading

(b) Any assistance given or knowledge acquired by a servant or agent of the Carriers in assisting the Trader, whether in connection with loading or unloading of goods into or out of any Container or otherwise, will be given or acquired on behalf of the Trader who shall be responsible for the acts and knowledge of such servant or agent as if he were the Trader's employee.

(c) Consignments requiring special appliances for loading onto or unloading a vehicle or Container are accepted for transit only on condition that the Sender undertakes that such appliances will be available at loading and unloading. Where special appliances are required for loading and unloading, but are not available, the Carriers shall nonetheless be at liberty (but not bound) to load or unload in such a manner as they may think fit, and in such case the Carriers shall be under no liability whatsoever to the Trader for any damage howsoever caused during the loading or unloading, whether or not by the negligence of the Carriers, and the Sender shall be responsible for and indemnify the Carriers against any loss, damage or claim which the Carriers may suffer or incur in connection with such loading or unloading.

(d) The Sender shall be responsible for the suitability of the means of access to and egress from any premises at which the Carriers are instructed to collect or deliver a Consignment, including delivery or collection of empty Containers.

Comments

2.634 Who is to be responsible for loading and unloading is a matter for party agreement, unless the transport is subject to CIM, Article 20. Further, Condition 10 makes it clear that, in the absence of special agreement, Freightliner has no duty to provide equipment. Condition 10 also states the corollary that it is for the sender to provide any special appliances required for (un)loading; and Condition 10(c) provides that, if the sender is in breach of the obligation to provide the necessary equipment and Freightliner nonetheless elects[1] to (un)load, it is entirely at the risk of the trader.

1. On this cf. the corresponding provision of the RHA Conditions of Carriage, Condition 4, para. 1.274, above.

11. Transit *2.635*

(a) Transit begins when the Consignment is handed to or collected by the Carriers for carriage, and ends (unless otherwise previously determined) when the Consignment is delivered, or as provided in Condition 11 (c) below.

(b) (i) Transit shall be suspended when at any time prior to the end of transit the Consignment is held by the Carriers at some place other than the destination at the request or for the convenience of the Trader (including detention for Customs purposes) or because the Trader has refused or has shown or stated that he is unable to take delivery at the destination.

(ii) If transit shall have ended under these Conditions, but Freightliner subsequently carries the Consignment for whatever reason, such subsequent carriage shall be treated as undertaken pursuant to a separate Contract for carriage subject to these Conditions.

(c) Transit shall (unless otherwise previously determined) end, notwithstanding that the Consignment has not been delivered:

(i) In the case of a Consignment to be delivered by the Carriers when it is tendered at the Consignee's premises within the customary cartage hours of the delivery district or at such other time or place as may be agreed between the Carriers and the Trader.

(ii) In the case of a Consignment to be collected by the Trader: (a) at the expiration of 11 hours from the arrival of the Consignment at the rail or other terminal, depot or place to which it has been consigned; or (b) at the time at which the goods are loaded aboard a trailer, wagon, vehicle or other conveyance belong to or operated by the Trader, his servants or agents; or (c) if the goods are already aboard a trailer or wagon, at the time the Trader, his servants or agents attach the tractor unit, engine or other mode of traction to such trailer or wagon; whichever be the earlier. Unless otherwise agreed between the Trader and Freightliner, it is the duty of the Sender to advise the Consignee of the expected time of arrival of the Consignment.

(iii) In the case of a Consignment consigned to a Private Siding, where such delivery is hindered or prevented by circumstances beyond the Carriers' control, the Carriers may give notice to the Sender or Consignee accordingly and transit shall end 11 hours thereafter.

Comment

Transit begins when possession, and hence custody and control, pass from the sender (or his agent) to Freightliner; and ends when tender of the consignment, and hence an offer of possession and control, is made by Freightliner to the consignee. The period of transit (and thus Condition 11) is important notably because, when transit ends, the nature and level of Freightliner's liability for the consignment changes under Condition 12(b). In the carriage of goods, whatever the mode of carriage, when custody and control change there is a significant change in the risk and usually therefore a change of legal regime[1]; so it is here. *2.636*

The primary rule for the ending of transit being actual delivery of the consignment to the consignee, provision has to be made for cases in which, through no fault of Freightliner, that cannot be done. Hence Condition 12(b) reflects the common law rule[2] that tender of the goods at the right time and place amounts to delivery for the purpose of ending transit. It is supplemented by Condition 12(c)(ii) and Condition 14(b) which give Freightliner a right to sell a consignment which has not been collected. Condition 14(b), however, is different from common law where the *2.637*

1. Clarke, *Insurance*, Chap. 16–2A6.
2. Glass/Cashmore, para. 1.67. See *Startup* v. *Macdonald* (1843) 6 Man. & G. 593; *Heugh* v. *L.N.W. Ry.* (1870) L.R. 5 Ex. 51.

general rule is that notice is not effective until it has been received,[3] whereas under Condition 21 the notice to the trader required by Condition 14(b) is operative earlier on transmission, such as posting.

2.638

12. Storage

Freightliner will store the Consignment after termination or during suspension of transit as defined in Condition 11 hereof (unless otherwise agreed) or if Freightliner accepts instructions for storage whether or not in connection with carriage of any Consignment. With the exception of Conditions 2, 5,16 and 18, all storage shall be subjected to the Conditions herein, and in addition to the following special provisions:

(a) The Carriers may at their option store Consignments either outside or under cover. Consignments must be adequately protected by the Trader for outside storage.

(b) The Carriers shall not be liable for any loss or mis-delivery or damage or delay of whatever nature or howsoever arising in the case of any consignment or part thereof:

- (i) except upon proof that such loss or mis-delivery or damage or delay has been caused by the neglect or default of the Carriers;
- (ii) caused either wholly or partially and either directly or indirectly by fire or flood, howsoever arising;
- (iii) in respect of which the Carriers have given notice that no suitable accommodation for storage is available;
- (iv) in respect of which the Carriers have given notice that the Consignment is or has become in their opinion unsuitable for storage;
- (v) in regard to storage unless a claim is made in writing to Freightliner within seven days of the date when the Trader first acquires knowledge of such loss or mis-delivery or damage or delay and unless suit is commenced within one year of the said date; but the Trader shall have the benefit of a like proviso to that in Condition 18(a) hereof in regard to any such claim and the benefit of a like condition to Condition 18(c) hereof in regard to the said commencement of suit.

(c) (i) Freightliner may at any time require the Trader to remove the Consignment and pay all charges thereon by giving him 48 hours notice of such requirements.

(ii) In the event of the whole or any part of the Consignment not being removed within 48 hours, the Carriers may after giving a further 28 days notice of their intention so to do sell the whole or any part of such Consignment and payment or tender of the proceeds of sale after deducting the expenses of sale and all other charges due in respect of the Consignment shall (without prejudice to any outstanding claim which the Sender may have against Freightliner) discharge Freightliner from all liability in respect of the Consignment.

(d) Upon the Sender or any person duly authorised by him giving adequate prior notice to Freightliner, Freightliner will permit the Sender or authorised person to enter upon the premises where the Consignment is stored for the purpose of inspecting the same at any reasonable time during the normal hours of business.

Comment

2.639 Condition 12 is central to the liability of Freightliner not as carrier but in its role as warehouseman and bailee. However, it cannot be divorced from its role as carrier because Condition 12 applies when transit is suspended and, in particular, when transit ends under Condition 11. Freightliner's underlying liability is that of a bailee at common law. In so far as that is a liability for negligence, Condition 12 is consonant with the common law rule. However, at common law, evidence at outturn of loss of or damage to goods in the custody of a bailee has led to a

3. *Holwell Securities Ltd.* v. *Hughes* [1974] 1 All E.R. 164 (C.A.).

presumption of liability unless the bailee disproves negligence,[1] and a court may be inclined to ignore Condition 12(b)(i) in so far as it puts the onus of proof on the claimant.

As regards the requirements of notice, see Condition 21. As regards periods of notice, see Condition 18. *2.640*

13. Charges *2.641*

(a) Freightliner's charges for carriage and storage together with services incidental thereto including the provision of Containers shall be payable by the Sender without prejudice to Freightliner's rights against the Consignee or any other person, provided that where Freightliner has accepted goods "carriage forward" the Sender shall only pay such charges if the consignee fails to pay on demand.

(b) A claim, counterclaim or set-off shall not be made the reason for deferring or withholding payment of monies otherwise due to Freightliner.

(c) The Sender shall pay Freightliner's charges for:

(i) detaining beyond the time allowed for their use wagons, vehicles, Containers, coverings and other equipment provided by the Carriers;

(ii) use or occupation of any siding or other accommodation; where such detention use or occupation is at the Trader's request or for his convenience.

(d) Subject to Condition 13(a) hereof charges shall be payable when the Consignment is received by Freightliner. Without prejudice to the foregoing, the Sender may pay periodically provided each and every invoice is paid within 28 days of the date thereon. In case of late payment, Freightliner in addition is entitled to interest at 2% above The Royal Bank of Scotland minimum lending rate or the equivalent thereof.

Comment

1. Who pays?

Condition 13(a) is consistent with but different from the related common law rules,[1] in that the charges are payable by the sender. At common law the person liable to pay charges is the person who contracts with the carrier; but the inference from the distinct mention in Condition 13(a) of the consignee is for a different rule here, because the common law position is that the person who contracts with the carrier is presumed to be the consignee.[2] *2.642*

The saving reference to the consignee is consistent with common law, where the rule is that even when the charges in a particular case are payable by a sender, if the goods are delivered to the consignee, common law implies a contract whereby unpaid charges become payable by the consignee.[3] However, the provision for consignments "carriage forward", which is also found in Condition 8(1) of the RHA Conditions, purports to change the common law rule.[4] *2.643*

1. *Travers, Joseph & Sons Ltd.* v. *Cooper* [1915] 1 K.B. 73. See also *Levison* v. *Patent Steam Carpet Cleaning Co. Ltd.* [1978] QB 69 (C.A.); applied in *Euro Cellular Ltd.* v. *Danzas Ltd.* [2004] 1 Lloyd's Rep. 521 at [65]. Palmer, p. 1104.

1. See Glass/Cashmore, para. 1.106; and Palmer, p. 1101.

2. See the Comment on Condition 1.

3. *World Transport Co.* v. *Tealing & Co.* [1936] 2 All E.R. 573; Clarke [1991] L.M.C.L.Q. 5.

4. Palmer, p. 1016.

2. The time for payment

2.644 The time for payment is a matter of contract and thus, in this case, Condition 13(d), that in principle charges are payable when the Consignment is first received by Freightliner. This displaces the common law rule that freight charges are payable at the time of delivery, provided that the goods have been delivered or tendered.[5]

2.645 As regards the "no set-off" provision in Condition 13(b), freight is payable at common law even if the goods are delivered short in quantity or damaged[6]; this too is a rule for carriage by sea but one which has been applied to carriage by road with "unconcealed reluctance"[7]; and the argument, that a "no set-off" clause in the BIFA Conditions was unreasonable under the Unfair Contract Terms Act 1977, has been rejected by the Court of Appeal because such clauses were common and, in the view of the court, that reflected a general view of what was reasonable in the trade.[8] The rule is controversial, however,[9] Condition 13(b) seeks to maintain it, as does Condition 7.6 of the EWS Conditions, as well as both the BIFA Conditions and Condition 8(2) of the RHA Conditions.

2.646 If the sender is obliged to pay charges and has not done so, Freightliner can simply refuse to carry the goods until freight has been paid or sufficient security given. In the event of non-payment by the consignee, Freightliner's primary remedy is a lien on the goods, which is provided for in Condition 14.

2.647

14. Lien

(a) The Consignment and each and every part thereof is accepted by Freightliner subject to a:

(i) lien upon such Consignment for monies, charges or expenses due to it in connection with the carriage or storage thereof;

(ii) general lien upon such Consignment for any other monies, charges or expenses due to it.

(b) In case all such monies, charges or expenses due are not paid in full within 28 days from the date upon which Freightliner first gives notice of the exercise of its lien to the Trader, the said Consignment or any part thereof may be sold and the proceeds of sale applied in or towards the satisfaction of such monies, charges or expenses and all costs incurred in relation to the exercise of Freightliner's lien and the sale, and Freightliner shall account for any surplus.

(c) The liens provided by clause (a) hereof shall be exercisable against the Trader and all other persons interested in the Consignment or any part thereof, and are exercisable to recover monies, charges and expenses due from any one or more of any such persons.

Comment

2.648 At common law every carrier or at least every common carrier,[1] which, however, according to Condition 24 Freightliner is not, has a "particular" lien on goods in its possession for freight and charges in relation to goods which it is ready and able to

5. Palmer, p. 1102.
6. *Aries Tanker Corp.* v. *Total Transport* [1977] 1 W.L.R. 185 (H.L.)
7. By May J. in *United Carriers Ltd.* v. *Heritage Food Group (UK) Ltd.* [1995] 4 All E.R. 95, 102.
8. In *Overland Shoes Ltd.* v. *Schenkers Ltd.* [1998] 1 Lloyd's Rep. 498.
9. See Clarke, *CMR*, para. 45g.
1. Cf. Glass/Cashmore, para. 1.110.

deliver. This "particular" lien is distinguished from a "general lien" in respect of debts due under previous contracts of carriage between the same parties. A general lien does not arise as a matter of law but is often granted by a provision of the contract of carriage. Condition 14(a)(ii) is such a provision. As is usual, Condition 14(b) gives Freightliner a right to sell the consignment if the debt is not paid within a certain time, in this case 28 days.

15. Liability for Loss, Mis-delivery, Damage or Delay [Liability of the Sender] *2.649*

(a) The Sender shall save harmless and keep Freightliner indemnified against all claims and demands of any kind whatsoever (including, without prejudice, to the generality of the foregoing, claims or demands based on alleged negligence by the Carriers) by whomsoever they are made, greater than or in addition to the liability of Freightliner under the Conditions.

(b) Without limiting the foregoing the Sender shall indemnify Freightliner against any such claims or demands of any nature whatsoever made by any Subcontractor, or by any servant or agent of Freightliner or of any Subcontractor, or by any other person whatsoever at any time concerned with any Consignment or Container or with the services the subject of the Contract, whether or not any such claim or demand shall arise out of any claim or demand made directly or indirectly by the Trader against any such Subcontractor, servant, agent or other person.

(c) The Sender hereby expressly undertakes to be responsible for and to indemnify Freightliner against all loss and damage and claims whatsoever arising in any way from any noncompliance by the Trader with any of these Conditions.

Comment

Concerning Condition 15(a) and 15(b), see Condition 4, Comment 1 and the Comment on Condition 9. Concerning Condition 15(c), see Conditions 7, 8 and 22. Concerning the meaning of "loss", "damage" and "delay", see CMR Article 17, Comment 4 (para. 1.91, above). Concerning the meaning of "mis-delivery" see Condition 16, Comment 1. *2.650*

[16.] [Liability of Freightliner] *2.651*

16.1 Subject to these Conditions Freightliner shall be liable for loss or mis-delivery of or damage or delay in respect of the Consignment or any part thereof occurring or caused otherwise than during storage as defined by Condition 12 above unless and except in so far as such loss or mis-delivery or damage or delay has arisen or resulted from:

(a) Act of God;
(b) Any consequence of war, invasion, act of foreign enemy, hostilities, civil war, rebellion, insurrection, military or usurped power or confiscation, requisition, destruction of or damage to property by or under the order of any Government or public or local authority, restraint of prices (including administrative or government action);
(c) Seizure under legal process;
(d) Error, act, omission, mis-statement or misrepresentation by the Trader or other owner of the Consignment or by servants or agents of either of them;
(e) Inherent liability to wastage in bulk or weight latent defect or inherent defect, vice or natural deterioration of the Consignment or any part thereof:
(f) Insufficient or improper packing;
(g) Insufficient or improper labelling or addressing;

(h) Riot, civil commotion, strikes, lockouts, stoppage or restraint of labour from whatever cause;
(i) The consignee not taking or accepting delivery within a reasonable time.
(j) Delay otherwise than during the course of storage upon proof that such delay has been caused by the neglect or default of the Carriers.

16.2 (a) Freightliner shall not incur liability of any kind to a Consignment where there has been fraud on the part of the Trader;
(b) Where under this Condition Freightliner is not under any liability in respect of some of the factors causing the loss or mis-delivery or damage or delay, it shall only be liable to the extent that those factors for which it is liable under this Condition have contributed to the said loss or mis-delivery or damage or delay.

16.3 Save as aforesaid Freightliner shall be under no liability whatsoever in connection with any Consignment or any instructions given to it.

Comments

1. Liability

2.652 Condition 16 is a central provision whereby Freightliner is liable for loss or mis-delivery of or damage or delay to the consignment. "Mis-delivery" is delivery other than to the right person or to a person who is reasonably believed to be the right person, and to the right place or what is reasonably believed to be the right place.[1] Concerning the meaning of "loss", "damage" and "delay", see CMR Article 17, Comment 4, paragraphs 1.91 *et seq.*, above.

2.653 This and the other Conditions must be read in context, i.e., as terms of a contract of carriage under which Freightliner, as carrier, undertakes to deliver the consignment at the agreed destination in the same order and condition in which it was received from the sender. In principle that undertaking is strict and absolute, however, in practice it is subject to contract terms such as these Conditions and, in particular, the exceptions found in Condition 16 and the limit on amount in Condition 17.

2. Exceptions to liability

2.654 Exceptions (a) to (j) are similar to exceptions (i) to (ix) in RHA Condition 9. Condition 16.1 stipulates, as would usually be the construction put on a condition of this kind, that, for the exception pleaded to be effective as such, the loss, mis-delivery, damage or delay in question must have "arisen or resulted from" the excepted cause. This is an instance of strict construction, construction *contra proferentem*: unless very clear from the contract, exceptions do not excuse a defendant carrier unless the excepted event caused the loss, damage or delay in issue. More than that, the event has been required to be the proximate cause, as understood in the law of insurance.[2] This means that the impact of the event on the

1. *M'Kean* v. *M'Ivor* (1870) L.R. 6 Ex. 36.

2. See *Reardon Smith Line* v. *Ministry of Agriculture, Fisheries and Food* [1960] 1 Q.B. 439, affirmed [1962] 1 Q.B. 42 (C.A.) affirmed on other grounds [1963] A.C. 691, re whether a strike, the exonerating event, had caused delay in loading. To resolve this issue, McNair J. (at 492) relied on a statement by Lord Dunedin in *Leyland Shipping Co.* v. *Norwich Union Fire Insurance Society* [1918] A.C. 350, 362 suggesting that the event must be the proximate cause of the loss; and in this regard the reasoning of McNair J. was approved by Willmer L.J. (at 102). See also in this sense: *Benjamin on Sale*, (para. 8–088 and cases cited) concerning "prevention" clauses in sales contracts.

consignment must have been for practical purposes inevitable, a very close causal connection indeed.[3]

(a) *An Act of God* is some elemental force of nature, which could not have been foreseen or, if foreseen, could not have been guarded against by any ordinary or reasonable precaution.[4] Such events are rare. Kahn-Freund suggested a consignment struck by lightning.[5] Past cases suggest also damage to a consignment when snow blocked the line.[6] *2.655*

(b) *War* connotes aggression on the part of a government which exists at least *de facto.* A formal declaration of war is not necessary and anyway, if there has been no declaration, the case is probably a case of "hostilities". Hostilities are situations in which, whether or not a state of war exists within the obscure sense of international law, there is "armed conflict between competing nations".[7] Acts of terrorists do not fall into this category, unless the terrorists can be said to represent or be sponsored by a government.[8] *2.656*

(c) *Seizure under legal process* is detention or interference by the courts as a result of legal proceedings and in this respect it has been distinguished from the orders of government, referred to at the end of exception (b). *2.657*

(d) *Error etc.* is a catch-all exception by reference to the conduct of the trader. On the one hand, it is not clear what "mis-statement" and "misrepresentation" add to "error".[9] On the other hand, it is clear that exception (d) overlaps with other exceptions, such as exceptions (f) and (g). A prime example of exception (d) is something done or omitted by the sender during loading or unloading, as to which, see also Condition 10. It seems that Freightliner is excused under exception (d) regardless of fault on the part of the trader.[10] Fraud on the part of the trader is the subject of a specific provision, Condition 16.2(a). *2.658*

(e) *Inherent defect* is the central feature of exception (e), which is another catch-all exception. It embraces "inherent liability to wastage in bulk or weight" and "natural deterioration".[11] It overlaps "latent defect", which is a defect of any kind at all which could not be expected to be discovered by any inspection or test which the person concerned could reasonably be expected to make.[12] *2.659*

Inherent defect means the same as the better known "inherent vice". "Inherent vice", both in contract conditions and international carriage regimes such as CMR, is taken to mean what it also means at common law[13]: some defect in the goods *2.660*

3. See Clarke, *Insurance*, Chap. 25–3.

4. Kahn-Freund, p. 243; *Nugent* v. *Smith* (1876) 1 C.P.D. 423, 437 concerning carriage by sea.

5. Kahn-Freund, p. 244.

6. *Briddon* v. *Great Northern Ry.* (1858) 28 L.J.Ex. 51.

7. *Kawasaki Kisen Kabushiki Kaisha* v. *Bantham S.S. Co. (No. 2)* (1938) 61 Ll.L.Rep. 131, 138, affirmed [1939] 2 K.B. 544 (C.A.).

8. *Pan American World Airways Inc.* v. *Aetna Casualty & Surety Co.* [1975] 1 Lloyd's Rep. 77 (U.S.C.A. 2 Cir., 1974).

9. Palmer, p. 1106.

10. Cf. CMR Article 17.2 (para. 1.77, above) which refers to the "wrongful" act of the sender or consignee.

11. Cf. however, *Donald & Son (Wholesale Meat Contractors) Ltd.* v. *Continental Freeze*, 1984 S.L.T. 182.

12. *The Amstelslot* [1963] 2 Lloyd's Rep. 223 (H.L.). On the distinction with "inherent vice", see further Clarke, *CMR*, para 89a.

13. For a relatively recent decision see *Noten* v. *Harding* [1990] 2 Lloyd's Rep. 283 (C.A.).

which by its development through ordinary processes going on in those goods tends to the injury or destruction of the goods.[14]

2.661 (f) *Insufficient or improper packing* is also a kind of inherent defect (exception (e)) and in most cases an instance of "act" or "omission" by the trader (exception (d)) as well. Packing probably refers to the packing of goods inside the container but might apply to the container itself when that has been supplied by the trader. Packing is insufficient if it does not enable the particular goods to withstand the normal dangers of the kind contemplated by the particular rail journey. These include the handling to be expected by Freightliner (see Condition 10); and this must be considered in the light of what Freightliner can be taken to know about the contents of the container, bearing in mind that it has neither a right nor a duty to open a container to investigate its contents, unless Condition 8(c) applies.

2.662 (g) *Insufficient or improper labelling or addressing* is often a particular kind of error etc. by the trader (exception (d)) and possibly of insufficient or improper packing (exception (f)). See also Condition 9(b) and Condition 9(c)(ii).

2.663 (h) *Riot etc.* is another catch-all exception taking in forms of public disorder of a lesser magnitude than those falling within exception (b). For a riot there must be 12 or more persons with a common purpose, which must have been at least incepted and in a manner which involves the use or threat of unlawful violence; and which was "such as would cause a person of reasonable firmness present at the scene to fear for his personal safety".[15] There is a presumption that contracts use terms which have a technical sense in criminal law, such as "riot", in that same sense.[16]

2.664 Civil commotion, which overlaps riot,[17] is "something considerably more serious than a leaderless mob"[18] and "is used to indicate a stage between riot and civil war".[19] It is a "rising of the people . . . for purposes of general mischief".[20]

2.665 A strike at common law is "a general concerted refusal by workmen to work in consequence of an alleged grievance".[21] For the purposes of labour law and industrial relations it also has a statutory definition.[22] A restraint of labour does not seem to have been defined but certainly includes a threat by employees not to move or handle certain goods.[23]

2.666 (i) *Failure by the consignee to take or accept delivery of the consignment within a reasonable time* appears to be covered also by exception (d). In such circumstances the liability of Freightliner would be that of an involuntary bailee.[24] See also Condition 11(c)(ii) and Condition 12.

14. See further CMR, Article 17, Comment 6, paras. 1.96 to 1.97, above.
15. Public Order Act 1986, s. 1. See Clarke, *Insurance*, Chap. 19–3E.
16. *London & Lancashire Fire Ins. Co.* v. *Bolands Ltd.* [1924] A.C. 836.
17. *Kuwait Airways* v. *Kuwait Ins. Co.* [1999] 1 Lloyd's Rep. 803 (H.L.).
18. *Spinney's (1948) Ltd.* v. *Royal Ins. Co. Ltd.* [1980] 1 Lloyd's Rep. 406, 437.
19. *Levy* v. *Assicurazioni Generali* [1940] A.C. 791, 800 (P.C.).
20. *Spinney's* case (above), p. 438.
21. *William* v. *Naamlooze* (1915) 21 Com. Cas. 253, 257. See also *Tramp Shipping Corp.* v. *Greenwich Marine Inc.* [1975] 2 All E.R. 989, 992 (C.A.).
22. See Deakin & Morris, *Labour Law* (3rd ed., London, 2001), Chap. 11.12.
23. *Young & Son (Wholesale Fish Merchants) Ltd.* v. *British Transport Commission* [1955] 2 Q.B. 177; Kahn-Freund, p. 249.
24. See Palmer, Chap. 15.

(j) *Delay* as an exception "otherwise than during the course of storage upon proof that such delay has been caused by the neglect or default of the Carriers", which is almost a verbatim repetition of Freightliner's liability for storage under Article 12(b)(i), appears to mean delay, except delay when Freightliner is storing a consignment in accordance with Article 12, i.e. that delay is an exception operating (only) when Freightliner is performing the contract of carriage. That leaves a *prima facie* reading of Article 16.1 as "Freightliner shall be liable for . . . delay . . . except in so far as . . . delay has arisen from . . . (j) Delay". *Sed quaere.* *2.667*

17. Limit of Liability *2.668*

(a) The liability (howsoever arising) of Freightliner to pay compensation in respect of any one Consignment shall in any case be limited in so far as the loss or mis-delivery or damage or delay howsoever sustained is in respect of:

(i) a Container to a sum calculated at a rate of £1,500 per tonne gross weight of the Container and in so far as it is in respect of the whole contents of a Container or the whole of goods not in a Container to a sum calculated at a rate of £1,500 per tonne of such contents or goods each calculation to be made separately;

(ii) part of the contents of a Container or part of goods not in a Container to the proportion of any sum ascertained separately in accordance with subclause (i) hereof for contents or goods which the value of the said part bears to the value of the whole of the contents or goods.

(b) Provided that:

(i) nothing in this Condition shall limit Freightliner's liability to a sum less than £10 in respect of any one Consignment;

(ii) Freightliner shall be entitled to require proof of the value of the whole Consignment, as well as of any part thereof to which the claim relates;

(iii) nothing in this condition shall limit Freightliner's liability in respect of any death or personal injury to any person.

(c) Freightliner shall not in any case be liable for loss of use of or payment of hire on or demurrage on Containers and/or vehicles or for loss of a particular market whether held daily or at intervals or for loss of profit or increased losses or for any other indirect or consequential damages of whatsoever kind.

(d) If the Trader is permitted to leave any tractor unit, trailer, or other property of whatever nature (other than the Consignment) it is agreed that such property is left at the Trader's own risk. Freightliner accepts no responsibility for any loss or damage of whatsoever nature and howsoever caused to such goods.

Comment

Freightliner's liability to pay compensation in respect of loss or mis-delivery of or damage or delay[1] to a consignment is limited in accordance with Condition 17. The liability is *prima facie* Freightliner's liability under Article 16.1; and Condition 17 also purports to limit Freightliner's liability "howsoever arising" in respect of "loss or mis-delivery or damage or delay howsoever sustained" in respect of a consignment. When the liability of a road carrier "howsoever sustained", under a pre-1989 *2.669*

1. For the meaning of loss, mis-delivery, damage and delay, see Condition 16, Comment 1.

version of the RHA Conditions, was considered by the Commercial Court,[2] the court held that, in spite of the well-known rules of construction *contra proferentem* stated in the *Canada Steamship* case,[3] the limit in question applied even when the loss or damage had been caused by the carrier's negligence. In contrast, although Condition 17(c) purports to limit the particular liability of Freightliner for "any other indirect or consequential damages of whatsoever kind", it should be noted that a restrictive view of similar wording in a pre-1989 version of the RHA Conditions was taken by Saville J. in *Shell* v. *P & O*.[4]

2.670 English courts have been slow to condemn standard conditions in widespread use as unreasonable under the Unfair Contract Terms Act 1977.[5] The Freightliner Conditions are new, however, they are sufficiently similar to conditions of longer lineage, such as the RHA Conditions, for their youth not to count against them. Moreover, courts are less hostile to limitation clauses such as Condition 17 than to exception clauses such as those in Condition 16.1.[6] However, one of the BIFA Conditions, not unlike Condition 17, was struck out in *Overseas Medical Supplies* v. *Orient Transport Services*.[7] The "carrier" in this case was a firm that specialised in the carriage of goods and "associated services". The condition was struck out because it was a case of "of a trading organisation which, under a single contract had agreed to combine at least two activities or functions in respect of which the nature of the work undertaken, the incidence of risk as between the parties, and the effect of a breach of duty by the ['carrier'] were all of different character, yet were treated without distinction as subject to a single [and relatively low] limitation of liability".[8] One can surmise that Freightliner's role as carrier and its role as warehouseman under Condition 12 are not "functions in respect of which the nature of the work undertaken, the incidence of risk as between the parties, and the effect of a breach of duty" by Freightliner were all of sufficiently "different character" for the ruling in *Medical Supplies* v. *Orient Transport Services* to count against Freightliner under this Condition. However, the levels of liability under Condition 12 and Condition 16.1 are sufficiently different to produce a different "incidence of risk as between the parties", so the ruling should not be ignored.

2.671

18. Limits

(a) Freightliner shall not in any event be liable for loss or mis-delivery of:
   (i) damage to the whole or any part of the Consignment, or physical loss, mis-delivery or non delivery of part of the Consignment unless advised thereof in writing within fourteen days after the termination of the transit;
   (ii) the whole of the Consignment unless it is advised of the loss, mis-delivery or non-delivery in writing by the Trader (otherwise than upon any of Freightliner's

2. *Cert plc* v. *George Hammond plc* [1999] 2 All E.R. (Comm.) 976.
3. *Canada Steamships Line Ltd.* v. *R.* [1952] A.C. 192 (P.C.). See also *Alderslade* v. *Hendon Laundry Ltd.* [1945] K.B. 189 (C.A.).
4. *Shell Chemicals UK Ltd.* v. *P & O Roadtanks Ltd.* [1993] 1 Lloyd's Rep. 114, 118, with reference to *Croudace Construction Ltd.* v. *Cawoods Concrete Products Ltd.* [1978] 2 Lloyd's Rep. 55 (C.A.).
5. See the Introduction to the RHA Conditions (paras. 1.251 *et seq.*, above).
6. *Ailsa Craig Fishing Co. Ltd.* v. *Malvern Fishing Co. Ltd.* [1983] 1 W.L.R. 964 (H.L.).
7. [1999] 2 Lloyd's Rep. 273 (C.A.).
8. *Per* Potter L.J. at [21].

documents) within 28 days and the claim is made in writing within 42 days after transit began.

(b) Provided that if in any particular case the claimant proves that:

(i) it was not reasonably possible to advise Freightliner or claim in writing within the aforesaid times; and

(ii) such advice or claim was given or made within a reasonable time; and

(iii) there has been no prejudice to Freightliner thereby:

Freightliner shall not have the benefit of sub-clause (a) of this Condition.

(c) Freightliner shall in any event be discharged from all liability whatsoever in respect of the Consignment unless suit is commenced within a period of time of one year from the termination of the transit or, in the case of loss, mis-delivery or non-delivery of the whole of the Consignment, from the said 28 days referred to in Condition 18 (a) (ii) hereof.

(d) If not later than 5 days before the expiration of the said period or any agreed extension thereof the claimant requests an extension of the said one year period, the said time shall continue until Freightliner's reply. If the said request is refused the said time shall continue for a further 13 days after the day when the claimant has been advised of such refusal.

Comments

1. Notice

Condition 18 contains "limits" on the liability of Freightliner in a sense different from those of Condition 17. Whereas the latter concerns limits on the amount of an established liability, those in Condition 18 rule out Freightliner's liability altogether unless the claimant notifies Freightliner of the claim within a specified time limit (Condition 18(a)) or commences proceedings against Freightliner within the specified limitation period (Condition 18(c)). In short the "limits" are time limits. *2.672*

If proceedings are commenced against Freightliner late in the limitation period, it will be badly placed to find evidence to mount a defence. Hence, it is generally regarded as reasonable for carriers such as Freightliner to require notice of some kind within a short time after the events that may give rise to a claim, followed, if the matter is to be taken further, by a more detailed claim within a certain time after that. Thus Condition 18(a)(i) requires any potential claimant to "advise" Freightliner in writing[1] within specified periods of time of the occurrence of certain kinds of loss. "Advice" means notification,[2] and notification means that the communication has been received, otherwise it is not effective.[3] The content of the "advice" is not that the potential claimant intends to claim but is the allegation of the specified kind of loss, so that Freightliner can investigate the allegation before the facts become obscure or evidence hard to obtain. Computation of time is in accordance with Condition 19. *2.673*

The requirements of Condition 18(a) are qualified by Condition 18(b) in a way not found in other conditions or carriage regimes discussed in Parts 1 to 3 of this book. Condition 18(b)(i) and Condition 18(b)(ii) combine to override Condition 18(a) when the claimant can prove that Freightliner has received reasonable notice. Condition 18(b)(iii) settles an issue which has vexed courts concerned with issues *2.674*

1. For the meaning of writing see, CMR Article 30, Comment 3, paras. 1.179 *et seq.*, above.
2. Kahn-Freund, p. 393.
3. *Holwell Securities Ltd.* v. *Hughes* [1974] 1 All E.R. 164 (C.A.).

of notice in other contexts[4] by confirming that Freightliner cannot defend a claim because it is late under Condition 18(a) if it has suffered no prejudice or, as one might say, if in terms of the effect of late notice the notice given was not unreasonable. This too must be proved by the claimant.

2. Claims

2.675 The periods for commencement of suit are those specified in Condition 18(c) with the possibility of extension in accordance with Condition 18(d). Computation of time is in accordance with Condition 19. Condition 18(c) amounts to a considerable restriction on the time allowed by statute. Claims against a carrier or warehouseman, whether based in contract, tort or bailment are subject to sections 2 and 5 of the Limitation Act 1980, and must be brought within six years of the date on which the cause of action accrued, subject to extension in certain cases.

2.676 Conditions such as Conditions 18(c) are found in other transport documents, notably, international Conventions. The provision of the BIFA Conditions corresponding to Condition 18, which requires notice of claims within 14 days and proceedings within 9 months, was held to be unreasonable under the Unfair Contract Terms Act 1977 at first instance in *Granville Oil*. On appeal, however, the provision was upheld.[5] See the Introduction to these Conditions, paragraphs 2.603 to 2.604, above.

2.677 **19. Computation of Time**

In the computation of time where any period provided by these Conditions is 7 days or less, Saturdays, Sundays and Public Holidays shall not be included.

2.678 **20. Other Published Regulations**

The Consignment is carried or stored subject to any other published bye-laws and regulations of Statutory force affecting directly or indirectly carriage or storage by Freightliner for the time being in force and in the event of conflict between such bye-laws and regulations and these Conditions the said byelaws and regulations shall prevail.

2.679 **21. Service of Notice**

Any notice to either the Sender or the Trader relating to any Consignment or part thereof or required by or referred to in any of the provisions of these Conditions shall be conclusively regarded as served on the Sender or Trader if the same has been sent by post to the Sender at the Sender's last known address. Such service shall be treated for all purposes as having been effected on the Sender or Trader at the time when such notice would in the ordinary course of post have been delivered at the Sender's last known address.

4. E.g. insurance claims: Clarke, *Insurance*, Chap. 26–2E2.
5. *Granville Oil & Chemicals Ltd.* v *Davis & Turner Ltd.* [2003] EWCA Civ 570, [2003] 2 Lloyd's Rep. 356.

22. Consignments in Bond *2.680*

The Sender will indemnify the Carriers against any claims made upon them by the Commissioners of Customs and Excise in respect of any dutiable Consignments delivered to the Carriers while in bond.

23. Application of these Conditions *2.681*

All carriage, all storage and the provision of Containers is undertaken by Freightliner on the basis of these Conditions and no servant or agent of Freightliner has any authority to vary or waive these Conditions or any part thereof.

24. Freightliner not a Common Carrier *2.682*

Freightliner is not a Common Carrier.

Comment

In an attempt to ensure that these Conditions are applied in preference to the common law rules for common carriers, Condition 24 asserts that Freightliner is not a common carrier, however, although such statements are indeed evidence of the status of the carrier concerned, they are not conclusive of the question which is one of law.[1] *2.683*

25. Law and Jurisdiction *2.684*

The Contract shall be governed by English law and United Kingdom courts alone shall have jurisdiction in any dispute between the Carrier and the Sender.

Comment

Clauses such as Condition 25 are commonplace. The purpose of submitting any dispute to the courts of the United Kingdom with an instruction to apply English law to the contract of carriage is to ensure a convenient forum and that the Conditions will be interpreted in a way that Freightliner intended. *2.685*

[*The next paragraph is 2–695*]

1. *Eastman Chemical AG* v. *NMT Trading Ltd.* [1972] 2 Lloyd's Rep. 25, 30–31.

IV. CARRIAGE OF GOODS BY RAIL WITHIN THE UNITED KINGDOM: ENGLISH WELSH & SCOTTISH RAILWAY LIMITED GENERAL CONDITIONS OF CARRIAGE (AUGUST 2004)

2.695 These Conditions set out the basis on which EWS transports goods for the Customer. EWS is not and does not contract as a common carrier. These Conditions shall apply to all transportation of goods by EWS. *A Copy of these terms is available at* www.ews-railway.co.uk.

Please note that these Conditions contain limitations or exclusions of liability on the part of EWS. In order to minimise its charges EWS considers it reasonable to limit its liability and to share risk with the Customer in the manner set out in these Conditions.

Customers are recommended to take professional advice and to consider their insurance arrangements for risks that fall to them under these Conditions.

Comment

2.696 In an attempt to ensure that they are applied in preference to the common law rules for common carriers, the Preamble asserts that EWS does not contract as a common carrier; however, although such statements are indeed evidence of the status of the carrier concerned, they are not conclusive of the question which is one of law.[1] Note also that, in an attempt to ensure that they are interpreted in a way that the drafter intended, Condition 19.11 refers disputes to English law and to the courts of the United Kingdom. English law includes the Unfair Contract Terms Act 1977 and this appears to have been in the mind of the drafter when writing the sentences in bold type in the Preamble.

2.697 Whereas contracts for the carriage of goods by sea were largely saved from the 1977 Act, contracts of carriage by rail and road were not. As the Conditions concern the business liability of EWS, they come within the scope of the Act: section 1. Being standard terms on which the customer is invited to contract, they will be enforced only to the extent that they are reasonable: section 3. That a term is reasonable is for the carrier, EWS, to prove: section 12. This depends on a number of factors, as follows.

2.698 On the one hand, if EWS is in a stronger negotiating position than the customer, that will count against EWS. Other factors counting against a carrier, such as EWS, are that the carrier is usually the best risk avoider as well as being party best placed to insure against loss of or damage to goods in transit.[2] On the other hand, one factor that counts in favour of a party such as EWS seeking to rely on standard terms is that the customer has been made actually aware that the document contains terms of this kind; it is this factor also that lies behind the words in bold type. Further, in the case of terms in established and widespread use in a particular trade context such as carriage, a court will be hesitant to declare that a term is

1. *Eastman Chemical AG* v. *NMT Trading Ltd.* [1972] 2 Lloyd's Rep. 25, 30–31.
2. Clarke, *Insurance*, Chap. 5–6.

unreasonable and hence unenforceable.[3] The EWS Conditions are new, however, as regards the exceptions and limitations they are sufficiently similar to conditions of longer lineage in other contracts for their youth not to count against them. Within the four corners of the contract clauses limiting the amount of liability (such as Condition 8.4) are more favourably viewed than clauses (such as Condition 8.2) that exclude liability altogether.[4]

The current attitude of the courts, largely one of non-interference, was expressed by Tuckey L.J. in *Granville Oil*: *2.699*

"The 1977 Act obviously plays a very important role in protecting vulnerable consumers from the effects of draconian contract terms. But I am less enthusiastic about its intrusion into contracts between commercial parties of equal bargaining strength, who should generally be considered capable of being able to make contracts of their choosing and expect to be bound by their terms. Here the transaction includes carriage of goods by sea and insurance. These spheres of commercial activity standing on their own are excluded from the Act (see Schedule 1, para. 1(a) (insurance) and 2(c) and 3 (carriage of goods by ship)). In this case the element of road transport was sufficient to render the transaction subject to the Act, but the mixed nature of the contract of carriage emphasizes the interest of the freight forwarder in having a time limitation which is applicable across the spectrum of his obligations."[5]

1. Definitions and Application *2.700*

1.1 In these Conditions the following words shall have the following meanings:

"Arrival Point" the location to which a Consignment is to be transported by EWS pursuant to the Contract;

"Claims" claims, Losses, damages, liabilities, demands, judgements, costs and expenses (including legal costs) incurred or suffered by a party (including death or personal injury);

"Conditions" these conditions;

"Confidential Information" all information in respect of the business of each of the parties including, without prejudice to the generality of the foregoing, business methods, prices, business, financial, marketing, development or manpower plans, or customer lists that arise through the negotiation or performance of the Contract;

"Consignee" the person (who may or may not be the Customer) to whom EWS delivers the Goods;

"Consignment" Goods in bulk or contained in one parcel, package or container, as the case may be, or any number of separate parcels, packages or containers sent at one time in one load by or for the Customer from one address to one address;

"Consignor" the person (who may or may not be the Customer) from whom EWS collects the Goods;

"Contract" the contract between EWS and the Customer for the carriage of the Goods, which includes any Specification agreed by the parties and to which these Conditions apply;

"Customer" the person who contracts with EWS for the carriage of Goods;

"Customer's Equipment" items falling within the terms of Condition 16;

"Dangerous Goods" goods of any nature falling within the definition of "dangerous goods" given in the Carriage of Dangerous Goods and Use of Transportable Pressure Equipment Regulations 2004 as amended or replaced from time to time;

3. *George Mitchell (Chesterhall)* v. *Finney Lock Seeds* [1983] 2 A.C. 803. See also *Schenkers Ltd.* v. *Overland Shoes Ltd.* [1998] 1 Lloyd's Rep. 498, (C.A.); but cf. *Overseas Medical Supplies Ltd.* v. *Orient Transport Services Ltd.* [1999] 2 Lloyd's Rep. 273 (C.A.).

4. Generally, see Clarke, *CMR*, para. 239a.

5. *Granville Oil & Chemicals Ltd.* v. *Davis & Turner Ltd.* [2003] EWCA Civ 570, [2003] 2 Lloyd's Rep. 356 at [31]; see also at [32]. The case concerned the BIFA Conditions (1989 edition).

"Departure Point" the location from which a Consignment is to be transported by EWS pursuant to the Contract;

"EWS" English Welsh & Scottish Railway Limited (registered number 2938988) and its successors and assignees;

"EWS Group" any holding company of EWS and any subsidiary of EWS or any such holding company from time to time ("holding company" and "subsidiary" having the meaning given in Section 736 of the Companies Act 1985);

"EWS Loading Standards" the standards for the loading and unloading of Wagons and any other equipment used to transport Goods, a copy of which is available upon request from EWS;

"Force Majeure" any circumstance beyond the resonable control of either party including, without limitation, acts of God, war, riot, terrorism, crime, civil commotion, compliance with any law or governmental order, rule, regulation or direction or any overriding emergency procedures, accident, fire, flood, severe weather conditions, failure of, material reduction in utility of or inability to use a third party's infrastructure or refusal due to a physical or operational impediment of any such third party to allow such use and strikes and any other industrial action or dispute;

"Goods" the goods which EWS is to carry pursuant to the Contract;

"Indemnified Amount" £5,000,000 or such other sum as shall be agreed in writing between EWS and the Customer;

"Loss" the actual loss or destruction of Goods;

"Network Rail" Network Rail Limited (no. 4402220) or Network Rail Infrastructure Limited (no. 2904587) each of whose registered office is at 40 Melton Street London NW1 2EE or either of their successor's or assigns;

"Private Siding" a railway or siding not owned by or leased to EWS or Network Rail;

"Railway Industry Standards" as the context requires the applicable published rules and regulations including codes of practice and conduct in force from time to time relating to any equipment or activity or service to be provided under or used in connection with the Contract;

"Specification" the completed EWS "specification" or other document, which sets out terms agreed between the parties' for the transport of Goods. (*A blank copy of an EWS specification document is available at www.ews-railway.co.uk*);

"Term" the duration of the Contract as set out in the Specification;

"Wagons" wagons or containers in which Goods are transported;

1.2 Any reference in these Conditions to a statute or statutory provision shall be construed as a reference to the same as amended, consolidated, modified, extended, re-enacted or replaced from time to time.

1.3 The headings in these Conditions are for convenience only and shall not affect the construction of these Conditions.

1.4 The expression "person" means any individual, firm, company, unincorporated association and partnership and vice versa.

1.5 The expression, Consignee, Consignor and Customer shall include such persons principals, agents, employees and sub-contractors.

Comments

1. Definitions

2.701 Condition 1 is of a common type which defines major terms used in the Conditions.

2.702 "Consignment" came before the court for interpretation in *Spectra*,[1] in which a similar definition appeared in the standard conditions of a contract of carriage of goods by road. The decision indicates that, if the customer's goods are spread over more than one truck, each truck will be regarded as a Consignment. For more

1. *Spectra International plc* v. *Hayesoak Ltd.* [1997] 1 Lloyd's Rep. 153.

detailed discussion of the decision, see the Comment on Condition 1 of the RHA Conditions of Carriage, paragraphs 1.261 to 1.262, above.

The "Contract" is defined as the contract between EWS and the customer for the carriage of goods, i.e., the contract of carriage under which EWS, as carrier, undertakes (in Condition 2.1.1 and Condition 8.1) to collect the Consignment from the Departure Point and deliver it without undue delay (Condition 10.1) at the Arrival Point, and in the same order and condition in which the Consignment was received from the consignor. In principle at common law that undertaking is strict and absolute, however, in practice it is subject to contract terms such as these Conditions and, in particular, to the exceptions found in Conditions 8, 9 and 10.3 and the limits on amount payable by EWS found in Conditions 8.4 and 10.3. The contract provides the context in which the Conditions must be read and construed. *2.703*

The "Customer" is defined as any person who contracts with EWS for the carriage of goods by EWS. That person may be the consignor but more commonly it is the consignee of the goods. "It is clear that where goods are despatched by a carrier, the contract for payment of carriage is between him and the consignee, even though the goods should have been booked by the consignor; and though the property in these goods turned out afterwards to be in the consignor."[2] This is still the common law rule but it applies only as long as the particular carrier is entitled to assume, as may well not be the case with goods carried by EWS, that the goods are the property of a consignee different from the Consignor.[3] *2.704*

"*Force majeure*" has an established meaning in Belgian and French law but not in English law, hence, if the expression is used at all, it is common to find a contract definition[4] of the kind found in Condition 1.1. See also Condition 9 (para. 2.748, below). The "definition" in Condition 1.1 is less a definition than a description by listing examples, many of which are specific and well-known exceptions to liability found in other conditions of carriage. For "act of God" and "governmental order", see the Freightliner Conditions, Condition 16.1(a) and (b) (para. 2.651, above); for "riot", "civil commotion", and "strike", see the Freightliner Conditions, Condition 16.1 (h) (para. 2.651, above). At common law "fire" requires ignition, light as well as heat[5]; and the meaning of "accident" depends to a degree on context but generally it connotes something fortuitous and unexpected.[6] *2.705*

"*Force majeure*" here, as in other contexts, sets a level of obligation lower than that required for the common law defence of impossibility; otherwise an exception of *force majeure* such as this would be of little practical importance. The distinguishing feature that unifies the list is that, whereas common law requires that there be "some unforeseen supervening event over which the parties to the contract have no control" at all,[7] here the event must be no more than "beyond the reasonable *2.706*

2. *Stephenson* v. *Hart* (1828) 4 Bing. 476, 487.

3. Clarke, *CMR*, para. 42; Palmer, pp. 959 *et seq.* and 1095; see also C. Cashmore, *Who Can Sue on a Contract of Carriage of Goods* (London, 1990), Chap. 3.

4. See Benjamin, para. 8–084 *et seq.* and para. 19–118 *et seq.*

5. *Everett* v. *London Assurance* (1865) 19 C.B. (N.S.) 126, 133.

6. E.g. *The Miss Jay Jay* [1987] 1 Lloyd's Rep. 32, 36 (C.A.).

7. *Paal Wilson & Co. A/s* v. *Partenreederei Hannah Blumenthal* [1983] 1 A.C. 854, 882; see also *The Super Servant Two* [1990] 1 Lloyd's Rep. 1, 10 (C.A.).

control" of the parties concerned. Nonetheless the condition will still be construed *contra proferentem* and Bingham L.J., as he then was, once observed of such a condition that "it naturally follows that the Court will imply the least onerous obligation necessary to give the contract business efficacy".[8] As to the precise difference, a copious case law can be found relating to the performance of commodity sales contracts.[9]

2. Exclusivity and fairness

2.707 An earlier version of the Conditions contained a Condition of a kind referred to as an "entire agreement" clause. The purpose of such clauses "is to preclude a party to a written agreement from threshing through the undergrowth and finding in the course of negotiations some (chance) remark or statement (often long forgotten or difficult to recall or explain) on which to found a claim such as the present to the existence of a collateral warranty".[10] Such clauses have been challenged under the Unfair Contract Terms Act 1977, and the 2004 version has omitted the Condition. Concerning the impact of the Act on standard carriage contracts, see also the Comment on the Preamble to these Conditions (paras. 2.696 *et seq.*, above).

3. Rights of third parties

2.708 At common law parties to a contract such as this are free to vary or rescind the contract agreed between them without the consent of anyone not party to the contract. However, that position was altered by the Contracts (Rights of Third Parties) Act 1999; see Comment 3 on Condition 2, paragraphs 2.712 *et seq.*, above.

[*The next paragraph is 2.715*]

2.715 **2. EWS' Obligations**

2.1 EWS shall for the Term and in consideration of payment of the Charges:

2.1.1 transport each Consignment from the Departure Point to the Arrival Point, subject to the terms of the Contract. EWS shall be entitled to transport each Consignment by such route and means as it shall decide;

2.1.2 be the Train Operator, as defined in the Railways Act 1993, for the purposes of the Contract;

2.1.3 provide the services specified in the Contract with reasonable skill and care and in accordance with applicable Railway Industry Standards;

2.1.4 provide any equipment specified in the Contract as to be provided by EWS, such equipment to be safe and functional in respect of its designed purpose and in accordance with applicable Railway Industry Standards;

8. *Pagnan SpA* v. *Tradax Ocean Transportation SA* [1987] 2 Lloyd's Rep. 342, 348 (C.A.).
9. Benjamin *loc. cit.*
10. *Intrepreneur Pub Co. (GL)* v. *East Crown Ltd.* [2000] 2 Lloyd's Rep. 611 at [7].

2.1.5 permit or procure access on the terms of Condition 15 for the Customer (provided the identity of any agents or subcontractors of the Customer is notified to EWS and approved by EWS in advance of them seeking such access) to EWS' land or premises for the purposes of fulfilling the Customer's obligations under the Contract;

2.1.6 if the Departure Point and/or Arrival Point is/are located at any land or premises owned or leased by EWS (save where such land is leased to EWS by the Customer, Consignee or Consignor), use its reasonable endeavours to ensure that:

2.1.6.1 such land or premises are safe, free from defects and, where appropriate, are kept and operated in an appropriate condition for use as part of a railway network and comply with applicable Railway Industry Standards; and

2.1.6.2 such land or premises are connected to Network Rail's network enabling safe transfer on to the Network Rail network; and

2.1.7 use its reasonable endeavours not to cause damage to the Customer's or any third party's infrastructure, land or premises in the performance of the Contract.

2.2 EWS may sub-contract any part(s) or the whole of the transport of the Goods.

Comment

Condition 2 lists in general terms the obligations undertaken by EWS, of which those in Condition 2.1.2 through to Condition 2.1.7 go beyond those necessarily or normally undertaken by a carrier, and which reflect the role of EWS as a carrier of goods in bulk. *2.716*

Condition 2.1.1 specifies, in a way that other carriage conditions such as those of Freightliner do not, the underlying contract of carriage under which EWS, as carrier, undertakes to collect the consignment from the Departure Point and deliver it at the Arrival Point. Condition 2.1.1 omits, however, to state the usual associated obligation to deliver the consignment in the same order and condition in which it was received from the consignor at the Departure Point. This aspect of the undertaking, however, has not been excluded but is an apparent feature of the liability assumed by EWS in Condition 8.1. *2.717*

In principle at common law the entire undertaking is strict and absolute, however, in practice it is subject to contract terms such as these Conditions and, in particular, to the exceptions found, notably, in Conditions 8, 9 and 10.3 and to the limits on amount found in Conditions 8.4 and 10.3. *2.718*

3. Loading/Unloading *2.719*

3.1 If EWS is to load the Goods on the Wagons, then the Customer shall make the Goods reasonably accessible to EWS at the Departure Point, packaged and labelled as set out in Condition 4 and at the times stated in the Specification.

3.2 If the Customer or its Consignor or Consignee loads or reloads the Wagons the Customer shall:

3.2.1 procure that each Wagon is loaded or reloaded in a manner which complies with all applicable laws, regulations, Railway Industry Standards and EWS Loading Standards;

3.2.2 procure that each Wagon is loaded or reloaded evenly (with the weight distributed evenly over the Wagon) and that each Wagon is not overloaded;

3.2.3 procure that each Wagon is loaded or reloaded in a manner which will not cause any injury or damage to any property or person during transportation of the Goods or any delay in transportation;

3.2.4 procure that any dunnage, stanchions, straps or other loose equipment is not damaged and is secured to the Wagons; and

3.2.5 without prejudice to any other provision of the contract be liable for and indemnify EWS in full against all Claims arising out of (1) the Customer's, breach of Conditions 3.2.1, 3.2.2, 3.2.3 and/or 3.2.4; (2) the Customer's, negligent or wilful act or omissions, or (3) any breach of statutory duty by the Customer in relation to loading, unloading or reloading the Goods.

3.3 EWS' employees have no authority to give assistance beyond that agreed in writing by EWS and EWS shall not be liable for any claims howsoever caused (including without limitation if caused by negligence) by the giving of any other assistance.

3.4 If the Customer, the Consignor, or the Consignee is to load, unload or reload Goods from the Wagons the Customer shall ensure that the same is carried out expeditiously, in sufficient time to enable EWS to perform the Contract and so as not to delay the use of EWS' equipment elsewhere by EWS.

3.5 EWS shall have the right to carry out a brief visual inspection of any Wagons loaded by or on behalf of the Customer and/or any Goods, which EWS is to transport. Any such brief visual inspection shall not relieve the Customer of any of its obligations under the Contract or at law in relation to loading or packaging of or otherwise relating to the Goods and shall not be deemed to be acceptance by EWS that the Customer has complied with such obligations.

Comment

2.720 The party to be responsible for loading and unloading is a matter for party agreement, unless the transport is subject to CIM, Article 20. This is reflected in the contingent wording of the opening words of Condition 3.2. which are followed by a list of overlapping duties to be observed by a customer when it is the customer's duty to load or unload the goods. In the attention to detail Condition 3 is more like the corresponding terms of a charterparty than the un/loading condition of a contract for carriage by land. Compare Condition 10 of the Freightliner Conditions (para. 2.633, above) and also Condition 4 of the RHA Conditions (para. 1.274, above). It is noteworthy, in particular, that in Condition 3 two significant practical problems are addressed.

2.721 First, according to Condition 3.3, EWS are not be liable, if employees of EWS assist the customer, "for any Claims howsoever caused (including without limitation if caused by negligence)". It seems that this Condition has been drawn to achieve a total exclusion of the liability of EWS notwithstanding the rules of construction *contra proferentem* developed in the *Canada S.S.* case.[1]

2.722 Secondly, Condition 3.5 addresses the dilemma of a carrier which, for obvious practical and safety reasons wishes to ensure that the customer has loaded a consignment properly but fears that, by intervening, it will be considered to have assumed some responsibility for the state of the packing or loading.[2] According to Condition 3.5 EWS may, if it so chooses, carry out a "brief visual inspection" but the customer is not thereby relieved of any of is obligations. It is clear from the final words of the Condition that EWS is not estopped from complaining about the

1. *Canada Steamships Line Ltd.* v. *R.* [1952] A.C. 192 (P.C.). See also *Alderslade* v. *Hendon Laundry Ltd.* [1945] K.B. 189 (C.A.).

2. See Comment 11 (paras. 1.110 *et seq.*, above) and Comment 12 (paras. 1.113 *et seq.*, above) on Art. 17 of CMR and, in particular, the Comments on Article 8 of CMR (paras. 1.37 *et seq.*, above).

packing or loading later; but whether EWS does not assume any co-responsibility at all in law, for instance to third parties, remains a question.

4. The Goods, Labelling and Packaging *2.723*

4.1 The Customer warrants that either it is the legal owner of the Goods or that it has the authority of the legal owner(s) and/or all persons having an interest in the Goods to enter into the Contract and to accept the Conditions for the transport of the Goods.

4.2 The Customer shall give EWS such details for each Consignment as EWS may require from time to time. The Customer will issue EWS with adequate forwarding instructions for each Consignment. The Customer shall procure that each Consignment shall be clearly and properly addressed and labelled in accordance with EWS' requirements. If the Customer should change any aspect of a Consignment after advising EWS of the information required in this Condition [4.2], then the Customer shall as soon as practicable notify EWS of such changes (and in any event shall notify EWS prior to the movement of such Consignment).

4.3 The Customer shall ensure that all Goods.

4.3.1 are adequately and properly packaged and that such packaging complies with all applicable laws, rules, regulations and Railway Industry Standards;

4.3.2 will be safe and fit to be transported; and

4.3.3 will not cause death or personal injury to any person or damage to any property or other Goods during transportation.

4.4 The Customer shall indemnify EWS against all Claims arising from a breach of Condition 4.3 by the Customer or its Consignor or Consignee and in the event that there is a dispute as to the cause of a Claim the Customer shall be required to establish to the reasonable satisfaction of EWS that the cause of the Claim was other than the Goods not being adequately and properly packaged and other than the Goods not being safe and fit to be transported. Where no cause of a Claim can be established to the reasonable satisfaction of EWS, the Customer shall be deemed to be in breach of Condition 4.3.

4.5 The Customers confirms that, other than as agreed in writing between it and EWS, there are and will be no special requirements for the transport of the Goods. Accordingly EWS shall have no liability for any deterioration or Loss of or damage to the Goods resulting from any such special requirement not so agreed in writing. If the Customer notifies EWS of any such special requirement EWS shall have no obligation to transport such Goods unless it agrees to do so in writing. If EWS agrees to carry any Goods for which there is a special requirement it may charge the Customer additional sums.

Comment

Concerning the obligation of the customer to furnish information and to properly package the consignment, imposed by Condition 4.1 and Condition 4.2, respectively, see the Comment on Condition 3 *in fine* (paras. 2.720 *et seq.*, above). Concerning the warranty that the goods are fit for transportation, the subject of Condition 4.3, see the Comment on Condition 5 (paras. 2.726 to 2.727, below). Concerning the obligation imposed on the customer by Condition 4.4, see Condition 8, Comment 2 (paras. 2.739 *et seq.*, below). *2.724*

5. Dangerous goods *2.725*

5.1 EWS shall have no obligation to accept any Dangerous Goods for carriage. EWS shall have no liability for any Claims (including without limitation in negligence) in respect of any Dangerous Goods unless, prior to loading, EWS has received in writing precise and correct identification of the Goods and has further agreed in writing to accept the same for carriage.

5.2 If EWS accepts any Dangerous Goods for carriage the Customer shall ensure that the Goods are safely packaged and labelled with the precise and correct identity of the relevant substances and/or articles and all other relevant information as specified by any statutory or regulatory requirements from time to time and that a certificate of readiness is issued by the Customer prior to carriage commencing and the Customer complies with any other requirements of EWS for the time being in force regarding carriage of Dangerous Goods.

5.3 Without prejudice to any other provision of the Contract the Customer shall indemnify EWS in full against all Claims arising out of or in connection with the carriage of Dangerous Goods which EWS has not expressly accepted for carriage in writing or in respect of which the Customer has not complied with its obligations under Condition 5.2 even where caused by the negligence of EWS.

5.4 EWS shall have the right to enter and have access to any premises not owned by EWS where Dangerous Goods are or are to be loaded or unloaded to audit the loading and unloading procedures that are in place and/or which occur in relation to Dangerous Goods and where such premises are not owned by the Customer, the Customer shall procure that EWS shall have such right to enter and access such premises.

Comment

2.726 Dangerous goods are defined in Condition 1.[1] Behind Condition 5 is the common law warranty that a person sending goods is liable for goods in a state that makes them unfit for carriage.[2] It is a strict warranty, breach of which does not depend on the knowledge or negligence of the sender.[3] Moreover, the sender is liable to a carrier, such as EWS, not only for damage done by the sender's goods to the property of the carrier but also faces the possibility of action by the carrier on behalf of others affected,[4] unless they have already been indemnified by the sender.[5] The EWS Conditions contain an indemnity to this effect in Condition 10.2.

2.727 If, however, EWS agrees in accordance with Condition 5.1 to accept dangerous goods and the customer delivers them to EWS in a state fit for carriage and in compliance with Condition 5.2, the liability of EWS for those goods is the same as that for any other class of goods, subject to Condition 5 and in particular Condition 5.3 and Condition 5.4. Concerning the latter, see the Comment on Condition 3 *in fine* (paras. 2.720 *et seq.*, above).

2.728 **6. Charges**

6.1 The Customer for the Term shall pay to EWS the charges agreed between the parties as shown in the Specification (and as may be varied in accordance with these Conditions or as otherwise agreed in writing between EWS and the Customer from time to time).

6.2 EWS may issue an invoice at any time in respect of any individual Consignment the subject of the Contract following carriage of such Consignment or as otherwise agreed in accordance with the terms of the Contract.

6.3 All charges shall be paid by the Customer to EWS in the currency of the invoice in cleared funds within 28 days of the date of the relevant invoice. All remittances should include a reference to the relative invoice (including its number). Payment should be made as follows (as may be varied from time to time by written notice from EWS):

1. But see now the Carriage of Dangerous Goods and Use of Transportable Pressure Equipment Regulations 2004 (S.I. 2004/568), which came into force on 10 May 2004.
2. See Palmer, pp. 999 *et seq.*
3. *Bamfield* v. *Goole and Sheffield Transport Co.* [1910] 2 K.B. 94 (C.A.).
4. *The Winkfield* [1902] P. 42; *G.N. Ry.* v. *L.E.P. Transport* [1922] 2 K.B. 742 (C.A.).
5. *O'Sullivan* v. *Williams* [1992] 3 All E.R. 385 (C.A.).

Payment by CHAPS or BACS should be made to the following:
Bank: Royal Bank of Scotland, Corporate Banking Office, PO Box 450, 5–10 Great Tower Street, London, EC3P 3HX
Swift: RBOSGB2L
Sort Code: 16 04 00
Account Number: 20095263 (for EWS Railway)
Account Name: English Welsh & Scottish Railway Revenue Account

All CHAPS/BACS remittance advices to be posted to EWS Credit Control, CSDC, Lakeside Business Park, Carolina Way, Doncaster, DN4 5PN.

6.4 If any charges payable by the Customer under the Contract are not paid on the due date for payment EWS shall be entitled to charge the Customer interest (accruing on a daily basis) at the rate of four percent above the base lending rate of Royal Bank of Scotland Bank PLC from time to time, from the due date of payment until payment (whether before or after judgment).

6.5 All charges and/or payments payable pursuant to the Contract are exclusive of value added tax and any other tax, duty or fee imposed from time to time by any government or other authority and are subject to the addition of value added tax and any other tax, duty or fee at the appropriate rate.

6.6 All payments to be made by the Customer to EWS under the Contract shall be made in full without any set-off, restriction or condition and without any deduction for or on account of any counterclaim unless such deduction has been agreed in advance in writing with EWS.

6.7 If EWS accepts any change to the Specification proposed by the Customer, EWS may charge the Customer an additional reasonable charge in respect of such change. EWS will inform the Customer as soon as reasonably practicable of such additional charges. The Customer agrees to pay such additional charges.

6.8 If (a) the Customer fails to make any Goods available for collection and/or loading at the specified time or (b) the Consignee fails to take delivery of any Goods immediately on arrival at the Delivery Point or (c) the Customer breaches its obligations under Condition 3.4 then EWS may charge the Customer additional charges.

6.9 During the Term EWS will not vary its charges or these Conditions without the prior consent of the Customer, save in circumstances where a change in charges arises as a consequence of a change in law, manner or rate of taxation or as a result of decision by any competent legal or regulatory authority. EWS will give as much notice as reasonably practicable of any such change in its charges or these Conditions. Details of changes may be published on *www.ews-railway.co.uk* from time to time.

Comments

1. Who pays?

Prima facie Condition 6.1 reaffirms the common law rule,[1] that the person liable to pay charges is the person (the customer) who contracts with the carrier. However, the common law position is that the person who contracts with the carrier is presumed to be the consignee[2]; and that when the charges in a particular case are payable by a sender and the goods are delivered to the designated consignee, a contract is implied that unpaid charges become payable by the consignee.[3] *2.729*

2. The time for payment

The time and manner of payment is a matter of contract and thus, in this case, Condition 6.3, that charges are payable in the invoice currency in cleared funds *2.730*

1. See Glass/Cashmore, para. 1.106; and Palmer, p. 1101.
2. See the Comment on Condition 1, paras. 2.701 *et seq.*, above.
3. *World Transport Co.* v. *Tealing & Co.* [1936] 2 All E.R. 573; Clarke [1991] L.M.C.L.Q. 5.

within 28 days of invoice. This displaces the common law rule that freight charges are payable at the time of delivery, provided that the goods have been delivered or tendered.[4]

2.731 As regards the "no set-off" provision in Condition 6.6, freight is payable at common law even if the goods are delivered short in quantity or damaged[5]; this is a rule for carriage by sea but one which has been applied to carriage by road with "unconcealed reluctance"[6]; and the argument, that a "no set-off" clause in the BIFA Conditions was unreasonable under the Unfair Contract Terms Act 1977, has been rejected by the Court of Appeal because such clauses were common and, in the view of the court, that reflected a general view of what was reasonable in the trade.[7] The rule is controversial, however,[8] Condition 6.6 seeks to maintain it, as does Condition 13(b) of Freightliner's Conditions, as well as both the BIFA Conditions and Condition 8(2) of the RHA Conditions.

2.732 If the sender is obliged to pay charges and has not done so, EWS can simply refuse to carry the goods until the charges have been paid or sufficient security given. In the event of non-payment by the consignee, EWS' primary remedy is a lien on the goods, which is provided for in Condition 7.

2.733

7. Financial Security

7.1 If EWS reasonably determines that it would be commercially prudent to obtain financial security against the Customer failing to perform any of its obligations hereunder, EWS shall be entitled to require the Customer to provide such financial security against the failure of the Customer to perform any of its obligations under the Contract as EWS deems appropriate. Failure to provide such security within the time period stipulated by EWS shall be deemed to be a material breach of this Contract.

7.2 EWS shall have a lien on all Consignments in EWS' possession for all charges due to EWS from the Customer. EWS shall be entitled to charge the Customer its costs associated with asserting and exercising its lien. If the lien is not satisfied within a reasonable period of time from the date upon which EWS first gives notice of its exercise to the Customer then the Goods the subject of the lien may be sold and the proceeds of sale applied in satisfaction of the lien and all proper and related charges and expenses of EWS in exercising the lien and EWS will account to the Customer for any surplus.

Comment

2.734 Condition 7.1 is less a contractual term than a pre-contractual warning. As regards Condition 7.2, at common law every carrier or at least every common carrier,[1] which, however, according to the preamble to the Conditions EWS is not, has a "particular" lien on goods in its possession for freight and charges in relation to goods which it is ready and able to deliver. This "particular" lien is distinguished from a "general lien" which extends to debts due under previous contracts of carriage between the same parties. A general lien does not arise as a matter of law

4. Palmer, p. 1102.
5. *Aries Tanker Corp.* v. *Total Transport* [1977] 1 W.L.R. 185 (H.L.).
6. *United Carriers Ltd.* v. *Heritage Food Group (UK) Ltd.* [1995] 4 All E.R. 95, 102.
7. In *Overland Shoes Ltd.* v. *Schenkers Ltd.* [1998] 1 Lloyd's Rep. 498.
8. See Clarke, *CMR*, para. 45g.
1. Cf. Glass/Cashmore, para. 1.110.

but is often granted by a provision of the contract of carriage. Condition 7.2 is such a provision. As is usual, Condition 7.2 gives EWS a right to sell the goods if the debt is not paid within a reasonable time.

8 Loss or Damage of Goods *2.735*

8.1 Subject to the other provisions of these Conditions and unless agreed otherwise in writing between EWS and the Customer, EWS shall be liable for any Loss of or damage to Goods which occurs whilst the Goods are in transit between the Departure Point and the Arrival Point.

8.2 EWS shall have no liability for any Loss of or damage to Goods which arises from any of the following:

8.2.1 inherent liability to wastage in bulk or weight, latent defect or inherent defect, vice or natural deterioration of the Goods;

8.2.2 any act or omission of the Customer, the Consignor or the Consignee; or

8.2.3 any event of Force Majeure.

8.3 EWS shall have no liability for any Loss of or damage to Goods caused by the manner in which the same are loaded or unloaded by a person other than EWS.

8.4 Unless otherwise agreed in writing between the Customer and EWS the liability of EWS for Loss of or damage to Goods whilst in transit in accordance with this Condition 8 shall be limited to, in the case of Loss, the cost (excluding VAT) to the Customer of the relevant Goods and in the case of damage, the reduction in value subject to (in all cases) a maximum of £1,300 per tonne of Goods. EWS shall have no other liability for any Loss of or damage to Goods even if caused by its negligence.

8.5 EWS shall be entitled to proof of the actual value or reduction in value (as the case may be) of any Goods the subject of Loss or damage.

Comments

1. The liability of EWS for loss or damage

Condition 8.1, together with Condition 2.1.1, is central to the contract of carriage under which EWS undertakes to collect the consignment from the Departure Point and deliver it without undue delay (Condition 10.1) at the Arrival Point in the same order and condition in which it was received from the consignor. EWS accepts liability for loss of or damage to the goods in question between collection and delivery, i.e., while they are in transit. *2.736*

Transit is more than the period of time in which the goods are being moved from one place to another; it is the entire period during which they are in the custody and control of EWS. Transit begins when possession, and hence custody and control, pass from the consignor to EWS; and ends when tender of the consignment is made by EWS to the consignee. The period (and thus Condition 8.1) is important notably because, when transit ends, Condition 12 purports to excuse the carrier in respect of any loss of or damage to the goods occurring later. In the carriage of goods, whatever the mode of carriage, when possession and hence control change there is a significant change in the risk and usually therefore a change of legal regime.[1] *2.737*

The key point being change of possession and control, the primary rule for the ending of transit is actual delivery of the consignment to the consignee. Commonly provision is made for cases in which, through no fault of the carrier, that cannot be *2.738*

1. Clarke, *Insurance*, Chap. 16–2A6.

done. For example, some conditions, such as Condition 11 of the Freightliner Conditions, reaffirm the common law rule[2] that tender of the goods at the right time and place amounts to delivery for the purpose of ending transit. This does not appear to been provided for expressly in the EWS Conditions but, presumably, the common law rule would apply by default.

2. Exceptions

2.739 "Inherent vice" is the central feature of the first exception set out in Condition 8.2.1, which is a catch-all exception. Inherent vice is essentially the same as "inherent defect" and also takes in "inherent liability to wastage in bulk or weight" and "deterioration".[3] Moreover, it overlaps "latent defect", which is a defect of any kind at all which could not be expected to be discovered by any inspection or test which the person concerned, here EWS, could reasonably be expected to make.[4]

2.740 "Inherent vice" in contract conditions, as well as international carriage regimes such as CMR,[5] is taken to mean what it also means at common law[6]: some defect in the goods which by its development through ordinary processes going on in those goods tends to the injury or destruction of the goods.[7]

2.741 "Act or omission" etc. in Condition 8.2.2 is an exception by reference to the conduct of the customer and, if not customers, the consignor and consignee. In effect there is a degree of potential overlap with other provisions, such as Condition 5.3. A prime example of this exception is something done or omitted by the customer during loading or unloading, which also excuses EWS in Condition 8.3; cf. Condition 3 (para. 2.719, above). *Prima facie* EWS is excused under Condition 8.2.2 regardless of whether there has been any fault in the act or omission in question.[8]

2.742 "*Force majeure*", which is a ground of exoneration for EWS in Condition 8.2.3, also excuses EWS as well as the customer in Condition 9. *Force majeure* is defined in Condition 1.

3. Causation

2.743 Condition 8.2 articulates what would be the usual interpretation of an exonerating Condition of this kind, that, for the exception pleaded to be effective as such, the loss or damage in question must be such as "arises from", i.e., is caused by, the excepted cause. Anyway, as an instance of strict construction, construction *contra proferentem*, exceptions do not excuse a defendant unless the excepted event caused

2. Glass/Cashmore, para. 1.67. See *Startup* v. *Macdonald* (1843) 6 Man. & G. 593; *Heugh* v. *L.N.W. Ry.* (1870) L.R. 5 Ex. 51.

3. Cf., however, *Donald & Son (Wholesale Meat Contractors) Ltd.* v. *Continental Freeze*, 1984 S.L.T. 182.

4. *The Amstelslot* [1963] 2 Lloyd's Rep. 223 (H.L.). On the distinction with "inherent vice", see further Clarke, *CMR*, para. 89a.

5. Paras. 1.1 *et seq.*, above.

6. For a relatively recent decision see *Noten* v. *Harding* [1990] 2 Lloyd's Rep. 283 (C.A.).

7. See further CMR, Art. 17, Comment 6, paras. 1.96 to 1.97, above.

8. Cf. CMR Art. 17.2 (paragraph 1.77, above) which refers to the "wrongful" act of the sender or consignee.

the loss, damage or delay in issue. More than that, some courts have required the event to be the proximate cause, as understood in the law of insurance.[9] This means that the impact of the event on the goods must have been for all practical purposes inevitable, a very close causal connection indeed.[10]

4. Limited liability

In the case of loss of goods the usual measure of indemnity at common law is the market value of the goods of that kind at destination[11] or, in the case of regimes such as CMR,[12] their value at the place and time at which they were accepted for carriage.[13] In the case of loss of goods under Condition 8.4, however , the liability of EWS is limited to the actual cost to the customer ex VAT, which may or may not be the CMR figure. *2.744*

In the case of damage to goods the usual measure of indemnity at common law is either the reduction in the market value of the goods, assessed as indicated above, or the cost of cure, as appropriate. However, like CMR, Condition 8.4. rules out the cost of cure and refers to the "reduction in value" of the goods but without specifying the measure of indemnity. *Prima facie* the context suggests that once again it is by reference to the actual cost to the customer ex VAT. *2.745*

Whether it is a case of loss or damage, the amount recoverable is limited to a maximum of £1,300 per tonne of goods. The limit by reference to weight probably includes the weight of packing inside the container, if any, but not that of the metal container itself, and applies whatever the actual value of the goods. Arbitrary as it might seem, the intention behind limits of this kind is to give the carrier, who will be aware of the weight of the standard container or of the truck, a rough idea of the potential liability for any one load without having to investigate further.[14] *2.746*

In addition, Condition 8.4 concludes that EWS shall have no other liability for any loss of or damage to goods even if caused by negligence. Presumably this provision is intended, as is Condition 3.3, to forestall the application of the rules of construction *contra proferentem* developed in the *Canada S.S.* case.[15] *2.747*

9. Force Majeure *2.748*

9.1 Neither party shall be deemed to be in breach of the Contract or otherwise liable to the other for any failure or delay in performing its obligations under the Contract due to Force

9. See *Reardon Smith Line* v. *Ministry of Agriculture, Fisheries and Food* [1960] 1 Q.B. 439, affirmed [1962] 1 Q.B. 42 (C.A.), affirmed on other grounds [1963] A.C. 691, re whether a strike, the exonerating event, had caused delay in loading. To resolve this issue, McNair J. (at 492) relied on a statement by Lord Dunedin in *Leyland Shipping Co.* v. *Norwich Union Fire Insurance Society* [1918] A.C. 350, 362 suggesting that the event must be the proximate cause of the loss; and in this regard the reasoning of McNair J. was approved by Willmer L.J. (at 102). See also in this sense: Benjamin, para. 8–088. and cases cited, concerning "prevention" clauses in sales contracts.

10. See Clarke, *Insurance*, Chap. 25–3.

11. *The Heron II, Koufos* v. *C. Czarnikow Ltd.* [1969] 1 A.C. 350.

12. Paras. 1.1 *et seq.*, above.

13. Art. 23.1.

14. *BGH 30.1.1981* (1981) 16 ETL 455, 458.

15. *Canada Steamships Line Ltd.* v. *R.* [1952] A.C. 192 (P.C.). See also *Alderslade* v. *Hendon Laundry Ltd.* [1945] K.B. 189 (C.A.).

Majeure. If a party's performance of its obligations under the Contract is affected by Force Majeure:

9.1.1 it shall give notice to the other party, specifying the nature and extent of the Force Majeure, as soon as reasonably possible upon becoming aware of the Force Majeure and will at all times use reasonable endeavours to mitigate the severity of the Force Majeure;

9.1.2 the date for performance of such obligation shall be deemed suspended only for a period equal to the delay caused by Force Majeure;

9.1.3 it shall not be entitled to payment from the other party in respect of extra costs and expenses incurred by virtue of the Force Majeure.

Comment

2.749 Condition 9 excuses both EWS and the customer, as the case may be, for any failure or delay in performing its obligations under the contract due to Force Majeure. EWS is also excused by *force majeure* under Condition 8.2.3, the only obvious difference being that the latter extends to liability in tort as well as contract. *Force majeure* is defined in Condition 1.

2.750 Condition 9 also prescribes the consequences of *force majeure*. Whereas at common law the contract is usually discharged automatically when performance becomes impossible, the effect of Condition 9.1.2 is that the contract is not discharged but suspended while performance is impossible as a result of the *force majeure*. From the perspective of common law therefore time is not "of the essence of the contract". Moreover "costs and expenses incurred by virtue of the Force Majeure" lie where they fall: Condition 9.1.3; and Condition 9.1.1 requires the party directly affected by the *force majeure* to "give notice to the other party". As to the meaning of "notice" see Condition 19.8 (paragraph 2.787, below).

2.751

10. Liability

10.1 Subject to Conditions 3.3, 3.4, 4.3, 4.5, 5.1, 8, 9, 10, 11, 12, 16.5, 16.6, 16.7 and 16.8 EWS shall be liable for any delay in delivery of a Consignment and shall be liable for and indemnify the Customer in full against all Claims, incurred or suffered by the Customer arising directly from any negligent or wrongful act or omission on the part of EWS.

10.2 The Customer shall be liable for and shall indemnify EWS in full against all Claims, incurred or suffered by EWS arising from any neligent or wrongful act or omission on the part of the Customer, the Consignee or the Consignor, or their suppliers or arising from any inherent defect in Wagons supplied by the Customer (or a third party nominated by the Customer).

10.3. The parties' liability to each other in respect of any breach of the Contract and breach of any other obligation whether in contract, tort, by statute or otherwise arising out of or in connection with the Contract or its performance (in each case whether caused by negligence or otherwise) and pursuant to the indemnities contained in the Contract shall be limited as follows:

10.3.1 neither party shall have liability to the other for loss of profit, customer claims, loss of business, loss of goodwill, loss of reputation, whether such loss or claims are direct or indirect or any consequential loss whatsoever (save that this Condition 10.3.1 shall not apply in respect of any loss of profit arising from the Customer's breach of the Contract or any payment due to be made by the Customer as a consequence of the Contract terminating or loss of profit or arising from any failure by the Customer to provide to EWS a required volume of Goods set out in the Contract);

10.3.2 EWS shall have no liability for any such breach which arises from the act or omission of the Customer, the Consignor, or the Consignee;

10.3.3 the Customer shall have no liability for any such breach which arises from the act or omission of EWS;

10.3.4 EWS' maximum liability for or arising out of or in connection with a failure by EWS to deliver a Consignment within the time stated in the Specification, or if no time is so specified, then within a reasonable period of time, shall be the price (excluding VAT) the Customer paid to EWS for carriage of such Consignment;

10.3.5 EWS' maximum liability for the Loss of or damage to Goods shall be as set out in Condition 8; and

10.3.6 where both parties to the Contract are signatories to the Claims Allocation and Handling Agreement (dated 1 April 1994 and as amended from time to time) ("CAHA") neither party's liability to the other in respect of the relevant matter shall exceed the liability of such party pursuant to or allocated in accordance with CAHA for such matter.

10.4 The maximum liability of either party to the other in respect of any breach of this Contract and breach of any other obligation whether in contract, tort, by statute or otherwise arising out of or in connection with the Contract or its performance (in each case whether caused by negligence or otherwise) and pursuant to the indemnities contained in the Contract shall be £5,000,000 for any claim or series of claims that arise from any one occurrence.

10.5 Nothing herein shall in any way diminish either party's common law duty to mitigate their respective losses (and each party shall be obliged to mitigate its losses where such losses are the subject of any indemnity contained in the Contract).

10.6 Each party's liability to indemnify the other under the Contract shall be reduced proportionally to the extent that the act or omission of the other party, its employees, agents or sub-contractors may have contributed to the event which gives rise to the liability to so indemnify.

10.7 Where either party (the "indemnitee") becomes aware that matters have arisen which will or are likely to give rise to a claim against it which will or is likely to give rise to a claim against the other the [*sic*] ("the indemnifier") under the indemnities contained in the Contract the indemnitee will:

10.7.1 as soon as practicable notify the indemnifier in writing of the potential claim and of the matters which will or are likely to give [rise] to such claim;

10.7.2 not make any admission of liability, agreement or compromise with any person, body or authority in relation to the potential claim without prior written agreement of the indemnifier; and

10.7.3 at all times disclose in writing to the indemnifier all information and documents relating to the potential claim or the matters which will or are likely to give rise to such claim.

10.8 Nothing in these Conditions shall exclude or restrict either party's liability for:

10.8.1 death or personal injury caused by its negligence; or

10.8.2 fraud or fraudulent representations made by it.

10.9 The exclusions and limitations of liability contained in these Conditions (including but not limited to those contained in Conditions 8, 9, 10, 11, 12, 16 and 19) shall extend to members of EWS Group and EWS' employees, agents and sub-contractors all of whom shall be entitled to the benefit of such exclusions and limitations and The Contracts (Rights of Third Parties) Act 1999 shall apply to all such persons and to their benefiting from such exclusions and limitations.

10.10 EWS does not accept liability for the acts or omissions of other carriers unless such other carriers have been specifically engaged by EWS as subcontractors or assignees in respect of performing EWS's obligations under this Contract.

Comments

1. The liability of EWS for delay

Whereas the liability of EWS for loss or damage to goods is dealt with in Condition 8, the liability of EWS for delay in delivery of a consignment is the concern of Condition 10.1. The liability is not for delay in the course of transit but for delay in delivery. On the one hand, that does not rule out the possibility of liability for breach *2.752* of the duty implied at common law to carry goods with reasonable despatch. On the other hand, there can be no delay in delivery without a yardstick to measure the matter, i.e. an agreed date for delivery or, if there has been no agreement, an implied obligation to deliver with in a reasonable time. However, the reference in Condition 10.3.4 to "the time stated in the Specification", defined in Condition 1, suggests that usually an agreed date will be entered in that document. Concerning the meaning of "delay", see also CMR, Article 17, Comment 4, paragraphs 1.91 *et seq.*, above.

2.753 EWS' liability under Condition 10.1 is limited. First, it is limited to losses "arising directly from any negligent or wrongful act or omission on the part of EWS". However, an exclusion of "any other indirect or consequential damages of whatsoever kind" was restrictively construed in *Shell* v. *P & O.*[1] Secondly, the liability is for negligence only thus excluding the usual construction of a carrier's undertaking to deliver goods in accordance with contract as being strict and absolute. However, if "wrongful" is to add anything to "negligent", it is possible that the liability of EWS under Condition 10.1 extends to breach of a strict statutory duty of some kind. The liability of EWS is further limited by Condition 10.3.1, not as here by reference to the nature of the cause of delay, but by reference to the kind of loss suffered by the customer in consequence.

2. *The liability of the customer*

2.754 The liability of the customer under Condition 10.2 is similarly limited to "negligent or wrongful" acts or omissions. The customer is also liable under Condition 3.2.5 in respect of losses to EWS caused by the way in which the customer loads or unloads the goods, and under Condition 5.3 in respect of dangerous goods. The liability of the customer is limited by Condition 10.3.1, not however as here by reference to the nature of the cause, but by reference to the kind of loss suffered by EWS in consequence.

3. *Liability limits*

2.755 Liability limits are the subject of Condition 10.3. The liability of each party is excluded altogether by Condition 10.3.1 not by reference to the nature of the cause, the domain of Condition 10.1 for EWS and Condition 10.2 for the customer, but by reference to the kind of loss complained of. It is comprehensively drawn and seeks to anticipate every possible suit, for example, by including proceedings based on loss of commercial reputation.

2.756 For liabilities that remain, the liability of each party is limited, where it applies, by Condition 10.3.6, and, in all cases, by Condition 10.4. The limit in Condition 10.4 applies to "any claim or series of claims that arise from any occurrence". Such wording and, in particular, the meaning of "occurrence" has been extensively litigated in respect of insurance policies. Broadly speaking, the proper interpretation

1. *Shell Chemicals UK Ltd.* v. *P & O Roadtanks Ltd.* [1993] 1 Lloyd's Rep. 114, 118, concerning similar wording in a pre-1989 version of the RHA Conditions.

in a particular case depends on the "degree of unity in relation to cause, locality, time and, if initiated by human action, the circumstances and purposes of the persons responsible".[2]

Further, the liability of EWS for delay is limited to the "price" of carriage: Condition 10.3.4. A similar limit is also found, for example, in CMR, Article 23.5 (para. 1.143, above) and CIM, Article 43 (para. 2.358, above) except that in CIM the limit is "four times the carriage charges". The liability of EWS for loss of or damage to the goods is limited by Condition 10.3.5 to that set out in Condition 8. *2.757*

Rules of general law are preserved, rules of mitigation by Condition 10.5 and rules about contributory causation (negligence) by Condition 10.6. Condition 10.7, the last of these provisions, contains an obligation on each party to give notice of impending claims. As to the meaning of "notice" see Condition 19.8 (para. 2.789, below). However, other aspects this kind of clause have been litigated in respect of "claims made" insurance cover in professional indemnity policies.[3] A distinct "notice of loss, damage or delay" provision is to be found in Condition 11, below. *2.758*

11. Claims Procedure *2.759*

11.1 EWS shall have no liability for any Loss of, damage to or delay in the delivery of any Goods unless it is advised of the same in writing within 7 days of the completion or termination of carriage by EWS of the relevant Consignment provided that if in any particular case:

11.1.1 the Customer proves that it was not reasonably possible for the Customer to advise EWS in writing within the above time period; and

11.1.2 the Customer did notify EWS of the same within a reasonable time;

then EWS shall not have the benefit of this Condition.

11.2 Notices of any Losses, damages or delays in the delivery of Goods should be sent by post to Risk Management Team, CSDC, Carolina Way, Doncaster, DN4 5PN or faxed on 01302 766421 or by e-mail to *Risk.management@ews-railway.co.uk* (or such other address, fax number or e-mail address as shall be notified by EWS from time to time) and marked for the attention of the Risk Management Team.

Comments

1. Claims

Condition 11 is a typical procedural condition. Although headed "Claims Procedure", it concerns just one aspect of what might be described broadly as "claims procedure": requirements for notice of loss, damage or delay within a specified time[1]; and there is distinct "notice of claims" provision in Condition 10.7.1. "Claim" usually refers to something more in the nature of a demand. Under Article 27 of CMR (para. 1.159, above) it has been a held that a claim is a general intimation that the claimant considers the carrier to be liable, albeit without *2.760*

2. *Kuwaiti Airway Corp.* v. *Kuwait Ins. Co.* [1996] 1 Lloyd's Rep. 664, 686; appeals on other grounds were dismissed: [1999] 1 Lloyd's Rep. 803 (H.L.). Clarke, *Insurance*, Chap. 17–4C3.

3. See Simpson (Ed.), *Professional Negligence and Liability* (London, 2000), para. 5.5.

1. See CMR, Art. 30, Comment 3, paras. 1.179 *et seq.*, above.

necessarily any quantification of the complaint.[2] Conditions commonly contain a "notice of loss" requirement to be met within a short time after the events that may give rise to a claim, to be followed, if the matter is to be taken further, by compliance with a "notice of claims" requirement within a certain time after that. In Condition 11 "claim" might be better described as "notice" or "advice".

2. Notice

2.761 Be that as it may, it is required by Condition 11.1 that EWS be "advised" of any loss etc. within seven working days (defined in Condition 1) of the occurrence of the loss etc. in question. Conditions commonly specify a longer period for non-apparent loss or damage but that is not the case here where, subject to the effect of Condition 11.1.1, the seven-day period appears to be absolute. The period runs from "completion" of carriage by EWS, which appears to mean the end of transit and delivery to the consignee; see Condition 8, Comment 1 (paras. 2.736 *et seq.*, above).

2.762 Alternatively, the period runs from "termination" of carriage by EWS, as to which see Condition 14, paragraph 2.774, below.

2.763 The "advice" required will be construed to mean notification,[3] as to which see Condition 19.8, paragraph 2.789, below. Conditions commonly specify that notice must be in writing,[4] and that is so here: Condition 19.8. The content of the "advice" is not that the customer intends to claim but the allegation of the specified kind of loss with enough information about it to enable EWS to investigate the allegation before the facts become obscure or evidence hard to obtain.

2.764 An issue which has vexed courts concerned with issues of notice in other contexts[5] is whether a defendant can defend a claim under a condition such as Condition 11.1, if it has suffered no prejudice as a result of late notice. Unlike Condition 18(b)(iii) of the Freightliner Conditions,[6] Condition 11 is silent on this point, however, prejudice is likely to be a factor that affects what is "reasonable" under the proviso in Condition 11.1.1. Other factors affecting what is "reasonable" will be the difficulties faced by the customer in satisfying the seven-day requirement of Condition 11.1, such as whether and to what extent the loss or damage was not apparent.

2.765

12. Storage and Sale of Goods after Transit

12.1 Where Goods are held by EWS after transit or whilst transit is suspended EWS shall store the Goods at the Customer's cost in such storage facility as EWS shall deem appropriate. EWS shall have no liability for any Loss of or damage to Goods (even if caused by negligence) occurring during the period of storage.

2. *William Tatton & Co.* v. *Ferrymasters* [1974] 1 Lloyd's Rep. 203, 207; see also *West Wake Price & Co.* v. *Ching* [1957] 1 W.L.R. 45.
3. Kahn-Freund, p. 393.
4. For the meaning of "writing" see CMR, Art. 30, Comment 3, paras. 1.179 *et seq.*, above.
5. E.g. insurance claims: Clarke, *Insurance*, Chap. 26–2E2.
6. Para. 2.671, above.

12.2 Where Goods which are held by EWS after transit or whilst transit is suspended are Dangerous Goods, then EWS will hold such Goods at the Customer's sole risk and expense and EWS may, if it is satisfied it is reasonable to do so, destroy the Goods and/or return them to the Customer or its Consignor or its Consignee (who shall receive them at once) or otherwise dispose of them.

Comment

Condition 12 concerns the role of EWS not as a carrier but as involuntary bailee. At common law even an involuntary bailee owes a duty of care in respect of goods in its possession, so Condition 12.1 amounts to a significant exclusion of EWS' liability and, therefore, one which will be strictly construed.[1] *2.766*

Condition 12.2 is a provision commonly found which governs the exercise of the carrier's lien on goods in its possession, see Condition 7.2, paragraph 2.733, above, and, in particular, the carrier's power to sell the goods. The power is conditional on prior notification to the customer. Given observance of these Conditions[2] the power granted by Condition 7.2 will be enforced by the courts.[3] *2.767*

13. Insurance *2.768*

13.1 The Customer shall maintain, at its own expense, comprehensive insurance (covering loss or damage to persons or property) to an amount which is not less than the Indemnified Amount together with employer's liability insurance in an amount no less than the statutory minimum. Such insurance is to be held with a reputable insurance company.

13.2 The insurance cover required to be held by the Customer shall be primary in respect of the Customer's liabilities arising under the Contract.

13.3 At EWS' request, the Customer shall provide current certificates of insurance in order to satisfy EWS that such insurance coverage is in effect. In the event of the required insurance cover being withdrawn or terminated the Customer will immediately inform EWS who can terminate the Contract forthwith without prejudice to any rights it may have under the Contract.

13.4 EWS shall maintain, at its own expense, insurance (covering loss or damage to persons or property) to an amount which is consistent with UK prudent railway practice and as required by all applicable laws and regulations. Such insurance shall include employer's liability insurance in an amount no less than the statutory minimum and is to be held with a reputable insurance company.

13.5 The insurance cover required to be held by EWS shall be primary in respect of EWS' liabilities arising under the Contract.

13.6 At the Customer's request, EWS shall provide a current certificate of insurance in order to satisfy the Customer that such insurance coverage is in effect. In the event of this insurance cover being withdrawn or terminated EWS will immediately inform the Customer who can terminate the Contract forthwith without prejudice to any rights it may have under the Contract.

13.7 In the event that liability is determined to be split in some proportion between EWS and the Customer then the insurance held by each party in compliance with this Condition 13 will be primary in respect of that party's liability.

1. See *Canada Steamships Line Ltd.* v. *R.* [1952] A.C. 192 (P.C.).
2. In particular, notification in the sense of Condition 19.8 (para. 2.789, below).
3. See the Comment on Condition 7 of the RHA Conditions, para. 1.283, above.

Comments

1. Certificates of insurance

2.769 The insurance cover that may be required under Condition 13 is of various kinds. Certificates of the insurance, which evidence compliance with the requirement and at least summarise the terms of the cover, are usually issued by insurers in appropriate cases and must be supplied by the customer (Condition 13.3) or EWS (Condition 13.6), as the case may be, on request.

2.770 In all cases insurance must be bought from "reputable insurance companies": Condition 13.1. This requirement is best observed by buying insurance through a qualified broker, it being one of the duties of a broker obtaining cover for clients to see that the recommended insurer has the means to pay and has a reputation for doing so with reasonable promptitude.[1]

2. The insurance duties of the customer

2.771 The customer may be required, according to Condition 13.1, to maintain "comprehensive insurance (covering loss or damage to persons or property) to an amount which is not less than the Indemnified Amount". As regards goods, cover is readily available in the form of All Risks or Transit insurance.[2] In some cases, when a contract requires party A to insure risk X or to pay the premium for such insurance, it is understood to mean that the other party, B, is to have the "benefit of insurance" and that risk X is to be born by A rather than B. In so far as the loss insured would otherwise be the responsibility of party B, the requirement amounts to an exclusion of B's liability.[3] Under international carriage regimes, such as CMR (Article 41.2, para. 1.236, above) and the Hague-Visby Rules on carriage by sea (Article III, rule 8), benefit of insurance clauses are null and void. However, in the context of the EWS Conditions as a whole albeit subject to the Specifications in a particular case, that does not appear to be the intended effect of Condition 13.1.

3. The insurance duties of EWS

2.772 EWS is required by Condition 13.5 to cover its liabilities arising under the contract. This is not surprising, however, it should be noted that comprehensive liability cover is normally construed as confined to tortious liability[4] and, in this case, the cover purchased by EWS must make it clear that cover extends to the contractual liabilities incurred by EWS in the course of its business.

2.773 EWS is also required by Condition 13.4 to maintain insurance "covering loss or damage to persons or property", whose property being unspecified. In the context of a contract with a customer such as this, the word appears to refer to the property of the customer, not least because insurance cover taken out by bailees not as agent

1. *Hurrell* v. *Bullard* (1863) 3 F. & F. 445, 453; Clarke, *Insurance*, Chap. 9–5B.
2. Needless to say perhaps, it does not literally cover "all risks"; see Clarke, *Insurance*, Chap. 17–3.
3. *Mark Rowlands Ltd.* v. *Berni Inns Ltd.* [1986] Q.B. 211 (C.A.).
4. See e.g. *James Longley & Co.* v. *Forest Giles Ltd.* [2001] EWCA Civ 1242; [2002] Lloyd's Rep. I.R. 421 at [17]; Clarke, *Insurance*, Chap. 17–4A.

but as insured on the property of bailors is commonplace: so much so that special rules to make it effective have been developed by the courts over nearly two centuries.[5]

14. Termination *2.774*

14.1 A party may by notice in writing served on the other party ("Defaulting Party") terminate the Contract forthwith if:

14.1.1 the Defaulting Party shall be in material breach of any of the terms of the Contract and, where the breach is capable of remedy, the Defaulting Party fails to remedy such breach within 28 days of service of a written notice from the party not in breach, specifying the breach and requiring the Defaulting Party to remedy such breach or;

14.1.2 bankruptcy or insolvency proceedings are brought against the Defaulting Party or if an arrangement with its creditors is made, or if a receiver or administrator is appointed over any of the Defaulting Party's assets or if the Defaulting Party goes into liquidation.

14.2 Without prejudice to Condition 14.1 EWS may by notice in writing served on the Customer terminate the Contract forthwith if the Customer fails to pay monies due under an invoice by the due date for payment of such invoice.

4.3 For the purposes of these Conditions a breach shall be capable of remedy if it can be remedied in all respects other than time of performance.

14.4 The termination of the Contract howsoever arising is without prejudice to the rights, duties and liabilities of the parties accrued prior to termination.

Comments

1. Termination

Condition 14 tailors the common law rules relating to "termination" of contract by one party. In Condition 14 the contract of carriage may be terminated on one or other of two grounds. The first is that the other party is in serious breach of its obligations under the contract, breach referred to in Condition 14.1.1 as "material" breach. The second is that, loosely speaking, the other party is insolvent: Condition 14.1.2. This condition corresponds, although not closely enough to assist, to the common law rules whereby a contracting party may have become unable to perform the contract and thus be in "anticipatory breach" of contract before the due date for performance. *2.775*

2. Material breach

Condition 14.1.1 posits but does not define a "material" breach. A material breach is likely to be interpreted as meaning what common law regards as a sufficiently serious breach to justify termination of the contract. To decide whether a breach is serious, common law has not one test but a series of points to be considered in order to assess whether, in the particular cases, a breach is serious. Not all are relevant to a contract such as this; the points relevant here are twofold. *2.776*

First, in commercial contracts there is a presumption that "time is of the essence", that is to say that performance on time is important and that, therefore if *2.777*

5. See Clarke, *Insurance*, Chap. 5–6.

one party is late the other is entitled to terminate the contract.[1] One common law qualification to this general rule concerns obligations to make payment,[2] however, this qualification is ruled out by Condition 14.3. An important qualification to the "time of essence" rule in the case of the EWS Conditions concerns non-performance excused by *force majeure* (defined in Condition 1) by Condition 9.

2.778 Secondly, for all kinds of contract the common law rule is that breach is serious if it "goes to root of the contract", i.e. if "the breach substantially deprives [the innocent party] of what he contracted for".[3] This rule looks less to the breach of contract than to the consequences of the breach. More specifically a breach is considered to be serious, if the innocent party would not have made the contract at all if that party had known how the other would (not) perform[4]; or if the innocent party would not have accepted the actual (non)performance of the other party without insisting on a reduction in payment.[5] In other cases the "substantial deprivation" test is applied by considering the ratio of breach to the performance promised.[6] Such would be the case, for example, if EWS had undertaken to make a series of deliveries over a period of time and had made some in conformity with the contract but not others.

3. *The consequences of material breach*

2.779 At common law the consequence of a serious breach of contract is that the innocent party is entitled without more ado to terminate the contract. This can be done without formality; any unequivocal expression of intention by the innocent party will suffice.[7] On this point the common law rules have been tailored to the situation by EWS in Condition 14.1, as regards procedural formality, by the insistence on "notice in writing" in order to trigger the intended consequences by way of termination of the contract. As to the meaning of "notice" see Condition 19.8, paragraph 2.789, below.

2.780 At common law the effect of an unequivocal expression of intention to terminate by the innocent party is that the contract is indeed terminated, i.e., discharged prospectively from the time of termination.[8] The prospective character of termination, as regards its effect on contractual duties, is confirmed by Condition 14.4. However, that apart, on this point too the common law rule has been tailored by EWS in Condition 14.1.1 as regards breach which, although material, is capable of remedy. A breach is capable of remedy if it can be "remedied in all respects other than time of performance": Condition 14.3. In that case, but *semble* not other cases, the party wishing to terminate the contract must send a written notice to the party in breach, specifying the breach and requiring it to be remedied. The party in

1. *Universal Bulk Carriers Ltd.* v. *André et Cie.* [2001] EWCA Civ 588; [2001] 2 Lloyd's Rep. 65 at [20].
2. E.g. *The Selene G* [1981] 2 Lloyd's Rep. 180, 185.
3. *Hong Kong Fir Shipping Co. Ltd.* v. *Kawasaki Kisen Kaisha Ltd.* [1962] 2 Q.B. 26 (C.A.).
4. *Flight* v. *Booth* (1834) 1 Bing. N.C. 370.
5. *Kendall (Henry) & Sons* v. *William Lillico & Sons Ltd.* [1969] 2 A.C. 31.
6. *Hong Kong Fir* (above).
7. *Vitol SA Ltd.* v. *Norelf Ltd.* [1966] A.C. 800.
8. *Johnson* v. *Agnew* [1980] A.C. 367.

breach then has 28 days to remedy the breach and only on its failure to do so within 28 days is the contract terminated. Moreover, the effect of termination at common law is that parties are discharged from performing all outstanding obligations except certain procedural duties such as arbitration.

15. Access to Premises *2.781*

15.1 The Customer shall procure that none of its employees, agents, sub-contractors or contractors or the Consignee or the Consignor enter onto any part of any land or premises owned or controlled by EWS without the prior consent of EWS and being accompanied by a member of EWS staff. The Customer shall procure that any person who enters onto EWS' land or premises complies with all applicable EWS regulations and instructions (including but not limited to those relating to alcohol and drugs) copies of which are available on request from EWS.

15.2 The Customer shall procure such access to its, its sub-contractor's, the Consignor's or the Consignee's land as is necessary for EWS to perform the Services. EWS shall procure that none of its employees, agents, sub-contractors or contractors enter onto any part of the Customer's, Consignor's or the Consignee's land without the Customer having procured the aforementioned consent. EWS shall procure that any person entering into the Customer's, its sub-contractor's, the Consignor's or the Consignee's land or premises on behalf of EWS shall comply with all applicable regulations and instructions that are brought to the attention of EWS in writing.

5.3 Each party shall take all reasonable steps to ensure the health and safety of the other party's employees, agents or sub contractors whilst on their premises and shall consult and liaise with each other with a view to maintaining a safe system of work at such premises.

5.4 No party shall acquire any interest (whether legal or equitable) in any land or premises belonging to the other party or any third party as a consequence of this Contract.

Comment

To control access to premises, evidently a matter of concern to EWS, is sometimes regulated in other kinds of contract but is not the subject of other conditions of carriage considered in this book. *2.782*

16. Customer's Equipment and Private Sidings *2.783*

16.1 This Condition shall apply where it is agreed between EWS and the Customer that:

16.1.1 the Customer or one of its contractors is to provide any equipment for EWS to use in transporting Goods including but not limited to Wagons (whether such equipment is owned by the Customer or any other person), in these Conditions such equipment shall be "Customer's Equipment"; and/or

16.1.2 where the Departure Point and/or the Arrival Point is located at any Private Sidings (save where access to such Private Sidings is governed by a separate private sidings agreement to which EWS is a party);

For the avoidance of doubt where Wagons are the subject of a separate contract of use agreement, such contract of use agreement shall take precedence over any conflicting term of this Condition 16.

16.2 The Customer shall:

16.2.1 ensure that the Customer's Equipment is registered with the appropriate authority and is safe and fit to run, is free from defects and complies with and is maintained in accordance with all applicable Railway Industry Standards;

16.2.2 ensure that the Private Sidings are safe, free from defects and are kept in an appropriate condition for use as part of a railway network and comply with all applicable Railway Industry Standards;

16.2.3 ensure that the Private Sidings are connected to the Network Rail network enabling safe transfer onto the Network Rail network and do not allow risk to be imported onto the Network Rail network; and

16.2.4 ensure that EWS has the access to the Private Sidings and to the Network Rail network from the Private Sidings reasonably required by EWS to enable it to carry Goods in accordance with the Contract.

16.3 EWS may refuse to accept any Customer's Equipment if it does not comply with Condition 16.2.1. The Customer shall not rely upon EWS carrying out any checks upon the Customer's Equipment and the Customer acknowledges that EWS relies upon the Customer's obligations under Condition 16.2.1.

16.4 EWS may refuse to collect or deliver any Consignment if there is any breach of Condition 16.2.2, 16.2.3 or 16.2.4. The Customer shall not rely upon EWS carrying out any checks upon Private Sidings and the Customer acknowledges that EWS relies upon the Customer's obligations in Conditions 16.2.2, 16.2.3 and 16.2.4.

16.5 EWS's liability for any loss of or damage to any Customer's Equipment caused by its proven negligence shall be limited to the reasonable cost of repair and in any event shall be limited to the depreciated value of that Customer's Equipment. EWS shall have no other liability arising from any loss or damage to Customer's Equipment even if caused by negligence. The Customer shall give EWS a reasonable opportunity to inspect any damage for which it is claimed EWS is responsible under this Condition.

16.6 Without prejudice to any other provision of the Contract the Customer shall indemnify EWS in full against all Claims and sums payable to Network Rail as a consequence of EWS' failure to meet performance standards suffered or incurred by EWS which arises from any Customer's Equipment not complying with Condition 16.2.1.

16.7 If EWS damages any Private Sidings by its proven negligence it shall be liable for the reasonable repair costs of the same. EWS shall have no other liability arising from damage to Private Sidings even if caused by its negligence.

16.8 Where any of the Goods, the Customer's Equipment or the Private Sidings are not the property of the Customer, the Customer shall procure that EWS has no liability for any loss or destruction of or damage to the same (whether caused by negligence or otherwise) to any other person owning or having an interest therein (including but not limited to any insurer of any such person) in addition to EWS' liability to the Customer under the express terms of the Contract and the Customer shall indemnify EWS from any Claim to any such person.

Comment

2.784 Condition 16 seeks to address the particular concerns of EWS' business and the context in which it operates. As regards Condition 16.5, see the Comments on Condition 8, paragraphs 2.736 *et seq.*, above.

2.785

17. Confidentiality

17.1 Each party shall keep confidential the terms of the Contract and any and all Confidential Information that it may acquire in relation to the other party. Neither party shall use the other party's Confidential Information for any purpose other than to perform its obligations under the Contract. Each party shall ensure that its agents and employees comply with the provisions of this Condition 17.1.

17.2 The obligations on a party set out in Condition 17.1 shall not apply to any information which:

17.2.1 is publicly available or becomes publicly available through no act or omission of that party; or

17.2.2 a party is required to disclose by law or by competent legal or regulatory authority.

Comment

Confidentiality, evidently a matter of concern and thus regulated in many other kinds of contract, is not the subject of other conditions of carriage considered in this book. *2.786*

18. Intellectual Property *2.787*

All intellectual property rights in the services provided by EWS (including any software supplied by EWS), all documents, drawings and information supplied by EWS to the Customer in connection with this Contract remain the absolute property of EWS. Such documents, drawings and information will not be copied, disclosed or used (except for the purpose for which they were supplied) without the prior written consent of EWS. No licence or other right is granted by EWS to the Customer with regard to the intellectual property of EWS except as expressly set out in this Contract and for the purpose of performing the services by EWS or as otherwise permitted at law.

Comment

Condition 18 can be read in conjunction with Condition 17 in that Condition 18 deals with a particular and important kind of confidentiality but one that has been the subject of legal developments such that the law speaks of "property" and protects ownership as such.[1] *2.788*

19. General *2.789*

19.1 If at any time any Condition or part of the Contract is found by any court, tribunal or administrative body of competent jurisdiction to be wholly or partly illegal, invalid or unenforceable in any respect that shall not affect or impair the legality, validity or enforceability of any other provision of these Conditions or the Contract. In any such circumstances the parties shall negotiate in good faith in order to agree the terms of a mutually satisfactory provision, achieving as nearly as possible the same commercial effect, to be substituted for the Condition or part of the Contract, which is found to be illegal, invalid or unenforceable.

19.2 The failure or delay by a party in exercising any right, power or remedy available to it under the Contract shall not in any circumstances impair such right, power or remedy nor operate as a waiver of it. The single or partial exercise by either party of any right, power or remedy under the Contract shall not in any circumstances preclude any other or further exercise of it or the exercise of any other right, power or remedy.

19.3 Any waiver of a breach of, or default under, any of the terms of the Contract shall not be deemed a waiver of any subsequent breach or default and shall in no way affect the other terms of the Contract.

19.4 The express terms of this Contract are in lieu of all warranties, conditions, terms, undertakings and obligations implied by statute, common law, custom, trade usage, course of dealing or otherwise, all of which are hereby excluded to the fullest extent permitted by law.

19.5 Each party warrants that it has not been induced to enter into the Contract by a statement or promise which the Contract does not contain save that this Condition shall not exclude any liability which a party would otherwise have to the other in respect of any statements made fraudulently by that party.

19.6 Subject to any variation agreed pursuant to Condition 19.7 these Conditions together with the Specification shall form the Contract and contain all the terms which the parties have

1. See Bently and Sherman, *Intellectual Property Law* (2nd ed., 2004).

agreed in relation to the subject matter of the Contract to the exclusion of all other terms and conditions. EWS shall not be deemed to accept any other conditions or any modification or waiver of these Conditions by failing to object to any conditions contained in a communication from the Customer.

19.7 Any variation to these Conditions shall have no effect unless expressly agreed in writing and signed by the authorised representatives of the parties.

19.8 Any demand, notice or other communication given or made under or in connection with the Contract will be in writing to the usual trading address or registered office of the party stipulated in such notice and will be deemed to have been given or made when delivered personally if properly addressed and if posted within three business days of posting and/or if sent by fax upon being sent or if sent by e-mail or other electronic means upon such communication being acknowledged has having been received.

19.9 The Contract may not be assigned by the Customer. The Customer may not sub-contract any of its obligations without EWS's prior written consent and if it does sub-contract its obligations it will not be relieved of any of its obligations as a result.

19.10 This Contract is personal to the parties and is not for the benefit of third parties. The Customer agrees that it will not assign or transfer any of its rights or obligations under this Contract and specifically that it will not re sell or seek to re sell services afforded to it by EWS under the Contract to any third party. Any rights of any person to enforce the terms of the Contract pursuant to the Contracts (Rights of Third Parties) Act 1999 are excluded save as expressly set out otherwise in Condition 10.9.

19.11 This Contract shall be considered as a contract made in England according to English law and subject to the exclusive jurisdiction of the English Courts to which the parties hereby submit.

Comment

2.790 Condition 19 contains a number of provisions dealing with different matters. Many of them, such as Condition 19.9, are designed to eliminate possible doubt or ambiguity. Other provisions, such as Condition 19.11, are to ensure that the contract receives a predictable construction. All are designed make the contractual relationship work smoothly. In this respect the opposite, however, is the likely effect of the second sentence of Condition 19.1. Sensible as they sound to businessmen, such is the uncertainty raised by provisions of this kind that the courts have held that such provisions are too vague to be enforceable.[1]

2.791 Certain provisions in Condition 19 confirm the interpretation of words or events likely to be drawn by the English courts. Thus Article 19.2, for example, confirms *inter alia* the application of decisions such as *Morrison*.[2] Again, Article 19.3 applies *The Scaptrade*[3] to relations between EWS and Customers, something which would not otherwise have been obvious to those concerned, with or without knowledge of the law.

2.792 Up to a point the same might be said of Condition 19.1. This provision restates the law but also goes further. The common law rule of severance[4] applies a "blue pencil" test, whereby the offending provision will be removed and the remainder of the contract enforced but only if, as severed, the contract still makes grammatical sense.[5] Condition 19.1 appears to be less strict. In another respect, however, a literal reading of the provision appears to go too far because it takes no account of the

1. *Walford* v. *Miles* [1992] 2 A.C. 128, 138. Treitel, Chap. 2.5.2(2)(e).
2. *Morrison* v. *Universal Marine Insurance Co.* (1872–73) L.R. 8 Ex. 197.
3. *Scandinavian Trading Tanker Co. AB* v. *Flota Petrolera Ecuatoriana* [1983] 2 A.C. 694.
4. E.g. *Goldsoll* v. *Goldman* [1915] 1 Ch. 292 (C.A.).
5. See e.g. *T. Lucas & Co. Ltd.* v. *Mitchell* [1974] Ch. 129, 135 (C.A.).

gravity of the particular case. Under certain circumstances a court might well take the view that the illegal transportation of toxic material or hard drugs was so serious, that public policy was so outraged, that the entire operation and the entire contact was "contaminated" and would refuse to enforce any part of the contract at all.[6] Moreover, it should be recalled that Condition 19.1 is concerned only with illegal terms of the contract. If a lawful contract is actually performed in an illegal manner, for example as regards weight and safety restrictions, a court might refuse to enforce (any part of) the contract on that ground.[7]

In contrast, Condition 19.5, concerning when notice and other kinds of communication are effective, replaces the courts' usual interpretation with a detailed provision that places the relevant time at a point between a receipt rule (the common law preference[8]) and a sending rule, according to the terms of the document.[9] Courts are likely to give effect to these provisions without demur. *Prima facie* the same might be said of Condition 19.6 seen as a Condition reinforcing the parol evidence rule. However, Condition 19.6 may also be viewed restrictively as an "entire agreement" clause and, as such, open to censure by the court.[10] The same is true *a fortiori* of Condition 19.5. *2.793*

6. *Bennett* v. *Bennett* [1952] 1 K.B. 249, 254 (C.A.).

7. E.g. *Ashmore Benson Pease & Co. Ltd.* v. *A.V. Dawson Ltd.* [1973] 1 W.L.R. 828 (C.A.).

8. *Holwell Securities Ltd.* v. *Hughes* [1974] 1 All E.R. 164 (C.A.) interprets "notification" to require receipt.

9. *Adams* v. *Lindsell* (1818) 106 E.R. 250: if the document is silent.

10. Enforced after scrutiny in, e.g., *Watford Electronics Ltd.* v. *Sanderson CFL Ltd.* [2001] 1 All E.R. (Comm) 696 (C.A.).

PART 3

CARRIAGE OF GOODS BY AIR

I. INTRODUCTION

1. Applicability of common form documents

Reference must always be made to the air waybill Conditions of Contract and to the conditions of carriage of particular carriers in conjunction with applicable law in the relevant jurisdiction. However, IATA documentation and procedures, whether arising pursuant to its resolutions or its recommended practices form the basis of the air waybill Conditions of Contract and of the conditions of carriage of cargo for many air carriers whether or not members of IATA. They are accordingly used in this text as common form documents for carriage of goods by air within the UK and for the cross-border carriage of goods by air. *3.1*

In some cases consignors or intermediaries may charter an aircraft and the charter terms will entail individual negotiations as no industry common form exists for the charter contract. Such charter contracts are, however, often separate from the contracts for the carriage by air of cargo. It is often an intermediary who is the charterer and the aircraft operator and consignors may not be in a contractual relationship with one another. At law, however, the operator may be the servant or agent of the charterer under the 1962 Act in so far as the consignor is concerned. In most cases carriage of cargo (whether of individual shipments or of intermediaries' "consolidations") will be upon the carrier's standard conditions and not generally subject to individual negotiation with consignors. *3.2*

2. Applicability of common form documents to cross-border carriage

An international Convention (see below, para. 3.4), from which there can be no "contracting-out", usually governs the legal relationship between carrier, consignor and consignee so far as the documents of carriage and liability for loss, damage and delay to cargo in the course of carriage by air are concerned. The common form documents (Conditions of Contract) have been drafted accordingly and must be interpreted in this light. *3.3*

3. Applicability of international Conventions under UK law

International conventions on carriage by air apply by operation of UK domestic legislation but take effect between the parties to the contract of carriage as terms of *3.4* the contract. The contract in a particular case is evidenced by the Conditions of Contract contained in the standard air waybill issued by the carrier in question. The Conditions used are usually those recommended by IATA in a standard waybill published by IATA, currently those contained in IATA Resolution 600b(ii). For some time the expectation has been that these would be replaced by those contained in IATA Resolution 600b, however, at the time of writing Resolution 600b had not been declared effective. The Conditions refer to "the Convention", however, being in standard form they do not indicate which Convention applies; that must be determined as described below.

3.5 The main Conventions are the Warsaw Convention 1929 (WC) (paras. 3.307 *et seq.*, below) and the amended version arising from the Hague Protocol 1955 (paras. 3.37 *et seq.*, below) officially named therein as the Warsaw Convention as amended at the Hague 1955 (HP), each as further amended.[1] WC and HP were each supplemented by the Guadalajara Convention 1961 (paras. 3.525 *et seq.*, below). WC was further amended by (Montreal) Additional Protocol No. 1 of 1975.[2] HP was further amended by (Montreal) Additional Protocol Nos. 2[3] and 4[4] of 1975. The version in force in the UK on 1 February 2004 is HP as yet further amended by the (Montreal) Additional Protocol No 4 (MP4) (paras. 3.219 *et seq.*, below). The entire web of instruments was codified into one new instrument, the Montreal Convention 1999 (MC) (paras. 3.555 *et seq.*, below), which provides in Article 55 that its provisions shall prevail over any rules which apply to international carriage by air between States parties to that Convention by virtue of those States commonly being party to the previous instruments referred to in this paragraph. MC came into force for those States that had ratified it, which did not then include the UK, on 4 November 2003. It came into force in the UK on 28 June 2004. In the UK the Conventions have been given force of law as follows:

(i) WC: the 1967 Order, Schedule 2.
(ii) WC Convention as amended by Additional Protocol No. 1: the 1967 Order, Schedule 3;
(iii) HP as amended by Additional Protocol No. 2: the 1961 Act, Schedule 1 (as amended by the 1979 Act);
(iv) MP4: the 1961 Act Schedule 1A[5];
(v) WC as supplemented by the Guadalajara Convention: 1967 Order, Schedule 2. Part 1 sets out the English text and Part 2 the French text.
(vi) HP as supplemented by the Guadalajara Convention: the 1961 Act as supplemented by the 1962 Act.
(vii) HP as amended by the Guatemala Protocol and as further amended by Montreal Protocol No. 3: the 1961 Act as amended by the 1979 Act (see

1. HP to be read and interpreted as one single instrument with WC: Hague Protocol, Art. 19.
2. For text of (Montreal) Additional Protocol No. 1 see HMSO Treaty Series No. 75 (1997) Cm 3823.
3. For text of (Montreal) Additional Protocol No. 2 see HMSO Treaty Series No. 76 (1997) Cm 3824.
4. For text of (Montreal) Additional Protocol No. 4 see HMSO Treaty Series No. 28 (1999) Cm 4337.
5. See also the Carriage by Air Acts (Implementation of Protocol No. 4 of Montreal 1975) Order 1999, S.I. 1999/1312.

1979 Act, section 1(1). The relevant parts of the 1979 Act are not likely to be brought into force.

(vii) MC.

The UK also makes provision for carriage to which the above Conventions do not apply, because the carriage is not international carriage, as follows: HP as amended by Additional Protocol No. 1 and as supplemented by the Guadalajara Convention, as modified by the 1967 Order, Schedule 1 (paras. 3.463 *et seq.*, below).

4. Application of the law in the UK

The law applied by UK courts to cases involving the carriage of goods by air is found in legislation which incorporates international Conventions into domestic law or is statute law based on such Conventions. In the case of incorporation, presumably the intention of Parliament is the same as that behind the Conventions, that, as regards liability, the text should be exclusive[6]: there will be no concurrent liability, for example, under the English law of tort. *3.6*

5. International carriage governed by the Conventions

The 1967 Order has three Schedules. Schedules 2 and 3 to the Order apply to international carriage as defined therein: carriage under WC. These schedules, in practice, apply to far fewer shipments over which the UK has jurisdiction than HP and subsequent versions of the regime. The Carriage by Air (Parties to Convention) Order 1999 certifies who, for the purposes of UK law, are the States party to WC and is conclusive evidence of the matters so certified. *3.7*

The widespread ratification of HP means that, for practical purposes, most cross-border shipments have been subject, under UK law, to the 1961 Act, s. 1, which gives effect to HP (paras. 3.37 *et seq.*, below). The expectation is that there will be a gradual shift from HP via MP4 to MC (paras. 3.555 *et seq.*, below). MC was signed in Montreal on 28 May 1999. It came into force internationally on 4 November 2003 and in the UK on 28 June 2004.[7] *3.8*

6. International carriage not governed by the Conventions

WC, by an Additional Protocol to Article 2, enabled a state to reserve the right to declare at the time of ratification or of accession that the Convention should not apply to international carriage by air performed by that state or by legally constituted public bodies.[8] If such a reservation has not been made, the Convention *3.9*

6. *Sidhu* v. *B.A.* [1997] A.C. 430, 443 *et seq.*; *Fellowes* v. *Clyde Helicopters* [1997] 1 All E.R. 775, 791 (H.L.). As regards the Conventions, the same view has been taken in other countries, e.g. Germany: *BGH 28.11.1978*, NJW 1.979.496; and the USA: *Shah* v. *Pan Am World Services, Inc.*, 148 F. 3d 84, 97–98 (2 Cir., 1998); *King* v. *American Airlines*, 284 F. 3d 352 (2 Cir., 2002).

7. See the Carriage by Air Acts (Implementation of the Montreal Convention 1999) Order 2002: S.I. 2002/263.

8. For such reservations, see the Carriage by Air (Parties to Convention) Order 1999, S.I. 1999/1313.

applies to carriage performed by such a state or by legally constituted public bodies and according to the 1961 Act, s. 8, every such High Contracting Party shall be deemed to have submitted to the jurisdiction of the courts in the United Kingdom. The 1961 and 1962 Acts and the 1967 Order apply to the Crown.[9]

3.10 The 1961 Act enables a statutory instrument from time to time to provide that Schedules 1 (HP) or 1A (MP4) to that Act shall not apply to the carriage of cargo for the military authorities of the UK or another state, in aircraft registered in that state, if the whole capacity of the aircraft has been reserved by or on behalf of those authorities.

7. Non-international carriage governed by UK legislation

3.11 Carriage by air which is neither international carriage for the purposes of the 1961 Act, Scheds. 1 or 1A, nor the 1967 Order, Scheds. 2 or 3, is carriage in respect of which the 1967 Order, Sched. 1 (paras. 3.463 *et seq.*, below), may apply. The 1967 Order provides, under the enabling provisions,[10] that it shall apply to all carriage by air not being carriage to which the 1961 Act, Schedule 1 (paras. 3.37 *et seq.*, below), applies. The text of Schedule 1 is a truncated version of HP as amended by the Guadalajara Convention. In particular, Chapter II (Documents of Carriage) does not apply. Accordingly, there is no requirement at law for the carrier to require the consignor to make out and hand over to him a document called an "air waybill", for any such air waybill to contain a notice drawing attention to limitations of liability, nor for the statements in the air waybill to constitute *prima facie* evidence of the facts stated. Nor, under the Order, does a consignor have a right of disposition over the cargo.

8. Non-international carriage governed by common law

3.12 The 1967 Order does not apply to gratuitous carriage of cargo if not performed by an air transport undertaking or by the Crown. Also, the Secretary of State may exempt any carriage of any person from the requirements of the 1967 Order. Since it is unlikely that such carriage would be performed under these air waybill conditions the common law rules are not here set out.

9. Applicability of the law in a particular case

3.13 In any matter potentially governed by these Conventions the applicable legal regime must first be identified by reference to the agreement made between the parties, as evidenced in the usual case by the air waybill having regard to the place of departure and of destination and of any agreed stopping places for the cargo concerned.[11] It is then necessary to establish the extent to which, if at all, those places are in territories of states that have ratified one or more of the Conventions and whether

9. 1961 Act, s. 13, 1967 Order, para. 7.
10. The 1961 Act, s. 10(1) and of that section as applied by s. 5(2) of the 1962 Act.
11. See HP, Art. 1, Comment 3, paras. 3.43 *et seq.*, below.

or not there exists a treaty relationship, by which is meant a set of rules, common to *both* states, between those states.[12]

Thus, for example, a carriage on 1 January 1999 from London to Lyon was governed by HP as both France and the UK were parties to HP. However, carriage on that date from London to Los Angeles was governed by WC because on that date the USA did not apply HP but WC. Although the UK repealed the Carriage by Air Act 1932, which gave effect to WC, when it enacted the Carriage by Air Act 1961, giving effect in the UK to HP, the set of rules contained in WC remained on the statute book[13] for cases such as carriage to the USA. 3.14

Further, the UK mode of implementation of the Guadalajara Convention and of the Montreal Protocol No. 2 (but not of the other instruments) complicates the position by providing that those instruments shall apply to any claims before the UK courts arising out of international carriage under HP and, in the case of the Guadalajara Convention, of international carriage under WC. 3.15

This analysis must be accomplished for each shipment: any one package may therefore be subject to a different legal regime from that applying to another package possibly within the same pallet or container, aboard any one aircraft. 3.16

10. The Convention history

The original Convention (WC) (paras 3.307 *et seq.*, below) arose mainly out of two sessions of the Conférence Internationale de Droit Privé Aérien and the work of its specialist Comité International Technique d'Experts Juridiques Aériens (CITEJA). It was signed on 12 October 1929 by Austria, Belgium, Brazil, Czechoslovakia, Denmark, France, Germany, Greece, Italy, Japan, Luxembourg, Netherlands, Norway, Poland, Romania, the Russian Federation, South Africa, Spain, Switzerland, United Kingdom and Yugoslavia. It entered into force on 13 February 1933, being 90 days after the deposit with the Government of Poland of the necessary five instruments of ratification. It entered into force in the UK on 15 May 1933, being given the force of law by the Carriage by Air Act 1932, which Act was repealed by the 1961 Act. 3.17

The Hague Protocol of 1955 (HP) (paras. 3.37 *et seq.*, below), which amended the Convention text of 1929 (WC), entered into force on 1 August 1963, being 90 days after the deposit with the Government of Poland of the thirtieth instrument of ratification: the UK deposited its instrument of ratification on 3 March 1967. HP was the form that generally applied throughout the world until the late 1990s. The HP amendments did not enter into force in the UK until 1 June 1967 pursuant to the 1961 Act.[14] Further amendments, set out in the Montreal Protocol No. 4 (MP4) (paras. 3.219 *et seq.*, below), came into force in the UK on 21 May 1999 and the new Convention, the Montreal Convention 1999 (MC) (paras. 3.555 *et seq.*, 3.18

12. For certification, in UK law, as to who are the Parties to the Convention, to the amended Convention and to the Convention as amended by Montreal Protocol No. 1 and the territories in respect of which they are parties see the Carriage by Air (Parties to Convention) Order 1999 (S.I. 1999/1313). NB: no such certification exists with respect to the parties to the amended Convention as amended by Montreal Protocol No. 2 and No. 4.

13. See Sched. 2 to the 1967 Order.

14. See Art. 1(3), Carriage by Air (Convention) Order 1967, S.I. 1967/479.

below) came into force in the UK in 2004. Article 53.6 of MC provides that it shall enter into force generally on the sixtieth day following the date of deposit of the thirtieth instrument of ratification, acceptance, approval or accession with the Depositary (ICAO) between the States which have deposited such instrument, which occurred in November 2003.

11. Outline of the law

3.19 The earlier regimes (whether WC or HP) (paras. 3.307 *et seq.* and 3.317 *et seq.*, below), as amended by MP4 (paras. 3.219 *et seq.*, below), as well as MC (paras. 3.555 *et seq.*, below), can be summarised thus:

(i) *Liability*: the carrier is liable for damage sustained upon proof of loss, damage or delay to cargo during the carriage by air (Articles 18 (para. 3.99) and 19 (para. 3.111), unless the carrier can prove one of the defences: the burden of establishing the defence is on the carrier.

(ii) *Defences*: the carrier is not liable if it is proved that the carrier and its servants and agents took all necessary measures to avoid the damage or that it was impossible for it or them to take such measures (Article 20 (para. 3.116)). The equivalent defence in MC applies only to damage occasioned by delay (Article 19 (para. 3.590)). There is also a defence of contributory negligence (Article 21 (para. 3.122); MC, Article 20 (para. 3.592)). In addition, although not a defence, the carrier has an indemnity in certain matters from the consignor (Article 10 (para. 3.68)).

(iii) *Jurisdiction*: an action for damages must be brought at the option of the plaintiff in the territory of one of the High Contracting Parties to the applicable legal instruments either before the court having jurisdiction where the carrier is ordinarily resident, or has its principal place of business, or has an establishment by which the contract has been made or before the court having jurisdiction at the place of destination (Article 28 (para. 3.173); MC, Article 33 (para. 3.614)).

(iv) *Limitation*: there are strict time limits for complaints to the carrier in the case of damage or delay to cargo (Article 26 (para. 3.169); MC, Article 31 (para. 3.610)). Furthermore the so-called "right to damages" in respect of loss damage or delay is extinguished within two years reckoned from the date of arrival at the destination, or from the date on which the aircraft ought to have arrived, or from the date on which the carriage stopped (Article 29 (para. 3.181), MC Article 35 (para. 3.618)).

(v) *Damages*: the damages that may be awarded against the carrier are limited by reference to the weight of the cargo concerned. The limit is the monetary equivalent of 17 SDRs per kilogramme (Article 22(2)(b) (para. 3.125); MC, Article 22.3 (para. 3.594)). The assessment of damages is left to the rules of the jurisdiction concerned. The possibility found in earlier versions of the regime (WC and HP, Article 25 (paras. 3.350 and 3.147)), that the limit would be removed in cases of damage done "with intent to cause damage or recklessly and with knowledge that damage would probably result", applies to passengers and their baggage but applies no longer to cargo. However, it is still possible for a consignor to declare a value for the cargo and, so far as that declaration is not for a value greater than the actual value, thereby to increase the carrier's liability to the sum declared (Article 22(2)(a) (para. 3.125); MC, Article 22.3 (para. 3.594)).

(vi) *Documentation*: certain particulars are required to be stated in the air waybill (Article 8 (para. 3.63); MC, Article 5 (para. 3.564)) but the trend in law reform has been to reduce the number of particulars required in law and to remove sanctions attached to any omission. Moreover, provision has been made for electronic documentation to be used instead of paper documents (MP4, Article 5 (para. 3.223); MC, Article 4 (para. 3.562)).

(vii) *General provisions*: any clause by which the parties purport to infringe the rules laid down by the applicable legal instruments is null and void (Article 32 (para. 3.198); MC, Article 49 (para. 3.646)). However nothing contained therein prevents a carrier either from refusing to enter into any contract of carriage or from making regulations which do not conflict with the provisions of the instrument concerned (Article 33 (para. 3.200)). MC does not contain a corresponding provision.

(viii) *Costs*: WC made no provision for the costs of any party. HP and MP4 (Article 22(4) (paras. 3.125 and 3.260)) and MC (Article 22.6 (para. 3.594)) expressly state that the limits of liability shall not prevent the court, in accordance with its own law, awarding in addition court costs and the expenses of litigation incurred by the plaintiff, upon terms. There is no mention of carrier's costs.

12. Contracting/actual carrier

Under WC, there was uncertainty as to the liability situation of an actual carrier who was not a contracting carrier or a successive carrier. A "supplementary" Convention, the Guadalajara Convention 1961 (paras. 3.525 *et seq.*, below), was signed noting that WC does not contain particular rules relating to international carriage by air performed by a person who is not a party to the agreement for carriage. It was enacted into English law by the 1962 Act, the provisions of the Guadalajara Convention being set out in the Schedule to that Act. It supplements the 1961 Act, Schedule 1 (HP) (paras. 3.37 *et seq.*, below), and, with minor amendments, the 1967 Order (WC) (paras. 3.307 *et seq.*, below), and is given force of law in the UK. As such it is applicable in the UK to nearly all air carriage. However, overseas a court might only apply the Guadalajara Convention where the places of departure and of destination are States party to that Convention, it having achieved relatively fewer ratifications than WC or HP. When MC applies, the Guadalajara Convention as such does not, however, Articles I to IX of the Guadalajara Convention have been incorporated as Articles 39 to 47 of MC (paras. 3.626 to 3.641, below). 3.20

13. Carrier's servant or agent

3.21 Under WC there was uncertainty as to the applicability of the limitation of liability to such persons. HP, MP4 (Article 25A (para. 3.266)) and MC (Article 43 (para. 3.634)) afford such protection for acts and omissions in "the scope of employment".

14. International Conventions: approach to construction

3.22 As the Conventions take the form of an international treaty, albeit as a technique of private law regulation in the international arena, the general rules on the interpretation of treaties apply.[15] Thus the House of Lords in *Fothergill*[16] took the view that, having ratified the Vienna Convention on the Law of Treaties 1969,[17] the United Kingdom has an international obligation to interpret later treaties as indicated in Articles 31 to 33 of that Convention.

3.23 In particular, according to Article 31.1, a "treaty shall be interpreted in good faith in accordance with the ordinary meaning to be given to the terms of the treaty in their context and in the light of its object and purpose". Moreover, according to Article 32, when the interpretation according to Article 31 "(a) leaves the meaning ambiguous or obscure; or (b) leads to a result which is manifestly absurd or unreasonable", recourse may be had to "supplementary means of interpretation", which include "the preparatory work of the treaty and the circumstances of its conclusion". According to Article 31.3(b), it is also legitimate to have regard to "any subsequent practice in the application of the treaty which establishes the agreement of the parties regarding its interpretation".

3.24 As regards preparatory work (*les travaux préparatoires*) resort by English courts will be rare and cautious.[18] As regards subsequent practice, English courts have often referred to decisions not only of the English courts but also those of other countries, in particular, the USA. This commentary follows that lead, however, clearly, "much must depend upon the status of each court and of the extent to which the point of issue has been subjected to careful analysis. Material of this kind, where it is found to be of the appropriate standing and quality, may be of some help in pointing towards an interpretation of the Convention which has received general acceptance in other countries."[19]

3.25 Some reference is also made to the work of commentators, however, "delegates cannot have taken them into account in agreeing on the text. . . . The persuasive effect of learned commentaries, like the arguments of counsel in an English court, will depend on the cogency of their reasoning".[20]

3.26 In addition, as a matter of interpretation, the court is not only entitled but obliged to consider the French text of the regime in question. The process has been described thus:

15. See further: Clarke, *Air*, Ch. 4
16. *Fothergill* v. *Monarch* [1981] A.C. 251, 283.
17. Cmnd 4140.
18. *Fothergill* (above), p. 278.
19. *Sidhu* v. *British Airways* [1997] A.C. 430, 443.
20. *Fothergill* (above), p. 283–284.

1. Interpretation of the English text, according to the principles upon which international Conventions are to be interpreted
2. Interpretation of the French text according to the same principles but with additional linguistic problems.
3. Comparison of these meanings.[21]

In case of conflict the UK legislation giving force of law to WC, HP and the Guadalajara Convention provides that if there is any inconsistency between the English text and the French text (each as therein set out) the text in French shall prevail (1961 Act and 1962 Act, section 1(2)).

15. UK law: meaning of and application to other territories

Reference is made throughout this text to "UK law" because the UK is the party to the relevant international legal instruments. The UK, of course, comprises the separate legal systems of England and Wales, Scotland, and Northern Ireland. The Channel Islands and the Isle of Man (IOM) are not part of the UK, but the principal UK legislation is also relevant to such territories. There may be differences as to procedure in the application of this legislation. 3.27

[*The next paragraph is 3.37*]

21. *Fothergill* (above), p. 272.

II. THE 1955 AMENDED CONVENTION AS GIVEN FORCE OF LAW IN THE UK BY THE 1961 ACT, SCHEDULE 1[1]

3.37 **Convention for the unification of certain rules relating to international carriage by air**

Chapter I: Scope—definitions

Article 1—Definitions

(1) This Convention applies to all international carriage of persons, baggage or cargo performed by aircraft for reward. It applies equally to gratuitous carriage by aircraft performed by an air transport undertaking.

(2) For the purposes of this Convention, the expression international carriage means any carriage in which, according to the agreement between the parties, the place of departure and the place of destination, whether or not there be a break in the carriage or a transhipment, are situated either within the territories of two High Contracting Parties or within the territory of a single High Contracting Party if there is an agreed stopping place within the territory of another State, even if that State is not a High Contracting Party. Carriage between two points within the territory of a single High Contracting Party without an agreed stopping place within the territory of another State is not international carriage for the purposes of this Convention.

(3) Carriage to be performed by several successive air carriers is deemed, for the purposes of this Convention, to be one undivided carriage if it has been regarded by the parties as a single operation, whether it had been agreed upon under the form of a single contract or of a series of contracts, and it does not lose its international character merely because one contract or a series of contracts is to be performed entirely within the territory of the same State.

Comments

1. Conclusion of the contract

3.38 Article 1, in particular Article 1(1), defines the physical operation to which HP applies. For cases falling within its scope HP is the exclusive source of liability on matters regulated by HP; there is no concurrent liability, for example, in tort. Article 1 is substantially the same as Article 1 of WC, MP4 and MC.

3.39 As to whether or not a contract has been made, Article 11(1), like Article 11(1) of WC, MP4 and MC, provides that the air waybill is *prima facie* evidence of the conclusion of the contract, and that the air waybill is *prima facie* evidence of the receipt of the cargo and of the conditions of carriage. The parties to the contract are those who made the contract, and not necessarily those shown as consignors or consignees on the air waybill, although often this is the case.[2]

2. The terms of the contract

3.40 Carriers' terms are part of the contract of carriage, if the customer has "sufficient notice", i.e. reasonable notice of the terms.[3] before or at the time that the contract

1. Being the English text of the Warsaw Convention as amended by the Hague Protocol (The 1955 Amended Convention) (HP).

2. *Grein* v. *Imperial Airways Ltd.* [1937] 1 K.B. 50, 77 (C.A.). The consignee has rights against the carrier under Art. 14 of the various regimes.

3. *Circle Freight International* v. *Medeast Gulf Exports* [1988] 2 Lloyd's Rep. 427, 430 (C.A.).

of carriage was concluded.[4] A customer has sufficient notice when the customer is or should be aware that the terms exist and that the carrier intends those terms to apply to the contract of carriage.[5] Awareness of terms is likely to be presumed of most of the carriers' customers.[6] Sufficient notice may be actual or constructive. Whether or not the customer has read the terms or knows what they say[7] or even knows that the terms exist, the customer will be held to have constructive notice of the existence of the terms, either as a matter of general commercial knowledge[8] or, in appropriate cases, as a result of past dealings with the carrier concerned.[9]

Exceptions arise, i.e., a term is not binding as written on these grounds, in any one of the following cases: *3.41*

(a) A complete copy of the terms (usually to be found in the air waybill) is not available to read[10] or the only available copy is illegible.[11]
(b) Although common law does not require the conditions to be intelligible to a person untrained in the law,[12] there is some suggestion that, if "the draughtsmanship is so convoluted and prolix that one almost needs an LL.B. to understand them",[13] conditions will be unreasonable under the Unfair Contract Terms Act 1977,[14] which, however, applies only if the carriage is within the UK or the place of business of each of the contracting parties is in the UK.[15]
(c) When the customer is a consumer and the term is unintelligible to such a person.[16] The Office of Fair Trading has ruled, for example, that an indication of the currency value of SDRs was required to make it comprehensible to consumers.[17] In other cases the Office has required that carrier conditions be redrafted to be in line with IATA Recommended Practice 1724.[18]
(d) A term will not be binding if the content of the term is both onerous and unusual, unless it has been specifically drawn to the attention of the

4. *Olley* v. *Marlborough Court Hotel* [1949] 1 K.B. 532 (C.A.).
5. *Parker* v. *S.E. Ry.* (1877) 2 C.P.D. 416 (C.A.). Cf. *Poseidon Freight Forwarding Co. Ltd.* v. *Davies Turner Southern Ltd.* [1996] 2 Lloyd's Rep. 388 (C.A.).
6. *William Teacher & Sons Ltd.* v. *Bell Lines Ltd.* 1991 S.L.T. 876 (Ct. Sess.).
7. *Circle Freight* (above).
8. *British Crane Hire Corp.* v. *Ipswich Plant Hire* [1975] Q.B. 303 (C.A.); *Lacey's Footwear (Wholesale) Ltd.* v. *Bowler Int. Freight Ltd.* [1997] 2 Lloyd's Rep. 369, 378 (C.A.).
9. *Henry Kendall & Sons* v. *William Lillico & Sons* [1969] 2 A.C. 31. *Cf. McCutcheon* v. *David MacBrayne Ltd* [1964] 1 W.L.R. 125 (H.L.); and *Poseidon Freight Forwarding Co. Ltd.* v. *Davies Turner Southern Ltd.* [1996] 2 Lloyd's Rep. 388, 392 (C.A.).
10. *Circle Freight* (above). E.g. *Poseidon* (above) and *Mertens* v. *Flying Tiger Lines* 1965 US Av.R. 1. *Papet* v. *Air France, Paris 7.12.1994*, BTL 1996.23.
11. *Chellaram & Co.* v. *China Ocean Shipping Co.* [1989] 1 Lloyd's Rep. 413 (N.S.W.).
12. *Derby Cables* v. Frederick Oldridge [1959] 2 Lloyd's Rep. 140, 149.
13. *The Zinnia* [1984] 2 Lloyd's Rep. 211, 222.
14. *Ibid.* See also *The Starsin* [2004] 1 A.C. 715 at [15] and at [77].
15. S. 26.
16. Unfair Terms in Consumer Contracts Regulations 1999, S.I. 1999/2083, reg. 7.
17. See OFT *Bulletins* Nos. 24 and 25, December 2003.
18. *Ibid.* Nos. 2 and 45.

customer.[19] However, this exception is not likely to apply to air waybills based on IATA Conditions.

3.42 Where a party has chartered an aircraft for the carriage of cargo the terms of that contract may, of course, be more fully or even exclusively[20] set out in the charter agreement so that the air waybill(s) will operate only to acknowledge receipt of the cargo. As between the parties to the charter, presumably the charter agreement would apply subject always to any mandatory law.

3. *International carriage by air*

3.43 Carriage includes not only transportation but also operations incidental to movement such as being in an aircraft standing waiting to take off,[21] as well as what occurs to goods while in custody of the airport authority after landing.[22] Moreover, the carriage contemplated is by air and thus by means of aircraft, which are not defined. Stressing the word "all" (international carriage) in Article 1(1) Lord Hope said that the Convention "was intended to be, and is, capable of accommodating changes in the practice of airlines and aircraft operators with regard to the purpose for which aircraft are used to carry people and goods".[23]

3.44 Carriage is international when the places of departure and destination and of any agreed stopping places for the cargo concerned are in different contracting States.[24] The route agreed is what counts even if the aircraft does not actually leave the state of departure.[25] So, to determine whether or not there is international carriage, reference must be had to the agreement made between the parties as evidenced by the air waybill. This analysis must be accomplished for each shipment: a package being carried on any one aircraft may therefore be subject to a different legal regime from that applying to an adjoining package albeit possibly on the same pallet or within the same container.

3.45 An agreed stopping place is any "place where according to the contract the machine by which the contract is to be performed will stop in the course of performing the contractual carriage, whatever the purpose of the descent may be".[26] It is sufficient that the place is identified only by its IATA airport code,[27] or by reference to "a published and readily available timetable".[28]

19. *Thornton* v. *Shoe Lane Parking* [1971] 2 Q.B. 163 (C.A.); *Interfoto Picture Library* v. *Stiletto Visual Programmes* [1989] Q.B. 433 (C.A.); *Lacey's Footwear (Wholesale) Ltd.* v. *Bowler Int. Freight Ltd.* [1997] 2 Lloyd's Rep. 369, 384 (C.A.); *O'Brien* v. *MGN Ltd.* [2001] EWCA Civ 1279; [2002] C.L.C. 33.

20. See e.g. *Post Office* v. *British World Airlines Ltd.* [2000] 1 Lloyd's Rep. 378.

21. *Clarke v Royal Aviation Group* (1997) 34 Ord. (3d) 481.

22. *OLG Frankfurt/Main 21.4.98.* TranspR 1999.24.

23. *Fellowes* v. *Clyde Helicopters* [1997] 1 All E.R. 775, 791 (H.L.); cf. *Disley* v. *Levine* [2001] EWCA Civ 1087, [2002] 1 W.L.R. 785.

24. See Clarke, *Air* Art. 1, note 1.

25. *Grein* v. *Imperial Airways* [1937] 1 K.B. 50, 78 (C.A.).

26. *Ibid.*

27. *Southern Electronic* v. *Air Express*, 994 F. Supp. 1472, 1476 (N.D. Ga., 1998).

28. *Kraus* v. *KLM*, 92 N.Y.S. 2d 315, 317 (1949).

4. Cargo

Cargo means anything that can be carried and which the carrier has agreed to carry, but which is not regarded as "baggage". The French translation of "goods" as *marchandises* has a narrower connotation confined to commerce, however, it is likely that the broader sense will be taken in courts in common law countries. The line between registered baggage and cargo, which also travels in the hold of the aircraft, is less a conceptual one than empirical. It depends on party intention which, in turn, depends mostly on how the carrier actually deals with the case. For example, in one case live dogs were checked in and treated as baggage,[29] whereas human remains always travel as cargo.[30] *3.46*

5. Reward

Reward is not defined in HP. However, according to the Civil Aviation Act 1982, s. 105(1), " 'reward' . . . includes any form of consideration received or to be received wholly or partly in connection with the flight irrespective of the person by whom or to whom the consideration has been or is to be given". For the purpose of domestic legislation it has been held to include a sharing of expenses.[31] *3.47*

6. Air transport undertaking

HP does not define an "air transport undertaking". However the Air Navigation (No. 2) Order 1995, art. 118(1) (repealed by the Air Navigation Order 2000, S.I. 2000/1562), defined it as "an undertaking whose business includes the carriage by air of passengers or cargo for valuable consideration". Thus it is likely to include the charterer of an aircraft.[32] The waybill may specify who is the carrier concerned. *3.48*

The relevant air transport undertaking is referred to throughout HP (as well as WC, MP4 and MC) as the "carrier". Later, the Guadalajara Convention distinguished the carrier which concluded the contract of carriage from the actual carrier which performed it, and regulated their rights *inter se*. Any one movement of goods may be performed by a series of carriers under a series of separate contracts of carriage. However, when the movement "has been regarded by the parties as a single operation" (HP, Article 1(3)) it is treated as a single "undivided carriage" undertaken by "successive carriers" (*ibid*).[33] In the case of successive carriage each carrier is deemed by Article 30 to be one of the contracting parties to the carriage in so far as the contract deals with that part of the carriage which is performed under his supervision. *3.49*

Note that courts in the USA, which is not a party to the Guadalajara Convention, have drawn a distinction between direct carriers which operate aircraft and indirect *3.50*

29. *Newell* v. *Canadian Pacific* (1976) 74 D.L.R. (3d) 574 (Ont.).

30. *Johnson* v. *American*, 834 F. 2d 721 (9 Cir., 1987).

31. *Corner* v. *Clayton* [1976] 2 Lloyd's Rep. 422 (Div. Ct.).

32. See *Gurtner* v. *Beaton* [1993] 2 Lloyd's Rep. 369 (C.A.). A German decision to this effect is *BGH 24.6.69*, (1970) 5 ETL 97.

33. See *Haldimann* v. *Delta*, 168 F. 3d 1324, 1326 (D.C. Cir., 1999). See also *Rotterdamsche Bank NV and Another* v. *British Overseas Airways Corporation and Another* [1953] 1 All E.R. 675.

air carriers which "hold out a transportation service to the public under which they utilize the services of a direct carrier for the actual transportation by air" and which, although they carry no goods themselves, "assume the responsibility of a carrier".[34]

3.51 **Article 2—Carriage by State/mail**

(1) This Convention applies to carriage performed by the State or by legally constituted public bodies provided it falls within the conditions laid down in Article 1.
(2) This Convention shall not apply to the carriage of mail and postal packages.

Comment

3.52 When the carriage of mail and postal packages is undertaken by the State or legally constituted public bodies, Article 2(2) qualifies Article 2(1). In the UK a modified version of HP, set out in the 1967 Order, Sched. 1 (paras. 3.463 *et seq.*, below), is stated to apply to the carriage of such matters.

3.53 **Chapter II: Documents of carriage**

Section 3—Air waybill

Article 5—Air waybill: requirement

(1) Every carrier of cargo has the right to require the consignor to make out and hand over to him a document called an "air waybill"; every consignor has the right to require the carrier to accept this document.
(2) The absence, irregularity or loss of this document does not affect the existence or the validity of the contract of carriage which shall, subject to the provisions of Article 9, be none the less governed by the rules of this Convention.

Comments

1. Role of the air waybill

3.54 The air waybill is the means whereby the fact that HP may apply to the contract is brought to the attention of the parties. For particulars that must be included, see Article 8. For sanctions against the carrier in the event of non-compliance with Article 8, see Article 9. For the shipper's responsibility to the carrier with regard to the air waybill and the carrier's sanctions against the shipper under HP, see Article 10 For circumstances where, these requirements are waived under HP, see Article 34.

3.55 As with other transport documents such as the consignment note required by CMR for international carriage of goods by road, the air waybill functions as a receipt for the goods, as evidence of the contract of carriage and as an authority to

34. *DHL* v. *Civil Aeronautics Board*, 584 F. 2d 914, 915 (9 Cir., 1978); see also Whalen, XXV *Air & Space*, L12, 15 (2000).

give disposal instructions over the goods, but has no role as a document of title, i.e., the air waybill is not a transferable document like the bill of lading used in maritime commerce.

2. *Electronic air waybills*

Those who drafted WC and HP contemplated an air waybill made of paper, whereas, in the light of developments in international trade, other means of preserving a record of carriage (e.g. electronic data interchange) were allowed for by those who drafted MP4 and MC. Standard forms of air waybill are made available by IATA. *3.56*

Article 6—Air waybill: form of *3.57*

(1) The air waybill shall be made out by the consignor in three original parts and be handed over with the cargo.

(2) The first part shall be marked "for the carrier", and shall be signed by the consignor. The second part shall be marked "for the consignee"; it shall be signed by the consignor and by the carrier and shall accompany the cargo. The third part shall be signed by the carrier and handed by him to the consignor after the cargo has been accepted.

(3) The carrier shall sign prior to the loading of the cargo on board the aircraft.

(4) The signature of the carrier may be stamped; that of the consignor may be printed or stamped.

(5) If, at the request of the consignor, the carrier makes out the air waybill, he shall be deemed, subject to proof to the contrary, to have done so on behalf of the consignor.

Comment

Article 6 contains the only guidance found in HP concerning the form of the air waybill save that, according to Article 5, it must be a document. The requirement of three original parts, like that in CMR for consignment notes for the international carriage of goods by road, probably reflects maritime practice in respect of bills of lading when WC and CMR were drafted. In principle it is for the consignor to make out the three parts, however, if, at the request of the consignor, the carrier makes out the air waybill, the carrier is presumed to have done so on behalf of the consignor. *3.58*

The first part is for carrier's file; and the purpose of requiring the consignor's signature on this part is to establish the responsibility of the consignor under Article 10(3). The second part is required by Article 13 to be handed over to the consignee *inter alia* for complaints to the carrier under Article 26(3). The third part is to facilitate disposal of the goods under Article 12. The carrier's signature,[1] which is to acknowledge receipt of the cargo as described in the air waybill in accordance with Article 11, must be affixed (Article 6(3)) at any time "prior to loading": ordinarily cargo is accepted by the carrier well before loading, even before it reaches the airport of departure. *3.59*

1. In France, even a typed entry may count as signature: *Cass. France 4.3.2003*, (2003) 38 E.T.L. 369.

3.60 For the mandatory contents of the air waybill see Article 8 For the IATA standard form and layout of an air waybill see IATA Resolution 600a (paras. 3.671 *et seq.*, below). Having regard to Article 9, which is concerned with documentary evidence of what the carrier has received by way of cargo, there is no alternative to an air waybill unless Article 34 applies.

3.61 **Article 7—Air waybill: multiple packages**

The carrier of cargo has the right to require the consignor to make out separate waybills when there is more than one package.

Comment

3.62 IATA carriers had resolved at the time (IATA Resolution 600) that one air waybill must be issued for one "consignment", whether comprising one or more pieces of goods, if accepted from one shipper at one time and at one address, receipted for in one lot.

3.63 **Article 8—Air waybill: mandatory contents**

The air waybill shall contain:

(a) an indication of the places of departure and destination;
(b) if the places of departure and destination are within the territory of a single High Contracting Party, one or more agreed stopping places being within the territory of another State, an indication of at least one such stopping place;
(c) a notice to the consignor to the effect that, if the carriage involves an ultimate destination or stop in a country other than the country of departure, the Warsaw Convention may be applicable and that the Convention governs and in most cases limits the liability of carriers in respect of loss of or damage to cargo.

Comment

3.64 Article 8 does not expressly require the shipper and consignee to be identified but instead Article 8(a) and (b) set out three matters designed to draw the parties' attention to facts that indicate whether the contract is for international carriage, and thus subject to the application of HP, and to put on notice any successive carriers. In practice the places may be sufficiently indicated by standard (IATA) abbreviations for airports such as LHR for London Heathrow. Moreover, an air waybill "that refers the shipper to readily available timetables provides sufficient information to notify the shipper" of these places.[1] See further Article 1, Comment 3, paragraphs 3.41 *et seq.*, above.

3.65 Article 8(c) requires a notice fundamental to carrier's liability: in the absence of notice the carrier is deprived of the benefit of limited liability; see Article 9, below. Such notice is also provided for in standard form IATA air waybills.

1. *Brinks* v. *SAA*, 93 F. 3d 1022, 1035 (2 Cir., 1996).

Article 9—Air waybill: non-compliance *3.66*

If, with the consent of the carrier, cargo is loaded on board the aircraft without an air waybill having been made out, or if the air waybill does not include the notice required by Article 8, paragraph (c), the carrier shall not be entitled to avail himself of the provisions of Article 22, paragraph (2).

Comment

The sanction for non-compliance is draconian; it reflects the importance attached to the specified particulars at the time, especially the notice required by Article 8(q). It is more draconian than, for example, the corresponding provision for international carriage of goods by road, CMR, Article 7(3). The sanction was dropped from MP4, Article 9 and MC, Article 9, the corresponding provisions of these Conventions. *3.67*

Article 10—Air waybill: shipper's responsibility *3.68*

(1) The consignor is responsible for the correctness of the particulars and statements relating to the cargo which he inserts in the air waybill.

(2) The consignor shall indemnify the carrier against all damage suffered by him, or by any other person to whom the carrier is liable, by reason of the irregularity, incorrectness or incompleteness of the particulars and statements furnished by the consignor.

Comment

Under Article 10, as well as Article 10 of MP4 and MC, the consignor is liable for the correctness of the particulars and statements in the air waybill relating to the cargo, i.e., for information that the consignor provides and not for the accuracy of other information contained in the air waybill such as stopping places.[1] See also Article 16. *3.69*

The consignor's liability is to the carrier, however, it is without any limitation equivalent to that enjoyed by the carrier under Article 22. The consignor's liability could theoretically be considerable, for example, to an unwitting carrier of illegal substances subject to fines, the seizure of its aircraft and release made subject to payment or the forfeiture of aircraft.[2] *3.70*

For the kind of particulars ordinarily incorporated in standard form air waybills, see IATA Resolution 600a (paras. 3.671 *et seq.*, below). Further particulars of the consignor's duty may be found in air waybill conditions such as IATA Conditions of Carriage for Cargo (RP 1601, CSC(19)), Article 4.5 (paras. 3.853 to 3.854, below). *3.71*

Article 11—Air waybill: as evidence of contract *3.72*

(1) The air waybill is prima facie evidence of the conclusion of the contract, of the receipt of the cargo and of the conditions of carriage.

1. *American Home* v. *Maeder*, 999 F. Supp. 543, 548 (S.D.N.Y., 1998).
2. See *Air Canada* v. *United Kingdom*, ECR 9/1994/456/537, (1995) 2 A.S.L.R. 156.

(2) The statements in the air waybill relating to the weight, dimensions and packing of the cargo, as well as those relating to the number of packages, are prima facie evidence of the facts stated; those relating to the quantity, volume and condition of the cargo do not constitute evidence against the carrier except so far as they both have been, and are stated in the air waybill to have been, checked by him in the presence of the consignor or relate to the apparent condition of the cargo.

Comments

1. The prima facie case

3.73 Article 11,which is the same as Article 11 of WC and substantially the same as Article 11 of MP4 and MC, concerns the evidential role of the air waybill. A rebuttable presumption is established by Article 11 as to the correctness of the particulars and statements in the waybill relating to the cargo that would be apparent to the carrier on acceptance of the cargo in the ordinary course of events.

3.74 To "make out a *prima facie* case" with respect to the carrier's liability for loss or damage, the claimant must establish on the balance of probabilities (1) that the cargo was delivered to the carrier in a certain condition, (2) that all or part of the cargo arrived in a different condition, and (3) that the difference resulted in financial loss to the claimant.[1] Likewise to make out a *prima facie* case with respect to carrier's liability for loss of cargo, the claimant must establish on the balance of probabilities (1) that a certain quantity of cargo was delivered to the carrier, (2) that some or all of the cargo was not delivered at destination, and (3) that that resulted in financial loss to the claimant. *Prima facie* evidence means rebuttable evidence. As for statements made in the air waybill which are not referred to in Article. 11.2, such as declarations of value under Article 22.2, the regime is silent on the evidential effect of such statements and, it seems, that must be determined by national law.

2. Apparent conformity

3.75 Whether the case be one of damage or loss, the first point about what was delivered to the carrier is established by a presumption as to the correctness of those particulars and statements in the waybill relating to the cargo, in so far as that would be apparent to the carrier on acceptance of the cargo in the ordinary course of events. As regards the condition of cargo, in particular, the carrier is not obliged to go beyond a superficial examination of the cargo without good reason, and not entitled to do so unless authorised under the carrier's contract terms.[2]

3.76 Moreover, unlike carriers by certain other modes of transport, the air carrier is not obliged to admit in the air waybill any of the particulars that might enable the claimant to make a *prima facie* case, except the weight of the goods: see Article 8. However, certain cargo, such as dangerous cargo, is acceptable only under prescribed conditions, see: IATA Conditions of Carriage for Cargo, Article 3—Acceptability of Goods for Carriage (para. 3.830, below). Although these

1. *Offshore Aviation* v. *Transcon*, 831 F. 2d 1013, 1014 (11 Cir., 1987). The precise amount of the loss can be specified later.

2. See *BRI* v. *Air Canada*, 725 F. Supp. 133, 139–140 (E.D.N.Y. 1989).

Conditions are mainly for the benefit of the carrier, their observance in practice is likely to result in acknowledgement of certain particulars by the carrier.

Further, unlike the carrier by road and CMR, Article 8, for example, the air carrier is not obliged to check the goods in accordance with HP, Article 11(2), with or without the presence of the consignor. In practice, however, certain goods will be acceptable only under prescribed conditions such as IATA Conditions of Carriage for Cargo (IATA RP1601, CSC(19)), Article 3—Acceptability of Goods for Carriage (para. 3.830, below). The carrier is likely to check that the goods in question are indeed acceptable. Moreover, cargo may be held and/or checked before departure for security reasons. *3.77*

Where cargo is subject to successive carriage there will ordinarily be no opportunity for the presence of the consignor in relation to the handing over of the cargo to a second or successive carrier: it seems that these provisions are designed only in relation to the original acceptance of the cargo. *3.78*

Article 12—Shipper's disposal instructions *3.79*

(1) Subject to his liability to carry out all his obligations under the contract of carriage, the consignor has the right to dispose of the cargo by withdrawing it at the aerodrome of departure or destination, or by stopping it in the course of the journey on any landing, or by calling for it to be delivered at the place of destination or in the course of the journey to a person other than the consignee named in the air waybill, or by requiring it to be returned to the aerodrome of departure. He must not exercise this right of disposition in such a way as to prejudice the carrier or other consignors and he must repay any expenses occasioned by the exercise of this right.

(2) If it is impossible to carry out the orders of the consignor the carrier must so inform him forthwith.

(3) If the carrier obeys the orders of the consignor for the disposition of the cargo without requiring the production of the part of the air waybill delivered to the latter, he will be liable, without prejudice to his right of recovery from the consignor, for any damage which may be caused thereby to any person who is lawfully in possession of that part of the air waybill.

(4) The right conferred on the consignor ceases at the moment when that of the consignee begins in accordance with Article 13. Nevertheless, if the consignee declines to accept the waybill or the cargo, or if he cannot be communicated with, the consignor resumes his right of disposition.

Comments

1. Exercise of rights of disposal

Article 12, which is the same as Article 12 of WC and substantially the same as Article 12 of MP4 and MC, confers a right of disposal on the consignor over cargo during the carriage by air. It is similar to CMR, Article 12. *3.80*

Article 12 confers the right of disposal on the consignor with regard to the cargo during the carriage by air by way of withdrawing it from any carriage or delivery, stopping it in the course of carriage or naming a person other than the consignee on the air waybill as the person to whom it should be delivered (Article 12(1)). The right appears to end once the consignee has accepted a copy of the air waybill from the carrier and required the carrier to deliver the cargo. *3.81*

Where carriage is actually performed by a carrier not party to the contract, the disposal instructions must be addressed to the contracting carrier but the definition *3.82* of carrier in the IATA Conditions of Carriage for Cargo (paras. 3.811 *et seq.*, below) is wide enough to cover both. The consignee also has right to dispose of cargo conferred by Article 13. Rights of suit in respect of disposition are the subject of Article 14.

2. The role of the air waybill

3.83 The right of disposal is linked to possession of the third part of the air waybill. The carrier is only obliged to comply with directions from the consignor on production of that air waybill: Article 12.2. Thus when, for example, cargo has been grouped with that of others and the (master) air waybill for the whole consignment is held by the forwarder who organised the groupage, the consignor usually has no right of disposal: the rule ensures operational efficiency. However, the rule requiring production of the air waybill also seeks to protect third persons who may be in possession of the original copy of the air waybill: not only buyers from the consignor but also lenders who may have taken the air waybill as security. The carrier that obeys the consignor's order without requiring production of the air waybill is liable under Article 12(2); however, liability is that of Article 18 and may be subject to carrier's limits of liability under Article 22. In any event, the consignor loses the right of disposal when that right is acquired by the consignee: Article 12.4.

3. Limits on the right of disposal

3.84 To protect the legitimate interests of the carrier, the consignor's right of disposal is constrained by Article 12(1) and (2). With one reservation mentioned below, the carrier can only be required to obey instructions of the kind specified. In particular, the repeated reference to "the course of the journey" indicates that the consignor cannot require the carrier to alter the route; and, whereas the corresponding Article 12.1 of CMR gives the sender the right "to change the place at which delivery is to take place", the air carrier can be required only to deliver the cargo "at the place of destination . . . to a person other than the consignee named" in the air waybill.

3.85 Moreover, the interests of the carrier are protected in more general terms by Article 12(1) *in fine*: the carrier must not be prejudiced. Although prejudice will not be presumed, it has been held[1] that the consignor, if called upon to do so, must show that the instruction will not (or did not) prejudice the carrier. However, the reservation is that, if they record it in the air waybill, carrier and consignor can agree a range of instructions, that may be given by the consignor, wider than those permitted by Article 12(1). These may include a change of route.

3.86 **Article 13—Delivery/non-arrival**

(1) Except in the circumstances set out in the preceding Article, the consignee is entitled, on arrival of the cargo at the place of destination, to require the carrier to hand over to him

1. *BGH 9.10.1964*, NJW 1964.2348, 2350.

the air waybill and to deliver the cargo to him, on payment of the charges due and on complying with the conditions of carriage set out in the air waybill.

(2) Unless it is otherwise agreed, it is the duty of the carrier to give notice to the consignee as soon as the cargo arrives.

(3) If the carrier admits the loss of the cargo, or if the cargo has not arrived at the expiration of seven days after the date on which it ought to have arrived, the consignee is entitled to put into force against the carrier the rights which flow from the contract of carriage.

Comment

Article 13, whereby the consignee acquires rights both to a copy of the air waybill and to the goods, unless the consignor has exercised the right to dispose of the goods under Article 12, is similar to CMR, Article 13. *3.87*

The effect of Article 13(1) is to bind the consignee, not an original party to the contract of carriage (in the ordinary course of business), to the contract of carriage. Under Article 13 the consignee acquires rights to a copy of the air waybill and it is on the basis of the conditions set out in the air waybill that the consignee becomes party to the contract of carriage. In fact the IATA standard form air waybill does not set out any conditions to be complied with by the consignee, although on appropriate facts the conditions of carriage for cargo incorporated by reference in the air waybill may refer. *3.88*

In particular, the consignee acquires the right to delivery of the goods, unless meanwhile the consignor has exercised the rights of disposal over the cargo in favour of a third party under Article 12. Delivery of the goods must be at the place of destination, which is *prima facie* the place recorded as such on the air waybill,[1] to the designated consignee. If the air waybill mentions person A as consignee and person B as "notify party", delivery to B is a misdelivery. Even if there is an industry practice of regarding the "notify party" as the agent of the consignee, the contract distinguishes clearly between the two persons and, absent ambiguity, to deliver to the notify party is a breach of the contract of carriage.[2] As to whether delivery to Customs is delivery to the consignee, see IATA Conditions of Carriage for Cargo, Article 8 (para. 3.878, below). *3.89*

In the absence of (proper delivery of) the goods in the circumstances described in Article 13(3), the consignee may claim damages against the carrier under Article 18(1). The consignee's right "to put into force against the carrier the rights which flow from the contract of carriage" under Article 13(3) is independent of the right to delivery under Article 1(1).[3] Note, however, that the consignee is not the only person entitled to rights against the carrier in such circumstances: see Article 14, below. *3.90*

Article 14—Shipper/consignee rights *3.91*

The consignor and the consignee can respectively enforce all the rights given them by Articles 12 and 13, each in his own name, whether he is acting in his own interest or in the interest of another provided that he carries out the obligations imposed by the contract.

1. See also IATA Conditions of Carriage for Cargo, Art. 8.3 (paras. 3.882 to 3.883, below).
2. *Kologel* v. *Down in the Village*, 17 Avi. 17,104 (S.D.N.Y., 1982).
3. *American Banana Co.* v. *VIASA*, 404 N.E. 2d 1330 (N.Y.C.A., 1980).

Comment

3.92 On the one hand, Article 14 side-steps the rule of some common law jurisdictions that a party can only recover compensation in respect of own loss[1]; and it enables the enforcement of rights "in the interest of another", not, however, all rights under the contract of carriage but "the rights given them by Articles 12 and Article 13". Thus, in one case, for example, the consignee originally designated could bring proceedings to recover the loss of a person to whom cargo was redirected when it had been rejected by the consignee[2]; however, it seems that a forwarder named as consignee in the air waybill has no such right.[3] The named consignee is the obvious person to sue the carrier although the consignee does not have exclusive title to do so.[4] On the other hand, under English common law the owner of the goods damaged or lost has rights, notably rights against the carrier, that are derived from his interest in the goods, rather than from either the consignor or the consignee.[5] Article 14 is the same as Article 14 of WC and MP4, and substantially the same as Article 14 of MC.

3.93

Article 15—Waiver

(1) Articles 12, 13 and 14 do not affect either the relations of the consignor or the consignee with each other or the mutual relations of third parties whose rights are derived either from the consignor or from the consignee.

(2) The provisions of Articles 12, 13 and 14 can only be varied by express provision in the air waybill.

(3) Nothing in this Convention prevents the issue of a negotiable air waybill.

Comment

3.94 Article 15, which wraps up some outstanding questions arising under Articles 12 to 14 of HP, is the same as Article 15 of WC. However, notwithstanding Article 15(3), the IATA standard form air waybill is now expressly not negotiable. Consequently neither Article 15 of MP4 and MC contain a provision corresponding to Article 15(3) but are substantially the same as Article 15(1) and (2) of HP.

3.95 Unlike most provisions in HP (or the other regimes), Articles 12 to 14 can be varied by agreement between consignor and carrier in order to be in accordance with agreements, notably those of the consignor, with other persons such as an agreement to sell to the consignee. Article 15(1) makes it clear that the rights of the consignor under Article 12, when exercised, cannot derogate from the consignor's obligations to the consignee. Moreover, what Article 15(1) does not make clear, is that, as regards third parties whose rights are derived either from the consignor or

1. In England see e.g. *The Albazero* [1977] A.C. 774.

2. *American Banana Co.* (above).

3. Cf. the controversial decision in *Johnson* v. *American*, 834 F. 2d 721 (9 Cir., 1987) that only the consignor and consignee named in the waybill can sue. However, the same decision can be found in France: *Versailles 4.9.2003*, BTL 2003.798; and in Germany: *OLG Düsseldorf 11.11.1993*, VersR 1994.1498.

4. *Western Digital Corporation* v. *British Airways* [2001] Q.B. 733 (C.A.).

5. He also has a right to sue in his own name: *Western Digital* (above).

from the consignee, Articles 12–14 do not affect their rights against the consignor or consignee. In the interests of those affected any variation agreed must be recorded in the air waybill for all to see: Article 15(2).

Article 16—Shipper's documents: customs etc. *3.96*

(1) The consignor must furnish such information and attach to the air waybill such documents as are necessary to meet the formalities of customs, octroi or police before the cargo can be delivered to the consignee. The consignor is liable to the carrier for any damage occasioned by the absence, insufficiency or irregularity of any such information or documents, unless the damage is due to the fault of the carrier or his servants or agents.

(2) The carrier is under no obligation to enquire into the correctness or sufficiency of such information or documents.

Comment

The consignor is the person best placed to obtain the relevant information and documentation and thus, if it is incorrect or insufficient, bears the responsibility under Article 16, which is the same as Article 16 of WC, and substantially the same as Article 16 of MP4 and MC. The consignor's liability is such that if, for example, loss or destruction of documents is entirely accidental or the incorrect information or documents came from another apparently reliable person other than the carrier, the consignor is liable nonetheless: liability is strict. Moreover, it is not limited in amount by Article 22 but such questions of the measure of damage are governed by national law.[1] If, however, the inaccuracy or insufficiency arises from advice provided by the carrier and (reasonably) relied on by the consignor, the consignor is excused by the proviso to Article 16(1). *3.97*

Chapter III: Liability of the carrier *3.98*

[Article 17 concerns liability for damage sustained in the event of death or injury to passengers.]

Article 18—Carrier's liability: loss, damage *3.99*

(1) The carrier is liable for damage sustained in the event of the destruction or loss of, or of damage to, any registered baggage or any cargo, if the occurrence which caused the damage so sustained took place during the carriage by air.

(2) The carriage by air within the meaning of the preceding paragraph comprises the period during which the baggage or cargo is in charge of the carrier, whether in an aerodrome or on board an aircraft, or, in the case of a landing outside an aerodrome, in any place whatsoever.

(3) The period of the carriage by air does not extend to any carriage by land, by sea or by river performed outside an aerodrome. If, however, such a carriage takes place in the performance of a contract for carriage by air, for the purpose of loading, delivery or transhipment, any damage is presumed, subject to proof of the contrary, to have been the result of an event which took place during the carriage by air.

1. See Clarke, *Air*, Comment on Art. 16.

Comments

1. Liability arising during carriage

3.100 Article 18, which sets out the liability regime of HP, is the same as Article 18 of WC. The main rule stated in Article 18(1), which is substantially the same as Article 18(2) of MP4 and Article 18(1) of MC, is that the carrier is liable for damage sustained during carriage unless the carrier can establish one of the defences set out in Article 20 or 21. Under other carriage Conventions, such as CMR, it is enough to make a case against the carrier that a physical change in cargo, which has taken place during the carriage, makes the goods less valuable than before. Under the air conventions, such as HP, however, that must be established but it is not enough. The claimant must also show that the damage was caused by an "occurrence" during the "period" of carriage by air as defined in Article 18(2).[1] The occurrence may be an event or a human act, as well as an omission such as failure to load or to deliver causing delay.[2]

2. Damage

3.101 The damage (mentioned in the first line of Article 18(1)) is the financial damage flowing from the physical loss of or damage to cargo (mentioned later in Article 18(1)) caused by the occurrence. The damage both physical and financial, in contrast to the occurrence which caused it, may be sustained not only during the period of carriage but also later.[3] Physical damage to cargo is not defined; the point is left to national law; and in England damage usually means a change in the physical condition of the cargo which reduces its value.[4] Damage includes an extreme change in the form of destruction, which embraces not only physical disintegration but also the case of cargo which exists in some form but has become commercially valueless.[5] Such was the case of dogs that departed alive but arrived dead.[6] English law, however, also acknowledges that the meaning of "damage" varies according to the context[7]; and even in the limited context of Article 18(1) the meaning of "damage" varies.[8]

3.102 The measure of damage is also left to national law. The rule of English law is that the carrier is liable for any kind of loss which, given what the carrier knew or should have known at the time of contracting about the claimant's situation, should have been in the reasonable contemplation of the carrier as likely to result from a breach of the kind that occurred.[9] In the case of damaged cargo the usual measure is the difference in value between the cargo as it was when taken over by the carrier and

1. *Winchester Fruit Ltd.* v. *American Airlines Inc.* [2002] 2 Lloyd's Rep. 265, C.L.C.C. (B.L.).
2. *Cohen* v. *Vaarig*, 405 N.Y.S. 2d 44 (App. Div., 1978).
3. *Nowell* v. *Quantas*, 22 Avi. 18,071 (W.D. Wash., 1990).
4. See *Promet Engineering (Singapore) Pte Ltd.* v. *Sturge* [1997] 2 Lloyd's Rep. 146, 151; also Clarke, *Air*, Art. 18, note 5.
5. I.e., cannot be used for the purposes intended by the consignee.
6. *Dalton* v. *Delta Air Lines Inc.*, 570 F. 2d 1244, 1247 (5 Cir., 1978).
7. *Swansea* v. *Harpur* [1912] 3 K.B. 493, 505 (C.A.).
8. See *Fothergill* v. *Monarch* [1981] A.C. 251, 273.
9. *Koufos* v. *Czarnikow* [1969] 1 A.C. 350, a case of carriage by sea, in which the carrier was liable for loss of market at destination.

the cargo in its damaged state. If there is no market where such cargo might be replaced and by reference to which its value can be assessed, the normal measure is the "cost of cure" unless that cost would be so great as to be unreasonable.[10] Moreover, if the carrier knew or should have known that the cargo was needed in the claimant's business, the carrier may be liable for loss of business such as loss of production.[11] In the case of lost cargo the carrier is liable for market value at destination or the cost of replacement, as appropriate.

3. The period of responsibility

The occurrence by which damage is sustained must take place "during the carriage by air" (Article 18(1)), which is "the period during which the . . . the cargo is in charge of the carrier" (Article 18(2)). Article 18(2) is substantially the same as Article 18(4) of MP4 and in essence the same as Article 18(3) of MC. *3.103*

Charge of cargo does not have to be exclusive charge; for example, a race horse is in charge of the carrier when on board the carrier's aircraft even though the horse is also attended by persons employed by the consignor.[12] What counts is that the carrier is still in a position to control the situation and protect the goods. It has been held that, having regard to the French text (*sous la garde du transporteur*), "in charge of the carrier" has "overtones of safe-keeping, custody and care".[13] *3.104*

In particular, sub-contractors employed to carry, handle or care for cargo, which are answerable to the carrier, represent the carrier in this respect. This principle has been extended to cargo lost while in the actual custody of an airport authority after landing, even where the authority is a monopoly and the carrier had no choice of custodian; the carrier had a relationship with the authority which the consignor and consignee did not.[14] Customs authorities, however, are not usually regarded as sub-contractors in this sense and goods in their hands are not in the charge of the carrier unless perhaps the carrier has undertaken to clear the goods through Customs.[15] *3.105*

Cargo may pass through various hands in succession. On arrival at the airport of destination there will ordinarily be a need for customs clearance and procedures for obtaining this differ from place to place. If cargo remains within carrier's warehouses at the airport pending inspection for customs purposes there, it seems that the cargo remains in the charge of the carrier.[16] There is no English legal authority, however, on the question whether carriage by air under HP (or one of the other regimes) can be suspended if in some way cargo is taken outside the carriage by air and then effectively brought back in, for example, when damage occurs just after carriage by air has ceased and cargo is brought back into the charge of the carrier at the airport of destination.[17] *3.106*

10. *Ruxley* v. *Forsyth* [1996] 1 A.C. 344.
11. *Hadley* v. *Baxendale* (1859) 9 Ex. 341, a case of carriage by road.
12. *United Stables* v. *Pacific Western* (1969) 5 D.L.R. 3d 67 (B.C.).
13. *Swiss Bank Corp. and Others* v. *Brink's-MAT Ltd.* [1986] 2 Lloyd's Rep. 79.
14. *OLG Frankfurt/Main 21.4.1998*, TranspR 1999.24, 25; affirmed on this point: *BGH 21.9.2000*, TranspR 2001.29.
15. *Alltransport* v. *Seaboard*, 349 N.Y.S. 2d 277 (1988).
16. See *The Thomas Cook Group Ltd.* v. *Air Malta Company Ltd.* [1997] 2 Lloyd's Rep. 399.
17. See *Federal Insurance Company* v. *Air Express International Corp.* (1994) 13 Avn. Law, No. 12.

3.107 As regards damage inflicted at the time of transfer of (custody of) cargo to or from the carrier, much depends on the facts of the case. Some parts of a consignment of cargo may and other parts may not be in the charge of the carrier at the time when the occurrence which caused the loss or damage occurs.[18] For example, when a carrier uses a fork-lift truck to unload cargo from the consignor's vehicle, the cargo is in the charge of the carrier once lifted clear of the vehicle and whether or not any delivery note has been handed over.[19] However, in the case of cargo that has been delivered to the wrong person it has been held that the carrier remains liable to the person entitled to it. The argument that Article 18(1) did not apply because the loss occurred only after the defendant released the cargo, was rejected. The court took the view that loss occurred when the cargo was wrongfully released, release being the last act of the carrier as carrier.[20]

4. Responsibility outside the airport

3.108 Article 18(1) and (2), making the carrier liable under HP for loss or damage sustained while "the cargo is in charge of the carrier", is qualified by Article 18(3) whereby "carriage by land, by sea or by river performed outside an aerodrome" (usually referred to today as an airport) is outside the scope of the regime. Article 18(3) is substantially the same as Article 18(5) of MP4 and the first two sentences of Article 18(4) of MC.

3.109 Even a short feeder service, which is operated by the air carrier by road to or from the aerodrome, is outside the scope of HP and the other air regimes, if it is proved that the loss or damage was the result of an occurrence outside the airport.[21] This rule reflects the unimodal practices of the early years of carriage by air; it is ill adapted to modern practice and the intermodal carriage of unit loads. It is not obvious to people today why an air carrier, which may routinely operate road vehicles in an integrated intermodal movement, should move from one liability regime to another when the vehicle crosses the boundary of the airport. The rule has been applied strictly by the High Court of Australia to a contract of carriage by air with delivery to a bonded warehouse 4 km.[22] from the airport, however, the Court also accepted the possibility that the Convention regime might be applicable outside the airport, not as such but as terms of the contract recorded in the air waybill.

3.110 On the one hand, the rule is not improved by literal interpretation in the USA of "aerodrome", that cargo is not in carriage by air when in a warehouse just outside the airport perimeter.[23] Better is a more purposive interpretation applied in the UK, that a cargo shed situated within the commercial area commonly known as the

18. See *Swiss Bank Corp. and Others* v. *Brink's-MAT Ltd.* [1986] 2 Lloyd's Rep. 79; further proceedings in same case reported at [1986] 2 All E.R. 188.

19. *Rolls-Royce Ltd.* v. *Heavylift-Volga Dnepr Ltd.* [2000] 1 Lloyd's Rep. 653.

20. *Hatzlachh* v. *Tradewinds*, 738 F. Supp. 714, 716 (S.D.N.Y., 1990).

21. E.g. *Read-Rite* v. *Burlington*, 186 F. 3d 1190 (9 Cir., 1999). See also *Quantum* v. *Plane Trucking* [2002] EWCA Civ 350, [2002] 1 W.L.R. 2678, [2002] 2 Lloyd's Rep. 25, in which CMR applied.

22. *Siemens* v. *Schenker Int.*, 205 ALR 232 (2004).

23. *Victoria Sales Corporation* v. *Emery Air Freight Inc.*, 917 F. 2d 705 (1990), followed in *Igudesman* v. *Aircargo Handling Services* (1995) W.L. 59486 (N.D. Cal. 1995), *Qualimetrics* v. *LEP Profit International Inc.* (1997) 16 Avn. Law 1.

airport, on land owned by the airport operating company but outside any "airside/landside" fence, is nevertheless within the "aerodrome".[24] On the other hand, the rule, however interpreted, applies only when it has been proved that "the occurrence which caused the damage" took place outside the airport. Otherwise, according to Article 18(3) *in fine*, "any damage is presumed, subject to proof of the contrary, to have been the result of an event [i.e. occurrence] which took place during the carriage by air".

Article 19—Carrier's liability: delay *3.111*

The carrier is liable for damage occasioned by delay in the carriage by air of passengers, baggage or cargo.

Comments

1. Liability

Under Article 19, which is the same as Article 19 of WC, and substantially the same as Article 19 of MP4 and the first sentence of Article 19 of MC, the carrier is liable for damage occasioned by delay unless the carrier can establish one of the defences set out in Articles 20 or 21. If the consignor is responsible for the delay, the carrier may be entitled to indemnity from the consignor under Article 10 or Article 16. *3.112*

2. Duty of dispatch

Liability for delay premises a breach on the part of the carrier of the contract of carriage. A duty to deliver on time is not provided for by the air regimes; it is a matter of contract. If the carrier promises to get cargo to destination by date X and does not do so, *prima facie* the carrier is liable under the terms of the contract of carriage in respect of the delay. Such a promise may be combined with (and qualified by) a commitment in the air waybill to exercise reasonable dispatch. What is reasonable may be affected by the carrier's awareness, if any, that the consignment is urgent, e.g., to arrive in time for the Christmas market.[1] Sometimes courts have been willing to infer urgency from the very fact that the goods were consigned by air.[2] Concerning the meaning of delay, see also Comment 1 on Condition 8 of the Conditions of Contract (IATA Resolution 600b (II) (paras. 3.741 *et seq.*, below)). *3.113*

If the carrier promises to deliver by date X, terms, such as one requiring reasonable dispatch, qualify what might otherwise be seen as a strict obligation to deliver by date X and to that extent such terms are exemption clauses. Such terms must have been effectively incorporated into the particular contract. Unless they have signed a contract containing the terms, persons contracting with air carriers must have sufficient notice of the terms.[3] *3.114*

24. *Rolls Royce plc* v. *HVD* (above).
1. *Panalpina* v. *Densil Underwear* [1981] 1 Lloyd's Rep. 187.
2. *Ibid.*
3. See Art. 1, Comment 2, paras. 3.40 *et seq.*, above.

3. Delay

3.115 Delay refers to delay not just in the flight itself (a view held in the past) but delay in any stage of the service undertaken by the carrier.[4] The damage occasioned by the delay is actionable although sustained later.[5] Nonetheless the immediate cause of the delay must be in some sense "operational" and associated with aviation, such as bad weather[6] or mechanical failure during the service even though the ultimate cause of the failure can be traced back to poor maintenance beforehand.[7] In contrast, delay caused by management "failure" is not subject to Article 19. Delay in commencing the flight because of staff shortage[8] or a power failure at the airport,[9] for example, is not an Article 19 delay but a case governed by national law. Staffing and power problems are risks facing most kinds of business.

3.116

Article 20—Defence

The carrier is not liable if he proves that he and his servants or agents have taken all necessary measures to avoid the damage or that it was impossible for him or them to take such measures.

Comments

1. The standard of care required

3.117 In England the commonly cited view is that of Bingham J., in the *Brink's-MAT* case,[1] that the phrase "all necessary measures" cannot be read entirely literally, but must, rather, be construed to mean "all reasonable measures"; and that Article 20 was "imposing a somewhat higher duty upon the carrier than a mere duty to take reasonable care". "Somewhat higher", however, has been argued[2] to have become appreciably higher; and that over time the requirement has been construed by the courts to be much less one of reasonable care and much more a duty like that of the "utmost care" required of road carriers under CMR.[3]

3.118 If such care can be established by the carrier, the effect of Article 20, which is the same as Article 20(1) of WC and essentially the same as the second part of Article 20 of MP4 and of MC, is to excuse the carrier altogether under HP and WC and to excuse the carrier for delay (only) under MP4 and MC.

4. *Air France* v. *Arlab, Aix 29.12.1983* (1985) 39 RFDA 478, 483; see also *Bart* v. *BWIA* [1967] 1 Lloyd's Rep. 239.
5. *Nowell* v. *Quantas*, 22 Avi. 18,071 (W.D. Wash., 1990).
6. *OLG Düsseldorf 13.6.96*, TranspR 1997.150, 151.
7. *Daniel* v. *Virgin Atlantic*, 59 F. Supp. 2d 986, 991 (N.D. Cal., 1998).
8. *Lg Bonn 14.1.1998*, TranspR 1999.109.
9. *OLG Düsseldorf 13.6.96*, TranspR 1997.150.

1. *Swiss Bank Corp. and Others* v. *Brink's-MAT Ltd.* [1986] 2 Lloyd's Rep. 79, 96–97. See also in this sense: *Manufacturers Hanover Trust Co.* v. *Alitalia*, 429 F. Supp. 964 (S.D.N.Y., 1977).
2. See Clarke, *Air*, p. 135.
3. On the basis of the judgment of Mustill J. in *Silber* v. *Islander Trucking* [1985] 2 Lloyd's Rep. 243.

2. The scope of proof required

As regards what the carrier must prove, two lines of approach have been observed. The first is an *a priori* approach, whereby, without particular regard to what actually went wrong later, the carrier is required to show that all the measures that could be expected in the circumstances were taken. Broadly speaking that means that the carrier must prove that an airworthy aircraft and competent personnel had been provided for the performance of the contract. This approach tends to decisions close to (or not much stricter than) a rule requiring (no more than) reasonable care and skill. The second approach, the one more likely to be taken in the UK, is an *a posteriori* approach in which the court focuses attention on the event that caused the loss (or damage) and asks what could or should the carrier have done to prevent it. The result is a stricter duty under the second line of approach than the first. In particular, if the cause of the loss is unknown on the second approach the carrier is unlikely to be excused.[4] *3.119*

Whichever approach is taken, the court posits a carrier with the standard of knowledge and skill of a competent professional carrier. The carrier is imputed with the state of knowledge in the air industry at the time. Insurers and others, directly or indirectly through trade associations, have offered information to carriers, for example, on security. This process of "education" has been reinforced here as in other contexts by insurance warranties, whereby the carrier loses liability cover, unless certain procedures are observed.[5] Having gained a picture of the model carrier, the court then asks what measures are to be expected of such a carrier in the light of key factors in the actual case. *3.120*

3. The measures required

One factor, which has a bearing on what the carrier should have done, is the likelihood of loss: the greater the likelihood of loss (the danger) the more that will be expected of the carrier by way of measures of prevention. *3.121*

(a) In cases of theft, for example, account will be taken of location[6] and of the attractiveness of the goods to thieves.[7]
(b) A second factor is the practicality of the measures which, according to the claimant, the carrier should have taken to avoid the loss in question.[8] The easier (and perhaps cheaper) it would have been to take a particular measure that would have prevented the damage, the greater the likelihood that it will be required of the carrier.

4. *Panalpina* v. *Densil Underwear* [1981] 1 Lloyd's Rep. 187, 190–191. E.g. *Air France* v. *Helvetia Assurance, Paris 20.12.2002*, BTL 2003.157.
5. See R. Margo, *Aviation Insurance* (3rd ed., 2000), 10.74 *et seq.*
6. E.g. *Norton McNaughton* v. *Polar*, 702 N.Y.S. 2d 759, 761 (Sup., 1999).
7. E.g. gold bars: *Cie. Le Languedoc* v. *Sté Hernu-Peron, Paris 17.11.1975* (1976) 30 RFDA 109: jeans: *B.G.H. 16.2.84*, VersR 1984.551.
8. *Silber* (above), p. 249 re CMR.

(c) A third factor is legality. Personnel such as pilots will not be expected to exceed the hours permitted by law—any more than drivers of road vehicles.[9]

(d) A fourth factor in some cases is current practice in the air industry at the time. This factor has been influential in a case of robbery,[10] in which the English court heeded evidence of industry procedures in general and from an aviation security consultant in particular, as well as an account of the security recommendations of IATA, albeit with some allowance for local conditions. In this connection personal injury cases governed by HP or the other regimes are of limited assistance because the courts put a greater value on life and limb than on property and require more of the carrier.

3.122 **Article 21—Contributory negligence**

If the carrier proves that the damage was caused by or contributed to by the negligence of the injured person, the court may, in accordance with the provisions of its own law, exonerate the carrier wholly or partly from his liability.

Comment

3.123 Article 21 provides the carrier with a defence based on the contributory negligence not of the claimant as such but "the injured person". Nonetheless, since the consignor and consignee are the only persons with a right of action for goods lost, damaged or delayed, the assumption from the context of the regime as a whole is that the "injured person" in question is the cargo claimant and that the negligence of any other person may not be taken into account. Examples are failure by the consignor to store goods at an appropriate temperature prior to being handed over for carriage[1] or to pack the goods adequately.[2] This is a matter of concern to those interested in cargo as standard insurance clauses, such as the Institute Cargo Clauses (Air), exclude cover for loss thus caused.

3.124 As regards the calculation of the amount of liability in cases of partial exoneration, it is unsettled whether the damages to be reduced are the damages that would be arrived at without application of the limit of liability set out in Article 22(1) or the damages that would result from the application of that limit before any such reduction. The issue is to be settled in accordance with the *lex fori*, therefore, see Law Reform (Contributory Negligence) Act 1945, s. 1(1), as applied by the 1961 Act, s. 6. In this central respect Article 21 of WC is the same, however in the corresponding provisions of MP4 (Article 21(2)) and MC (Article 20) the reference to "its own law" i.e. the *lex fori*, has been omitted.

9. *Silber loc. cit.*
10. *Thomas Cook* v. *Air Malta* [1997] 2 Lloyd's Rep. 399, 411, 415, 416. See also *Republic Nat. Bank* v. *Eastern*, 815 F. 2d 232 (2 Cir., 1987) and *Ospina* v. *TWA*, 24 Avi. 17, 109 (2 Cir., 1992).
1. *AG World Exports* v. *Arrow Air*, 22 Avi. 18,221 (S.D. Fla., 1990).
2. *Lg Hamburg 3.12.1992*, TranspR 1995.76.

Article 22—Limitation of liability 3.125

(1) [Concerns passengers.]
(2) (a) In the carriage of registered baggage and of cargo, the liability of the carrier is limited to a sum of 17 special drawing rights per kilogramme, unless the passenger or consignor has made, at the same time when the package was handed over to the carrier, a special declaration of interest in delivery at destination and has paid a supplementary sum if the case so requires. In that case the carrier will be liable to pay a sum not exceeding the declared sum, unless he proves that that sum is greater than the passenger's or consignor's actual interest in delivery at destination.
(b) In the case of loss, damage or delay of part of registered baggage or cargo, or of any object contained therein, the weight to be taken into consideration in determining the amount to which the carrier's liability is limited shall be only the total weight of the package or packages concerned. Nevertheless, when the loss, damage or delay of a part of the registered baggage or cargo, or of an object contained therein, affects the value of other packages covered by the same baggage check or the same air waybill, the total weight of such package or packages shall also be taken into consideration in determining the limit of liability.
(3) [Concerns passengers' hand luggage.]
(4) The limits prescribed in this Article shall not prevent the court from awarding, in accordance with its own law, in addition, the whole or part of the court costs and of the other expenses of the litigation incurred by the plaintiff. The foregoing provision shall not apply if the amount of the damages awarded, excluding court costs and other expenses of the litigation, does not exceed the sum which the carrier has offered in writing to the plaintiff within a period of six months from the date of the occurrence causing the damage, or before the commencement of the action, if that is later.
(5) The sums mentioned in terms of the special drawing right in this Article shall be deemed to refer to the special drawing right as defined by the International Monetary Fund. Conversion of the sums into national currencies shall, in case of judicial proceedings, be made according to the value of such currencies in terms of the special drawing right at the date of the judgment.

Comments

1. The limits

Article 22, central to the liability regime, affords the carrier a monetary limit on the liability established under Articles 18 and 19. Article 22 sets limits not tariffs. Each claimant must prove actual loss up to the relevant limit. The limit can be exceeded only when the loss has been caused intentionally or recklessly as contemplated by Articles 25 and 25A; or when, in accordance with Article 22.2(a), there is a declaration of special interest. 3.126

A declaration of special interest is not required to be made in writing[1] but an English court has required it to be in the box for such declarations on the front of the air waybill.[2] It has been held that such declaration was "a limit of liability specified in Article 22" which would not apply if the consignor was able to bring his case within Article 25. Accordingly, the consignor was not estopped, by reason of his 3.127

1. *KLM* v. *Hamman*, Uni. L. Rev. 2003.924 (High Ct. S. Africa). Cf. *OLG Köln 16.2.1990*, TranspR 1990.199.

2. *Westminster Bank* v. *Imperial Airways* [1936] 2 All E.R. 890. Also in this sense: *Air France* v. *Uni Europe, Paris 19.12.2001*, BTL 2002.149. See also *Eurocopter Deutschland* v. *DHL, Versailles 4.4.2002*, BTL 2002.287. But cf. *Redha Al-Ansari Exchange Est.* v. *KLM Royal Dutch Airline*, Dubai Civil Suit No. 162/94, Cassation Appeal No. 292/95, [1996] *Air Law* No. 4/5.

declaration, from seeking the full value of the cargo even if, on the facts, no supplementary fee had been paid either with respect to the market value or at all.[3]

3.128 In addition to the amount of loss recoverable in this way, the claimant may get an award for costs and interest (see Comments 4 and 5, below) but that is all. It has been held, for example, that a claimant cannot recover prepaid freight charges in addition to the "sum" by way of compensation determined by Article 22(2)(a).[4]

2. Beneficiaries of the limits

3.129 The "carrier" with limited liability under Article 22 means not only the corporate legal entity contracting the carriage but also its employees who, in practice, insist that their employer provides indemnity protection. Moreover, the category includes all "agents who perform services fundamental to, or in furtherance of, the carriage enterprise, and which the carrier itself would be bound to perform . . . pursuant to its contract with its customers", although not in direct contractual relation with the carrier.[5] On the meaning of "servants" and "agents", see also Article 25A, Comment 2, below.

3. Calculation of the limit

3.130 The limit is calculated as so much money per (kilogramme) unit of weight. Limits referable to the weight of the cargo are commonplace in carriage Conventions. See also the Comment on Condition 6 (paragraphs 3.765 *et seq.*, below) and Condition 8 of the Conditions of Contract (IATA Resolution 600b (II) (para. 3.771, below).

3.131 The reference to "17 special drawing rights" per unit was substituted, for "two hundred and fifty francs", by the 1979 Act.[6] In case of damage where the functionality of a whole shipment is prevented due to damage to part, the ability of a claimant to eliminate or mitigate damage by early replacement of that part is relevant to the measure of damages but not to determination of the limitation sum. That must be assessed by reference to the state of affairs at the end of the carriage by air during which damage was sustained, i.e. upon the weight of the whole shipment.

3.132 The point arose in *Applied Implants Technology Ltd.* v. *Lufthansa Cargo*,[7] in which the carrier argued that the limit should be fixed under Article 22.2(a) by reference only to the part (£X) rather than the whole (nearly £4X) under Article 22.2(b) because a replacement part arrived only five days after the rest of the machine. One of the difficulties about this argument was that it would mean that the enhanced

3. *Antwerp United Diamond B.V.B.A.* v. *Air Europe* [1996] Q.B. 317; but cf. *BRI* v. *Air Canada*, 725 F. Supp 133 (E.D.N.Y., 1989). See Clarke, *Air*, note 5 to Art. 22(2).

4. *O'Rourke* v. *Eastern*, 730 F. 2d (2 Cir., 1984).

5. *Waxman* v. *CIS Mexicana de Avacion*, 13 F. Supp. 2d 508, 515 (S.D.N.Y., 1998).

6. S. 4(1)(a)(i) brought into force on 1 December 1997 by the Carriage by Air and Road Act 1979 (Commencement No. 2) Order 1997 (S.I. 1997/2565 (c. 97)). This implements (Montreal) Additional Protocol (No. 2) but in a way so as to apply to all claims subject to UK law.

7. [2000] 2 Lloyd's Rep. 46.

limitation figure would never apply to the delay of a part, which is contrary to the actual wording of Article 22.2(b). The court concluded that the carrier's argument confused two separate matters, the appropriate limit and the measure of actual loss, and confirmed that the limit of liability must be assessed by reference to the state of affairs as at the end of the carriage by air in which the damage was sustained.[8]

4. *Costs*

Sight should not be lost of the importance of the cost of litigation and associated interest charges, which vary from jurisdiction to jurisdiction. The corresponding provision of WC, Article 22, made no mention of such costs. This important factor was addressed by HP in the proviso set out in Article 22(4) and later in the corresponding provisions of MP4 (Article 22(4)) and MC (Article 22(6)). The costs, incurred by the carrier or its servant or agent, are those that might, under English law, be awarded against a claimant on any basis, e.g. for failing at trial to be awarded damages exceeding a prior payment into court. *3.133*

5. *Interest*

The court is empowered by Article 22(4) to make an award "according to its own law" in respect of "the other expenses of the litigation". The power, which is not found in WC, is found in Article 22(4) of MP4 and, with one significant difference,[9] Article 22(6) of MC. The wording of this provision has provided some basis for the argument that interest may be awarded in respect of the time during which the claimant was without his due as a result of litigation. In general the English courts can and usually do exercise their statutory discretion in favour of awarding pre-judgment interest. However, the fact that HP does not make any express reference in Article 22(4) to interest to be awarded in addition to the limits prescribed in Article 22(2) has led the English court in the *Brink's-MAT* case[10] to hold that it is not permissible to add interest onto the Article 22(2) amounts. The court stressed[11] "the basic principle that . . . air carriers should be protected from having to pay out more than a fixed and definite sum"; and that, in the interests of uniformity, nothing should be read into the Convention which was not clearly implied. *3.134*

Arguably the decision in the *Brink's-MAT* case does not rule out an award of interest in a case where the Article 22(2) limits would not apply by reason of the application of Articles 25 or 25A. Moreover, the foregoing does not affect the statutory interest that runs from the date of pronouncement of any court judgment. In the event that a judgment or order is made for damages to be assessed, however, the statutory rate will apply only as from the date when damages are finally *3.135*

8. At [17]. See also *Deere* v. *Lufthansa*, 621 F. Supp. 721 (N.D. Ill., 1984), affirmed 855 F. 2d 385 (7 Cir., 1988).

9. See this Comment *in fine*.

10. *Swiss Bank Corp. and Others* v. *Brink's-MAT Ltd. and Others* [1986] Q.B. 853; USA *idem* under WC: *O'Rourke* v. *Eastern*, 730 F. 2d (2 Cir., 1984).

11. [1986] Q.B. at pp. 852–853.

assessed.[12] Note that Article 22(6) of MC puts the point beyond doubt by reference to "the other expenses of litigation incurred by the plaintiff, including interest".

6. Offer in writing

3.136 As regards the offer in writing referred to in Article 22(4), the exception has been applied literally and, for example, an offer accidentally made later than six months after the occurrence does not trigger the exception and costs can be awarded.[13] The exception is intended to encourage provisional payments, however, some commentators are sceptical. Their advice to claimants is not to institute suit for six months but to wait for an offer from the carrier, thus compelling the carrier to make an offer without discovery about the claimant's financial situation. On the one hand, the carrier's only source of information is the claimant's (legal) representative. On the other hand, the carrier has little incentive to pursue that source lest the cost mount up.[14]

3.137 **Article 23—Convention: liability paramount**

(1) Any provision tending to relieve the carrier of liability or to fix a lower limit than that which is laid down in this Convention shall be null and void, but the nullity of any such provision does not involve the nullity of the whole contract, which shall remain subject to the provisions of this Convention.

(2) Paragraph (1) of this Article shall not apply to provisions governing loss or damage resulting from the inherent defect, quality or vice of the cargo carried.

Comments

1. Article 23(1): mandatory rules

3.138 Article 23, taken in conjunction with Article 32, makes clear that there can be no "contracting out" of HP on the part of the carrier. Article 23(1) is substantially the same as Article 23 of WC. Both Article 23(1) and Article 23(2) are to be found together in Article 23 of MP4, whereas in MC Article 23(1) is repeated in Article 27 but the "inherent defect" defence in HP, Article 23(2), is located in the more limited context of Article 18(2).[1]

3.139 The effect of Article 23 is to prevent the carrier from purporting to exclude liability for particular goods or for particular heads of damage, unless caught by Article 23(2), or shortening the notice period stated in Article 29.[2] However, "tending to relieve" suggests something operative in the future, with the corollary that an agreement having that effect after the event is not invalidated by Article 23.1, i.e., Article 23.1 does not invalidate agreements to settle or compromise past

12. *Thomas* v. *Bunn* [1991] 1 A.C. 32.
13. *GKN Westland Helicopters* v. *Korean Air Lines* [2003] 2 Lloyd's Rep. 629.
14. Whalen, 25 *Air & Space Law* 12, 19 (2000).
1. Note that the "inherent defect" defence is also stated in Art. 18(2) of MP4.
2. *Nissan* v. *Fritz*, 210 F. 3d 1099, 1106 (9 Cir., 2000).

claims.[3] Moreover, Article 23 does not prevent the parties agreeing in advance that the carrier shall perform the contract by reference to special conditions, e.g., particular stipulations as to the care and security to be given to the consignment.

2. Article 23(2): inherent defect, quality or vice

The meaning of "inherent defect, quality or vice" is determined by national law, however, some degree of uniformity has developed: not least because it has been interpreted to mean what it does in other transport contexts. For example, *Albacora*,[4] a leading English case on the Hague Rules that govern carriage by sea, has been applied in Canada to carriage by air.[5] However the Hague Rules do not, any more than HP and the air regimes, define "inherent defect, quality or vice" and English courts have resorted to the common law understanding of the words. *3.140*

At common law an inherent vice is some defect in the cargo which by its development through ordinary processes within the cargo itself tends to the injury or destruction of the cargo, to such an extent that it does not survive the normal rigours of the journey in question and remain suitable for use in commerce for a reasonable time after the end of the journey.[6] The concept therefore is relative—relative to features of the particular cargo (fragility, sensitivity to temperature or humidity), relative to the journey (length) and to the mode of transportation (pressurisation, temperature of cargo space, any special care to be expected from the carrier). *3.141*

On the one hand, live animals do not suffer from "inherent . . . quality" simply because they are alive and thus difficult passengers.[7] Carriers that have agreed to carry animals can be expected to take measures to deal with all but the most unexpected. In contrast other carriage Conventions such as Article 18.5 of CMR contain special rules for live animals. On the other hand, if goods need special care, such as temperature control, but the carrier has not been made aware of this, the goods which suffer in consequence do so as a result of inherent defect, quality or vice. In *Albacora* Lord Reid said that, if the contract of carriage "had required refrigeration there would have been no inherent vice. But as it did not there was inherent vice because the goods could not stand the treatment which the contract authorized or required".[8] That was also "the case of flowers which froze during carriage because the aircraft was not heated and there was no reason for the shipper to believe it would be heated".[9] Again, there was a "defect" in "the case of a machine which fell apart during the flight because it was so constructed as to be unable to stand the normal incidents of flight".[10] *3.142*

3. To this effect with reference to Art. 24: *Tokyo District Court, 25.9.2000*, Unif. L. Rev. 2002–3.922.

4. *Albacora* v. *Westcott & Laurance* [1966] 2 Lloyd's Rep. 53 (H.L.).

5. *A.-G. of Canada* v. *Flying Tiger Line* (1987) 61 O.R. (2d) 673, 677.

6. *Blower* v. *GWR* (1872) L.R. 7 C.P. 655, 662; *Noten* v. *Harding* [1990] 2 Lloyd's Rep. 283 (C.A.).

7. *Flying Tiger Line* (above).

8. Above, p. 59.

9. *Flying Tiger Line* (above). Likewise deep frozen shrimps: *Paris 31.3.1995*, BTL.1995.377.

10. *Flying Tiger Line* (above), p 677.

3. Packing

3.143 Packing, according to English common law, is part of the "cargo" and thus cargo packed in such a way that it will not survive the expected transit is regarded as suffering from inherent vice.[11] However, in some countries the view has been taken that questions of the (in)sufficiency of packing should be decided under Article 20, i.e., that the carrier would be excused only if the carrier could show that all necessary measures had been taken to avoid the damage or that such measures were impossible. Indeed the English courts may take a similar view in relation to the air regimes, because other carriage Conventions provide expressly for a defence of defective packing in addition to one for inherent defect etc.

3.144 **Article 24—Convention: conditions and limits paramount**

(1) In the cases covered by Article 18 and 19 any action for damages, however founded, can only be brought subject to the conditions and limits set out in this Convention.

[(2) Concerns passengers.]

Comment

3.145 The primacy of the conditions and limits set out in HP is the subject of Article 24(1); it is identical to Article 24 of WC and the similar corresponding provisions of MP4 (Article 24(2)) and MC (Article 29). There is no uniformity internationally on the question whether HP (or, when applicable, WC, MP4 and MC) provides the only cause of action in disputes arising out of the (international) carriage of cargo by air. With one reservation, however, there is clear authority in the UK in the affirmative as between passenger and carrier.[1] In *Sidhu*,[2] the House of Lords held, adopting a purposive approach to construction, that HP provides a uniform code, prescribing the (only) circumstances and cause of action in which a carrier will be liable in damages (to a consignor or consignee) arising out of international carriage by air.

3.146 The reservation lies in the reference to "cases covered by Article 18 and 19" and thus to actions *against* the carrier. On the one hand, such cases include extra-contractual (restitutionary) claims against the carrier,[3] something that appears more clearly from the corresponding provisions of MP4 (Article 24(2)) and MC (Article 29), which refer to any action for damages "whether under this Convention or in contract or in tort or otherwise". On the other hand, it is a clear corollary that Article 24 does not apply to claims by a carrier against the consignor or consignee, e.g. for freight charges or for indemnity under HP (as well as MP4 and MC) Articles

11. *L.N.W. Ry.* v. *Hudson* [1920] A.C. 324, 333.

1. *Sidhu* v. *British Airways plc, aka Abnett* v. *British Airways plc* [1997] A.C. 430. *Idem* in Germany (*BGH 28.11.*1978, NJW 1979.496) and the USA (*Re Air Disaster at Lockerbie*, 928 F. 2d 1267 (2 Cir., 1991); *King* v. *American Airlines*, 284 F. 3d 352 (2 Cir., 2002)).

2. Above.

3. *Western Digital Corp.* v. *British Airways plc* [2001] Q.B. 733 (C.A.). In France, however, such actions have been entertained but the amount recoverable was limited in line with the relevant Convention: e.g. *Air France* v. *Zagureb, Cass. 2.4.1996* (1997) 50 RFDA 448.

12(1) and 16(1). A further reservation might be thought to stem from the reference to "actions for damages". These are indeed the usual means of redress but remedies other than damages, if available in national law, might be awarded to claimants successful under HP or the other regimes on the basis that such remedies are covered by the authentic French version of the text, in which the phrase "action en responsabilité" is used.[4]

Article 25—Disapplication of limitation of liability *3.147*

The limits of liability specified in Article 22 shall not apply if it is proved that the damage resulted from an act or omission of the carrier, his servants or agents, done with intent to cause damage or recklessly and with knowledge that damage would probably result; provided that, in the case of such act or omission of a servant or agent, it is also proved that he was acting within the scope of his employment.

Comments

1. Wording and effect

Article 25 concerns particularly grave conduct on the part of the carrier, his servants or agents.[1] The corresponding provision of WC is also Article 25 (para. 3.350, below), however, the conduct in question was there described differently. In particular, the phrase in WC is "wilful misconduct", which was replaced by "done with intent to cause damage or recklessly and with knowledge that damage would probably result" in HP and the corresponding provisions of MP4 and MC. However, the latter provisions affect only the carriage of passengers and baggage and not, unlike Article 25 of HP, the carriage of cargo. *3.148*

Under HP the effect of Article 25 is that, in cases of grave misconduct, the carrier loses the benefit of the limits of liability set out in Article 22, both those calculated by reference to the weight of the goods and those based on any special declaration of interest in delivery at destination,[2] and must pay the actual loss suffered by the claimant; but, however outrageous the conduct, note that Article 25 does not authorise or allow an award of punitive damages.[3] *3.149*

2. "Wilful misconduct"

"Wilful misconduct" is an expression of English common law origin brought in to Article 25 of WC. It gave rise to diverse interpretations in other jurisdictions and for that reason was replaced by the wording in Article 25 of HP, which purports to spell out the true sense of "wilful misconduct", i.e., a change of wording but not of true meaning. Similar provisions are found in other Conventions concerning the *3.150*

4. Cf. Leffers (1997) 22 A. & S.L. 312.
1. See Art. 25A, below.
2. *Antwerp United Diamonds BVBA* v. *Air Europe* [1966] Q.B. 317.
3. *Re Air Disaster at Lockerbie*, 928 F. 2d 1267 (2 Cir., 1991).

international carriage of goods, such as Article IV, r. 5(e), of the Hague-Visby Rules on carriage by sea.[4]

3.151 Reported decisions on Article 25 involving death or injury to passengers are not irrelevant but should be regarded with caution. On the one hand, some courts are slow to conclude that a pilot of good record and in good health will deliberately risk his own life and that of his passengers.[5] On the other hand, in the past many courts in the USA where the question has often been raised, putting a high value on human life while also regarding the Article 22 limits as too low, have been more ready than most to apply Article 25.

3.152 *Prima facie* the burden of proof is on the claimant to prove that, on the balance of probability, Article 25 applies. However, at common law when there is a *prima facie* case of grave misconduct (fundamental breach) against a bailee such as a carrier, the matter being something squarely in the carrier's sphere, it is for the carrier to explain what happened; and if the carrier "leaves the cause of damage undiscovered and unexplained" the carrier is liable.[6] A similar position has been taken as regards cargo movements regulated by HP by the Austrian and German Supreme Courts[7] and by the Superior Court of Ontario in *Connaught Laboratories* v. *British Airways*,[8] in which the judge noted that the claimant gave timely notice to the carrier which, however, took no steps to investigate or preserve evidence until two years later when proceedings were issued. In these circumstances the judge concluded that it was appropriate "to draw an adverse inference from the failure of British Airways to call any evidence as to why the cargo came to be stored" without the requisite refrigeration. He noted that the information was solely "within the power British Airways to obtain"[9] and held that Article 25 applied.

3.153 In *Thomas Cook Group Ltd.* v. *Air Malta*,[10] a case on the old wording "wilful misconduct" found in WC, Cresswell J. outlined the approach of the English court to the issue and to the evidence before it:

> "1. The starting point . . . is an enquiry about the conduct ordinarily to be expected in the particular circumstances. 2. The next step is to ask whether the acts or omissions of the defendant were so far outside the range of such conduct as to be properly regarded as 'misconduct'. . . . 3. It is next necessary to consider whether the misconduct was wilful. 4. What does not amount to wilful misconduct? Wilful misconduct is far beyond negligence, even gross or culpable negligence. 5. What does amount to wilful misconduct?. . . . 6. The final step is to consider whether the wilful misconduct (if established) caused the loss of or damage to the goods."

4. Cf. CMR, Art. 29, which still speaks of "wilful misconduct".

5. See e.g. *Johnson Estate* v. *Pischke* [1989] 3 W.W.R. 207, 220; and *Connaught Laboratories* v. *British Airways* (2002) 217 D.L.R. (4th) 717 at [33].

6. *Levison* v. *Patent Steam Carpet Cleaning Co.* [1978] Q.B. 69, 82 (C.A.).

7. *BGH 21.9.2000*, TranspR 2001.29, applied in e.g. *OLG München 13.12.2001*, TranspR 2004.35, *OLG Köln 26.3.2002*, TranspR 2003.111 and *OLG Frankfurt 28.5.2002*, TranspR 2003.169, in application of the procedural *lex fori*. Austria in this sense: *OGH 29.11.2001*, TranspR 2004.36; (2002) 37 ETL 825.

8. (2002) 217 D.L.R. (4th) 717.

9. At [61].

10. *The Thomas Cook Group Ltd.* v. *Air Malta Company Ltd.* [1997] 2 Lloyd's Rep. 399, 407–408. See also *Goldman* v. *Thai Airways International Ltd.* [1983] 3 All E.R. 693 at 698.

However, courts in other countries are likely to distinguish motive and intent, and what counts under Article 25 of HP is intent. If the pilot changes course to save the life of a passenger with inevitable damage to sensitive cargo, that is scarcely misconduct but in such a case under HP in other countries, it is likely nonetheless that Article 25 applies. In England the decision may be different. *3.154*

When the cause of damage has been discovered and explained, there may still be the difficulty of deciding whether the critical acts or omissions were intentional or reckless, a state of mind. This "must inevitably be determined by reference to the data of practical experience . . . Assessment of state of mind is essentially a factual inquiry."[11] On that courts agree. However, the approach to the facts in different jurisdictions varies. *3.155*

The classic illustration of the UK view, which has been widely quoted, is that of Barry J. in *Horobin*.[12] According to this view, the claimant must establish actual awareness of the risk being taken,[13] but with emphasis on awareness: the approach is subjective in that it focuses on the mind of the person and the wrongfulness of the act or omission. See Comment 3, below. In other countries, notably the USA, the approach is more objective in that it focuses on awareness of results by taking an objective view of the circumstances. For example, in *Ospina*,[14] the court asked whether there was evidence of behaviour "in a manner which *implied* a reckless disregard of the probable consequences". Recently, however, there have been some signs in the UK of a move to the US position. For example, in *Nugent* Auld L.J. said that the "greater the obviousness of the risk the more likely the tribunal is to infer recklessness and that, the defendant, in so doing, knew that he would probably cause damage".[15] *3.156*

A typical damage case is one decided in Australia, *SS Pharmaceuticals* v. *Qantas*,[16] in which the carrier's agents could see marks on the cargo indicating that it should be stored in the dry, as well as the poor state of the plastic wrapping. Moreover, it was raining at the time and apparent that a typical Sydney summer thunderstorm was likely. Nonetheless they left the cargo uncovered in the open in the storm. From this evidence the court inferred that "such servants and agents must also have known that such 'deplorably bad handling' of the cargo would probably result in damage to the cargo".[17] Another typical case is that of the agent or employee who *3.157*

11. *Koirala* v. *Thai Airways*, 126 F. 3d 1205, 1210 (9 Cir., 1997).

12. *Horobin* v. *BOAC* [1952] 2 All E.R. 1016, 1022. Cf. *Glen* v. *Korean Airlines* [2003] Q.B. 1386. Under the Civil Aviation Act 1982 s. 76(2), damages "shall be recoverable without proof of negligence or intention or other cause of action, as if the loss or damage had been caused by the wilful act, neglect, or default of the owner of the aircraft". At [37] Simon J. held that "the effect of section 76(2) is that the claimant is absolved from having to show either a deliberate act or carelessness. In this context, 'wilful act' means a deliberate act and not 'intentional wrongdoing'."

13. *Gurtner* v. *Beaton* [1993] 2 Lloyd's Rep. 369, 387 (C.A.).

14. *Ospina* v. *TWA*, 24 Avi. 17,109 (2 Cir., 1192) (emphasis added); see also *Cortes* v. *American*, 177 F. 3d 1272, 1291 (11 Cir., 1999).

15. *Nugent* v. *Michael Goss Aviation Ltd.* [2000] 2 Lloyd's Rep. 222, 227 (C.A.). Also in this sense *Connaught Laboratories* v. *British Airways* (2002) 217 D.L.R. (4th) 717 at [62]. See also *R.* v. *Reid* [1992] 3 All E.R. 673, 675 (H.L.).

16. [1991] 1 Lloyd's Rep. 288 (C.A.N.S.W.)

17. P. 1016. See also *Connaught Laboratories* (above). Moreover, there are many French decisions like this: Clarke, *Air*, Art. 25, note 4.

deliberately disobeys clear instructions evidently designed to protect the cargo in his charge.[18]

3. Probable results

3.158 Probable results are results which are likely to happen.[19] Hence it is not enough that resulting damage should be merely "foreseeable".[20] For example, if the carrier has an unsafe system for handling cargo, without more, damage to cargo is (reasonably) foreseeable but it is not probable and Article 25 does not apply.[21] It has been held, however, that, if there is awareness that some damage is probable, the claimant does not have to establish awareness of (the probability of) the (greater) degree of damage that actually occurred,[22] and Article 25 applies. Although this was a case of passenger death decided in California, which may have been influenced by local notions of causation, the French text ("*le dommage résulte d'un acte . . . avec l'intention de provoquer un dommage*") does suggest that only "some" damage has to be intended.

3.159 That is certainly likely to be the decision in the UK, however, perhaps for the wrong reasons. What counts, according to some statements, is that there was actual awareness of (some) risk-taking, almost regardless of the degree of risk. Read like that they go too far. For example, the act or omission must be one "which he knows and appreciates is wrong, and is done or omitted regardless of the consequences, not caring what the result of his carelessness may be".[23] Again, a person "wilfully misconducts himself if he knows and appreciates that it is misconduct on his part in the circumstances to do or to fail or omit to do something and yet (a) intentionally does or fails or omits to do it or (b) persists in the act, failure or omission regardless of the consequences or (c) acts with reckless carelessness, not caring what the results of his carelessness may be".[24] Taken with an English decision that rejected the relevance of constructive knowledge,[25] the UK approach is difficult to reconcile with the reference in Article 25 to "knowledge that *damage* would probably result". The subjective emphasis in English courts on the (wrongfulness of the) carrier's act or omission (see Comment 2, above) was not surprising under WC, in which Article 25 refers to "wilful misconduct" but harder to justify when the words were substituted in HP (and the later regimes), which refers to what "would probably result".

18. See *The Thomas Cook Group Ltd.* v. *Air Malta Company Ltd.* [1997] 2 Lloyd's Rep. 399, 407; and *Laceys Footwear* v. *Bowler* [1997] 2 Lloyd's Rep. 369, 375–6 (C.A.), a case concerning the corresponding provision of CMR, Art. 29.

19. *Goldman* v. *Thai Airways International Ltd.* [1983] 3 All E.R. 693, 700 (C.A.).

20. *Koufos* v. *Czarnikow* [1969] 1 A.C. 350.

21. *Rolls-Royce* v. *HVD* [2000] 1 Lloyd's Rep. 653.

22. *Husain* v. *Olympic*, 116 F. Supp. 2d 1121, 1140 (N.D. Cal., 2000).

23. *Rustenburg* v. *South African Airways* [1977] 1 Lloyd's Rep. 564, 569 with reference to a similar statement in the judgment of Barry J. in *Horabin* v. *BOAC* [1952] 2 All E.R. 1016, 1022.

24. *The Thomas Cook Group Ltd.* v. *Air Malta Company Ltd.* [1997] 2 Lloyd's Rep. 399, 407–8.

25. *Nugent* v. *Michael Goss Aviation Ltd.* [2000] 2 Lloyd's Rep 222 (C.A.).

4. Theft

Theft cases are broadly of two kinds, "inside jobs" and "outside jobs". When theft is an "inside job", i.e., theft by the carrier's own agents or employees, typically a court will conclude that "any thief or thieves must be aware that damage would probably result even though that was not their specific intent when they stole the package in question".[26] When theft is an "outside job", a typical Article 25 case is that of a carrier, who has been made well aware of the high value of goods, but takes no special steps to protect them from thieves.[27] Moreover, a German court has held that, if a sealed parcel turns out to be empty on delivery, that is *prima facie* a case of Article 25.[28] 3.160

Article 25A—Servant or agent of carrier 3.161

(1) If an action is brought against a servant or agent of the carrier arising out of damage to which this Convention relates, such servant or agent, if he proves that he acted within the scope of his employment, shall be entitled to avail himself of the limits of liability which that carrier himself is entitled to invoke under Article 22.

(2) The aggregate of the amounts recoverable from the carrier, his servants and agents, in that case, shall not exceed the said limits.

(3) The provisions of paragraphs (1) and (2) of this Article shall not apply if it is proved that the damage resulted from an act or omission of the servant or agent done with intent to cause damage or recklessly and with knowledge that damage would probably result.

Comments

1. Actions against servant or agents

WC established a right of action against the carrier but not expressly against any other person. Some jurisdictions would not permit an action against the servant and agent but clearly, if such an action is possible (as it is in the UK) and the carrier's limitation of liability did not apply for the benefit of that servant or agent, the purpose of internationally agreed limits of liability could have been defeated in some cases. To prevent this Article 25A was added by HP and corresponding provisions retained by MP4 (Article 25A) and MC (Article 30). As to questions of jurisdiction over the servant and agent see Article 28 3.162

2. The identity of servants and agents

Servants are those with whom the carrier has entered a contract of employment. Agents are those with whom the carrier has contracted for the performance of a specified task. The distinction between servants and agents depends on national 3.163

26. *Rustenburg* (above) at 574; *Swiss Bank* v. *Air Canada* (1982) 129 D.L.R. (3d) 85, 104–5 (Fed. Ct. Canada).

27. *British Airways* v. *UAP, Cass. France 9.7.1991,* (1992) 27 ETL 279; *Finnair* v. *Winterthur,* Unif. L. Rev. 2003.776 (Swiss Fed. Ct.)

28. *LG Darmstadt 25.9.2002,* TranspR 2003.114.

law. The difficulty in drawing this distinction in the context of carriage by air produces significant differences between jurisdictions.

3.164 The authentic French text refers to (both) servants and agents as *préposés* which, according to decisions of the French courts, is a limited category of persons over whom the carrier has control. Usually, it refers to a person who is part of the enterprise, who has been given a contract of employment (*embauché*), and who is subject to the orders of the employer as regards the way he or she does the work.[1] Thus, for example, French courts have ruled out of the category firms with a significant role in the movement of cargo such as those employed to handle cargo between different stages of its transportation (*transitaires*).[2]

3.165 The English translation of *préposés* as "servants or agents" is not exact and brings in a wider range of persons than *préposés*. Indeed the reference to "agent" is one that finds no counterpart in most translations of Article 25A into other languages.[3] However, the English translation does find some support in the *travaux* of the WC.[4] Moreover, "servants or agents" has nonetheless been retained in Article 30 of MC and is also found in the corresponding provision of other transport Conventions, such as CMR Article 3, not least because it is better suited to the modern practice of carriers in outsourcing traditional carriage functions to a web of independent contractors.

3.166 Uniformity of law has been further impaired because courts in the USA have taken a particularly broad view of agents, which goes beyond persons who undertake tasks "essential" to the operation of carriage, and extends to persons whose work is "in furtherance" of the contract of carriage, for example, firms employed to maintain and repair the aircraft.[5] It is doubtful that this was the intention of the drafters of WC, however, it does accommodate well the modern practice of carriers in outsourcing, at least, when the carrier chooses the contractor; and perhaps also when, although that contractor has a functional monopoly at the place in question, the carrier is still able to choose the time schedule for handling and give specific directions about how the work should be done.[6] More difficult cases are those beyond any such control by the carrier such as those involving Air Traffic Control.

3. *Scope of employment*

3.167 A person is a servant or agent for the purpose of immunity under Article 25A only when acting within the scope of employment, which is determined by national law. Strike action is usually outside the scope of anyone's employment in any jurisdiction.[7] UK courts are likely to draw on rules of vicarious liability associated with the

1. Schmid (1986) 40 R.F.D.A. 165, 167.
2. *Paris 7.10.98*, BTL 1998.820.
3. Schmid (above) at 168.
4. Schmid at 169.
5. *Lear* v. *New York Helicopter Co.*, 597 N.Y.S. 2d 411 (1993). Cf. the view that the category does not include agents working for more than one carrier: *Dazo* v. *Global Airport Security Services*, 295 F. 3d 934 (9 Cir., 2002); noted critically by Brown, 68 J. Air L. & Com. 639 (2003).
6. *BGH 21.9.2000*, TranspR 2001.29.
7. E.g. *OLG Stuttgart 24.2.1993*, TranspR 1995.74.

common law of tort. The critical case is theft; it is "accepted law that a master is liable for the dishonesty or fraud of his servant if it was done in the course of his employment and for his master's benefit".[8] Similarly, a bailee for reward, such as an air carrier, "is not answerable for a theft by one of its servants but only for a theft by such of them as are deputed by him to discharge some part of his duty of taking reasonable care. A theft by any servant who was not employed to do anything in relation to the goods is entirely outside the scope of his employment and cannot make the master liable".[9] Accordingly, for the purposes of WC and HP the English courts have been prepared to hold that the theft of goods by a cargo loader was within the scope of his employment for it "was clearly part of his duty to take reasonable care of the package during the operation of loading and stowing it on the aircraft".[10] *Prima facie* the employee, who does not steal during working hours but who profits from knowledge then acquired about the location of valuable cargo to steal after hours, is not acting within the scope of employment.[11] However, some courts, such as the Federal Court of Canada, have held otherwise.[12]

In cases of theft there is likely to be little dispute that the theft was "an act or omission of the servant or agent done with intent to cause damage or recklessly and with knowledge that damage would probably result". As to what this means see the Comments on Article 25, above. *3.168*

Article 26—Complaint *3.169*

(1) Receipt by the person entitled to delivery of baggage or cargo without complaint is prima facie evidence that the same have been delivered in good condition and in accordance with the document of carriage.

(2) In the case of damage, the person entitled to delivery must complain to the carrier forthwith after the discovery of the damage, and, at the latest, within seven days from the date of receipt in case of baggage and fourteen days from the date of receipt in the case of cargo. In the case of delay the complaint must be made at the latest within twenty-one days from the date on which the baggage or cargo have been placed at his disposal.

(3) Every complaint must be made in writing upon the document of carriage or by separate notice in writing despatched within the times aforesaid.

(4) Failing complaint within the times aforesaid, no action shall lie against the carrier, save in the case of fraud on his part.

Comments

1. Presumption of performance

For an action to lie against the carrier, a complaint must have been addressed within the time periods set out in Article 26, which are longer than those stipulated by the corresponding provision (Article 26) of WC. In that regard Article 26 is the same as *3.170*

8. *Morris* v. *C.W. Martin & Sons Ltd.* [1965] 2 Lloyd's Rep. 63 at 69 (C.A.).

9. *Morris* v. *C.W. Martin* at 78, applied to carriage by air in *Swiss Bank Corp. and Others* v. *Brink's-MAT Ltd.* [1986] 2 Lloyd's Rep. 79. See also *Frans Maas (UK)* v. *Samsung Electronics* [2004] 2 Lloyd's Rep. 251.

10. *Rustenburg* v. *South African Airways* [1977] 1 Lloyd's Rep. 564 at 576.

11. In this sense: *Saint-Paul Fire Co.* v. *Air France, Cass. France 22.7.1986*, (1986) 40 RFDA 428.

12. *Swiss Bank* v. *Air Canada* (1982) 129 D.L.R. (3d) 85, 104–105.

Article 26 of MP4 and Article 31 of MC. The duty is distinct from and independent of the obligation to file any legal proceedings that are required in accordance with Article 29. Article 26(1) states a presumption, that delivery has been made in accordance with the contract of carriage, a presumption in favour of the carrier unless a complaint is made. Obviously, the timeous making of a proper complaint is important if the cargo interest is to preserve its position against the carrier. Equally obviously, the time limits do not apply in a case of fraud. Fraud is a matter for national law; for the law of England, see the Comment on Condition 10 of the RHA Conditions, paragraphs 1.318, *et seq.*, above.

2. Complaint

3.171 No particular form of complaint is prescribed by HP (or by WC, MP4 or MC). However, it has been argued that the complaint will not be valid if merely verbal.[1] In practice most carriers have standard form "freight inspection claim" forms to facilitate capture of relevant information and promote any applicable salvage procedures. To constitute a valid complaint it must sufficiently state the damage to which the subsequent action relates. For example, a complaint of physical damage will not suffice for Article 26(2) in respect of an action for partial loss of cargo.[2] Nonetheless, it may be be sufficient that the complaint is in "general terms".[3] If goods arrive damaged, it is enough to stamp the waybill "Received damaged". That indicates the line of inquiry; and it may be difficult to do more as "writing space may be limited on such a document" and "succinct complaints are often a necessity".[4] As to the meaning of delay, see Comment 1 on Condition 8 of the Conditions of Contract (IATA Resolution 600b (II)), paragraphs 3.772 *et seq.*, below.

3. The purpose of Article 26

3.172 As it is for a claimant to prove a case against the carrier anyway, it seems to lawyers in common law countries that this presumption adds little or nothing to the underlying legal position.[5] However, it may be difficult to ascertain when cargo was damaged, and how. Thus the main purpose of Article 26 "is (a) to enable the airline to check the nature of the damage, (b) to enable it to make enquiries how and when it occurred, (c) to enable it to assess its possible liability, to make provision in its accounts and if necessary to claim on its insurance, (d) to enable it to ensure that relevant documents (e.g. the air waybill) are retained until the issue of liability is disposed of".[6]

1. Leshem (1990) *Air Law*, Vol. XV, No. 2, 100.
2. *Western Digital Corporation* v. *British Airways plc* [2001] Q.B. 733 (C.A.).
3. *Ibid.* at [88].
4. *Schmoldt* v. *Pan Am*, 767 P. 2d 411, 415 (Okl., 1989). See Clarke, *Air*, Art. 26, notes 3 and 5; also the corresponding provision of CMR, Art. 30, para. 1.176, above.
5. E.g. *Scrutton on Charterparties* (20th ed., 1996), p. 434. concerning the parallel provision of Art. III, Rule 6, of the Hague Rules.
6. *Fothergill* v. *Monarch Airlines Ltd.* [1981] A.C. 251, 272. See also in this sense *Connaught Laboratories* v. *Air Canada* (1979) 94 D.L.R. 3d 586, 593 (Ont.).

Article 28—Jurisdiction *3.173*

(1) An action for damages must be brought, at the option of the plaintiff, in the territory of one of the High Contracting Parties, either before the court having jurisdiction where the carrier is ordinarily resident, or has his principal place of business, or has an establishment by which the contract has been made or before the court having jurisdiction at the place of destination.

(2) Questions of procedure shall be governed by the law of the court seised of the case.

Comments

1. Exclusivity

Article 28, which is substantially the same as Article 28 of WC and MP4 and Article 33(1) and (4) of MC, provides for jurisdiction in places connected with the carrier but which are also likely to be convenient for the claimant. No basis of jurisdiction is given in places connected with servants or agents of the carrier. However, the imperative language of Article 28, that an action "must be brought" in one of the four places, is intended as a constraint on the claimant; it is nonetheless open to the defendant to waive any valid objection and allow a matter to proceed notwithstanding that it is not one of the above four places.[1] Subject to this Article 28 is the only basis on which jurisdiction can be founded in respect of cargo actions under HP, MP4 and MC. The "fifth jurisdiction" provided for by Article 33(2) of MC applies only to "damage resulting from the death or injury of a passenger". Moreover, the Civil Jurisdiction and Judgments Act 1982 does not apply, as the Brussels Convention 1968 does not affect any Conventions which in relation to particular matters govern jurisdiction.[2] *3.174*

In *Rothmans*[3] Roskill L.J. referred to the four places for jurisdiction and observed that it is possible *3.175*

> "that any two of them might coincide. Thus, for example the contract might be made at the carrier's principal place of business or the place of destination might be a place where the carrier is ordinarily resident, but it is for the plaintiff to select where he wishes to sue, subject to the limitation that he can only sue . . . in one of [those] four places. Article 28 creates a self-contained code within the limits of which the plaintiff must found his jurisdiction."

If the claimant has correctly founded the action in the UK, a claim is validly brought in any part of the several jurisdictions comprised within the UK as the High Contracting Party, subject to its own internal rules.[4] In the UK there is no scope for the carrier to stay the action on the ground of *forum non conveniens*.[5] It is noteworthy, however, that many courts in the USA take a different view.[6] Moreover, *3.176*

1. See Art. 32 (below) and *Rothmans Ltd.* v. *Saudi Arabian Airlines Corporation* [1981] Q.B. 368, 375.

2. See Sched. 1, Title VII, Relationship to other Conventions, Art. 57.

3. Above, at p. 385.

4. See *Abnett* v. *British Airways plc*, 1996 S.L.T. 529, 532 with reference to *Mertens* v. *Flying Tiger Line*, 341 F. 2d 851 (2 Cir., 1965), cert. den. 382 U.S. 816. *Abnett* was affirmed on other grounds *sub. nom. Sidhu* v. *British Airways plc* [1997] A.C. 430.

5. *Milor SRL and Others* v. *British Airways plc* [1996] Q.B. 702.

6. See Mendelsohn and Lieux, 68 JALC 75 (2003); Tompkins, 28 Air & Space Law 54 (2003); and Clarke, *Air*, Art. 28, Comment (c).

in certain civil law countries it is open to carriers, if the courts concerned should have jurisdiction under Article 28, to apply there for a declaration concerning the extent of their liability: a potent weapon having regard to different questions of procedure as between jurisdictions.

2. Connecting points

3.177 The "ordinary residence" of a carrier is not the same as either his place of business in the UK, which is registered under the Companies Act for service of process on the carrier, or a branch office of the carrier. Carriers tend to have branch offices, not merely agencies or local subsidiaries, throughout the world and, if a branch office were a place where the carrier was "ordinarily resident", it would have been unnecessary to juxtapose the two phrases "ordinarily resident" and "principal place of business" in Article 28: the former would have been sufficient.[7]

3.178 The "principal place of business" of a carrier is the carrier's "operational headquarters".[8] In practice this is usually also the place of incorporation.[9] However, if these are in different places, the "operational headquarters" is what counts.

3.179 The "establishment by which the contract has been made" is the place, branch or agency, where the original contract was made. No account is taken of where any subsequent variations of the contract were agreed.[10] Divergent views have been expressed about how significant the connection with the branch or agency must be.

3.180 The "place of destination" is the place stipulated as such by the contract of carriage and thus, usually, the place designated as such in the air waybill.[11]

3.181 **Article 29—Time bar**

(1) The right to damages shall be extinguished if an action is not brought within two years reckoned from the date of arrival at the destination, or from the date on which the aircraft ought to have arrived, or from the date on which the carriage stopped.

(2) The method of calculating the period of limitation shall be determined by the law of the court seized of the case.

Comments

1. The commencement of the limitation period

3.182 Article 29, which is the same as Article 29 of WC and MP4 and substantially the same as Article 35 of MC, states the period of limitation during which any action arising under HP must be brought. For claims against a servant or agent of the carrier the 1961 Act, s. 5(1), contains a similar rule.

7. See *Rothmans* (above) at 374–375, *per* Mustill J. Cf. USA: courts usually locate ordinary residence at the place of incorporation, e.g. *Recumar* v. *KLM*, 608 F. Supp. 795 (D.C.N.Y., 1985).

8. *Recumar* at 798.

9. E.g. *Osborne* v. *British Airways plc*, 198 F. Supp. 2d 901 (S.D. Tex., 2002).

10. *Boyar* v. *Korean Airlines*, 664 F. Supp. 1481 (D.C., 1987).

11. *OLG Celle 24.10.2002*, TranspR 2003.201. See Art. 1, Comment 3, above.

The period runs from one of three trigger points, the time of actual or putative arrival, and the time when the carriage stopped. These are largely questions of fact which in most cases give rise to no special difficulty. If more than one point is applicable, it appears that, as three starting dates are identified, the latest would be the relevant one; but there has been some uncertainty in individual cases.[1] *3.183*

Since the cause of action expires at the end of the period it may be held that the period cannot be suspended or extended.[2] This is the view of courts in the USA,[3] whereas in Germany the Supreme Court has held that, although the period cannot be shortened, it can be extended by party agreement.[4] Although there is no English authority on the point, analogy with decisions on insurance cover suggest the same result: cover, which has ended by operation of law, may nevertheless continue in effect by agreement on the basis that, by the agreement, the insurer is estopped from pleading the rule of law.[5] *3.184*

2. *Arrival*

In a large airport with many movements of cargo it may be unclear when exactly goods arrived. If a date of arrival cannot be ascertained for the cargo, at latest the period "begins to run once a party with enforceable rights under a carriage knows or has reason to know something has gone wrong with this shipment, be it misdelivery, loss or delay".[6] Even when the location of cargo is known, there being more than one stage in its progress from runway to the hands of the consignee, a disputed point of law concerns the stage in that progress which counts as arrival. On the one hand, cargo which has reached the agreed destination but has been refused entry by Customs authorities, it has been held, has not properly arrived; its arrival is no more than provisional.[7] On the other hand, that cargo has arrived when it is handed over to the consignee might be thought beyond doubt, however, it is not so. *3.185*

One view indeed is that there can be no arrival until actual delivery to the consignee; thus, if an aircraft arrives at the airport one day but the cargo is not handed over physically until the next day, time does not begin to run until then—when physical possession is taken by the consignee.[8] But another view is that arrival occurs before that when the consignee has been informed that he is entitled to take physical possession of the cargo.[9] Yet another view, however, which follows from reasoning of the kind found in *Balani*,[10] is that time should not start to run *3.186*

1. See *All Transport Inc.* v. *Seaboard World Air Lines*, 349 NYS 2d 277 (1973).
2. Generally, see Hughes and Couturier (1985) *Air Law*, Vol. X; and Goldhirsch (1987) *Air Law*, Vol. XII, No. 2, 94.
3. See *Magnus Electronics* v. *Royal Bank of Canada*, 19 Avi. 17,944 (N.D. Ill., 1985); *Fishman* v. *Delta*, 132 F. 2d 138, 144 (2 Cir., 1998); and *Fireman's Fund* v. *Alpina*, 27 Avi. 18,402 (N.D. Ill., 2001).
4. *BGH 22.4.1982*, NJW 1983.516.
5. *HIH* v. *Axa* [2003] Lloyd's Rep. IR 1 (C.A.) at [29].
6. *Balani* v. *Malaysian Airline System*, 24 Avi. 18,078 (S.D.N.Y., 1994).
7. *Eggink* v. *TWA*, 22 Avi. 17,731 (S.D.N.Y., 1990).
8. *Air Afrique* v. *Scac Frigo, Cass. (France) 3.6.97* (1998) 205 RFDA 142.
9. *Lg Stuttgart 19.8.1997,* TranspR 1998.196; ULR 1998.884.
10. Above.

against a consignee until the consignee has had an opportunity to inspect the cargo in question.[11]

3.187 In any event, sooner or later carriage and the carrier's role and responsibility as carrier must come to an end. On the one hand, if, after a reasonable time the consignee has not come for the cargo, the carrier holds it not as carrier but as warehouseman, and a different limitation rule may apply.[12] On the other hand, the period may begin to run before arrival in any sense at all if, as it is stated in Article 29(1), carriage has stopped. Most obviously that is the case if the cargo is destroyed in transit or, being damaged, is disposed of where it is.

3. *Rights extinguished*

3.188 Article 29 fixes a two-year period after which the right of action against the carrier is extinguished. Strictly speaking, Article 29 does not need to be pleaded. "Extinguished" means more than merely unenforceable: the "two year period is not a mere period of limitation operating at its expiration to bar a remedy. It is an integral part of a right."[13] In the (governing) French text *"déchéance"* means loss of a right.[14] If a person's right has been lost, it is "non-existent . . . finished, gone forever".[15] Moreover, in this respect Article 29(1) applies separately to each cause of action against a carrier. Accordingly, if a case is pleaded within two years but an alternative ground is available then but not pleaded until after the two year-period has ended, even though both grounds may relate to the same cargo and damage, action based on the first ground will be in time but action based on the second will not.[16]

4. *Claims for contribution*

3.189 The Civil Liability Contribution Act 1978, s. 1(3) provides that a "person shall be liable to make contribution . . . notwithstanding that he has ceased to be liable in respect of the damage in question since the time when the damage occurred, unless he ceased to be liable by virtue of the expiry of a period of limitation or prescription which extinguished the right on which the claim against him in respect of the damage was based". *Prima facie* the latter is the effect of Article 29. However, in the UK that is overridden by the more specific provisions of the 1961 Act. Section 5(2) provides that the two-year period of Article 29 does not apply to claims for contribution between persons liable for any damage to which HP relates. Claims against other persons are subject to the Limitation Act 1980, s. 10. There appears to be no uniformity of interpretation on this point in other jurisdictions.

11. *Korba* v. *TWA*, 508 N.E. 2d 48, 53 (Ind. App., 1987).

12. *Belgian Endive* v. *American*, 673 N.Y.S. 2d 817 (N.Y., 1998).

13. *Timeny* v. *British Airways* (1991) 102 ALR 565 (Sup. Ct. S.A.).

14. Cornu, *Vocabulaire juridique*, p. 232.

15. *Proctor* v. *Jetway* [1982] 2 NSWLR 264, 271. As regards the effect on defences such as deduction or abatement, see CMR, Art. 32, Comment 3, para. 1.203, above.

16. *Western Digital Corporation* v. *British Airways plc* [2001] QB 733 (C.A.).

Article 30—Successive carriage 3.190

(1) In the case of carriage to be performed by various successive carriers and falling within the definition set out in the third paragraph of Article 1, each carrier who accepts passengers, baggage or cargo is subjected to the rules set out in this Convention, and is deemed to be one of the contracting parties to the contract of carriage in so far as the contract deals with that part of the carriage which is performed under his supervision.

(2) [Concerns claims by passengers.]

(3) As regards baggage or cargo, the passenger or consignor will have a right of action against the first carrier, and the passenger or consignee who is entitled to delivery will have a right of action against the last carrier, and further, each may take action against the carrier who performed the carriage during which the destruction, loss, damage or delay took place. These carriers will be jointly and severally liable to the passenger or to the consignor or consignee.

Comments

1. Successive carriage

Article 30, which is substantially the same as Article 30 of WC and MP4 and Article 36 of MC, concerns liability for cargo when transportation is undertaken by two or more successive carriers. More specifically, successive carriage, according to Article 1(3), is carriage which the parties regard as a single operation, whether "agreed upon under the form of a single contract or of a series of contracts". However, Article 30 regulates only the case of successive carriage under a single contract. In the case of successive carriage under a series of contracts, carriers actually are contracting parties from the beginning and need not be deemed contracting parties by virtue of Article 30. What counts in this regard is party intention at the time of the contract.[1] 3.191

2. Successive carriers

Although Article 30 does not refer to *air* carriers.[2] This can be inferred from the general context and, in particular, from Article 1(3). The "first carrier", it has been held, is *prima facie* the person identified as being the first carrier in the air waybill.[3] However, it has been forcefully argued that the first carrier should be the one who actually contracted with the consignor, even when that carrier did not actually perform any part of the carriage and is not mentioned in the waybill.[4] 3.192

If the contracting carrier substitutes another carrier to perform a carriage, which is subject to HP, WC or MP4 (but not MC), the case is not one of successive carriage but one subject to the 1962 Act, which in the UK enacts the Guadalajara Convention (paras. 3.525 *et seq.*, below). Under MC the corresponding rules are in MC itself: Articles 39 *et seq.* (paras. 3.626 *et seq.*, below). When part of the transportation is to be performed by a non-air carrier, that part is outside the scope 3.193

1. *Rotterdamsche Bank NV and Another* v. *British Overseas Airways Corporation and Another* [1953] 1 All E.R. 675. *Cass.com. (France) 13.11.2002*, BTL 2002.771.

2. For a contractual definition of "carrier" see Art. 1.6 of the Conditions of Carriage for Cargo: IATA Recommended Practice 1601 CSC(19), para. 3.812, below.

3. *OLG Hamburg 2.9.1982*, RIW 1983.874.

4. See Clarke, *Air*, Art. 30, note 4.

of the Conventions altogether. However, when the contract is a contract for carriage by successive air carriers, the substitution of a non-air carrier for one stage, e.g. a land carrier when aircraft are grounded by fog, does not deprive a subsequent air carrier of its role as a successive carrier under Article 30.

3. Entitlement to sue

3.194 Are the consignee and the consignor, the only persons mentioned in Article 30, the only persons entitled to sue in respect of lost or damaged cargo? The question arose in *Western Digital*,[5] in which the question was whether a claim could be brought by a cargo owner not named in the waybill. In line with an earlier English decision[6] an affirmative answer was given by the Court of Appeal. A similar conclusion has been reached in New Zealand.[7] In certain other countries, however, the decisions have been more restrictive.[8] This difference in opinion reflects not only differing interpretation of the relevant Convention but also differences in related rules of the *lex fori*.

3.195 Article 30 is the only provision of HP (or WC, MP4 and MC) that addresses the question of entitlement to sue, and then only in relation to successive carriage. Other carriage Conventions such as CMR are the same in this respect. Under the CMR there seems to be a consensus that, in the absence of a rule in the Convention that is clearly exclusive, national law still applies; and, as regards CMR claims brought in the UK, the common law rule referable to ownership survives.[9] The same appears to be true of HP.[10]

3.196 **Chapter IV: Provisions relating to combined carriage**

Article 31—Combined carriage

(1) In the case of combined carriage performed partly by air and partly by any other mode of carriage, the provisions of this Convention apply only to the carriage by air, provided that the carriage by air falls within the terms of Article 1.

(2) Nothing in this Convention shall prevent the parties in the case of combined carriage from inserting in the document of air carriage conditions relating to other modes of carriage, provided that the provisions of this Convention are observed as regards the carriage by air.

Comment

3.197 Combined carriage (sometimes referred to as multimodal or intermodal carriage) is carriage of goods by more than one mode of transport, when the contract provides

5. *Western Digital* v. *B.A.* [1999] 2 Lloyd's Rep. 380.

6. *Gatewhite* v. *Iberia* [1990] 1 Q.B. 326.

7. *Tasman Pulp* v. *Brambles* [1981] 2 N.Z.L.R. 225.

8. France: *Cass.Com. 13.11.2002*, BTL 2002.771, and South Africa: *Pan Am* v. *S.A. Fire* [1965] 3 S.A.L.R. 150.

9. See CMR, Art. 17, Comment 2, paras. 1.85, *et seq.*, above.

10. That was assumed without, it seems, discussion by Cresswell J. in *Thomas Cook* v. *Air Malta* [1997] 2 Lloyd's Rep. 399, 400.

for the employment of more than one mode of transport. The carrier cannot convert single mode (unimodal) air carriage into combined carriage by substitution of another mode without the consent of the other party. In the case of combined transport the regime for the other mode applies to that stage of the carriage. In Europe that is most likely to be CMR or national for carriage by road: see, paragraphs 1.1 *et seq.*, above.

Chapter V: General and final provisions *3.198*

Article 32—Prohibition on contracting-out

Any clause contained in the contract and all special agreements entered into before the damage occurred by which the parties purport to infringe the rules laid down by this Convention, whether by deciding the law to be applied, or by altering the rules as to jurisdiction shall be null and void. Nevertheless for the carriage of cargo arbitration clauses are allowed subject to this Convention, if the arbitration is to take place within one of the jurisdictions referred to in the first paragraph of Article 28.

Comment

Article 32 reiterates the underlying policy of any uniform regime relating to international carriage that, to be uniform, it must be largely mandatory. See also Article 23, above. Article 32 of WC and of MP4 and Article 49 of MC are substantially the same. It is uncertain what "special agreements" may be entered into *after* damage has occurred that might infringe the rules. However, the prohibition applies to any "clause contained in the contract" of carriage. This suggests something operative in the future, with the corollary that an agreement having that effect after the event is not invalidated by Article 29. *3.199*

Article 33—Freedom to contract *3.200*

Nothing contained in this Convention shall prevent the carrier either from refusing to enter into any contract of carriage, or from making regulations which do not conflict with the provisions of this Convention.

Comment

Article 33, which is substantially the same as Article 30 of WC, allows states to provide different rules for internal flights. Moreover, although the air Conventions are exclusive within their domain, they do not provide comprehensive regimes. Carriers are free therefore to supplement the rules of the Conventions with contract terms. In practice there is widespread use of terms and regulations drafted by IATA. A qualified version of Article 33 is to be found in Article 33 of MP4 but there is no corresponding provision in MC. *3.201*

3.202 **Article 34—Extraordinary carriage**

The provisions of Articles 3 to 9 inclusive relating to documents of carriage shall not apply in the case of carriage performed in extraordinary circumstances outside the normal scope of an air carrier's business.

Comment

3.203 Article 34 is a saving provision for non-commercial flights for which a commercial regime is inappropriate. In particular, the documented legislative history of WC "reveals that Article 34 was adopted to protect a carrier who, for a benevolent purpose, undertakes a flight which *from its inception* is to be performed under 'extraordinary circumstances' and outside the normal scope of a carrier's business".[1] Cases suggested include the carriage of cargo to territory affected by hostilities or in other circumstances in which the transportation is likely to be unsafe, including mercy flights.

3.204 Corresponding but differing provisions are to be found in Article 34 of WC and MP4, and Article 51 of MC. This is also the position with respect to non-international carriage by air under the 1967 Order, Schedule 1, where in the UK Chapter 2 of HP is not applied, *viz.*, there is no requirement for an air waybill or for it to contain the particulars set out in Article 8. Carriers' liability is subject to the other provisions of HP including the limitation of liability provisions.

3.205 **Article 35—Days: meaning**

The expression "days" when used in this Convention means current days not working days.

Comment

3.206 This provision, which is the same as Article 35 of WC and MP4 and substantially the same as Article 52 of MC, is relevant to the degree of delay which triggers consignee rights under Article 13 and to the time allowed for making complaints under Article 26.

3.207 **Article 36—Governing language**

The Convention is drawn up in French in a single copy which shall remain deposited in the archives of the Ministry of Foreign Affairs of Poland and of which one duly certified copy shall be sent by the Polish Government to the Government of each of the High Contracting Parties.

3.208 **Article 40A—Application**

(1) [Concerns the definition of "High Contracting Party".]

(2) For the purposes of the Convention the word territory means not only the metropolitan territory of a State but also all other territories for the foreign relations of which that State is responsible.

[*The next paragraph is 3.219*]

1. *Karfunkel* v. *Air France*, 427 F. Supp. 971, 978 (S.D.N.Y., 1977).

III. THE MP4 CONVENTION AS GIVEN FORCE OF LAW IN THE UK BY THE 1961 ACT, SCHEDULE 1A[1]

International Carriage under the MP4 amended Convention 3.219

Chapter I: Scope—Definitions

Article 1—Definitions

(1) This Convention applies to all international carriage of persons, baggage or cargo performed by aircraft for reward. It applies equally to gratuitous carriage by aircraft performed by an air transport undertaking.

(2) For the purposes of this Convention, the expression *international carriage* means any carriage in which, according to the agreement between the parties, the place of departure and the place of destination, whether or not there be a break in the carriage or a transhipment, are situated either within the territories of two High Contracting Parties, or within the territory of a single High Contracting Party if there is an agreed stopping place within the territory of another State, even if that State is not a High Contracting Party. Carriage between two points within the territory of a single High Contracting Party without an agreed stopping place within the territory of another State is not international carriage for the purposes of this Convention.

(3) Carriage to be performed by several successive air carriers is deemed, for the purposes of this Convention, to be one undivided carriage if it has been regarded by the parties as a single operation, whether it had been agreed upon under the form of a single contract or of a series of contracts, and it does not lose its international character merely because one contract or a series of contracts is to be performed entirely within the territory of the same State.

Comment

Article 1 of MP4 defines the contract to which it applies. It is identical to Article 1 of HP (para. 3.37, above). 3.220

Article 2—State/postal items 3.221

1. This Convention applies to carriage performed by the State or by legally constituted public bodies provided it falls within the conditions laid down in Article 1.
2. In the carriage of postal items, the carrier shall be liable only to the relevant postal administration in accordance with the rules applicable to the relationship between the carriers and the postal administrations.
3. Except as provided in paragraph (2) of this Article, the provisions of this Convention shall not apply to the carriage of postal items.

Comment

Article 2(1) and (3) are substantially similar to Article 2 of HP (para. 3.51, above). 3.222

1. Being the English text of the Warsaw Convention with the Hague Protocol amendments as amended by Montreal Additional Protocol No. 4 as supplemented by the Guadalajara Convention.

3.223

Chapter II: Documents of Carriage

Section 3—Documentation Relating to Cargo

Article 5—Air waybill/record: requirement

(1) In respect of the carriage of cargo an air waybill shall be delivered.
(2) Any other means which would preserve a record of the carriage to be performed may, with the consent of the consignor, be substituted for the delivery of an air waybill. If such other means are used, the carrier shall, if so requested by the consignor, deliver to the consignor a receipt for the cargo permitting identification of the consignment and access to the information contained in the record preserved by such other means.
(3) The impossibility of using, at points of transit and destination, the other means which would preserve a record of the carriage referred to in paragraph (2) of this Article does not entitle the carrier to refuse to accept the cargo for carriage.

Comment

3.224 The air waybill and, more recently, the receipt for cargo are the documents widely used for the carriage of goods by air. The provision in Article 5(2) for substituting other means which would preserve a record of the carriage to be performed in lieu of the traditional air waybill was an innovation in MP4, a possibility not envisaged by the drafters of WC and HP. In other respects Article 5 is similar to Article 5 of HP (para. 3.53, above).

3.225

Article 6—Air waybill: form of

(1) The air waybill shall be made out by the consignor in three original parts.
(2) The first part shall be marked "for the carrier"; it shall be signed by the consignor. The second part shall be marked "for the consignee"; it shall be signed by the consignor and the carrier. The third part shall be signed by the carrier and handed by him to the consignor after the cargo has been accepted.
(3) The signature of the carrier and that of the consignor may be printed or stamped.
(4) If, at the request of the consignor, the carrier makes out the air waybill, he shall be deemed, subject to proof to the contrary, to have done so on behalf of the consignor.

Comment

3.226 Article 6 is substantially the same as Article 6(1), (2), (4) and (5) of HP (para. 3.57, above). The contents of the air waybill that are mandatory are stated in Article 8. For the IATA standard form and layout of an air waybill see IATA Resolution 600a (para. 3.671, below).

3.227

Article 7—Air waybill: multiple packages

Where there is more than one package:
(a) the carrier of the cargo has the right to require the consignor to make out separate air waybills;
(b) the consignor has the right to require the carrier to deliver separate receipts when the other means referred to in paragraph (2) of Article 5 are used.

Comment

Article 7(a) is the same as Article 7 of HP (para. 3.61, above). 3.228

Article 8—Contents of air waybill/receipt 3.229

The air waybill and receipt for the cargo shall contain:
(a) an indication of the places of departure and destination;
(b) if the places of departure and destination are within the territory of a single High Contracting Party, one or more agreed stopping places being within the territory of another State, an indication of at least one such stopping place; and
(c) an indication of the weight of the consignment.

Comment

Article 8(a) and (b) are substantially the same as Article 8(a) and (b) of HP (para. 3.63, above). Accommodation is made for such information in standard form IATA air waybills. 3.230

Article 9—Non-compliance 3.231

Non-compliance with the provisions of Articles 5 to 8 shall not affect the existence or the validity of the contract of carriage, which shall, nonetheless, be subject to the rules of this Convention including those relating to limitation of liability.

Comment

Article 9 differs from the corresponding provision of HP, Article 9, in that under Article 9 of MP4, like Article 9 of MC, the non-compliant carrier remains subject to the rules of MP4 relating to limitation of liability, Article 22, whereas under Article 9 of HP, as well as Article 9 of WC, the carrier loses the right of limitation. 3.232

Article 10—Responsibility for particulars 3.233

(1) The consignor is responsible for the correctness of the particulars and statements relating to the cargo inserted by him or on his behalf in the air waybill or furnished by him or on his behalf to the carrier for insertion in the receipt for the cargo or for insertion in the record preserved by the other means referred to in paragraph (2) of Article 5.

(2) The consignor shall indemnify the carrier against all damage suffered by him, or by any other person to whom the carrier is liable, by reason of the irregularity, incorrectness or incompleteness of the particulars and statements furnished by the consignor or on his behalf.

(3) Subject to the provisions of paragraphs (1) and (2) of this Article, the carrier shall indemnify the consignor against all damage suffered by him, or by any other person to whom the consignor is liable, by reason of the irregularity, incorrectness or incompleteness of the particulars and statements inserted by the carrier or on his behalf in the receipt for the cargo or in the record preserved by the other means referred to in paragraph (2) of Article 5.

Comment

3.234 Article 10(1) and (2) are substantially the same as Article 10(1) and (2) of HP (para. 3.68, above). Article 10(3) was new but in substance it is also found in Article 10 of MC. Note that the consignor is liable under Article 10 without any limitation equivalent to that enjoyed by the carrier under Article 22(2) save that the carrier's liability to other persons may be subject to a limit of liability at law, such as that under Article 22(2), that could inure for the benefit of the consignor. However, the consignor is responsible only for the correctness of the particulars and statements relating to the cargo and not for other information contained in the air waybill, such as stopping places.[1] Note that the liability of the consignor under Article 10 is in addition to that of the consignor under Article 16 for such information and such documents as are necessary to meet the formalities of Customs, octroi or police

3.235

Article 11—Air waybill: evidentiary value

(1) The air waybill or the receipt for the cargo is prima facie evidence of the conclusion of the contract, of the acceptance of the cargo and of the conditions of carriage mentioned therein.

(2) Any statements in the air waybill or the receipt for the cargo relating to the weight, dimensions and packing of the cargo, as well as those relating to the number of packages, are prima facie evidence of the facts stated; those relating to the quantity, volume and condition of the cargo do not constitute evidence against the carrier except so far as they both have been, and are stated in the air waybill to have been, checked by him in the presence of the consignor, or relate to the apparent condition of the cargo.

Comment

3.236 Article 11 is substantially the same as Article 11 of HP (para. 3.72, above).

3.237

Article 12: Shipper's disposal instructions

(1) Subject to his liability to carry out all his obligations under the contract of carriage, the consignor has the right to dispose of the cargo by withdrawing it at the airport of departure or destination, or by stopping it in the course of the journey on any landing, or by calling for it to be delivered at the place of destination or in the course of the journey to a person other than the consignee originally designated, or by requiring it to be returned to the airport of departure. He must not exercise this right of disposition in such a way as to prejudice the carrier or other consignors and he must repay any expenses occasioned by the exercise of this right.

(2) If it is impossible to carry out the orders of the consignor, the carrier must so inform him forthwith.

(3) If the carrier obeys the orders of the consignor for the disposition of the cargo without requiring the production of the part of the air waybill or the receipt for the cargo delivered to the latter, he will be liable, without prejudice to his right of recovery from the consignor, for any damage which may be caused thereby to any person who is lawfully in possession of that part of the air waybill or the receipt for the cargo.

(4) The right conferred on the consignor ceases at the moment when that of the consignee begins in accordance with Article 13. Nevertheless, if the consignee declines to accept the

1. *American Home* v. *Maeder*, 999 F. Supp. 543, 548 (S.D.N.Y., 1998).

cargo, or if he cannot be communicated with, the consignor resumes his right of disposition.

Comment

Article 12 is substantially the same as Article 12 of HP (para. 3.79, above). Moreover, it has significant similarities to Article 12 of CMR (para. 1.53, above). *3.238*

Article 13—Delivery/non-arrival *3.239*

(1) Except when the consignor has exercised his right under Article 12, the consignee is entitled, on the arrival of the cargo at the place of destination, to require the carrier to deliver the cargo to him, on payment of the charges due and on complying with the conditions of carriage.

(2) Unless it is otherwise agreed, it is the duty of the carrier to give notice to the consignee as soon as the cargo arrives.

(3) If the carrier admits the loss of the cargo, or if the cargo has not arrived at the expiration of seven days after the date on which it ought to have arrived, the consignee is entitled to enforce against the carrier the rights which flow from the contract of carriage.

Comment

Article 13 is substantially the same as Article 13 of HP (para. 3.86, above). Note, however, that Article 13 differs from Article 13 of HP in that the carrier is no longer required by Article 13(1) to hand over the (second) air waybill when delivering the cargo. The usefulness of that requirement had been questioned for some time. *3.240*

Article 14—Shipper/consignee rights *3.241*

The consignor and the consignee can respectively enforce all the rights given them by Articles 12 and 13, each in his own name, whether he is acting in his own interest or in the interest of another, provided that he carries out the obligations imposed by the contract of carriage.

Comment

Article 14 is the same as Article 14 of HP (para. 3.91, above). *3.242*

Article 15—Waiver *3.243*

(1) Articles 12, 13 and 14 do not affect the relations of the consignor and the consignee with each other or the mutual relations of third parties whose rights are derived either from the consignor or from the consignee.

(2) The provisions of Articles 12, 13 and 14 can only be varied by express provision in the air waybill or the receipt for the cargo.

Comment

Article 15(1) and (2) are essentially the same as Article 15(1) and (2) of HP (para. 3.93, above). However, Article 15(3) of HP, which permits a negotiable air waybill, *3.244* was omitted from MP4 as negotiable air waybills are not required in modern practice.

3.245

Article 16—Shipper's documents: customs etc.

(1) The consignor must furnish such information and such documents as are necessary to meet the formalities of customs, octroi or police before the cargo can be delivered to the consignee. The consignor is liable to the carrier for any damage occasioned by the absence, insufficiency or irregularity of any such information or documents, unless the damage is due to the fault of the carrier, his servants or agents.

(2) The carrier is under no obligation to enquire into the correctness or sufficiency of such information or documents.

Comment

3.246 Article 16 is the same as Article 16 of HP (para. 3.96, above).

3.247

Chapter III Liability of the Carrier and Extent of Compensation for Damage

Article 18—Damage to cargo

(1) [Concerns registered baggage.]

(2) The carrier is liable for damage sustained in the event of the destruction or loss of, or damage to, cargo upon condition only that the occurrence which caused the damage so sustained took place during the carriage by air.

(3) However, the carrier is not liable if he proves that the destruction, loss of, or damage to, the cargo resulted solely from one or more of the following:

(a) inherent defect, quality or vice of that cargo;

(b) defective packing of that cargo performed by a person other than the carrier or his servants or agents;

(c) an act of war or an armed conflict;

(d) an act of a public authority carried out in connection with the entry, exit or transit of the cargo.

(4) The carriage by air within the meaning of the preceding paragraphs of this Article comprises the period during which the cargo is in the charge of the carrier, whether in an airport or on board an aircraft, or, in the case of a landing outside an airport, in any place whatsoever.

(5) The period of the carriage by air does not extend to any carriage by land, by sea or by river performed outside an airport. If, however, such carriage takes place in the performance of a contract for carriage by air, for the purpose of loading, delivery or transhipment, any damage is presumed, subject to proof to the contrary, to have been the result of an event which took place during the carriage by air.

Comments

1. The liability regime

3.248 Article 18 is the provision central to the liability regime of MP4. The carrier is liable if an occurrence by which damage is sustained took place during the carriage by air, which is the period defined by Article 18(4) and (5), unless the carrier can establish one of the defences set out in Article 18(3), Article 20 or Article 21. The defences found in HP were reformulated in MP4: Article 18(2), Article 18(4) and Article

18(5) are substantially the same as Article 18(1), Article 18(2) and Article 18(3) respectively of HP (para. 3.99, above). Article 18(3) of MP4 was new and is not found in (WC or) HP.

3.249 The defences, exonerating causes, listed in Article 18 excuse the carrier if, in the language of Article 18(3), the destruction, loss of, or damage to, the cargo resulted "solely" from one of the exonerating causes. Clearly, if the word "solely" were to be applied literally the carrier's defence would not often succeed. However, in *Winchester Fruit*, having stated that the right approach was "to look at the adventure as whole", the judge concluded that it was sufficient for a successful defence by the carrier that the inherent vice in the fruit was the "dominant cause of their deterioration".[1] In the corresponding provision of MC, Article 18(2), the word "solely" was omitted.

2. Inherent defect, quality or vice

3.250 Article 18(3) contains defences widely encountered in other transport Conventions, notably inherent defect, quality or vice, and defective packing. The meaning of these phrases is determined by national law, however, some degree of uniformity in interpretation has developed because the words are found in other transport contexts. Thus *Albacora* v. *Wescott & Laurance*,[2] a leading English shipping case on the meaning of "inherent defect, quality or vice" in Article IV.2(m) of the Hague Rules, has been applied in Ontario to carriage by air.[3]

3.251 An inherent vice (or defect) is a defect in cargo which by its development through ordinary processes within the cargo itself tends to the injury or destruction of that same cargo, to such an extent that it does not survive the normal rigours of the journey in question and remain suitable for use in commerce for a reasonable time after the end of the journey.[4] The concept is relative to features of the particular cargo such as fragility, sensitivity to temperature or humidity; to features of the journey such as length and weather conditions; and to the manner of transportation such as pressurisation, temperature of cargo space, and any special care to be expected from the carrier. For example, in one case no special care having been promised by the carrier, flowers which froze during carriage because the aircraft was not heated suffered from inherent vice, there being no reason for the shipper to expect that it would be heated.[5]

3. Defective packing

3.252 Packing is defective if its state is such that the particular goods are unable to withstand the dangers of normal transit of the kind contemplated by the particular contract of carriage. English law sees the packing as part of the cargo so that cargo

1. *Winchester Fruit Ltd.* v. *American Airlines Inc.* [2002] 2 Lloyd's Rep. 265 at [55], C.L.C.C. (B.L.)
2. [1966] 2 Lloyd's Rep. 53 (H.L.).
3. *A.-G. of Canada* v. *Flying Tiger Line* (1987) 61 O.R. (2d) 673, 677. See *Soya* v. *White* [1983] 1 Lloyd's Rep. 122, 126 (H.L.).
4. *Noten* v. *Harding* [1990] 2 Lloyd's Rep. 283 (C.A.), concerning carriage by sea.
5. *A.-G. of Canada* v. *Flying Tiger Line* (1987) 61 O.R. (2d) 673, 677.

packed in such a way that it will not survive the expected transit suffers from inherent vice.[6] In other countries that may not be the case.

4. Acts of war or of public authorities

3.253 Act of war and armed conflict is a reference to armed hostilities between *de jure* or *de facto* states and their governments.[7] Acts of a public authority are those directed at the enforcement of customs, excise, trade, embargo or quarantine regulations.

3.254

Article 19—Delay

The carrier is liable for damage occasioned by delay in the carriage by air of passengers, baggage or cargo.

Comment

3.255 Article 19 is the same as Article 19 of HP (para. 3.111, above). It must be read with Article 20, which excuses the carrier in respect of damage caused by delay which could not be avoided.

3.256

Article 20—Defence

In the case of passengers and baggage, and in the case of damage occasioned by delay in the carriage of cargo, the carrier shall not be liable if he proves that he and his servants and agents have taken all necessary measures to avoid the damage or that it was impossible for them to take such measures.

Comment

3.257 Articles 18 and 19 of MP4 impose a *prima facie* liability on the carrier subject to a limitation rule in Article 22, as qualified by Article 25A, and subject to the "necessary measures" defence in Article 20. Liability is not founded on any notion of want of care or fault but the carrier may escape liability by proving observance of the high duty of care apparently contemplated by Article 20. In that respect Article 20 of MP4 is the same as Article 20 of HP (para. 3.116, above) except that, as regards cargo, the defence in Article 20 of MP4 has been restricted to damage occasioned by delay.

3.258

Article 21—Contributory fault

(1) [Concerns passengers and baggage.]

(2) In the carriage of cargo, if the carrier proves that the damage was caused by or contributed to by the negligence or other wrongful act or omission of the person claiming

6. *L.N.W. Ry.* v. *Hudson* [1920] A.C. 323, 333.

7. *Pan-Am* v. *Aetna* [1975] 1 Lloyd's Rep. 77 (2 Cir., 1974).

compensation, or the person from whom he derives his rights, the carrier shall be wholly or partly exonerated from his liability to the claimant to the extent that such negligence or wrongful act or omission caused or contributed to the damage.

Comments

Article 21 is largely the same as Article 21 of HP (para. 3.122, above). Among the differences is that the reference in Article 21 of MP4 to "omission" is not found in Article 21 of HP, although it is found in the corresponding provision of CMR, Article 17(2) (para. 1.77, above). Examples of contributory fault under Article 21 of MP4 are false declarations (of weight or contents) giving rise to delay in Customs clearance; or a knowing failure to provide documents essential if the cargo is not to be seized on arrival by Customs.[1] Moreover, it seems that Article 21 refers to acts which are deliberate rather than negligent. *3.259*

Article 22—Limits of liability *3.260*

(1) [Concerns passengers.]

(2) (a) [Concerns registered baggage.]

(b) In the carriage of cargo, the liability of the carrier is limited to a sum of 17 Special Drawing Rights per kilogramme, unless the consignor has made, at the same time when the package was handed over to the carrier, a special declaration of interest in delivery at destination and has paid a supplementary sum if the case so requires. In that case the carrier will be liable to pay a sum not exceeding the declared sum, unless he proves that that sum is greater than the consignor's actual interest in delivery at destination.

(c) In the case of loss, damage or delay of part of registered baggage or cargo, or of any object contained therein, the weight to be taken into consideration in determining the amount to which the carrier's liability is limited shall be only the total weight of the package or packages concerned. Nevertheless, when the loss, damage or delay of a part of the registered package or cargo, or of an object contained therein, affects the value of other packages covered by the same baggage check or the same air waybill, the total weight of such package or packages shall also be taken into consideration in determining the limit of liability.

(3) [Concerns unregistered baggage.]

(4) The limits prescribed in this Article shall not prevent the court from awarding, in accordance with its own law, in addition, the whole or part of the court costs and of the other expenses of the litigation incurred by the plaintiff. The foregoing provision shall not apply if the amount of the damages awarded, excluding court costs and other expenses of the litigation, does not exceed the sum which the carrier has offered in writing to the plaintiff within a period of six months from the date of the occurrence causing the damage, or before the commencement of the action, if that is later.

(5) The sums mentioned in terms of the Special Drawing Right in this Article shall be deemed to refer to the Special Drawing Right as defined by the International Monetary Fund. Conversion of the sums into national currencies shall, in case of judicial proceedings, be made according to the value of such currencies in terms of the Special Drawing Right, at the date of the judgment.

(6) The value of a national currency, in terms of the Special Drawing Right, of a High Contracting Party which is a Member of the International Monetary Fund shall be calculated in accordance with the method of valuation applied by the International Monetary Fund, in effect at the date of the judgment, for its operations and transactions. The value of a national currency, in terms of the Special Drawing Right, of a High Contracting Party which is not a Member of the International Monetary Fund, shall be calculated in a manner determined by

1. *KLM* v. *Tannerie des Cuirs, Paris 6.6.2001*, BTL 2001.664.

that High Contracting Party. Nevertheless, those States which are not Members of the International Monetary Fund and whose law does not permit the application of the provisions of paragraph 2(b) of Article 22 may, at the time of ratification or accession or at any time thereafter, declare that the limit of liability of the carrier in judicial proceedings in their territories is fixed at a sum of 250 monetary units per kilogramme. This monetary unit corresponds to sixty-five and a half milligrammes of gold of millesimal fineness nine hundred. This sum may be converted into the national currency concerned in round figures. The conversion of this sum into national currency shall be made according to the law of the State concerned.

Comment

3.261 Article 22 is substantially the same as Article 22(1) to (5) of HP (para. 3.125, above). Article 22(6), for which there is no corresponding provision in HP, addresses a question that had become more problematical since 1955. As is commonplace, the limits are referable to the weight of the cargo. See Comment on Condition 6 of the Conditions of Contract (IATA Resolution 600b (II) (para. 3.763, below).

3.262

Article 23—Invalidity of contractual provisions

(1) Any provision tending to relieve the carrier of liability or to fix a lower limit than that laid down in this Convention shall be null and void, but the nullity of any such provision does not involve the nullity of the whole contract, which shall remain subject to the provisions of this Convention.

(2) Paragraph 1 of this Article shall not apply to provisions governing loss or damage resulting from the inherent defect, quality or vice of the cargo carried.

Comment

3.263 Article 23 is the same as Article 23 of HP (para. 3.157, above).

3.264

Article 24—Convention paramount

(1) [Concerns passengers and baggage.]

(2) In the carriage of cargo, any action for damages, however founded, whether under this Convention or in contract or in tort or otherwise, can only be brought subject to the conditions and limits of liability set out in this Convention without prejudice to the question as to who are the persons who have the right to bring suit and what are their respective rights. Such limits of liability constitute maximum limits and may not be exceeded whatever the circumstances which give rise to the liability.

Comment

3.265 Article 24(2) corresponds to Article 24 of HP (para. 3.144, above), however, the essence of the rule is fortified in MP4 by express reference to extra-contractual actions and by the last sentence of Article 24(2).

3.266

Article 25A—Servants, agents

(1) If an action is brought against a servant or agent of the carrier arising out of damage to which this Convention relates, such servant or agent, if he proves that he acted within the

scope of his employment, shall be entitled to avail himself of the limits of liability which that carrier himself is able to invoke under Article 22.

(2) The aggregate of the amounts recoverable from the carrier, his servants or agents, in that case, shall not exceed the said limits.

(3) [Concerns the carriage of passengers and baggage.]

Comment

Article 25A is the same as Article 25A of HP (para. 3.161, above). *3.267*

Article 26—Complaint *3.268*

(1) Receipt by the person entitled to delivery of baggage or cargo without complaint is prima facie evidence that the same have been delivered in good condition and in accordance with the document of carriage.

(2) In the case of damage, the person entitled to delivery must complain to the carrier forthwith after the discovery of the damage, and, at the latest, within seven days from the date of receipt in the case of baggage and fourteen days from the date of receipt in the case of cargo. In the case of delay, the complaint must be made at the latest within twenty-one days from the date on which the baggage or cargo has been placed at his disposal.

(3) Every complaint must be made in writing upon the document of carriage or by separate notice in writing and despatched within the times aforesaid.

(4) Failing complaint within the times aforesaid, no action shall lie against the carrier, save in the case of fraud on his part.

Comment

Article 26 is the same as Article 26 of HP (para. 3.169, above). *3.269*

Article 27—Death of person liable *3.270*

In the case of the death of the person liable, an action for damages lies in accordance with the terms of this Convention against those representing his estate.

Comment

There is no provision corresponding to Article 27 to be found in HP. It is unlikely that the carrier will be an individual, however, Article 27 may well be applicable if an action is brought against a servant or agent. *3.271*

Article 28—Jurisdiction *3.272*

(1) An action for damages must be brought, at the option of the plaintiff, in the territory of one of the High Contracting Parties, either before the court having jurisdiction where the carrier is ordinarily resident, or has his principal place of business, or has an establishment through which the contract has been made or before the court having jurisdiction at the place of destination.

(2) Questions of procedure shall be governed by the law of the court seised of the case.

Comment

3.273 Article 28 is substantially the same as Article 28 of HP (para. 3.173, above).

3.274

Article 29—Limitation of actions

(1) The right to damages shall be extinguished if an action is not brought within two years, reckoned from the date of arrival at the destination or from the date on which the aircraft ought to have arrived, or from the date on which the carriage stopped.

(2) The method of calculating the period of limitation shall be determined by the law of the court seised of the case.

Comment

3.275 Article 29 is the same as Article 29 of HP (para. 3.181, above).

3.276

Article 30—Successive carriage

(1) In the case of carriage to be performed by various successive carriers and falling within the definition set out in the third paragraph of Article 1, each carrier who accepts cargo is subjected to the rules set out in this Convention and is deemed to be one of the contracting parties to the contract of carriage in so far as the contract deals with that part of the carriage which is performed under his supervision.

(2) [Concerns only claims by passengers.]

(3) As regards baggage or cargo, the consignor will have a right of action against the first carrier, and the consignee who is entitled to delivery will have a right of action against the last carrier, and further, each may take action against the carrier who performed the carriage during which the destruction, loss, damage or delay took place. These carriers will be jointly and severally liable to the consignor or consignee.

Comment

3.277 Article 30 is substantially the same as Article 30 of HP (para. 3.190, above).

3.278

Article 30A—Recourse

Nothing in this Convention shall prejudice the question whether a person liable for damage in accordance with its provisions has a right of recourse against any other person.

Comment

3.279 The purpose of Article 30A is to ensure that questions of subrogation and contribution between carriers, which arise *inter alia* out of successive carriage, are resolved not by MP4 but by national law. The provision also found in Article 37 of MC but not in WC or HP.

Chapter IV: Combined Carriage *3.280*

Provisions relating to Combined Carriage

Article 31—Combined carriage

(1) In the case of combined carriage performed partly by air and partly by any other mode of carriage, the provisions of this Convention apply only to the carriage by air, provided that the carriage by air falls within the terms of Article 1.

(2) Nothing in this Convention shall prevent the parties in the case of combined carriage from inserting in the document of air carriage conditions relating to other modes of carriage, provided that the provisions of this Convention are observed as regards the carriage by air.

Comment

Article 31 is the same as Article 31 of HP (para. 3.196, above). *3.281*

Chapter V: General and Final Provisions *3.282*

Article 32—Mandatory application

Any clause contained in the contract and all special agreements entered into before the damage occurred by which the parties purport to infringe the rules laid down by this Convention, whether by deciding the law to be applied, or by altering the rules as to jurisdiction, shall be null and void. Nevertheless for the carriage of cargo arbitration clauses are allowed subject to this Convention if the arbitration is to take place within one of the jurisdictions referred to in the first paragraph of Article 28.

Comment

Article 32 is the same as Article 32 of HP (para. 3.198, above). *3.283*

Article 33—Freedom to contract *3.284*

Except as provided in paragraph (3) of Article 5, nothing in this Convention shall prevent the carrier from either refusing to enter into any contract of carriage, or from making regulations which do not conflict with the provisions of this Convention.

Comment

Apart from the reference to Article 5(3) Article 33 is the same as Article 33 of HP *3.285*
(para. 3.200, above).

Article 34—Extraordinary carriage *3.286*

The provisions of Articles 3 to 8 inclusive relating to documents of carriage shall not apply in the case of carriage performed in extraordinary circumstances outside the normal scope of an air carrier's business.

Comment

3.287 Article 34 is the same as Article 34 of HP (para. 3.202, above).

3.288

Article 35—Days: meaning

The expression "days" when used in this Convention means current days not working days.

Comment

3.289 Article 35 is the same as Article 35 of HP (para. 3.205, above).

3.290

Article 36—Governing language

The Convention is drawn up in French in a single copy which shall remain deposited in the archives of the Ministry of Foreign Affairs of Poland and of which one duly certified copy shall be sent by the Polish Government to the Government of each of the High Contracting Parties.

Comment

3.291 Article 36 is the same as Article 36 of HP (para. 3.207, above).

3.292

Articles 37–40

[*Articles 37, 38, 39 and 40 are not reproduced. They deal with the coming into force of the Convention.*]

3.293

Article 40A—Application

(1) [Defines "High Contracting Party".].

(2) For the purposes of the Convention the word *territory* means not only the metropolitan territory of a State but also all other territories for the foreign relations of which that State is responsible.

Comment

3.294 Article 40A is substantially the same as Article 40A of HP (para. 3.208, above).

3.295

Article 41

[*Article 41 and the concluding words of the Convention are not reproduced. They deal with the coming into force of the Convention.*]

Additional Protocol (with reference to Article 2) 3.296

The High Contracting Parties reserve to themselves the right to declare at the time of ratification or of accession that the first paragraph of Article 2 of this Convention shall not apply to international carriage by air performed directly by the State, its colonies, protectorates or mandated territories or by any other territory under its sovereignty, suzerainty or authority.

Comment

The Additional Protocol is not found in HP. 3.297

[*The next paragraph is 3.307*]

IV. THE CONVENTION AS GIVEN FORCE OF LAW IN THE UK BY THE 1967 ORDER, SCHEDULE 2[1]

3.307 **International Carriage under the unamended Warsaw Convention**

Chapter I: Scope—definitions

Article 1—Definitions

(1) This Schedule applies to all international carriage of persons, baggage or cargo performed by aircraft for reward. It applies equally to gratuitous carriage by aircraft performed by an air transport undertaking.

(2) "International carriage" means any carriage in which, according to the contract made by the parties, the place of departure and the place of destination, whether or not there be a break in the carriage or a transhipment, are situated either within the territories of two States Parties to the Convention for the Unification of Certain Rules relating to International Carriage by Air signed at Warsaw on behalf of His Majesty on 12th October 1929, or within the territory of a single such State, if there is an agreed stopping place within the territory subject to the sovereignty, suzerainty, mandate or authority of another State, even though that State is not a party to the said Convention of 1929.

(3) A carriage to be performed by several successive air carriers is deemed for the purposes of this Schedule, to be one undivided carriage, if it has been regarded by the parties as a single operation, whether it had been agreed upon under the form of a single contract or of a series of contracts, and it does not lose its international character merely because one contract or a series of contracts is to be performed entirely within a territory subject to the sovereignty, suzerainty, mandate or authority of the same High Contracting Party.

Comment

3.308 Article 1 is the same as Article 1 of HP (para. 3.37, above), apart from minor differences. For example, the latter refers to "This Convention" where Article 2 refers to "This Schedule": a reference to this version of the Convention (WC) as enacted in the UK by Schedule 2 of the 1961 Act. For the carriage of mail and postal packages see the 1967 Order, Schedule 1, applicable to Non-International Carriage and the Carriage of Mail and Postal Packages (paras. 3.463 *et seq.*, below).

3.309 **Article 2—Carriage by State/mail**

(1) This Schedule applies to carriage performed by the State, not being a State which has availed itself of the Additional Protocol to the Warsaw Convention, or by legally constituted public bodies, provided it falls within the conditions laid down in Article 1.

(2) This Schedule does not apply to carriage performed under the terms of any international postal Convention.

Comment

3.310 Article 2 is substantially the same as Article 2 of HP (para. 3.51, above).

1. Being the English text of the Warsaw Convention 1929 without the Hague Protocol amendments but as supplemented by the Guadalajara Convention.

Chapter II: Documents of carriage *3.311*

Section 3—Air Waybill

Article 5—Air waybill: requirement

(1) Every carrier of cargo has the right to require the consignor to make out and hand over to him a document called an "air waybill", every consignor has the right to require the carrier to accept this document.

(2) The absence, irregularity or loss of this document does not affect the existence or the validity of the contract of carriage which shall, subject to the provisions of Article 9, be none the less governed by the rules of this Schedule.

Comment

Article 5 is substantially the same as Article 5 of HP (para. 3.53, above). For the particulars that must be included in the air waybill see Article 8. For the sanctions against the carrier in the event of non-compliance with Article 8 see Article 9. For the shipper's responsibility to the carrier with regard to the air waybill and the carrier's sanctions against the shipper, see Article 10. For when these requirements are waived, see Article 34. *3.312*

Article 6—Air waybill: form of *3.313*

(1) The air waybill shall be made out by the consignor in three original parts and be handed over with the cargo.

(2) The first part shall be marked "for the carrier", and shall be signed by the consignor. The second part shall be marked "for the consignee"; it shall be signed by the consignor and by the carrier and shall accompany the cargo. The third part shall be signed by the carrier and handed by him to the consignor after the cargo has been accepted.

(3) The carrier shall sign on acceptance of the cargo.

(4) The signature of the carrier may be stamped; that of the consignor may be printed or stamped.

(5) If, at the request of the consignor, the carrier makes out the air waybill, he shall be deemed, subject to proof to the contrary, to have done so on behalf of the consignor.

Comment

Apart from Article 6(3) Article 6 is the same as Article 6 of HP (para. 3.57, above). *3.314*

Article 7—Air waybill: multiple packages *3.315*

The carrier of cargo has the right to require the consignor to make out separate waybills when there is more than one package.

Comment

Article 7 is the same as Article 7 of HP (para. 3.61, above). *3.316*

3.317 **Article 8—Air waybill: mandatory contents**

The air waybill shall contain the following particulars:

(a) the place and date of its execution;
(b) the place of departure and of destination;
(c) the agreed stopping places, provided that the carrier may reserve the right to alter the stopping places in case of necessity, and that if he exercises that right the alteration shall not have had the effect of depriving the carriage of its international character;
(d) the name and address of the consignor;
(e) the name and address of the first carrier;
(f) the name and address of the consignee, if the case so requires;
(g) the nature of the cargo;
(h) the number of the packages, the method of packing and the particular marks or numbers upon them;
(i) the weight, the quantity and the volume or dimensions of the cargo;
(j) the apparent condition of the cargo and of the packing;
(k) the freight, if it has been agreed upon, the date and place of payment, and the person who is to pay it;
(l) if the cargo is sent for payment on delivery, the price of the cargo, and, if the case so requires, the amount of the expenses incurred;
(m) the amount of the value declared in accordance with Article 22(2);
(n) the number of parts of the air waybill;
(o) the documents handed to the carrier to accompany the air waybill;
(p) the time fixed for the completion of the carriage and a brief note of the route to be followed, if these matters have been agreed upon;
(q) a statement that the carriage is subject to the rules relating to liability established by the Warsaw Convention.

Comment

3.318 WC does not require the shipper and consignee to be identified but instead Article 8 sets out a lengthy list of matters (that was reduced to only three in Article 6 of HP) that must be stated in the air waybill. Observance of Article 8(a)–(i) and (q) is fundamental to the carriers' liability: see Article 9 as well as the Comments on the Notice required in the air waybill by the Conditions of Contract (IATA Resolution 600b (II) (paras. 3.742 *et seq.*, below) and the Comments on Condition 3 *ibid.* (paras. 3.756 *et seq.*, below). However, in the USA an appellate court has ruled that it is the unambiguous requirements, Articles 8(a)–(g) (but not of Article 8(h) and (i) which were considered ambiguous and not required unless commercially significant), that must be contained in the air waybill.[1]

3.319 **Article 9—Air waybill: non-compliance**

If the carrier accepts cargo without an air waybill having been made out or if the air waybill does not contain all the particulars set out in Article 8(a) to (i) inclusive and (q), the carrier shall not be entitled to avail himself of the provisions of this Schedule which exclude or limit his liability.

1. *Maritime Insurance Co. Ltd.* v. *Emery Freight Corp.*, 983 F. 2d 437, 24 Avi. Cas. 17,831 (2d Cir., 1993).

Comment

Article 9 is substantially the same as Article 9 of HP (para. 3.66, above). Decisions under WC confirm that the rest of the Convention applies nonetheless.[1] *3.320*

Article 10—Air waybill: shipper's responsibility *3.321*

(1) The consignor is responsible for the correctness of the particulars and statements relating to the cargo which he inserts in the air waybill.

(2) The consignor will be liable for all damage suffered by the carrier or any other person by reason of the irregularity, incorrectness or incompleteness of the said particulars and statements.

Comment

Article 10 is the same as Article 10 of HP (para. 3.68, above), except that the liability for all damage suffered by the carrier or any other person was replaced by an obligation to indemnify the carrier against all damage suffered by the carrier or any other person to whom the carrier is liable. *3.322*

Article 11—Air waybill: as evidence of contract *3.323*

(1) The air waybill is prima facie evidence of the conclusion of the contract, of the receipt of the cargo and of the conditions of carriage.

(2) The statements in the air waybill relating to the weight, dimensions and packing of the cargo, as well as those relating to the number of packages, are prima facie evidence of the facts stated; those relating to the quantity, volume and condition of the cargo do not constitute evidence against the carrier except so far as they both have been, and are stated in the air waybill to have been, checked by him in the presence of the consignor or relate to the apparent condition of the cargo.

Comment

Article 11 is the same as Article 11 of HP (para. 3.72, above). *3.324*

Article 12—Shipper's disposal instructions *3.325*

(1) Subject to his liability to carry out all his obligations under the contract of carriage, the consignor has the right to dispose of the cargo by withdrawing it at the aerodrome of departure or destination, or by stopping it in the course of the journey on any landing, or by calling for it to be delivered at the place of destination or in the course of the journey to a person other than the consignee named in the air waybill, or by requiring it to be returned to the aerodrome of departure. He must not exercise this right of disposition in such a way as to prejudice the carrier or other consignors and he must repay any expenses occasioned by the exercise of this right.

(2) If it is impossible to carry out the orders of the consignor the carrier must so inform him forthwith.

1. E.g. *Hitachi Data Systems Corp.* v. *United Parcel Service Inc.*, 76 F. 3d 276 (9th Cir., 1996).

(3) If the carrier obeys the orders of the consignor for the disposition of the cargo without requiring the production of the part of the air waybill delivered to the latter he will be liable, without prejudice to his right of recovery from the consignor, for any damage which may be caused thereby to any person who is lawfully in possession of that part of the air waybill.

(4) The right conferred on the consignor ceases at the moment when that of the consignee begins in accordance with Article 13. Nevertheless, if the consignee declines to accept the waybill or the cargo, or if he cannot be communicated with, the consignor resumes his right of disposition.

Comment

3.326 Article 12, which confers this right of disposal on the consignor with regard to his cargo during the carriage by air, is the same as HP, Article 12 (para. 3.79, above).

3.327 **Article 13—Delivery/non-arrival**

(1) Except in the circumstances set out in the preceding Article, the consignee is entitled, on arrival of the cargo at the place of destination, to require the carrier to hand over to him the air waybill and to deliver the cargo to him, on payment of the charges due and on complying with the conditions of carriage set out in the air waybill.

(2) Unless it is otherwise agreed, it is the duty of the carrier to give notice to the consignee as soon as the cargo arrives.

(3) If the carrier admits the loss of the cargo, or if the cargo has not arrived at the expiration of seven days after the date on which it ought to have arrived, the consignee is entitled to put into force against the carrier the rights which flow from the contract of carriage.

Comment

3.328 Article 13 is the same as HP, Article 13 (para. 3.86, above).

3.329 **Article 14—Shipper/consignee rights**

The consignor and consignee can respectively enforce all the rights given them by Articles 12 and 13, each in his own name, whether he is acting in his own interest or in the interest of another provided that he carries out the obligations imposed by the contract.

Comment

3.330 Article 14 is the same as Article 14 of HP (para. 3.91, above).

3.331 **Article 15—Waiver**

(1) Articles 12, 13 and 14 do not affect either the relations of the consignor or the consignee with each other or the mutual relations of third parties whose rights are derived either from the consignor or from the consignee.

(2) The provisions of Articles 12, 13 and 14 can only be varied by express provision in the air waybill.

(3) [No longer applicable.]

Comment

Article 15 is the same as Article 15 of HP (para. 3.93, above). *3.332*

Article 16—Shipper's documents: customs etc. *3.333*

(1) The consignor must furnish such information and attach to the air waybill such documents as are necessary to meet the formalities of customs, octroi or police before the cargo can be delivered to the consignee. The consignor is liable to the carrier for any damage occasioned by the absence, insufficiency or irregularity of any such information or documents, unless the damage is due to the fault of the carrier or his servants or agents.

(2) The carrier is under no obligation to enquire into the correctness or sufficiency of such information or documents.

Comment

Article 16 is the same as Article 16 of HP (para. 3.96, above). *3.334*

Chapter III: Liability of the carrier *3.335*

Article 18—Carrier's liability: loss, damage

(1) The carrier is liable for damage sustained in the event of the destruction or loss of, or of damage to, any registered baggage or any cargo, if the occurrence which caused the damage so sustained took place during the carriage by air.

(2) The carriage by air within the meaning of the preceding paragraph comprises the period during which the baggage or cargo is in charge of the carrier, whether in an aerodrome or on board an aircraft, or, in the case of a landing outside an aerodrome, in any place whatsoever.

(3) The period of the carriage by air does not extend to any carriage by land, by sea or by river performed outside an aerodrome. If, however, such a carriage takes place in the performance of a contract for carriage by air, for the purpose of loading, delivery or transhipment, any damage is presumed, subject to proof of the contrary, to have been the result of an event which took place during the carriage by air.

Comment

Under Article 18, which is the central provision of the liability regime, the carrier is liable unless the carrier can establish one of the defences set out in Articles 20 or 21. Article 18 is the same as HP, Article 18 (para. 3.99, above). *3.336*

Article 19—Carrier's liability: delay *3.337*

The carrier is liable for damage occasioned by delay in the carriage by air of passengers, baggage or cargo.

Comment

Article 19 is the same as Article 19 of HP (para. 3.111, above). Under Article 19 the carrier is liable for damage occasioned by delay unless the carrier can establish one *3.338* of the defences set out in Article 20 or Article 21. If the consignor is responsible for the delay, the carrier may be entitled to indemnity from the consignor under Article 10 or Article 16. Concerning the meaning of delay, see Comment 1 on Condition 8 of the Conditions of Contract (IATA Resolution 600b (II)), paragraphs 3.772, *et seq.*, below.

3.339 **Article 20—Defence**

(1) The carrier is not liable if he proves that he and his servants or agents have taken all necessary measures to avoid the damage or that it was impossible for him or them to take such measures.

(2) In the carriage of cargo and baggage the carrier is not liable if he proves that the damage was occasioned by negligent pilotage or negligence in the handling of the aircraft or in navigation and that, in all other respects, he and his servants or agents have taken all necessary measures to avoid the damage.

Comment

3.340 Article 20(1) is the same as Article 20 of HP (para. 3.116, above), in which, however, Article 20(2) of WC was not reproduced as it had become unnecessary in view of advances in aviation.

3.341 **Article 21—Contributory negligence**

If the carrier proves that the damage was caused or contributed to by the negligence of the injured person, the court may, in accordance with the provisions of its own law, exonerate the carrier wholly or partly from his liability.

Comment

3.342 Article 21 is the same as Article 21 of HP (para. 3.122, above).

3.343 **Article 22—Limitation of liability**

(1) [Concerns the limit of liability to passengers.]

(2) In the carriage of registered baggage and of cargo, the liability of the carrier is limited to a sum of 250 francs per kilogramme, unless the consignor has made, at the time when the package was handed over to the carrier, a special declaration of the value at delivery and has paid a supplementary sum if the case so requires. In that case the carrier will be liable to pay a sum not exceeding the declared sum, unless he proves that that sum is greater than the actual value to the consignor at delivery.

(3) [Concerns the limit of liability of which the passenger takes charge.]

(4) The sums mentioned above shall be deemed to refer to the French franc consisting of $65\frac{1}{2}$ milligrammes of gold of millesimal fineness 900. These sums may be converted into any national currency in round figures.

Comments

3.344 As regards cargo Article 22(2) is in substance similar to Article 22(2)(a) of HP (para. 3.125, above). Article 22(4) is substantially the same as Article 22(5) and (6) of MP4. Article 22, which is central to the liability regime, should be read in conjunction with Article 23, Article 24 and Article 25. See also the Comments on Condition 7 of the Conditions of Contract (IATA Resolution 600b (II)), paragraphs 3.772 *et seq.*, below.

The francs referred to in Article 22 are a currency unit having a gold value set out in Article 22(4): this (now notional) currency unit derives from the gold value of the French franc at the time that WC came into force. For conversion into pounds sterling see the Carriage by Air (Sterling Equivalents) Order 1999 (S.I. 1999 No. 2881). The unit was replaced in subsequent versions of the regime such as HP by SDRs. *3.345*

Article 23—Convention paramount *3.346*

Any provision tending to relieve the carrier of liability or to fix a lower limit than that which is laid down in this Schedule shall be null and void, but the nullity of any such provision does not involve the nullity of the whole contract, which shall remain subject to the provisions of this Schedule.

Comment

Article 23 is the same as Article 23(1) of HP (para. 3.137, above). *3.347*

Article 24—Convention paramount *3.348*

In the cases covered by Articles 18 and 19 any action for damages, however founded, can only be brought subject to the conditions and limits set out in this Schedule.

Comment

Article 24 is the same as Article 24(1) of HP (para. 3.144, above). *3.349*

Article 25—Disapplication of limitation of liability *3.350*

(1) The carrier shall not be entitled to avail himself of the provisions of this Schedule which exclude or limit his liability, if the damage is caused by his wilful misconduct or by such default on his part as, in accordance with the law of the Court seised of the case, is considered to be equivalent to wilful misconduct.

(2) Similarly the carrier shall not be entitled to avail himself of the said provisions, if the damage is caused as aforesaid by any servant or agent of the carrier acting within the scope of his employment.

Comment

Article 25 has the same role as Article 25 of HP. However, the wording is significantly different in that the test of grave conduct is different from that found in Article 25 of HP, in which "wilful misconduct" was replaced by wording intended to have the same meaning but believed to be better understood, in particular, by *3.351* non-common law courts; see Comment 2 on Article 25 of HP (paras. 3.150 *et seq.*, above). Similar provisions referring to "wilful misconduct" are still found in other Conventions concerning the international carriage of goods such as CMR (Article 29) and CIM (Article 44). Concerning the way courts conduct the inquiry into the alleged misconduct, see Comment 2 on Article 25 of HP (paras. 3.150 *et seq.*, above). Concerning the identity of servants and agents, see Comment 2 on Article 25A of HP (paras. 3.163 *et seq.*, above).

3.352 **Article 26—Complaint**

(1) Receipt by the person entitled to delivery of the baggage or cargo without complaint is prima facie evidence that the same has been delivered in good condition and in accordance with the document of carriage.

(2) In the case of damage, the person entitled to delivery must complain to the carrier forthwith after the discovery of the damage and, at the latest, within three days from the date of receipt in the case of baggage and seven days from the date of receipt in the case of cargo. In the case of delay the complaint must be made at the latest within fourteen days from the date on which the baggage or cargo has been placed at his disposal.

(3) Every complaint must be made in writing upon the document of carriage or by separate notice in writing despatched within the times aforesaid.

(4) Failing complaint within the times aforesaid, no action shall lie against the carrier, save in the case of fraud on his part.

Comment

3.353 Article 26 is the same as HP Article 26 (para. 3.169, above) except that in HP the periods of time were changed from three days to seven days (damage to baggage), from seven days to four days (damage to cargo) and 14 days to 21 days (delay). As to the meaning of days, see Article 35. As to the meaning of delay, see Comment 1 on Condition 8 of the Conditions of Contract (IATA Resolution 600b (II)), paragraphs 3.772 *et seq.*, below.

3.354 **Article 28—Jurisdiction**

(1) An action for damages must be brought, at the option of the plaintiff, in the territory of one of the High Contracting Parties to the Warsaw Convention, either before the court having jurisdiction where the carrier is ordinarily resident, or has his principal place of business, or has an establishment by which the contract has been made or before the court having jurisdiction at the place of destination.

(2) Questions of procedure shall be governed by the law of the court seised of the case.

Comment

3.355 Article 28 is the same as Article 28 of HP (para. 3.173, above).

3.356 **Article 29—Time bar**

(1) The right to damages shall be extinguished if an action is not brought within two years reckoned from the date of arrival at the destination or from the date on which the aircraft ought to have arrived, or from the date on which the carriage stopped.

(2) The method of calculating the period of limitation shall be determined by the law of the Court seised of the case.

Comment

Article 29 is the same as Article 29 of HP (para. 3.181, above). *3.357*

Article 30—Successive carriage *3.358*

(1) In the case of carriage to be performed by various successive carriers and falling within the definition set out in the third paragraph of Article 1, each carrier who accepts passengers, baggage or cargo is subjected to the rules set out in this Schedule, and is deemed to be one of the contracting parties to the contract of carriage in so far as the contract deals with that part of the carriage which is performed under his supervision.

(2) [Concerns successive carriage of passengers.]

(3) As regards baggage or cargo, the passenger or consignor will have a right of action against the first carrier, and the passenger or consignee who is entitled to delivery will have a right of action against the last carrier, and further, each may take action against the carrier who performed the carriage during which the destruction, loss, damage or delay took place. These carriers will be jointly and severally liable to the passenger or to the consignor or consignee.

Comment

Article 30 is substantially the same as Article 30 of HP (para. 3.190, above). The rights of action referred to are subject to Article 28. *3.359*

Chapter IV: Provisions relating to combined carriage *3.360*

Article 31—Combined carriage

(1) In the case of combined carriage performed partly by air and partly by any other mode of carriage, the provisions of this Schedule apply only to the carriage by air, provided that the carriage by air falls within the terms of Article 1.

(2) Nothing in this Schedule shall prevent the parties in the case of combined carriage from inserting in the document of air carriage conditions relating to other modes of carriage, provided that the provisions of this Schedule are observed as regards the carriage by air.

Comment

Article 31 is substantially the same as Article 31 of HP (para. 3.196, above). *3.361*

Chapter V: General and final provisions *3.362*

Article 32—Prohibition on contracting-out

Any clause contained in the contract and all special agreements entered into before the damage occurred by which the parties purport to infringe the rules laid down by this Schedule, whether by deciding the law to be applied, or by altering the rules as to jurisdiction shall be null and void. Nevertheless for the carriage of cargo arbitration clauses are allowed subject to this Schedule, if the arbitration is to take place within one of the jurisdictions referred to in the first paragraph of Article 28.

Comment

3.363 Article 32 is substantially the same as Article 32 of HP (para. 3.198, above). Article 32 reiterates the policy of an intended uniform code of law relating to international carriage by air. See also Article 23.

3.364

Article 33—Freedom to contract

Nothing contained in this Schedule shall prevent the carrier from refusing to enter into any contract of carriage, or from making regulations which do not conflict with the provisions of this Schedule.

Comment

3.365 Article 33 is substantially the same as Article 33 of HP (para. 3.200, above).

3.366

Article 34—Extraordinary carriage

This Schedule does not apply to international carriage by air performed by way of experimental trial by air navigation undertakings with the view to the establishment of a regular line of air navigation, nor does it apply to carriage performed in extraordinary circumstances outside the normal scope of an air carrier's business.

Comment

3.367 Article 34 is a provision which evidently reflects the conditions in which commercial aviation was developing at the time that WC was agreed. The corresponding provision of HP, Article 34, does not include the case of experimental trial by air navigation undertakings with the view to the establishment of a regular line of air navigation.

3.368

Article 35—Days: meaning

The expression "days" when used in this Schedule means current days not working days.

Comment

3.369 Article 35 is relevant to consignee rights under Article 13 and to complaints under Article 26. Apart from one unimportant difference of wording it is the same as Article 35 of HP (para. 3.202, above).

APPLICATION OF THE GUADALAJARA CONVENTION

The Guadalajara Convention[1] is applicable to carriage to which this version of WC applies in the following form: *3.370*

Article I *3.371*

In the Guadalajara Convention as applied by this Schedule:

(a) "The Warsaw Convention" means the 1955 amended Convention as applied by this Schedule;

(b) "contracting carrier" means a person who as a principal makes an agreement for carriage governed by the Warsaw Convention with a passenger or consignor or with a person acting on behalf of the passenger or consignor;

(c) "actual carrier" means a person, other than the contracting carrier, who, by virtue of authority from the contracting carrier, performs the whole or part of the carriage contemplated in paragraph (b) but who is not with respect to such part a successive carrier within the meaning of the Warsaw Convention. Such authority is presumed in the absence of proof to the contrary.

Article II *3.372*

If an actual carrier performs the whole or part of carriage which, according to the agreement referred to in Article I, paragraph (b), is governed by the Warsaw Convention, both the contracting carrier and the actual carrier shall, except as otherwise provided in the Guadalajara Convention as applied by this Schedule, be subject to the rules of the Warsaw Convention, the former for the whole of the carriage contemplated in the agreement, the latter solely for the carriage which he performs.

Article III *3.373*

1. The acts and omissions of the actual carrier and of his servants and agents acting within the scope of their employment shall, in relation to the carriage performed by the actual carrier, be deemed to be also those of the contracting carrier.

2. The acts and omissions of the contracting carrier and of his servants and agents acting within the scope of their employment shall, in relation to the carriage performed by the actual carrier, be deemed to be also those of the actual carrier. Nevertheless, no such act or omission shall subject the actual carrier to liability exceeding the limits specified in Article 22 of the Warsaw Convention. Any special agreement under which the contracting carrier assumes obligations not imposed by the Warsaw Convention or any waiver of rights conferred by that Convention or any special declaration of interest in delivery at destination contemplated in Article 22 of the said Convention, shall not affect the actual carrier unless agreed by him.

Article IV *3.374*

Any complaint to be made or order to be given under the Warsaw Convention to the carrier shall have the same effect whether addressed to the contracting carrier or to the actual carrier. Nevertheless, orders referred to in Article 12 of the Warsaw Convention shall only be effective if addressed to the contracting carrier.

1. Paras. 3.463 *et seq.*, below.

3.375 **Article V**

In relation to the carriage performed by the actual carrier, any servant or agent of that carrier or of the contracting carrier shall, if he proves that he acted within the scope of his employment be entitled to avail himself of the limits of liability which are applicable under the Guadalajara Convention as applied by this Schedule to the carrier whose servant or agent he is unless it is proved that he acted in a manner which, under the Warsaw Convention, prevents the limits of liability from being invoked.

3.376 **Article VI**

In relation to the carriage performed by the actual carrier, the aggregate of the amounts recoverable from that carrier and the contracting carrier, and from their servants and agents acting within the scope of their employment, shall not exceed the highest amount which could be awarded against either the contracting carrier or the actual carrier under the Guadalajara Convention as applied by this Schedule, but none of the persons mentioned shall be liable for a sum in excess of the limit applicable to him.

3.377 **Article VII**

In relation to the carriage performed by the actual carrier, an action for damages may be brought, at the option of the plaintiff, against that carrier or the contracting carrier, or against both together or separately. If the action is brought against only one of those carriers, that carrier shall have the right to require the other carrier to be joined in the proceedings, the procedure and effects being governed by the law of the Court seised of the case.

3.378 **Article VIII**

Any action for damages contemplated in Article VII of the Guadalajara Convention as applied by this Schedule must be brought, at the option of the plaintiff, either before a Court in which an action may be brought against the contracting carrier, as provided in Article 28 of the Warsaw Convention, or before the Court having jurisdiction at the place where the actual carrier is ordinarily resident or has his principal place of business.

3.379 **Article IX**

1. Any contractual provision tending to relieve the contracting carrier or the actual carrier of liability under the Guadalajara Convention as applied by this Schedule or to fix a lower limit than that which is applicable according to the Guadalajara Convention as applied by this Schedule shall be null and void, but the nullity of any such provision does not involve the nullity of the whole agreement, which shall remain subject to the provisions of the Guadalajara Convention as applied by this Schedule.

2. In respect of the carriage performed by the actual carrier, the preceding paragraph shall not apply to contractual provisions governing loss or damage resulting from the inherent defect, quality or vice of the cargo carried.

3. Any clause contained in an agreement for carriage and all special agreements entered into before the damage occurred by which the parties purport to infringe the rules laid down by the Guadalajara Convention as applied by this Schedule, whether by deciding the law to be applied, or by altering the rules as to jurisdiction, shall be null and void. Nevertheless, for the carriage of cargo arbitration clauses are allowed, subject to the Guadalajara Convention as applied by this Schedule, if the arbitration is to take place in one of the jurisdictions referred to in Article VIII.

Article X *3.380*

Except as provided in Article VII, nothing in the Guadalajara Convention as applied by this Schedule shall affect the rights and obligations of the two carriers between themselves.

[*The next paragraph is 3.389*]

V. THE CONVENTION AS AMENDED BY ADDITIONAL PROTOCOL NO. 1 AS GIVEN FORCE OF LAW IN THE UK BY THE 1967 ORDER, SCHEDULE 3[1]

3.389 **Convention for the Unification of Certain Rules Relating to International Carriage by Air**

Chapter 1: Scope—Definitions

Article 1—Definitions

(1) This Schedule applies to all international carriage of persons, baggage or cargo performed by aircraft for reward. It applies equally to gratuitous carriage by aircraft performed by an air transport undertaking.

(2) For the purposes of this Schedule, "international carriage" means any carriage in which, according to the contract made by the parties, the place of departure and the place of destination, whether or not there be a break in the carriage or a transhipment, are situated either within the territories of two States Parties to the Convention for the Unification of Certain Rules relating to International Carriage by Air signed at Warsaw on behalf of His Majesty on 12th October 1929 as amended by Additional Protocol No. 1 of Montreal 1975 or within the territory of a single such State, if there is an agreed stopping place within the territory subject to the sovereignty, suzerainty, mandate or authority of another State, even though that State is not a party to the said Convention of 1929.

(3) A carriage to be performed by several successive air carriers is deemed for the purposes of this Schedule, to be one undivided carriage, if it has been regarded by the parties as a single operation, whether it had been agreed upon under the form of a single contract or of a series of contracts, and it does not lose its international character merely because one contract or a series of contracts is to be performed entirely within a territory subject to the sovereignty, suzerainty, mandate or authority of the same High Contracting Party.

Comment

3.390 Article 1 defines the contracts to which the regime applies. The Carriage by Air (Parties to Convention) Order 1999, Schedule 1 (S.I. 1999/1313), is conclusive evidence of who are the High Contracting Parties to this version of the regime. The text set out here was incorporated into the 1967 Order by the Carriage by Air Acts (Application of Provisions) (Fourth Amendment) Order 1998, in force 2 May 1998. That 1998 Order gives force of law to the English text of the Convention incorporating a modified version of the supplementary Convention done at Guadalajara[2] to contracts that are governed by the Additional Protocol No. 1[3] which introduces a new unit of account—the special drawing right—for the purposes of such carriage. Accordingly, in the UK, such carriage is governed by a version of the Convention amended in these respects. The other principal differences from the 1967 Order, Schedule 2, are the deletion herein of Articles 15(3) and 25A. For further comments on this text reference should be made to the corresponding provisions of WC (without the amendments made by Montreal

1. Being the English text of the Warsaw Convention without the Hague Protocol amendments but as amended by Montreal Additional Protocol No. 1 and as supplemented by the Guadalajara Convention.

2. Paras. 3.525 *et seq.*, below.

3. Cm. 3823.

Additional Protocol No. 1) and the supplementary Convention done at Guadalajara.[4]

In particular, it will be seen that Article 1 is the same as Article 1 of HP (para. 3.37, above), apart from minor differences. For example, the latter refers to "This Convention" where Article 2 refers to "This Schedule": a reference to this version of the Convention (WC) as enacted in the UK by Schedule 3 to the 1967 Order. For the carriage of mail and postal packages see the 1967 Order, Schedule 1.[5] *3.391*

Article 2—State/mail *3.392*

(1) This Schedule applies to carriage performed by the State, not being a State which has availed itself of the Additional Protocol to the Warsaw Convention, or by legally constituted public bodies, provided it falls within the conditions laid down in Article 1.

(2) This Schedule does not apply to carriage performed under the terms of any international postal Convention.

Comment

Article 2 is substantially the same as Article 2 of HP (para. 3.51, above). As regards Article 2(2), see the Carriage by Air (Parties to Convention) Order 1999, Schedule 2 (S.I. 1999/1313). Article 2 here is not referring to Additional Protocol No. 1. *3.393*

Chapter II: Documents of Carriage *3.394*

Section 3—Air Waybill

Article 5—Air waybill requirement

(1) Every carrier of cargo has the right to require the consignor to make out and hand over to him a document called an "air waybill", every consignor has the right to require the carrier to accept this document.

(2) The absence, irregularity or loss of this document does not affect the existence or the validity of the contract of carriage which shall, subject to the provisions of Article 9, be none the less governed by the rules of this Schedule.

Comment

Article 5 is substantially the same as Article 5 of HP (para. 3.53, above). For the particulars that must be included in the air waybill, see Article 8. For the sanctions against the carrier in the event of non-compliance with Article 8, see Article 9. For the shipper's responsibility to the carrier with regard to the air waybill and the carrier's sanctions against the shipper, see Article 10. For when these requirements are waived, see Article 34. *3.395*

4. Paras. 3.525 *et seq.*, below.
5. Paras. 3.463 *et seq.*, below.

3.396 **Article 6—Air waybill: form of**

(1) The air waybill shall be made out by the consignor in three original parts and be handed over with the cargo.

(2) The first part shall be marked "for the carrier", and shall be signed by the consignor. The second part shall be marked "for the consignee"; it shall be signed by the consignor and by the carrier and shall accompany the cargo. The third part shall be signed by the carrier and handed by him to the consignor after the cargo has been accepted.

(3) The carrier shall sign on acceptance of the cargo.

(4) The signature of the carrier may be stamped; that of the consignor may be printed or stamped.

(5) If, at the request of the consignor, the carrier makes out the air waybill, he shall be deemed, subject to proof to the contrary, to have done so on behalf of the consignor.

Comment

3.397 Article 6 is the same as Article 6 of HP (para. 3.57, above), except for a slight change in the wording of Article 6(3).

3.398 **Article 7—Air waybill: multiple packages**

The carrier of cargo has the right to require the consignor to make out separate waybills when there is more than one package.

Comment

3.399 Article 7 is the same as Article 7 of HP (para. 3.61, above).

3.400 **Article 8—Mandatory contents**

The air waybill shall contain the following particulars:

(a) the place and date of its execution;
(b) the place of departure and of destination;
(c) the agreed stopping places, provided that the carrier may reserve the right to alter the stopping places in case of necessity, and that if he exercises that right the alteration shall not have the effect of depriving the carriage of its international character;
(d) the name and address of the consignor;
(e) the name and address of the first carrier;
(f) the name and address of the consignee, if the case so requires;
(g) the nature of the cargo;
(h) the number of the packages, the method of packing and the particular marks or numbers upon them;
(i) the weight, the quantity and the volume or dimensions of the cargo;
(j) the apparent condition of the cargo and of the packing;
(k) the freight, if it has been agreed upon, the date and place of payment, and the person who is to pay it;
(l) if the cargo is sent for payment on delivery, the price of the cargo, and, if the case so requires, the amount of the expenses incurred;
(m) the amount of the value declared in accordance with Article 22(2);
(n) the number of parts of the air waybill;
(o) the documents handed to the carrier to accompany the air waybill;
(p) the time fixed for the completion of the carriage and a brief note of the route to be followed, if these matters have been agreed upon;

(q) a statement that the carriage is subject to the rules relating to liability established by the Warsaw Convention.

Comment

Article 8 has the same role as Article 8 of HP, however, the latter requires fewer entries in the air waybill. *3.401*

Article 9—Air waybill: non-compliance *3.402*

If the carrier accepts cargo without an air waybill having been made out or if the air waybill does not contain all the particulars set out in Article 8(a) to (i) inclusive and (q), the carrier shall not be entitled to avail himself of the provisions of this Schedule which exclude or limit his liability.

Comment

Article 9 is essentially the same as Article 9 of HP (para. 3.66, above). *3.403*

Article 10—Air waybill: shipper's responsibility *3.404*

(1) The consignor is responsible for the correctness of the particulars and statements relating to the cargo, which he inserts in the air waybill.

(2) The consignor will be liable for all damage suffered by the carrier or any other person by reason of the irregularity, incorrectness or incompleteness of the said particulars and statements.

Comment

Article 10 is the same as Article 10 of HP (para. 3.68, above), except that the liability for all damage suffered by the carrier or any other person was replaced by an obligation to indemnify the carrier against all damage suffered by the carrier or any other person to whom the carrier is liable. *3.405*

Article 11—Air waybill: as evidence of contract *3.406*

(1) The air waybill is prima facie evidence of the conclusion of the contract, of the receipt of the cargo and of the conditions of carriage.

(2) The statements in the air waybill relating to the weight, dimensions and packing of the cargo, as well as those relating to the number of packages, are prima facie evidence of the facts stated; those relating to the quantity, volume and condition of the cargo do not constitute evidence against the carrier except so far as they both have been, and are stated in the air waybill to have been, checked by him in the presence of the consignor, or relate to the apparent condition of the cargo.

Comment

Article 11 is the same as Article 11 of HP (para. 3.72, above). *3.407*

3.408 **Article 12—Shipper's disposal instructions**

(1) Subject to his liability to carry out all his obligations under the contract of carriage, the consignor has the right to dispose of the cargo by withdrawing it at the aerodrome of departure or destination, or by stopping it in the course of the journey on any landing, or by calling for it to be delivered at the place of destination or in the course of the journey to a person other than the consignee named in the air waybill, or by requiring it to be returned to the aerodrome of departure. He must not exercise this right of disposition in such a way as to prejudice the carrier or other consignors and he must repay any expenses occasioned by the exercise of this right.

(2) If it is impossible to carry out the orders of the consignor the carrier must so inform him forthwith.

(3) If the carrier obeys the orders of the consignor for the disposition of the cargo without requiring the production of the part of the air waybill delivered to the latter he will be liable, without prejudice to his right of recovery from the consignor, for any damage which may be caused thereby to any person who is lawfully in possession of that part of the air waybill.

(4) The right conferred on the consignor ceases at the moment when that of the consignee begins in accordance with Article 13. Nevertheless, if the consignee declines to accept the waybill or the cargo, or if he cannot be communicated with, the consignor resumes his right of disposition.

Comment

3.409 Article 12 is the same as Article 12 of HP (para. 3.79, above).

3.410 **Article 13—Delivery/non-arrival**

(1) Except in the circumstances set out in the preceding Article, the consignee is entitled, on arrival of the cargo at the place of destination, to require the carrier to hand over to him the air waybill and to deliver the cargo to him, on payment of the charges due and on complying with the conditions of carriage set out in the air waybill.

(2) Unless it is otherwise agreed, it is the duty of the carrier to give notice to the consignee as soon as the cargo arrives.

(3) If the carrier admits the loss of the cargo or if the cargo has not arrived at the expiration of seven days after the date on which it ought to have arrived, the consignee is entitled to put into force against the carrier the rights which flow from the contract of carriage.

Comment

3.411 Article 13 is the same as Article 13 of HP (para. 3.86, above).

3.412 **Article 14—Shipper/consignee rights**

The consignor and the consignee can respectively enforce all the rights given them by Articles 12 and 13, each in his own name, whether he is acting in his own interest or in the interest of another, provided that he carries out the obligations imposed by the contract.

Comment

3.413 Article 14 is the same as Article 14 of HP (para. 3.91, above).

Article 15—Waiver *3.414*

(1) Articles 12, 13 and 14 do not affect either the relations of the consignor or the consignee with each other or the mutual relations of third parties whose rights are derived either from the consignor or from the consignee.

(2) The provisions of Articles 12, 13 and 14 can only be varied by express provision in the air waybill.

Comment

Article 15 is the same as Article 15(1) and (2) of HP (para. 3.93, above). *3.415*

Article 16—Shipper's documents: customs etc. *3.416*

(1) The consignor must furnish such information and attach to the air waybill such documents as are necessary to meet the formalities of customs, octroi or police before the cargo can be delivered to the consignee. The consignor is liable to the carrier for any damage occasioned by the absence, insufficiency or irregularity of any such information or documents, unless the damage is due to the fault of the carrier or his servants or agents.

(2) The carrier is under no obligation to enquire into the correctness or sufficiency of such information or documents.

Comment

Article 16 is the same as HP Article 16 (para. 3.96, above). *3.417*

Chapter III: Liability of the Carrier *3.418*

Article 17

[Article 17 concerns liability for damage sustained in the event of death or injury to passengers.]

Article 18—Carrier's liability: loss, damage *3.419*

(1) The carrier is liable for damage sustained in the event of the destruction or loss of, or of damage to, any registered baggage or any cargo, if the occurrence which caused the damage so sustained took place during the carriage by air.

(2) The carriage by air within the meaning of the preceding paragraph comprises the period during which the baggage or cargo is in charge of the carrier, whether in an aerodrome or on board an aircraft, or, in the case of a landing outside an aerodrome, in any place whatsoever.

(3) The period of the carriage by air does not extend to any carriage by land, by sea or by river performed outside an aerodrome. If, however, such a carriage takes place in the performance of a contract for carriage by air, for the purpose of loading, delivery or transhipment, any damage is presumed, subject to proof of the contrary, to have been the result of an event which took place during the carriage by air.

Comment

Article 18 is the same as HP Article 18 (para. 3.99, above). *3.420*

3.421 **Article 19—Carrier's liability: delay**

The carrier is liable for damage occasioned by delay in the carriage by air of passengers, baggage or cargo.

Comment

3.422 Article 19 is the same as Article 19 of HP (para. 3.111, above). Concerning the meaning of delay, see also Comment 1 on Condition 8 of the Conditions of Contract (IATA Resolution 600b (II)), paragraphs 3.772 *et seq.*, below.

3.423 **Article 20—Defence**

(1) The carrier is not liable if he proves that he and his servants or agents have taken all necessary measures to avoid the damage or that it was impossible for him or them to take such measures.

(2) In the carriage of cargo and baggage the carrier is not liable if he proves that the damage was occasioned by negligent pilotage or negligence in the handling of the aircraft or in navigation and that, in all other respects, he and his servants or agents have taken all necessary measures to avoid the damage.

Comment

3.424 Article 20(1) is the same as Article 20 of HP (para. 3.116, above), in which, however, Article 20(2) was not reproduced as it had become unnecessary in view of advances in aviation. Concerning the identity of servants and agents, see Article 25A of HP, Comment 2, paragraphs 3.163 *et seq.*, above.

3.425 **Article 21—Contributory fault**

If the carrier proves that the damage was caused by or contributed to by the negligence of the injured person, the court may, in accordance with the provisions of its own law, exonerate the carrier wholly or partly from his liability.

Comment

3.426 Article 21 is the same as HP, Article 21 (para. 3.122, above).

3.427 **Article 22—Limitation of liability**

(1) [Concerns passengers.]

(2) In the carriage of registered baggage and of cargo, the liability of the carrier is limited to a sum of 17 Special Drawing Rights per kilogramme, unless the consignor has made, at the time when the package was handed over to the carrier, a special declaration of the value at delivery and has paid a supplementary sum if the case so requires. In that case the carrier will be liable to pay a sum not exceeding the declared sum, unless he proves that that sum is greater than the actual value to the consignor at delivery.

[(3) Concerns passengers' hand luggage.]

(4) The sums mentioned in terms of the Special Drawing Rights in this Article shall be deemed to refer to the Special Drawing Right as defined by the International Monetary Fund. Conversion of the sums into national currencies shall, in case of judicial proceedings, be made according to the value of such currencies in terms of the Special Drawing Right at the date of the judgment. The value of a national currency, in terms of the Special Drawing Right, of a High Contracting Party which is a Member of the Monetary Fund, shall be calculated in accordance with the method of valuation applied by the International Monetary Fund, in effect at the date of the judgment, for its operations and transactions. The value of national currency, in terms of the Special Drawing Right, of a High Contracting Party which is not a Member of the International Monetary Fund, shall be calculated in a manner determined by that High Contracting Party.

Nevertheless, those States which are not Members of the International Monetary Fund and whose law does not permit the application of the provisions of paragraphs 1, 2 and 3 of Article 22 may at the time of ratification or accession or at any time thereafter declare that the limit of liability of the carrier in judicial proceedings in their territories is fixed at a sum of 125,000 monetary units per passenger with respect to paragraph 1 of Article 22; 250 monetary units per kilogramme with respect to paragraph 2 of Article 22; and 5,000 monetary units per passenger with respect to paragraph 3 of Article 22. This monetary unit corresponds to sixty-five and a half milligrammes of gold of millesimal fineness nine hundred. These sums may be converted into the national currency concerned in round figures. The conversion of these sums into national currency shall be made according to the law of the State concerned.

Comment

As regards cargo Article 22(2) is in substance similar to Article 22(a) of HP (para. 3.125, above). Article 22(4) is substantially the same as Article 22(5) and (6) of MP4 (para. 3.260, above). Article 22, which is central to the liability regime, should be read in conjunction with Article 23, Article 24 and Article 25. *3.428*

Article 23—Convention paramount *3.429*

Any provision tending to relieve the carrier of liability, or to fix a lower limit than that which is laid down in this Schedule shall be null and void, but the nullity of any such provision does not involve the nullity of the whole contract, which shall remain subject to the provisions of this Schedule.

Comment

Article 23 is the same as Article 23(1) of HP (para. 3.137, above). *3.430*

Article 24—Convention paramount *3.431*

In the cases covered by Articles 18 and 19 any action for damages, however founded, can only be brought subject to the conditions and limits set out in this Schedule.

Comment

Article 24 is the same as Article 24(1) of HP (para. 3.144, above). *3.432*

Article 25—Disapplication of limitation of liability *3.433*

(1) The carrier shall not be entitled to avail himself of the provisions of this Schedule which exclude or limit his liability, if the damage is caused by his wilful misconduct or by such default

on his part as, in accordance with the law of the Court seised of the case, is considered to be equivalent to wilful misconduct.

(2) Similarly the carrier shall not be entitled to avail himself of the said provisions, if the damage is caused as aforesaid by any servant or agent of the carrier acting within the scope of his employment.

Comment

3.434 Article 25 has the same role as Article 25 of HP. However, the wording is significantly different in that the test of grave conduct is different from that found in Article 25 of HP, in which "wilful misconduct" was replaced by wording intended to have the same meaning but believed to be better understood, in particular, by non-common law courts; see HP, Article 25, Comment 2, paragraphs 3.150 *et seq.*, above. Similar provisions referring to "wilful misconduct" are still found in other Conventions concerning the international carriage of goods such as CMR (Article 29, para. 1.164, above) and CIM (Article 44, para. 3.265, above). Concerning the identity of servants and agents, see Article 25A of HP, Comment 2, paragraphs 3.163 *et seq.*, above.

3.435

Article 26—Complaint

(1) Receipt by the person entitled to delivery of baggage or cargo without complaint is prima facie evidence that the same has been delivered in good condition and in accordance with the document of carriage.

(2) In the case of damage, the person entitled to delivery must complain to the carrier forthwith after the discovery of the damage, and, at the latest, within three days from the date of receipt in the case of baggage and seven days from the date of receipt in the case of cargo. In the case of delay the complaint must be made at the latest within fourteen days from the date on which the baggage or cargo has been placed at his disposal.

(3) Every complaint must be made in writing upon the document of carriage or by separate notice in writing despatched within the times aforesaid.

(4) Failing complaint within the times aforesaid, no action shall lie against the carrier, save in the case of fraud on his part.

Comment

3.436 Article 26 is the same as HP, Article 26 (para. 3.169, above), except that in HP the periods of time were changed from three days to seven days (damage to baggage), from seven days to four days (damage to cargo) and 14 days to 21 days (delay). As to the meaning of days, see Article 35. Concerning the meaning of delay, see Comment 1 on Condition 8 of the Conditions of Contract (IATA Resolution 600b (II)) (paras. 3.772 *et seq.*, below).

3.437

Article 28—Jurisdiction

(1) An action for damages must be brought, at the option of the plaintiff, in the territory of one of the High Contracting Parties to the Warsaw Convention as amended by Additional Protocol No. 1 of Montreal 1975 either before the court having jurisdiction where the carrier is ordinarily resident, or has his principal place of business, or has an establishment by which

the contract has been made or before the court having jurisdiction at the place of destination.

(2) Questions of procedure shall be governed by the law of the court seised of the case.

Comment

Article 28 is the same as Article 28 of HP (para. 3.173, above) except that the latter does not include the words "as amended by Additional Protocol No. 1 of Montreal 1975". *3.438*

Article 29—Time bar *4.439*

(1) The right to damages shall be extinguished if an action is not brought within two years reckoned from the date of arrival at the destination, or from the date on which the aircraft ought to have arrived, or from the date on which the carriage stopped.

(2) The method of calculating the period6 of limitation shall be determined by the law of the court seised of the case.

Comment

Article 29 is the same as Article 29 of HP (para. 3.181, above). *3.440*

Article 30—Successive carriage *3.441*

(1) In the case of carriage to be performed by various successive carriers and falling within the definition set out in the third paragraph of Article 1, each carrier who accepts passengers, baggage or cargo is subjected to the rules set out in this Schedule, and is deemed to be one of the contracting parties to the contract of carriage in so far as the contract deals with that part of the carriage which is performed under his supervision.

[(2) Concerns passengers' rights of action in certain cases.]

(3) As regards baggage or cargo, the passenger or consignor will have a right of action against the first carrier, and the passenger or consignee who is entitled to delivery will have a right of action against the last carrier, and further, each may take action against the carrier who performed the carriage during which the destruction, loss, damage or delay took place. These carriers will be jointly and severally liable to the passenger or to the consignor or consignee.

Comment

Article 30 is substantially the same as Article 30 of HP (para. 3.190, above). The rights of action referred to are subject to Article 28. *3.442*

Chapter IV: Provisions Relating to Combined Carriage *3.443*

Article 31—Combined carriage

(1) In the case of combined carriage performed partly by air and partly by any other mode of carriage, the provisions of this Schedule apply only to the carriage by air, provided that the carriage by air falls within the terms of Article 1.

(2) Nothing in this Schedule shall prevent the parties in the case of combined carriage from inserting in the document of air carriage conditions relating to other modes of carriage, provided that the provisions of this Schedule are observed as regards the carriage by air.

Comment

3.444 Article 31 is substantially the same as Article 31 of HP (para. 3.196, above).

3.445

Chapter V: General and Final Provisions

Article 32—Prohibition on contracting out

Any clause contained in the contract and all special agreements entered into before the damage occurred by which the parties purport to infringe the rules laid down by this Schedule, whether by deciding the law to be applied, or by altering the rules as to jurisdiction, shall be null and void. Nevertheless for the carriage of cargo arbitration clauses are allowed, subject to this Schedule, if the arbitration is to take place within one of the jurisdictions referred to in the first paragraph of Article 28.

Comment

3.446 Article 32 is substantially the same as Article 32 of HP (para. 3.198, above). Article 32 reiterates the policy of an intended uniform code of law relating to international carriage by air. See also Article 23.

3.447

Article 33—Freedom to contract

Nothing contained in this Schedule shall prevent the carrier either from refusing to enter into any contract of carriage, or from making regulations which do not conflict with the provisions of this Schedule.

Comment

3.448 Article 33 is substantially the same as Article 33 of HP (para. 3.200, above).

3.449

Article 34—Extraordinary carriage

This Schedule does not apply to international carriage by air performed by way of experimental trial by air navigation undertakings with the view to the establishment of a regular line of air navigation, nor does it apply to carriage performed in extraordinary circumstances outside the normal scope of an air carrier's business.

Comment

3.450 Article 34 is a provision which evidently reflects the conditions in which commercial aviation was developing at the time of WC. The corresponding provision of HP, Article 34, does not include the case of experimental trial by air navigation undertakings with the view to the establishment of a regular line of air navigation.

Article 35—Days: meaning of *3.451*

The expression "days" when used in this Schedule means current days not working days.

Comment

Article 35 is relevant to consignee rights under Article 13 and to complaints under Article 26. Apart from one unimportant difference of wording it is the same as Article 35 of HP (para. 3.202, above). *3.452*

APPLICATION OF THE GUADALAJARA CONVENTION

The Guadalajara Convention[1] is applicable to carriage to which the above regime applies in the form as set out above.[2] *3.453*

[*The next paragraph is 3.463*]

1. Paras. 3.525 *et seq.*, below.
2. See the final provisions of WC, as set out above at paras. 3.370 *et seq.*

VI. 1967 ORDER, SCHEDULE 1, AS IT APPLIES TO NON-INTERNATIONAL CARRIAGE AND THE CARRIAGE OF MAIL AND POSTAL PACKAGES[1]

3.463

Chapter I: Scope—definitions

Article 1—Definitions

(1) This Schedule applies to all carriage of persons, baggage or cargo performed by aircraft for reward. It applies equally to gratuitous carriage by aircraft performed by an air transport undertaking.

Comments

3.464 This regime was substituted by the Carriage by Air Acts (Application of Provisions) (Fifth Amendment) Order 1999 (S.I. 1999/1737). It applies a modified version of MP4, supplemented by the Guadalajara Convention to contracts for the carriage of goods by air which are not contracts for international carriage within the meaning of the 1967 Order, Schedule 2 or Schedule 3 nor of the 1961 Act, Schedule 1 (HP) or Schedule 1A (MP4). Note, however, that S.I. 1999/1737 was revoked by S.I. 2004/1899 which came into effect on 6 August 2004. The latter applies MC (below, paras. 3.555 *et seq.*) to carriage by air within the UK or carriage outside the scope of WC, WC as amended by Additional Protocol No. 1, HP, MP4 or MC. Note also, however, that S.I. 2004/1899, unlike earlier regulations of this kind, does not extend to the carriage of mail or postal packages.

3.465 This regime also applies to the carriage of mail and postal packets being a class of goods expressly excluded from Article 2 of WC and Article 2 of HP. The 1967 Order, paragraph (b), states that this modified version of the regime applies to the carriage of such matters. This does not expressly refer to mail or postal packages, and so presumably the provisions relating to cargo refer. However, the 1967 Order is overridden where a carrier acts as an agent or subcontractor of the Royal Mail which is effecting postal services under the Post Office Act 1969. Then the carrier is entitled to the immunity from proceedings in tort and bailment given to the Royal Mail except at the instance of the Royal Mail.[2]

3.466 The scope of the (non-international) carriage to which this regime might apply has been judicially considered, in the context of its possible extraterritorial application, as follows[3]:

(i) Carriage in which the places of departure and destination and agreed stopping places are all within the United Kingdom or other British territory is clearly within its scope. Reference to British territory is to the application of the provisions of the 1961 Act and of the 1967 Order to certain overseas territories: see Carriage by Air (Overseas Territories)

1. Being the English text of the Warsaw Convention as amended by the Hague Protocol and Montreal Protocol No. 4 (with modifications) and as supplemented by the Guadalajara Convention.

2. See the Post Office Act 1969, s. 29(1) and (3); and *American Express Co.* v. *British Airways Board* [1983] 1 W.L.R. 701.

3. *Holmes* v. *Bangladesh Biman Corp.* [1989] A.C. 1112, 1131.

Order 1967, S.I. 1967/809, and Carriage by Air Acts (Application of Provisions) (Overseas Territories) Order 1967, S.I. 1967/810.

(ii) Non-Convention carriage involving a place of departure or destination or agreed stopping place in a foreign state and a place of departure or destination or an agreed stopping place in the UK or other British territory. This Schedule applies "for relevant purposes" being presumably the determination of any claim before a court in the UK or relevant British territory.

(iii) Non-Convention carriage between places of departure and destination in two foreign states with no agreed stopping place in the UK or other British territory is not within the scope of the regime, as otherwise the Order would be asserting a jurisdiction over foreign firms which have done nothing to bring themselves within the jurisdiction of the UK courts.

(iv) Carriage in which the places of departure and destination and any agreed stopping places are all within the territory of a single foreign state, whether it is a Convention country or not, is not within the scope of the regime.

Accordingly carriage within categories (i) and (ii) is subject to the regime whereas carriage within categories (iii) and (iv) above is excluded from it: the enabling provisions in the 1961 Act (s. 10) have to be construed in conformity with the rule against giving extraterritorial effect to UK legislation. Persons and goods carried under a time charter of an aircraft where there are no fixed points of departure and of destination have, on particular facts (carriage within category (i)), been held to be within the scope of the regime.[4] *3.467*

Article 1 is substantially the same as Article 1 of HP except that the latter applies to international carriage whereas this regime does not. It should be recalled that where carriage is performed gratuitously and other than by an air transport undertaking it is not this regime but English common law rules that apply; see the Introduction to Part 3, Comment 8, paragraph 3.12, above. *3.468*

Article 2—Carriage by the State *3.469*

(1) This Schedule applies to carriage performed by the State or by legally constituted public bodies provided it falls within the conditions laid down in Article 1.

Comment

Article 2 is the same as Article 2 of MP4 (para. 3.221, above). *3.470*

Chapter II: Documents of carriage *3.471*

[This regime does not include provisions on carriage documents corresponding to those found in HP or MP4. Therefore an air waybill is not required in order to invoke the limitation of liability provisions contained in Article 22.]

4. *Herd* v. *Clyde Helicopters Ltd.* [1997] A.C. 534.

3.472

Chapter III: Liability of the carrier

Article 18—Carrier's liability: loss, damage

(2) The carrier is liable for damage sustained in the event of the destruction or loss of or of damage to cargo upon condition only that the occurrence which caused the damage so sustained took place during the carriage by air.

(3) However, the carrier is not liable if he proves that the destruction, loss of, or damage to, the cargo resulted solely from one or more of the following:

(a) inherent defect, quality or vice of that cargo;
(b) defective packing of that cargo performed by a person other than the carrier or his servants or agents;
(c) an act of war or an armed conflict;
(d) an act of a public authority carried out in connection with the entry, exit or transit of the cargo.

(4) The carriage by air within the meaning of the preceding paragraphs of this Article comprises the period during which the baggage or cargo is in charge of the carrier, whether in an airport or on board an aircraft, or, in the case of a landing outside an airport, in any place whatsoever.

(5) The period of the carriage by air does not extend to any carriage by land, by sea or by river performed outside an airport. If, however, such carriage takes place in the performance of a contract for carriage by air, for the purpose of loading, delivery or transhipment, any damage is presumed, subject to proof of the contrary, to have been the result of an event which took place during the carriage by air.

Comment

3.473 Under Article 18, which is the same as Article 18 of MP4 (para. 3.247, above), the carrier is liable unless it can establish one of the defences set out in Article 20 or 21.

3.474

Article 19—Carrier's liability: delay

The carrier is liable for damage occasioned by delay in the carriage by air of passengers, baggage or cargo.

Comment

3.475 Article 19, which is the same as Article 19 of MP4 (para. 3.254, above), establishes the liability rule for delay. The carrier is liable unless it can establish one of the defences set out in Articles 20 and 21. Note that the carrier is not entitled to indemnity from the consignor, as it is under WC and HP.

3.476

Article 20—Defence

In the carriage of passengers and baggage, and in the case of damage occasioned by delay in the carriage of cargo, the carrier shall not be liable if he proves that he and his servants or agents have taken all necessary measures to avoid the damage or that it was impossible for them to take such measures.

Comment

Article 20 is the same as Article 20 of MP4 (para. 3.256, above). *3.477*

Article 21—Contributory negligence *3.478*

(1) [Concerns passengers and luggage.]

(2) In the carriage of cargo, if the carrier proves that the damage was caused by or contributed to by the negligence or other wrongful act or omission of the person claiming compensation, or the person from whom he derives his rights, the carrier shall be wholly or partly exonerated from his liability to the claimant to the extent that such negligence or wrongful act or omission caused or contributed to the damage.

Comment

Article 21(2) is the same as Article 21(2) of MP4 (para. 3.258, above). *3.479*

Article 22—Limitation of liability *3.480*

(2) (a) In the carriage of cargo, the liability of the carrier is limited to a sum of 17 special drawing rights per kilogramme, unless the consignor has made, at the same time when the package was handed over to the carrier, a special declaration of interest in delivery at destination and has paid a supplementary sum, if the case so requires. In that case the carrier will be liable to pay a sum not exceeding the declared sum, unless he proves that that sum is greater than the consignor's actual interest in delivery at destination.

(b) In the case of loss, damage or delay of part of registered baggage or cargo, or of any object contained therein, the weight to be taken into consideration in determining the amount to which the carrier's liability is limited shall be only the total weight of the package or packages concerned. Nevertheless, when the loss, damage or delay of a part of the registered package or cargo, or of an object contained therein, affects the value of other packages covered by the same baggage check or the same air waybill, the total weight of such package or packages shall also be taken into consideration in determining the limit of liability.

(4) The limits prescribed in this Article shall not prevent the court from awarding, in accordance with its own law, in addition, the whole or part of the court costs and of the other expenses of the litigation incurred by the plaintiff. The foregoing provision shall not apply if the amount of the damages awarded, excluding court costs and other expenses of the litigation, does not exceed the sum which the carrier has offered in writing to the plaintiff within a period of six months from the date of the occurrence causing the damage, or before the commencement of the action, if that is later.

(5) The sums mentioned in terms of the special drawing rights in this Article shall be deemed to refer to the special drawing right as defined by the International Monetary Fund. Conversion of the sums into national currencies shall, in case of judicial proceedings, be made according to the value of such currencies in terms of the special drawing right at the date of judgment.

(6) The value on a particular day of one special drawing right shall be treated as equal to such a sum in sterling as the International Monetary Fund have fixed as being the equivalent of one special drawing right:

(a) for that day or

(b) if no sum has been so fixed for that day, for the last day before that day for which a sum has been so fixed.

(7) A certificate given by or on behalf of the treasury stating:

(a) that a particular sum in sterling has been fixed by the International Monetary Fund as referred to in paragraph (6) for a particular day; or

(b) that no sum has been so fixed for a particular day and that a particular sum in sterling has been so fixed for a day which is the last day for which a sum has been so fixed before the particular day,

shall be conclusive evidence of those matters for the purposes of this Article; and a document purporting to be such a certificate shall in any proceedings be received in evidence and, unless the contrary is proved, be deemed to be such a certificate.

Comment

3.481 Article 22(2)–(5) is substantially the same as Article 22(2)–(5) of MP4 (para. 3.260, above). It should be read in conjunction with Article 23, Article 24 and Article 25A. The regime is silent as to costs, costs incurred by the carrier or his servant or agent, of the kind that might be awarded under English law against a claimant, e.g. for failing at trial to be awarded damages exceeding a prior payment into court.

3.482

Article 23—Convention paramount

(1) Any provision tending to relieve the carrier of liability or to fix a lower limit than that which is laid down in this Schedule shall be null and void, but the nullity of any such provision does not involve the nullity of the whole contract, which shall remain subject to the provisions of this Schedule.

(2) Paragraph (1) of this Article shall not apply to provisions governing loss or damage resulting from the inherent defect, quality or vice of the cargo carried.

Comment

3.483 Article 23(1) is substantially the same as Article 23 of MP4 (para. 3.262, above).

3.484

Article 24—Convention paramount

(2) In the carriage of cargo, any action for damages, howsoever founded, whether under this Schedule or in contract or in tort or otherwise, can only be brought subject to the conditions and limits of liability set out in this Schedule without prejudice to the question as to who are the persons who have the right to bring suit and what are their respective rights. Such limits of liability constitute maximum limits and may not be exceeded whatever the circumstances which give rise to the liability.

Comment

3.485 Article 24(2) is the same as Article 24(2) of MP4 (para. 3.264, above).

3.486

Article 25A—Servant or agent of carrier

(1) If an action is brought against a servant or agent of the carrier arising out of damage to which this Schedule relates, such servant or agent, if he proves that he acted within the scope of his employment, shall be entitled to avail himself of the limits of liability which that carrier himself is able to invoke under Article 22.

(2) The aggregate of the amounts recoverable from the carrier, his servants and agents, in that case, shall not exceed the said limits.

Comment

Article 25A is substantially the same as Article 25A(1) and (2) of MP4 (para. 3.266, above). *3.487*

Article 26—Complaint *3.488*

(1) Receipt by the person entitled to delivery of baggage or cargo without complaint is prima facie evidence that the same has been delivered in good condition.

(2) In the case of damage, the person entitled to delivery must complain to the carrier forthwith after the discovery of the damage, and, at the latest, within seven days from the date of receipt in case of baggage and fourteen days from the date of receipt in the case of cargo. In the case of delay the complaint must be made at the latest within twenty-one days from the date on which the baggage or cargo have been placed at his disposal.

(3) Every complaint must be made in writing despatched within the times aforesaid.

(4) Failing complaint within the times aforesaid, no action shall lie against the carrier, save in the case of fraud on his part.

Comment

Article 26 is the same as Article 26 of MP4 (para. 3.268, above). *3.489*

Article 29—Time bar *3.490*

(1) The right to damages shall be extinguished if an action is not brought within two years reckoned from the date of arrival at the destination, or from the date on which the aircraft ought to have arrived, or from the date on which the carriage stopped.

(2) The method of calculating the period of limitation shall be determined by the law of the court seised of the case.

Comment

Article 29 is the same as Article 29 of MP4 (para. 3.274, above). *3.491*

Article 30—Successive carriage *3.492*

(1) In the case of carriage to be performed by various successive carriers, each carrier who accepts passengers, baggage or cargo is subjected to the rules set out in this Schedule and is deemed to be one of the contracting parties to the contract of carriage in so far as the contract deals with that part of the carriage which is performed under his supervision.

[(2) Concerns passengers.]

(3) As regards baggage or cargo, the passenger or consignor will have a right of action against the first carrier, and the passenger or consignee who is entitled to delivery will have a right of action against the last carrier, and further, each may take action against the carrier who performed the carriage during which the destruction, loss, damage or delay took place. These carriers will be jointly and severally liable to the passenger or to the consignor or consignee.

Comment

Article 30 is the same as Article 30 of MP4 (para. 3.276, above), except that the latter contains a cross-reference to Article 1 which would be inappropriate here. *3.493*

3.494 Note that, if a carrier substitutes another carrier to perform carriage the matter is not one of successive carriage, but dealt with under the provisions of the Guadalajara Convention[1] as applied to this regime.

3.495

Article 30A—Recourse

Nothing in this Schedule shall prejudice the question whether a person liable for damage in accordance with its provisions has a right of recourse against any other person.

Comment

3.496 Article 30A is the same as Article 30A of MP4 (para. 3.278, above)

3.497

Chapter IV: Provisions relating to combined carriage

Article 31—Combined carriage

(1) In the case of combined carriage performed partly by air and partly by any other mode of carriage, the provisions of this Schedule apply only to the carriage by air, provided that the carriage by air falls within the terms of Article 1.

(2) Nothing in this Schedule shall prevent the parties in the case of combined carriage from inserting in the document of air carriage conditions relating to other modes of carriage, provided that the provisions of this Schedule are observed as regards the carriage by air.

Comment

3.498 Article 31 is substantially the same as Article 31 of MP4 (para. 3.280, above).

3.499

Chapter V: General and final provisions

Article 32—Prohibition on contracting-out

Any clause contained in the contract and all special agreements entered into before the damage occurred by which the parties purport to infringe the rules laid down by this Schedule, whether by deciding the law to be applied, or by altering the rules as to jurisdiction, shall be null and void. Nevertheless for the carriage of cargo, arbitration clauses are allowed subject to this Schedule.

Comment

3.500 Article 32 is the same as Article 32 of MP4 (para. 3.282, above), except that the latter contains a cross-reference to Article 28 which would be inappropriate here. See also, however, Article 23, above.

1. Paras. 3.525 *et seq.*, below.

Article 33—Freedom to contract *3.501*

Except as provided in paragraph 3 of Article 5, nothing contained in this Schedule shall prevent the carrier either from refusing to enter into any contract of carriage or from making regulations which do not conflict with the provisions of this Schedule.

Comment

Article 33 is substantially the same as Article 33 of MP4 (para. 3.284, above). *3.502*

Article 35—Days: meaning *3.503*

The expression "days" when used in this Schedule means current days not working days.

Comment

Article 35 is substantially the same as Article 35 of MP4 (para. 3.288, above). *3.504*

APPLICATION OF THE GUADALAJARA CONVENTION

The Guadalajara Convention[1] is applicable to carriage to which this regime applies in the following form: *3.505*

Article I *3.506*

In the Guadalajara Convention as applied by this Schedule:

(a) "The Warsaw Convention" means the MP4 amended Convention as applied by this Schedule;

(b) "contracting carrier" means a person who as a principal makes an agreement for carriage governed by the Warsaw Convention with a passenger or consignor or with a person acting on behalf of the passenger or consignor;

(c) "actual carrier" means a person, other than the contracting carrier, who, by virtue of authority from the contracting carrier, performs the whole or part of the carriage contemplated in paragraph (b) but who is not with respect to such part a successive carrier within the meaning of the Warsaw Convention. Such authority is presumed in the absence of proof to the contrary.

Article II *3.507*

If an actual carrier performs the whole or part of carriage which, according to the agreement referred to in Article I, paragraph (b), is governed by the Warsaw Convention, both the contracting carrier and the actual carrier shall, except as otherwise provided in the Guadalajara Convention as applied by this Schedule, be subject to the rules of the Warsaw Convention, the former for the whole of the carriage contemplated in the agreement, the latter solely for the carriage which he performs.

1. Paras. 3.525 *et seq.*, below.

3.508

Article III

1. The acts and omissions of the actual carrier and of his servants and agents acting within the scope of their employment shall, in relation to the carriage performed by the actual carrier, be deemed to be also those of the contracting carrier.

2. The acts and omissions of the contracting carrier and of his servants and agents acting within the scope of their employment shall, in relation to the carriage performed by the actual carrier, be deemed to be also those of the actual carrier. Nevertheless, no such act or omission shall subject the actual carrier to liability exceeding the limits specified in Article 22 of the Warsaw Convention. Any special agreement under which the contracting carrier assumes obligations not imposed by the Warsaw Convention or any waiver of rights conferred by that Convention or any special declaration of interest in delivery at destination contemplated in Article 22 of the said Convention, shall not affect the actual carrier unless agreed by him.

3.509

Article IV

Any complaint to be made or order to be given under the Warsaw Convention to the carrier shall have the same effect whether addressed to the contracting carrier or to the actual carrier.

3.510

Article V

In relation to the carriage performed by the actual carrier, any servant or agent of that carrier or of the contracting carrier shall, if he proves that he acted within the scope of his employment be entitled to avail himself of the limits of liability which are applicable under the Guadalajara Convention as applied by this Schedule to the carrier whose servant or agent he is unless it is proved that he acted in a manner which, under the Warsaw Convention, prevents the limits of liability from being invoked.

3.511

Article VI

In relation to the carriage performed by the actual carrier, the aggregate of the amounts recoverable from that carrier and the contracting carrier, and from their servants and agents acting within the scope of their employment, shall not exceed the highest amount which could be awarded against either the contracting carrier or the actual carrier under the Guadalajara Convention as applied by this Schedule, but none of the persons mentioned shall be liable for a sum in excess of the limit applicable to him.

3.512

Article VII

In relation to the carriage performed by the actual carrier, an action for damages may be brought, at the option of the plaintiff, against that carrier or the contracting carrier, or against both together or separately.

3.513

Article IX

1. Any contractual provision tending to relieve the contracting carrier or the actual carrier of liability under the Guadalajara Convention as applied by this Schedule or to fix a lower limit than that which is applicable according to the Guadalajara Convention as applied by this Schedule shall be null and void, but the nullity of any such provision does not involve the nullity of the whole agreement, which shall remain subject to the provisions of the Guadalajara Convention as applied by this Schedule.

2. In respect of the carriage performed by the actual carrier, the preceding paragraph shall not apply to contractual provisions governing loss or damage resulting from the inherent defect, quality or vice of the cargo carried.

3. Any clause contained in an agreement for carriage and all special agreements entered into before the damage occurred by which the parties purport to infringe the rules laid down by the Guadalajara Convention as applied by this Schedule, whether by deciding the law to be applied, or by altering the rules as to jurisdiction, shall be null and void. Nevertheless, for the carriage of cargo arbitration clauses are allowed, subject to the Guadalajara Convention as applied by this Schedule.

Article X *3.514*

Except as provided in Article VII, nothing in the Guadalajara Convention as applied by this Schedule shall affect the rights and obligations of the two carriers between themselves.

Article XI *3.515*

Nothing herein shall impose any liability on the Postmaster General or any authority for the time being established by or under any Act of Parliament with power to provide postal services.

[*The next paragraph is 3.525*]

VII. THE GUADALAJARA CONVENTION AS GIVEN FORCE OF LAW IN THE UK BY THE 1962 ACT[1]

3.525 **Convention Supplementary to the Warsaw Convention, for the unification of certain rules relating to international carriage by air performed by a person other than the contracting carrier**

Article 1—Definitions

In this Convention:

(a) [defines the "Warsaw Convention" to mean the WC or HP or MP4, according to whether the carriage under the agreement referred to in paragraph (b) is governed by one or by the other;]

(b) "contracting carrier" means a person who as a principal makes an agreement for carriage governed by the Warsaw Convention with a passenger or consignor or with a person acting on behalf of the passenger or consignor;

(c) "actual carrier" means a person, other than the contracting carrier, who, by virtue of authority from the contracting carrier, performs the whole or part of the carriage contemplated in paragraph (b) but who is not with respect to such part a successive carrier within the meaning of the Warsaw Convention. Such authority is presumed in the absence of proof to the contrary.

Comments

3.526 The Guadalajara Convention makes provision for the situation where carriage is performed by a carrier not party to the contract of carriage . The regime does not apply (without more) where one carrier issues an air waybill as agent for another; see the Conditions of Carriage for Cargo: IATA Recommended Practice 1601 CSC(19), Article 11.10 (para. 3.902, below). Distinguish also successive carriage: see HP, Article 30, Comment 1 (para. 3.191, above).

3.527 Article 1 defines the roles of the carrier with which the regime is concerned. The regime is given force of law in the UK in relation to carriage to which it applies by the 1962 Act, s. 1(1).

3.528 **Article 2—Application of Convention to actual carrier**

If an actual carrier performs the whole or part of carriage which, according to the agreement referred to in Article 1, paragraph (b), is governed by the Warsaw Convention, both the contracting carrier and the actual carrier shall, except as otherwise provided in this Convention, be subject to the rules of the Warsaw Convention, the former for the whole of the carriage contemplated in the agreement, the latter solely for the carriage which he performs.

Comment

3.529 Article 2 provides, for the avoidance of doubt, that the actual carrier obtains the benefit of the regime as set out in WC, HP or MP4, as the case may be.

1. Being the English text of the Guadalajara Convention.

Article 3—Liability *3.530*

(1) The acts and omissions of the actual carrier and of his servants and agents acting within the scope of their employment shall, in relation to the carriage performed by the actual carrier, be deemed to be also those of the contracting carrier.

(2) The acts and omissions of the contracting carrier and of his servants and agents acting within the scope of their employment shall, in relation to the carriage performed by the actual carrier, be deemed to be also those of the actual carrier. Nevertheless, no such act or omission shall subject the actual carrier to liability exceeding the limits specified in Article 22 of the Warsaw Convention. Any special agreement under which the contracting carrier assumes obligations not imposed by the Warsaw Convention or any waiver or rights conferred by that Convention or any special declaration of interest in delivery at destination contemplated in Article 22 of the said Convention, shall not affect the actual carrier unless agreed to by him.

Comment

This is to be contrasted with the position in successive carriage as regulated by Article 30 of HP (para. 3.190, above). *3.531*

Article 4—Complaint *3.532*

Any complaint to be made or order to be given under the Warsaw Convention to the carrier shall have the same effect whether addressed to the contracting carrier or to the actual carrier. Nevertheless, orders referred to in Article 12 of the Warsaw Convention shall only be effective if addressed to the contracting carrier.

Comment

As regards complaints, see the Comments on Article 26 of HP, paragraphs 3.170 *et seq.*, above. *3.533*

Article 5—Servant or agent *3.534*

In relation to the carriage performed by the actual carrier, any servant or agent of that carrier or of the contracting carrier shall, if he proves that he acted within the scope of his employment, be entitled to avail himself of the limits of liability which are applicable under this Convention to the carrier whose servant or agent he is unless it is proved that he acted in a manner which, under the Warsaw Convention, prevents the limits of liability from being invoked.

Comment

Article 5 mirrors Article 25A of HP (para. 3.161, above) to the end that the limits of liability are not circumvented. *3.535*

Article 6—Limitation of liability *3.536*

In relation to the carriage performed by the actual carrier, the aggregate of the amounts recoverable from that carrier and the contracting carrier, and from their servants and agents acting within the scope of their employment, shall not exceed the highest amount which could be awarded against either the contracting carrier or the actual carrier under this Convention, but none of the persons mentioned shall be liable for a sum in excess of the limit applicable to him.

Article 7—Claims

In relation to the carriage performed by the actual carrier, an action for damages may be brought, at the option of the plaintiff, against that carrier or the contracting carrier, or against both together or separately. If the action is brought against only one of those carriers, that carrier shall have the right to require the other carrier to be joined in the proceedings, the procedure and effects being governed by the law of the court seised of the case.

Comment

3.538 Article 7 is silent as to the time limitation for such an action but the 1961 Act, s. 5(1), applies the two-year period to an actual carrier. Concerning jurisdiction see Article 8, below.

Article 8—Jurisdiction

Any action for damages contemplated in Article 7 of this Convention must be brought, at the option of the plaintiff, either before a court in which an action may be brought against the contracting carrier, as provided in Article 28 of the Warsaw Convention, or before the court having jurisdiction at the place where the actual carrier is ordinarily resident or has his principal place of business.

Comment

3.540 See the Comments on Article 25 of HP (paras. 3.148 *et seq.*, above), to which Article 8 is similar.

3.541 **Article 9—Prohibition against contracting-out**

(1) Any contractual provision tending to relieve the contracting carrier or the actual carrier of liability under this Convention or to fix a lower limit than that which is applicable according to this Convention shall be null and void but the nullity of any such provision does not involve the nullity of the whole agreement, which shall remain subject to the provisions of this Convention.

(2) In respect of the carriage performed by the actual carrier, the preceding paragraph shall not apply to contractual provisions governing loss or damage resulting from the inherent defect, quality or vice of the cargo carried.

(3) Any clause contained in an agreement for carriage and all special agreements entered into before the damage occurred by which the parties purport to infringe the rules laid down by this Convention, whether by deciding the law to be applied, or by altering the rules as to jurisdiction, shall be null and void. Nevertheless, for the carriage of cargo arbitration clauses are allowed, subject to this Convention, if the arbitration is to take place in one of the jurisdictions referred to in Article 3.

Comment

3.542 Article 9(1) and (2) contain rules similar to Article 23 of HP (para. 3.137, above) and Article 9(3) is similar to Article 32 of HP (para. 3.198, above).

Article 10—Relations between carriers *3.543*

Except as provided in Article 7, nothing in this Convention shall affect the rights and obligations of the two carriers between themselves.

Comment

Successive (and, for that matter, substitute) carriage by air is facilitated by interline traffic agreements between carriers by which each party is authorised to accept cargo for carriage over the routes of other carriers upon terms *inter alia* that each uses (generally) IATA forms and procedures for cargo handling, that each agrees to detailed provisions relating to acceptance, transfer routing and delivery of cargo, commissions, charges, interline settlement of amounts as between the carriers concerned and regarding claims handling and settlement. Each carrier agrees to indemnify other carriers with regard to loss, damage or delay incurred whilst cargo is, pursuant to the agreement, under the control or in the custody of that party. Carriers may further agree to a proration of amounts to be paid in settlement of claims on cargo where loss or damage is not detected at time of transfer between carriers: the proration on the claim settlement amount being made by reference to transportation charges received by each carrier as a proportion of all such charges. Dispute under such agreements may be subject to binding arbitration by IATA. Article 10 is intended to ensure respect for such agreements between carriers. *3.544*

[*The next paragraph is 3.555*]

VIII. THE MONTREAL CONVENTION 1999 FOR THE UNIFICATION OF CERTAIN RULES FOR INTERNATIONAL CARRIAGE BY AIR

3.555 THE STATES PARTIES TO THIS CONVENTION

RECOGNIZING the significant contribution of the Convention for the Unification of Certain Rules Relating to International Carriage by Air signed in Warsaw on 12 October 1929, hereinafter referred to as the "Warsaw Convention", and other related instruments to the harmonization of private international air law;

RECOGNIZING the need to modernise and consolidate the Warsaw Convention and related instruments;

RECOGNIZING the importance of ensuring protection of the interests of consumers in international carriage by air and the need for equitable compensation based on the principle of restitution;

REAFFIRMING the desirability of an orderly development of international air transport operations and the smooth flow of passengers, baggage and cargo in accordance with the principles and objectives of the Convention on International Civil Aviation, done at Chicago on 7 December 1994;

CONVINCED that collective State action for further harmonization and codification of certain rules governing international carriage by air through a new Convention is the most adequate means of achieving an equitable balance of interests;

HAVE AGREED AS FOLLOWS:

Comment

3.556 The earlier Conventions on carriage by air were codified, modified and updated[1] in the Montreal Convention 1999 (MC). Article 55 provides that its provisions shall prevail over any rules which apply to international carriage by air between States Parties to that Convention by virtue of those States commonly being party to the previous instruments. MC came into force for those states that had ratified it, which did not then include the UK, on 4 November 2003. It came into force in the UK on 28 June 2004.

3.557 Many of the provisions of MC that differentiate it from HP were already to be found in MP4 (paras. 3.219 *et seq.*, above). The most important provisions that differentiate MC from MP4, concerning limitation and jurisdiction, affect passengers but not cargo. As regards cargo MC and MP4 are similar.[2]

3.558 **Chapter I: General Provisions**

Article 1—Scope of application

1. This Convention applies to all international carriage of persons, baggage or cargo performed by aircraft for reward. It applies equally to gratuitous carriage by aircraft performed by an air transport undertaking.

1. See Bin Cheng, ZLW, Vol. 49 (2000), pp. 287–307 and pp. 484–499; Balfour, 4 (2) S. & T.L.I. 38 (2003); Clarke, *Air*, Chaps. 1.2 and 3.

2. For comparative commentary on MP4 and MC see Clarke, *Air*.

2. For the purposes of this Convention, the expression *international carriage* means any carriage in which, according to the agreement between the parties, the place of departure and the place of destination, whether or not there be a break in the carriage or a transhipment, are situated either within the territories of two States Parties, or within the territory of a single State Party if there is an agreed stopping place within the territory of another State, even if that State is not a State Party. Carriage between two points within the territory of a single State Party without an agreed stopping place within the territory of another State is not international carriage for the purposes of this Convention.

3. Carriage to be performed by several successive carriers is deemed, for the purposes of this Convention, to be one undivided carriage if it has been regarded by the parties as a single operation, whether it had been agreed upon under the form of a single contract or of a series of contracts, and it does not lose its international character merely because one contract or a series of contracts is to be performed entirely within the territory of the same State.

4. This Convention applies also to carriage as set out in Chapter V, subject to the terms contained therein.

Comment

Article 1 is in substance the same as Article 1 of MP4 (para. 3.219, above). *3.559*

Article 2—State/postal items *3.560*

1. This Convention applies to carriage performed by the State or by legally constituted public bodies provided it falls within the conditions laid down in Article 1.

2. In the carriage of postal items, the carrier shall be liable only to the relevant postal administration in accordance with the rules applicable to the relationship between the carriers and the postal administrations.

3. Except as provided in paragraph 2 of this Article, the provisions of this Convention shall not apply to the carriage of postal items.

Comment

Article 2 is the same as Article 2 of MP4 (para. 3.221, above). *3.561*

Chapter II: Documentation and Duties of the Parties Relating to the Carriage of Cargo *3.562*

Article 4—Cargo

1. In respect of the carriage of cargo, an air waybill shall be delivered.

2. Any other means which preserves a record of the carriage to be performed may be substituted for the delivery of an air waybill. If such other means are used, the carrier shall, if so requested by the consignor, deliver to the consignor a cargo receipt permitting identification of the consignment and access to the information contained in the record preserved by such other means.

Comment

Article 4 is in substance the same as Article 5(1) and (2) of MP4 (para. 3.223, *3.563*
above).

3.564

Article 5—Air waybill/cargo receipt: contents

The air waybill or the cargo receipt shall include:
(a) an indication of the places of departure and destination;
(b) if the places of departure and destination are within the territory of a single State Party, one or more agreed stopping places being within the territory of another State, an indication of at least one such stopping place; and
(c) an indication of the weight of the consignment.

Comment

3.565 Article 5 is in substance the same as Article 8 of MP4 (para. 3.229, above).

3.566

Article 6—Document relating to the nature of the cargo

The consignor may be required, if necessary, to meet the formalities of customs, police and similar public authorities to deliver a document indicating the nature of the cargo. This provision creates for the carrier no duty, obligation or liability resulting therefrom.

Comment

3.567 Article 6 has the same role as Article 16(1) of MP4, however, in substance it differs in obvious and significant respects.

3.568

Article 7—Air waybill: form of

1. The air waybill shall be made out by the consignor in three original parts.
2. The first part shall be marked "for the carrier"; it shall be signed by the consignor. The second part shall be marked "for the consignee"; it shall be signed by the consignor and by the carrier. The third part shall be signed by the carrier who shall hand it to the consignor after the cargo has been accepted.
3. The signature of the carrier and that of the consignor may be printed or stamped.
4. If, at the request of the consignor, the carrier makes out the air waybill, the carrier shall be deemed, subject to proof to the contrary, to have done so on behalf of the consignor.

Comment

3.569 Article 7 is in substance the same as Article 6 of MP4 (para. 3.225, above).

3.570

Article 8—Multiple packages

When there is more than one package:
(a) the carrier of the cargo has the right to require the consignor to make out separate air waybills;
(b) the consignor has the right to require the carrier to deliver separate cargo receipts when the other means referred to in paragraph 2 of Article 4 are used.

Comment

3.571 Article 8 is in substance the same as Article 7 of MP4 (para. 3.227, above).

Article 9—Non-compliance *3.572*

Non-compliance with the provisions of Articles 4 to 8 shall not affect the existence or the validity of the contract of carriage, which shall, nonetheless, be subject to the rules of this Convention including those relating to limitation of liability.

Comment

Article 9 is in substance the same as Article 9 of MP4 (para. 3.231, above). *3.573*

Article 10—Responsibility for particulars *3.574*

1. The consignor is responsible for the correctness of the particulars and statements relating to the cargo inserted by it or on its behalf in the air waybill or furnished by it or on its behalf to the carrier for insertion in the cargo receipt or for insertion in the record preserved by the other means referred to in paragraph 2 of Article 4. The foregoing shall also apply where the person acting on behalf of the consignor is also the agent of the carrier.

2. The consignor shall indemnify the carrier against all damage suffered by it, or by any other person to whom the carrier is liable, by reason of the irregularity, incorrectness or incompleteness of the particulars and statements furnished by the consignor or on its behalf.

3. Subject to the provisions of paragraphs 1 and 2 of this Article, the carrier shall indemnify the consignor against all damage suffered by it, or by any other person to whom the consignor is liable, by reason of the irregularity, incorrectness or incompleteness of the particulars and statements inserted by the carrier or on its behalf in the cargo receipt or in the record preserved by the other means referred to in paragraph 2 of Article 4

Comment

Article 10 is in substance the same as Article 10 of MP4 (para. 3.233, above), except that the second sentence of Article 10.1 of MC is new. *3.575*

Article 11—Evidentiary value of documentation *3.576*

1. The air waybill or the cargo receipt is prima facie evidence of the conclusion of the contract, of the acceptance of the cargo and of the conditions of carriage mentioned therein.

2. Any statements in the air waybill or the cargo receipt relating to the weight, dimensions and packing of the cargo, as well as those relating to the number of packages, are prima facie evidence of the facts stated; those relating to the quantity, volume and condition of the cargo do not constitute evidence against the carrier except so far as they both have been, and are stated in the air waybill or the cargo receipt to have been, checked by it in the presence of the consignor, or relate to the apparent condition of the cargo.

Comment

Article 11 is in substance the same as Article 11 of MP4 (para. 3.235, above). *3.577*

Article 12—Shipper's right of disposition *3.578*

1. Subject to its liability to carry out all its obligations under the contract of carriage, the consignor has the right to dispose of the cargo by withdrawing it at the airport of departure

or destination, or by stopping it in the course of the journey on any landing, or by calling for it to be delivered at the place of destination or in the course of the journey to a person other than the consignee originally designated, or by requiring it to be returned to the airport of departure. The consignor must not exercise this right of disposition in such a way as to prejudice the carrier or other consignors and must reimburse any expenses occasioned by the exercise of this right.

2. If it is impossible to carry out the instructions of the consignor, the carrier must so inform the consignor forthwith.

3. If the carrier carries out the instructions of the consignor for the disposition of the cargo without requiring the production of the part of the air waybill or the cargo receipt delivered to the latter, the carrier will be liable, without prejudice to its right of recovery from the consignor, for any damage which may be caused thereby to any person who is lawfully in possession of that part of the air waybill or the cargo receipt.

4. The right conferred on the consignor ceases at the moment when that of the consignee begins in accordance with Article 13. Nevertheless, if the consignee declines to accept the cargo, or cannot be communicated with, the consignor resumes its right of disposition.

Comment

3.579 Article 12 is in substance the same as Article 12 of MP4 (para. 3.237, above).

3.580

Article 13—Delivery

1. Except when the consignor has exercised its right under Article 12, the consignee is entitled, on arrival of the cargo at the place of destination, to require the carrier to deliver the cargo to it, on payment of the charges due and on complying with the conditions of carriage.

2. Unless it is otherwise agreed, it is the duty of the carrier to give notice to the consignee as soon as the cargo arrives.

3. If the carrier admits the loss of the cargo, or if the cargo has not arrived at the expiration of seven days after the date on which it ought to have arrived, the consignee is entitled to enforce against the carrier the rights which flow from the contract of carriage.

Comment

3.581 Article 13 is in substance the same as Article 13 of MP4 (para. 3.239, above).

3.582

Article 14—Consignor/consignee's rights

The consignor and the consignee can respectively enforce all the rights given to them by Articles 12 and 13, each in its own name, whether it is acting in its own interest or in the interest of another, provided that it carries out the obligations imposed by the contract of carriage.

Comment

3.583 Article 14 is in substance the same as Article 14 of MP4 (para. 3.241, above).

3.584

Article 15—Waiver

1. Articles 12, 13 and 14 do not affect either the relations of the consignor and the consignee with each other or the mutual relations of third parties whose rights are derived either from the consignor or from the consignee.

2. The provisions of Articles 12, 13 and 14 can only be varied by express provision in the air waybill or the cargo receipt.

Comment

Article 15 is in substance the same as Article 15 of MP4 (para. 3.243, above). *3.585*

Article 16—Customs etc. *3.586*

1. The consignor must furnish such information and such documents as are necessary to meet the formalities of customs, police and any other public authorities before the cargo can be delivered to the consignee. The consignor is liable to the carrier for any damage occasioned by the absence, insufficiency or irregularity of any such information or documents, unless the damage is due to the fault of the carrier, its servants or agents.

2. The carrier is under no obligation to enquire into the correctness or sufficiency of such information or documents.

Comment

Article 16 is in substance the same as Article 16 of MP4 (para. 3.245, above). *3.587*

Chapter III: Liability of the Carrier and Extent of Compensation for Damage *3.588*

Article 18—Liability: damage

1. The carrier is liable for damage sustained in the event of the destruction or loss of, or damage to, cargo upon condition only that the event which caused the damage so sustained took place during the carriage by air.

2. However, the carrier is not liable if and to the extent it proves that the destruction, or loss of, or damage to, the cargo resulted from one or more of the following:

(a) inherent defect, quality or vice of that cargo[1];
(b) defective packing[2] of that cargo performed by a person other than the carrier or its servants or agents;
(c) an act of war or an armed conflict;
(d) an act of public authority carried out in connection with the entry, exit or transit of the cargo.

3. The carriage by air within the meaning of paragraph 1 of this Article comprises the period during which the cargo is in the charge of the carrier.

4. The period of the carriage by air does not extend to any carriage by land, by sea or by inland waterway performed outside an airport. If, however, such carriage takes place in the performance of a contract for carriage by air, for the purpose of loading, delivery or transhipment, any damage is presumed, subject to proof to the contrary, to have been the result of an event which took place during the carriage by air. If a carrier, without the consent of the consignor, substitutes carriage by another mode of transport for the whole or part of a carriage intended by the agreement between the parties to be carriage by air, such carriage by another mode of transport is deemed to be within the period of carriage by air.

Comment

Article 18, which is similar to Article 18 of MP4 (para. 3.247, above) in most respects, is significantly more favourable to the carrier in one. Whereas MP4 *3.589*

1. See Comment 2 on Article 23 of HP, paras. 3.140 *et seq.*, above.
2. See Comment 3 on Article 23 of HP, paras. 3.143 *et seq.*, above.

requires the loss or damage to be "solely" the result of one of the exonerating causes specified in Article 18.3, "solely" has been deleted from Article 18.3 of MC and the implication is that the defences are also available to the extent that they were a partial cause of loss or damage. Thus evidence that the carrier was or should have been aware, for example, of defective packing, does not defeat the defence in question altogether.

3.590

Article 19—Liability: delay

The carrier is liable for damage occasioned by delay in the carriage by air of cargo. Nevertheless, the carrier shall not be liable for damage occasioned by delay if it proves that it and its servants and agents took all measures that could reasonably be required to avoid the damage or that it was impossible for it or them to take such measures.

Comment

3.591 The first sentence of Article 19 is substantially the same as Article 19 of MP4 (para. 3.254, above). The second sentence of Article 19 is substantially the same as Article 20 of MP4 (para. 3.256, above).

3.592

Article 20—Defence

If the carrier proves that the damage was caused or contributed to by the negligence or other wrongful act or omission of the person claiming compensation, or the person from whom he or she derives his or her rights, the carrier shall be wholly or partly exonerated from its liability to the claimant to the extent that such negligence or wrongful act or omission caused or contributed to the damage. . . . [1]

Comment

3.593 Article 20 is substantially the same as Article 21(2) of MP4 (para. 3.258, above).

3.594

Article 22—Limits of liability

1. [Concerns delay in the carriage of persons.]
2. [Concerns limited liability for passengers' baggage.]
3. In the carriage of cargo, the liability of the carrier in the case of destruction, loss, damage or delay is limited to a sum of 17 Special Drawing Rights per kilogramme, unless the consignor has made, at the time when the package was handed over to the carrier, a special declaration of interest in delivery at destination and has paid a supplementary sum if the case so requires. In that case the carrier will be liable to pay a sum not exceeding the declared sum, unless it proves that the sum is greater than the consignor's actual interest in delivery at destination.
4. In the case of destruction, loss, damage or delay of part of the cargo, or of any object contained therein, the weight to be taken into consideration in determining the amount to which the carrier's liability is limited shall be only the total weight of the package or packages concerned. Nevertheless, when the destruction, loss, damage or delay of a part of the cargo,

1. The rest of Art. 20 concerns death or injury to passengers.

or of an object contained therein, affects the value of other packages covered by the same air waybill, or the same receipt or, if they were not issued, by the same record preserved by the other means referred to in paragraph 2 of Article 4, the total weight of such package or packages shall also be taken into consideration in determining the limit of liability.

6. The limits prescribed in Article 21 and in this Article shall not prevent the court from awarding, in accordance with its own law, in addition, the whole or part of the court costs and of the other expenses of the litigation incurred by the plaintiff, including interest. The foregoing provision shall not apply if the amount of the damages awarded, excluding court costs and other expenses of the litigation, does not exceed the sum which the carrier has offered in writing to the plaintiff within a period of six months from the date of the occurrence causing the damage, or before the commencement of the action, if that is later.

Comment

The rules in MP4 that correspond to those in this Article are to be found in Article 22(2) and (4) (para. 3.260, above). The content of the rules is largely the same. *3.595*

Article 23—Conversion of monetary units *3.596*

1. The sums mentioned in terms of Special Drawing Rights in this Convention shall be deemed to refer to the Special Drawing Right as defined by the International Monetary Fund. Conversion of the sums into national currencies shall, in case of judicial proceedings, be made according to the value of such currencies in terms of the Special Drawing Right, at the date of the judgment. The value of a national currency, in terms of the Special Drawing Right, of a State Party which is a Member of the International Monetary Fund shall be calculated in accordance with the method of valuation applied by the International Monetary Fund, in effect at the date of the judgment, for its operations and transactions. The value of a national currency, in terms of the Special Drawing Right, of a State Party which is not a Member of the International Monetary Fund, shall be calculated in a manner determined by that State.

2. Nevertheless, those States which are not Members of the International Monetary Fund and whose law does not permit the application of the provisions of paragraph 1 of this Article may, at the time of ratification or accession or at any time thereafter, declare that the limit of liability of the carrier prescribed in Article 21 is fixed at a sum of 250 monetary units per kilogramme with respect to paragraph 3 of Article 22. This monetary unit corresponds to sixty-five and a half milligrammes of gold of millesimal fineness nine hundred. These sums may be converted into the national currency concerned in round figures. The conversion of these sums into national currency shall be made according to the law of the State concerned.

3. The calculation mentioned in the last sentence of paragraph 1 of this Article and the conversion method mentioned in paragraph 2 of this Article shall be made in such manner as to express in the national currency of the State Party as far as possible the same real value for the amounts in Articles 21 and 22 as would result from the application of the first three sentences of paragraph 1 of this Article. States Parties shall communicate to the Depositary the manner of calculation pursuant to paragraph 1 of this Article, or the result of the conversion in paragraph 2 of this Article as the case may be, when depositing an instrument of ratification, acceptance, approval of or accession to this Convention and whenever there is a change in either.

Article 24—Review of limits *3.597*

1. Without prejudice to the provisions of Article 25 of this Convention and subject to paragraph 2 below, the limits of liability prescribed in Articles 22 and 23 shall be reviewed by the Depositary at five-year intervals, the first such review to take place at the end of the fifth year following the date of entry into force of this Convention, or if the Convention does not

enter into force within five years of the date it is first open for signature, within the first year of its entry into force, by reference to an inflation factor which corresponds to the accumulated rate of inflation since the previous revision or in the first instance since the date of entry into force of the Convention. The measure of the rate of inflation to be used in determining the inflation factor shall be the weighted average of the annual rates of increase or decrease in the Consumer Price Indices of the States whose currencies comprise the Special Drawing Right mentioned in paragraph 1 of Article 23.

2. If the review referred to in the preceding paragraph concludes that the inflation factor has exceeded 10 per cent, the Depositary shall notify States Parties of a revision of the limits of liability. Any such revision shall become effective six months after its notification to the States Parties. If within three months after its notification to the States Parties a majority of the States Parties register their disapproval, the revision shall not become effective and the Depositary shall refer the matter to a meeting of the States Parties. The Depositary shall immediately notify all States Parties of the coming into force of any revision.

3. Notwithstanding paragraph 1 of this Article, the procedure referred to in paragraph 2 of this Article shall be applied at any time provided that one-third of the States Parties express a desire to that effect and upon condition that the inflation factor referred to in paragraph 1 has exceeded 30 per cent since the previous revision or since the date of entry into force of this Convention if there has been no previous revision. Subsequent reviews using the procedure described in paragraph 1 of this Article will take place at five-year intervals starting at the end of the fifth year following the date of the reviews under the present paragraph.

Comment

3.598 Article 24 is not found in earlier versions of the regime.[1] The point at which legislation becomes most rapidly outdated is often any provision that is vulnerable to erosion by monetary inflation. Moreover, one of the objections in the past to uniform law through treaties such as the air Conventions has been that the process of modification is slow and cumbersome; and, once original agreement is achieved, the regime is written in stone and impervious to the winds of change. To meet this kind of problem, Article 24 provides a mechanism for the revision of limits which does not require a diplomatic Convention.

3.599 **Article 25—Higher limits**

A carrier may stipulate that the contract of carriage shall be subject to higher limits of liability than those provided for in this Convention or to no limits of liability whatsoever.

Comment

3.600 Article 25, which is not found in earlier versions of the regime, should be read with Article 26.

3.601 **Article 26—Convention paramount**

Any provision tending to relieve the carrier of liability or to fix a lower limit than that which is laid down in this Convention shall be null and void, but the nullity of any such provision does not involve the nullity of the whole contract, which shall remain subject to the provisions of this Convention.

1. For commentary, see Bin Cheng, ZLW 2000.287, 300 *et seq.*

Comment

Article 26, taken in conjunction with Article 49, makes clear that there can be no "contracting out" of MC on the part of the carrier, except as provided in Article 25. Article 26 does not prevent the parties agreeing that the carrier shall perform the contract by reference to special conditions governing, e.g. the care and security to be given to the shipment, as long as the result is not a standard of care and security lower than that indicated by MC. Moreover, the words "tending to relieve" suggest something operative in the future, with the corollary that an agreement having that effect after the event is not invalidated by Article 26. This, of course, means that Article 26 does not invalidate agreements to settle or compromise claims. *3.602*

Article 27—Freedom to contract *3.603*

Nothing contained in this Convention shall prevent the carrier from refusing to enter into any contract of carriage, from waiving any defences available under the Convention, or from laying down conditions which do not conflict with the provisions of this Convention.

Comment

Article 27 is an expanded version of Article 33 of MP4 (para. 3.284, above). *3.604*

Article 28 *3.605*

[Concerns advance payments to passengers.]

Article 29—Basis of claims *3.606*

In the carriage of passengers, baggage and cargo, any action for damages, however founded, whether under this Convention or in contract or in tort or otherwise, can only be brought subject to the conditions and such limits of liability as are set out in this Convention without prejudice to the question as to who are the persons who have the right to bring suit and what are their respective rights. In any such action, punitive, exemplary or any other non-compensatory damages shall not be recoverable.

Comment

Article 29 is substantially the same as Article 24(2) of MP4 (para. 3.264, above). *3.607*

Article 30—Servants, agents *3.608*

1. If an action is brought against a servant or agent of the carrier arising out of damage to which the Convention relates, such servant or agent, if they prove that they acted within the scope of their employment, shall be entitled to avail themselves of the conditions and limits of liability which the carrier itself is entitled to invoke under this Convention.

2. The aggregate of the amounts recoverable from the carrier, its servants and agents, in that case, shall not exceed the said limits.

3. [Concerns passengers and baggage.]

Comment

3.609 Article 30.1 and Article (30.2) are substantially the same as Article 25A of MP4 (para. 3.266, above). See also below, MC, Article 43 (para. 3.634) and Article 44 (para. 3.635), for which there are no corresponding provisions in MP4, which extend such protection to actual carriers.

3.610

Article 31—Complaints

1. Receipt by the person entitled to delivery of cargo without complaint is prima facie evidence that the same has been delivered in good condition and in accordance with the document of carriage or with the record preserved by the other means referred to in paragraph 2 of Article 4.

2. In the case of damage, the person entitled to delivery must complain to the carrier forthwith after the discovery of the damage, and, at the latest, within fourteen days from the date of receipt in the case of cargo. In the case of delay, the complaint must be made at the latest within twenty-one days from the date on which the cargo has been placed at his or her disposal.

3. Every complaint must be made in writing and given or dispatched within the times aforesaid.

4. If no complaint is made within the times aforesaid, no action shall lie against the carrier, save in the case of fraud on its part.

Comment

3.611 Article 31 is substantially the same as Article 26 of MP4 (para. 3.268, above).

3.612

Article 32—Death of person liable

In the case of the death of the person liable, an action for damages lies in accordance with the terms of this Convention against those legally representing his or her estate.

Comment

3.613 Article 32 is substantially the same as Article 27 of MP4 (para. 3.270, above).

3.614

Article 33—Jurisdiction

1. An action for damages must be brought, at the option of the plaintiff, in the territory of one of the States Parties, either before the court of the domicile of the carrier or of its principal place of business or where it has a place of business through which the contract has been made or before the court at the place of destination.

2. [Concerns jurisdiction in cases of the death or injury of passengers.]

3. [Concerns jurisdiction in cases of the death or injury of passengers.]

4. Questions of procedure shall be governed by the law of the court seised of the case.

Comment

3.615 Article 28.1 is largely the same as Article 28.1 of MP4 (para. 3.272, above), however, here "domicile" replaces "ordinary residence", which is the connecting factor found in Article 28.1 of MP4. Domicile is the word used in the equivalent legislation in the USA; and the original French is "domicile". Article 28.4 is the same as Article 28.2 of MP4.

Article 34—Arbitration *3.616*

1. Subject to the provisions of this Article, the parties to the contract of carriage for cargo may stipulate that any dispute relating to the liability of the carrier under this Convention shall be settled by arbitration. Such agreement shall be in writing.

2. The arbitration proceedings shall, at the option of the claimant, take place within one of the jurisdictions referred to in Article 33.

3. The arbitrator or arbitration tribunal shall apply the provisions of this Convention.

4. The provisions of paragraphs 2 and 3 of this Article shall be deemed to be part of every arbitration clause or agreement, and any term of such clause or agreement which is inconsistent therewith shall be null and void.

Comment

There is no such provision in WC, HP or MP4. A reference to the possibility of arbitration, however, is to be found in the last sentence of Article 32 of WC, HP and MP4 and, given the importance of arbitration in modern commercial practice, this possibility has been regulated by Article 34 of MC. *3.617*

Article 35—Time bar *3.618*

1. The right to damages shall be extinguished if an action is not brought within a period of two years, reckoned from the date of arrival at the destination, or from the date on which the aircraft ought to have arrived, or from the date on which the carriage stopped.

2. The method of calculating that period shall be determined by the law of the court seised of the case.

Comment

This provision is substantially the same as Article 29 of MP4 (para. 3.274, above). Under each provision, if the action is not brought in time, the right is "extinguished". Extinguished means more than merely unenforceable, it means "non-existent . . . finished, gone forever".[1] Although Article 35 is headed "Time bar" and Article 29 of MP4, is headed "Limitation of actions", it does not appear that any substantial change was intended. *3.619*

Article 36—Successive carriage *3.620*

1. In the case of carriage to be performed by various successive carriers and falling within the definition set out in paragraph 3 of Article 1, each carrier which accepts cargo is subject to the rules set out in this Convention and is deemed to be one of the parties to the contract

1. *Proctor* v. *Jetway* [1982] 2 NSWLR 264, 271.

of carriage in so far as the contract deals with that part of the carriage which is performed under its supervision.

2. [Concerns claims by passengers.]

3. As regards cargo, the consignor will have a right of action against the first carrier, and the passenger or consignee who is entitled to delivery will have a right of action against the last carrier, and further, each may take action against the carrier which performed the carriage during which the destruction, loss, damage or delay took place. These carriers will be jointly and severally liable to the passenger or to the consignor or consignee.

Comment

3.621 Article 36 is substantially the same as Article 30 of MP4 (para. 3.276, above).

3.622

Article 37—Recourse

Nothing in this Convention shall prejudice the question whether a person liable for damage in accordance with its provisions has a right of recourse against any other person.

Comment

3.623 Article 37 is the same as Article 30A of MP4 (para. 3.278, above).

3.624

Chapter IV: Combined Carriage

Article 38—Combined carriage

1. In the case of combined carriage performed partly by air and partly by any other mode of carriage, the provisions of this Convention shall, subject to paragraph 4 of Article 18, apply only to the carriage by air, provided that the carriage by air falls within the terms of Article 1.

2. Nothing in this Convention shall prevent the parties in the case of combined carriage from inserting in the document of air carriage conditions relating to other modes of carriage, provided that the provisions of this Convention are observed as regards the carriage by air.

Comment

3.625 Apart from the addition of the cross-reference to Article 18.4, Article 38 is the same as Article 31 of MP4 (para. 3.280, above).

3.626

Chapter V: Carriage by Air Performed by a Person other than the Contracting Carrier

Article 39—Contracting/actual carrier

The provisions of this Chapter apply when a person (hereinafter referred to as "the contracting carrier") as a principal makes a contract of carriage governed by this Convention with a consignor or with a person acting on behalf of the consignor, and another person (hereinafter referred to as "the actual carrier") performs, by virtue of authority from the contracting carrier, the whole or part of the carriage, but is not with respect to such part a successive carrier within the meaning of this Convention. Such authority shall be presumed in the absence of proof to the contrary.

Comment

This and the following provisions incorporate the provisions of the Guadalajara Supplementary Convention 1961[1] into MC. *3.627*

Article 40—Liability: contracting/actual carrier *3.628*

If an actual carrier performs the whole or part of carriage which, according to the contract referred to in Article 39, is governed by this Convention, both the contracting carrier and the actual carrier shall, except as otherwise provided in this Chapter, be subject to the rules of this Convention, the former for the whole of the carriage contemplated in the contract, the latter solely for the carriage which it performs.

Comment

Article 40 is substantially the same as Article 2 of the Guadalajara Supplementary Convention 1961. *3.629*

Article 41—Mutual liability *3.630*

1. The acts and omissions of the actual carrier and of its servants and agents acting within the scope of their employment shall, in relation to the carriage performed by the actual carrier, be deemed to be also those of the contracting carrier.

2. The acts and omissions of the contracting carrier and of its servants and agents acting within the scope of their employment shall, in relation to the carriage performed by the actual carrier, be deemed to be also those of the actual carrier. Nevertheless, no such act or omission shall subject to the actual carrier to liability exceeding the amounts referred to in Articles 22, 23 and 24. Any special agreement under which the contracting carrier assumes obligations not imposed by this Convention or any waiver of rights or defences conferred by this Convention or any special declaration of interest in delivery at destination contemplated in Article 22 shall not affect the actual carrier unless agreed to by it.

Comment

Article 41 is substantially the same as Article 3 of the Guadalajara Supplementary Convention 1961. *3.631*

Article 42—Complaints: contracting/actual carrier *3.632*

Any complaint to be made or instruction to be given under this Convention to the carrier shall have the same effect whether addressed to the contracting carrier or to the actual carrier. Nevertheless, instructions referred to in Article 12 shall only be effective if addressed to the contracting carrier.

1. See paras. 3.525 *et seq.*, above.

Comment

3.633 Article 42 is substantially the same as Article 4 of the Guadalajara Supplementary Convention 1961.

3.634

Article 43—Servants and agents

In relation to the carriage performed by the actual carrier, any servant or agent of that carrier or of the contracting carrier shall, if they prove that they acted within the scope of their employment, be entitled to avail themselves of the conditions and limits of liability which are applicable under this Convention to the carrier whose servant or agent they are, unless it is proved that they acted in a manner that prevents the limits of liability from being invoked in accordance with this Convention.

Comment

3.635 Article 43 is substantially the same as Article 5 of the Guadalajara Supplementary Convention 1961.

3.636

Article 44—Aggregation of damages

In relation to the carriage performed by the actual carrier, the aggregate of the amounts recoverable from that carrier and the contracting carrier, and from their servants and agents acting within the scope of their employment, shall not exceed the highest amount which could be awarded against either the contracting carrier or the actual carrier under this Convention, but none of the persons mentioned shall be liable for a sum in excess of the limit applicable to that person.

Comment

3.637 Article 44 is substantially the same as Article 6 of the Guadalajara Supplementary Convention 1961.

3.638

Article 45—Addressee of claims

In relation to the carriage performed by the actual carrier, an action for damages may be brought, at the option of the plaintiff, against that carrier or the contracting carrier, or against both together or separately. If the action is brought against only one of those carriers, that carrier shall have the right to require the other carrier to be joined in the proceedings, the procedure and effects being governed by the law of the court seised of the case.

Comment

3.639 Article 45 is substantially the same as Article 7 of the Guadalajara Supplementary Convention 1961.

3.640

Article 46—Additional jurisdiction

Any action for damages contemplated in Article 45 must be brought, at the option of the plaintiff, in the territory of one of the States Parties, either before a court in which an action may be brought against the contracting carrier, as provided in Article 33, or before the court having jurisdiction at the place where the actual carrier has its domicile or its principal place of business.

Comment

Article 46 is substantially the same as Article 8 of the Guadalajara Supplementary Convention 1961. *3.641*

Article 47—Convention paramount *3.642*

Any contractual provision tending to relieve the contracting carrier or the actual carrier of liability under this Chapter or to fix a lower limit than that which is applicable according to this Chapter shall be null and void, but the nullity of any such provision does not involve the nullity of the whole contract, which shall remain subject to the provisions of this Chapter.

Comment

Article 47 is substantially the same as Article 9(1) of the Guadalajara Supplementary Convention 1961. *3.643*

Article 48—Waiver *3.644*

Except as provided in Article 45, nothing in this Chapter shall affect the rights and obligations of the carriers between themselves, including any right of recourse or indemnification.

Comment

Article 48 is substantially the same as Article 9 of the Guadalajara Supplementary Convention 1961. *3.645*

Chapter VI: Other Provisions *3.646*

Article 49—Convention paramount

Any clause contained in the contract of carriage and all special agreements entered into before the damage occurred by which the parties purport to infringe the rules laid down by this Convention, whether by deciding the law to be applied, or by altering the rules as to jurisdiction, shall be null and void.

Comment

Article 49 is substantially the same as the first sentence of Article 32 of MP4. The second sentence of Article 32 concerns arbitration clauses which are the subject of Article 34 of MC. *3.647*

3.648 **Article 50—Insurance**

States Parties shall require their carriers to maintain adequate insurance covering their liability under this Convention. A carrier may be required by the State Party into which it operates to furnish evidence that it maintains adequate insurance covering its liability under this Convention.

Comment

3.649 Article 50 is a provision of public law which is without direct effect on the contract of carriage and which has no counterpart in WC, HP or MP4.

3.650 **Article 51—Extraordinary carriage**

The provisions of Articles 3 to 5, 7 and 8 relating to the documentation of carriage shall not apply in the case of carriage performed in extraordinary circumstances outside the normal scope of a carrier's business.

Comment

3.651 Article 51 is substantially the same as Article 34 of MP4 (para. 3.286, above).

3.652 **Article 52—Definition of days**

The expression "days" when used in this Convention means calendar days, not working days.

Comment

3.653 Article 52 is substantially the same as Article 35 of MP4 (para. 3.288, above).

3.654 **Chapter VII: Final Clauses**

Article 53—Signature, ratification and entry into force

1. This Convention shall be open for signature in Montreal on 28 May 1999 by States participating in the International Conference on Air Law held at Montreal from 10 to 28 May 1999. After 28 May 1999, the Convention shall be open to all States for signature at the Headquarters of the International Civil Aviation Organization in Montreal until it enters into force in accordance with paragraph 6 of this Article.

2. This Convention shall similarly be open for signature by Regional Economic Integration Organisations. For the purpose of this Convention a "Regional Economic Integration Organisation" means any organisation which is constituted by sovereign States of a given region which has competence in respect of certain matters governed by this Convention and has been duly authorised to sign and to ratify, accept, approve or accede to this Convention. A reference to a "State Party" or "States Parties" in this Convention, otherwise than in paragraph 2 of Article 1, paragraph 1(b) of Article 3, paragraph (b) of Article 5, Articles 23, 33, 46 and paragraph (b) of Article 57, applies equally to a Regional Economic Integration Organisation. For the purpose of Article 24, the references to "a majority of the States

Parties" and "one third of the States Parties" shall not apply to a Regional Economic Integration Organisation.

3. This Convention shall be subject to ratification by States and by Regional Economic Integration Organisations which have signed it.

4. Any State or Regional Economic Integration Organisation which does not sign this Convention may accept, approve or accede to it at any time.

5. Instruments of ratification, acceptance, approval or accession shall be deposited with the International Civil Aviation Organisation, which is hereby designated the Depositary.

6. This Convention shall enter into force on the sixtieth day following the date of deposit of the thirtieth instrument of ratification, acceptance, approval or accession with the Depositary between the States which have deposited such instrument. An instrument deposited by a Regional Economic Integration Organisation shall not be counted for the purpose of this paragraph.

7. For other States and for other Regional Economic Integration Organisations, this Convention shall take effect sixty days following the date of deposit of the instrument of ratification, acceptance approval or accession.

8. The Depositary shall promptly notify all signatories and States Parties of:

(a) each signature of this Convention and date thereof;
(b) each deposit of an instrument of ratification, acceptance, approval or accession and date thereof;
(c) the date of entry into force of this Convention;
(d) the date of the coming into force of any revision of the limits of liability established under this Convention;
(e) any denunciation under Article 54.

Comment

MC came into force in some countries on 4 November 2003. It came into force in the UK on 28 June 2004. *3.655*

Article 54—Denunciation *3.656*

1. Any State Party may denounce this Convention by written notification to the Depositary.

2. Denunciation shall take effect one hundred and eighty days following the date on which notification is received by the Depositary.

Article 55—Relationship with other Warsaw Convention instruments *3.657*

This Convention shall prevail over any rules which apply to international carriage by air:

1. between States Parties to this Convention by virtue of those States commonly being Party to
   (a) the *Convention for the Unification of Certain Rules Relating to International Carriage by Air* signed at Warsaw on 12 October 1929 (hereinafter called the Warsaw Convention);
   (b) the *Protocol to Amend the Convention for the Unification of Certain Rules Relating to International Carriage by Air* signed at Warsaw on 12 October 1929, Done at The Hague on 28 September 1955 (hereinafter called The Hague Protocol);
   (c) the *Convention, Supplementary to the Warsaw Convention, for the Unification of Certain Rules Relating to International Carriage by Air Performed by a Person Other than the Contracting Carrier*, signed at Guadalajara on 18 September 1961 (hereinafter called the Guadalajara Convention);
   (d) the *Protocol to Amend the Convention for the Unification of Certain Rules Relating to International Carriage by Air Signed at Warsaw on 12 October 1929*

as Amended at the Protocol Done at The Hague on 28 September 1955 signed at Guatemala City on 8 March 1971 (hereinafter called the Guatemala City Protocol);

(e) Additional Protocol Nos. 1 to 3 and Montreal Protocol No. 4 to amend the Warsaw Convention as amended by The Hague Protocol or the Warsaw Convention as amended by both The Hague Protocol and the Guatemala City Protocol Signed at Montreal on 25 September 1975 (hereinafter called the Montreal Protocols); or

2. within the territory of any single State Party to this Convention by virtue of that State being Party to one or more of the instruments referred to in sub-paragraphs (a) to (e) above.

3.658 **Article 56—States with more than one system of law**

1. If a State has two or more territorial units in which different systems of law are applicable in relation to matters dealt with in this Convention, it may at the time of signature, ratification, acceptance, approval or accession declare that this Convention shall extend to all its territorial units or only to one or more of them and may modify this declaration by submitting another declaration at any time.

2. Any such declaration shall be notified to the Depositary and shall state expressly the territorial units to which the Convention applies.

3. In relation to a State Party which has made such a declaration:

(a) references in Article 23 to "national currency" shall be construed as referring to the currency of the relevant territorial unit of that State; and

(b) the reference in Article 28 to "national law" shall be construed as referring to the law of the relevant territorial unit of that State.

3.659 **Article 57—Reservations**

No reservation may be made to this Convention except that a State Party may at any time declare by a notification addressed to the Depositary that this Convention shall not apply to:

(a) international carriage by air performed and operated directly by that State Party for non-commercial purposes in respect to its functions and duties as a sovereign State; and/or

(b) the carriage of cargo for its military authorities on aircraft registered in or leased by that State Party, the whole capacity of which has been reserved by or on behalf of such authorities.

3.660 IN WITNESS WHEREOF the undersigned Plenipotentiaries, having been duly authorised, have signed this Convention.

DONE at Montreal on the 28th day of May of the year one thousand nine hundred and ninety-nine in the English, Arabic, Chinese, French, Russian and Spanish languages, all texts being equally authentic. This Convention shall remain deposited in the archives of the International Civil Aviation Organisation, and certified copies thereof shall be transmitted by the Depositary to all States Parties to this Convention, as well as to all States Parties to the Warsaw Convention, The Hague Protocol, the Guadalajara Convention, the Guatemala City Protocol, and the Montreal Protocols.

[*The next paragraph is 3.671*]

IX. AIR WAYBILL: FORM AND LAYOUT (IATA RESOLUTION 600a)[1] 3.671

Comments

1. Desirability of an air waybill

Whether under English common law or UK legislation concerned with the carriage of goods by air, it is not necessary for an air waybill to be drawn up (or "cut") in order for there to be a contract for the carriage of cargo by air. The absence of an air waybill will therefore not affect the existence or validity of a subsisting contract which may have been made verbally or in writing upon any other document. However, an air waybill is usually made out in order that all particulars ordinarily required to be agreed upon between the parties are recorded and relevant terms incorporated into the contract. Where carriage of cargo is international, however, the carrier is given the right to require the consignor to make out and hand over to him a document called an "air waybill" and every consignor has the right to require the carrier to accept this document.[2] 3.672

Moreover, in the case of international carriage, a carrier would ordinarily be foolish not to require an air waybill containing the stipulated particulars. Without an air waybill having been made out containing such particulars as required by WC and HP , the carrier is not entitled to avail himself of the limitation of liability provisions in Article 22(2); see HP, Article 9 (para. 3.66, above). However for non-international carriage or for international carriage under MP4 or MC no air waybill is required for such purposes; but the practical need for an agreed record of the contract of carriage, whether in the form of the traditional paper waybill or the more recent (electronic) "means which would preserve a record of the carriage to be performed",[3] remains. 3.673

2. Form of air waybill

None of the regimes governing contracts for the carriage of goods by air stipulates the detail or the form and layout of an air waybill except that it shall have three original parts: Article 6 of WC, HP and MP4, and MC Article 7. However, IATA has resolved that its members shall, in the case of international carriage by air of cargo, use a pre-printed air waybill of stipulated measurements and layout as set out in Attachments "A" and "B" of Resolution 600a. The IATA form air waybill has become adopted as the international norm because, for the convenience of consignors and air carriers, its layout and wording enables all particulars required by the various Conventions to be incorporated. 3.674

IATA has resolved that the outside measurements of the air waybill shall be between 208mm (8.2in.) and 230mm (9in.) in width and between 274mm (10.8in.) and 305mm (12in.) in length. The size of the boxes and their distance from the 3.675

1. See IATA, Air Waybill Handbook (26th ed., Montreal 2003).
2. See e.g. Art. 5 of HP, para. 3.533, above.
3. Art. 5 of MP4 and Art. 4 of MC.

upper and left-hand paper edge are set out in IATA Resolution 600a, Attachment "A", Appendix "A" (para. 3.677, below).

3. Terminology

3.676 In practice air waybills are either pre-printed airline air waybills issued by or on behalf of a particular air carrier or they are "neutral air waybills". Air waybills issued by intermediaries are known, by custom, as "house air waybills", unless for the carriage of "consolidations" of cargo when they are known as "master air waybills". IATA have defined the latter as a consignment of multi-packages which has been originated by more than one person, each of whom has made an agreement for carriage by air with another person other than a scheduled air carrier (IATA RP 1601 CSC(19) (paras. 3.811 *et seq.*, below)).

4. Notice on face of the air waybill

3.677 A notice on the face of the air waybill states that it is agreed that the goods described are accepted in apparent good order and condition (except as noted). Such a statement is *prima facie* evidence of the fact stated. If the word "apparent" did not appear then, the carrier's signature to the air waybill would not be construed as *prima facie* evidence that the cargo was in good order and condition. The current notice has amended earlier versions so as to refer to carriage other than by air. This notice also serves to incorporate into the air waybill all the conditions set out on the reverse of the document. The bold upper case typeface and direct language are simple and effective for this purpose (see box 1E).

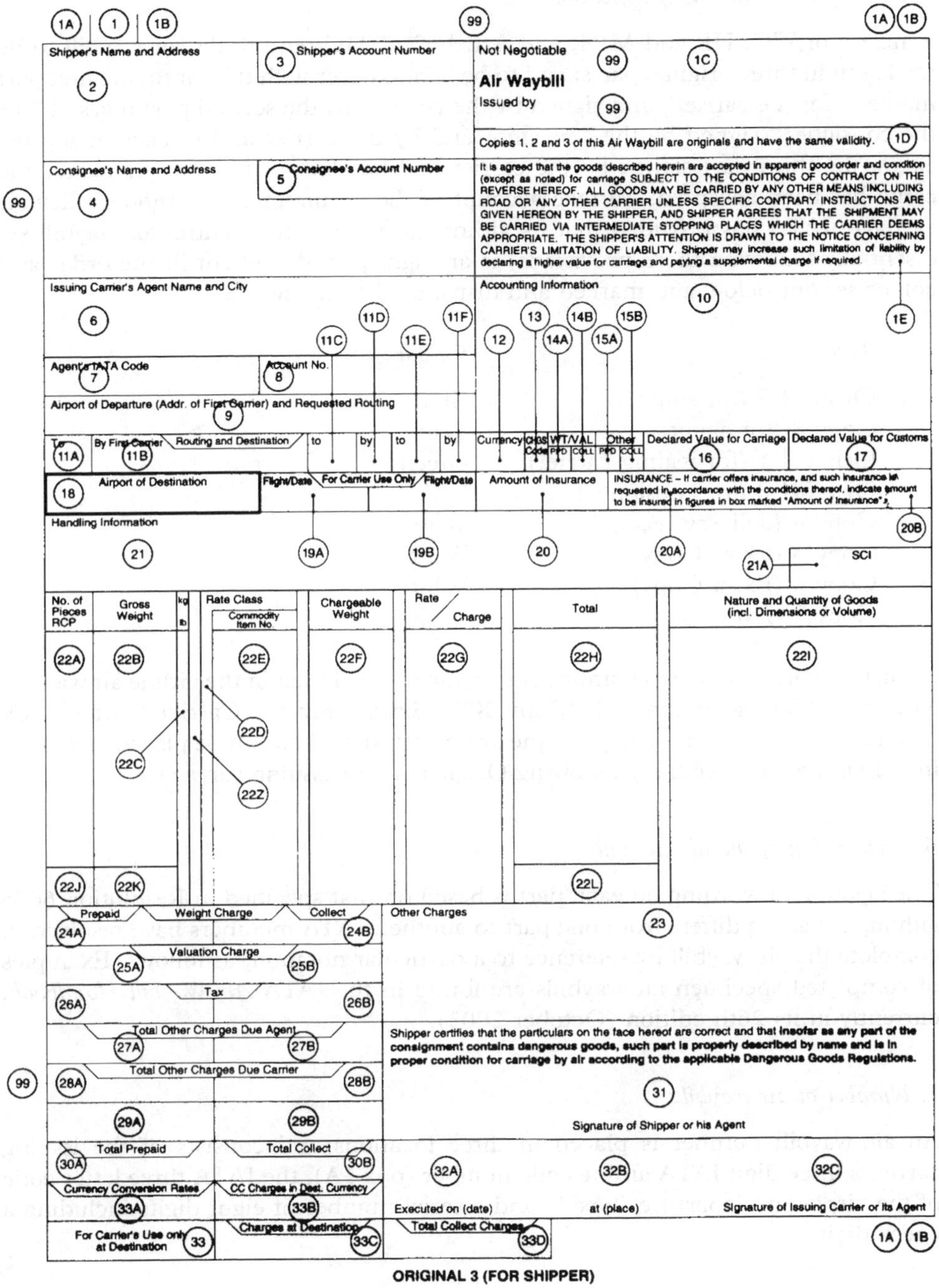
1A 1 1B 99 1A 1B

Shipper's Name and Address 2

3 Shipper's Account Number

Not Negotiable 99 1C

Air Waybill

Issued by 99

Copies 1, 2 and 3 of this Air Waybill are originals and have the same validity. 1D

Consignee's Name and Address 4 99

5 Consignee's Account Number

It is agreed that the goods described herein are accepted in apparent good order and condition (except as noted) for carriage SUBJECT TO THE CONDITIONS OF CONTRACT ON THE REVERSE HEREOF. ALL GOODS MAY BE CARRIED BY ANY OTHER MEANS INCLUDING ROAD OR ANY OTHER CARRIER UNLESS SPECIFIC CONTRARY INSTRUCTIONS ARE GIVEN HEREON BY THE SHIPPER, AND SHIPPER AGREES THAT THE SHIPMENT MAY BE CARRIED VIA INTERMEDIATE STOPPING PLACES WHICH THE CARRIER DEEMS APPROPRIATE. THE SHIPPER'S ATTENTION IS DRAWN TO THE NOTICE CONCERNING CARRIER'S LIMITATION OF LIABILITY. Shipper may increase such limitation of liability by declaring a higher value for carriage and paying a supplemental charge if required.

Issuing Carrier's Agent Name and City 6

Accounting Information 10 1E

11C 11D 11E 11F 12 13 14A 14B 15A 15B

Agent's IATA Code 7

Account No. 8

Airport of Departure (Addr. of First Carrier) and Requested Routing 9

To 11A | By First Carrier 11B | Routing and Destination | to | by | to | by | Currency | CHGS Code | WT/VAL PPD COLL | Other PPD COLL | Declared Value for Carriage 16 | Declared Value for Customs 17

Airport of Destination 18 | Flight/Date | For Carrier Use Only | Flight/Date | Amount of Insurance | INSURANCE – If carrier offers insurance, and such insurance is requested in accordance with the conditions thereof, indicate amount to be insured in figures in box marked "Amount of Insurance".

Handling Information 21 19A 19B 20 20A 20B

21A SCI

No. of Pieces RCP | Gross Weight | kg lb | Rate Class Commodity Item No. | Chargeable Weight | Rate / Charge | Total | Nature and Quantity of Goods (incl. Dimensions or Volume)

22A 22B 22E 22F 22G 22H 22I

22C 22D 22Z

22J 22K 22L

Prepaid 24A | Weight Charge | Collect 24B

Other Charges 23

Valuation Charge 25A 25B

Tax 26A 26B

Total Other Charges Due Agent 27A 27B

Total Other Charges Due Carrier 99 28A 28B

Shipper certifies that the particulars on the face hereof are correct and that **insofar as any part of the consignment contains dangerous goods, such part is properly described by name and is in proper condition for carriage by air according to the applicable Dangerous Goods Regulations.**

31

29A 29B

Signature of Shipper or his Agent

Total Prepaid 30A | Total Collect 30B

32A 32B 32C

Currency Conversion Rates 33A | CC Charges in Dest. Currency 33B

Executed on (date) | at (place) | Signature of Issuing Carrier or its Agent

For Carrier's Use only at Destination 33 | Charges at Destination 33C | Total Collect Charges 33D

1A 1B

ORIGINAL 3 (FOR SHIPPER)

Resolution 600a, Attachment 'B', Appendix 'A'

5. Multi-part document specification

3.678 Article 6 of WC, HP and MP4, and Article 7 of MC require the air waybill to be made out in three original parts; and to be handed over with the cargo, the first part marked "for the carrier" and signed by the consignor, the second part marked "for the consignee" signed by the consignor and by the carrier and to accompany the cargo, the third part signed by the carrier and handed to the consignor after the cargo has been accepted. To take account of the requirements of modern day air carriage, IATA has provided that its airline air waybill (the neutral air waybill set essentially following these provisions) is an eight part document in the order and colour set out below and marked and distributed as follows:

Title	*Colour*
Original 3 (for shipper)	Blue
Copy 8 (for agent)	White
Original 1 (for issuing carrier)	Green
Original 2 (for consignee)	Pink
Copy 4 (delivery receipt)	Yellow
Copy 5 (Extra Copy)	White
Copy 6 (Extra Copy)	White
Copy 7 (Extra Copy)	White

3.679 Further parts, up to a maximum of five, may be included in the airline air waybill, each on white paper marked "Copy XX (Extra copy for Carrier)" where XX denotes the number of the copy of the airline air waybill and to be placed anywhere in the airline air waybill set following Original 1 (for issuing carrier).

6. Preparation of the air waybill

3.680 The layout and wording on each part is based on that specified in Resolution 600a although shading differs from one part to another. IATA members have resolved to complete the air waybill by reference to a particular notation, as follows. Examples of completed specimen air waybills are found in the IATA *Air Waybill Handbook*, currently in its 26th edition (October 2003).

7. Number of air waybills

3.681 An air waybill number is placed in three locations and consists of the issuing carrier's three digit IATA airline code number (box 1A), the IATA three letter code of the airport of departure (box 1) and a serial number of eight digits including a check digit.

8. Consignor and consignee details

3.682 The name, address and country of the consignor and the consignee will be inserted at box 2 and box 4 respectively and a telephonic contact method and number may be inserted below such entries. None of the regimes require such particulars to be recorded. If either party has an account with the air carrier this will be inserted at box 3 and/or box 5, respectively.

9. Issuing carrier's agent

When not pre-printed, the name and location (airport or city) of the carrier's IATA cargo agent entitled to commission and its IATA seven digit code and account number will be inserted at box 6, box 7 and box 8, respectively. *3.683*

10. Routing information

The airport of departure, identified by the IATA three letter code, will be entered at box 9, with any requested routing shown in the same code. At box 11A the IATA three letter code identifying the airport of destination or first transfer point (or city when the name of the airport is unknown or because the city is served by more than one airport) may be inserted. The full name or IATA two character code of the first carrier will be inserted at box 11B with any further information relevant to second and third carriers inserted at boxes 11C–11F inclusive, the airport of destination of the last carrier or city when the name of the airport is unknown being inserted at box 18. Reference should be made to any agreed stopping places for carriage governed by WC. *3.684*

11. Accounting information, currency and charges

Accounting information required by the participating carriers may be inserted at box 10, the currency applicable in the country of departure (by reference to the ISO three letter currency code) will be inserted at box 12 and a two letter code may be inserted at box 13. For charges, an "X" is inserted as appropriate in boxes 14A or 14B according to whether charges by reference to the weight or valuation of the goods are prepaid or collect and similarly, in respect of other charges at origin, in either boxes 15A or 15B. If such information is in conflict with boxes 24A–24B, 25A–25B, 26A–26B, 27A–27B and 28A–28B, the latter take precedence over 14A–14B (as appropriate). *3.685*

12. Declared value for carriage/Customs

The declared value should be specified in box 16 and where no value is declared "N.V.D." is inserted. A value may be inserted for Customs, in box 17, which may be no value declared ("N.C.V."). *3.686*

13. Insurance

Insurance is not offered by all carriers. Where the issuing carrier offers insurance the amount insured or failing that an "XXX" is entered at box 20. *3.687*

14. Handling information

3.688 Handling information may be inserted in box 21, being such marks and any numbers which appear on the cargo, method of packing, name, address, country, or two letter country code and one or more methods of telephonic contact and number of any person to be notified of the arrival of the shipment in addition to the consignee, the name of documents accompanying the air waybill such as any "Consignors' Certification for Live Animals" and special handling instructions that may be required. If the air waybill is issued in the USA, the statement "These commodities licensed by USA for ultimate destination . . . diversion contrary to USA law prohibited" may also appear. Special customs information for shipments from and within the European Union is inserted at Box 21A.

3.689 In the case of dangerous goods, special requirements apply. IATA require either the statement "Dangerous Goods as per attached Consignors' Declaration" followed by "Cargo Aircraft Only" if applicable; or the statement "Dangerous Goods —Consignors' Declaration not required" to be inserted as the first entry. UK Regulations provide that an aircraft shall not carry dangerous goods as cargo unless, *inter alia*, the consignor of the goods has furnished the operator of the aircraft with a dangerous goods transport document, except that such a document shall not be required in respect of such categories of dangerous goods as may be specified in the current English language edition of the *Technical Instructions for the Safe Transport of Dangerous Goods by Air*, approved and published by decision of the Council of ICAO.

15. Shipment information

3.690 The number and gross weight of the pieces of cargo for the applicable rating entry will be inserted in boxes 22A and 22B and the unit of weight used (in kg or lb) inserted in box 22C. A small shaded strip (box 22Z) enables coded entries to reflect services to be provided which are additional to those normally associated with the rate class stipulated in box 22D. Examples include "D" (door to door service) and "J" (priority service).

3.691 One of several designated letter codes will be inserted in box 22D, e.g. "C" (specific commodity rate), "M" (minimum charge) or "Y" (unit load device discount). Specific information relating to rates may also be required to be completed in boxes 22E, 22F and 22G. The total charge or discount for each line entry is to be inserted in box 22H.

3.692 The nature and quantity of the goods will be described in box 22I and due account taken of Dangerous Goods Regulations and with respect to "live animals". For "consolidated shipments" the entry will show "consolidation as per attached list". When the chargeable weight is calculated by reference to the volume of the shipment either the greatest length, greatest width, greatest height, unit of measurement and number of pieces concerned or the volume and unit of measurement will be inserted.

3.693 Provision is made for "Other Charges" in box 23, whether the charge is incurred at origin, en route or at destination. There is a two letter code for particular charges, e.g. "BR" (bank release), "FC" (charges collect fee), "IN" (insurance premium),

"SD" (surface charge—destination). When a consignment is returned because of non-delivery, the new air waybill for the returning carriage should have all charges which should have been but were not collected from the original consignee, inserted in this box.

The weight/volume charge for air carriage, the valuation charge for any value declared for carriage, any tax and any other charges should be inserted as either wholly prepaid or wholly collect in boxes 24A–30B inclusive. 3.694

16. Consignor's certification

The consignor signs in box 31 certifying that the particulars on the face of the air waybill are correct and that in so far as any part of the consignment contains dangerous goods, such part is properly described by name and is in proper condition for carriage by air according to the applicable dangerous goods regulations. 3.695

17. Carrier's signature

The carrier issuing the air waybill[4] or his agent signs in box 32 entering the date and the name of the place concerned. 3.696

18. Conditions of Contract

The currently effective IATA Cargo Conference Resolutions have alternative form Conditions of Contract, being Resolutions 600b (paras. 3.707 *et seq.*, below) and 600b(II) (paras. 3.741 *et seq.*, below). In each case the Conditions are to be printed on the reverse of the three original copies of the air waybill, separately from any "domestic" Conditions of Contract of the carrier concerned. 3.697

[*The next paragraph is 3.707*]

4. See boxes 1A and 1C.

3.707 # X. AIR WAYBILL—CONDITIONS OF CONTRACT (IATA RESOLUTION 600b)

Notice

3.708 **I. Notice appearing on the face of the air waybill**

It is agreed that the goods described herein are accepted for carriage in apparent good order and condition (except as noted) and SUBJECT TO THE CONDITIONS OF CONTRACT ON THE REVERSE HEREOF, ALL GOODS MAY BE CARRIED BY ANY OTHER MEANS INCLUDING ROAD OR ANY OTHER CARRIER UNLESS SPECIFIC CONTRARY INSTRUCTIONS ARE GIVEN HEREON BY THE SHIPPER, AND SHIPPER AGREES THAT THE SHIPMENT MAY BE CARRIED VIA INTERMEDIATE STOPPING PLACES WHICH THE CARRIER DEEMS APPROPRIATE. THE SHIPPER'S ATTENTION IS DRAWN TO THE NOTICE CONCERNING CARRIER'S LIMITATION OF LIABILITY.

3.709 **II. Conditions of contract on the reverse side of the air waybill**

Notice concerning carriers' limitation of liability

If the carriage involves an ultimate destination or stop in a country other than the country of departure, the Warsaw Convention may be applicable and the Convention governs and in most cases limits the liability of carrier in respect of loss of, damage or delay to cargo to 250 Convention Gold Francs per kilogramme which shall be deemed to be equivalent to either 17 special drawing rights, or USD 20, or an amount to be determined under applicable law.

Comment

3.710 These Notices are set out on the face and reverse of the air waybill. They update alternative version 600b(II),[1] which is to be rescinded when Resolution 600b becomes effective. Resolution 600b has not been declared effective.

3.711 **Conditions of Contract**

Condition 1—Definitions

1. In this contract:
   CARRIER includes the air carrier issuing this air waybill and all carriers that carry or undertake to carry the cargo or perform any other services related to such carriage:
   WARSAW CONVENTION means whichever of the following instruments is applicable to the contract of carriage:
   the Convention for the Unification of Certain Rules Relating to International Carriage by Air, signed at Warsaw, 12 October 1929;
   that Convention as amended at The Hague on 28 September 1955;
   that Convention as amended at The Hague 1955 and by Montreal Protocol No. 1, 2, or 4 (1975) as the case may be.

Comment

3.712 This definitions clause updates Condition 1 in the alternative version 600b(II).[1] This version of the clause also sets out various legal regimes that may apply to carriage.

1. For commentary see paras. 3.741 *et seq.*, below.
1. Paras. 3.741 *et seq.*, below.

Condition 2—Incorporation of Conditions of Carriage *3.713*

2.1 Carriage is subject to the rules relating to liability established by the Warsaw Convention unless such carriage is not "international carriage" as defined by that Convention.

2.2 To the extent not in conflict with the foregoing carriage and other related services performed by each carrier are subject to:

2.2.1 applicable laws and government regulations;

2.2.2 provisions contained in the air waybill, Carrier's Conditions of carriage and related rules, regulations, and time tables (but not the times of departure and arrival stated therein) and applicable tariffs of such carrier, **which are made part hereof, and which** may be inspected at any airport or other cargo sales offices from which it operates regular services. When carriage is to/from the USA, the shipper and the consignee are entitled, upon request, to receive a free copy of the conditions of carriage. **The Conditions of Carriage include, but are not limited to:**

2.2.2.1 limits on the carrier's liability for loss, damage or delay of goods, including fragile or perishable goods;

2.2.2.2 claim restrictions, including time periods within which shippers or consignees must file a claim or bring an action against the carrier for its acts or omissions, or those of its agents;

2.2.2.3 rights, if any, of the carrier to change the terms of the contract;

2.2.2.4 rules about the Carrier's right to refuse to carry;

2.2.2.5 rights of the Carrier and limitations concerning delay or failure to perform service, including schedule changes, substitution of alternate carrier or aircraft and rerouting.

Comment

This is the updated version of Condition 2 in the alternative version 600b(II) (para. 3.750, below). *3.714*

Condition 3—Agreed stopping places *3.715*

3. The agreed stopping places (which may be altered by the carrier in case of necessity) are those places, except the place of departure and place of destination, set forth on the face hereof or shown in carrier's timetables as scheduled stopping places for the route. Carriage to be performed hereunder by several successive carriers is regarded as a single operation.

Condition 4—Limitation of liability *3.716*

4. Except as otherwise provided in Carrier's general conditions of carriage and applicable tariffs, in carriage to which the Warsaw Convention does not apply, carrier's liability shall not exceed 17 Special Drawing Rights, as defined by the International Monetary Fund, per kilogramme of cargo lost, damaged or delayed.

Comment

This is the updated version of Condition 4 in the alternative version 600b(II) (para. 3.757, below). *3.717*

3.718 **Condition 5—Declaration of value**

5.1 For cargo accepted for carriage, the Convention permits shipper to increase the limitation of liability by declaring a higher value for carriage and paying a supplemental charge if required.

5.2 In carriage to which the Warsaw Convention does not apply carrier shall, subject to its conditions of carriage and applicable tariffs, permit shipper to increase the limitation of liability by declaring a higher value for carriage and paying a supplemental charge if so required.

Comment

3.719 This is the updated version of Condition 5 in the alternative version 600b(II) (para. 3.759, below). WC and HP apply only to carriage by air subject to Article 18(3) of the Convention in each case; and, in the case of MP , subject to Article 18(4).

3.720 **Condition 6—Package weight**

6.1 In cases of loss of, damage or delay to part of the cargo, the weight to be taken into account in determining carrier's limit of liability shall be only the weight of the package or packages concerned.

6.2 Notwithstanding any other provisions, for "foreign air transportation" as defined by the U.S. Federal Aviation Act:

6.2.1 in the case of loss of, damage or delay to a shipment, the weight to be used in determining carrier's limit of liability shall be the weight which is used to determine the charge for carriage of such shipment; and

6.2.2 in the case of loss of, damage or delay to a part of a shipment, the shipment weight in 6.2.1 shall be prorated to the packages covered by the same air waybill whose value is affected by the loss, damage or delay. The weight applicable in the case of loss of or damage to one or more articles in a package shall be the weight of the entire package.

Comment

3.721 Condition 6.1 repeats what is set out as Condition 6 in the alternative version 600b(II) (para. 3.762, below). To the extent that Condition 6.2 infringes the rules of Article 22 of WC, HP, MP4, MC or other UK law it will be null and void. To the extent in any case that it increases the claimant's damages, it may be upheld.

3.722 **Condition 7—Carrier's servants and agents**

7. Any exclusion or limitation of liability applicable to carrier shall apply to carrier's agents, employees, and representatives and to any person whose aircraft or equipment is used by carrier for carriage and such person's agents, employees and representatives.

Comment

3.723 This is the updated version of Condition 7 in the alternative version 600b(II) (para. 3.766, below).

Condition 8—Delay/deviation, reservation as to mode of carriage *3.724*

8. Carrier undertakes to complete the carriage with reasonable dispatch. Where permitted by applicable laws, tariffs and government regulations, carrier may use alternative carriers, aircraft or modes of transport without notice but with due regard to the interests of the shipper. Carrier is authorised by the shipper to select the routing and all intermediate stopping places that it deems appropriate or to change or deviate from the routing shown on the face hereof.

Comment

This is the updated version of Condition 9 in the alternative version 600b(II) (para. 3.784, below). *3.725*

Condition 9—Complaint *3.726*

9. Receipt by the person entitled to delivery of the cargo without complaint shall be prima facie evidence that the cargo has been delivered in good condition and in accordance with the contract of carriage.

9.1 In the case of loss of, damage or delay to cargo a written complaint must be made to carrier by the person entitled to delivery. Such complaint must be made:

9.1.1 in the case of damage to or partial loss of the cargo, immediately after discovery of the damage and at the latest within 14 days from the date of receipt of the cargo;

9.1.2 in the case of delay, within 21 days from the date on which the cargo was placed at the disposal of the person entitled to delivery;

9.1.3 in the case of non-delivery of the cargo, within 120 days from the date of issue of the air waybill, or if an air waybill has not been issued, within 120 days from the date of receipt of the cargo for transportation by the carrier

9.2 Such complaint may be made to the carrier whose air waybill was used, or to the first carrier or to the last carrier or to the carrier, which performed the carriage during which the loss, damage or delay took place.

9.3 Unless a written complaint is made within the time-limits specified in 9.1 no action may be brought against carrier.

9.4 Any rights to damages against carrier shall be extinguished unless an action is brought within two years from the date of arrival at the destination, or from the date on which the aircraft ought to have arrived, or from the date on which the carriage stopped.

Comment

This is the updated version of Condition 12 in the alternative version 600b(II) (para. 3.793, below). *3.727*

Condition 10—Compliance with law/indemnity *3.728*

10. Shipper shall comply with all applicable laws and government regulations of any country to, from, through or over which the cargo may be carried, including those relating to the packing, carriage or delivery of the cargo, and shall furnish such information and attach such documents to the air waybill as may be necessary to comply with such laws and regulations. Carrier is not liable to shipper and shipper shall indemnify carrier for loss or expense due to shipper's failure to comply with this provision.

Comment

3.729 Condition 10 is identical to Condition 13 in the alternative version 600b(II) (para. 3.796, below).

3.730 **Condition 11—Waiver: prohibition**

11. No agent, employee or representative of carrier has authority to alter, modify or waive any provisions of this contract.

Comment

3.731 This is identical to Condition 14 in the alternative version 600b(II) (para. 3.798, below).

[*The next paragraph is 3.741*]

XI. AIR WAYBILL—CONDITIONS OF CONTRACT (IATA RESOLUTION 600b(II))

Notice 3.741

Notice concerning Carriers' limitation of liability

If the carriage involves an ultimate destination or stop in a country other than the country of departure, the Warsaw Convention may be applicable and the Convention governs and in most cases limits the liability of the carrier in respect of loss, damage, or delay to cargo to 250 French gold francs per kilogram, unless a higher value is declared in advance by the shipper and a supplementary charge paid if required.

The liability limit of 250 French gold francs per kilogram is approximately USD 20.00 per kilogram on the basis of USD 42.22 per ounce of gold.

Comments

1. The purpose of the notice

This Notice, which satisfies the notice requirement of Article 8(q) of WC and HP,[1] prefaces the actual Conditions of Contract in order to give the Notice due prominence. The Notice is the equivalent of the "clause paramount" statement required by the Conventions on carriage by sea. An amended Notice is set out in the IATA alternative form air waybill 600b.[2] *3.742*

The first paragraph of the Notice, is to alert those concerned to the possibility that the carriage may be governed by an international Convention on carriage by air. Whether it is so depends, of course, on the scope provisions of the Conventions concerned. However, all of the air Conventions (WC, HP, MP4 and MC) are similar in this respect. By Article 1 of each Convention it is potentially applicable if, as reiterated by the Notice, the particular carriage "involves an ultimate destination or stop in a country other than the country of departure".[3] Whether it is actually applicable depends on whether it has been adopted by the states concerned in the particular carriage. *3.743*

The first paragraph ends by indicating the importance of the question: the carrier's liability is limited and the limit is then stated in the second and last paragraph of the Notice. Such was the perception in the past of the importance of the Notice that, if the air waybill does not include such a Notice, under Article 9 of WC and HP (but not the subsequent MP4 and MC) the carrier is not entitled to avail himself of the provisions by which the liability of the carrier is limited. *3.744*

2. The unit of account

The unit of account in terms of French gold francs is now only relevant in UK law to carriage subject to WC. In the UK an amount is specified to be taken for the *3.745*

1. *Samuel Montagu & Co. Ltd.* v. *Swiss Air Transport Co. Ltd.* [1966] 2 Q.B. 306 (C.A.); and *Exim Industries* v. *Pan Am World Airways*, 754 F. 2d 106 (2 Cir., 1985).

2. Para. 3.709, above.

3. See, in particular, Comment 3 on Art. 1 of HP (paras. 3.43 *et seq.*, above); and Condition 3 of Conditions of Contract (IATA Resolution 600b), para. 3.715, above.

purposes of Article 22 of WC as being equivalent to the sums expressed in such francs (Carriage by Air (Sterling Equivalents) Order 1999), although the application of that sum being specified in pounds sterling, to a judgment given in a foreign currency where appropriate, is not entirely clear. It may be that the existence of the said Order precludes same.

3.746 For carriage subject to HP, MP4 or MC the carrier's limitation (in respect of liabilities arising out of an occurrence which took place on or after the relevant provisions came into force) is no longer be expressed in gold francs but by reference to SDRs, 17 SDRs (per kilogramme) being substituted for 250 French gold francs.

3.747 **Condition 1—Definitions**

As used in this contract " carrier" means all air carriers that carry or undertake to carry the goods hereunder or perform any other services incidental to such air carriage, "Warsaw Convention" means the Convention for the Unification of certain Rules relating to International Carriage by Air, signed at Warsaw, 12 October 1929,[1] or that Convention as amended at The Hague, 28h September 1955,[2] which ever may be applicable, and "French gold francs" means francs consisting of $65\frac{1}{2}$ milligrams of gold with a fineness of nine hundred thousandths.

Comment

3.748 As well as defining French gold francs, Condition 1 defines the carriers to which the Conditions apply, however, Condition 1 does not define carriers as such but, assuming a definition is to be found elsewhere, it limits the applicability of the Conditions to cases of carriage regulated by WC or HP.[3] WC and HP, however, refer to carriers but do not define them. Moreover, Article 1 of WC and HP mentions but does not define "air transport undertaking".[4] "Carrier" is defined contractually by Article 1.6 of the Conditions of Carriage for Cargo: IATA Recommended Practice 1601 CSC(19), paragraph 3.812, below.

3.749 Note that Condition 1 has been amended in IATA's alternative air waybill 600b, Condition 1 (para. 3.711, above) to include reference to the further legal regimes created by the Convention as amended by Montreal Protocols Nos. 5, 1, 2 and 4 of 1975, now in force and implemented into UK law. Also, in the UK, the Guadalajara Convention will apply. It has been resolved by IATA that, when Air Waybill 600b becomes effective, Air Waybill 600b(II) shall be rescinded.

3.750 **Condition 2—Governing rules**

2.1 Carriage hereunder is subject to the rules relating to liability established by the Warsaw Convention unless such carriage is not "international carriage"[1] as defined by that Convention.

1. Paras. 3.307 *et seq.*, above.
2. Paras. 3.37 *et seq.*, above.
3. As to which may be applicable see the Introduction, Comment 9, paras. 3.13 *et seq.*, above.
4. See Comment 6 on Art. 1 of HP, paras. 3.48 *et seq.*, above.

1. For the meaning of international carriage see Art. 1(2) of HP, para. 3.37, above.

2.2 To the extent not in conflict with the foregoing, carriage hereunder and other services performed by each carrier are subject to:

2.2.1 applicable laws (including national laws implementing the Convention), government regulations, orders and requirements;

2.2.2 provisions herein set forth; and

2.2.3 applicable tariffs, rules, conditions of carriage, regulations and timetables (but not the times of departure and arrival therein) of such carrier, which are made part hereof and which may be inspected at any of its offices and at airports from which it operates regular services. In transportation between a place in the United States or Canada and any place outside thereof the applicable tariffs are the tariffs in force in those countries.

Comments

1. Terms of the contract as evidenced by the waybill

Condition 2 affirms that the carriage to which the air waybill relates is governed by the Warsaw Convention, i.e. in this instance, WC or HP. Additionally, carriers' tariffs, conditions of carriage and other provisions are incorporated by reference. The Notice provisions on the face and highlighted on the reverse of the air waybill, underline the fact that it is a document of carriage obviously containing conditions[1]—including some that exclude and restrict liability—and the common form nature of the IATA conditions in the industry, all support their incorporation into the contract.[2] However, for cases falling within the scope of the relevant Convention, the Convention is the exclusive source of liability on matters regulated by the Convention; there is no concurrent liability, for example, in tort.[3] *3.751*

It would be highly unusual for a party to vary the conditions set out in this text and which are printed on the reverse of the air waybill. However, various overstamped endorsements may be made on the face of the document. Sometimes they have the effect of varying the terms on the reverse in order to record matters agreed upon, e.g., that cargo be carried on a particular flight date. More often various overstamped endorsements are put onto the face of the air waybill evidencing steps in the course of carriage, especially timings with respect to the handling of cargo at particular locations. The latter do not actually form terms of the contract but evidence its performance or not, as the case may be. *3.752*

Moreover, Condition 2.2.3 incorporates such further, more detailed, terms not only of the carrier issuing the air waybill but also of any other carrier performing carriage services.[4] As regards timetables, however, the words in brackets are to avoid time being fixed for carriage by reference to timetables. The carrier may otherwise agree to cargo being consigned on a particular flight date and/or by a particular *3.753*

1. See *Poseidon Freight Fowarding Co. Ltd.* v. *Davies Turner Southern Ltd.* [1996] 2 Lloyd's Rep. 388 (C.A.).

2. As regards incorporation of contractual terms, see further Comment 2 on Art. 1 of HP, paras. 3.40 *et seq.*, above.

3. See the Introduction, Comment 4, para. 3.6, above; also Comment 1 on Art. 28 of HP, paras. 3.174 *et seq.*, above.

4. By such reference on the air waybill this provision incorporates such further, more detailed, terms not only of the carrier issuing the air waybill but also of any other carrier performing carriage and other services thereunder. In the event of dispute, there will be an argument as to whether or not those further terms have been effectively incorporated into the contract, see Comment 2 on Art. 1 of HP, paras. 3.40 *et seq.*, above.

aircraft type and/or route but not fix a time for carriage. On the other hand, express shipments, especially of documents, sent by some specialist carriers on non-IATA terms may agree to fix a time for carriage and/or offer a money-back undertaking in event of delay.

2. Applicable competition law

3.754 As regards applicable public law regulation listed in Condition 2.2.1, a current feature is the evolution of European Community competition law applicable to air transport, both within the European Community and between the European Community and third countries, and the challenge to Member State approval of tariffs established in concert between carriers as anti-competitive and so null and void under the Treaty of Rome Article 85(1) and 85(2).[5] In particular "Government" is not defined in Resolution 600b(ii), and the involvement of European Community level legislation should be recognised. Moreover, "Applicable tariffs" can be complicated, varying according to *inter alia* carrier, route, nature of cargo and jurisdiction. It is clearly impractical for a common form air waybill to set out all these provisions. In so far as rates and charges are concerned, it is those in effect on date of issuance of the air waybill which apply: conceivably this could give rise to a dispute in the event of an earlier booking on a falling market: the carrier would presumably argue that the consignor accepted the new rate in the event of accepting the air waybill without complaint.

3.755 **Condition 3—Identity of carrier(s), place of departure/destination**

The first carrier's name may be abbreviated on the face hereof, the full name and its abbreviation being set forth in such carrier's tariffs, conditions of carriage, regulations and timetables. The first carrier's address is the airport of departure shown on the face hereof. The agreed stopping places (which may be altered by carrier in case of necessity) are those places, except the place of departure and the place of destination, set forth on the face hereof or shown in carrier's timetables as scheduled stopping places for the route. Carriage to be performed hereunder by several successive carriers is regarded as a single operation.

Comment

3.756 This Condition, which is deleted in the alternative IATA air waybill 600b, sets out some of the particulars that Article 8 of WC requires that the air waybill should contain. The requirement for those particulars was deleted from HP and is not found in MP4 or MC either.

3.757 **Condition 4—Limitation of liability**

Except as otherwise provided in carrier's tariffs or Conditions of Carriage, in carriage to which the Warsaw Convention does not apply, carrier's liability shall not exceed U.S.D. 20.00 or the

5. See Whish, *Competition Law* (5th ed., London, 2003), Chap. 23.

equivalent per kilogramme of goods lost, damaged or delayed, unless a higher value is declared by the shipper and a supplementary charge paid.

Comment

In the UK this clause has practically no application since the common law rules are unlikely to apply and the 1967 Order (now replaced by the 2004 Order) has legislated for non-international carriage and the carriage of mail and postal packets being a class of cargo not within the scope of WC or HP. IATA seems to have been concerned to provide for a limitation of liability in those jurisdictions which do not have such all-embracing legislation in carriage by air. Conceivably it could apply to non-Convention international carriage and to non-international carriage performed gratuitously and other than by an air transport undertaking. The substance of the Condition has been retained in IATA alternative air waybill 600b but IATA has deleted the reference to US $20.00 and substituted 17 SDRs. *3.758*

Condition 5—Declaration of value for carriage *3.759*

If the sum entered on the face of the air waybill as "Declared Value for Carriage" represents an amount in excess of the applicable limits of liability referred to in the above Notice and in these Conditions and if the shipper has paid any supplementary charge that may be required by the Carrier's tariffs, Conditions of Carriage or Regulations, this shall constitute a special declaration of value and in this case Carrier's limit of liability shall be the sum so declared. Payment of claims shall be subject to proof of actual damages suffered.

Comment

This Condition corresponds to Article 22(2) of WC (para. 3.343, above) and HP (para. 3.125, above). The value declared will be entered in box 16.[1] Any amount entered in box 17 would not constitute a declaration of value.[2] Carriers' conditions may, and IATA Resolution 612 (Shipper's Request for Changes of Air Waybill Amounts) does, provide that the declared value for carriage entered on the air waybill shall not be amended after despatch of the consignment from the airport of departure shown on the air waybill. *3.760*

Carriers' conditions of carriage or regulations may stipulate values in excess of which carrier may refuse carriage of the cargo concerned.[3] They may also stipulate that consignors may not declare a value for part only or differentiate between different value declarations as between parts of any one shipment. Individual carriers may stipulate limits that may be declared for carriage both with respect to individual consignments and with respect to one aircraft. Typically, valuation limits for one consignment may differ according to whether the shipment is to be carried *3.761*

1. See Comment 1 on Art. 22 of HP, paras. 3.126 *et seq.*, above.
2. See *Corocraft Ltd.* v. *Pan American Airways Inc.* [1969] 1 Q.B. 616.
3. See IATA Conditions of Carriage for Cargo, Recommended Practice 1601, Condition 3.2, paras. 3.831/3.832 *et seq.*, below.

solely over the lines of one carrier or to be the subject of interline carriage, when the limit may be lower. Limits may vary considerably from carrier to carrier.

3.762

Condition 6—Package weight

In cases of loss, damage or delay of part of the consignment, the weight to be taken into account in determining Carrier's limit of liability shall be only the weight of the package or packages concerned.

Comment

3.763 Condition 6 sets out the weight to be taken into consideration in calculating the carrier's limit of liability and accords with the approach commonly adopted to claims adjustment. However, carriers today ordinarily prefer not to issue a waybill for each package. Moreover, freight forwarder's consolidation of cargo, whereby many individual consignments and an equal or greater number of packages are consigned under one air waybill and loaded aboard aircraft, either as one integral unit or intermixed with other cargo, will be one consignment or "package". Whereas Condition 6 is in conformity with the practice of 1930 and the law under WC, under the later versions of the regime such as HP it may be null and void under Article 23.

3.764 Under Condition 6 the carrier's liability in respect of loss of or damage to a package forming part of a consignment of cargo is limited to 250 French gold francs per kilogramme of the lost or damaged package and not to 250 French gold francs per kilogramme of the total consignment of which the lost or damaged package forms part, nor to 250 French gold francs per kilogramme of the part of the total consignment which has its value affected by the loss of or damage to the package.[1] However, Article 22(2)(c) of HP and MP4, and Article 22(4) of MC provide that when the loss, damage or delay of part of registered cargo, or of an object contained therein, affects the value of other packages covered by the same air waybill, the total weight of such other package or packages shall also be taken into consideration in determining the limit of liability. In the UK this rule also applied to non-international carriage under the 1967 Order, Sched. 1.[2] See now S.I. 2004/1899.

3.765 Consequently, in the IATA alternative air waybill 600b[3] an extra and different condition has been added for "foreign air transportation"; and the United States Government acting by Civil Aeronautics Board Order has stipulated[4] that:

"For transportation to/from the United States, Article 6 shall be stated in the following language: notwithstanding any other provision for foreign air transportation as defined in the US Federal Aviation Act as amended, in case of loss or damage or delay of a shipment or part thereof, the weight to be used in determining the Carrier's limit of liability shall be the weight

1. *Datacard Corp.* v. *Air Express International Corp.* [1983] 2 Lloyd's Rep. 81.
2. *Applied Implants Technology Ltd.* v. *Lufthansa Cargo* [2000] 2 Lloyd's Rep. 46.
3. Paras. 3.707 *et seq.*, above.
4. CAB 79–10-101.

which is used (or a pro rata share in the case of part shipment loss, damage or delay) to determine the transportation charge for such shipment."

Condition 7—Carrier's servants and agents *3.766*

Any exclusion or limitation of liability applicable to Carrier shall apply to and be for the benefit of Carrier's agents, servants and representatives and any person whose aircraft is used by Carrier for carriage and its agents, servants and representatives. For purpose of this provision, Carrier acts herein as agent for all such persons.

Comments

1. The benefit of exclusions or limitations

Condition 7 is a potentially wide-ranging contractual provision going beyond but not necessarily conflicting with the provisions of the Conventions. By stipulating that the carrier is the agent for the class of persons referred to, Condition 7 excludes or limits liability of the persons who may not, but in practice often under the Guadalajara Convention would, be able to limit their liability as if carrier. Under English law the agency device is now unnecessary as the same result can be achieved under the Contracts (Rights of Third Parties) Act 1999. *3.767*

Moreover, on the one hand, Condition 7 appears to apply, for the benefit of the persons concerned, not only the limits of liability set out in Article 22 of WC, HP, MP4 and MC but also to apply the other rules relating to liability applicable to the carrier, including the Conditions of Contract. On the other hand, the benefit extended is limited to "any exclusion or limitation of liability applicable to Carrier". Moreover, under certain circumstances no exclusion or limitation of liability is applicable at law in international carriage under WC and HP: *3.768*

(i) where the carrier accepts cargo without an air waybill,[1]
(ii) where the air waybill does not contain all the particulars required by WC or HP, whichever is applicable, under Article 8(a)(i) to (q) inclusive,[2]
(iii) where Article 25 or 25A of WC or HP applies or
(iv) where there is a declaration of value.[3]

Note that for carriage under MP4 and MC the limitation sum is no longer disapplied on these grounds.

2. Persons who benefit in addition to the carrier

Servants are employees. Representatives are not defined. An agent has been defined by Article 1 of Conditions of Carriage for Cargo: IATA Recommended Practice 1601 CSC(19)[4] as "any person who has authority, express or implied, to act for or on behalf of Carrier in relation to the carriage of cargo". Cases decided with respect *3.769*

1. See Art. 9 of WC (para. 3.319, above) and HP (para. 3.66, above).
2. *Ibid.*
3. See Condition 5, para. 3.759, above.
4. Para. 3.812, below.

to WC and HP have given a wide meaning to the phrase "servant or agent" in the context of security and handling services: the exact ambit of the phrase being a matter for the facts of individual cases.[5] Persons whose aircraft is used by the carrier might encompass any aircraft manufacturer, owner or operator whether or not an air carrier, albeit that in most countries it is unlikely to be held to apply so widely as this would extend the regime beyond the class of persons within its ambit.

3.770 Under Condition 7 all these persons, in addition to the carrier, benefit from the exclusions or limitations. However, the benefit of this Condition for such other persons cannot be better than the underlying effectiveness of the Conditions for the carrier. It may not therefore extend to any acts or omissions outside performance of the contract for the carriage by air. Where the class of persons sought to be treated as if the carrier goes beyond those for whom statute has intervened in the legislation implementing the Conventions, as well as the Contracts (Rights of Third Parties) Act 1999, the effectiveness of this benefit might also be challenged for want of consideration from those other persons and/or want of authority, although presumably such a person would usually ratify the carrier's authority at least in the face of a claim. The wide definition of carrier and the provisions of the Guadalajara Convention,[6] which extended the regime to an actual non-contracting carrier, create difficulties in the application of this Condition. Although carrier A's limitation will apply for the benefit of carrier A's agents, when the cargo is passed for onward carriage to carrier B, it does not follow that anyone other than carrier B's agents have the benefit of B's limitation. If B is an air carrier, special provisions apply at law, under the Guadalajara Convention, as between carriers A and B where e.g. B is not a carrier who has been contracted by the consignor to carry the cargo successively to A but is instead a carrier who has so agreed with carrier A.[7] Then carrier A cannot subject carrier B to liability exceeding the Article 22 limit nor, unless carrier B agrees, can carrier A bind carrier B to any assumption of obligations not imposed by the various Conventions or any waiver of rights conferred therein or any declaration of value of cargo However, carrier B and its servants and agents can subject carrier A to liability without the Article 22 limits, in the event of damage caused by their intentional or reckless acts done with knowledge that damage would probably result and/or by their wilful misconduct under Article 25, because B's acts and omissions are deemed to be also those of A but only if in carriage by air.

3.771 **Condition 8—Delay/deviation**

8.1 Carrier[1] undertakes to complete the carriage[2] hereunder with reasonable despatch. Carrier may use alternate Carriers or aircraft and may, without notice and with due regard to

5. See Art. 25A, Comment 2, paras. 3.163 *et seq.*, above. Also *Reed* v. *Wiser*, 555 F. 2d 1079 (2 Cir., 1977); 434 U.S. 922 (1977); *Julius Young Jewellery Manufacturing Co. Inc.* v. *Delta Air Lines Inc.*, 414 N.Y.S. 2d 528 (1979). "Agent" may be given a wider meaning in the USA than in other countries: Clarke, *Air*, Art. 20, note 1.

6. Paras. 3.525 *et seq.*, above.

7. For the authority of carrier A, see Condition 8, para. 3.771, below.

1. See Condition 1 (para. 3.747, above) and Art. 1 of the Conditions of Carriage for Cargo: IATA Recommended Practice 1601 CSC(19), para. 3.812, below.

2. See Condition 10, para. 3.786, below.

the interests of the shipper use other means of transportation. Carrier is authorised to select the routing and all intermediate stopping places that it deems appropriate or to change or deviate from the routing shown on the face hereof. This sub-paragraph is not applicable to/from U.S.A.

8.2 Carrier undertakes to complete the carriage hereunder with reasonable despatch. Except within U.S.A. where carrier tariffs will apply, carrier may substitute alternate carriers or aircraft and may without notice and with due regard to the interests of the shipper use other means of transportation. Carrier is authorised by shipper to select the routing and all intermediate stopping places that it deems appropriate or to change or deviate from the routing on the face hereof. This sub-paragraph is applicable only to/from U.S.A.

Comments

1. Reasonable despatch

Condition 8 has the effect of imposing a qualified obligation of speed, reasonable despatch, one which would usually be implied at common law anyway and which complements and qualifies Article 19 of WC whereby the carrier is liable for delay. Condition 8 has been read as an implied contractual disclaimer against a strict interpretation of Article 19 coupled, in the case of WC[1] (but not HP, MP4 or MC) with the requirement to fix times for commencement or completion of carriage and to state the route. *3.772*

The modern IATA air waybill still provides (box 19 headed "For Carrier use only") for one or more particular flights/dates to be inserted but, it is submitted, this does not prevent the carrier from relying on any defences to liability under the applicable regime or Conditions of Contract such as Condition 8. Thus when particular flights/dates have been entered in box 19 or otherwise agreed upon, this would give rise to an obligation to perform carriage on those flights with reasonable, but not utmost, despatch. Alternatively, where no particular flights/dates have been agreed upon, there is nonetheless an obligation to complete carriage within a reasonable time. *3.773*

In one case a shipment of garments was consigned by air from London-Gatwick to Nigeria in two loads, which arrived respectively 16 and 19 days later than agreed between the consignor and carrier—in so far as there was an agreement that the cargo should go on a flight intended to leave Gatwick on a particular date. It was conceded that, in the context of a charter operation, a delay of five days would have been acceptable but the court held that a delay of 16 or 19 days, "dealing as we are with air traffic, which people employ because they wish to enjoy the advantages of speed which air travel offers . . . is an undue and unreasonable delay and there is a breach of the obligation to deliver within a reasonable time".[2] The measure of damage for breach is not regulated by WC (or the other air Conventions) and is left to national law.[3] Condition 8 also clarifies the associated question of substitution and sub-contracting. *3.774*

1. Art. 8(p).
2. *Panalpina International Transport Ltd.* v. *Densil Underwear Ltd.* [1981] 1 Lloyd's Rep. 187, 190.
3. See Comment 2 on Art. 18 of HP, paras. 3.101 to 3.102, above.

2. Sub-contracting

3.775 In common law unauthorised sub-contracting has been sometimes characterised as deviation.[4] Here it is authorised in principle. However, there will be cargoes, particularly those where special handling may be required and where a particular air carrier may hold out particular expertise, aircraft or other equipment suitable to consignors' goods, for which the identity of a particular carrier is important to the consignor. This is more likely to arise in the context of charters of aircraft than of a contract for the carriage of goods over the lines of the carrier, whether scheduled or non-scheduled.

3.776 Where the contract allows it and the carrier substitutes another air carrier, the provisions of the Guadalajara Convention[5] or MC,[6] as the case may be, will apply, defining the respective liabilities of and defences available to each carrier. In particular, the damages recoverable from the actual and the contracting carrier and from their servants or agents, acting within the scope of their employment, shall not exceed the highest amount which could be awarded against either the contracting or the actual carrier but none of these persons shall be liable for a sum in excess of the limit applicable to him.

3. Substitution: aircraft

3.777 The provision for alternate aircraft is unusual in that no particular aircraft is normally stipulated on the face of the air waybill. However, carriers' tariffs may refer to flights being performed by a particular aircraft type. Substitution of one aircraft type for another, both being operated by the same carrier, will generally be of little concern to the consignor save in cases where the cargo, perhaps by reason of its volume, can only be carried in a particular aircraft type.

3.778 In some circumstances substitution of aircraft can result in cargo being unable to be loaded. Condition 8 does not give a contractual right qualifying the earlier undertaking in the Condition to carry cargo "with reasonable dispatch" allowing it temporarily to withhold cargo from onward carriage and so the carrier's liability in such circumstances will depend upon what the parties have agreed.[7]

4. Substitution: other means of transportation

3.779 Using other means of transportation, i.e. carriage other than by air, may have been agreed upon so that no question should arise of the carrier being in breach of contract. Nonetheless disputes can arise where the agreement concerned is unclear by reason of a multiplicity of parties being concerned with the carriage and/or because it is only upon careful analysis of the carrier's tariff and conditions of carriage that its services (denoted by a particular set of characters that may appear

4. A recent road case on the point is *MRS Distribution Ltd.* v. *D.S. Smith (UK) Ltd.*, 2004 S.L.T. 631.

5. See paras. 3.525 *et seq.*, above.

6. See paras. 3.555 *et seq.*, above.

7. See the Conditions of Carriage for Cargo: IATA Recommended Practice 1601 CSC(19), Art. 6 at 6.3, paras. 3.867/3.868, below.

in box 19 of the air waybill under the heading flight/date) in fact denote carriage other than by air, most usually by road. It must also be remembered that under WC (and other Conventions) persons other than those named in the air waybill as consignor and consignee may have a right of action against the carrier.[8]

If they have not expressly agreed to a mode of carriage other than by air, the carrier must rely on Condition 8. It gives a wide authority because the carrier, by definition, includes *inter alia* all carriers that carry cargo and no notice to and therefore consultation with the consignor or, it would seem, anyone else is required. However, the carrier must act "with due regard to the interests of the shipper". The carrier may well not know what is in the interests of a shipper/consignee, save facilitating performance of the contract of carriage as originally agreed by some means of carriage other than by air.[9] *3.780*

Where, as is most often the case, the alternative mode, carriage by road, the CMR Convention may be applicable.[10] Disputes commonly arise in the context of the interface between carriage by air and carriage by road. Where the parties have expressly agreed that their contract should be partly for carriage by air and partly for carriage by road, it may be the case that, conceptually, the contract is not one for carriage by air but a contract for combined transportation, partly by air and partly by road. If so, the law can provide traps for the unwary by reason of the different rules of liability that may apply to the various Conventions. For example, the documentary formalities of CMR are almost satisfied by the provisions of the air waybill, but the air waybill does not contain the statement required by CMR Article 6(1)(k) that carriage is subject, notwithstanding any clause to the contrary, to Article 6 *et seq.* of CMR. However, the biggest trap is the possibility of higher monetary limits.[11] In such a case the solution in the alternative IATA air waybill 600b[12] is to allow carriage by any means and limit liability to SDR 17 per kilogramme which is higher than under Article 23 of CMR. *3.781*

5. *Route*

Condition 8 also clarifies the question of route. The route agreed upon is that stated on the face of the air waybill at box 9, if completed, or at box 11B. Accordingly, it is possible for the air waybill to record little information evidencing any agreement on route.[13] In carriage by sea alteration of the contractually agreed upon route may give rise to the doctrine of deviation, disentitling a shipowner from relying on exclusions in his contract.[14] Its relevance to carriage by air is in some doubt even at *3.782*

8. See e.g. HP Art. 26, para. 3.169, above; also Clarke, *Air*, Art. 18, note 1, and cases cited.
9. The clause does not, though, provide for shippers' interests to be the only matters to which regard must be paid; see Muller-Röstin (1992) *Air Law*, Vol. XVII, No. 6 at 295.
10. See paras. 1.8 *et seq*, above.
11. See *Quantum Ltd.* v. *Plane Trucking Ltd.* [2002] 2 Lloyd's Rep. 24 (C.A.), discussed in connection with Art. 2 of CMR, para. 1.20, above.
12. Paras. 3.707 *et seq.*, above. See Conditions 4 and 8, paras. 3.716 and 3.724, above.
13. However, see the Conditions of Carriage for Cargo: IATA Recommended Practice 1601 CSC(19), Art. 6 at 6.3, paras. 3.867/3.868, above.
14. Carver, *Bills of Lading* (London, 2001), para. 9–213.

common law; its application to a contract of carriage governed by uniform law of the kind established by the air Conventions is highly undesirable.[15]

3.783 Note that in the corresponding Condition of IATA air waybill 600b,[16] Condition 8, the text has been considerably amended. In particular, Condition 8.2 has been deleted.

3.784 **Condition 9—Carrier's liability**

Subject to the Conditions herein, the Carrier shall be liable for the goods during the period they are in its charge or the charge of its agent.

Comment

3.785 Condition 9 adds little to the effect of Article 18 of WC and HP, however, when WC or HP apply, it should be recalled that there is also the potential for other carriers to be liable as successive carriers under Article 30. That is why Condition 9 has been deleted from the alternative IATA air waybill 600b. Condition 9 is important only in the limited circumstances where WC and HP do not apply and the common law rules apply instead.[1]

3.786 **Condition 10—Payment**

10.1 Except when the Carrier has extended credit to the Consignee without the written consent of the shipper, the shipper guarantees payment of all charges for carriage due in accordance with Carrier's tariffs, Conditions of Carriage and related Regulations, applicable laws (including national laws implementing the Convention), Government Regulations, Orders and requirements.

10.2 When no part of the consignment is delivered, a claim with respect to such consignment will be entertained even though transportation charges thereon are unpaid.

Comment

3.787 The carrier's conditions of carriage, regulations and tariffs detail the rates and charges from time to time applying, being those published by the carrier and in effect on the date of issue of the air waybill. These documents also detail the basis of the rates and charges and the services that are and are not included. Conditions of carriage may stipulate whether rates and charges may be paid in any particular currency.[1]

3.788 Condition 10, which was deleted from the alternative IATA air waybill 600b, concerns the liability of the consignor. In some cases it is agreed that charges shall be payable on a charges collect basis (payable by the consignee). However, in

15. See the Comments on Art. 6 of CMR, and citations, paras. 1.29 *et seq.*, above.

16. Paras. 3.724, above.

1. See the Introduction, Comment 8, para. 3.12, above.

1. See e.g the Conditions of Carriage for Cargo: IATA Recommended Practice 1601 CSC(19), Art. 5 at 5.4, paras. 3.862/3.863, below.

practice restrictions are often placed on the nature of cargo (e.g. perishables) that may be accepted on a charges collect basis. Other cases of such restrictions relate to the value of the cargo (and thereby the worth of the carrier's lien), the identity of the last carrier, the identity of the consignee, and the effect of any currency regulations in the country of destination; for example, a country where regulations prevent the conversion of funds into other currencies or the transfer of funds to other countries. Indeed, the carrier's conditions of carriage generally provide that cargo will not be accepted unless charges have been prepaid unless otherwise arranged. Moreover, against the possibility of charges for carriage not having been paid by a consignor, the carrier may be given a lien on the cargo and be given the right to dispose of the cargo at public or private sale in or towards satisfaction of any liability to it.[2]

The carrier's conditions of carriage are further likely to provide that the consignor *3.789*
is liable for all charges and expenses resulting from or in connection with the failure of the consignee to take delivery of the shipment after its arrival at the airport of destination. Such liability is to include but not be limited to carriage charges incurred in returning the shipment if so required by the consignor's instructions.

Condition 11—Delivery *3.790*

Notice of arrival of goods will be given promptly to the Consignee or to the person indicated on the face hereof as the person to be notified. On arrival of the goods at the place of destination, subject to the acceptance of instructions from the shipper prior to arrival of the goods at the place of destination, delivery will be made to, or in accordance with, the instructions of the Consignee. If the Consignee declines to accept the goods or cannot be communicated with, disposition will be in accordance with instructions of the shipper.

Comment

Condition 11, which was deleted from the alternative IATA air waybill 600b,[1] *3.791*
concerns the practicalities of delivery. The consignee is entitled on arrival of the cargo at the place of destination to require the carrier to hand over the air waybill and to deliver the cargo, on payment of any charges due and on complying with the conditions of carriage set out in the air waybill: Article 13(2) of WC and HP. The consignee may not be the consignor's intended ultimate recipient as goods may be consigned to a third party, such as a bank, for the financial security of the consignor or another party. However, the carrier's obligation is not to deliver to any party other than the consignee named on the air waybill, unless the consignee has so provided, or the carrier will be liable for loss sustained. In the event of breach of this obligation the consignee's claim against the carrier is in respect of "loss" of the cargo under Article 18 of WC or HP.[2]

2. See e.g. Art. 5, para. 3.759, above. Concerning the possibility of set-off, see *Panalpina International Transport Ltd.* v. *Densil Underwear Ltd.* [1981] 1 Lloyd's Rep. 187.

1. Paras. 3.707 *et seq.*, above.

2. E.g. *Hatzlachh* v. *Tradewinds*, 738 F. Supp. 714 (S.D.N.Y., 1990); see Clarke, *Air*, Art. 18, note 4.

3.792 As regards delivery "in accordance with the instructions of the Consignee", under Article 10(2) of the Conventions[3] the consignor must indemnify the carrier against all damage suffered by the carrier or by another person to whom the carrier is liable, by reason of the irregularity, incorrectness or incompleteness of the particulars and statements furnished by the consignor. However, this indemnity does not relieve the carrier of its obligation to seek disposition instructions from the consignor in appropriate cases and to act upon them within a reasonable time. For so long as the cargo remains in charge of the carrier any breach by the carrier of the consignor's disposition instructions is governed by Articles 18(1) and 19 of the Conventions. In practice the carrier will wish to impose terms on the consignor if practicable.

3.793 **Condition 12—Complaint**

12.1 The person entitled to delivery must make a complaint to the Carrier in writing in the case:

12.1.1 Of visible damage to the goods, immediately after discovery of the damage, and at the latest within fourteen days from receipt of the goods;

12.1.2 Of other damage to the goods, within fourteen days from the date of receipt of the goods;

12.1.3 Of delay, within 21 days of the date the goods are placed at his disposal; and

12.1.4 Of non-delivery of the goods within 120 days from the date of the issue of the air waybill.

12.2 For the purpose of 12.1 complaint in writing may be made to the Carrier whose air waybill was used or to the First Carrier or to the Last Carrier or to the Carrier who performed the transportation during which the loss, damage or delay took place.

12.3 Any rights to damages against Carrier shall be extinguished unless an action is brought within two years from the date of arrival at the destination, or from the date of which the aircraft ought to have arrived, or from the date on which the transportation stopped.

Comment

3.794 Condition 12 concerns complaints and, in particular, the time periods for complaints. Article 26 of WC stipulates shorter periods; those stipulated in Condition 12 derive from HP Article 26(2),[1] and have been retained in the corresponding provisions of MP4 and MC, except for the 120 day rule in Condition 12.1.4. That is not found in any of the Conventions and is thus open to challenge as being null and void under Article 32 of e.g. HP.[2] Another difference concerns the scope of the Condition: whereas Condition 12.3 substantially repeats Article 29(1) of WC, HP, and MP4, and Article 35 of MC, it differs by limiting it to actions against, rather than actions brought by, the carrier.

3.795 With respect to carriage not governed by any of the Conventions, a time limit is imposed that would not exist at common law: for non-international carriage, and for carriage governed by common law rules in their entirety, there is no provision equivalent to Article 26. The ordinary rules in the Civil Jurisdiction and Judgments Act 1982 apply.

3. See paras. 3.66, 3.321, above.

1. As regards detail of the notice requirement, see the Comments on Art. 26, paras. 3.170 *et seq.*, above.

2. See also *Western Digital Corporation* v. *British Airways plc* [2001] Q.B. 733 (C.A).

Condition 13—Compliance with law *3.796*

The shipper shall comply with all applicable laws and Government regulations of any country to, from, through or over which the goods may be carried, including those relating to the packing, carriage or delivery of the goods, and shall furnish such information and attach such documents to this air waybill as may be necessary to comply with such laws and regulations. Carrier is not liable to the shipper for loss or expense due to the shipper's failure to comply with this provision.

Comment

Condition 13, while purporting to exempt the carrier from liability to the consignor (shipper) for loss or expense arising from the consignor's failure to comply with such law(s), stops at that: it does not expressly stipulate an indemnity in respect of any loss suffered by the carrier arising from non-compliance by the consignor, in addition to any indemnity in favour of the carrier otherwise existing at law.[1] However, Condition 10 of the alternative IATA air waybill 600b,[2] whilst generally maintaining the above language, expressly adds in the last sentence of this condition, an indemnity in carrier's favour for loss or expense. *3.797*

Condition 14—Waiver: prohibition *3.798*

No agent, servant or representative of Carrier has authority to alter, modify or waive any provisions of this contract.

Condition 15—Insurance *3.799*

If Carrier offers insurance and such insurance is requested, and if the appropriate premium is paid and the fact recorded on the face hereof, the goods covered by this air waybill are insured under an open policy for the amount requested as set out on the face hereof (recovery being limited to the actual value of goods lost or damaged provided that such amount does not exceed the insured value). The insurance is subject to the terms, conditions and coverage (from which certain risks are excluded) of the open policy, which is available for inspection at an office of the Issuing Carrier by the interested party. Claims under such policy must be reported immediately to an office of Carrier.

Comment

Not all carriers offer first party insurance and the Conventions do not require them to do so, however, Article 50 of MC[1] requires carriers to maintain adequate insurance covering their liability under that Convention. Condition 15 has been deleted from the alternative IATA air waybill 600b.[2] *3.800*

[*The next paragraph is 3.811*]

1. Notably under Art. 10(2) of WC, HP and MP4, and Art. 10(3) of MC.
2. Paras. 3.707 *et seq*, above.
1. Para. 3.648, above.
2. Paras. 3.707 *et seq*, above.

XII. CONDITIONS OF CARRIAGE FOR CARGO: IATA RECOMMENDED PRACTICE 1601 CSC(19)

3.811 *[Text in italics (to be shaded) are changed conditions yet to receive final regulatory approval from the US Dept. of Transportation referred to as (CSC(23) 1601) except those marked with an asterisk (referred to as (CSC(24) 1601) and those marked with a double asterisk (CSC(19) 1601).]*

3.812

Article 1—Definitions

1.1 "AGENT." Except when the context otherwise requires any person who has authority, express or implied, to act for or on behalf of carrier in relation to the carriage of cargo.

1.2 "AIR WAYBILL." The document entitled "Air Waybill" made out by or on behalf of the shipper, which evidences the contract between the shipper and carrier for carriage of cargo over routes of carrier.

1.3 "APPLICABLE CONVENTION." Unless the context requires otherwise, whichever of the following instruments is applicable to the contract of carriage.

1.1 "AGENT." Except when the context otherwise requires any person who has authority, express or implied, to act for or on behalf of CARRIER in relation to the CARRIAGE of CARGO.

1.2 "AIR WAYBILL." Any document made out by or on behalf of the SHIPPER, which evidences the contract between the SHIPPER and CARRIER of cargo.

1.3 "APPLICABLE CONVENTION." Unless the context requires otherwise, whichever of the following instruments is applicable to the CARRIAGE.

- 1.3.1 The Convention for the Unification of Certain Rules Relating to International Carriage by Air, signed at Warsaw 12 October 1929; (hereinafter referred to as the Warsaw Convention);
- 1.3.2 The Warsaw Convention as amended at The Hague on 28 September 1955;
- 1.3.3 The Warsaw Convention as amended by Additional Protocol No.1 of Montreal 1975;
- 1.3.4 The Warsaw Convention as amended at The Hague 1955 and by Additional Protocol No.2 of Montreal 1975;
- 1.3.5 The Warsaw Convention as amended at the Hague 1955 and by Protocol No.4 of Montreal 1975.
- *1.3.6 the Montreal Convention 1999.*

1.4 "CARGO" (which is equivalent to the term "Goods"). Anything carried or to be carried in an aircraft except mail, or baggage carried under a passenger ticket and baggage check, but includes baggage moving under an air waybill or shipment record.

1.5 "CARRIAGE" (which is equivalent to the term "Transportation"). Carriage of cargo by air or by another means of transport, whether gratuitously or for reward.

1.6 "CARRIER." Includes the air carrier issuing the air waybill or preserving the shipment record and all carriers that carry or undertake to carry the cargo or to perform any other services related to such air carriage.

1.7 "CHARGES COLLECT." The charges entered on the air waybill or shipment record for collection from the consignee against delivery of the shipment.

1.8 "CONSIGNEE." The person whose name appears on the air waybill or shipment record, as the party to whom the shipment is to be delivered by carrier.

1.4 "CARGO" (which is equivalent to the term "GOODS"). Anything carried or to be carried in an aircraft or by any other means of transportation except mail, or baggage carried under a passenger ticket and baggage check, and includes any item moving under an AIR WAYBILL or SHIPMENT record.

1.5 "CARRIAGE" (which is equivalent to the term "Transportation"). CARRIAGE of CARGO by air or by another means of transportation, whether gratuitously or for reward.

1.6 "CARRIER." Includes the air carrier designated in the AIR WAYBILL or the SHIPMENT RECORD and all carriers that carry or undertake to carry the CARGO or to perform any other services related to such CARRIAGE.

1.7 "CHARGES COLLECT." The charges entered on the AIR WAYBILL or SHIPMENT RECORD for collection from the CONSIGNEE against delivery of the SHIPMENT.

1.8 "CONSIGNEE." The person whose name appears on the AIR WAYBILL or SHIPMENT RECORD, as the party to whom the SHIPMENT is to be delivered by CARRIER.

1.9 "DAYS." Full calendar days, including Sundays and legal holidays; provided that for purposes of notification the balance of the day upon which notice is despatched shall not be counted.

1.10 "DELIVERY SERVICE." The surface carriage of inbound shipments from the airport of destination to the address of the consignee or that of his designated agent or to the custody of the appropriate government agency when required, including any incidental surface carriage between airports.

1.11 "PICK-UP SERVICE." The surface carriage of outbound shipments from the point of pickup at the address of the shipper or that of his designated agent to the airport of departure, including any incidental surface carriage between airports.

1.12 "SHIPMENT" (which is equivalent to the term "Consignment"). Except as otherwise provided herein, one or more packages, pieces or bundles of cargo accepted by carrier from one shipper at one time and at one address receipted for in one lot and under a single air waybill or a single shipment record, for carriage to one consignee at one destination address.

1.10 "DELIVERY SERVICE." The surface CARRIAGE of inbound SHIPMENTS from the airport of destination to the address of the CONSIGNEE or that of his designated agent or to the custody of the appropriate government agency when required.

1.11 "PICK-UP SERVICE." The surface CARRIAGE of outbound SHIPMENTS from the point of pickup at the address of the SHIPPER or that of his designated agent to the airport of departure.

1.12 "SHIPMENT" (which is equivalent to the term "Consignment"). Except as otherwise provided herein, one or more packages, pieces or bundles of CARGO accepted by CARRIER from one SHIPPER at one address receipted for in one lot and under a single AIR WAYBILL, for CARRIAGE to one CONSIGNEE at one destination address.

1.13 "SHIPMENT RECORD." Any record of the contract of carriage preserved by carrier, evidenced by means other than an air waybill.

1.14 "SHIPPER" (which is equivalent to the term "Consignor"). The person whose name appears on the air waybill or shipment record, as the party contracting with carrier for the carriage of cargo.

1.13 "SHIPMENT RECORD." Any record of the contract of carriage preserved by CARRIER, evidenced by means other than an AIR WAYBILL.

1.14 "SHIPPER" (which is equivalent to the term "Consignor"). The person whose name appears on the AIR WAYBILL or SHIPMENT RECORD, as the party contracting with CARRIER for the CARRIAGE of CARGO.

1.15 "SPECIAL DRAWING RIGHT." A Special Drawing Right as defined by the International Monetary Fund.

Comments

Article 1.6, containing an inclusive definition of carrier, is important because the Conventions refer to carriers but do not define them. Article 1.6 is designed to be all-embracing with the intention of affording as wide a class of carriers as possible the benefit of the provisions and limitations of liability in the applicable Convention. In order to identify the carrier on the air waybill it is necessary to look in a number of places. *3.813*

Reference is made to the carrier issuing the air waybill (a) in coded form (intelligible only to the experienced consignor or his agent) at box 1A; (b) in terms of preprinted information or, failing that, by the name and head office address *3.814* corresponding to the Box 1A airline code number at box 1C; and (c) by the issuing carrier's signature at box 32C. However, the carrier's agent may sign, and the pro-forma air waybill makes it clear on the face that he is signing as such, his full details being set out in box 6. Moreover, if the carrier issuing the air waybill is not solely to effect the carriage, but merely issues the air waybill for carriage over the lines of another carrier, the issuing carrier does so as agent for the other carrier.[1]

3.815 For those carriers, who are contracted to perform carriage and against whom an action may lie at law, see Article 30(1) and (2) of the applicable Convention. For the purposes of identifying the first carrier, reference should be made to box 11 where the full name or IATA two character code of the carrier concerned will be found inserted; this will not be the issuing carrier unless that carrier is also first to perform carriage. Successive carriers should also each be identified there. In the case of carriage being performed by a carrier other than by a contracting carrier, the identity of that carrier will not be found on the air waybill copy of the consignor although it will be endorsed on the air waybill accompanying the cargo.

3.816 It is important to note that persons coming within the definition of carrier, as above, may not be the only persons who are regarded by the law as carriers engaged in the carriage by air of the cargo concerned. Freight forwarders may act simply as the agent of the consignor and/or of the carrier when, subject to the applicable law, their acts will be governed by the law of agency and any particular contractual provisions. However, they will be carriers in relation to their customers, if they issue their own air waybills to consignors providing for carriage by air and then, most obviously having consolidated several consignments of cargo, subsequently contract, as consignor, with another carrier to effect such carriage, most obviously also then naming themselves or an overseas agent as consignee on the air waybill of that other carrier.

3.817

Article 2—Applicability

2.1 General

These conditions shall apply to all carriage of cargo, including all services incidental thereto, performed by or on behalf of carrier; provided however that if such carriage is "International Carriage" as defined in the applicable Convention (see 1.3) such carriage shall be subject to the provisions of the applicable Convention and to these conditions to the extent that these conditions are not inconsistent with the provisions of such Convention.

These conditions shall apply to all CARRIAGE OF CARGO, including all services incidental thereto, performed by or on behalf of CARRIER; provided however that if such CARRIAGE is "International Carriage" as defined in the APPLICABLE CONVENTION such CARRIAGE shall be subject to the provisions of the APPLICABLE CONVENTION and to these conditions to the extent that these conditions are not inconsistent with the provisions of such APPLICABLE CONVENTION.

3.818 **2.2 Applicable laws and Carrier's tariffs**

To the extent not in conflict with 2.1 all carriage and other services performed by carrier are subject to:

1. See Art. 11.10, para. 3.902, below.

2.2.1 applicable laws (including national laws implementing a Convention or extending the rules of the applicable Convention to carriage which is not "International Carriage" as defined in the applicable Convention) government regulations, orders and requirements;

2.2.2 these conditions and other applicable tariffs, rules, regulations and timetables (but not the times of departure and arrival therein specified) of carrier which may be inspected at any of its offices and at airports from which it operates regular services.

To the extent not in conflict with 2.1 all CARRIAGE and other services performed by CARRIER are subject to:

2.2.1 applicable laws (including national laws implementing a Convention or extending the rules of the APPLICABLE Convention to CARRIAGE which is not "International CARRIAGE" as defined in the APPLICABLE CONVENTION) government regulations, orders and requirements;

2.2.2 these conditions and other applicable tariffs, rules, regulations and timetables (but not the times of departure and arrival therein specified) of CARRIER which may be inspected at any of its offices and at airports from which it operates regular services.

2.3 Application to United States and Canada *3.819*

These conditions do not apply to carriage between places in the United States or in Canada or between a place in the United States or in Canada and any place outside thereof to which tariffs in force in those countries apply. The tariffs applicable to such carriage are available for inspection at the offices of carrier.

2.3 Application to United States and Canada *3.820*

These conditions do not apply to CARRIAGE between places in the United States or in Canada or between a place in the United States or in Canada and any place outside thereof to which tariffs in force in those countries apply. The tariffs applicable to such CARRIAGE are available for inspection at the offices of CARRIER.

2.4 Gratuitous carriage *3.821*

With respect to gratuitous carriage, carrier reserves the right to exclude the application of all or any part of these conditions.

2.4 Gratuitous carriage *3.822*

To the extent permitted by law with respect to gratuitous CARRIAGE, CARRIER reserves the right to exclude the application of all or any part of these conditions.

2.5 Charters *3.823*

With respect to carriage of cargo performed pursuant to a charter agreement with carrier, such carriage shall be subject to carrier's charter tariffs applicable thereto (if any) and these conditions shall not apply except to the extent provided in said charter tariff. Where carrier has no charter tariff applicable to such charter agreement, these conditions shall apply to such agreement except that carrier reserves the right to exclude the application of all or any part of these conditions and, in case of divergence between the applicable provisions of these conditions and the conditions contained or referred to in the charter agreement, the latter shall prevail and the shipper, by accepting carriage pursuant to a charter agreement, whether or not concluded with the shipper, agrees to be bound by the applicable terms thereof.

2.5 Charters *3.824*

With respect to CARRIAGE of CARGO performed pursuant to a charter agreement with CARRIER, such CARRIAGE shall be subject to CARRIER's charter tariffs applicable thereto (if any) and these conditions shall not apply except to the extent provided in said charter tariff.

Where CARRIER has no charter tariff applicable to such charter agreement, these conditions shall apply to such agreement except that CARRIER reserves the right to exclude the application of all or any part of these conditions and, in case of divergence between the applicable provisions of these conditions and the conditions contained or referred to in the charter agreement, the latter shall prevail and the SHIPPER, by accepting CARRIAGE pursuant to a charter agreement, whether or not concluded with the SHIPPER, agrees to be bound by the applicable terms thereof.

3.825 **2.6 Change without notice**

These conditions and the published rates and charges are subject to change without notice except to the extent otherwise provided by applicable law or government regulations or order; provided however that no such change shall apply to a contract of carriage after the date of issuance of the air waybill by carrier or after the date the rate or charge for the carriage has been entered in the shipment record.

3.826 *2.6 Change without notice*

These conditions and the published rates and charges are subject to change without notice except to the extent otherwise provided by applicable law or government regulations or order; provided however that no such change shall apply to a contract of CARRIAGE after the date of conclusion of the contract of CARRIAGE or after the date the rate or charge for the CARRIAGE has been entered in the SHIPMENT RECORD.

3.827 **2.7 Effective rules**

All carriage of cargo governed by these conditions shall be subject to carrier's rules, regulations and tariffs in effect on the date of issuance of the air waybill by carrier or on the date of the shipment record, whichever is applicable, provided that in the event of inconsistency between these conditions and carrier's rules, regulations and tariffs, these conditions shall prevail.

3.828 *2.7 Effective rules*

All CARRIAGE of CARGO governed by these conditions shall be subject to CARRIER's rules, regulations and tariffs in effect on the date of the conclusion of the contract of CARRIAGE, provided that in the event of inconsistency between these conditions and CARRIER's rules, regulations and tariffs, these conditions shall prevail.

Comment

3.829 Although Article 2 regulates the applicability of the Conditions of Carriage for Cargo (IATA RP 1601) they cannot be considered in isolation. They will usually fall to be considered in conjunction with IATA air waybill Conditions of Contract version 600b or 600b(II).[1] Moreover, as is recognised by Condition 2.2, to the extent that other means of transportation are used, other mandatory law, including international Conventions such CMR,[2] may apply; and these Conditions will apply only to the extent that they are not in conflict with any other mandatory law.

3.830 **Article 3—Acceptability of goods for carriage**

3.1 Cargo acceptable

3.1.1 Carrier undertakes to transport, subject to the availability of suitable equipment and space, all shipments unless otherwise excluded by carrier's regulations and provided:

1. Paras. 3.707 *et seq.* and 3.741 *et seq.*, above.
2. For which see paras. 1.8, *et seq.*, above.

3.1.1 CARRIER undertakes to transport, subject to the availability of suitable equipment and space, all SHIPMENTS unless otherwise excluded by CARRIER's regulations and provided:

3.1.1.1 the transportation, or the exportation or importation thereof is not prohibited by the laws or regulations of any country to be flown from, to or over;

3.1.1.2 they are packed in a manner suitable for carriage by aircraft;

3.1.1.2 they are packed in a manner ready for CARRIAGE as required by the issuing CARRIER and any subsequent CARRIER;

3.1.1.3 they are accompanied by the requisite shipping documents;

3.1.1.4 they are not likely to endanger aircraft, persons or property, or cause annoyance to passengers.

3.1.1.4 they are not likely to endanger aircraft or any other means of transportation, persons or property, or cause annoyance to passengers.

3.1.2 Carrier reserves the right without assuming any liability to refuse carriage of cargo when circumstances so require.

3.2 Valuation limit of shipment *3.831*

Carrier may refuse carriage of shipments having a declared value for carriage in excess of the amount specified in carrier's regulations.

3.2 Valuation limit of shipment *3.832*

CARRIER may refuse CARRIAGE of SHIPMENTS having a declared value for CARRIAGE in excess of the amount specified in CARRIER's regulations.

3.3 Packing and marking of cargo *3.833*

3.3.1 Shipper is responsible for ensuring that the cargo is packed in an appropriate way for carriage so as to ensure that it can be carried safely with ordinary care in handling and so as not to injure or damage any persons, goods or property. Each package shall be legibly and durably marked with the name and full address of the shipper and consignee.

3.3.2 Packages containing valuables as defined in carrier's regulations must be sealed if so requested by carrier.

3.3 Packing and marking of cargo *3.834*

3.3.1 SHIPPER is responsible for ensuring that the CARGO is packed in an appropriate way for CARRIAGE so as to ensure that it can be carried safely with ordinary care in handling and so as not to injure or damage any persons, goods or property. Each package shall be legibly and durably marked so as to identify the SHIPPER and CONSIGNEE.

3.3.2 The CARRIER reserves the right to refuse the transportation of cargo that is not suitably marked packed and/or marked.

3.4 Cargo acceptable only under prescribed conditions *3.835*

Dangerous goods, live animals, perishables, fragile goods, human remains, and other special cargo are acceptable only under the conditions set forth in carrier's regulations applicable to the carriage of such cargo.

3.4 Special Cargo *3.836*

Special CARGO, including but not limited to valuables, dangerous goods, live animals, perishables, fragile goods, and human remains, is acceptable only under the conditions set forth in CARRIER's regulations applicable to the CARRIAGE of such CARGO.

3.5 Responsibility for non-observance of conditions relating to special cargo *3.837*

Responsibility for non-observance of the conditions relating to the carriage of cargo rests upon the shipper who shall indemnify carrier for any loss, damage, delay, liability or penalties carrier may incur because of carriage of any such cargo.

3.838 *3.5 Responsibility for non-observance of conditions relating to special cargo*

Responsibility for non-observance of the conditions relating to the CARRIAGE of CARGO rests upon the SHIPPER who shall indemnify CARRIER for any loss, damage, delay, liability or penalties CARRIER may incur because of CARRIAGE of any such CARGO.

3.839 **3.6 Carrier's right of inspection**

Carrier reserves the right to examine the packaging and contents of all shipments and to enquire into the correctness or sufficiency of information or documents tendered in respect of any shipment but carrier shall be under no obligation to do so.

3.840 *3.6 Carrier's right of inspection*

CARRIER reserves the right to examine the packaging and contents of all SHIPMENTS and to enquire into the correctness or sufficiency of information or documents tendered in respect of any SHIPMENT but CARRIER shall be under no obligation to do so.

3.841 **3.7 Unit Load Devices**

When shipper undertakes to load a unit load device (ULD) he must comply with carrier's loading instructions and shall be liable for and indemnify carrier against all consequences of any non-compliance with such instructions.

3.842 *3.7 Unit Load Devices*

When SHIPPER undertakes to load a unit load device (ULD) he must comply with CARRIER's loading instructions and shall be liable for and indemnify CARRIER against all consequences of any non-compliance with such instructions.

Comment

3.843 Both carriers' conditions and government regulations[1] prescribe many matters with regard to what is acceptable for carriage and, in particular, to the carriage of dangerous goods.

3.844 **Article 4—Documentation**

4.1 Air waybill

The shipper shall make out or have made out on his behalf an air waybill in the form, manner and number of copies prescribed by carrier, and shall deliver such air waybill to carrier simultaneously with the acceptance of the cargo by carrier for carriage. However, charges for carriage and other charges, insofar as they have been ascertained, shall be inserted in the air waybill by carrier. Carrier may require the shipper to make out, or have made out on his behalf, separate air waybills when there is more than one package.

3.845 *4.1 Air waybill*

The SHIPPER shall make out or have made out on his behalf an AIR WAYBILL in the form, manner and number of copies prescribed by CARRIER, and shall deliver such AIR WAYBILL to CARRIER simultaneously with the acceptance of the CARGO by CARRIER for CARRIAGE. However, charges for CARRIAGE and other charges, insofar as they have been ascertained, shall be inserted in the AIR WAYBILL by CARRIER. CARRIER may require the SHIPPER to make

1. See Air Navigation Order 2000 (S.I. 2000/1562), the ICAO Technical Instructions for the Safe Transport of Dangerous Goods by Air and the Air Navigation (Dangerous Goods) Regulations 2000 (S.I. 2000/2786).

out, or have made out on his behalf, separate AIR WAYBILLS when there is more than one package.

4.2 Shipment record *3.846*

Carrier, with the express or implied consent of the shipper, may substitute for the delivery of an air waybill a shipment record to preserve a record of the carriage to be performed. If such shipment record is used carrier shall, if so requested by the shipper, deliver to the shipper in accordance with carrier's regulations a Receipt permitting identification of the shipment and access, in accordance with carrier's regulations, to the information contained in the shipment record.

*4.2 Shipment record*** *3.847*

Carrier, with the express or implied consent of the shipper, may substitute for the delivery of an air waybill a shipment record to preserve a record of the carriage to be performed. If such shipment record is used carrier shall, if so requested by the shipper, deliver to the shipper in accordance with carrier's regulations a Receipt for the Cargo permitting identification of the shipment and access, in accordance with carrier's regulations, to the information contained in the shipment record.

4.2 Shipment record *3.848*

CARRIER, with the express or implied consent of the SHIPPER, if required by the APPLICABLE CONVENTION, may substitute for the delivery of an AIR WAYBILL a SHIPMENT RECORD to preserve a record of the CARRIAGE to be performed. If such SHIPMENT RECORD is used CARRIER shall, if so requested by the SHIPPER, deliver to the SHIPPER in accordance with CARRIER's regulations a Receipt for the CARGO permitting identification of the SHIPMENT and access, in accordance with CARRIER's regulations, to the information contained in the SHIPMENT RECORD.

4.3 Apparent condition/packing of the cargo *3.849*

If the apparent order and condition of the cargo and/or packing is in any way defective the shipper shall, if an air waybill is delivered, include on the air waybill a statement of such apparent order and condition. If no air waybill is delivered the shipper shall advise carrier of the apparent order and condition of the cargo, to enable carrier to insert an appropriate reference thereto in the shipment record. However, if the shipper fails to include such statement in the air waybill or to advise carrier of the apparent order and condition of the cargo, or if such statement or advice is incorrect, carrier may include in the air waybill or insert in the shipment record a statement of the apparent order and condition of the cargo, or note a correction thereto.

4.3 Apparent condition/packing of the cargo *3.850*

If the apparent order and condition of the CARGO and/or packing is in any way defective the SHIPPER shall, if an AIR WAYBILL is delivered, include on the AIR WAYBILL a statement of such apparent order and condition. If no AIR WAYBILL is delivered the SHIPPER shall advise CARRIER of the apparent order and condition of the CARGO, to enable CARRIER to insert an appropriate reference thereto in the SHIPMENT RECORD. However, if the SHIPPER fails to include such statement in the AIR WAYBILL or to advise CARRIER of the apparent order and condition of the CARGO, or if such statement or advice is incorrect, CARRIER may include in the AIR WAYBILL or insert in the SHIPMENT RECORD a statement of the apparent order and condition of the CARGO, or note a correction thereto.

4.4 Preparation, completion or correction by Carrier *3.851*

Carrier may at the request of the shipper expressed or implied, make out the air waybill in which event, subject to proof to the contrary, carrier shall be deemed to have done so on behalf of the shipper. If the air waybill handed over with the cargo or if the particulars and statements relating to the cargo furnished by or on behalf of the shipper to carrier for insertion in the shipment record do not contain all the required particulars, or if the air waybill or such particulars or statements contain any error, carrier is authorised to complete or correct the air waybill or particulars or statements to the best of carrier's ability without being under any obligation to do so.

3.852 *4.4 Preparation, completion or correction by Carrier*

CARRIER may at the request of the SHIPPER expressed or implied, make out the AIR WAYBILL in which event, subject to proof to the contrary, CARRIER shall be deemed to have done so on behalf of the SHIPPER. If the AIR WAYBILL handed over with the CARGO or if the particulars and statements relating to the CARGO furnished by or on behalf of the SHIPPER to CARRIER for insertion in the SHIPMENT RECORD do not contain all the required particulars, or if the AIR WAYBILL or such particulars or statements contain any error, CARRIER is authorised to complete or correct the AIR WAYBILL or particulars or statements to the best of CARRIER's ability without being under any obligation to do so.

3.853 **4.5 Responsibility for particulars**

The shipper is responsible for the correctness of the particulars and statements relating to the cargo inserted by him or on his behalf in the air waybill or furnished by him or on his behalf to carrier for insertion in the shipment record. Where such information is provided by means of Electronic Data Interchange, it is the responsibility of the shipper or the shipper's agent to verify contents, accuracy and completeness of the EDI messages and subsequent messages according to the agreed standards and specifications. The shipper shall indemnify carrier against all damage suffered by him or by any other person to whom carrier is liable, by reason of the irregularity, incorrectness or incompleteness of the particulars and statements furnished by the shipper or on his behalf.

3.854 *4.5 Responsibility for particulars*

The SHIPPER is responsible for the correctness of the particulars and statements relating to the CARGO inserted by him or on his behalf in the AIRWAYBILL or furnished by him or on his behalf to CARRIER for insertion in the SHIPMENT RECORD. Where such information is provided by means of Electronic Data Interchange (EDI), it is the responsibility of the SHIPPER or the SHIPPER's agent to verify contents, accuracy and completeness of the EDI messages and subsequent messages according to the agreed standards and specifications. The SHIPPER shall indemnify CARRIER against all damage suffered by him or by any other person to whom CARRIER is liable, by reason of the irregularity, incorrectness or incompleteness of the particulars and statements furnished by the SHIPPER or on his behalf.

3.855 **4.6 Alterations**

Air waybills, the writing on which has been altered or erased, need not be accepted by carrier.

3.856 *4.6 Alterations*

AIR WAYBILLS, the writing on which has been altered or erased, need not be accepted by CARRIER.

3.857

Article 5—Rates and charges

5.1 Applicable rates and charges

Rates and charges for carriage governed by these conditions are those duly published by carrier and in effect on the date of issuance of the air waybill by carrier, or on the date the rate or charge for the carriage has been entered in the shipment record.

Rates and charges for CARRIAGE governed by these conditions are those duly published by CARRIER and in effect on the date the contract of carriage has been concluded.

5.2 Basis of rates and charges *3.858*

Rates and charges will be based on the units of measurement and subject to the rules and conditions published in carrier's regulations and rate tariffs.

5.2 Basis of rates and charges *3.859*

Rates and charges will be based on the units of measurement and subject to the rules and conditions published in CARRIER's regulations and rate tariffs.

5.3 Services not included in published rates and charges *3.860*

Except as otherwise provided in carriers' regulations, rates and charges apply only from airport to airport and do not include any ancillary service given by carrier in connection with the air carriage.

5.3 Services not included in published rates and charges *3.861*

Except as otherwise provided in CARRIERS' regulations, rates and charges apply only from airport to airport and do not include any ancillary service given by CARRIER in connection with the air CARRIAGE.

5.4 Payment of charges *3.862*

5.4.1 Rates and charges are published in the currency shown in the applicable rate tariffs, and may be paid in any currency acceptable to carrier. When payment is made in a currency other than in the currency in which the rate or charge is published, such payment will be made at the rate of exchange established for such purpose by carrier, the current statement of which is available for inspection at carrier's office where payment is made.

5.4 Payment of charges *3.863*

5.4.1 Rates and charges are published in the currency shown in the applicable rate tariffs, and may be paid in any currency acceptable to CARRIER. When payment is made in a currency other than in the currency in which the rate or charge is published, such payment will be made at the rate of exchange established for such purpose by CARRIER, the current statement of which is available for inspection upon first request at CARRIER's office where payment is made. The provisions of this paragraph are subject to applicable exchange laws and government regulations

5.4.2 Full applicable charges, whether prepaid or collect fees, duties, taxes, charges, advances and payments, made or incurred or to be incurred by carrier and any other sums payable to carrier will be deemed fully earned, whether or not the cargo is lost or damaged, or fails to arrive at the destination specified in the contract of carriage. All such charges, sums and advances will be due and payable upon receipt of the cargo by carrier, except that they may be collected by carrier at any stage of the service performed under the contract of carriage.

5.4.2 Full applicable charges, whether prepaid or collect fees, duties, taxes, charges, advances and payments, made or incurred or to be incurred by CARRIER and any other sums payable to CARRIER will be deemed fully earned, whether or not the CARGO is lost or damaged, or fails to arrive at the destination specified in the contract of CARRIAGE. All such charges, sums and advances will be due and payable upon receipt of the CARGO by CARRIER, except that they may be collected by CARRIER at any stage of the service performed under the contract of carriage and may be collected at any time upon demand of CARRIER.

5.4.3 The Shipper guarantees payment of all unpaid charges, unpaid charges collect, advances and disbursements of carrier. The shipper also guarantees payment of all costs, expenditures, fines, penalties, loss of time, damage and other sums which carrier may incur or suffer by reason of the inclusion in the shipment of articles the carriage of which is prohibited by law, or the illegal, incorrect or insufficient marking, numbering, addressing or packing of packages or descriptions of the cargo, or the absence, delay or incorrectness of any export or import licence or any required certificate or document, or any improper customs valuation, or incorrect statement of weight or volume. Carrier shall have a lien on the cargo for each of the foregoing and, in the event of non payment thereof, shall have the right to dispose of the cargo at public or private sale (provided that prior to such sale carrier shall have mailed notice thereof to the shipper or to the consignee at the address stated in the air waybill) and to pay itself out of the proceeds of such sale any and all such amounts. No such sale shall, however, discharge any liability to pay any deficiencies, for which the shipper and the consignee shall remain jointly and severally liable. By taking delivery or exercising any other right arising from the contract of carriage, the consignee agrees to pay such charges, sums and advances, except pre-paid charges.

***5.4.3 The Shipper guarantees payment of all unpaid charges, unpaid charges collect, advances and disbursements of carrier. The shipper also guarantees payment of all costs, expenditures, fines, penalties, loss of time, damage and other sums which carrier may incur or suffer by reason of the inclusion in the shipment of articles the carriage of which is prohibited by law, or the illegal, incorrect or insufficient marking, numbering, addressing or packing of packages or descriptions of the cargo, or the absence, delay or incorrectness of any export or import licence or any required certificate or document, or any improper customs valuation, or incorrect statement of weight or volume. Carrier shall have a lien on the cargo for each of the foregoing and, in the event of non payment thereof, shall have the right to dispose of the cargo at public or private sale (provided that prior to such sale carrier shall have mailed notice thereof to the shipper or to the consignee at the address stated in the air waybill or in the shipment record) and to pay itself out of the proceeds of such sale any and all such amounts. No such sale shall, however, discharge any liability to pay any deficiencies, for which the shipper and the consignee shall remain jointly and severally liable. By taking delivery or exercising any other right arising from the contract of carriage, the consignee agrees to pay such charges, sums and advances, except pre-paid charges.*

5.4.3 The SHIPPER guarantees payment of the freight rate, storage charges, and all other unpaid charges, unpaid CHARGES COLLECT, advances and disbursements of CARRIER. The SHIPPER also guarantees payment of all costs, expenditures, fines, penalties, loss of time, damage and other sums which CARRIER may incur or suffer by reason of the inclusion in the SHIPMENT of articles the CARRIAGE of which is prohibited by law, or the illegal, incorrect or insufficient marking, numbering, addressing or packing of packages or descriptions of the CARGO, or the absence, delay or incorrectness of any export or import licence or any required certificate or document, or any improper customs valuation, or incorrect statement of weight or volume. CARRIER shall have a lien on the CARGO for each of the foregoing and, in the event of non payment thereof, shall have the right to dispose of the CARGO at public or private sale (provided that prior to such sale CARRIER shall have mailed notice thereof to the SHIPPER or to the CONSIGNEE at the address stated in the AIR WAYBILL) and to pay itself out of the proceeds of such sale any and all such amounts. No such sale shall, however, discharge any liability to pay any deficiencies, for which the SHIPPER and the CONSIGNEE shall remain jointly and severally liable. By taking delivery or exercising any other right arising from the contract of CARRIAGE, the CONSIGNEE agrees to pay such charges, sums and advances, except pre-paid charges.

5.4.4 If the gross weight, measurement, quantity or declared value of the cargo exceeds the gross weight, measurement, quantity or declared value on which charges for carriage have been previously computed, carrier shall be entitled to require payment of the charge on such excess.

5.4.5 Charges collect shipments will be accepted only to countries listed in carrier's regulations and subject to the conditions contained therein. In any event carrier reserves the right to refuse shipments on a charges collect basis to any country where regulations prevent the conversion of funds into other currencies or the transfer of funds to other countries. Information on countries to which charges collect service is available may be obtained from offices and representatives of carrier.

5.4.6 All charges applicable to a shipment are payable in cash at the time of acceptance thereof by the carrier in the case of a prepaid shipment, i.e. a shipment on which the charges are to be paid by the shipper, or at the time of delivery thereof by the carrier in the case of a collect shipment, i.e. a shipment on which the charges are to be paid by the consignee.

5.4.4 If the gross weight, measurement, quantity or declared value of the CARGO exceeds the gross weight, measurement, quantity or declared value on which charges for CARRIAGE have been previously computed, CARRIER shall be entitled to require payment of the charge on such excess.

5.4.5 CHARGES COLLECT SHIPMENTS will be accepted only to countries listed in CARRIER's regulations and subject to the conditions contained therein. In any event CARRIER reserves the right to refuse SHIPMENTS on a CHARGES COLLECT basis to any country where regulations prevent the conversion of funds into other currencies or the transfer of funds to other countries. Information on countries to which CHARGES COLLECT service is available may be obtained from offices and representatives of CARRIER.

**5.4.6 All charges applicable to a SHIPMENT are payable in cash at the time of acceptance thereof by the CARRIER in the case of a prepaid SHIPMENT, i.e. a SHIPMENT on which the charges are to be paid by the SHIPPER, or at the time of delivery thereof by the CARRIER in the case of a collect shipment, i.e. a SHIPMENT on which the charges are to be paid by the CONSIGNEE. If the CONSIGNEE fails to pay said charges, when such charges are to be collected, the SHIPPER remains obligated to pay these charges.*

5.4.6 All charges applicable to a SHIPMENT are payable in cash at the time of acceptance thereof by the CARRIER in the case of a prepaid SHIPMENT, i.e. a SHIPMENT on which the charges are to be paid by the SHIPPER, or at the time of delivery thereof by the CARRIER in the case of a collect shipment, i.e. a SHIPMENT on which the charges are to be paid by the CONSIGNEE. If the CONSIGNEE fails to pay said charges, when such charges are to be collected, the SHIPPER remains obligated to pay these charges, except when the CARRIER has extended credit to the CONSIGNEE without the written consent of the SHIPPER.

5.4.7 Carrier may cancel the carriage of the shipment upon refusal by the shipper, after demand by carrier, to pay the charges or portion thereof so demanded, without carrier being subject to any liability therefore.

5.4.7 CARRIER may cancel the CARRIAGE of the SHIPMENT upon refusal by the SHIPPER, after demand by CARRIER, to pay the charges or portion thereof so demanded, without CARRIER being subject to any liability therefor.

Article 6—Shipments in course of carriage 3.864

6.1 Compliance with Government requirements

6.1.1 The shipper shall comply with all applicable laws, customs and other government regulations of any country to, from, through or over which the cargo may be carried, including those relating to the packing, carriage or delivery of the cargo, and shall, together with the shipment, furnish such information and deliver such documents as may be necessary to comply with such laws and regulations. Carrier shall not be obliged to inquire into the correctness or sufficiency of such information or documents. Carrier shall not be liable to the shipper or any other person for loss or expense due to shipper's failure to comply with this provision. The shipper shall be liable to carrier for any damage occasioned by the failure of the shipper to comply with this provision.

6.1.2 Carrier shall not be liable for refusing to carry any shipment if carrier reasonably determines in good faith that such refusal is required by any applicable law, government regulation, demand, order or requirement.

6.1.1 The SHIPPER shall comply with all applicable laws, customs and other government regulations of any country to, from, through or over which the CARGO may be carried, including those relating to the packing, CARRIGE or delivery of the CARGO, and shall, together with the SHIPMENT, furnish such information and deliver such documents as may be necessary to comply with such laws and regulations. CARRIER shall not be obliged to inquire into the correctness or sufficiency of such information or documents. CARRIER shall not be liable to the SHIPPER or any other person for loss or expense due to SHIPPER's failure to comply with this provision. The SHIPPER shall be liable to CARRIER for any damage occasioned by the failure of the SHIPPER to comply with this provision.

6.1.2 CARRIER shall not be liable for refusing to carry any SHIPMENT if CARRIER reasonably determines in good faith that such refusal is required by any applicable law, government regulation, demand, order or requirement.

3.865 **6.2 Disbursements and customs formalities**

Carrier is authorised (but shall be under no obligation) to advance any duties, taxes or charges and to make any disbursement with respect to the cargo and the shipper and consignee shall be jointly and severally liable for the reimbursement thereof. No carrier shall be under obligation to incur any expense or make any advance in connection with the forwarding or reforwarding of the cargo except against pre-payment by the shipper. If it is necessary to make customs entry of the cargo at any stopping place, and no customs clearance agent has been named on the face of the air waybill or in the shipment record, the cargo shall be deemed to be consigned to the carrier carrying the cargo to such place. For any such purpose a copy of the air waybill, or of the shipment record, certified by the carrier, shall be deemed original.

3.866 ***6.2 Disbursements and customs formalities***

CARRIER is authorised (but shall be under no obligation) to advance any duties, taxes or charges and to make any disbursement with respect to the CARGO and the SHIPPER and by taking delivery or exercising any other right arising out of the contract of CARRIAGE the CONSIGNEE shall be jointly and severally liable for the reimbursement thereof. No CARRIER shall be under obligation to incur any expense or make any advance in connection with the forwarding or reforwarding of the CARGO except against pre-payment by the SHIPPER. If it is necessary to make customs entry of the CARGO at any stopping place, and no customs clearance AGENT has been named on the face of the AIR WAYBILL or in the SHIPMENT record, the CARGO shall be deemed to be consigned to the CARRIER carrying the CARGO to such place. For any such purpose a copy of the AIR WABILL, or of the SHIPMENT record, certified by the CARRIER, shall be deemed original.

3.867 **6.3 Schedules, routings and cancellations**

6.3.1 Times shown in carrier's timetables or elsewhere are approximate and are not guaranteed and form no part of the contract of carriage. No time is fixed for commencement or completion of carriage or delivery of cargo. Unless specifically agreed otherwise and so indicated in the air waybill or shipment record, carrier undertakes to deliver the cargo with reasonable dispatch but assumes no obligation to carry the cargo by any specified aircraft or over any particular route or routes, or to make connections at any point according to any particular schedule. Carrier is hereby authorised to select or deviate from the route or routes of the shipment, notwithstanding that the same may be stated on the face of the air waybill or in the shipment records. Carrier is not responsible for errors or omissions either in timetables or other representations of schedules. No employee, agent or representative of carrier is authorised to bind carrier by any statements or representations of the dates or times of departure or arrival, or of operation of any flight.

6.3.2 Carrier is authorised to carry the consignment without notice wholly or partly by any means of surface transportation or to arrange such carriage.

6.3.3 Carrier reserves the right without notice, to cancel, terminate, divert, postpone, delay or advance any flight, or the further carriage of any cargo, or to proceed with any flight without all or any part of the cargo, if it considers that it would be advisable to do so because of any fact beyond its control or not reasonably to be foreseen, anticipated, or predicted at the time the cargo was accepted: or if it considers that any other circumstances so require.

6.3.4 In the event any flight is cancelled, diverted, postponed, delayed or advanced or is terminated at a place other than the place of destination or in the event the carriage of any shipment is so cancelled, diverted, postponed, delayed, advanced or terminated, carrier shall not be under any liability with respect thereto. In the event the carriage of the shipment or any part thereof is so terminated, delivery thereof by carrier by any transfer agent for transfer or delivery or the placing of such shipment in storage shall be deemed complete delivery under the contract of carriage, and carrier shall be without any further liability with respect thereto, except to give notice or the disposition of the shipment to the shipper or to the consignee, at the address stated in the air waybill or shipment record. Carrier may, but shall not be obligated to, forward the shipment for carriage by any other route or forward the shipment as agent for the shipper or the consignee for onward carriage by any transportation service on behalf of the shipper or the consignee. The cost of doing so attaches to the cargo.

6.3.5 Subject to applicable laws, regulations and orders, carrier is authorised to determine the priority of carriage as between shipments, and as between cargo and mail or passengers. Carrier may likewise decide to remove any articles from a shipment, at any time or place whatsoever, and to proceed with the flight without them. If as a result of determining such priority, cargo is not carried or carriage thereof is postponed or delayed or if any articles are removed from a shipment, carrier will not be liable to shipper or consignee or to any other party for any other consequences therefor.

6.3 Schedules, routings and cancellations *3.868*

6.3.1 Unless specifically agreed otherwise and so indicated in the AIR WAYBILL or SHIPMENT RECORD, CARRIER undertakes to carry the cargo with reasonable despatch but assumes no obligation to carry the CARGO by any specified aircraft or over any particular route or routes, or to make connections at any point according to any particular schedule. Times shown in CARRIER's timetables or elsewhere are approximate and not guaranteed and form no part of the contract of CARRIAGE. No time is fixed for commencement or completion of CARRIAGE or delivery of CARGO. CARRIER is hereby authorised to select or deviate from the route or routes of the SHIPMENT, notwithstanding that the same may be stated on the face of the AIR WAYBILL or in the SHIPMENT RECORD. CARRIER is not responsible for errors or omissions either in timetables or other representations of schedules. No employee, AGENT or representative of CARRIER is authorised to bind CARRIER by any statements or representations of the dates or times of departure or arrival, or of operation of any flight.

6.3.2 CARRIER is authorised to carry the consignment without notice wholly or partly by any means of surface transportation or to arrange such CARRIAGE.

6.3.3 If it consider that it would be advisable to do so because of any fact beyond its control or not reasonably to be foreseen, anticipated, or predicted at the same time the CARGO was accepted; or it reasonably considers that any other circumstances so require, taking into account the interests of the SHIPPER, CARRIER reserves the right without notice, to cancel, terminate, divert, postpone, delay or advance any flight, or the further CARRIAGE of any CARGO, or to proceed with any flight without all or any part of the CARGO.

6.3.4 Provided that no regulations/laws to the contrary are applicable, in the event any flight is, pursuant to 6.3.3, cancelled, diverted, postponed, delayed or advanced or is terminated at a place other than the place of destination or in the event the CARRIAGE of any SHIPMENT is so cancelled, diverted, postponed, delayed, advanced or terminated, CARRIER shall only be liable for gross negligence and wilful misconduct. In the event the CARRIAGE of the SHIPMENT or any part thereof is so terminated, delivery thereof by CARRIER by any transfer agent for transfer or delivery or the placing of such SHIPMENT in storage shall be deemed complete delivery under the contract of CARRIAGE, and CARRIER shall be without any further liability with respect thereto, except to give notice or the disposition of the SHIPMENT to the SHIPPER or to the CONSIGNEE, at the address stated in the AIR WAYBILL or SHIPMENT RECORD. CARRIER may, but shall not be obligated to, forward the SHIPMENT for CARRIAGE by any other route or forward the SHIPMENT as AGENT for the SHIPPER or the CONSIGNEE for onward CARRIAGE by any transportation service on behalf of the SHIPPER or the CONSIGNEE. The cost of doing so attaches to the CARGO.

6.3.5 Unless otherwise agreed and subject to applicable laws, regulations and orders, CARRIER is authorised to determine the priority of CARRIAGE as between SHIPMENTS, and as between CARGO and mail or passengers. CARRIER may likewise decide to remove any articles from a SHIPMENT, at any time or place whatsoever, and to proceed with the flight without them. If as a result of determining such priority, CARGO is not carried or CARRIAGE thereof is postponed or delayed or if any articles are removed from a SHPMENT, CARRIER will not be liable to SHIPPER or CONSIGNEE or to any other party for any other consequences therefor.

6.4 Certain rights of Carrier over shipment in course of carriage *3.869*

If in the opinion of carrier it is necessary to hold the shipment at any place for any reasonable purpose, either before, during or after carriage, carrier may, upon giving notice thereof to the shipper, store the shipment for the account and at the risk and expense of the shipper, in any warehouse or other available place, or with the customs authorities: or carrier may deliver the shipment to another transportation service for onward carriage to the consignee. The shipper shall indemnify carrier against any expense or risk so incurred.

3.870 *6.4 Certain rights of Carrier over shipment in course of carriage*

If in the opinion of CARRIER it is necessary to hold the SHIPMENT at any place for any reasonable purpose, either before, during or after CARRIAGE, CARRIER may, upon giving notice thereof to the SHIPPER, store the SHIPMENT for the account and at the risk and expense of the SHIPPER, in any warehouse or other available place, or with the customs authorities: or CARRIER may deliver the SHIPMENT to another transportation service for onward CARRIAGE to the CONSIGNEE. The SHIPPER shall indemnify CARRIER against any expense or risk so incurred.

3.871 **Article 7—Shipper's right of disposition**

7.1 Exercise of right of disposition

Every exercise of the right of disposition must be made by the shipper or his designated agent, if any, and must be applicable to the whole shipment under a single air waybill, or under a single shipment record. The right of disposition over the cargo may only be exercised if the shipper or such agent produces the part of the air waybill that was delivered to him, or communicates such other form of authority as may be prescribed by carrier's regulations. Instructions as to disposition must be given (in writing) in the form prescribed by carrier. In the event that the exercise of the right of disposition results in a change of consignee, such new consignee shall be deemed to be the consignee appearing on the air waybill or in the shipment record.

3.872 *7.1 Exercise of right of disposition*

Every exercise of the right of disposition must be made by the SHIPPER or his designated AGENT, if any, and must be applicable to the whole SHIPMENT under a single AIR WAYBILL, or under a single shipment record. The right of disposition over the CARGO may only be exercised if the SHIPPER or such AGENT produces the part of the AIR WAYBILL that was delivered to him, or communicates such other form of authority as may be prescribed by CARRIER's regulations. Instructions as to disposition must be given in writing in the form prescribed by CARRIER. In the event that the exercise of the right of disposition results in a change of CONSIGNEE, such new CONSIGNEE shall be deemed to be the CONSIGNEE appearing on the AIR WAYBILL or in the SHIPMENT record.

3.873 **7.2 Shipper's option**

7.2.1 Subject to his liability to carry out all his obligations under the contract of carriage and provided that this right of disposition is not exercised in such a way as to prejudice carrier or other shippers, the shipper may at his own expense dispose of the cargo either:

7.2.1.1 by withdrawing it at the airport of departure or of destination; or

7.2.1 To the extent permitted by law and APPLICABLE CONVENTION, and subject to his liability to carry out all his obligations under the contract of CARRIAGE and provided that this right of disposition is not exercised in such a way as to prejudice CARRIER or other SHIPPERS, or the CONSIGNEE's right to delivery, the SHIPPER may at his own expense dispose of the CARGO either:

7.2.1.1 by withdrawing it at the airport of departure; or

7.2.1.2 by stopping it in the course of the journey on any landing; or

7.2.1.3 by calling for it to be delivered at the place of destination or in the course of the journey to a person other than the consignee named in the air waybill or shipment record; or

7.2.1.3 by calling for it in course of the journey to be delivered at the place of destination to a person other than the CONSIGNEE named in the AIR WAYBILL or SHIPMENT RECORD; or

7.2.1.4 by requiring it to be returned to the airport of departure.

7.2.2 Provided that if, in the opinion of carrier, it is not reasonably practicable to carry out the order of the shipper, carrier shall so inform him promptly and carrier shall thenceforward be under no obligation to carry out any such order.

7.2.2 Provided that if, in the opinion of CARRIER, it is not reasonably practicable to carry out the order of the SHIPPER, CARRIER shall so inform him promptly and CARRIER shall thenceforward be under no obligation to carry out any such order.

7.3 Payment of expenses *3.874*

The shipper shall be liable for and shall indemnify carrier for all loss or damage suffered or incurred by carrier as a result of the exercise of his right of disposition. The shipper shall reimburse carrier for any expenses occasioned by the exercise of his right of disposition.

7.3 Payment of expenses *3.875*

The SHIPPER shall be liable for and shall indemnify CARRIER for all loss or damage suffered or incurred by CARRIER as a result of the exercise of his right of disposition. The SHIPPER shall reimburse CARRIER for any expenses occasioned by the exercise of his right of disposition.

7.4 Extent of shipper's right *3.876*

The shipper's right of disposition shall cease at the moment when, after arrival of the cargo at the destination, the consignee takes possession or requests delivery of the cargo or air waybill, or otherwise shows his acceptance of the cargo. Nevertheless, if the consignee declines to accept the air waybill or the cargo, or if he cannot be communicated with, such right of disposition shall continue to vest in the shipper.

7.4 Extent of shipper's right *3.877*

Provided that no regulations to the contrary are applicable, the SHIPPER's right of disposition shall cease at the moment when, after arrival of the CARGO at the destination, the CONSIGNEE takes possession or requests delivery of the CARGO or AIR WAYBILL, or otherwise shows his acceptance of the CARGO. Nevertheless, if the CONSIGNEE declines to accept the AIR WAYBILL or the CARGO, or if he cannot be communicated with, such right of disposition shall continue to vest in the SHIPPER.

Article 8—Delivery *3.878*

8.1 Notice of arrival

Notice of arrival of the shipment will, in the absence of other instructions be sent to the consignee and any other person whom carrier has agreed to notify as evidenced in the air waybill or shipment record: such notice will be sent by ordinary methods. Carrier is not liable for non-receipt or delay in receipt of such notice.

8.1 Notice of arrival *3.879*

Notice of arrival of the SHIPMENT will, in the absence of other instructions be sent to the CONSIGNEE and any other person whom CARRIER has agreed to notify as evidenced in the AIR WAYBILL or SHIPMENT record: such notice will be sent by ordinary methods. CARRIER is not liable for non-receipt or delay in receipt of such notice.

8.2 Delivery of shipment *3.880*

Except as otherwise specifically provided in the air waybill or shipment record, delivery of the shipment will be made only to the consignee named therein, or his agent. Delivery to the consignee shall be deemed to have been effected:

8.2.1 when carrier has delivered to the consignee or his agent any authorisation from carrier required to enable the consignee to obtain release of the shipment; and

8.2.2 when the shipment has been delivered to customs or other government authorities as required by applicable law or customs regulation.

3.881 *8.2 Delivery of shipment*

Except as otherwise specifically provided in the AIR WAYBILL or SHIPMENT RECORD, delivery of the SHIPMENT will be made only to the CONSIGNEE named therein, or his agent. Delivery to the CONSIGNEE shall be deemed to have been effected:

8.2.1 when CARRIER has delivered to the CONSIGNEE or his agent any authorisation from CARRIER required to enable the CONSIGNEE to obtain release of the SHIPMENT; and

8.2.2 when the SHIPMENT has been delivered to customs or other government authorities as required by applicable law or customs regulation.

3.882 **8.3 Place of delivery**

Except as provided in 9.3, the consignee must accept delivery of and collect the shipment at the airport of destination or the respective facility designated by the carrier.

3.883 *8.3 Place of delivery*

Except as provided in 9.3, the CONSIGNEE must accept delivery of and collect the SHIPMENT at the airport of destination or the respective facility designated by the CARRIER.

3.884 **8.4 Failure of Consignee to take delivery**

8.4.1 Subject to the provisions of 8.5 hereof, if the consignee refuses or fails to take delivery of the shipment after its arrival at the airport of destination, carrier will endeavour to comply with any instructions of the shipper set forth on the face of the air waybill, or in the shipment record. If such instructions are not set forth or cannot reasonably be complied with, carrier shall notify the shipper of the consignee's failure to take delivery and request his instructions. If no such instructions are received within thirty (30) days, carrier may sell the shipment in one or more lots at public or private sale, or destroy or abandon such shipment.

8.4.2 The shipper is liable for all charges and expenses resulting from or in connection with the failure to take delivery of the shipment including, but not limited to, carriage charges incurred in returning the shipment if so required by the shipper's instructions. If the shipment is returned to the airport of departure and the shipper refuses or neglects to make such payments within fifteen (15) days after such return, carrier may dispose of the shipment or part thereof at public or private sale after giving the shipper ten days notice of its intention to do so.

3.885 *8.4 Failure of Consignee to take delivery*

8.4.1 Subject to the provisions of 8.5 hereof, if the CONSIGNEE refuses or fails to take delivery of the SHIPMENT after its arrival at the airport of destination, CARRIER will endeavour to comply with any instructions of the SHIPPER set forth on the face of the AIR WAYBILL, or in the SHIPMENT record. If such instructions are not set forth or cannot reasonably be complied with, CARRIER shall notify the SHIPPER of the CONSIGNEE's failure to take delivery and request his instructions. If no such instructions are received within thirty (30) days, CARRIER may sell the SHIPMENT in one or more lots at public or private sale, or destroy or abandon such SHIPMENT.

8.4.2 The SHIPPER is liable for all charges and expenses resulting from or in connection with the failure to take delivery of the SHIPMENT including, but not limited to, CARRIAGE charges incurred in returning the SHIPMENT if so required by the SHIPPER's instructions. If the SHIPMENT is returned to the airport of departure and the SHIPPER refuses or neglects to make such payments within fifteen (15) days after such return, CARRIER may dispose of the SHIPMENT or part thereof at public or private sale after giving the SHIPPER ten (10) DAYS notice of its intention to do so.

8.5 Disposal of perishables *3.886*

8.5.1 When a shipment containing perishable articles as defined in carrier's regulations is delayed in the possession of carrier, is unclaimed or is refused at place of delivery, or other for reasons is threatened with deterioration, carrier may immediately take such steps as it sees fit for the protection of itself and other parties in interest, including but not limited to the destruction or abandonment of all or any part of the shipment, the sending of communications for instructions at the cost of the shipper, the storage of the shipment or any part thereof at the risk and cost of the shipper, or the disposition of the shipment or any part thereof at public or private sale without notice.

8.5.2 In the event of the sale of the shipment as provided for above, either at the place of destination or at the place to which the shipment has been returned, carrier is authorised to pay to itself and other transportation services out of the proceeds of such sale all charges, advances, and expenses of the carrier and other transportation services plus costs of sale, holding any surplus subject to the order of the shipper. A sale of any shipment shall, however, not discharge the shipper and/or owner of any liability hereunder to pay any deficiencies.

8.5 Disposal of perishables *3.887*

8.5.1 When a SHIPMENT containing perishable articles as defined in CARRIER's regulations is delayed in the possession of CARRIER, is unclaimed or is refused at place of delivery, or other for reasons is threatened with deterioration, CARRIER may immediately take such steps as it sees fit for the protection of itself and other parties in interest, including but not limited to the destruction or abandonment of all or any part of the SHIPMENT, the sending of communications for instructions at the cost of the SHIPPER, the storage of the SHIPMENT or any part thereof at the risk and cost of the SHIPPER, or the disposition of the SHIPMENT or any part thereof at public or private sale without notice.

8.5.2 In the event of the sale of the SHIPMENT as provided for above, either at the place of destination or at the place to which the SHIPMENT has been returned, CARRIER is authorised to pay to itself and other transportation services out of the proceeds of such sale all charges, advances, and expenses of the CARRIER and other transportation services plus costs of sale, holding any surplus subject to the order of the SHIPPER. A sale of any SHIPMENT shall, however, not discharge the SHIPPER and/or owner of any liability hereunder to pay any deficiencies.

8.6 Responsibility for charges *3.888*

By accepting delivery of the air waybill and/or the shipment the consignee shall become liable for payment of all costs and charges in connection with the carriage. Unless otherwise agreed the shipper shall not be released from his own liability for these costs and charges and will remain jointly and severally liable with the consignee. Carrier may make delivery of the shipment or the air waybill conditional upon payment of these costs and charges.

8.6 Responsibility for charges *3.889*

By accepting delivery of the SHIPMENT the CONSIGNEE shall become liable for payment of all costs and charges in connection with the CARRIAGE. Unless otherwise agreed the SHIPPER shall not be released from his own liability for these costs and charges and will remain jointly and severally liable with the CONSIGNEE. CARRIER may make delivery of the SHIPMENT or the AIR WAYBILL conditional upon payment of these costs and charges.

Article 9—Pick-up and delivery services *3.890*

9.1 Shipments

Are accepted for carriage from their receipt at carrier's cargo terminal or airport office at the place of departure to the airport at the place of destination.

3.891 *9.1 Shipments*

Are accepted for CARRIAGE from their receipt at CARRIER's CARGO terminal or airport office at the place of departure to the airport at the place of destination or the respective facility as designated by the CARRIER.

3.892 **9.2 Availability of service**

Pick-up service and delivery service will be available at the points, to the extent and subject to the rates and charges established for such services in accordance with the applicable regulations of carrier.

3.893 *9.2 Availability of service*

PICK-UP and DELIVERY SERVICE will be available at the points, to the extent and subject to the rates and charges established for such services in accordance with the applicable regulations of CARRIER.

3.894 **9.3 Request for service**

Pick-up service, if available, will be provided when requested by the shipper. Except when otherwise provided by carrier's tariffs, delivery service may be provided unless contrary instructions are given by the shipper or by the consignee. Such contrary instructions must be received by carrier prior to removal of the shipment from carrier's airport terminal at destination.

3.895 *9.3 Request for service*

PICK-UP SERVICE, if available, will be provided when requested by the SHIPPER. Except when otherwise provided by CARRIER's tariffs, DELIVERY SERVICE may be provided unless contrary instructions are given by the SHIPPER or by the CONSIGNEE. Such contrary instructions must be received by CARRIER prior to removal of the SHIPMENT from CARRIER's airport terminal at destination.

3.896 **9.4 Shipment for which service is unavailable**

Pick-up service and delivery service will not be provided by carrier without special arrangement for any shipment which, in the opinion of carrier, because of its volume, nature, value or weight is impractical for carrier to handle in normal course.

3.897 *9.4 Shipment for which service is unavailable*

PICK-UP SERVICE and DELIVERY SERVICE will not be provided by CARRIER without special arrangement for any SHIPMENT which, in the opinion of CARRIER, because of its volume, nature, value or weight is impractical for CARRIER to handle in normal course.

3.898 **9.5 Liability**

If pick-up service or delivery service is performed by or on behalf of carrier, such surface transportation shall be upon the same terms as to liability as set forth in Article 11 hereof.

3.899 *9.5 Liability*

If PICK-UP SERVICE or DELIVERY SERVICE is performed by or on behalf of CARRIER, such surface transportation shall be upon the same terms as to liability as set forth in Article 11 hereof unless otherwise provided by mandatory regulations.

3.900 **Article 10—Successive carriers**

10.1 Carriage to be performed under one contract of carriage by several successive carriers is regarded as a single operation.

10.1 CARRIAGE to be performed under one contract of CARRIAGE by several successive CARRIERS is regarded as a single operation.

Comment

Article 10 reflects Article 1(3) of HP and WC, paragraphs 3.37 and 3.307, above, respectively. *3.901*

Article 11—Carrier's liability *3.902*

11.1 Carrier is liable to the shipper, consignee or any other person for damage sustained in the event of destruction or loss of, or damage to, or delay in the carriage of cargo only if the occurrence which caused the damage so sustained took place during the carriage as defined under Article 1.

11.2 Except as may be otherwise provided in any applicable Convention, carrier is not liable to the shipper, consignee or any other person for any damage, delay or loss of whatsoever nature arising out of or in connection with the carriage of cargo or other services performed by carrier, unless such damage, delay or loss is proved to have been caused by the negligence or wilful default of carrier and there has been no contributory negligence on the part of the shipper, consignee or other claimant.

11.3 Carrier is not liable if the destruction, loss of or damage to cargo is proved to have resulted solely from the inherent defect, quality, nature or vice of that cargo.

11.4 Carrier will not be liable for any loss, damage or expense arising from death due to natural causes or death or injury of any animal caused by the conduct or acts of the animal itself or of other animals such as biting, kicking, goring or smothering, nor for that caused or contributed to by the condition, nature or propensities of the animal, or by defective packing of the animal, or by the inability of the animal to withstand unavoidable changes in its physical environment inherent in the carriage by air.

11.5 Carrier shall not be liable in any event for any consequential loss or damage arising from carriage subject to these conditions, whether or not carrier had knowledge that such loss or damage might be incurred.

11.6 If the damage was caused or contributed to by the negligence or other wrongful act or omission of the person claiming compensation, or the person from whom he derives his rights, the carrier shall be wholly or partly exonerated from liability to the claimant to the extent that such negligence or wrongful act or omission caused or contributed to the damage.

11.7 Unless the shipper has made a special declaration of value for carriage and has paid the supplementary sum applicable, liability of carrier will not exceed the applicable Convention limit or, if no Convention applies, 17 Special Drawing Rights per kilogram of cargo destroyed, lost, damaged or delayed. If the shipper has made a special declaration of value for carriage, it is agreed that any liability shall in no event exceed such declared value for carriage as stated on the face of the air waybill or included in the shipment record. All claims shall be subject to proof of value.

11.8 In the case of loss, damage or delay of part of the shipment or of any object contained therein, the weight to be taken into consideration in determining the amount to which carrier's liability is limited shall be only the weight of the package or packages concerned. Nevertheless, when the loss, damage or delay of part of the shipment or of any object contained therein, affects the value of other packages covered by the same air waybill, the total weight of such package or packages shall also be taken into consideration in determining the limit of liability. In the absence of proof to the contrary, the value of any such part of the shipment lost, damaged or delayed as the case may be, shall be determined by reducing the total value of the shipment in the proportion that the weight of that part of the shipment lost, damaged or delayed has to the total weight of the shipment.

11.9 The shipper, owner and consignee whose property causes damage to or destruction of another shipment or of the property of carrier, shall indemnify carrier for all losses and expenses incurred by carrier as a result thereof. Cargo which, because of inherent defect, quality or vice or because of defective packing is likely to endanger aircraft, persons or property may be abandoned or destroyed by carrier at any time without notice and without liability therefor attaching to carrier.

11.10 A carrier issuing an air waybill for carriage over the lines of another carrier does so as agent for such other carrier. Any reference in a shipment record to carriage to be performed by another carrier shall be deemed to refer to carriage to be provided as a principal by such other carrier. No carrier shall be liable for the loss, damage or delay of cargo not occurring on its own line except that the shipper shall have a right of action for such loss, damage or delay on terms herein provided against the first carrier and the consignee or the person entitled to delivery shall have such a right of action against the last carrier under the contract of carriage.

11.11 Whenever the liability of carrier is excluded or limited under these conditions, such exclusion or limitation shall apply to agents, servants or representatives of carrier and also to any carrier whose aircraft is used for carriage.

11.1 CARRIER is liable to the SHIPPER, CONSIGNEE or any other person for damage sustained in the event of destruction or loss of, or damage to, or delay in the CARRIAGE of CARGO only if the occurrence which caused the damage so sustained took place during the CARRIAGE as defined under Article 1.

11.2 To the extent provided by APPLICABLE CONVENTION, CARRIER's liability shall be limited to the amount stipulated in such APPLICABLE CONVENTION notwithstanding the existence of gross negligence of wilful misconduct on the part of the CARRIER.

11.3 Except as may be otherwise provided for in any APPLICABLE CONVENTION, CARRIER is not liable to the SHIPPER, CONSIGNEE or any other person for any damage, delay or loss of whatsoever nature arising out of or in connection with the CARRIAGE of CARGO or other services performed by CARRIER or its AGENTS unless such damage, delay or loss is proved to have been caused by the negligence or wilful default of CARRIER.

11.4 CARRIER is not liable if the destruction, loss of or damage to CARGO is proved to have resulted solely from the inherent defect, quality, nature or vice of that CARGO.

11.5 CARRIER will not be liable for any loss, damage or expense arising from death due to natural causes or death or injury of any animal caused by the conduct or acts of the animal itself or of other animals such as biting, kicking, goring or smothering, nor for that caused or contributed to by the condition, nature or propensities of the animal, or by defective packing of the animal, or by the inability of the animal to withstand unavoidable changes in its physical environment inherent in the CARRIAGE.

11.6 To the extent not in conflict with applicable law, the CARRIER shall not be liable in any event for any consequential loss or damage arising from CARRIAGE subject to these conditions, whether or not CARRIER had knowledge that such loss or damage might be incurred.

11.7 Contributory negligence on the part of the SHIPPER, CONSIGNEE or other claimants releases the CARRIER of its liability to the extent provided by APPLICABLE CONVENTION and applicable law.

11.8 Liability of CARRIER will not exceed the APPLICABLE CONVENTION limit or, if no Convention applies, 17 SPECIAL DRAWING RIGHTS per kilogram of CARGO destroyed, lost, damaged or delayed. If, with the agreement of the CARRIER, the SHIPPER has made a special declaration of value for CARRIAGE and has paid the supplementary sum applicable, it is agreed that any liability shall in no event exceed such declared value for CARRIAGE stated on the face of the AIR WAYBILL or included in the SHIPMENT RECORD. All claims shall be subject to proof of value.

11.9 In the case of loss, damage or delay of part of the SHIPMENT or of any object contained therein, the weight to be taken into consideration in determining the amount to which CARRIER's liability is limited shall be only the weight of the package or packages concerned. Nevertheless, when the loss, damage or delay of part of the SHIPMENT, or of an object contained therein, affects the value of other packages covered by the same AIR WAYBILL, the total weight of such package or packages shall also be taken into consideration in determining the limit of liability. In the absence of proof to the contrary, the value of any such part of the SHIPMENT lost, damaged or delayed as the case may be, shall be determined by reducing the total value of the SHIPMENT in the proportion that the weight of that part of the SHIPMENT lost, damaged or delayed has to the total weight of the SHIPMENT.

11.10 The SHIPPER, and to the extent permitted by applicable law, the owner and CONSIGNEE, whose property or SHIPMENT causes damage to or destruction of another SHIPMENT or of the property of CARRIER, shall indemnify CARRIER for all losses and expenses incurred by CARRIER as a result thereof. CARGO which, because of inherent defect, quality or vice or because of defective packing, is likely to endanger aircraft, persons or property may be abandoned or destroyed by CARRIER at any time without notice and without liability therefor attaching to CARRIER.

11.11 A CARRIER issuing an AIR WAYBILL for CARRIAGE over the lines of another CARRIER does so as AGENT for such other CARRIER. Any reference in a SHIPMENT RECORD to CARRIAGE to be performed by another CARRIER shall be deemed to refer to CARRIAGE to be provided as principal by such other CARRIER. No CARRIER shall be liable for the loss, damage or delay of CARGO not occurring on its own line except that the SHIPPER shall have a right of action for such loss, damage or delay on terms herein provided against the first CARRIER and the CONSIGNEE or other person entitled to delivery shall have such a right of action against the last CARRIER under the contract of CARRIAGE.

11.12 Whenever the liability of CARRIER is excluded or limited under these conditions, such exclusion or limitation shall apply to AGENTS, servants or representatives of CARRIER and also to any CARRIER whose aircraft or other means of transportation is used for CARRIAGE.

Comment

As Article 1.6 defines carriage as "carriage of cargo by air or by another means of transport", under Condition 11.1 the carrier is liable for any loss etc., to cargo to a degree that goes beyond the liability, under UK law, of the carrier by air under the Conventions. The latter is also true of Condition 11.2 which in effect applies to gratuitous carriage other than by an air transport undertaking. However, Condition 11.5 goes not only further but too far as it infringes Article 32 of both HP and WC. *3.903*

Condition 11.3 reflects Article 23(2) of HP (para. 3.137, above), as well as UK law for non-international carriage by air, but not WC which contains no such provision. Condition 11.4 is not found in WC or HP, which contain no provision aimed specifically at live animals. Animals have always been passengers regarded with some caution by carriers[1] and this is the reason for Condition 11.4. Conditions 11.6, 11.7, and 11.8 substantially repeat and amplify Articles 21, 22(a), 22(b) of WC and HP. The first sentence of Condition 11.9 does the same for Article 10(2) of WC and HP; and Condition 11.11 has the same relationship to Article 25A of HP (WC has no such provision) but extends the immunity beyond the liability limits, to which Article 25A refers, to all exclusions of or limits on liability.

Article 12—Limitations on claims and actions *3.904*

12.1 Receipt by the person entitled to delivery of the cargo without complaint is prima facie evidence that the same has been delivered in good condition and in accordance with the contract of carriage.

12.2 No action shall be maintained in the case of loss or damage to goods unless a complaint is made to carrier in writing by the person entitled to delivery. Such complaint shall be made:

12.2.1 in the case of visible damage to or partial loss of the goods, immediately after its discovery and at the latest within fourteen (14) days from the date of receipt of the goods;

12.2.2. in the case of other damage to the goods, within fourteen (14) days from the date of receipt of the goods;

1. See e.g. Art. 17.4(f) of CMR (para. 1.77, above) and Art. 34.3(f) of CIM (para. 2.253, above).

12.2.3 in the case of delay, within twenty-one (21) days from the date on which the goods were placed at the disposal of the person entitled to delivery;

12.2.4 in the case of non delivery of the goods, within one hundred and twenty (120) days of the date of issue of the air waybill or the date of the shipment record, whichever is applicable.

12.3 Any right to damages against carrier shall be extinguished unless an action is brought within two years after the occurrence of the events giving rise to the claim.

12.1 Receipt by the person entitled to delivery of the CARGO without complaint is prima facie evidence that the same has been delivered in good condition and in accordance with the contract of CARRIAGE.

12.2 No action shall be maintained in the case of loss or damage to goods unless a complaint is made to CARRIER in writing by the person entitled to delivery. Such complaint shall be made:

12.2.1 in the case of visible damage to or partial loss of the goods, immediately after its discovery and at the latest within fourteen (14) DAYS from the date of receipt of the goods;

12.2.2. in the case of other damage to the goods, within fourteen (14) DAY from the date of receipt of the goods;

12.2.3 in the case of delay, within twenty-one (21) DAYS from the date on which the goods were placed at the disposal of the person entitled to delivery;

12.2.4 in the case of non delivery of the goods, within twenty-one (21) DAYS of the date the date the goods ought to have arrived at destination.

12.3 The right to damages shall be extinguished if an action is not brought within two years, reckoned from the date of arrival at the destination, or from the date on which the aircraft ought to have arrived, or from the date on which the transportation stopped. The method of calculating that period shall be determined by the law of the court seized of the case.

Comment

3.905 Condition 12 repeats Article 26(1) of HP and WC, as well as the UK law that applies to non-international carriage by air. It is in line with Condition 12 of the IATA standard form air waybill 600b(II). However, the rule in Condition 12.3 differs from the corresponding rule in Article 29 of HP (para. 3.181, above) and WC (para. 3.356, above) as regards the moment at which time begins to run.[1]

3.906 **Article 13—Overriding law**

13.1 Insofar as any provision contained or referred to in the air waybill or shipment record or these conditions may be contrary to mandatory law, government regulations, orders or requirements, such provision shall remain applicable to the extent that it is not overridden thereby. The invalidity of any such provision shall not affect any other parts.

13.1 To the extent that any provision contained or referred to herein is contrary to anything contained in the APPLICABLE CONVENTION, and in any applicable laws, government regulations, orders or requirements, that cannot be waived by agreement of the parties, such provision shall not apply. The invalidity of any provision shall not affect the validity of any other provision contained herein.

Comment

3.907 Except in so far as the Conditions refer to the Conventions, the Conditions make no provision relating to governing law. This is left to the court of the jurisdiction seised

1. See *Belgian Endive Marketing Board* v. *American Airlines* (1996) 15 Avn. Law, No. 18.

of the matter. In the UK, in the case of a dispute about a carriage of goods within the scope of one of the air Conventions, the court will characterise the case as such and apply a unilateral conflicts rule in favour of the *lex fori*[1] and thus apply the appropriate Convention as enacted in the UK,[2] e.g. the 1961 Act (including Scheds. 1 and 1A) or the 1967 Order (Scheds. 1, 2 or 3) as the case may be.

Article 14—Modification and waiver 3.908

14.1 No agent, servant or representative of carrier has authority to alter, modify or waive any provision of the contract of carriage or of these conditions.

14.1 No AGENT, servant or representative of CARRIER has authority to alter, modify or waive any provision of the contract of CARRIAGE or of these conditions.

1. See Clarke, *Air*, Chap. 2.1.
2. See the Introduction, Comment 3, paras. 3.4 *et seq.*, above.

PART 4

CARRIAGE OF GOODS BY INLAND WATER WITHIN THE UK

I. INTRODUCTION

An "inland waterway" includes both a river and a canal[1] but, in practice, many of the navigable parts of rivers are tidal and transport upon them is therefore governed by the rules relating to the carriage of goods by sea.[2] Canals constitute part of the inland transport system but the more detailed rules are more closely allied to those applicable to the carriage of goods by road and rail than they are to carriage by sea. Indeed, in the case of the railways most of the leading cases were decided at a time when the track was owned by the operator of the freight services and ownership could not therefore (with the exception of CMR) be separated from the provision of the means of transport. In the case of canal carriage it is necessary to distinguish between the "public" owner of the canals—the British Waterways Board[3] and those private firms which carry on a business of carriage by canal barge.[4] However, since *4.1*

1. Transport Act 1962, s. 90.
2. British Waterways Carriage of Freight Conditions 2003, Cond. 2.1, defines a "waterway" for the purposes of the Conditions, unless the context otherwise requires, as "any canal or inland navigation belonging to or under the control of British Waterways and includes any works, land or premises belonging to or under the control of British Waterways and held or used by them in connection with such canal or inland navigation".
3. Transport Act 1962, s. 31(5). The Carriage of Freight Conditions 2003, Cond. 2.1, defines the term "British Waterways" for the purposes of the Conditions as meaning "the British Waterways Board and its successors".
4. Several "private" carriers by inland water operate their own barge services for their own commodities (e.g. Shell Transport & Trading plc or Blue Circle) or are traders involved either in modest inland water carriage operations or operators of inland water and coaster trade. There are, therefore, particular terms of business adopted by these individual firms. Today, British Waterways no longer acts as a carrier itself and there are only a relatively small number of private carriers operating inland water freight services. British Waterways requires all freight carried on its waterways by a freight vessel, to be carried subject to the Carriage of Freight Conditions 2003. Cond. 2.1 defines a freight operator as "the person using or intending to use a waterway for the carriage of goods by a Freight Vessel whether as the Owner of a Freight Vessel or of the Goods or in any other capacity". The same condition applies the definition of Freight Vessel contained in the British Waterways Freight Vessel Conditions 2003. There were special conditions of carriage used in the old port of Hull and on the waterway between Hull and Goole produced by the Hull River Craft and Lighter Owners' Carriage Conditions (1984 edition) but these are no longer in general use. There were also special conditions under which British Waterways handles freight at its docks, ship wharves, barge wharves, depots and other facilities: see British Waterways Terms and Conditions of Handling Goods, 1980 edition. The main carriers today are J.J. Prior Transport; Wood, Hall & Heward; Robert Wynn & Sons; Alan Oliver Workboats; K.D. Marine (UK) Ltd.; River Sea Trading Ltd.; Humber Barges; John H. Whitakers (Tankers) Ltd. A more complete list is available from the Association of Inland Shipping Operators and from the Commercial Boat Operators Association.

the British Waterways Board was also the transferee of the former British Transport Commission of the shares in a number of canal carrier and warehousing companies,[5] it is given express power to carry goods by inland waterway and road, as well as to store goods.[6] Notwithstanding these powers, however, British Waterways no longer operates a freight-carrying barge fleet and all freight carried on their inland waterways is now carried by private concerns. There are still some canals in private ownership, the most important being the Manchester Ship Canal and the Bridgewater Canal. As to the rest, they are usually short branches linking with national canals.[7]

4.2 It is the duty of the Secretary of State for the Environment, Food and Rural Affairs to whom the British Waterways Board is responsible, to promote a national policy for the use of inland waterways for commercial transport. Britain's inland waterways carried around 96,000 (25 tonne) lorry loads of freight in 2003–04, earning £0.7 million in freight tolls and dues.[8] This is a tiny proportion of the total freight carried within the UK by road, rail and air but the plan is to double the volume of freight carried by inland water by 2010, largely by concentrating on container carriage and the carriage of minerals and waste.[9]

4.3 The Secretary of State may make grants or other payments for the purpose of securing or encouraging the carriage of goods by inland waterway or sea rather than by road where he is satisfied that it is in the public interest.[10] Such grants or payments may, in particular, be made in respect of facilities for or in connection with the carriage of goods by inland waterway or sea, including facilities for loading or unloading goods.[11] Grants or payments under this provision must be of such amounts and subject to such conditions (including conditions requiring their repayment in specified circumstances) as the Secretary of State may determine.[12] These grants are, in practice, largely made from environmental considerations. The grant programme is known as the "Freight Facility Scheme" and is available from the Department of Transport. A number of projects have been successful in transferring freight from road to water through the grant aid system, including the refurbishment of a fuel distribution terminal at Leeds; the development of aggregate distribution sites; the refurbishment of wharf facilities for the transfer of vegetable

5. Transport Act 1962, s. 31(6), Sched. IV, Pt III.

6. *Ibid.* s. 10(3).

7. The main navigations controlled by British Waterways that are capable of carrying major freight barges and seagoing vessels are the Aire & Calder, the River Ouse, the Caledonian, the Trent/Mersey, the Severn/Trent, the Crinan, the Gloucester & Sharpness, the Grand Union, and the Weaver. The main ports/terminals are Caldaire, Howden, Selby, Corpach, Arishaig, Sharpness and Weston Point.

8. British Waterways Annual Report & Accounts 2002/2003, p. 19.

9. See *Freight on Water*: a report by the Freight Study Group, Department of the Environment, Food and Rural Affairs, 2002. The major loads now carried by water are bulk goods (dry cargoes such as minerals, grain, waste and recyclable materials) liquid cargoes (such as petroleum, now moved from refineries or coastal terminals to inland distribution terminals by water) and aggregates which are regularly taken by water from quarries to distribution centres or concrete batching plants. Water is also used to carry abnormal "invisible" loads such as prefabricated sections of the Flue Gas Desulphurisation Plant carried to the Drax power complex on the River Ouse navigation.

10. Transport Act 2000, s. 272(1).

11. *Ibid.* s. 272(2).

12. *Ibid.* s. 272(3).

oils; a new steel handling wharf facility and the building or refurbishment of barges.[13]

The British Waterways Board succeeded to the canal and inland navigation undertakings carried on by the former British Transport Commission, with the exception of the Lower Ouse Improvement (transferred to the British Transport Docks Board) and six harbours listed in the Transport Act 1962.[14] The British Waterways Board is a body corporate with perpetual succession and a common seal.[15] It is under a statutory duty in exercise of its statutory powers to provide to such extent as it may think expedient (1) services and facilities on the inland waterways owned and managed by it, and (2) port facilities at any harbour owned or managed by it and to have due regard to efficiency, economy and safety of operation as respects the services and facilities it provides.[16] These statutory duties do not impose any form of obligation enforceable by court proceedings which would not otherwise be enforceable.[17] The Board is also required to maintain the inland waterways owned or managed by it to certain prescribed standards for prescribed purposes.[18] The existence of these obligations could have resulted, in the past, in terms to like effect being implied into contracts of carriage where the Board is the carrier, though, despite the fact that the Board does have powers to be a carrier,[19] it no longer, in practice, exercises them. Today the Board merely permits others to use their waterways subject to the operational requirements agreed between the Board and the freight operator, and the observance by the freight operator of the Carriage of Freight Conditions, the Freight Vessel Conditions and the Board's bye-laws.[20] If there is a failure to comply with these requirements the Board can give written notice to the "offender" requiring remedial action to be taken within a reasonable time. Serious or persistent failure to adhere to requirements will result in permission to carry freight on the waterways being withdrawn, as will any action that compromises the safety or "significant waterway operational requirements".[21] 4.4

In the performance of its statutory duties the British Waterways Board (BWB) has a range of powers. The following are the most significant: 4.5

(1) to carry goods by inland waterways and to provide facilities for traffic on the inland waterways owned or managed by it[22];

13. See *Freight on our Waterways* (British Waterways, 2003), p. 10.
14. Sched. 3, Pt. III; Transport Act 1962, s. 31(5).
15. *Ibid.* s. 1(2), Sched. 1, para. 1.
16. *Ibid.* s. 10(1).
17. *Ibid.* s. 10(4).
18. For further details see *Halsbury's Laws of England*, 5th ed., Vol 39(1), paras. 398 *et seq.*
19. Transport Act 1962 s. 10(3)(a).
20. See below, para. 4.13.
21. "A Freight Operator may use those Waterways detailed in the Operational Schedule for the purposes of transporting Goods by Freight Vessel subject to the observance by the Freight Operator of these conditions, any requirements specified in the Operational Schedule and the bye-laws. In the event of any serious or persistent failure by the Freight Operator to comply with any of the provisions of these conditions, the Operational Schedule or the bye-laws, British Waterways may withdraw its consent given under the terms of the Operational Schedule. The consent may be terminated immediately if safety or significant Waterway operational requirements are compromised. Otherwise the Freight Operator will be notified in writing and given a reasonable time to effect a remedy prior to the consent being terminated": Carriage of Freight Conditions 2003, Conds. 4.1, 4.2.
22. Transport Act, 1962, s. 10(3)(a).

(2) to operate harbours owned or managed by it and to provide port facilities at those harbours[23];
(3) to provide transport services by road
  (a) for the carriage of goods which have been or are to be carried by the BWB by inland waterway,[24] and
  (b) for the carriage of goods where the use of an inland waterway owned or managed by the Board has been temporarily interrupted[25] and to carry goods by these services[26];
(4) to consign goods on behalf of others on routes wholly or partly owned or managed by the BWB, or to or from, or on routes through, any of the harbours owned or managed by it[27];
(5) to store goods which have been or are to be carried on any of the inland waterways owned or managed by the Board, or which have been or are to be loaded or unloaded in or carried through any of the harbours owned or managed by it and, in so far as any premises provided for the purpose of that or any other part of its business are not required for those purposes, to use them to provide facilities for the storage of other goods[28];
(6) to enter into and carry out agreements
  (a) with carriers outside Great Britain for the through carriage of goods and passengers under one contract or at a through rate or in the same vessels or containers,[29] and
  (b) with any person engaged in coastal shipping for co-ordinating the activities of that person with those of the Board and, in particular, for facilitating the through carriage of goods, for the quoting of through rates and for the pooling of receipts or expenses.[30]

4.6 The Board has ceased to be a common carrier.[31] There is, therefore, no duty to accept consignments offered to it for carriage. Carriers by water such as hoymen,[32] bargemen[33] and ferrymen[34] if any such still exist, are common carriers if they hold themselves out as ready to carry goods for the public, and are subject to the same liabilities as is the common carrier by land.[35] The provisions of the Carriers Act 1830 do not, however, apply to common carriers by water. Carriers by inland water impliedly warrant that their craft is seaworthy, the warranty of seaworthiness being

23. *Ibid.* s. 10(3)(b).
24. *Ibid.* s. 10(3)(c)(i).
25. *Ibid.* s. 10(3)(c)(ii).
26. *Ibid.* s. 10(3)(c)(iii).
27. *Ibid.* s. 10(3)(e).
28. *Ibid.* s. 10(3)(f).
29. *Ibid.* s. 10(3)(g)(i).
30. *Ibid.* s. 10(3)(g)(ii).
31. *Ibid.* s. 43(6).
32. *Dale* v. *Hall* (1750) 1 Wils. 281.
33. *Rich* v. *Kneeland* (1613) Cro. Jac. 330.
34. *Southcote's Case* (1601) 4 Co. Rep. 83b.
35. See Palmer, *Bailment* (2nd ed., London, Sweet & Maxwell, 1991), pp. 969 *et seq.*

interpreted as a warranty that the vessel is fit for the purpose for which it is to be used.[36]

4.7 It might be thought that contracts for the carriage of goods by inland water, if concluded on the basis of standard terms of business, would need to satisfy the requirement of reasonableness set out in the Unfair Contract Terms Act 1977, s. 11. However, it is provided by Schedule 1, paragraph 3 to that Act that where goods are carried by ship, over the whole or part of the journey, the provisions of sections 2(2), 3 and 4 do not, except in favour of a person dealing as a consumer, apply to the contract in so far as it operates in relation to the carriage by ship. Accordingly, aside from attempts to exclude or restrict liability for death or personal injury (covered by section 2(1)) or exclusions in consumer contracts (which inland water carriage of goods contracts are, in practice, unlikely to be) the Unfair Contract Terms Act 1977 may be safely ignored[37] save in so far as the inland water carrier's terms purport to cover the part of the journey undertaken by road, rail or warehousing.

4.8 The major concern over this restrictive application of the Unfair Contract Terms Act 1977 arises over the meaning of the word "ship" in Schedule 1, paragraph 3. In some statutes the word "ship" is defined in such a way as to include barges (even if needing a tow for propulsion) and other small craft.[38] However, in contrast, some legislation defines a ship by reference to its sea-going capability, which presumably might exclude canal barges.[39] At common law, Erle J. said[40] "that the word 'ship', in common use, may denote either a mere frame, or a ship with its apparatus ready for sea". In *Ex parte Ferguson*[41] Blackburn J. thought that the word "ship" connoted a vessel that went to sea. A similar construction was adopted by Sir Robert Phillimore in *The C. S. Butler.*[42] On the other hand, a more liberal construction was adopted by Lord Coleridge C.J. in *The Mac*[43] where he thought the word "ship" included any vessel used to convey merchandise by water, provided the cargo was protected from water and the weather. It therefore included a hopper barge and possibly even a mud barge used in conjunction with a dredger. Finally, Atkinson J. in *Polpen Shipping Co. Ltd.* v. *Commercial Union Assurance Co. Ltd.*[44] said that a ship "was any hollow structure intended to be used in navigation, i.e. intended to do its real work on the seas *or other waters*" (italics supplied). It is therefore submitted that the balance of authority is in favour of construing the word "ship" in the Unfair Contract Terms Act 1977, Sched. 1, para. 3, as including vessels used for inland water carriage though the matter cannot be said to be entirely free from doubt.

36. See *Paterson Steamships* v. *Canadian Co-operative Wheat Producers* [1934] A.C. 538, *per* Lord Wright at p. 545.

37. As may be the Unfair Terms in Consumer Contract Regulations: S.I. 1999/2083, implementing Council Directive 93/13/EEC of 5 April 1993.

38. See e.g. the Naval Prize Act 1864, s. 7; Foreign Enlistment Act 1870, s. 30; Territorial Waters Jurisdiction Act 1878, s. 7; Merchant Shipping Act 1894 s. 742 (which only excludes vessels propelled by oars); Marine Insurance Act 1906, Sched. 1; Petroleum (Consolidation) Act 1928, s. 23; Harbours Act 1964, s. 57; Trade Descriptions Act 1968, s. 39(1).

39. See e.g. the Explosives Act 1875, s. 108.

40. In *Gibson* v. *Small* (1853) 4 H.L. Cas. 353 at 384.

41. (1871) 40 L.J.Q.B. 105.

42. (1874) L.R. 4 A. & E. 238.

43. (1882) 7 P.D. 126 at 128, 129.

44. [1943] 1 K.B. 161 at 167.

4.9 Article 1 of the Hague-Visby Rules provides that the Rules apply only to the carriage of goods under bills of lading or similar documents, including those issued under a charterparty.[45] Article I(d) makes the Rules applicable to carriage in "ships". Perhaps, therefore, the Rules do not apply to carriage in small boats. In *Wirth Ltd.* v. *S.S. Arcadia Forest*[46] it was held that a barge was not a "ship" for the purposes of the Hague-Visby Rules. The case was reversed on appeal[47] but on other grounds. The issue is not, therefore, settled, even as a point of US law, although it has been held by the Supreme Court of Canada that where a barge is used for the purposes of unloading cargo from a vessel to the shore, then it is a "ship" within the Rules.

4.10 A further point of difficulty arises in the fact that Article I(b) refers to carriage by "sea" and even if the disputed proposition that a barge is a "ship" for the purposes of the Rules could be sustained, there is the further question of whether carriage by "sea" would include the non-tidal parts of rivers or canals such as to attract application of the Rules. The double unlikelihood of a barge being regarded as a "ship" for the purposes of the Rules and a canal being regarded as "sea" probably means that for practical purposes a contract for the carriage of goods by inland water will not be treated as incorporating the Hague-Visby Rules, at least where the waters are not tidal.

4.11 By virtue of the British Waterways Act 1983[48] the British Waterways Board may serve a notice on any person reasonably believed by it to be the master or owner, or to have been the master or owner at any date specified in the notice, requiring the recipient to give the Board within the time specified in the notice (which must not be less than 14 days beginning with the day on which the notice is served), the following information:

(i) the name and address of any person whom the recipient of the notice believes to be the master or owner of the vessel, or to have been such at any date specified in the notice[49]; or

(ii) the capacity in which such master has or takes command, charge, possession or management of the vessel, or had or took such command, charge, possession or management at any date specified in the notice[50]; or

(iii) the nature of the interest in or control over the vessel of any such owner at any date specified in the notice.[51]

45. Somewhat misleading since a bill of lading given by a shipowner to a charterer is a mere receipt for the goods and not evidence of the contract of carriage. The Hague-Visby Rules thus only apply compulsorily by statute to bills of lading issued under a charterparty if the bill is transferred by endorsement to a third party. If the third party collects the cargo at the point of discharge and finds it damaged his claim against the shipowner will then be subject to the Hague-Visby Rules. The Rules only apply to the charterparties themselves if the charterparty contractually incorporates the Rules.

46. [1974] 2 Lloyd's Rep. 563 (US State District Court, Eastern District of Louisiana).

47. See 537 F. (2d) 1272.

48. S. 6(1).

49. *Ibid.* s. 6(2)(a).

50. *Ibid.* s. 6(2)(b).

51. *Ibid.* s. 6(2)(c).

The Board can exercise this power where, with a view to performing any of its statutory functions, it forms the view that it ought to have information as to the master or owner of any vessel which is or has been on any inland waterway or reservoir owned or managed by the Board. Any notice served under these powers must name or otherwise identify the vessel in respect of which it is served, specify the particular statutory function of the Board to which the notice relates and specify the enactment by or under which that function is to be performed.[52] A valid notice cannot be served under this provision on anyone who is no longer the master or owner of the named vessel at the date of service of the notice if more than six months have elapsed since the recipient ceased to be the master or owner.[53] It is a criminal offence to fail to provide the information requested in the notice or to give false or fraudulently misleading information in response to it.[54] 4.12

The British Waterways Act 1983 also contains powers permitting the Board to control unsafe vessels found on navigations owned or controlled by the British Waterways Board. A duly authorised officer of the Board[55] may at any reasonable time enter any vessel on any of the Board's inland waterways for the purpose of inspecting the condition of the vessel so as to ascertain whether the vessel is unsafe.[56] The Act contains requirements as to the service of notice,[57] unless the officer believes that safety considerations call for an immediate inspection.[58] The officer, on completion of the inspection, must issue a notice specifying the defects, the measures required to remedy them, the time within which defects must be remedied or, in serious cases, to remove the vessel altogether.[59] There are penalties for disobeying instructions in the notice or undertaking forbidden movements of the vessel[60] and provisions allowing an appeal to a magistrates' court by any person aggrieved by the notice or by the refusal of the Board to issue the relevant certificate stating that the vessel is not, or is no longer, unsafe.[61] The Board has the power to remove any sunk, stranded or abandoned vessel, or any vessel which is left moored on a waterway without authority on giving 28 days' notice to the owner.[62] 4.13

All expenses incurred by the Board in removing, storing or destroying the relevant craft, or the removing or storing of any furniture, tackle and apparel of the vessel, or any cargo, goods, chattels and effects on board, or the marking, watching, buoying or otherwise controlling the vessel, may be recovered from the owner.[63] If within six weeks of its removal by the Board any vessel cannot be proved to the Board's reasonable satisfaction to belong to any claimant it, together with any 4.14

52. *Ibid.* s. 6(3).
53. *Ibid.* s. 6(4).
54. *Ibid.* s. 6(5).
55. *Ibid.* s. 7(1)(a)(iv).
56. *Ibid.* s. 7(2)(a). A vessel is unsafe if its condition is such as to constitute a danger to persons on board, to other persons or to any property: s. 7(1)(a)(ii).
57. *Ibid.* s. 7(1)(b)(i).
58. *Ibid.* s. 7(1)(b)(ii).
59. *Ibid.* s. 7(3).
60. *Ibid.* s. 7(4)–(6).
61. *Ibid.* s. 7(7).
62. *Ibid.* s. 8(1)(2).
63. *Ibid.* s. 8(3).

tackle, cargo, goods etc. vests in the Board.[64] However, if within 12 months of its removal a claim to the relevant craft is made by a person who subsequently proves that he is the owner of it, the Board must, if the relevant craft is unsold, permit the owner to retake it together with any tackle, cargo, goods etc. on payment of the Board's expenses.[65] If the vessel and the tackle, cargo, goods etc. on board have been sold then the Board must pay the owner an amount equivalent to the proceeds of sale, less the Board's expenses.[66] The Board also has the power, at any time, to move without notice any vessel that is an obstruction or a source of danger.[67]

4.15 These powers are further reinforced by the Board's Freight Vessel Conditions.[68] These Conditions contain a definition of a freight vessel and set out the circumstances and conditions it is necessary to observe before a vessel can be used for the carriage of goods on any of British Waterways' navigations. The relevant provisions of the Freight Vessel Conditions 2003 are set out in section II, below.

[*The next paragraph is 4.25*]

64. *Ibid.* s. 8(4).

65. *Ibid.* s. 8(4) proviso.

66. *Ibid.*

67. *Ibid.* s. 8(5). Note also the power of British Waterways to deal with obstructions or hindrances to navigation on its canals: British Waterways Act 1995, s. 18. It also has the power to remove vessels to permit works (*ibid.* s. 19) and to control moorings (*ibid.* s. 21).

68. Made by British Waterways under the Transport Act 1962, s. 43 and under its bye-laws. They apply to any freight vessel used or kept on a waterway on or after 1 April 2003: British Waterways Freight Vessel Conditions 2003, Cond. 1. A new draft set of standards of fitness for purpose requirements for registration are currently under consideration by the Maritime & Coastguard Agency in respect of freight vessels for use on inland navigations, pursuant to a consideration of the implementation of EC Directive 82/714/EC. A Community certificate would allow operators to move vessels to any Community waters.

II. BWB FREIGHT VESSEL CONDITIONS 2003

2. Interpretation 4.25

2.1 In these conditions, unless the context otherwise requires:

"approved person" has the meaning given in condition 7.8.

"British Waterways" means the British Waterways Board and its successors.

"category of water", "category A water", "category B and C waters" have the meanings given by the Merchant Shipping (Categorisation of Waters) Regulations 1992 (S.I. 1992/2356).

"freight vessel" means any ship, boat, barge, tug, lighter, raft or any other description of craft (whether or not capable of navigation) other than:

(a) Business Craft licensed under the BW Craft Licence Scheme as:

(i) a "leisure business craft" including holiday hire boat, day hire boat, hotel boat, passenger boat, trip boat, restaurant boat, shared ownership or time share boat, or

(ii) a "trading craft" including floating shops and offices, floating workshop, work boat (tugs, dredgers etc. for work taking place on or close to the waterway), cargo carrying boat (not registered as a freight vessel and subject to BW Carriage of Freight Conditions), or

a houseboat for which a houseboat certificate under the British Waterways Act 1971 is in force, or

a pleasure boat, within the meaning given by the bye-laws of British Waterways from time to time in force, and licensed under the BW Craft License Scheme, or

a work boat belonging to or under the control of British Waterways or an authorised contractor being subject to the BW Work Boat Safety Scheme.

"Inspection Certificate" has the meaning given in Condition 6.

"Insurance Policy" has the meaning given in Condition 8.

"master" means the person having for the time being the command, charge or management of a freight vessel.

"registered" has the meaning given in Condition 4.

"Waterway" means any canal or inland navigation belonging to or under the control of British Waterways.

2.2 The headings in these conditions are for convenience only and shall not affect their interpretation.

2.3 Reference to any provision of any Act of Parliament or subordinate legislation (including bye-laws) shall be deemed to be a reference to such Act of Parliament, subordinate legislation or bye-laws as amended, modified, re-enacted or replaced, whether before or after the date specified in Condition 1.

2.4 Reference to the singular shall include the plural and vice versa.

3. Conditions of Use 4.26

A freight vessel may not be kept or used on a waterway unless:

3.1 The vessel is registered, and its registration number, or its name and port of registration, is clearly displayed.

3.2 A Fitness-for-Purpose Inspection Certificate or equivalent is in force in relation to that vessel.

3.3 An Insurance Policy is in force in respect of that vessel, and

3.4 When navigated, the vessel is under the command of a competent master and, when necessary to ensure safe operation, there is in attendance an adequate and competent crew.

4. Registration 4.27

A freight vessel is registered for the purposes of Condition 3.1 if:

4.1 It is registered with British Waterways in accordance with Condition 5 below; or

4.2 It is registered with the Port of London Authority under the provisions of section 124 of the Port of London Act 1968 as a lighter or tug; or

4.3 It is a British Vessel registered under Part II of the Merchant Shipping Act 1995; and which possesses either of the certificates detailed in Condition 6.3 or 6.4; or

4.4 It is a vessel for which a Community Inland Navigation Certificate has been issued by a member State of the European Union (other than the United Kingdom) in accordance with Council Directive 82/714/EC and that licence is then in force and is applicable to the category of waters being navigated, or

4.5 It is a vessel to which part 1 of the Merchant Shipping (Port State Control) Regulations 1995 applies.

4.28

5. Registration with British Waterways

5.1 An application to register a freight vessel with British Waterways shall be made in such form as British Waterways shall from time to time require and shall include:

(i) the name, address and (if different) usual place of business of the owner,
(ii) the name of the vessel,
(iii) a statement for the purposes for which the vessel is, or is to be, used by reference to the nature or type of goods carried and the category of waters navigated,
(iv) a statement of the dimensions of the vessel in such form as may be specified by British Waterways,
(v) a copy of the Fitness for Purpose Inspection Certificate relating to the vessel,
(vi) a copy (or other acceptable evidence) of the Insurance Policy relating to the vessel,
(vii) such other information as British Waterways may consider relevant to the application,
(viii) and shall be accompanied by such fee as British Waterways shall from time to time determine.

5.2 The owner of a freight vessel registered with British Waterways shall immediately notify British Waterways of any change of address or change of usual place of business.

5.3 A registration of a freight vessel with British Waterways shall cease to be in force on the earlier of;

(i) the end of any period specified in the confirmation of registration, or the date on which

the ownership of the vessel changes, or
the vessel is altered in any material respect, or
the purposes for which the vessel is to be used changes from that specified in the application for registration.

5.4 Immediately a registration of a freight vessel with British Waterways ceases to be in force, the owner must notify British Waterways, stating in writing the reason it has ceased to be in force and the location of the vessel. Such notification may be accompanied by an application for re-registration.

4.29

6. Inspection Certificate

An Inspection Certificate, for the purposes of Condition 3.2 means:

6.1 In relation to a vessel registered with British Waterways, a certificate of inspection of fitness for purpose issued in accordance with the provisions of Condition 7 below; or

6.2 In relation to a vessel registered with the Port of London Authority (and not also registered under the Merchant Shipping Act 1995), a Certificate of Registration issued under the Bye-law 8.4 of the Craft and Boat Registration and Regulation Bye-laws 2000 made by that Authority provided the inspection under Bye-law 5 or Bye-law 6 of those Bye-laws took place within the last 12 months; or

6.3 A certificate issued under the Merchant Shipping (Survey and Certification) Regulations 1995, as amended; or

6.4 A Load Line Exemption Certificate issued under the Merchant Shipping (Vessels in Commercial Use for Sport or Pleasure) Regulations 1998 (S.I. 1998/2771 as amended by S.I. 2000/482) or under the Merchant Shipping (Small Workboats and Pilot Boats) Regulations 1998 (S.I. 1998/1609); or

6.5 A Community Inland Navigation Certificate issued in accordance with Council Directive 82/714/EC;

6.6 In relation to a vessel in which part 1 of the Merchant Shipping (Port State Control) Regulations 1995 applies an inspection or survey certificate issued by a Competent Authority of Approved Classification Society which is, as a minimum, the equivalent standard of the British Waterways Fitness-for-Purpose Certificate.

7. Inspection of Fitness for Purpose *4.30*

7.1 A certificate of inspection of fitness for purpose may be issued (and may be revoked) in the circumstances set out in this condition.

7.2 The owner of a freight vessel shall at his own expense arrange for it to be inspected by an approved person and shall provide all reasonably necessary facilities for the approved person to enter, inspect, measure, survey and examine the vessel to enable him to determine the vessel's fitness for the purpose or purposes specified (or intended to be specified) in the registration of the vessel. The approved person shall record the results of his inspection in such form and by reference to any guidance notes as British Waterways shall from time to time require or provide.

7.3 If, following an inspection, an approved person determines that works are required to the vessel before a certificate may properly be issued, then provided these works are completed within 28 days of the date of the inspection, the approved person may re-inspect the vessel by reference to those works alone in order to be satisfied that a certificate may properly be issued.

7.4 If, following an inspection or re-inspection, the approved person is satisfied that the vessel is fit for its purpose he shall issue a certificate to that effect in a form approved by British Waterways. Unless earlier revoked, such certificate shall be valid for a period of one year.

7.5 British Waterways may at any time revoke a certificate issued under this condition by notice in writing to the owner of the vessel if it becomes aware that the vessel has been altered in any material way in respect of its fitness-for-purpose since the last inspection.

7.6 This provision applies where, within a period of 28 days prior to the expiry of the validity of a certificate issued under Condition 7.5, a vessel is inspected by an approved person for the purpose of a replacement certificate, and the approved person is satisfied as a result of that inspection that a replacement certificate may properly be issued. In those circumstances, the period of validity of the replacement certificate shall be one year from the date of expiry of the validity of the certificate being replaced.

7.7 An approved person for the purpose of this condition means a person who is a member of such bodies concerned with the examining and surveying of vessels or otherwise approved for the purpose of examination of vessels as shall from time to time be included in a list published by British Waterways. British Waterways may in that list indicate the necessary qualification, experience or level of skill necessary (in addition to membership of, or approval by, the specified body) to be an approved person. British Waterways may additionally or alternatively specify approved persons by reference to criteria published from time to time by the Maritime and Coastguard Agency.

8. Insurance Policy[1] *4.31*

An Insurance Policy for the purposes of Condition 3.3 means an insurance policy complying with Part I of Schedule 2 to the British Waterways Act 1995 but provided that:

1. Vessel owners using British Waterways' navigations are required to hold insurance policies and certificates for each of their vessels using the canals: British Waterways Act 1995, s. 17(3) and Sched. 2, Part I.

8.1 The exclusion in Paragraph 3(c) of a requirement for insurance cover for liability for goods shall not apply so far the liability relates to persons other than the owners or consignees of those goods.

8.2 The exclusion in Paragraph 3(e) of a requirement for insurance cover for contractual liability shall not apply in respect of contractual liability to British Waterways.

8.3 British Waterways may prescribe a sum under paragraph 3(f) that applies only to freight vessels, and may prescribe different sums by reference to the nature of the goods carried.

4.32

9. Competency of Master and Crew

9.1 The minimum competencies required for the purposes of Condition 3.4 are:

(i) for a master in command of a freight vessel being navigated in Category A waters, a British Waterways Helmsman's Certificate;

(ii) for a master in command of a freight vessel being navigated in Category B and C waters, Maritime and Coastguard Agency Boatmaster Licence;

(iii) a European Community Boatmaster's licence (with appropriate local knowledge)

(iv) for crew in attendance on freight vessels being navigated on any Waterway, British Waterways Deckhand's Certificate.

9.2 British Waterways may from time to time, by published list or by individual notification, recognise other maritime qualifications that meet the minimum competencies specified above.

9.3 British Waterways may, in any conditions of carriage, require levels of competency greater than the minimum specified in Condition 9.1 where the nature or type of goods carried are such that the safe operation of the freight vessel or the waterway to be navigated may otherwise be at risk.

4.33

10. Vessels Laid Up

10.1 An owner of a freight vessel registered with British Waterways may notify British Waterways in writing that such vessel is laid up, specifying the location at which it is laid up.

10.2 Where notification under 10.1 above is given it shall not be necessary for a certificate of fitness for purpose under condition 7 to be in force in respect of that vessel. Such vessel shall nevertheless remain subject to the provisions Section 7 British Waterways Act 1983 (Control of unsafe vessels).

10.3 A freight vessel that is laid up in accordance with the condition must be capable of navigation, or be under active repair to make it so within a reasonable time. Such vessel may not be navigated on a Waterway except with the prior consent of British Waterways for the purpose only to take it to a place of repair or to an appropriate place for inspection under Condition 7.

[*The next paragraph is 4.45*]

III. BWB CARRIAGE OF FREIGHT CONDITIONS 2003

British Waterways has also published a set of Carriage of Freight Conditions 2003.[1] Despite their name these conditions do not govern the terms of the contract between the trader and the carrier (though, as we shall see, they can have implications for that contract) but instead set out the terms upon which any freight operator (carrier) is permitted to use British Waterways' navigations for the carriage of goods. These Conditions are as follows: 4.45

2. Interpretation 4.46

2.1 In these conditions, unless the context requires otherwise:

"British Waterways" means the British Waterways Board and its successors;

"Bye-laws" means the bye-laws of British Waterways;

"Charges" means all tolls, dues or any other charges payable to British Waterways for or in relation to the carriage of Goods on a Waterway by or on behalf of a Freight Operator;

"Dangerous Substances" means any substance defined as such in the Dangerous Substances in Harbour Areas Regulations 1987;

"Environmental Damage" means any perceptible injury or damage to living organisms or property or any pollution or impairment of the environment (being air, water and land) resulting from the discharge, emission, escape or migration or any substance, energy, noise or vibration, other than any such injury or damage of a minor nature that is ordinarily incidental to the normal and well-managed operation of a Freight Vessel by a competent person;

"Freight Operator" means the person using or intending to use a Waterway for the carriage of Goods by a Freight Vessel whether as the Owner of a Freight Vessel or of the Goods or in any other capacity;

"Freight Vessel" has the meaning given in the British Waterways Freight Vessel Conditions 2003;

"Freight Vessel Conditions" means the British Waterways Freight Vessel Conditions 2003;

"Goods" means each and every cargo of any description whatsoever being transported by a Freight Vessel together with any package, case, pallet, container, vehicle or other thing which conveys, carries, contains, protects or supports cargo or is designed or made to do so;

"Owner" Means:

(1) in relation to Goods, the legal owner of the Goods or person, from time to time, in charge or and/or with physical possession of the Goods including, without limitation, a consignor, consignee, shipper, broker or the agents or any of the foregoing; and

(2) in relation to a Freight Vessel, the legal owner or any person, from time to time, in charge of, and/or operating, a Freight Vessel including without limitation, a Master, broker, charterer, hirer, mortgagee in possession or the agents of any of the foregoing;

"Operational Schedule" means the schedule of operational requirements (including details of the Freight Vessel and Waterway permitted to be used) agreed by British Waterways and the Freight Operator in respect of a particular carriage of Goods or a series of carriages of like nature;

"Master" means the person for the time being having command, charge or management of a Freight Vessel;

1. Made under the Transport Act 1962, s. 43 and the British Waterways Bye-laws and are specified to apply to any carriage of goods by a freight vessel (as defined in the Freight Vessel Conditions 2003) on a waterway on or after 1 April 2003.

"Normal Working Hours" means the usual working hours of the waterway(s) identified in the Operational Schedule;

"Waterway" means any canal or inland navigation belonging to or under the control of British Waterways and includes any works, land or premises belonging to or under the control of British Waterways and held or used by them in connection with such canal or inland navigation;

"Week" means the 7 days running from Sunday to Saturday inclusive.

2.2 The headings in these conditions are for convenience only and shall not affect their interpretation.

2.3 Reference to any provision of any Act of Parliament or subordinate legislation (including bye-laws) shall be deemed to be a reference to such Act of Parliament, subordinate legislation or bye-laws as amended, modified, re-enacted or replaced whether before or after the date hereof and any reference to any provision of any such Act or legislation shall also include, where appropriate, any provision of which it is a re-enactment (whether with or without modification).

2.4 Reference to the singular shall include the plural and vice versa.

4.47 **3. General**

3.1 The carriage of Goods by a Freight Vessel on a Waterway shall be subject to these conditions and the terms of any Operational Schedule agreed from time to time.

3.2 Any Freight Operator intending to carry Goods on a Waterway by Freight Vessel shall first notify British Waterways. The notification shall be in such form and give such details as British Waterways may reasonably require, including without limitation, details of the nature or type of Goods intended to be carried, of the route intended to be taken and of the Freight Vessel to be used.

3.3 The agreement of an Operational Schedule shall be based on the information given in the notification. An Operational Schedule may be agreed for a particular carriage of Goods or for a series of carriages of like nature. British Waterways shall not be under any obligation to issue an Operational Schedule or otherwise permit the carriage of Goods by a Freight Operator. If British Waterways refuses to agree an Operational Schedule or otherwise to permit the carriage of Goods it shall give its reasons in writing.

3.4 These conditions, and the terms of any Operational Schedule, cannot be varied except in writing signed by an authorised officer of British Waterways.

3.5 The loading and/or unloading of Goods by or on behalf of a Freight Operator onto or over any land owned by or under the control of British Waterways (excluding land let to third parties) is not permitted under these conditions and shall require a separate agreement between British Waterways and the Freight Operator.

4.48 **4. Use of Waterways**

4.1 A Freight Operator may use those Waterways detailed in the Operational Schedule for the purposes of transporting Goods by Freight Vessel subject to the observance by the Freight Operator of these conditions, any requirements specified in the Operational Schedule and the bye-laws.

4.2 In the event of any serious or persistent failure by the Freight Operator to comply with any of the provisions of these conditions, the Operational Schedule or the bye-laws, British Waterways may withdraw its consent given under the terms of the Operational Schedule. The consent may be terminated immediately if safety or significant Waterway operational requirements are compromised. Otherwise the Freight Operator will be notified in writing and given a reasonable time to effect a remedy prior to the consent being terminated.

4.49 **5. Declaration of Goods**

5.1 To enable the correct calculation of charges and for similar purposes, the Freight Operator shall complete a declaration in writing in respect of all Goods transported on a Waterway in the form prescribed by British Waterways for this purpose from time to time.

5.2 The declaration shall be completed by or on behalf of the Freight Operator and submitted to the British Waterways Office prescribed on the Operational Schedule by post or facsimile within 7 days of the end of the Week in which the relevant Freight Vessel carrying the Goods arrives at its destination in a Waterway or leaves a Waterway for a destination other than one in a Waterway.

5.3 Compliance by the Freight Operator with Condition 5.1 above shall be deemed sufficient to satisfy the declaration requirements of the bye-laws.

5.4 Upon the reasonable request of British Waterways, the Freight Operator shall make available for inspection by an authorised officer of British Waterways or its nominated representative all relevant and/or material documentation relating to the loading, unloading and carriage of Goods by the Freight Operator on a Waterway.

6. Charges *4.50*

6.1 The Freight Operator shall pay to British Waterways the Charges applicable to the carriage of the Goods and such other charges as may be specified in the Operational Schedule.

6.2 The call-out service referred to in Condition 7.3 shall be provided by British Waterways at the Charges for individual Waterways set out in the Operational Schedule. Charges will be payable in respect of any call-out requested by or on behalf of a Freight Operator and subsequently not taken up by a Freight Operator.

6.3 Charges will be payable in respect of all emergency call-outs made by or on behalf of a Freight Operator except where the emergency call-out is attributable to the breakdown or malfunctioning of any of British Waterways' manned locks, moveable bridges and other operational structures provided for the purpose of navigating a Waterway which prevents or impedes the passage of a Freight Vessel by or on behalf of a Freight Operator.

6.4 Payment of all Charges shall be due 30 days from the date of invoice. All charges will be subject to VAT where applicable.

6.5 British Waterways reserves the right to charge interest on all overdue Charges. Such interest shall be calculated on a day-to-day basis on the amount outstanding at the rate of 3% above the base rate from time to time of National Westminster Bank plc from due date (after as well as before judgement) until the outstanding amount is paid in full.

7. Navigation *4.51*

7.1 Subject to Condition 7.2 below, the Waterways specified in the Operational Schedule shall be available for navigation by a Freight Operator provided that British Waterways shall be free to close all or any part of a Waterway where closure is necessary to carry out maintenance to a Waterway or in the case of an emergency. Except in the case of an emergency, notice will be given and closure will be kept as short as is reasonably practical.

7.2 Subject to Condition 7.3, manned locks and moveable bridges will normally be available for navigation by a Freight Operator during the normal working hours of such structures as indicated in the Operational Schedule.

7.3 Navigation of manned locks and moveable bridges will be possible outside the normal working hours of such structures on a call-out basis provided that a minimum of 24 hours prior notice, or as otherwise agreed in the Operational Schedule, is given to the relevant local BW Office of the Freight Operator's desire to navigate through such structures outside its normal working hours. Such notice must be received by the relevant BW Office during the normal working hours of that BW Office indicated on the Operational Schedule.

8. Freight Operators Obligations *4.52*

8.1 The Freight Operator shall:

8.1.1 ensure that all Freight Vessels used by the Freight operator, the Owners of such Freight Vessels and any of their agents, employees and sub-contractors comply with the provisions of the Freight Vessel Conditions, the bye-laws and any other legislation and/or regulations relevant to the movement of Goods and carriage of Dangerous Substances by a vessel on a Waterway; and

8.1.2 be responsible for the competency of the Master and crew of the Freight Vessel; and

8.1.3 be responsible for the condition of the Goods and the adequate and safe storage of the Goods on the Freight Vessel.

8.1.4 Without prejudice to the generality of the provisions of Condition 8.1 the Freight Operator shall not do or fail to do, or permit others to do or fail to do anything which may cause or result in any Environmental Damage.

8.1.5 The Freight Operator shall comply with any specific instruction of British Waterways with regard to the Freight Operator's use of a Waterway that may properly be given and which affects or is likely to affect performance or any health and safety duties of British Waterways.

4.53

9. Indemnity

9.1 Without prejudice to any other rights or remedies available to British Waterways; the Freight Operator shall indemnify British Waterways and keep it indemnified against all damages, losses, claims, proceedings, demands, liabilities, costs, orders and out-of-pocket expenses (including all costs incurred in investigating or defending any claim, proceedings, demand or order and any expenses incurred in preventing, avoiding or mitigating loss, liability or damage) including without limitation:

9.1.1 damage to a Waterway or loss of or damage to any other property of British Waterways;

9.1.2 loss of or damage to property of a third party;

9.1.3 death or personal injury of an employee and/or representative of British Waterways;

9.1.4 death or personal injury of any other person;

9.1.5 loss of or damage arising from Environmental Damage;

9.1.6 loss of profits, indirect, special or consequential losses incurred or suffered by or claimed against British Waterways as a result of the acts or omissions of the Freight Operator, its employees, servants, agents or sub-contractors including any failure by the Freight Operator, its employees, servants, agents or sub-contractors to comply with these terms and conditions.

9.1.7 British Waterways shall as soon as reasonably practicable inform the Freight Operator of any circumstances of which British Waterways is aware whereby British Waterways may seek to enforce the indemnity provided by condition 9.1.1 British Waterways shall not admit liability to, or settle any claims or proceeding brought by, any other party in respect of which it may seek to enforce the said indemnity without first consulting with the Freight Operator.

4.54

10. Insurance

The Freight Operator shall at its own expense effect and maintain such insurance as required by any applicable law including (where it is the Owner of the Freight Vessel) in respect of its obligations under the Freight Vessel Conditions.

Where by reason of the nature of the Goods to be carried or by any other circumstances where British Waterways reasonably determines there to be additional risk, British Waterways may specify additional insurance requirements (as to nature or level of cover) to that referred to in condition 10.1, in the Operational Schedule.

4.55

11. Liability of British Waterways

British Waterways shall be liable for damage to property caused by the negligence of British Waterways, its employees, servants or agents provided that the aggregate liability of British

Waterways to the Freight Operator for damage to property arising out of any one incident shall not exceed:

(i) in the case of loss or damage to Goods, the cost of repairing, recovering or replacing such Goods; and

(ii) in the case of damage to a Freight Vessel, the lesser of the cost of repairing such damaged Freight Vessel or in the case of total loss, replacing such damaged Freight Vessel.

But, the maximum aggregate liability of British Waterways under (i) and/or (ii) above arising out of any one incident shall not exceed £10 million.

Save for the provisions of Condition 11.1 and for liability for death or personal injury resulting from the negligence of British Waterways, British Waterways shall not be liable to the Freight Operator, its employees, servants, agents or subcontractors by reason of any representation (unless fraudulent), or any implied warranty, condition, or other term or any duty at statute or common law in contract or in tort for any damages, losses, liabilities, costs, expenses including any loss of profit or any indirect, special or consequential loss which arise out of or in connection with the use by the Freight Operator, its employees, servants, agents or sub-contractors of a Waterway.

British Waterways shall not be liable to the Freight Operator by reason of any non-availability or all or any part of a Waterway or any delay in the performance or failure to perform its obligations in relation to a Waterway if such delay or failure was due to any cause beyond British Waterways reasonable control.

12. Assignment and Subcontracting 4.56

None of the consents or permissions given to the Freight Operator under these conditions by way of the Operational Schedule or otherwise may be assigned or transferred in whole or in part without the prior written consent of British Waterways.

13. Notices 4.57

Any notice or other communication to be given by British Waterways under these conditions may be given in accordance with the provisions of section 17 of the British Waterways Act 1983.

14. Invalidity 4.58

The invalidity, illegality or unenforceability of any provision of these conditions shall not affect the other conditions.

15. Law and Jurisdiction 4.59

These conditions (and any proceedings whereby one party might be entitled to join the other as a third party) shall be governed by and construed in all respects in accordance with English Law and the parties hereby submit to the exclusive jurisdiction of the English Courts.

[*The next paragraph is 4.69*]

IV. THE GOODS[1] AND THEIR DOCUMENTATION

4.69 Clauses commonly found in carriage contracts dealing with the warranty of authority of the trader[2] to consign the goods and the requirement for a consignment note generally observe the following pattern:

> (1) The Carrier contracts upon the condition that the Trader warrants that he is either the owner or authorised agent of the owner of the merchandise to be carried and accepts these Conditions of Carriage on his own behalf and on behalf of any owner and any subsequent owners interested in such merchandise.
>
> (2) Every consignment of merchandise shall (except as agreed otherwise in writing) be accompanied by a consignment note or be the subject of some other documentation which clearly identifies the consignment.
>
> (3) The Carrier shall, if so required, sign a document prepared by the Trader acknowledging the receipt of the consignment but no such document shall be evidence of the condition or the correctness of the declared nature, quantity or weight of the consignment at the time it is received by them.

4.70 A contract for inland water carriage is a contract between a carrier and the owner of the consignment. Normally, but not always, the consignee is the owner of the goods while they are in transit. However, if the owner is not one of the contracting parties he will, nevertheless be regarded as such at common law by virtue of an implied warranty of authority to the effect that the contracting party is the authorised owner of the merchandise.[3]

4.71 The contract will also normally specify that every consignment be accompanied by a consignment note or be the subject of some other documentation (such as correspondence) that clearly identifies the consignment. The carrier will then generally sign a document prepared by the owner of the goods or his agent acknowledging receipt. It is usually provided, however, that such a receipt is not to be regarded as evidence of the condition or of the correctness of the declared nature, quantity or weight of the consignment at the time it is received. Sometimes the carrier will also require conforming addressing and labelling and also require that the consignment note follows a specified form. Although bills of lading are not used for inland water carriage it was held, *obiter*, in *Bryans* v. *Nix*[4] that there is no reason in principle why a canal receipt should not be treated as a document of title if it was accepted as such by the "custom of merchants". However, there seems to be no evidence of such a custom having been established in the inland water trade. Under the Factors Act 1889, s. 1(4), the expression "documents of title" includes "any bill of lading and warrant or order for the delivery of goods, and any other document used in the ordinary course of business as proof of the possession or control of goods, or authority or purporting to authorise, either by endorsement or by delivery,

1. "Goods" are defined by s. 1(3) of the Factors Act 1889 to include "wares and merchandise".

2. The contract will need to contain a definition of "Trader". This will generally mean "the person with whom the carrier contracts for the carriage of merchandise or for arranging for the carriage of merchandise by an independent carrier or carriers". At common law the term "trader" has been interpreted to include consignor, consignee and carrier (*Master Lightermen and Barge Owners' Assn.* v. *Southern Ry. Co. (No. 2)* (1934) 21 Ry. & Can. Tr. Cas. 126, *per* Maugham L.J. at p. 155). The clause set out here provides a more practical limited definition though it can, depending upon the circumstances, include both the consignor and the consignee.

3. *Colleen* v. *Wright* (1857) 8 E. & B. 647. Accordingly the express warranty of authority found in contracts, including the clause quoted (which is the "common form" clause), is probably otiose.

4. (1839) 4 M. & W. 7754.

the possessor of the document to transfer or receive the goods thereby represented".

4.72 An inland water carriage consignment note, although it may incorporate the terms of the contract, is not generally a document of title.[5] Accordingly, merely possessing a consignment note is not proof that its holder is entitled to the goods. So, the trader cannot substitute a third party for himself by delivery of documents by anything less than a new contract in the form of a novation.[6] On the other hand, the document that the carrier sends to consignees where goods are "to be called for", informing them that the goods have arrived,[7] may constitute a document authorising delivery of the goods to the possessor.[8]

4.73 A document of title represents goods in the sense that it can be used to obtain possession of the goods. So, a delivery order is an order for the delivery of the goods either immediately or at a later date: it can be used to obtain possession of the goods from the carrier, a warehouseman or other bailee.[9] However, with the exception of bills of lading, the transfer of documents such as dock warrants and delivery orders do not transfer property in the goods *per se*. In order to effect constructive delivery of the goods via the medium of a document such as a delivery order it is also necessary that the person in possession of the goods attorns to their new owner. Attornment can take place by the bailee acknowledging that he now holds the goods to the new owner's order, but it is vital that the bailee communicates with the holder of the delivery order. There is no attornment where the bailee merely receives the delivery order and notes its contents.[10] The essential characteristic that distinguishes documents of title from other documents is that the object of the document of title is the *disposal* of the goods. Consequently, as an invoice merely provides proof of payment, it is not a document of title.[11] The standard form carriage contract is not concerned with documents of title as such, merely with a warranty of ownership or agency. However, if the carrier is in possession of a document of title, or is to attorn to the consignee (perhaps in its capacity as warehouseman) the nature of the documentation that the carrier holds will be of significance.

[*The next paragraph is 4.83*]

5. Cf. *Official Assignee of Madras* v. *Mercantile Bank of India* [1935] A.C. 53.
6. *London & South Western Ry. Co. & Great Northern Ry. Co.* v. *Bishop* (1898) 42 S.J. 255.
7. See para. 4.229, below.
8. *Heugh* v. *London & North Western Ry. Co.* (1870) 5 Ex. 51.
9. *Gunn* v. *Bolckow Vaughan & Co.* (1875) L.R. 10 Ch. App. 491, *per* Mellish L.J. at p. 502; *Capital & Counties Bank Ltd* v. *Warriner* (1896) 12 T.L.R. 216.
10. *Laurie & Morewood* v. *Dudin & Sons* [1926] 1 K.B. 223, *per* Scrutton L.J. at p. 237; *D.F. Mount Ltd.* v. *Jay (Provisions) Ltd.* [1980] 1 Q.B. 159, *per* Salmon L.J. at p. 169; *Jenkyns* v. *Usborne* (1844) 7 Man. & G. 678; *McEwan* v. *Smith* (1849) H.L.C. 309.
11. *Anglo-Irish Asset Finance* v. *D.S.G. Financial Services* [1995] C.L.Y. 4491.

V. LIABILITIES

4.83 There are normally standard provisions in the carriage contract dealing with the allocation of liabilities where goods are carried either at the carrier's risk or at the trader's risk.

A. CARRIER'S RISK

4.84 The carrier shall be liable for any loss, misdelivery of or damage to the goods occurring during transit unless the carrier shall prove that such has been occasioned by:

(a) Act of God;
(b) Act of war, invasion, hostilities (whether war be declared or not), terrorist acts or actions by or of the Queen's enemies;
(c) Arrest or restraint of Princes, or Rulers, or seizure under legal process;
(d) Orders or restrictions imposed by the Government[1] or any Government Department, or by any local or public authority;
(e) Act or omission of the trader, his servants or agents;
(f) Inherent liability to wastage in bulk or weight, latent or inherent defect, vice or natural deterioration or the merchandise;
(g) Casualty (including fire, flood, explosion or other casualty);
(h) Riot, civil commotion, strikes, lockouts, stoppage or restraint of labour from whatever cause;
(i) And all and every other Dangers and Accidents of the Seas, Rivers and Navigations of whatsoever nature and kind.

Provided that:

(i) where loss, misdelivery or damage arises and the Carrier has failed to prove that they used all reasonable foresight and care in the carriage of the goods the Carrier shall not be relieved from liability for such loss, misdelivery or damage;
(ii) the Carrier shall not incur liability of any kind in respect of goods where there has been fraud on the part of the Trader.

4.85 Carriage at the carrier's risk at common law involves the carrier, when met with a claim, proving a specific exemption (e.g. Casualty). It is then up to the trader to defeat that defence by proving that the carrier has been negligent. However current custom and practice in relation to insurance arrangements can involve a modification to this common law position, as in the above clause where, in addition to proving a specific exempting event the carrier must also establish that it has not been negligent. However, the carrier does not automatically accept liability in those cases in which its employees have failed to use all reasonable foresight and care unless this is proved by the claimant.[2]

4.86 Liability in the clause set out above is contractual strict liability subject to the establishment of one of the exceptions. "Loss" for this purpose refers to physical rather than pecuniary loss[3] and "misdelivery" is delivery to anyone but the correct addressee (or a person who is reasonably believed to be the correct addressee) at the

1. For the meaning of the word "government" in a commercial document see *Luigi Monta of Genoa* v. *Cechofracht Co. Ltd.* [1956] 2 Q.B. 522.

2. *Coldman* v. *Hill* [1919] 1 K.B. 443; *Brook's Wharf & Bull Wharf Ltd.* v. *Goodman Bros.* [1937] 1 K.B. 534; *Houghland* v. *R.R. Low (Luxury Coaches) Ltd.* [1962] 1 Q.B. 694; *Firestone Tyre Co. Ltd.* v. *Vokins* [1951] 1 Lloyd's Rep. 32; *Hunt & Winterbotham (West of England Ltd.* v. *BRS Parcels Ltd.* [1962] 1 Q.B. 617; *Ulster-Swift Ltd.* v. *Taunton Meat Haulage Ltd.* [1977] 1 W.L.R. 625 (Megaw L.J. at 633).

3. *Young & Son (Wholesale Fish Merchants) Ltd.* v. *British Transport Commission* [1955] 2 Q.B. 177.

correct address (or what is reasonably believed to be the correct address).[4] If misdelivery actually occurs the carrier will be liable to the trader not for misdelivery as such but because that misdelivery has caused loss of or damage or delay to the goods. Railway cases have established that misdelivery does not include wrongful detention by the carrier.[5] The claimant must establish, of course, that the goods have been damaged in the first place. "Damage" in this context includes deterioration in the goods as a result of delay[6] i.e. either total loss, a reduction in quantity or a reduction in the quality of the goods i.e. any change in the goods as a result of which their value has been reduced. It does not include consequential losses.

A loss by Act of God means a loss by the forces of nature which were the direct cause of the loss or damage and which were either unforeseeable or, if foreseeable, not capable of being prevented by any reasonable precautions. The carrier is not liable for any accident where it can be shown that such accident was due directly and exclusively to natural causes, with no human intervention contributing, and that it could not have been prevented by any amount of foresight and reasonable care,[7] such as heavy icing-up of a canal, or rain and frost which might do harm to certain types of goods.[8] 4.87

In general the meaning of "Act of war or of the Queen's enemies" is reasonably clear though for the avoidance of doubt some "war clauses" now also expressly include a reference to terrorist activities.[9] The Court of Appeal considered the definition of war in *Kawasaki Kisen Kaisha Kobe* v. *Bantham S.S. Co. Ltd.*[10] This case concerned a cancelling clause under a 12-month time charterparty which allowed "Charterers and owners to have liberty of cancelling the charterparty if war breaks out involving Japan". The Court of Appeal took the view that the words "outbreak of war" and similar phrases should be given a common sense meaning and that it was not necessary for war to have broken out within the technical sense that it has in the public international law context. 4.88

"Warlike operations" were defined by Atkinson J. in *Clan Line Steamers Ltd.* v. *Liverpool and London War Risks Association Ltd.*[11] as 4.89

> "[an operation] which forms part of an actual or intended belligerent act or series of acts by combatant forces, . . . part may be performed preparatory to the actual act or acts of belligerency, but there must be a connection sufficiently close between the act in question and the belligerent act or acts to enable a tribunal to say with at least some modicum of common sense . . . that it formed part of the acts of belligerency".

4. *McKean* v. *McIvor* (1870) L.R. 6 Ex. 36; *Heugh* v. *LNW Ry.* (1870) L.R. 5 Ex. 51.

5. *LNW Ry.* v. *Neilson* [1922] 1 K.B. 192, 202, although unlawful detention may amount to the tort of conversion: *Perry & Co. Ltd.* v. *BRB* [1980] 2 All E.R. 579. Misdelivery would appear to mean, in the context of exceptional perils, delivery by mistake and thus does not cover deliberate misdelivery to the wrong address: *Alexander* v. *Railway Executive* [1951] 2 K.B. 882.

6. *Hartstoke Fruiterers Ltd.* v. *LMS Ry. Co.* [1943] K.B. 362.

7. *Nugent* v. *Smith* (1876) 1 C.P.D. 423.

8. However, some adverse weather conditions can be foreseen and must be guarded against by the carrier, provided he is not thereby required to take extraordinary precautions: *Briddon* v. *Great Northern Ry.*: (1858) L.J.Ex. 51; *Ryan* v. *Youngs* [1938] 1 All E.R. 522. See also footnote 17, below.

9. The acts of terrorists would not fall within this clause without an express reference on the basis of existing case law unless the act of terrorism can be proved to be state-sponsored: *Pan American World Airways Inc.* v. *Aetna Casualty & Surety Co.* [1975] 1 Lloyd's Rep. 77 (USCA, 2d Cir., 1974).

10. [1939] 2 K.B. 544.

11. [1943] K.B. 209 at 221.

It is likely that "hostilities" has a similar meaning to "warlike operations". It is possible for there to be hostilities without the outbreak of war. "Hostilities" refers to particular acts or operations of hostility, rather than the existence of a state of war.

4.90 Reference to "arrest or restraint of Princes etc. etc." appears to be an adaptation of the traditional maritime risks exception. The clause is modified for inland water carriage from the "traditional" charterparty clause to allow for the exception to cover detention or interference by the courts as a consequence of legal proceedings. "Arrest or restraint" does not, however, have to be accompanied by force.[12] Judicial action is covered under sub-clause (c) above whereas sub-clause (d) concerns executive action. It includes action taken by the British Government as well as other governments and by the agents of British and foreign governments. Executive action by order of the Government or any local or public authority may go so far as confiscation or even destruction of the goods, e.g. for health or environmental reasons.

4.91 It would be unreasonable if the trader could require an innocent carrier to pay where the loss was caused entirely by his own fault. A common example at common law would be where goods are liable to be damaged in transit if they are not properly protected by packing. In such a case it is the duty of the trader to pack them properly.[13] Another example arises where the real nature of the goods is concealed from the carrier so that he has no opportunity of exercising the usual care when the particular nature of the goods so requires. Here it is only bound to use such ordinary care as the goods appear to need and, if it does so it is not liable for damage due to any want of extraordinary care. These circumstances are expressly covered by sub-clause (e) though the burden is on the carrier to prove the excepted peril. If the exception is proved it becomes irrelevant whether the act or omission of the trader, his servants or agents is negligent or not. On the face of it this clause does not make it clear whether the common law rule that the carrier is to remain liable for the negligence of its own employees contributing to the loss will apply, hence it is usual to include a clause in the standard terms of carriage to the effect that: "Unless these conditions otherwise expressly state the rights and liabilities of the Trader and the Carrier respectively, whether at Common Law or under any Statute, shall remain unaffected."[14]

4.92 Sub-clause (f) deals with latent defects, inherent vice and wastage as an excepted peril. At common law inherent vice means some default or defect latent to the goods themselves which, by its operation, tends to the damage or destruction of the goods. Clearly the carrier cannot be expected to undertake the risk of loss from such a cause. Accordingly, it is not liable for injury to agricultural or market garden produce from heating or natural decay during transit, provided it has taken all reasonable care of the goods as appropriate such as, for example, ensuring that there

12. *British & Foreign Marine Insurance Co.* v. *Sanday* (1916) 21 Com. Cas. 154; *Miller* v. *Law Accident Insurance Co.* (1903) 8 Com. Cas. 161.

13. See paras. 4.197 *et seq.*, below.

14. This provision, formerly very common in contracts of inland water carriage (e.g. Cond. 25 of the now obsolete British Waterways Board General Merchandise Conditions 1973) is intended both to import relevant statutory provisions and to encourage the implication of terms from the common law rules which might not, but for this clause, have been made.

is proper ventilation. Again, a carrier is not responsible for evaporation of liquids or reduction of leakage, provided all ordinary and reasonable care has been taken to prevent this. A defect in goods may be harmless provided the goods are not moved, but may cause injury as soon as they are carried from place to place, such as particularly volatile liquids or delicate chemicals. Provided the carrier uses all reasonable care it will not be liable for damage caused by such a defect.

Many of the cases of "inherent vice" concern animals.[15] However, the principles are equally applicable to other cargoes. If the cause of destruction or injury comes from something in the goods themselves which the carrier cannot reasonably be expected to foresee or to guard against, or from the ordinary wear and tear of the goods which cannot be avoided if the goods are carried in the ordinary way, and which is in no way due to the carrier's negligence, the carrier is not responsible for the damage. The inclusion within this excepted peril of "inherent liability to wastage in bulk or weight" indicates that "inherent vice" covers characteristics of a qualitative nature which result in a reduction in quantity. This is, therefore, no more than an express articulation of what is, in any event, covered by the closing words of the sub-clause. It would seem that an "inherent defect" is the same thing as "inherent vice". A "latent" defect is one that one would not expect to discover on any reasonable examination or test which the carrier could be expected to carry out.[16] 4.93

The "casualty" excepted peril covers certain "natural" perils, such as fire or explosion as a consequence of accidents that are not classed as Acts of God at common law.[17] As soon as there is any human intervention contributing to the causation of the loss, Act of God cannot be invoked as an exception. Although the word "casualty" as an excepted peril is a frequently encountered word in standard form carriage contracts, its meaning is not entirely clear. Obviously, it does not simply mean "accident" for, if it did, the whole basis of the carrier's liability under "carrier's risk" terms would be illusory. As Professor Kahn-Freund pointed out[18]: "This construction would be to the effect that the carrier is liable for accident except where the cause of damage is an accident." Aside from the express reference to fire, flood and explosion, the sub-clause is probably intended to cover the kind of casualty which, in common parlance, would be termed a disaster. In other words, provided the carrier can prove reasonable care and foresight, it will not be responsible for the consequences of major catastrophes, even if they do not fall within the narrow definition given by the courts to the phrase "Act of God". 4.94

15. *Blower* v. *Great Western Ry.* (1872) L.R. 7 C.P. 655; *Kendall* v. *London & South Western Ry.* (1872) L.R. 7 Ex. 373; *Lister* v. *Lancashire & Yorkshire Ry.* [1903] 1 K.B. 878; cf. *Donald & Son (Wholesale Meat Contractors)* v. *Continental Freeze*, 1984 S.L.T. 182.

16. *Union of India* v. *N.V. Reederij, Amsterdam* [1963] 2 Lloyd's Rep. 223.

17. See *Ryan* v. *Youngs* [1938] 1 All E.R. 522; *Forward* v. *Pittard* (1785) 1 T.R. 33; Act of God means not a mere misfortune but something overwhelming (*per* Martin B. in *Oakley* v. *Portsmouth Steam Packet Co.* (1856) 11 Ex. 623). Lord Mansfield, in *Trent Navigation* v. *Wood* (1785) 4 Doug. K.B. 286 defined Act of God as "a natural necessity, as wind and storms, which arise from natural causes, and is distinct from inevitable accident". See also *Pandorf* v. *Hamilton* (1886) 17 Q.B.D. 675; *Nichols* v. *Marsland* (1875–76) L.R. 10 Ex. 255; *Nitro-Phosphate Co.* v. *L & S Katherine's Dock Co.* (1878) 9 Ch.D. 503; *R.* v. *Essex Commissioners of Sewers* (1885) 14 Q.B.D. 561; *Baldwins Ltd.* v. *Halifax Corp.* (1916) 85 L.J.K.B. 1769; *Makin* v. *L.&N.E. Ry.* [1943] 1 K.B. 467.

18. O. Kahn-Freund, *The Law of Carriage by Inland Transport* (4th ed., Stevens, 1965), p. 245.

4.95 "Riot" is defined in the Public Order Act 1986.[19] "Civil Commotion" is "considerably more serious than a leaderless mob"[20] and "is used to indicate a stage between riot and Civil war".[21] The "classic" definition was provided by Lord Mansfield in *Langdale* v. *Mason*[22] as "an insurrection of the people for general purposes, though it may not amount to a rebellion, where there is usurped power". It is clear, therefore, that something more than a mere general civil disturbance of a transient character is required, so a general and vague proof of a disturbance at the place of loading which may have interrupted or impeded but which did not actually prevent the loading is not civil commotion for this purpose.[23]

4.96 A strike is a "general concerted refusal by workmen to work in consequence of an alleged grievance".[24] A strike must involve an element of *simultaneous* cessation of work on the part of workers.[25] For this purpose the strike must be against the employer, not merely a refusal to work because an infectious disease is prevalent, or the weather is hot or wet or such like excuses.[26] A strike is also "distinct from a stoppage which is brought about by some external event, such as a bomb scare or by apprehension of danger".[27] A restraint of labour would include a threat by employees not to move or handle certain goods.[28] The sub-clause specifies that the excepted peril covers all the designated circumstances "from whatever cause". These words would, on their face, appear wide enough to cover negligence by the carrier.[29] However, a more likely construction here, in the light of the proviso whereunder the carrier is obliged to use "all reasonable foresight and care", is that these words will be given a narrower meaning.

19. S. 1: "Where 12 or more persons who are present together use or threaten unlawful violence for a common purpose and the conduct of them (taken together) is such as would cause a person of reasonable firmness present at the scene to fear for his personal safety, each of the persons using unlawful violence for the common purpose is guilty of riot" (s.1.(1)).

20. *Spinney's (1948) Ltd.* v. *Royal Insurance Co. Ltd.* [1980] 1 Lloyd's Rep. 406.

21. *Levy* v. *Assicurazioni Generali* [1940] A.C. 791, *per* Luxmore L.J. at p. 800.

22. (1781) Park 968.

23. See *The Village Bell* (1874) 30 L.T. 232; *Bolivia Republic* v. *Indemnity Mutual Marine Insurance Co.* [1909] 1 K.B. 785.

24. *Williams Bros Ltd.* v. *Naamlooze Berghuys Kolenhandel* (1915) 21 Com. Cas. 253, 257, applied in *Tramp Shipping Corp* v. *Greenwich Marine Inc.* [1975] 2 All E.R. 989. See also Kelly C.B. in *King* v. *Parker* (1876) 34 L.T. 889.

25. *Farrer* v. *Close* (1869) L.R. 4 Q.B. 612, *per* Hannen J.

26. *Stephens* v. *Harris* (1887) 57 L.J.Q.B. 203; *Re Richardsons and Samuel* (1898) 66 L.J.Q.B. 868; *Re Allison & Co. and Richards* (1904) 20 T.L.R. 584; *Steel, Young & Co* v. *Grand Canary Coaling Co.* (1904) 20 T.L.R. 542.

27. *Per* Lord Denning M.R. in *Tramp Shipping Corp.* v. *Greenwich Marine Inc.*, [1975] 2 All E.R. 989. In *B. & S. Contracts and Designs Ltd.* v. *Victor Green Publications Ltd.* [1984] I.C.R. 419, the Court of Appeal held that the claimant could not rely on a *force majeure* clause that included "strikes" because it had not acted reasonably when it had refused to pay its workforce the additional money demanded by them, which additional payment would have been facilitated by the claimants using the money advanced by its customer to pay the workforce, the more especially since the customer had advanced that money to avert the threatened strike.

28. See *Young & Son (Wholesale Fish Merchants) Ltd.* v. *British Transport Commission* [1955] 2 Q.B. 177.

29. See *Travers & Sons Ltd.* v. *Cooper* [1915] 1 K.B. 73; *Smith* v. *South Wales Switchgear* [1978] 1 W.L.R. 165. See also: Yates & Hawkins, *Standard Business Contracts* (London, Sweet & Maxwell, 1986), pp. 103–116 and Treitel, *The Law of Contract* (11th ed., London, Sweet & Maxwell, 2003), pp. 223–225.

At common law a claimant is able to make a case against a carrier without proof of the cause of the loss or injury and without proof of negligence on the carrier's part. However, should the carrier prove an excepted peril it was then up to the claimant to defeat that defence by proving that the carrier had been negligent and this would usually involve proof of the cause of the loss or damage. Modern inland water carriage contracts, as in the case of the proviso in the clause set out above, generally reverse the onus of proof in favour of the claimant trader; it is therefore for the carrier to prove that it was not negligent as a condition precedent to exculpation and not for the claimant to prove that the carrier was negligent.[30] However, the proviso goes on to state that the carrier shall not be liable where the trader has been guilty of fraud. The most common circumstance where fraud can arise is the case of a fraudulent declaration about the nature or value of the goods which are the subject of carriage. 4.97

B. TRADER'S RISK

Conditions of inland water carriage will generally offer a choice of carriage either at the Carrier's Risk (see above) or at the Trader's (owner's) Risk. The majority of carriers by inland waterway carrying cement, coal, aggregate, waste and general cargo normally accept goods for carriage and storage only at trader's risk. A common form of clause is as follows: 4.98

> Where notice is given by the Carrier that merchandise will be accepted for carriage by the Carrier at Trader's Risk only, the Carrier shall not be liable for damage to or for loss arising from damage to, a consignment of such merchandise or any part thereof except upon proof that such damage or loss arose from the wilful misconduct of the Carrier, its servants or agents.

The effect of this clause is to make the carriage of the goods subject to trader's risk. It does so in a somewhat curious fashion and the construction of this clause is not entirely free from doubt. 4.99

Where notice is given by the carrier under this condition, the carrier will only be liable on proof of wilful misconduct, as against carriage at carrier's risk, where it is up to the carrier to prove one of the excepted perils and disprove negligence. In *Young & Son (Wholesale Fish Merchants) Ltd.* v. *British Transport Commission*[31] it was argued that a clause, drafted in similar terms to the above, positively imposed liability on the carrier where the loss or damage had arisen from the wilful misconduct of the carrier's employees. McNair J. rejected this construction. Professor Kahn-Freund observed, in connection with this type of clause, that it "should be read against a background of the common law". At common law the carrier was liable. The Condition says that he shall not be liable in principle, but, by way of an exception to this exception from the common law, it says that he shall be liable for wilful misconduct. This is couched in negative language in view of the distribution of the burden of proof but it is nevertheless a provision which in an 4.100

30. For similar analogous provisions in a contract for carriage by rail see *Robert Hutchinson & Co.* v. *British Railways Board*, 1970 S.L.T. 72.

31. [1955] 2 Q.B. 177.

affirmative way imposes liability.[32] So, if there is carriage at trader's risk the carrier is only liable in the case of wilful misconduct. It is, of course, arguable that this clause would simply fail the reasonableness test under the Unfair Contract Terms Act 1977,[33] were it applicable, although it is likely that it could be made "reasonable" by the carrier offering the trader a reduction in freight rates for carriage at trader's risk.

4.101 No particular form of notice is required by this clause. Presumably, therefore, oral notice will suffice, though the carrier will carry the burden of proving that the requisite notice invoking trader's risk provisions was given. The word "loss" in the clause appears to mean "financial loss" and not "loss of the goods" and thus covers the financial loss the owner has suffered both through the physical loss of and physical damage to his goods.

4.102 The burden of proving wilful misconduct is a heavy one as in most cases the owner of the damaged or lost goods will be unable to discover how the goods were damaged or what caused their loss. In so far as information is discoverable in such circumstances it will usually be information in the exclusive possession of the carrier and the carrier will be under no obligation to inform the owner. Failure to offer an explanation of the loss raises no presumption of wilful misconduct.[34] On the other hand, "proof beyond reasonable doubt" is not required. It is enough for the owner to prove that the loss was, on a balance of probabilities, more likely to have been due to wilful misconduct than to mere carelessness. Thus, where misconduct such as malicious damage on the part of some unknown person has been proved and the owner can show that no member of the outside public but only the carrier's employees had effective access to the goods while in transit, it is reasonable to infer that the misconduct was committed by the carrier's employees.[35] While a series of acts of carelessness, however numerous, cannot of themselves add up to wilful misconduct, the fact that other similar acts were committed by the same person may raise an inference as to the wrongdoer's state of mind when he committed each act.[36]

4.103 For an act to amount to wilful misconduct the person who commits it must realise he is doing something wrong or must do it recklessly, without caring whether it is wrong or not and regardless of its consequences.[37] While a deliberate omission may constitute wilful misconduct, negligence, however gross, will not.[38] The test of wilful misconduct is subjective and knowledge cannot be imputed in order to satisfy it.[39] A carrier's employee will not be guilty of wilful misconduct simply by breaking his employer's instructions or rules. For his act to constitute wilful misconduct he

32. Kahn-Freund, *The Land of Carriage By Inland Transport* (4th ed., Stevens, 1965), p. 257.

33. Ss.3, 11(1). See also *Waldron-Kelley* v. *British Rail* [1981] C.L.Y. 303; *Wight* v. *British Rail* [1983] C.L.Y. 424.

34. *H.C. Smith Ltd.* v. *Great Western Ry.* [1922] 1 A.C. 178.

35. *H.C. Smith Ltd.* v. *Midland Ry.* (1919) 88 L.J.K.B. 868.

36. *Horabin* v. *BOAC* [1952] 2 All E.R. 1016, *per* Barry J. at 1024.

37. *Bastable* v. *North British Ry.* 1912 S.C. 555; *Graham* v. *Belfast & N. Counties Ry.* [1905] 2 I.R. 13; *Forder* v. *Great Western Ry.* [1905] 2 K.B. 532, *per* Lord Alverstone at 535; *Jones Ltd.* v. *Bencher* [1986] 1 Lloyd's Rep. 54; *Rustenburg Platinum Mines Ltd.* v. *South African Airways* [1977] 1 Lloyd's Rep. 564, *per* Ackner J. at 569, aff'd at [1979] Lloyd's Rep. 19.

38. See *Lewis* v. *Great Western Ry.* (1877) 3 Q.B.D. 195.

39. *Forder* v. *Great Western Ry.* [1905] 2 K.B. 532.

must be aware that the breach will result in greater risk of loss or damage to the cargo than would otherwise be the case.[40] Cases involving carriage by rail indicate that "wilful misconduct" includes theft by employees of the railway. By analogy, therefore, theft by employees of the inland water carrier should similarly constitute wilful misconduct. However, doubt arises from the decision of Bingham J. in *Swiss Bank Corp.* v. *Brink's-Mat Ltd.*[41] in which the learned judge, considering Condition 13(1) of the then current edition of the Institute of Freight Forwarders Trading Conditions providing that the defendant company would be liable for loss only where it was proved that the loss "was due to the wilful neglect or default of the company or its own servants" held that words "wilful default" meant wilful default in the course of an employee's employment. Clearly theft, or indeed other criminal conduct, at least if it involves *mens rea* as against strict liability, would not be within the course of employment. However, this decision appears to have been *per incuriam* in that it failed to consider the relevant railway cases to the opposite effect.[42]

[*The next paragraph is 4.115*]

40. *Horabin* v. *BOAC* [1952] 2 All E.R. 1016; *Jones* v. *Bencher* [1986] 1 Lloyd's Rep. 54.
41. [1986] 2 Lloyd's Rep. 79.
42. *H.C. Smith* v. *Midland Ry.* (1919) 88 L.J.K.B. 868; *W. Young & Son (Wholesale Fish Merchants) Ltd.* v. *British Transport Commission* [1955] 2 Q.B. 177. Cf. *Re City Equitable Fire Insurance Co. Ltd.* [1925] 1 Ch. 407; *Monarch Airlines* v. *Luton Airport* [1998] 1 Lloyd's Rep. 403.

VI. LIMITATIONS OF LIABILITY AND NOTICE PROVISIONS

4.115 Statutory controls on exclusion and limitation clauses are imposed by the Unfair Contract Terms Act 1977.[1] It has, however, been argued in section I of this Part that this Act has no application to carriage by inland water.[2] The standard conditions for inland water carriage do include limitations on liability, but they almost certainly lie outside the ambit of the 1977 Act except in so far as they cover warehousing, or carriage of the goods on part of the route by road or rail.

> The liability of the carrier in respect of any one consignment (irrespective of the nature of the merchandise) shall in any case be limited:
> (i) where the loss, however sustained, is in respect of the whole of a consignment to a sum at the rate of £1,000 per metric ton of the gross weight of the consignment;
> (ii) where the loss, however sustained, is in respect of part of a consignment, to the proportion of the sum ascertained in accordance with (i) of this clause which the actual value of that part of the consignment bears to the actual value of the whole consignment;
> unless the nature and value thereof be declared in writing at the time of delivery to the Carrier and a charge over and above the charge for carriage be paid as compensation for the greater risk incurred, in which case the Carrier will, subject to the terms of this contract, accept liability for the loss actually sustained, not exceeding the amount so declared provided that if the actual value of the consignment is greater than the declared value the Carrier shall be liable only in the proportion which the declared value bears to the actual value. The Carrier shall be entitled under this clause to require proof of the value of the whole consignment.

4.116 At common law the consignor is not under a duty to inform a carrier of the contents or value of the package, and the carrier has no right to open it unless the contract conditions so provide. The liability of the carrier under this clause is limited "in respect of the whole of the consignment" to a sum "at the rate of £1,000 per metric ton of the gross weight of the consignment". Hence, if the loss is sustained in respect of the whole of the consignment, the trader cannot, in the absence of a special contract, recover more than this maximum amount. The value amount is remarkably low, in modern terms, but this is quite deliberate. If the clause stopped at this point it is probable that it would be declared unreasonable and thus unenforceable by a court under the Unfair Contract Terms Act 1977[3] in the unlikely event, and contrary to the argument advanced above, that this Act applies to carriage by inland water. However, even were the Act applicable, given the fact that the carrier cannot open a package to inspect and ascertain its value itself, that without a declared value insurance arrangements become difficult, that a low value amount is likely to encourage traders to declare value and finally, that by paying additional freight charges the trader can raise these limits, it is likely that this clause could be proved by the carrier to have been a reasonable one to have included in the contract.[4] If the trader does not declare value and pay the additional charge any

1. See para. 4.116, below.
2. See para. 4.7, above.
3. Ss.3(1)(2), 11(1)(4).
4. *Phillips Products Ltd.* v. *Hyland and Hamstead Plant Hire Co. Ltd.* [1987] 2 All E.R. 60; *George Mitchell (Chesterhall) Ltd.* v. *Finney Lock Seeds* [1983] 2 A.C. 803; *Stag Line* v. *Tyne Ship Repair Group* [1984] 2 Lloyd's Rep. 211; *Rees Hough Ltd.* v. *Redland Reinforced Plastics Ltd.* [1984] C.I.L.L. 84; *Photo Production Ltd.* v. *Securicor Transport Ltd.* [1980] A.C. 827, *per* Lords Wilberforce and Diplock; *Stewart Gill Ltd.* v.

compensation payable for loss or damage is limited to £1,000 per metric ton of gross weight. To ascertain the amount of the limit, it is necessary to find the weight of the consignment and calculate what it represents in terms of multiples or fractions of one metric ton. The trader can get no more than the identical number of multiples or fractions of £1,000. This is the maximum he can get but in order to receive anything he may have to prove the value of the consignment.

The loss may be sustained in respect only of part of the consignment i.e. part of the consignment may have been lost or damaged or delayed. In that case the calculation of the maximum which can be claimed in the absence of a special contract is more complex. It is then necessary to find the maximum which could have been claimed if the entire consignment had been lost, damaged or delayed. Next, the "actual value" of the whole of the consignment must be ascertained, along with the actual value of the part lost, damaged or delayed. The maximum amount payable is the same proportion of the maximum which would have been payable for the whole. Thus, whereas the amount payable for a total consignment depends on weight, the proportion of it that is payable depends on value. Quite deliberately no exception is normally provided from these limitations for cases of wilful default.[5] 4.117

The word "loss" in the context of this clause refers to financial loss, not to "loss" as distinguished from "damage" or "delay".[6] If, for example, the whole consignment is damaged in transit or delayed, the limits represent the maximum recoverable, just as they do when the consignment is "lost" in the physical sense of having disappeared. The trader can, by adopting the declared value procedure laid down in the clause, obtain the right to claim beyond the specified maximum in the event of loss, damage or delay. To do this he must declare the nature and value of the goods consigned and he must do so in writing at the time of delivery of the goods to the carrier. Further, he must pay a charge over and above the normal freight charges as compensation for the greater risk incurred by the carrier. If he does this the carrier accepts liability for the loss actually sustained but not exceeding the amount declared. If the "actual value" of the consignment is greater than the declared value, then the carrier is only liable in the proportion which the declared value bears to the "actual value". However, any statement the trader makes of the value of the goods, whether in the consignment note or otherwise, does not prevent the carrier from requiring proof of such value. 4.118

It is customary, besides the usual "excepted perils"[7] for the contract to contain other general exclusions of liability in the following terms: 4.119

Horatio Meyer & Co. Ltd. [1992] Q.B. 600; *Watford Electronics Ltd.* v. *Sanderson CFL Ltd.* [2001] 1 All E.R. (Comm.) 696; *Britvic Soft Drinks Ltd.* v. *Messer UK Ltd.* [2002] 1 Lloyd's Rep. 20, at pp. 57–58; *The Flamar Pride* [1990] 1 Lloyd's Rep. 434; *Moores* v. *Yakely Associates Ltd.* (1999) 62 Con. L.R. 76; *Lease Management Services Ltd.* v. *Purnell Secretarial Services Ltd.* [1994] Tr. L.R. 337; *Schenkers Ltd.* v. *Overland Shoes Ltd.* [1998] 1 Lloyd's Rep. 498; *Overseas Medical Supplies Ltd.* v. *Orient Transport Services Ltd.* [1999] 2 Lloyd's Rep. 273; *St Albans City & District Council* v. *I.C.L.* [1996] 4 All E.R. 481; *The Salvage Association* v. *C.A.P. Financial Services Ltd.* [1995] F.S.R. 655. See also paras. 4.232, *et seq.*, below.

5. But see the discussion below, at paras. 4.145 *et seq.*, on breach of a fundamental term.
6. *G.H. Renton & Co. Ltd.* v. *Palmyra Trading Corp. of Panama* [1957] A.C. 149.
7. See section V, above, paras. 4.83 *et seq.*

The Carrier shall not in any case[8] be liable for:
(a) loss of a particular market, whether held daily or at intervals; or
(b) indirect or consequential damages;
(c) loss, damage or delay to the extent to which the same is caused by or arises from the consignee not taking or accepting delivery within a reasonable time.

4.120 This set of limitations is most likely to be operable when goods are carried at carrier's risk but they are also theoretically applicable to carriage at trader's or owner's risk. There is, in the case of claims in respect of loss, damage or delay, a likelihood of some overlap between the clause (c) above and that set out below in section X (paras. 4.221 *et seq.*). When the Carrier is acting as warehouseman, this condition will be subject to the statutory test of reasonableness contained in the Unfair Contract Terms Act 1977, s. 11.[9]

4.121 Under the common law the carrier would not be liable, in any event, for damages that are too remote under the rule in *Koufos* v. *C. Czarnikow Ltd (The Heron II)*[10] or which are not within the special knowledge of the carrier under the second limb of the rule in *Hadley* v. *Baxendale.*[11] A carrier is only liable at common law for those kinds of loss or damage which, given the actual or imputed knowledge of that carrier, should have been in the reasonable contemplation of that carrier as not unlikely to result in the event of a breach of the kind that occurred.[12] This condition is even more restrictive, in that liability for loss of profit at a particular market is expressly excluded, as is liability for consequential loss in general.

4.122 The carrier is not liable for loss, damage or delay which is due to the event specified in sub-clause (c). This circumstance is outside the control of the carrier. To claim the exemption the carrier must prove that the loss, damage or delay arise as a direct consequence of the excepted circumstance and without wilful misconduct or default on the part of the carrier or its employees. At common law also a carrier is not liable for delay unless the delay results from its negligence or it has assumed responsibility contractually for such an event irrespective of personal fault. This obligation is simply to exercise reasonable care and skill to deliver the goods at the agreed time or (failing any express agreement) within a reasonable time.[13] Thus, even at common law, and without this clause, the carrier would not be answerable for a failure to deliver within a reasonable time where this was a consequence of acts by a third party, or of adverse circumstances over which the carrier had no control.[14]

4.123 A relevant issue may be whether the consignee knew or should have been aware that the goods were available for delivery. At common law the carrier was obliged to give notice to the consignee.[15] The clauses commonly found in modern contracts of

8. Cf. *The Chanda* [1989] 2 Lloyd's Rep. 494, which seems to suggest that, at least on the basis of similar wording in the Hague Rules, that these words do not protect in the case of wilful misconduct.
9. See above, note 3 and below, paras. 4.232 *et seq.*
10. [1969] 1 A.C. 350.
11. (1854) 9 Exch. 341. See further, *Chitty on Contracts* (29th ed.), paras. 27.01 *et seq.*
12. See *Horne* v. *Midland Ry. Co.* (1873) L.R. 8 C.P. 131; *Simpson* v. *London & North Western Ry. Co.* (1876) 1 Q.B.D. 274.
13. *Panalpina International Transport Ltd.* v. *Densil Underwear Ltd.* [1981] 1 Lloyd's Rep. 187.
14. *Taylor* v. *Great Northern Ry. Co.* (1866) L.R. 1 C.P. 385; *Briddon* v. *Great Northern Ry. Co.* (1858) 28 L.J.Ex. 51.
15. *Mitchell* v. *Lancashire & Yorkshire Ry. Co.* (1875) L.R. 10 Q.B. 256.

carriage by inland water tend to be silent on the issue of notice and, on one construction, this may mean that the carrier is not obliged to give the consignee notice that the goods are available for delivery. However, it is clearly in the carrier's interest to give such notice as this has the effect of terminating transit under a separate clause of the contract defining the circumstances when transit begins and ends.[16] The responsibilities of the carrier in relation to the cargo are, of course, reduced from the time transit ends.

Most contracts for the carriage of goods by inland water contain procedural limitations on claims or actions brought against the carrier, such as the following example: 4.124

> The Carrier shall not be liable[17]:
> (a) (i) for loss from a package or from an unpacked consignment; or
> (ii) for damage, deviation, misdelivery, delay or detention unless it is advised thereof in writing (otherwise than upon any of the Carrier's documents) within three days, and the claim be made in writing within seven days, succeeding the date of determination of transit of the consignment, or the part of the consignment in respect of which the claim arises;
> (b) for non-delivery of the whole of a consignment, or of any separate package forming part of a consignment, unless it is advised of the non-delivery in writing (otherwise than upon any of the Carrier's documents) within 28 days and the claim be made in writing within 42 days after the consignment was handed to the Carrier by the Trader.
>
> Provided that if in any action brought against the Carrier in pursuance of a claim the Court shall be satisfied that:
> (i) it was not reasonably possible for the Carrier to be advised in writing or for the claim to be made in writing within the aforesaid times; but
> (ii) such advice or claim was made or given within a reasonable time; and
> (iii) having regard to all the circumstances it is equitable to adjudicate upon the claim;
>
> the Carrier shall not have the benefit of this clause.

Under this clause there are different time limits laid down for "advice of loss" and "notification of claims". The carrier must be told almost immediately that merchandise has been lost or damaged but, once this has been done, the claimant is given a little more time to submit the claim in detail. The clause distinguishes between loss from a package or from an unpacked consignment or of any separate package forming part of a consignment. The former (clause (a)(i)) requires advice of loss within three days and notification of claims within seven days. The latter (clause (b)) calls for advice of loss within 28 days and notification of claims within 42 days. Damage, deviation, misdelivery, delay or detention resulting in anything less than total or partial loss through non-delivery carry the three and seven days' limit (clause (a)(ii)).[18] 4.125

16. See below section X, paras. 4.221 *et seq.*

17. It is possible that a court would construe a clause drafted in this fashion as one that imposes a condition precedent to liability i.e. notification of claims is a necessary pre-condition for the incidence of any right, remedy, duty or liability at all: see *The Aries* [1988] 1 W.L.R. 185; *Acme Transport Co. Ltd.* v. *Betts* [1981] 1 Lloyd's Rep. 131; Cf. *The Virgo* [1978] 1 W.L.R. 986.

18. Well-drafted contracts of carriage will contain a clause determining which days shall and shall not be included for this and other purposes in the contract for which time needs to be computed. The standard clause is: "In the computation of time, the following days shall be included: In England and Wales: Saturday, Sunday, New Year's Day, Good Friday, Easter Monday, the May Day Bank Holiday, the Spring Bank Holiday, the Summer Bank Holiday, Christmas Day and Boxing Day; in Scotland, the holidays designated for England and Wales and January 2nd and the early August Bank Holiday."

4.126 No advice and no claim have any validity so as to preserve the rights of the owner of the goods against the carrier unless they are in writing. The writing must not be on the carrier's own documents: recording missing or damaged items on the delivery note will therefore not do. It is desirable that the advice is given, and the claim made, at the place where those employees or agents of the carrier who deal with such claims are located, i.e. at the port, depot, forwarding or delivery station or whatever. In general it is desirable to include a clause somewhere in the Carrier's Conditions of Carriage clarifying the address to which all written notices required by the contract should be sent in order to avoid the possibility of dispute as to whether a written notice has been sent to the correct place. It is also desirable to include a clause governing the service of notices by post in terms similar to the following:

> When a notice given in compliance with any of the Conditions is sent by post, service of such a notice shall be deemed to be made by properly addressing, prepaying, posting by first class post and producing a post office-certified "proof of posting" of that notice and, unless the contrary is proved, in such circumstances service shall be deemed to have been effected at the time at which the notice should be delivered in the ordinary course of post.

Such a clause removes disputes not only as to when notice was sent, but also when it was deemed to have been received, as use of the word "advised" in the notice clause generally means "notified" and "notification" clearly means that the notice has been received or has been deemed to have been received.[19]

4.127 Claims against the carrier, whether in contact or tort, are subject to the Limitation Act 1980.[20] No action can therefore be brought after the expiration of six years from the date[21] when the cause of action accrued.[22] It will be necessary under the 1980 Act for the carrier actually to plead the defence of limitation because the court itself will not take the point against the claimant. Time runs from the earliest date when an action could have been brought, but various provisions allow for some postponement when the claimant neither knew nor ought to have known crucial facts or was the "victim" of mistake, fraud or concealment. If action were brought late in the limitation period the carrier would find it difficult to obtain evidence sufficient to amount to a defence. Hence, these contractually imposed short notice periods are necessary to avoid hardship to the carrier.

4.128 However, this clause also contains a provision designed to ensure that the tight time limits do not result in hardship to the trader. Accordingly, if it can be shown (a) that it was not reasonably possible to observe the time limits and (b) that the advice of loss was given and the notice of claim was made within a reasonable time, the restrictive time limits will not apply and, presumably, the general statutory

19. *Holwell Securities Ltd.* v. *Hughes* [1974] 1 All E.R. 164. The notice does not need to have come to the attention of the relevant employee to have been "received": *The Brimnes* [1975] Q.B. 929.

20. Ss. 2 and 5.

21. The claim form must be issued within this period but may be served any time within four months after issue: C.P.R. 7.5.

22. It is submitted that the special limitation period for accidents at sea (Merchant Shipping Act 1995, Sched. 6) has no application to inland water—see above section I. However, note that for contribution between tortfeasors the limitation period is two years from the date when the right to contribution accrued: Limitation Act 1980, s. 10.

provisions under the Limitation Act 1980 will then alone operate.[23] It is for the court to be satisfied that the two conditions set out in the clause apply and that it is equitable, having regard to all the circumstances, to adjudicate on the claim. It is, of course, always open to the carrier to accede to a request for an extension of the time limits and, if it fails to do so, it is open to the court to hold that it should have done so. It is always for the trader to prove the facts he advances in support of his claim for an extension of the time limits. It is unlikely that the time limits will be extended if the trader made it impossible by his own course of business to raise the complaint in time.[24] If, therefore, the trader has arranged for the goods to be delivered to a third party's wharf, having made no or inadequate arrangements to discover if the goods arrived at all, or arrived late or damaged, he cannot use his own sloppy business practices as an excuse to obtain an extension of time.[25]

The time limits will almost certainly operate as substantive defences, thus effectively extinguishing the cause of action.[26] It could be argued that where legal action is required to be brought in a foreign jurisdiction and no suit is brought there in time, proceedings should be stayed in England even if brought within time. Such authority as exists suggests, however, that it is not necessary, in order to succeed in the English courts in such circumstances, to show a strong case for jurisdiction in England apart from the time limit, but rather, provided the claimant has acted reasonably in commencing the English proceedings, a stay will only be granted on terms that the defendant waives the foreign time bar.[27] *4.129*

Contracts of carriage will normally contain an obvious "anti-fraud" clause such *4.130*
as:

> "The Carrier shall not incur liability of any kind in respect of any consignment in relation to which there has been fraud on the part of the Trader."

The main instance of fraud on the part of the trader is likely to be where there has been a fraudulent declaration about the nature or value of the goods consigned. At common law a statement is fraudulent if it is made (a) knowing it to be false or (b)

23. As to the unlikely operation of the Unfair Contract Terms Act 1977 to this provision see para. 4.5, above. If that Act does, however, apply, the importation of a concept of reasonableness into the drafting of the clause is likely to result in the clause as a whole being upheld as reasonable within s.11(1) of the 1977 Act (see para. 4.143, below). In any event, even were this argument, on its own, insufficiently persuasive, courts have been hesitant to strike down as unreasonable terms in standard conditions of business that are in widespread use within the particular trade or industry: *Sonicare International Ltd.* v. *East Anglia Freight Terminals Ltd.* [1997] 2 Lloyd's Rep. 48; *Monarch Airlines Ltd.* v. *Luton Airport Ltd.* [1998] 1 Lloyd's Rep. 403; *Overland Shoes Ltd.* v. *Schenkers Ltd.* [1998] 1 Lloyd's Rep. 498.

24. See *Wapnah* v. *London, Midland and Scottish Ry.* (1933) 22 Ry. & Can. Tr. Cas. 87; *H.B. Bernard & Son Ltd.* v. *London, Midland and Scottish Ry.* (1943) 28 T.C. 93; *Frydon Bros & Co. Ltd.* v. *London & North Eastern Ry. Co.* (1946) 28 T.C. 113.

25. But note *Sully* v. *Southern Ry. Co.* (1942) 28 T.C. 108 where station staff at the arrival point knew that a consignment had disappeared but failed to let the consignee know of this. The carrier was held to have acted inequitably in relying on the fact that the consignee inevitably failed to give notice of his claim in due time.

26. *The Jay Bola* [1992] 2 Lloyd's Rep. 48. Barring the remedy or claim is distinct from barring the right to arbitrate: *The Seki Rolette* [1998] 2 Lloyd's Rep. 638; *Thyssen* v. *Calypso* [2000] 2 Lloyd's Rep. 243.

27. *Mahavir Minerals Ltd.* v. *Cho Yang Shipping Co. Ltd. (The MC Pearl)* [1997] 1 Lloyd's Rep. 566; *Citi-March Ltd.* v. *Neptune Orient Lines* [1997] 1 Lloyd's Rep. 72; *Baghlaf Al Zafer Factory Co.* v. *Pakistan National Shipping Co.* [1998] 2 Lloyd's Rep. 224. Cf. *Continental Fertilizer Co. Ltd.* v. *Pionier Shipping CV (The Pionier)* [1995] 1 Lloyd's Rep. 223.

without belief in its truth or (c) recklessly, careless of whether it be true or false.[28] The carrier will undertake a heavy onus of proof if it wishes to allege fraud on the trader's part.

4.131 The carrier may be asked to collect "paid on" charges at the time of delivery. If the carrier undertakes this service it needs to have a protection in place to protect it against any failure or oversight to pay by the entity that is to make the payment. A suitable clause is, therefore, usually inserted into the contract of carriage:

> Where the Carrier agrees to perform the service of collecting "Paid On" charges it shall not be liable for failure to collect such charges in any case where, either before or after delivery, the person from whom such charges are to be collected fails to pay after reasonable demands have been made for the payment thereof.

This clause provides that if the carrier's employees try but fail to collect the charges, the carrier will not be liable where, either before or after delivery, the person from whom the charges are to be collected fails to pay after reasonable demands have been made to pay them.

[*The next paragraph is 4.141*]

28. *Derry* v. *Peek* (1889) 14 App. Cas. 337.

VII. DELAYED TRANSIT AND DEVIATION

> The Carrier shall be liable for loss or damage to the goods proved by the Trader to have been caused by delay unless the Carrier proves that such delay has arisen without negligence on the part of the Carrier. 4.141

Although the Unfair Contract Terms Act 1977 does not apply to a contract for the carriage of goods by inland water, one more general effect of that Act has been to encourage limited exclusions of liability for loss or damage caused by delays in transit to be drafted "positively", rather than negatively in the form of limitation or exclusion clauses. As has been pointed out earlier[1] the proviso at the end of this clause reverses the common law onus of proof in favour of the trader. If the trader can prove that the loss or damage arose from a delay in transit the carrier will be liable unless it can prove that such loss or damage was not occasioned by a want of care on its part. 4.142

Goods are considered to have been "delayed" if they are not delivered within the time agreed or, if there is no agreed time within which delivery should take place, within a reasonable time. What constitutes a reasonable time depends upon the circumstances of the case.[2] If delay is the result of a deviation from the normal route then it is possible that the maritime law doctrine of deviation could be applied.[3] It has been applied to carriage by rail contracts in the past[4] most notably in *Gunyon* v. *South Eastern & Chatham Ry.*[5] In this case a perishable cargo of cherries was contracted to be sent by fast passenger train. It travelled part of the route by slow goods train and the cherries deteriorated as a consequence. The court held that the railway was disentitled from relying on exclusion clauses in the contract because when "the cherries were shipped on a goods train this contract was no longer being performed and the goods were no longer being carried at owner's risk". The case was treated as being analogous to the maritime doctrine of deviation from route. The normal consequence of a deviation is the loss of the right to rely on any exclusion or limitation clause. The clause quoted above is not, of course, such a clause but any deviation might well affect any limits or exclusions found elsewhere in the contract of carriage. This is discussed in more detail later in this section. 4.143

When a carrier undertakes to carry goods, it undertakes to carry them by the ordinary route (unless a precise itinerary is agreed) provided that such route is in the ordinary course of business. If the carrier unnecessarily deviates from the usual route, and delivery is delayed in consequence, it is liable at common law, though reasonable deviation, such as that which may be necessary to safeguard the goods is 4.144

1. See para. 4.97, above.

2. The leading cases on delay in this context all relate to carriage by rail: see *Caledonian Ry.* v. *Hunter* (1858) 20 Sess. Cas. 2nd Ser. 1097; *Taylor* v. *Great Northern Ry.* (1866) L.R. 1 C.P. 385; *Briddon* v. *Great Northern Ry.* (1858) 28 L.J. Ex. 51. In *Sims & Co.* v. *Midland Ry. Co.* [1913] 1 K.B. 103 Scrutton J. held that a strike by employees of a railway company must be taken into account as one of the factors affecting whether goods had been delivered within a reasonable time.

3. See Kahn-Freund, *The Law of Carriage by Inland Transport* (4th ed., Stevens, 1965), p. 287. See also Yates & Hawkins, *Standard Business Contracts* (Sweet & Maxwell, 1986), pp. 341–347; cf. Debattista [1989] J.B.L. 22; Livermore (1990) 2 J.C.L. 241.

4. See *Mallett* v. *Great Eastern Ry.* [1899] 1 Q.B. 309; *London & North Western Ry.* v. *Neilson* [1922] 2 A.C. 263.

5. [1915] 2 K.B. 370.

permissible.[6] The goods may be carried by as long and circuitous a route as the carrier pleases, provided no delay or loss or damage is thereby caused and provided also that no specific route has been agreed between the parties. At common law, in so far as deviation leads to delay, the carrier is liable to compensate the owner for any financial loss caused to him by the delay. The customary way of dealing with this problem is for the contract of carriage to provide that the carrier shall not be liable for loss or damage to merchandise arising from accidental or unavoidable delay in transit,[7] i.e. the claimant must prove that the delay was due either to wilful misconduct or, depending upon the construction placed upon the word "accidental", negligence on the part of the carrier. In a further attempt to ensure that the contract (together with its exclusions and limitations) continues to govern the relationship between carrier and owner, even in the event of a deviation, a clause to the following effect is also frequently included:

> These conditions shall apply by whatever route the merchandise is carried.

4.145 There are, nevertheless, circumstances in which, on one view of the law, neither of the clauses set out in this section will be of much assistance. Where a deviation is such as to amount to a breach of a fundamental term[8] there is at least an arguable issue as to whether these clauses could apply at all. In order to understand how this doctrine might apply to deviation it is necessary to examine some complex case law concerned largely with contracts for the supply of services or the sale, rather than the carriage, of goods. Their relevance will, it is hoped, become apparent later in this section. Whether or not there has been a breach of a fundamental term depends upon whether the promisor has performed the obligation which forms the essential character and base of the contract. The most famous example is that of Lord Abinger in *Chanter* v. *Hopkins*[9] where he observed "if a man offers to buy peas off another, and he sends beans, he does not perform his contract . . . the contract is to sell peas, and if he sends him anything else in their stead, it is non-performance of it". The same idea was expressed by Devlin J. in *Smeaton Hanscomb & Co.* v. *Sassoon I. Setty & Son & Co.*[10] where the learned judge thought that the supply of pine logs under a contract for the sale of mahogany logs would have been a breach of a fundamental term, which he defined as "something which underlines the whole contract so that, if it is not complied with, the performance becomes something totally different from that which the contract contemplates".[11]

4.146 A breach of fundamental term then, results in performance so "totally different" that there cannot, in effect, be any performance at all of the actual obligation agreed. If any goods, services or facilities are proffered, they are so different from those stipulated for that they are not referable to the fundamental obligation undertaken

6. *Kish* v. *Taylor* [1912] A.C. 604.
7. See paras. 4.141 to 4.142, above.
8. Not the same as the now discredited doctrine of fundamental breach.
9. (1834) 4 M. & W. 399, amended to chalk and cheese by Pearson L.J. in *UGS Finance* v. *National Mortgage Bank of Greece* [1964] 1 Lloyd's Rep. 446 at p. 453.
10. [1953] 1 W.L.R. 1468.
11. *Ibid.* at p. 1470.

by the contract.[12] Put another way, there will be a breach of fundamental term when the consideration contracted for has totally failed. In *Pinnock Bros.* v. *Lewis & Peat*[13] the defendants agreed to purchase 100 bags of copra cake for use as cattle food. The feed contained such a high proportion of castor beans as to render it dangerous to cattle. Roche J. said[14]: " . . . I hold that the delivery in this case could not properly be described as copra cake at all." The plaintiffs had delivered a substance quite different from that contracted for. They had not performed their contract in a fundamental respect and the breach of this fundamental term resulted in their failure to supply the consideration contracted for.

The principle was considered in *George Mitchell (Chesterhall) Ltd.* v. *Finney Lock Seeds.*[15] There was a contract for the sale of winter cabbage seeds with a clause limiting the liability of the vendor to the purchase price and excluding all other liability. Parker J.[16] held that the seed supplied was not, in fact, winter cabbage seed and the crop was not fit for consumption. It was, in the learned judge's view, in no commercial sense vegetable seed at all. He saw no distinction between this and not supplying anything at all. The House of Lords decided otherwise. Lord Bridge, delivering the only speech of length, considered it was not a different in kind "peas and beans" case. However, in reaching this conclusion he relied heavily on the wording of the exclusion clause, which simply referred to supplying "seeds". Seeds had in fact been sold and delivered. The exclusion clause therefore covered the event.[17] The implication from the reliance by Lord Bridge on the precise wording of the exclusion clause is that, had the goods supplied been sufficiently different from the goods promised he would have agreed with Parker J. at first instance and Oliver L.J. in the Court of Appeal on the common law issue.[18] 4.147

There are, of course, problems with this "different in kind" approach. How does one define the *genus* contracted for? What if the vendor attempts to reserve to himself some latitude by incorporating a clause conferring an option to vary the description? What degree of seriousness can be tolerated in defects before the *genus* becomes different? What is the relationship between the fundamental term of the contract and the description attached to the subject-matter? A failure to comply with the contract description can be a breach of an express term of the contract, implied and fundamental terms notwithstanding.[19] 4.148

If non-performance may be equated with a total failure of consideration, then the difficulties of identifying the *genus*, the contractual "kind" from which the tendered performance differs, become less acute. In the end the solution to these problems 4.149

12. There are many other examples: thus, failure by a seller to transfer title in goods subject to a contract of sale may amount to a breach of the Sale of Goods Act 1979, s. 12(1)(a) which, in turn, will involve the seller in a breach of a fundamental term of the contract: *Rowland* v. *Divall* [1923] 2 K.B. 500.

13. [1923] 1 K.B. 690.

14. *Ibid.* at p. 697.

15. [1983] 2 A.C. 803.

16. [1981] 1 Lloyd's Rep. 476.

17. Lord Bridge reached the same result as Parker J., however, by holding that the exclusions were unreasonable under the Sale of Goods Act 1979, s. 55.

18. [1983] Q.B. 284 at pp. 304–305.

19. *Andrews Bros (Bournemouth) Ltd.* v. *Singer & Co.* [1934] 1 K.B. 17; *Porter* v. *General Guarantee Corp. Ltd.* [1982] R.T.R. 384.

will come down to the particular construction of the contract. So, for example, the subject-matter of a contract for the supply of winter cabbage seed may, on a true construction of that contract, including an exclusion clause referring to or defining the contract subject-matter, be (i) winter cabbage seed, (ii) cabbage seed which may be a winter variety or may be some other type, (iii) seed which may or may not be cabbage seed, (iv) something which may or may not be seed.[20] A contract for the fourth kind would be void, either for uncertainty or because it lacked contractual content, if it enabled the supplier to supply anything he wished, but it might be perfectly valid if it was a contract to supply some specific object (such as the findings of an archaeological "dig"). To some extent, therefore, the subject-matter of the contract will be determined by the context of the transaction. If the contract is construed as being of the kind described in (i), then supplying seeds of a different variety, or of another vegetable altogether, may well be a breach of a fundamental term.[21] The court is less and less likely to reach this conclusion, depending upon whether it adopts construction (ii), (iii) or (iv) and, in determining what exactly the promisor has promised to provide, negative definitions (in the shape of exclusions and limitations) will be as relevant as positive ones.[22]

4.150 Where there is a total failure of consideration arising as a result of a total non-performance, or arising from a purported performance so different in kind from that contracted for that is equivalent to non-performance, a breach of fundamental term is committed. The courts have in the past held that where a party commits a breach of a fundamental term he will, for a variety of reasons, be prevented from relying upon any clause of exemption of limitation in subsequent proceedings arising out of the contract.[23]

20. *George Mitchell (Chesterhall) Ltd.* v. *Finney Lock Seeds* [1983] 2 A.C. 803, *per* Lord Bridge at p. 813.

21. See *Porter* v. *General Guarantee Corp. Ltd.* [1982] R.T.R. 384.

22. *George Mitchell (Chesterhall) Ltd.* v. *Finney Lock Seeds* [1983] 2 A.C. 803; see also *Photo Production Ltd.* v. *Securicor Transport Ltd.* [1980] A.C. 827, *per* Lord Diplock, at p. 851. Perhaps the most common cases in which this problem has arisen are commodity contracts and contracts for the supply of motor vehicles. In the latter case, for example, it may be that a car is so defective that it cannot be made to go without extensive repairs: can it then properly be described as a "car" at all? See, *e.g. Karsales (Harrow) Ltd.* v. *Wallis* [1956] 1 W.L.R. 936, *per* Birkett L.J. at p. 942 and Parker L.J. at p. 943; *George Mitchell (Chesterhall) Ltd.* v. *Finney Lock Seeds*, above, *per* Lord Bridge at p. 813. Whether or not it can will depend on whether the court, taking account of all the clauses, including the exclusion clause, forms the view that the contract is one for a car capable of self-propulsion, a car that may be capable of self-propulsion, or something that may or may not be a car. Supplying a car incapable of self-propulsion may well place the supplier in breach of a fundamental term if the contract is construed as being of the first type but the court is less likely to reach this conclusion if the contract is of the second type, and most unlikely to reach it in the third case.

23. *Pinnock Bros* v. *Lewis & Peat Ltd.* [1923] 1 K.B. 690. See also *Nichol* v. *Godts* (1854) 10 Ex. 191; *Smeaton Hanscomb & Co.* v. *Sassoon I. Setty & Son & Co.* [1953] 1 W.L.R. 1468, *per* Devlin J. at p. 1470; *Karsales (Harrow) Ltd.* v. *Wallis* [1956] 1 W.L.R. 936, *per* Birkett L.J. at p. 942 and *per* Parker L.J. at p. 943; *Yeoman Credit Ltd.* v. *Apps* [1962] 2 Q.B. 508, *per* Holroyd Pearce L.J. at p. 520; *Astley Industrial Trust* v. *Grimley* [1963] 1 W.L.R. 584, *per* Upjohn J. at p. 598; *Charterhouse Credit Co.* v. *Tolly* [1963] 2 Q.B. 683, *per* Donovan L.J. at p. 701 and *per* Upjohn L.J. at p. 710; *Suisse Atlantique Société d'Armement Maritime S.A.* v. *N.V. Rotterdamsche Kolen Centrale* [1967] 1 A.C. 361, *per* Viscount Dilhorne at p. 393, Lord Reid at pp. 397–398, 404; *George Mitchell (Chesterhall) Ltd.* v. *Finney Lock Seeds Ltd.* [1983] 2 A.C. 803 where, at p. 817, Lord Bridge accepted the principle although he did not regard it as applicable to the instant case.

4.151 What is supplied may not literally be a different thing from what was bargained for, but may be so seriously defective as to be different in substance. There will be a total failure of consideration if the goods delivered or the services supplied are so defective that they cannot properly be described as the goods or services promised under the contract: such defective performance is equivalent to non-performance.[24] There can be nothing of the consideration contracted for in the original contract now available to accept. There is, therefore, an *automatic* termination in the event of a breach of a fundamental term. That being so, acceptance of what is proffered will amount to acceptance of a new entirely separate contract and the courts will not necessarily imply into this new contract, or construe to be applicable, an exclusion or limitation clause that was present in the old one. The right to damages for breach of the original contract, however, still survives (disregarding, for the moment, any problems with the exclusion clause) because the promisee's rights under the contract have not been surrendered. Should the new, totally different, performance be accepted as a new contract, then the promisee will be required to pay on a *quantum meruit* or *quantum valebat*, but will be entitled to set-off from this the damages due to him for non-performance of the original contract.

4.152 Although the original contract is, of necessity, repudiated by non-performance as a result of breach of a fundamental term, until termination the contract remains on foot and binding. All its terms, including exclusion or limitation clauses, continue to operate as agreed between the parties. It therefore follows that the innocent party's damages will accrue at a time when the exclusion or limitation clauses, along with all the other terms of the contract, are still on foot, and success or failure in any claim to damages on the original contract will depend upon how that clause is construed.

4.153 The cases before 1980 appear to suggest that a breach of a fundamental term produces an automatic termination of the contract with the possible result that an exclusion or limitation clause will not apply. It is clear that affirmation cannot take place where there has been a breach of a fundamental term since there is nothing of the contractual performance promised left to affirm. However, it is not the law that an exclusion clause can never, in these circumstances, apply. In *Photo Production Ltd.* v. *Securicor Transport Ltd.*[25] Lord Wilberforce said: "I have no second thoughts as to the main proposition [in the *Suisse Atlantique* case[26]] that the question whether, and to what extent, an exclusion clause is to be applied to a fundamental breach, or a breach of a fundamental term, or indeed to any breach of contract, is a matter of construction of the contract."

4.154 In the same case Lord Diplock expressed the view[27] that both the primary and secondary obligations of a contract can be excluded or modified by an appropriately

24. See the example given by Upjohn J. in *Astley Industrial Trust* v. *Grimley* [1963] 1 W.L.R. 584 at p. 598, of the delivery of Suffolk Punch horses in purported performance of a contract for the sale of a tractor. Acceptance of the horses cannot be regarded as affirmation of a contract for the sale of a tractor. Lord Reid, in the *Suisse Atlantique* case felt, [1967] 1 A.C. 361 at p. 404, that such conduct as that described by Upjohn J. would not be delivery under the contract at all but would be an offer of a new contract on terms to be implied.

25. [1980] A.C. 827 at pp. 842–843.

26. [1967] 1 A.C. 361.

27. [1980] A.C. 827 at p. 849.

drafted clause. If exclusion clauses may be drafted so as to operate on the primary obligations of the contract as well as the secondary, then a clause might, in an appropriate form and on a proper construction, give the *proferens* such latitude that it prevented his performance (or lack of it) from amounting to a total failure of consideration,[28] however remote that performance might be from what might be considered "performance" were the exclusions not present. Against this it must be remembered that in the *Suisse Atlantique* case it was said[29] that a clause which, in effect, absolved a party from the consequences of failing to provide any performance at all makes the entire contract illusory.[30] There is no doubt, nevertheless, that the clause may radically modify the primary obligations so as to give considerable latitude to the *proferens* in circumstances where, but for the clause, he would have committed a breach of a fundamental term.

4.155 Where the court holds the *proferens* to have committed a breach of a fundamental term, the contract will be terminated for total failure of consideration, notwithstanding the exclusion clause, *only* where that exclusion clause does not, on its construction, prevent the court from finding that there has been a failure to perform the fundamental obligation of the contract. The success of any consequent action in damages for breach will, again, be dependent upon whether the exclusion or limitation clause can be construed to apply to the secondary obligation under the contract to pay compensation,[31] and whether, in an appropriate case, it satisfies any reasonableness test applicable under statute or common law.

4.156 Thus, the matter appears to reduce to two questions: first, can a *proferens* contract out of primary obligations? The answer to this would appear to be "yes" though it requires the most careful and rigorous drafting. Secondly, does a breach of a primary obligation, or a serious breach of a secondary obligation always give rise to a repudiatory breach? The answer to this is also "yes" though it must be remembered that whether or not a breach has taken place may well depend itself upon a construction of the contract as a whole, including the exclusion clause. The occurrence of a repudiatory breach does not, as a rule of law, prevent reliance on an exclusion clause, which must, nevertheless be construed in the light of the events which have occurred.

4.157 Assuming that, notwithstanding the presence of an exclusion or limitation clause, a breach of a fundamental term is established, the success of any action in damages will depend, in part, upon the construction placed upon the clause and the extent to which it modifies the secondary obligation to compensate. However, this reasoning does not apply in respect of actions to recover money paid over in advance under a contract, the consideration for which has totally failed. For example, if a consignee of goods wishes merely to recover the freight charges he has paid in advance to a carrier who has committed a breach of a fundamental term, he does

28. I.e. breach of a fundamental term.

29. [1967] 1 A.C. 361, *per* Lords Reid and Wilberforce at pp. 398 and 432, respectively.

30. It may be argued, *contra*, that the effect of such a clause would be to convert a seemingly bilateral contract into a unilateral one. The *proferens* promises nothing and hence non-performance gives rise to no liability. Should the *proferens* choose, however, to render some performance, the other party is then bound by his promises: *United Dominions Trust (Commercial) Ltd.* v. *Eagle Aircraft Ltd.* [1968] 1 All E.R. 104, *per* Diplock, L.J. at pp. 108–109.

31. *Photo Production Ltd.* v. *Securicor Transport Ltd.* [1980] A.C. 827.

not need to rely on the contract of carriage for an action in damages, and hence he need not be concerned with any exclusion or limitation clause. The "innocent" party can recover any money paid by a restitutionary action for money had and received and, not being an action based upon the contract, there seems no reason why the quasi-contractual action should not proceed free of any trammels imposed by exclusion or limitation clauses in the contract.[32]

Before proceeding in restitution the innocent party must, as a general rule, have brought the contract to an end. If he does not do so, the contract continues to govern the situation and the plaintiff must then seek his remedy on the contract and not in restitution.[33] Moreover if, with knowledge of the breach, the innocent party affirms the contract, he will have lost his right to determine the contract for that breach, unless it is of a continuous nature.[34] Since a breach of a fundamental term involves such defective performance of the core primary obligations of the contract that it is equivalent to non-performance, it is hard to see how the contract can be anything but terminated. Purported affirmation would simply be the equivalent of accepting a new offer.[35] *4.158*

The conditions laid down for the availability of the restitutionary claim would, therefore, almost invariably apply in the case of a breach of a fundamental term to enable any money already paid by the innocent party to be recovered. *4.159*

However, while the victim of a breach of a fundamental term can recover any money he has paid over to the party in breach, usually despite the presence of an exclusion clause, he may not necessarily recover by way of compensation, in contract, damages for any other property handed over, e.g., pursuant to a contract of carriage or other contractually based bailment, nor can he recover damages for his loss of bargain. This is because at the time when the secondary obligation to compensate arises, which is the time of the breach, the contract, including the exemption clause, is still in force. Logically, therefore, the exclusion clause ought to protect the "guilty" party against all actions for damages unless it can, on its construction, be regarded as not covering the events that occurred. It will not protect where the clause is found not to cover the particular loss sustained by the innocent party, or where it purports only to affect the right to terminate for breach but not the right to damages, i.e. where it is drafted to operate only on the primary obligations and not the secondary.[36] *4.160*

32. *Fibrosa Spolka Akcyjna* v. *Fairbairn Lawson Combe Barbour Ltd.* [1943] A.C. 32, *per* Viscount Simon L.C. at p. 46, and Lord Wright at p. 65. See also Sale of Goods Act 1979, s. 54.

33. *Weston* v. *Downes* (1778) 1 Doug. 23.

34. *Kwei Tek Chao* v. *British Traders and Shippers Ltd.* [1954] 2 Q.B. 459, *per* Devlin, J. at p. 475.

35. Although, if the circumstances were right, the court might conceivably imply a release of the guilty party from liability under the first contract as a result of acceptance of the second, only the very clearest evidence would raise such an inference and, in the absence of consideration clear action in reliance on the release is necessary. *Fontana N.V.* v. *Mautner* (1979) 254 E.G. 199; *Raiffeisen Hauptgenossenschaft* v. *Louis Dreyfus & Co.* [1981] 1 Lloyd's Rep. 345; *Cook Industries Ltd.* v. *Meunerie Liégeois S.A.* [1981] 1 Lloyd's Rep. 359; *The Scaptrade* [1983] 1 All E.R. 301; *Etablissements Soules & Cie.* v. *International Trade Development Co. Ltd.* [1980] 1 Lloyd's Rep. 129; *Brikom Investments* v. *Carr* [1979] Q.B. 467.

36. *Suisse Atlantique Société d'Armement Maritime S.A.* v. *N.V. Rotterdamsche Kolen Centrale* [1967] 1 A.C. 361, *per* Viscount Dilhorne at p. 395, Lord Reid at p. 398, Lord Upjohn at p. 419 and Lord Wilberforce at p. 432.

4.161 The doctrine of breach of a fundamental term can apply in the event of a deviation and, as we have seen, since the maritime doctrine of deviation has been applied to carriage by rail, there is no reason to suppose that it is not equally applicable to carriage by inland water. A geographic deviation occurs when a vessel departs from the contract route for an unjustified reason. The contract route is defined by the contract in the context of its commercial purpose and may be modified or widened in scope by a liberty to deviate clause.[37] These clauses may so widen the contract voyage as to permit the master great flexibility as to the vessel's route. Custom may be adduced as parole evidence to define the contractual route, unless it is inconsistent with the express words of the contract.

4.162 If a deviation is "justified" at common law, it is, in effect, not a deviation at all. It has long been recognised that deviations are justified to avoid danger. There is, further, a duty to use skill and care in avoiding hazards and in mitigating the consequences of any disaster which may be met.[38] This duty may necessitate a stop for repairs but the master must only depart from the contract route to the extent and for the length of time that the occasion demands.[39] However, the putting in for repairs will not, it seems, be a deviation even if the repairs are necessary on account of unseaworthiness of the vessel for which the vessel's owner is, in any event, liable.[40] It is justified to deviate to save life, but not merely to save property not on board the vessel.[41] If the property is on board, on the other hand, then whether or not the deviation is justified will be determined by balancing the interests of all the cargo owners and the vessel owner.[42]

4.163 Whether or not deviation constitutes a breach of a fundamental term depends upon whether it constitutes non-performance, which in turn depends upon the intention of the parties. The starting point will be an assumption that the parties did not intend the bailee to be protected on a journey not contemplated by the contract. This assumption derives from policy considerations applied in four different areas of the law in the last two centuries: carriage of goods by sea, insurance,[43] bailment,[44] and contract. If the liability for deviation arises from a breach of contract, of course, it would seem that whether it was intentional or negligent would be irrelevant, assuming it was not justified at common law. In *Rio Tinto Co.* v. *Seed Shipping Co.*[45]

37. See *Berger & Co. USA* v. *Vegoil* [1984] 1 Lloyd's Rep. 440. The clause quoted in para. 4.144, above, is not, technically, a "liberty to deviate" clause but a clause purporting to apply all the contract terms regardless of the route taken, even if that is not "the agreed route". It could well, therefore, be a clause affected by, rather than controlling, the application of the doctrine of breach of a fundamental term.

38. *Worms* v. *Storey* (1855) 11 Ex. 427; *Phelps* v. *Hill* [1891] 1 Q.B. 605.

39. *Phelps* v. *Hill*, above; *The Rona* (1884) 51 L.T. 28.

40. *Kish* v. *Taylor* [1912] A.C. 604.

41. *Scaramanga* v. *Stamp* (1880) 5 C.P.D. 295.

42. *Notara* v. *Henderson* (1870) L.R. 5 Q.B. 354.

43. Deviation was regarded as a breach of the duty *uberrimae fidei*. The insurer is absolved from liablity to pay when this duty is breached by an increase in the risk to the insured interest—a breach of a continuing warranty given by the insured: *Green* v. *Young* (1702) 2 Salkeld 444; *Max* v. *Roberts* (1810) 12 East 88; *Parker* v. *James* (1814) 4 Comp. 112; *Davies* v. *Garrett* (1830) 6 Bing. 716.

44. See *Coggs* v. *Bernard* (1703) 2 Ld. Raym. 909, *per* Holt C.J. at p. 915.

45. (1926) 42 T.L.R. 381.

the master sailing out of the Clyde negligently gave the order to steer south-east instead of south-west. The ship was wrecked as a result of this error yet it was held that there had been no deviation. However, in *Hain S.S. Co. Ltd.* v. *Tate & Lyle*,[46] as a result of the non-delivery of a telegram by the Cuban Post Office, the master set off for home instead of for the next port of loading. On receiving the correct information by wireless, he altered course to the correct port. The House of Lords held that there was a deviation. One conclusion to be drawn from these cases may be that there will be a deviation, given the geographical requirements, whatever the state of mind of the carrier, with the possible exception of negligent navigation. These cases could be reconciled by arguing that the carrier must intend to go on a route other than the contractual one, whether or not he knows what that route is, before a deviation in the legal sense occurs.[47] In *Hain S.S. Co. Ltd.* v. *Tate & Lyle* the House of Lords made it clear that a deviation, whatever else it may also be, does amount to a breach of a condition of the contract,[48] although their Lordships are less clear about whether the cause of action which gave rise to the claim for substantial damages was based on the contract or some other common law duty.

One possible view of the cause of action is that it arises from deviation being treated as non-performance.[49] Clearly it is a special kind of non-performance since it is very far from the case that the carrier has done nothing under the contract. It is non-performance in the sense in which the term is understood by the Court of Appeal in *Rowland* v. *Divall*[50] in a contract for the sale of a car under which the buyer, while getting four months' use of the car, did not get title and was thus enabled to recover the full purchase price with no deduction for intermediate use and enjoyment. Atkin L.J. observed[51]: "The buyer has not received any part of that which he contracted to receive—namely the property and right to possession—and that being so, there has been a total failure of consideration." In deviation cases, unless the exclusion clause, on its construction, conferred on the carrier a liberty to deviate,[52] a finding of non-performance by reason of deviation thus enables the 4.164

46. (1936) 41 Com. Cas. 350.

47. There is support for this distinction in *Foscolo Mango* v. *Stag Line* (1931) 39 Ll.L.R. 101, *per* Slesser L.J. at p. 108; in *Tait* v. *Levi* (1811) 14 East. 481, Lord Ellenborough considered that going innocently to the wrong port as a result of mistaking the coastline would be a deviation but the other two members of the court appeared to disagree, basing liability instead on breach of warranty of the crew's competence.

48. (1936) 41 Com. Cas. 350, *per* Lord Atkin at pp. 354–355, Lord Wright at pp. 362–363 and Lord Maugham at p. 371. See also *Berger & Co USA* v. *Vegoil* [1984] 1 Lloyd's Rep. 440.

49. *Davies* v. *Garrett* (1830) 6 Bing. 716, *Scaramanga* v. *Stamp* (1880) 5 C.P.D. 295; *Leduc* v. *Ward* (1888) 20 Q.B.D. 475; *Balian* v. *Joly* (1890) 6 T.L.R. 345; *The Dunbeth* [1897] P. 133; *International Guano* v. *Macandrew* [1909] 2 K.B. 360; *US Shipping Board* v. *Masters* (1992) 10 Ll.L.R. 573 at p. 575. See also *Wibau Maschinenfabrik Hartmann S.A. and another* v. *Mackinnon Mackenzie & Co. (The Chanda)* [1989] 2 Lloyd's Rep. 494, overruled by *Daewoo Heavy Industries Ltd.* v. *Klipriver Shipping Ltd.*, *The Times*, 17 April 2003.

50. [1923] 2 K.B. 500; see also *Karflex Ltd.* v. *Poole* [1933] 2 K.B. 251; *Butterworth* v. *Kingsway Motors Ltd.* [1954] 1 W.L.R. 1286.

51. [1923] 2 K.B. 500 at p. 507; Bankes L.J. also uses the terminology of, and cites authority on, the quasi-contractual remedy of an action for money had and received.

52. See the approach to such construction adopted in *Connolly, Shaw Ltd.* v. *A/S Det Nordenfjeldske D/S* (1934) 49 Ll.L.R. 183 and *G.H. Renton & Co.* v. *Palmyra Trading Corp. of Panama* [1957] A.C. 149.

trader to take advantage of the resultant automatic termination of the contract.[53] The bailor is then in a position to recover his further, post-breach losses from the bailee by virtue of the bailee's duty in bailment.[54]

4.165 Given that there is a deviation from the contract route the contract will, on the above reasoning and in the absence of a liberty to deviate clause or a common law justification, be terminated automatically. The continued custody of the goods gives rise to a new set of obligations in bailment, the breach of which, by failure to redeliver in a condition similar to that in which the goods were received, gives rise to liability.[55] It seems to be implicit that the termination of the contract in this manner is peculiar to deviation and that the contract cannot affect either this termination (except indirectly by modifying the duty, i.e. preventing there being a deviation) or the new obligations (usually in bailment) which arise.[56]

4.166 There is some doubt as to whether deviation still constitutes a breach of a fundamental term and, if it does, whether it brings the contract automatically to an end. The better view appears to be that both rules survive though it is only in contracts for the carriage of goods by sea or by inland water which, in general fall outside the provisions of the Unfair Contract Terms Act 1977, that the point is likely to have much practical effect.

4.167 In summary, therefore, whether or not deviation constitutes breach of a fundamental term, thus bringing the entire contract to an end, depends upon whether that deviation constitutes non-performance, which in turn depends upon the intention of the parties. The starting point will be the assumption that the parties to the carriage contract did not intend the carrier to be covered by the contract (including the exceptions, exemptions and limitations) on a journey not contemplated by the contract.[57]

4.168 In the same way that terms as to route, depending upon the construction of the contract, are usually regarded as fundamental, so also may terms as to time also be so regarded. Although it is the duty of the carrier to carry goods expeditiously to their destination, the question of whether the carrier's delay is regarded as going to

53. The view that deviation automatically terminates the contract of carriage is first articulated in *Balian* v. *Joly* (1890) 6 T.L.R. 345 but was applied with the utmost rigour some 35 years later *US Shipping Board* v. *Bunge & Born* (1925) 42 T.L.R. 174, where the effect of a deviation was to disentitle the shipowner from relying on the demurrage provisions of his contract. See also *Cooper* v. *Willomat* (1845) 1 C.B. 672; *Fenn* v. *Bittleston* (1851) 7 Ex. 152; *Bryant* v. *Wardell* (1848) 2 Ex. 479; *R.* v. *Poyser* (1851) 2 Den. 233; *Plasycoed Collieries Ltd.* v. *Partridge, Jones & Co.* [1912] 2 K.B. 345; *Whitely* v. *Hilt* [1918] 2 K.B. 808; *North General Wagon & Finance Co. Ltd.* v. *Graham* [1950] 2 K.B.; *Reliance Car Facilities* v. *Roding Motors* [1952] 2 Q.B. 844; *Union Transport Finance* v. *British Car Auctions* [1978] 2 All E.R. 385; *Joseph Thorley Ltd.* v. *Orchis S.S. Co. Ltd.* [1907] 1 K.B. 560; *Suisse Atlantique Société d'Armement Maritime S.A.* v. *N.V. Rotterdamsche Kolen Centrale* [1967] 1 A.C. 361, *per* Lord Reid at p. 399.

54. But see the judgment of Lloyd L.J. in *State Trading Corporation of India Ltd.* v. *M. Golodetz Ltd.* [1989] 2 Lloyd's Rep. 277 at p. 288.

55. In *Photo Production* v. *Securicor Transport Ltd.* [1980] A.C. 827, Lord Diplock said (at p. 850): "The bringing to an end of all primary obligations under the contract may also leave the parties in a relationship, typically that of bailor and bailee, in which they owe one another by operation of law fresh primary obligations of which the contract is not the source" (official corrected version).

56. *Ibid.* at pp. 847 *et seq.*, *per* Lord Diplock. See also the cogent explanation of this phenomenon by Judge Learned Hand in *Farr* v. *Hain* (1941) 121 F. 2d 940 at p. 944.

57. *State Trading Corporation of India Ltd.* v. *M. Golodetz Ltd.* [1989] 2 Lloyd's Rep. 277, *per* Kerr L.J. at p. 287.

the root of the contract, thus effecting a terminating breach of a fundamental term, will depend upon how the obligation-defining terms of the contract are construed.[58] Delay may be sufficient to amount to a total failure of the consideration contracted for where the parties cannot be taken to have intended the contract to relieve the obligation to perform for the period of the delay[59] or to alleviate a risk consequent upon the delay which is wholly at variance with the contract of carriage.[60] In *Gibaud* v. *Great Eastern Ry. Co.*[61] the claimant left his bicycle at the defendant's station and received a ticket containing a clause purporting to exempt the defendants from liability. The bicycle was not put in the cloakroom but was left in the booking hall, from where it was stolen. The Court of Appeal held that if the contract had been to keep the bicycle in the cloakroom and nowhere else, the defendants would have stepped outside the "four corners" of the contract and would not have been protected by the exemption clause.[62]

Once the contract of carriage loses its force by reason of a breach of a fundamental term, the clauses within it can no longer operate. They can only operate as terms of the contract or not at all. It is therefore impossible for a term contained in the carriage contract to be so drafted as to enable the carrier to rely upon it in circumstances in which the contract as a whole no longer operates. For this reason, unless the loss due to delay or deviation at the precise moment when the breach of fundamental term giving rise to the automatic termination occurs, when presumably the contract can still govern (and the carrier would carry an extraordinarily difficult burden of proof in that regard) it is difficult to see how any exculpatory clause in the carriage contract could be relied upon by the carrier once it has, without lawful excuse, deviated or delayed to the point of going to the root of the obligation to carry the goods. At that moment all the contractual terms have lost their force, including the term that purports to make the contractual conditions applicable irrespective of the route by which the consignment is carried. Where, however, the clause is considered *as a matter of construction*, to be incapable of applying to a delay or a deviation the question of the burden of proving the breach of fundamental term must be considered without regard to the clause. In such a case the weight of authority appears to place the burden of proof on the defendant bailee.[63] 4.169

[*The next paragraph is 4.179*]

58. See *A.F. Colverd & Co. Ltd.* v. *Anglo-Overseas Transport Co. Ltd.* [1962] 2 Lloyd's Rep. 352.

59. *The Cap Palos* [1921] P. 458.

60. *Bontex Knitting Works Ltd.* v. *St. John's Garage* [1943] 2 All E.R. 690, affirmed [1944] 1 All E.R. 381n.

61. [1921] 2 K.B. 246.

62. See also *London & N. Western Ry.* v. *Neilson* [1922] A.C. 263.

63. *Hunt & Winterbotham (West of England) Ltd.* v. *BRS (Parcels) Ltd.* [1962] 1 Q.B. 617; *United Fresh Meat Co. Ltd.* v. *Charterhouse Cold Storage Ltd.* [1974] 2 Lloyd's Rep. 286; Handford, 38 M.L.R. 577; Males [1978] C.L.J. 24; Treitel, *The Law of Contract* (11th ed., Sweet & Maxwell, 2003), p. 241; *Levinson* v. *Patent Steam Carpet Cleaning Co.* [1978] Q.B. 68, following *Woolmer* v. *Delmer Price* [1955] 1 Q.B. 291 and distinguishing the *Hunt & Winterbotham* case (above). See also Palmer, *Bailment* (2nd ed., Sweet & Maxwell, 1991), p. 1552. Cf. the observations of Lord Buckmaster in *H.C. Smith* v. *Great Western Ry. Co.* [1922] 1 A.C. 178 at p. 185.

VIII. CARRIER AS FORWARDING AGENT

4.179 In most contracts for carriage by inland water, especially now that both carriers and loads are significantly less numerous than in former times, cargo consolidation is quite common. Accordingly the carrier will frequently reserve the right in the contract to act as forwarding agent rather than carrier.

> (i) The Carrier shall be at liberty to arrange for the whole or part of the carriage to be performed by an independent carrier or carriers and the Carrier and any such carrier or carriers are authorised as agents for the Trader and/or his principal or principals, if any, to contract for such carriage upon the terms of any Bill of Lading or Conditions usually required by any such independent carrier or carriers. When the Carrier arranges and contracts for the whole or part of the carriage to be so performed the Carrier at all times contracts as agents of the Trader and/or his principal or principals, if any.
>
> (ii) Where the Carrier contracts for the whole of the carriage to be performed by an independent carrier or carriers the obligations and liability of the Carrier shall cease on the Carrier so contracting. Where the Carrier contracts for part of the carriage to be performed by an independent carrier or carriers the obligations and liability of the Carrier shall be deemed to terminate during the period commencing when the merchandise is either accepted into the possession of any independent carrier or, if tendered to any such carrier and not accepted, when the merchandise is so tendered and ending when the merchandise is received back into the possession of the Carrier and its servants.
>
> (iii) The Carrier shall not be liable for any loss, damage or delay caused by or arising from any defect in or unseaworthiness of any vessel or craft not belonging to the Carrier howsoever or wheresoever, such loss, damage or delay may have been caused.

4.180 A forwarding agent is one who makes contract of carriage for a principal (in this case the trader) and, though he may be a carrier of goods at the same time and may be responsible for the goods under the contract of carriage in so far as and as long as he acts as a carrier, he is not responsible for what happens to the goods once they are handed over to the independent carrier with whom he has made a contract for the trader.[1] A clause such as this is necessary since at common law it is by no means clear that a carrier is entitled to sub-contract. Indeed, in one case it was held that sub-contracting the carriage of goods that were particularly attractive to thieves was a fundamental breach of the contract.[2] However, common law always accepted that vicarious performance with the consent of the trader was permitted and this clause amounts to such consent. Nevertheless, as an agent the carrier must select any subcontractors with due care and skill[3] but where the whole of the carriage is subcontracted, the carrier acts merely as the trader's agent and the clause expressly provides that all the carrier's obligations and liabilities shall, on making the subcontract, forthwith cease. If only a part of the journey is sub-contracted then the carrier's obligations and liabilities are terminated for the period from when the

1. *Jones* v. *European & General Express Co. Ltd.* (1920) 4 Ll.L.Rep. 127. A discussion of the detailed law of freight forwarding contracts is beyond the scope of this part of this book. Reference should be made to specialist works on the subject: see Glass, *Multimodal Transport and Freight Forwarding* (Informa 2004), Chap. 2, *passim*; Bugden, *Freight Forwarding and Goods in Transit* (Sweet & Maxwell, 1999), especially Parts I and V.

2. See *Garnham, Harris & Elton Ltd.* v. *Alfred W. Ellis (Transport) Ltd.* [1967] 1 W.L.R. 940.

3. *Gillette Industries* v. *Martin* [1966] 1 Lloyd's Rep. 57.

goods are offered to the independent carrier and accepted into its possession until they are received back (if at all) by the carrier. If the goods are tendered to an independent carrier but it does not accept them (because, for instance, of their condition, packing or dangerous nature) then the carrier's obligations and liabilities are suspended until it resumes possession.

There will be circumstances in which the independent carrier, as a sub- 4.181
contractor, will be entitled to the benefit of any defences in the contract of carriage. Little help can be derived directly from the Contracts (Rights of Third Parties) Act 1999 since the above-quoted clause does not purport to make the independent carrier a party to the contract of carriage between the "lead" carrier and the trader.[4] However, given that the carrier's duty of care as a bailee for reward is modified by the terms of the contract of carriage and the trader has clearly consented to those terms of the bailment contained in the contract of carriage, he will normally be bound by the terms of the sub-bailment, provided that there is nothing especially unusual about them.[5]

It is essential to the efficacy of this theory of "bailment on terms" that the trader 4.182
consents to the sub-bailment[6] which he does by virtue of this clause. However, if the carrier also contracts with the sub-contractor on the basis that the latter shall enjoy the benefit of the carrier's conditions, the trader too is bound by that arrangement. If the independent contractor is sued in tort for negligence by the trader the carriage conditions will also come into play. As the trader and the independent carrier have encountered one another as a consequence of a contractual structure (the "lead" carriage contract) which provides for certain compensation arrangements in the event of the failure of one of the two parties in that contract to perform as promised, the law will not superimpose an added duty of care beyond that which was contemplated in the contract when the original parties to it reached agreement.[7]

The clause spells out the consequences for the carrier acting as forwarder in the 4.183
capacity of trader's agent. The terms of the contract make it expressly clear that the

4. Contracts of carriage by road and rail do sometimes contain such clauses in terms such as: "The Carrier enters into the contract of carriage for itself and on behalf of sub-contractors, agents and employees, all of whom shall have the benefit of the contract and shall be under no liability to the Trader in respect of the goods greater than or in addition to that of the Carrier under the contract." For a discussion of the extent to which such a clause is capable of conferring on sub-contractors the benefit of defences in the contract of carriage or subjecting then to the "burdens" arising therefrom see Treitel, *The Law of Contract* (11th ed., Sweet & Maxwell, 2003), pp. 638–645.

5. *Morris* v. *Martin & Sons* [1966] 1 Q.B. 716; *Port Swettenham Authority* v. *T. W. Wu & Co.* [1979] A.C. 580; *The Kapetan Markos NL (No. 2)* [1987] 2 Lloyd's Rep. 323; *Singer (UK) Ltd.* v. *Tees & Hartlepool Port Authority* [1988] 2 Lloyd's Rep. 164; *The Captain Gregos (No. 2)* [1990] 2 Lloyd's Rep. 395; *The Pioneer Container* [1994] 2 A.C. 324; *Johnson Matthey & Co.* v. *Constantine Terminals Ltd.* [1976] 2 Lloyd's Rep. 215; *Dresser UK Ltd.* v. *Falconbridge Management Ltd.* [1992] Q.B. 502; *The Gudermes* [1993] 1 Lloyd's Rep. 311; *Sonicare International Ltd.* v. *EAFT Ltd.* [1997] 2 Lloyd's Rep. 48; cf. *The Agia Skepi* [1992] 2 Lloyd's Rep. 467; *The Termagent* (1914) Com. Cas. 239; *The Rigoletto* [2000] 2 Lloyd's Rep. 532.

6. *The Aliakmon* [1986] A.C. 785. The trader may be bound by reason *both* of a bailment on terms and of a contract between the trader and the independent carrier made through the agency of the carrier: see *Sandeman Comprimar S.A.* v. *Transitos Integrales S.L.* [2003] EWCA Civ 113; *East West Corp.* v. *DKBS* [2003] EWCA Civ 83.

7. *The Aliakmon* [1986] A.C. 785; *Pacific Associates Inc.* v. *Baxter* [1990] 1 Q.B. 993; *Mayfair Photographic Supplies (London)* v. *Baxter Hoare & Co.* [1972] 1 Lloyd's Rep. 410; *London Drugs* v. *Kuehne & Nagel* (1993) 97 D.L.R. (4th) 261; *Norwich County Council* v. *Harvey* [1989] 1 W.L.R. 828; *British Telecommunications plc* v. *James Thomson & Sons (Engineering) Ltd.* [1999] 2 All E.R. 241.

carrier acts only as forwarding agent in respect of that part of the carriage not physically carried out by it. The form of words used in this version of the clause is likely to be conclusive of the matter[8] and those cases in which the courts have construed the contract as placing the forwarder in the position of principal *vis-à-vis* the trader will not apply[9] nor will the carrier be treated as an agent giving a warranty of performance.[10]

4.184 The clause makes it clear that privity of contract exists between the trader and the carrier, whether that be the "third party" carrier, or the "lead" carrier in respect of that part of the carriage which it performs itself.[11] It should be noted that if the "lead" carrier issues a through bill of lading, that is a bill covering the whole transit, it will be liable as a carrier under the bill for all sections of the carriage, whether the loss occurs during the period of transit by that carrier or not, regardless of this clause.[12]

4.185 On the face of it forwarding agent clauses containing provisions such as that in (iii) appear entirely reasonable in so far as they protect the carrier from liability for defective or unseaworthy vessels upon which the goods are carried pursuant to the arrangement envisaged in this clause more generally. However, the clause will also, on its face, absolve the carrier from any liability to exercise care in choosing other carriers when the cause of loss is the chosen carrier's unseaworthy vessel. On the other hand, in such circumstances the trader could probably rely on the common law duty of care owed by the carrier as forwarder to exercise all reasonable due care and skill in the selection of a carrier rather than upon any duty to provide a seaworthy vessel.[13] The clause might also appear to absolve the lead carrier from liability for providing an unseaworthy vessel even where that carrier is the actual carrier of the goods, in cases where the vessel is not owned by that carrier but merely chartered by it. It is unlikely, however, given the context of the rest of this clause, that a court would be favourably disposed towards such a construction.

4.186 It is also worth noting in this context that Condition 8 of British Waterways' Carriage of Freight Conditions 2003 provides:

> The Freight Operator shall:
>
> 8.1.1. ensure that all Freight Vessels used by the Freight operator, the Owners of such Freight Vessels and any of their agents, employees and sub-contractors comply with the provisions of the Freight Vessel Conditions, the bye-laws and any other legislation and/or regulations relevant to the movement of Goods and carriage of Dangerous Substances by a vessel on a Waterway; and
>
> 8.1.2. be responsible for the competency of the Master and crew of the Freight Vessel.

4.187 The British Waterways Freight Vessel Conditions 2003 require that vessels authorised by the relevant British Waterways agreed Operational Schedule carry a

8. *Victoria Fur* v. *Roadline* [1981] 1 Lloyd's Rep. 570.

9. *Harris* v. *Continental Express Ltd.* [1961] 1 Lloyd's Rep. 251; *Colverd & Co. Ltd.* v. *Anglo-Overseas Transport Co. Ltd.* [1961] 2 Lloyd's Rep. 352; *Salsi* v. *Jetspeed Air Services* [1977] 2 Lloyd's Rep. 57; *Landauer & Co.* v. *Smits & Co.* (1921) 6 Ll.L.R. 577; *Lynch Bros* v. *Edwards & Fase* (1921) 6 Ll.L.R. 371; *J. Evans & Son (Portsmouth) Ltd.* v. *Andrea Merzaro Ltd.* [1976] 1 W.L.R. 1078.

10. See *Harlow & Jones* v. *P.J. Walker Shipping & Transport* [1986] 2 Lloyd's Rep. 141.

11. Cf. *Lee Cooper Ltd.* v. *C.H. Jenkins & Sons Ltd.* [1967] 2 Q.B. 1.

12. *Moore* v. *Harris* (1886) 1 App. Cas. 318.

13. See *Gillette Industries* v. *W.H. Martin Ltd.* [1966] 1 Lloyd's Rep. 57; cf. *Marston Excelsior Ltd.* v. *Arbuckle Smith & Co. Ltd.* [1971] 2 Lloyd's Rep. 306.

"fitness for purpose inspection certificate".[14] While this is not, *per se*, an obligation imported into the freight forwarding condition of the contract of carriage, breach of the condition in 8.1.1. of the Carriage of Freight Conditions 2003 will enable the sanctions mechanisms in Condition 4 of those Conditions[15] to be invoked.

[*The next paragraph is 4.197*]

14. British Waterways Freight Vessel Conditions 2003, Condition 3.2: "A freight vessel may not be kept or used on a Waterway unless . . . a Fitness-for-Purpose Inspection Certificate [further provided for in Conditions 6 and 7] or equivalent is in force in relation to the vessel."
15. See paras. 4.8 to 4.10, above.

IX. PACKING AND DANGEROUS AND ENVIRONMENTALLY DAMAGING GOODS

4.197 At common law a carrier does not become responsible to the full extent of possible liabilities unless the goods, if they are of a nature to require packing, are securely packed. This is not a duty imposed on the consignors. The carrier has no claim against the consignor as a consequence of his neglect to provide proper packing, unless the goods are dangerous.[1] It is only a precaution to be taken by the consignor in order to enable the owner to claim damages in the cases of loss, injury or delay. Accordingly, contracts for the carriage of goods by inland water will contain a clause dealing with liability in the event of imperfect or inappropriate packing in terms similar to the following:

> The Carrier shall be liable for loss of or damage to merchandise not properly protected by packing only where it can be proved that the same (a) arose from the wilful misconduct of the Carrier or of its employees or (b) would have been suffered if the goods had been properly protected by packing and the Carrier would otherwise have been liable under this Contract.

4.198 This clause will be of primary significance where carriage is at carrier's risk.[2] At carrier's risk the general principle is that the carrier escapes liability if it can prove that the loss or injury was caused or arose from insufficient or improper packing. This may be sufficient protection against claims arising from the carriage of merchandise which does not require special packing. In the case of goods that are likely to be damaged unless protected by packing, but which are not in fact properly packed, it is for the trader to prove that the lack of adequate packing was not the cause of the loss.

4.199 If goods susceptible to damage and not properly protected by packing are lost or damaged during transit the trader can make the carrier liable in two cases. First, if it can prove wilful misconduct, the carrier is liable even though the wilful misconduct of its employees may have been facilitated by the improper packing. The trader can preclude the carrier from relying on the improper packing as a defence by putting himself in the position he would have been in if the goods had been carried at trader's risk. Secondly, if the trader cannot prove wilful misconduct, he must show that the loss or damage would have been suffered even if the goods had been properly protected by packing and that the carrier would have been liable if the goods had been carried under the standard terms applicable to ordinary merchandise transported at carrier's risk. If, for example, drums of non-dangerous chemicals insufficiently protected by packing are broken during transit, the trader can obtain damages if he can prove that the way in which the carrier's employees or agents loaded or unloaded the drums showed reckless indifference towards the consequences of rough handling. The carrier could not, in these circumstances, argue that even the rough treatment would not have damaged the goods if they had been properly packed (e.g. with padding) since proof of recklessness (i.e. wilful misconduct) overrides this defence. If, however, the trader is able to prove no more than carelessness on the part of the carrier's employees or agents, then he would

1. On which see paras. 4.200 *et seq.*, below.
2. See paras. 4.83 *et seq.*, above.

have to prove that the way in which the drums were loaded or unloaded would have led to damage even with proper packing. If the drums exploded as a result of a fire during transit, the trader would first have to prove that proper packing would not have protected the contents from damage by fire. After he had succeeded in this proof it would be for the carrier to show that reasonable foresight and care was applied because this would be a case of "casualty" under carrier's risk terms.[3]

Contracts for the carriage of goods by inland water will contain special terms dealing with the carriage of dangerous goods and the rights and duties of the parties in respect of the carriage of dangerous goods. British Waterways does require carriers on its waterways to make a "notification" of the nature of the goods being carried (including, of course, dangerous goods). The relevant condition of British Waterways Carriage of Freight Conditions 2003 (Condition 3.2) is set out at paragraph 4.47. *4.200*

Further, sub-conditions 8.1.1. to 8.1.3. of the same Conditions[4] require the freight operator to take certain precautions with regard to the movement and carriage of "dangerous substances". *4.201*

Although dangerous goods can be carried on the inland waterways, subject to the relevant provisions of British Waterways Carriage of Freight Conditions 2003 set out above (paragraphs 4.46 *et seq.*), the suitability of the barge transport as certified in accordance with British Waterways Freight Vessel Conditions 2003, and the provisions of British Waterways General Canal Bye-Laws 1965 (as amended), they will not, under the normal terms used for carriage, be carried entirely on normal trader's or owner's risk terms.[5] The carriage contract will contain a clause in the terms following or in terms to like effect: *4.202*

Dangerous Goods: Special Conditions *4.203*

(1) In this Condition the expression "Dangerous Merchandise" means such merchandise as either the Carrier or the British Waterways Board may from time to time have declared to be a dangerous substance.[6]

(2) The Carrier is under no obligation to convey Dangerous Merchandise by inland waterway or road transport and will only do so subject to these Conditions, to the special Conditions contained sub-paragraph 3 hereof and to such other special Conditions as it may think fit from time to time to make in any particular case, and in the event of any conflict

3. Para. 4.84, above, sub-clause (g).

4. See para. 4.15, above.

5. Every canal undertaker which carries or intends to carry explosives must make bye-laws for regulating their conveyance, loading and unloading: Explosives Act 1875, s. 35. Further, every canal company has power to make bye-laws regulating the loading, conveyance and landing of petroleum spirit in and upon a canal and the precautions to be observed with respect to it: Regulation of Railways Act 1873, ss. 3 and 9, as amended by the Petroleum (Condition) Act 1928, s. 23. See also British Waterways Board, General Canal Bye-Laws 1965.

6. British Waterways Carriage of Freight Conditions 2003 define dangerous substances as "any substance defined as such in the Dangerous Substances in Harbour Areas Regulations 1987". These require prior notice to be given before carriers bring dangerous substances into ports. See also the Carriage of Dangerous Goods Regulations 1994, SI 1994/670. See also *Schedule of Dangerous Goods: The Green Book* and *The Transport of Dangerous Goods on the Board's Waterways and Docks*, both publications by British Waterways. See also the United Nations' *Recommendations on the Transport of Dangerous Goods*, otherwise known as the "Orange Book".

between any such special Conditions and these Conditions the special Conditions shall prevail.

(3) The special Conditions relating to the conveyance of Dangerous Merchandise by inland waterways or road transport are as follows:

(a) Previous arrangements shall be made with the carrier for the carriage of the merchandise.

(b) A label shall be securely attached to each package describing the nature of the merchandise.

(c) The merchandise shall be marked and packed safely for conveyance by inland waterway and road transport in accordance with any requirement of the Carrier, any requirements of the British Waterways Board or other inland waterway operator and with any statutory requirement for the time being in force, or if there are no such requirements then in accordance with such requirements as may be agreed between the Carrier and the Trader.

(d) The Carrier will not be responsible for any loss of or damage to the merchandise and the Trader will be responsible for and will indemnify the Carrier in respect of any injury (fatal or otherwise) loss or damage sustained by the Carrier or third parties whilst the merchandise is in the custody of the Carrier for conveyance or storage, except and to the extent only that any such loss, injury or damage shall be proved to have been caused by the negligence of the Carrier or of their servants. Provided that if such loss, injury or damage is caused by non-compliance with any special Conditions or with any of the requirements with regard to packing subject to which the merchandise is being conveyed, the exclusion of liability in favour of the Carrier contained in this paragraph shall not apply when it is proved that the loss, injury or damage is due to the wilful misconduct of the Carrier's servants.

Under the British Waterways Freight Conditions 2003, Condition 9,[7] the carrier in turn agrees to indemnify British Waterways against loss or damage caused as a consequence of, *inter alia*, the carriage of dangerous goods or substances on British Waterways' navigations.

4.204 So, as a consequence of clauses such as those found in British Waterways Freight Conditions 2003, dangerous goods are carried subject to the general terms of carriage, and the Special Conditions set out in the above clause and any other special conditions the carrier sees fit to apply in particular cases. In the case of conflict between the carrier's general conditions of carriage and any special conditions, the special conditions should generally be drafted so as to prevail. It is a condition precedent to the carrier's liability for dangerous goods that the trader shows that the conditions specified in 3(a), (b) and (c) of the "special conditions" above have been complied with or, if they have not been complied with, that such non-compliance is due to the wilful misconduct of the carrier's employees. If the trader can overcome that hurdle, he will then need to prove further that the loss or damage was caused by the negligence of the carrier or its employees. The carrier may then be able, where relevant, to plead the excepted perils that will be contained in the carrier's risk provision described earlier in this Part[8] and the limitations contained elsewhere in the contract.[9]

4.205 The Special Conditions lay down that the trader "will be responsible for" and "will indemnify the carrier in respect of" any injury, loss or damage. The word "indemnify" in the above clause may refer to an obligation to reimburse the carrier for money paid by it to others, in contrast to compensation for damage to the carrier's vessel, equipment etc., to which the words "responsible for" may be

7. See para. 4.15, above.
8. Paras. 4.83 *et seq.*, above.
9. Described above, paras. 4.115 *et seq.*

construed to relate.[10] On the other hand it could be argued that the intention in this Special Condition, when coupled with the opening words of the Dangerous Goods clause, is only to impose a responsibility on the trader not to consign dangerous goods without special arrangements, thus putting the trader in breach of contract should he do so.[11] A further possible construction of the provision, if all parts of the Dangerous Goods clause are read together, is that it provides both for an obligation and an indemnity.[12] In this last circumstance it may be necessary to distinguish between whether an event calling for indemnification is a loss, damage or expense incurred by another, or whether it is a liability for a breach of contract, act or omission of the trader.[13] In the former case the time limit under the Limitation Act 1980, s. 5, runs from the time the amount to be indemnified is ascertained[14] whereas, in the latter, time will run as from the breach itself.[15]

At common law the consignor warrants that the goods are fit to be carried in the condition in which they are delivered to the carrier.[16] This is a warranty that can be varied by express contractual provision.[17] The warranty is strict and does not depend on negligence or knowledge of the dangerous nature of the goods on the part of the consignor.[18] In addition to the special conditions governing the carriage of dangerous goods there is, at common law, a general warranty of fitness of the goods for carriage, usually reinforced by an express condition in the following terms: *4.206*

> In the absence of written notice[19] to the contrary given to the Carrier at the time the goods are delivered to it, all merchandise is (apart from the want of proper protection by packing[20] in the case of damaged goods not properly protected by packing) warranted by the Trader:
> (a) to be fit to be carried in the condition in which it is handed to the Carrier; and
> (b) not to be dangerous merchandise as so defined by the terms of this Contract.

The arbiters of whether goods are dangerous are the carrier itself or British Waterways, or other canal operators, on whose navigations the goods will have to be transported. However, lack of knowledge of their dangerous nature on the trader's part will not prevent the application of the warranty given by the trader, as consignor, either at common law or under an express term of the contract, that the *4.207*

10. Cf. *Dock Services Ltd.* v. *Caledonian Stevedoring Co. Ltd.* (1949) 82 Ll.L.R. 179.

11. See in contrast the wording used in *Micada Compania Naviera S.A.* v. *Texim* [1968] 2 Lloyd's Rep. 57.

12. Breach of contract does not carry, in itself, an implied indemnity (*Nederlandsch-Amerikaansche Stoomvaart Maatschappij N.V.* v. *Royal Mail Lines Ltd. (The Nieuw Amsterdam)* [1958] 1 Lloyd's Rep. 412, although an indemnity may express the measure of damages available for a breach: *ibid.*; see also *Total Transport Corporation* v. *Arcadia Petroleum Ltd. (The Eurus)* [1996] 2 Lloyd's Rep. 408.

13. See *County & District Properties Ltd.* v. *C. Jenner & Son Ltd.* [1976] 2 Lloyd's Rep. 728, *per* Swanwick J.; cf. *Bosma* v. *Larsen* [1966] 1 Lloyd's Rep. 22.

14. *Cathiship S.A.* v. *Allanasons Ltd. (The Catherine Helen)* [1998] 3 All E.R. 714. Similar principles apply in the case of implied indemnities: *Telfair Shipping Corp.* v. *Intersea Carriers S.A.* [1984] 2 Lloyd's Rep. 467.

15. For a general discussion of indemnity provision, their construction and operation, see Yates & Hawkins, *Standard Business Contracts* (Sweet & Maxwell, 1986), Chap. 8.

16. *Burley* v. *Stepney Corporation* [1947] 1 All E.R. 507.

17. *Acatos* v. *Burns* (1878) 3 Ex. D. 282.

18. *Bamfield* v. *Goole & Sheffield Transport Co. Ltd.* [1910] 2 K.B. 94; *Great Northern Ry.* v. *L.E.P. Transport Ltd.* [1922] 2 K.B. 742.

19. See para. 4.126, above.

20. See para. 4.197, above.

goods are fit for carriage. However, special Condition 3(b) in paragraph 4.203, above, does require the goods to carry a label describing their nature.[21] However, the requirement of labelling, unlike the condition of disclosure imposed on the carrier by British Waterways under Condition 3.2 of British Waterways Carriage of Freight Conditions 2003, may be construed as only referring to a bare description of the goods and not necessarily a statement that they are dangerous. This latter statement under the variants of the standard terms in general use appears to be one for others to make. This does, however, leave open the question of what the position would be if neither the carrier nor the relevant canal operator had designated the contents of any part of the cargo as a dangerous substance but the trader (accurately) had done so as part of his labelling of the consignment. Would the special conditions apply in such a case? On a strict construction of the "usual terms" they would probably not—certainly such a declaration on the label would be sufficient to prevent the more general express or implied warranty of fitness for carriage from being given. It should be noted that under standard terms of inland water carriage the term "The Trader" can include a consignee buyer who has become the owner of the goods when the contract of carriage is made.[22]

4.208 An express term and special conditions dealing with dangerous goods should replace the common law implied warranty as to fitness for carriage (which is not simply limited to dangerous goods in the technical sense but also to goods likely to cause harm because of their vicious or harmful propensities, such as certain types of livestock—unlikely cargoes to be seen on Britain's canals these days). Such an express term will also take the place of the more general warranty of fitness for carriage that will normally be a separate express term of the carriage contract. Goods that are not physically dangerous in the accepted sense may nevertheless still be regarded as dangerous if they are liable to give rise to loss of other cargo carried in the same vessel. An example would be a part cargo infested with insects that was capable of contaminating other cargo on board.[23] At common law the consignor of such cargo is liable even if he did not know or have the means of knowing of the attribute in the cargo which was likely to cause danger.[24]

4.209 At common law, if dangerous goods damage goods belonging to other customers of the carrier, the carrier, as a bailee in possession may, subject to the effects of the Torts (Interference with Goods) Act 1977,[25] sue on behalf of such customers, and

21. See also British Waterways Carriage of Freight Conditions 2003 which require the freight operator to provide details of the goods to be carried. The relevant provision is set out at para. 4.47, above.

22. Most standard terms for carriage by inland water contain, in the definition clause, words to the effect that "Trader" means the person with whom the carrier contracts for the carriage of merchandise or for arranging the carriage of merchandise by "an independent carrier or carriers". Under the common law the term "trader" has been interpreted to include consignor, consignee and, in appropriate circumstances, the carrier: *Master Lightermen & Barge Owners' Association* v. *Southern Ry. Co. (No. 2)* (1934) 21 Ry. & Can. Tr. Cas. 126, *per* Maugham L.J. at 155.

23. *Effort Shipping Ltd.* v. *Linden Management S.A. (The Giannis NK)* [1998] 1 Lloyd's Rep. 337.

24. *Mitchell Colts & Co.* v. *Steel Bros & Co. Ltd.* [1916] 2 K.B. 610, *per* Atkin J. at p. 614; *Effort Shipping Ltd.* v. *Linden Management S.A. (The Giannis NK)* [1994] 2 Lloyd's Rep. 557, Longmore J., upheld by C.A. at [1996] 1 Lloyd's Rep. 577 and by H.L., above, note 23.

25. S. 8. The defendant in an action for wrongful interference with goods is entitled to show by way of defence that a third party had a better right than the claimant as respects all or any part of the interest claimed by the claimant or in right of which he sues; *ibid.* s. 8(1). See Palmer, *Bailment* (2nd ed., Sweet & Maxwell, 1991), pp. 283 *et seq.*

recover full damages under the rule in *The Winkfield*.[26] It does not seem to matter whether the bailee is liable to his customers under his contract with them or not; he can still recover full damages.[27] Obviously, in such a case he cannot pocket the damages he recovers but must hold the proceeds for the benefit of the owners of the goods.[28] It is therefore reasonably clear that a carrier may sue the consignor at common law. If the consignor of dangerous goods has been negligent, the owner of the consignment damaged in transit by those goods can sue the consignor in negligence. If, however, the consignor is an innocent freight forwarder who is unaware of the dangerous nature of the goods, no action in negligence is likely to succeed. Nevertheless, there does appear to be authority[29] to the effect that the strict nature of the common law warranty of fitness for carriage will extend to an action brought directly by the carrier's employees for their own injuries against a non-negligent consignor. Under the clause in the carriage contract relating to dangerous goods the liability of the consignor in respect of "third party" damage (whether to goods or personnel) is extended to include the consignee in those circumstances where the consignee is "The Trader"[30] where the claimant maintains a cause of action directly against the carrier, unless the trader can prove that the injury or damage was due to the carrier's own negligence. This is by virtue of the express indemnity included in sub-clause 3(d) of the special conditions. The indemnity probably extends to loss, damage or injury sustained either by the carrier or third parties.[31]

The contract of carriage is also likely to contain an express warranty, to complement the express fitness for carriage warranty, that the goods to be carried will not cause any environmental damage to the navigations nor infringe any relevant environmental protection or pest control legislation, though as has been explained earlier in this section, infested cargo which is likely to cause damage, at least to other cargo carried on the same barge or vessel, may be regarded as dangerous cargo. Clauses 8.1.4 and 8.1.5 of British Waterways Carriage of Freight Conditions 2003 impose the following obligations on all freight carriers using the Board's waterways: *4.210*

> 8.1.1 Without prejudice to the generality of the provisions of Condition 8.1 the Freight Operator shall not do or fail to do, or permit others to do or fail to do anything which may cause or result in any Environmental Damage.
>
> 8.1.2 The Freight Operator shall comply with any specific instruction of British Waterways with regard to the Freight Operator's use of a Waterway that may properly be given and which affects or is likely to affect performance or any health and safety duties of British Waterways.

In the context of these provisions, "environmental damage" is defined as "any perceptible injury or damage to living organisms or property or any pollution or impairment of the environment (being air, water and land) resulting from the discharge, emission, escape or migration of any substance, energy, noise or *4.211*

26. [1920] P. 42; see also *Great Northern Ry.* v. *L.E.P. Transport Co. Ltd.* [1922] K.B. 742, especially Scrutton L.J. at 765.
27. *Ibid.*
28. *Ibid.*
29. *Bamfield* v. *Goode and Sheffield Transport Co.* [1910] 2 K.B. 94.
30. See note 22, above.
31. But see para. 4.205, above.

vibration, other than any such injury or damage of a minor nature that is ordinarily incidental to the normal and well-managed operation of a Freight vessel by a competent person".[32]

[The next paragraph is 4.221]

32. British Waterways Carriage of Freight Conditions 2003, Cond. 2.1. Note also British Waterways Act 1995, s. 22, which places certain statutory duties on British Waterways, *inter alia*, to exercise its powers having due regard to a variety of statutorily laid down environmental issues.

X. COLLECTION, DELIVERY AND TERMINATION OF TRANSIT AND WAREHOUSING

Contracts for the carriage of goods by inland water will contain clauses to determine what amounts to proper collection and delivery of the goods. However, both of these provisions will themselves be dependent on the clause defining when transit of the goods is to be regarded as at an end. Accordingly, the definition of "termination of transit" is pivotal to this particular set of clauses. A common form transit clause is as follows: 4.221

(1) The transit shall (unless otherwise previously determined) be deemed to be at an end:

(a) In the case of merchandise to be delivered to the Trader's premises by a road vehicle of the Carrier, when it is tendered at the place of delivery, as defined by Condition (–)[1] within the customary hours of the Carrier for delivery in the district or as such other times as may be agreed between the Carrier and the Trader.

(b) In the case of merchandise not to be delivered to the Trader's premises, or consigned to premises to which there is no serviceable road or adequate approach, or to be kept till called for, or awaiting order or in the case of merchandise to be delivered by vessel to premises under the control and management of the Carrier, at the expiration of one clear day after notice of arrival is given in writing (or by telephone or email if so agreed in writing) to or at the address of the consignee or, where the address of the Trader or, where the address of both the Trader and the consignee are not known, at the expiration of one clear day after the arrival of the merchandise at the place to which it is consigned.

(c) In the case of merchandise to be carried by vessel to a wharf not under the control or management of the Carrier:

(i) when the vessel is placed alongside the wharf, or at the place where, by arrangement, the Trader takes delivery;

or

(ii) if the consignee is prevented from taking delivery through the act or omission of the Carrier when the cause which has prevented him from taking delivery has been removed and either the merchandise is delivered in accordance with paragraph (c)(i) of this Condition or on the expiration of one clear day after receipt by the consignee of notice in writing (or by telephone or email if so agreed in writing) that the Carrier is ready and willing to deliver, whichever be the earlier.

(d) In any other case when delivery takes place.

(2) When in the course of delivery goods are lifted from any vessel of the Carrier by crane chain or other tackle not under the control of the carrier, delivery shall be deemed to take place at the moment when the goods are attached to and suspended from such crane, chain or other tackle.

The end of transit does not necessarily coincide with the end of the journey. Though transit is always at an end when the goods are actually delivered, the contrary is not the case and transit may end though there has been no delivery, for example if the carrier tenders the goods to the consignee and acceptance is refused. Transit will then normally end under most carriers' standard terms with the procedure set out in sub-clause (1)(b), above. Transit may even be at an end when the carrier refuses to deliver, for example because the consignee has declined to pay the carriage. This is equivalent to a refusal by the consignee to accept delivery of the 4.222

1. The relevant Condition number for the clause dealing with delivery (see below) should be inserted here.

goods. The general principle, then, is that transit ends when the goods have been tendered to the consignee, whether he has accepted them or not.[2]

4.223 When goods have been tendered in accordance with these rules (which must be read in conjunction with the clauses dealing with collection and delivery)[3] transit ends. Goods which are to be delivered to the trader's premises but which the consignee refuses will not be in transit while being carried back to the carrier's depot and the carrier is then only liable as a warehouseman for whatever happens while they are returning.[4] If merchandise is not to be delivered by the carrier, or is to be retained by the carrier awaiting order, or if the merchandise is consigned to premises not served by appropriate access routes, or is consigned "to be kept until called for", or is merchandise to be delivered by vessel to the carrier's premises, transit does not end until one day after notice of arrival has been given. The carrier is not under a contractual obligation to give notice, but if the carrier knows the address of either the consignee or the trader, transit cannot be brought to an end without giving such notice.[5] The normal common law rule laid down in *Chapman* v. *Great Western Ry. Co.*[6] that transit ends a reasonable time after arrival at a depot will not apply if there is an appropriately worded transit clause in the contract. The notice must be given to or at the address of the consignee (if known). If the consignee's address is not known but the trader's address is, then notice must be given to or at the address of the trader. Writing for this purpose includes fax, but not e-mail. The parties can, however, expressly agree in writing that e-mail or even verbal notice will suffice. If the carrier does not know the address of the consignee or that of the trader (a circumstance that is almost impossible to arise in practice today, at least in respect of carriage on navigations operated by British Waterways because of the disclosure requirements imposed on freight carriers under British Waterways Carriage of Freight Conditions 2003) it cannot give notice and transit ends one clear day after the merchandise has arrived at the place to which it was consigned.

4.224 There are special rules applicable under the transit clause if the cargo is to be carried to a wharf not owned by the carrier. In this case delivery takes place, and thus transit ends, when the vessel is alongside the wharf or is alongside the place where, by special arrangement, the parties have agreed that delivery takes place. If the consignee is prevented from taking delivery, and if his inability to accept the goods is not due to the fault of the carrier, transit ends one clear day after the consignee has received notice of arrival. If, owing to an act or omission of the carrier, the consignee cannot take delivery, transit does not end before the cause which prevented him from taking delivery has been removed and the merchandise is either delivered on the wharf by arrangement or one clear day has expired after the receipt by the consignee of notice that the carrier is now ready and willing to deliver.

2. For a discussion of the circumstances when transit ends at common law, and an explanation of the legal basis upon which the carrier then continues to hold the goods, see Palmer, *Bailment* (2nd ed., Sweet & Maxwell, 1991), pp. 1002–1013.
3. Para. 4.227, below.
4. Paras. 4.230 *et seq.*, below.
5. For the meaning of "notice" see para. 4.126, above.
6. (1880) 5 Q.B.D. 278.

In all other cases transit ends either by delivery in accordance with the clause defining delivery[7] or as agreed. Normally delivery takes place, and thus transit ends when the goods cross the ship's rail. However, where the lifting gear used does not belong to the carrier, delivery is deemed to take place when the goods are attached to and suspended from the tackle, even though they may be occupying air space above the hold floor or barge deck. It is also customary for the contract to contain a clause such as the following: 4.225

> The delivery on board any boat or vessel of the carrier of any merchandise loaded from any ship, lighter, barge or wharf shall not be complete until such merchandise is actually on board.

Goods are "on board" when they cross the ship's rail.[8] To invoke this clause the contract must specify delivery "on board", otherwise delivery to the wharf or dock may be sufficient to terminate transit. 4.226

It is necessary to include a clause dealing with collection or delivery alongside that dealing with transit: 4.227

> When collection or delivery by road vehicle takes place at the Trader's premises the place of collection or delivery shall be the usual place of loading or unloading the merchandise into or from the road vehicle, but the Carrier shall not be under any obligation to provide any plant, power and/or labour which, in addition to the Carrier's driver, may be required for loading or unloading at such premises. In the case of merchandise collected from or delivered to any place in a dock or wharf, including any ship, boat, vessel or barge, berthed in such dock or wharf, such place shall be deemed to be the Trader's premises for the purposes of both this clause and any other clause in this contract providing for when transit shall be deemed to be at an end for the purposes of this agreement.

As has been explained, transit ends, in general, when the goods are delivered to the trader's premises. Similarly, transit begins, in general, when the goods are collected from the trader's premises i.e. when they are delivered to the carrier's custody for transport.[9] Accordingly, it is important to know what constitutes the trader's premises for these purposes. The immediately above-quoted clause provides that definition. It should be noted that aside from a vehicle and a driver, the carrier is not obliged to provide any plant, power or labour where the goods are delivered to or collected from the trader's premises by road. Where the goods are delivered to or collected from a dock or wharf or a berthed vessel these will, as the case may be, constitute "trader's premises" for the purposes of delivery or collection. 4.228

> The Carrier shall, in every case when merchandise is consigned to a wharf or depot of the carrier, and is not to be delivered by the Carrier's road vehicle or vessel, give notice in writing (or by telephone or email if so agreed in writing) of arrival to the consignee or, where his address is not known, or he refuses to take delivery, to the Trader where it is reasonable and practicable to do so. 4.229

Where transit does not end, as it normally would do under the contractual terms as to transit, with delivery to the trader's premises,[10] but is to end with delivery to a wharf or depot owned by the carrier,[11] then the carrier must give the consignee

7. Para. 4.221, above, and para. 4.227, below.
8. See *Petersen* v. *Freebody* [1895] 2 Q.B. 294.
9. See *Plischke* v. *Allisons Bros.* [1936] 2 All E.R. 1009.
10. See para 4.221, clause (1)(a), above.
11. See para 4.221, clause (1)(b), above.

notice in writing[12] of the arrival of the consignment. If the consignee's address is unknown or the consignee refuses to take delivery, then written notice must be given to the trader, where it is reasonable and practicable to do so. This is a condition precedent to the termination of transit under the "transit" clause set out earlier in this section.[13]

4.230 It is possible that a period of time could arise during or after transit has ended under the contract but before delivery of the cargo to the consignee when the carrier holds the goods, not as a carrier under carrier's or trader's risk terms but as a warehouseman. A well-drawn contract of carriage must provide for this eventuality.

> (1) Where after termination of the transit as defined herein the Carrier remains in possession of the merchandise it shall, unless otherwise agreed in writing, hold the merchandise as warehouseman, subject to the Carrier's Charges and Terms and Conditions of Storage copies of which may be obtained upon application to any office of the Carrier and further subject to the Condition that the Carrier will not be liable for any loss or damage to merchandise which has arrived at the destination wharf or depot and for which the Carrier gave notice that it has no suitable accommodation, no matter by whomsoever and howsoever such loss or damage may be caused and whether or not occasioned by the neglect or default of the Carrier. This condition shall not relieve the Carrier from any liability the Carrier might otherwise incur under these Conditions in the unloading of the goods.
>
> (2) The Carrier's liability for any loss or damage to goods held by it as warehouseman pursuant to this Condition shall in any case by subject to the limits and exclusions in Conditions [–].[14]
>
> (3) Dangerous goods held by the Carrier after termination or during suspension of transit will be subject to:
>
> (a) the Condition that the Carrier will not be liable for any loss or damage to the goods except upon proof by the Trader that such loss or damage arose from the wilful misconduct of the Carrier; and
>
> (b) the provisions of Condition [–][15] hereof.

4.231 The carrier's duty under this provision is that of a common law bailee for reward.[16] As such he must take reasonable care of the goods, with the corollary of liability for negligence, subject (a) to the relevant contractual provision setting limits on liability and (b) the clause providing that the carrier shall not be liable if merchandise not properly protected by packing is lost, misdelivered, detained or damaged, unless the owner proves that this mishap was occasioned by the wilful misconduct of the carrier's employees or that it would have occurred even if the goods had been properly protected by packing and (c) to a different level of duty entirely as regards dangerous merchandise.[17]

4.232 The limitations identified at (a), (b) and (c) of the previous paragraph being, as they now are, applied to a warehousing contract rather than a contract for the carriage of goods by inland water, will in this context be subject to the statutory test

12. See para. 4.126, above. Again, written notice will include fax. Telephonic or e-mail notice must be specifically agreed to in writing.

13. In para. 4.221, above.

14. The clause number corresponding to the clauses set out in paras. 4.115 and 4.141, above, will be inserted here.

15. The clause number corresponding to clause 3(d) set out in para. 4.203, above, will be inserted here.

16. See further Palmer, *Bailment* (2nd ed., Sweet & Maxwell, 1991), Chaps. 8 and 13.

17. See paras. 4.202 *et seq.*, above.

of reasonableness contained in section 11 of the Unfair Contract Terms Act 1977. The reasonableness of these limitations will be determined in part by reference to section 11(4) of the 1977 Act which requires consideration of the resources available to the carrier/warehouseman to meet the liability and the extent to which it was possible for him to obtain insurance cover. This is a major factor in evaluating reasonableness in this context.[18] So, it is possible that whether or not limitations of this kind will be upheld will depend upon who is in the best position to insure, which in turn will involve the availability of insurance to the trader and even the appropriateness of requiring him to insure. Lack of knowledge of the carrier as to the nature of the goods is also relevant,[19] as is the fact that at the time the carriage and thus the warehousing contract was made most cargoes carried by inland water transport were stored under similar limits.[20]

The factors to be considered are those relevant at the time the contract is made[21] 4.233
and it may be permissible to have regard to the guidelines set out in the 1977 Act for application to exclusion of the implied terms in sales of goods, even though they are not technically applicable to warehousing.[22] In respect of the criteria in these guidelines an important factor pointing towards the reasonableness of financial limits on claims is the fact that an increase is available to the trader subject to a declaration of value and payment of an increased charge,[23] although the fact that the notification of value and payment of the extra charge is to take place at the time of delivery of the goods to the carrier (the standard provision) could be a source of difficulty. Since the test of reasonableness under the 1977 Act has to be applied at the time the contract is made[24] that may pre-date delivery of the goods. It is then possible that any subsequent arrangement made on delivery could, in theory, be ignored in assessing reasonableness.[25] In any event, it is important that the additional charge must present a genuine opportunity to increase the carrier/

18. *Singer Co. (UK) Ltd.* v. *Tees & Hartlepool Port Authority* [1988] 2 Lloyd's Rep. 164 at 169 (where it was also observed that indemnity insurance is, by and large, less expensive than liability insurance); *Flamar Interocean Ltd.* v. *Denmac Ltd. (The Flamar Pride)* [1990] 1 Lloyd's Rep. 434.

19. *Wight* v. *British Railways Board* [1983] C.L.Y. 424.

20. In *Sonicare International Ltd.* v. *East Anglia Freight Terminal* [1997] 2 Lloyd's Rep. 48 a limit characterised as "derisory" was nevertheless held to be reasonable in the light of commercial reality and the allocation of risk by insurance. Equality of bargaining power of the parties, alongside the cost and availability of insurance, probably remain the most significant factors in assessing the reasonableness of limitations in commercial standard terms of business: *Stewart Gill Ltd.* v. *Horatio Myer & Co. Ltd.* [1992] Q.B. 600 (this case also makes it clear that the court has no power, under the 1977 Act, to sever the unreasonable parts of a clause from the reasonable, leaving the latter in force). See also *Watford Electronics Ltd.* v. *Sanderson CFL Ltd.* [2001] 1 All E.R. (Comm.) 696, *per* Chadwick L.J. Cf. *Britvic Soft Drinks Ltd.* v. *Messer UK Ltd.* [2002] 1 Lloyd's Rep. 20. A sensibly drawn limitation clause, such as the one under discussion, is more likely to pass the reasonableness test than a total exclusion of liability: *St Albans City and District Council* v. *International Computers Ltd.* [1996] 4 All E.R. 481.

21. Unfair Contract Terms Act 1977, s. 11(1).

22. *Ibid.* Sched. 2. See *Granville Oil & Chemicals Ltd.* v. *Davis Turner & Co. Ltd.* [2003] 1 All E.R. (Comm.) 819; Cf. *Stag Line Ltd.* v. *Tyne Shiprepair Group Ltd.* [1984] 2 Lloyd's Rep. 211, *per* Staughton J. at 222; *Moores* v. *Yakely Associates Ltd.* (1999) 62 Con. L.R. 76; *The Salvage Association* v. *C.A.P. Financial Services* [1995] F.S.R. 655.

23. See *Patec* v. *Translink*, 3 December 2002, Singapore High Court.

24. Unfair Contract Terms Act 1977, s. 11(1).

25. Cf. *Phillips Products Ltd.* v. *Hyland* [1987] 1 W.L.R. 659.

warehouseman's liability and not one that is so high that is discourages traders from opting for it.[26]

4.234 The procedural time limits on the making of claims set out earlier[27] clearly fall within the Unfair Contract Terms Act 1977, s. 13(1), and the clause containing them is thus subject to the reasonableness test under that Act. The burden of proving the impracticability of complying with the time limit is on the trader but, should that burden be discharged the court has a discretion to grant the trader relief. It is likely that this element of the clause would enable the condition as a whole to satisfy the reasonableness test in section 11(1) of the 1977 Act by seeking to ensure that the trader should find it practicable to comply.[28]

4.235 A warehouseman is one who, as part of his business, has the care and custody of another's goods. He is a bailee and, as such, is bound to take all reasonable care of the goods and is answerable for injury or loss caused by his own negligence and that of his employees. He is not liable for loss or injury if the goods are lost, injured or destroyed through no want of care on his part. Hence, if goods are in the hands of a carrier after the transit is at an end, and they are stolen from its warehouse or destroyed by fire without any negligence on its part, the carrier/warehouseman is not liable. It is for the warehouseman to prove that the loss or damage to the goods is not due to its employees' negligence.[29] In this situation the carrier becomes a bailee for reward who is bound, on the one hand, to take good care and, on the other, is entitled to charge a reasonable sum for taking care. The levying of a charge makes it completely clear that the carrier is a bailee for reward.[30] Thus, although there is much academic debate as to the need to establish the extent of the voluntary assumption of risk on the bailee's part, and the consensual nature, in general, of such bailments,[31] the traditional and usual liability of bailees for reward is almost certainly applicable in these circumstances. The carrier, of course, will not, in most standard form carriage contracts, assume responsibility for any loss, misdelivery or detention of or damage to merchandise when it has no proper facilities for storage, provided that it gives notice of the lack of suitable facilities to store the goods.

4.236 It is comparatively rare today for inland water carriage to be an entirely "discreet" transaction (though sometimes it is). Frequently carriage of goods by inland water will involve multimodal transport, i.e. the linking of two or more transport modes (such as road, inland water and sea carriage) under a dedicated contractual arrangement normally making use of a unit load device such as a container. Although containers are ideally suited to movement by canal barge, there are some physical restrictions, such as locks, low bridges and tunnels, that can severely limit the number of containers that can be carried on an individual vessel. Multimodal

26. Cf. *Peek* v. *North Staffordshire Ry. Co.* (1863) 10 H.L.C. 473. The need for such opportunity to be an effective one was noted in *Overseas Medical Supplies Ltd.* v. *Orient Transport Services* [1999] 2 Lloyd's Rep. 273.

27. See para. 4.124, above.

28. Cf. *R.W. Green Ltd.* v. *Cade Bros. Farm* [1978] 1 Lloyd's Rep. 602.

29. *Chapman* v. *Great Western Ry. Co.* (1880) 5 Q.B.D. 278. *Mitchell* v. *Lancashire & Yorkshire Ry. Co.* (1875) L.R. 10 Q.B. 256, in which the bailee was liable for storing bales of flax outside where they were damaged by water because it had insufficient "under cover" storage. See also *Joseph Travers & Sons Ltd.* v. *Cooper* [1915] 1 K.B. 73; *Port Swettenham Authority* v. *Wu (T.W.) & Co.* [1979] A.C. 580.

30. *Brooks Wharf & Bull Wharf Ltd.* v. *Goodman Bros.* [1937] 1 K.B. 534.

31. See Palmer, *Bailment* (2nd ed., Sweet & Maxwell, 1991), pp. 125–126, 506–523.

transport (sometimes referred to by its older label of "combined transport") is beyond the scope of this part of this book. A detailed examination of the principles of multimodal transport can be found fully discussed elsewhere.[32]

[*The next paragraph is 4.245*]

32. See Glass, *Multimodal Transport and Freight Forwarding* (Informa 2004), Chap. 3; De Wit, *Multimodal Transport, Carrier Liability and Documentation* (LLP Ltd, 1995), pp. 11 and 12 and *passim*.

XI. CHARGES, LIENS AND RIGHTS OF DISPOSAL

4.245 Normally, but not invariably, the consignee is the owner of the goods while they are in transit and hence a party to the contract with the carrier, made by the trader as his agent. There are also many cases in which the trader acts for his own account as principal and is thus himself a party to the contract. The question of who is liable for freight charges must be determined in this light. The owner of the goods is obligated to pay the freight charges if they remain unpaid. It follows, therefore, that at common law the carrier has the right to claim freight from the consignee. However, the consignee is not necessarily the only party so liable. The consignor, though frequently not a party to the contract, acting merely as the consignee's agent, may impliedly promise the carrier to cover its charges if the consignee refuses to pay or if for some reason the carrier chooses to demand charges from him. In *Great Western Ry.* v. *Bagge*[1] the consignment note provided that the consignee would pay the charges. However, the court held that there was a "resulting contract" and implied an undertaking by the consignor to pay the freight.[2] A carrier has, at common law, no right to sue for freight before it has performed its services and transit has come to an end. The standard clauses in use do not, in general, require prepayment of charges as a condition precedent to carriage in every case, though most reserve the right to impose such a condition. In practice prepayment may be required, even though transit may actually commence before that payment has been received as cleared funds. The standard conditions set out below give the carrier alternative sources from which to seek payment.

4.246 It is usual for the standard terms of carriage by inland water to contain a provision as to charges that reflects the common law position:

> The Carrier's charges for carriage shall be payable by the Trader without prejudice to the Carrier's rights against the Consignee or any other person. Provided that when the Carrier does not require prepayment of the carriage charges and the merchandise is consigned carriage forward, the Trader shall not be required to pay such charges unless the Consignee fails to pay after reasonable demands have been made by the Carrier for payment thereof.

4.247 So, except in those cases where the carrier has insisted on prepayment of the charges, the trader expressly undertakes to pay the carrier's charges for carriage (though not for any other services performed). It is also provided in the above clause that this liability on the part of the trader is not to prejudice the carrier's rights against the consignee or any other person. The carrier may, by accepting merchandise "carriage forward", intimate that it does not in the first instance intend to make the trader liable. In that event the carrier cannot demand freight from the trader unless it has first made a reasonable attempt to get the money from the consignee and this attempt has failed.

1. (1885) 15 Q.B.D. 625.

2. Cf. *World Transport Co.* v. *Tealing & Co.* [1936] 2 All E.R. 573 where, in a contract for the carriage of fruit from Spain to England under which the consignee accepted the goods, paid the purchase price to the consignor but refused to pay the carrier, the court held acceptance of the consignor's goods from the carrier for onward sale without notice to the contrary was evidence of an implied contract with the carrier to pay its charges; see also Clarke [1991] L.M.C.L.Q. 5.

At common law the carrier must be ready and willing to deliver the goods before being entitled to payment,[3] in the absence of agreement to the contrary between the parties, whether implied by custom, trade usage or express term. Where freight is earned in one way or another but the amount of freight has not been agreed by the parties the carrier may be able to secure a reasonable sum by way of freight.[4] The standard conditions of most carriers by inland water do not provide that freight is earned on shipment or acceptance of the goods for carriage and is payable whether the goods are lost or damaged or not (invariable provisions in bills of lading and air waybills). When there is no reference in the contract to the stage at which freight is earned but freight is to be payable in advance, it will be a matter of construction as to whether the freight is also earned at that time or whether the payment is an advance by the trader to be considered as a loan to be reimbursed if transit is not completed.[5] There is a distinction between nonfeasance and misfeasance. The former disentitles the carrier at common law from claiming freight but the latter does not. In the absence of express provisions the question is whether the delivery of damaged goods by the carrier is to be regarded as nonfeasance disentitling the carrier to claim for freight, or a mere misfeasance. The better view is that it is probably the latter.[6] It is important to remember that although freight may be earned on shipment or consignment it may become due for payment only on arrival. The freight charges will normally be payable to the contracting carrier or any agent duly authorised to receive payment. 4.248

The liability in contact to pay the freight charges is normally that of the entity with whom the carrier has contracted to carry the goods. This is normally the consignor[7] but not necessarily so. The consignor may consign the goods as the disclosed agent of the consignee or some other party, in which case the contract of carriage will be with the consignee or that other party.[8] However, even if the consignor acts as agent he may incur a liability if he contracts as undisclosed principal or, more generally, under a collateral contract. Furthermore, even where the primary liability to pay the freight charges rests with the consignor, the consignee may also be liable to pay the freight under an implied contract.[9] At common law, there is no right of abatement in the case of a claim for freight[10] nor is there a right of set-off, but merely a right of counterclaim not precluding the counterclaimant's immediate obligation to pay the freight charges.[11] It is not permissible for the court to avoid this rule by granting judgment for freight subject to a stay pursuant to the Civil Procedure Rules. For the 4.249

3. *Barnes* v. *Marshall* (1852) 18 Q.B. 785.

4. *Harris* v. *Parkwood* (1810) 3 Taunt. 264; Supply of Goods and Services Act 1982, s. 15.

5. See *Allison* v. *Bristol Marine Insurance Co.* (1876) 1 App. Cas. 209.

6. See the clear exposition of the law by Donaldson J. in *Montedison SpA* v. *Icroma SpA* [1980] 1 W.L.R. 48 at p. 50.

7. *Domett* v. *Beckford*, 5 B. & Ad. 521.

8. *Fragano* v. *Long* 4 B. & C. 219; *Dickenson* v. *Lano*, 2 F. & F. 188.

9. See *Brandt* v. *Liverpool, Brazil & River Plate Navigation Co.* [1924] 1 K.B. 575.

10. See *Hanak* v. *Green* [1958] 2 All E.R. 141, *per* Morris L.J. at pp. 145–146, 149–150; cf. *Gilbert-Ash (Northern) Ltd.* v. *Modern Engineering (Bristol) Ltd.* [1974] A.C. 689.

11. *Aries Tanker Corporation* v. *Total Transport Ltd.* [1977] 1 W.L.R. 185; *R.H. & D. International Ltd.* v. *I.A.S. Animal Air Services Ltd.* [1984] 1 W.L.R. 573; *United Carriers Ltd.* v. *Heritage Food Group (UK) Ltd.* [1995] 2 Lloyd's Rep. 269; *Colonial Bank* v. *European Grain and Shipping Ltd (The Dominique)* [1989] 1 Lloyd's Rep. 431.

court to act in this manner under its discretion would involve it in using the rules of procedure to bring about a result contrary to the rights of the parties under the substantive law.[12] The rule against abatement and set-off applies equally to a claim brought by the legal assignee of the carrier as the defendant cannot be in any better position by reason of an assignment of freight than he would otherwise be.[13] It is always possible for the parties to exclude the rule against abatement and set-off in the case of freight by an express provision in the contract of carriage.[14]

4.250 It is prudent for the conditions of carriage to contain express provisions for a carrier's lien, rather than relying purely on the common law. At common law the carrier is generally thought to have a lien over the consigned goods in respect of freight, though the authorities are inconclusive. In any event, common law grants, at most, a "passive" lien in that it confers no powers of sale on the carrier.[15] All it arguably permits the carrier to do is to hold a consignment of goods solely for charges relating to that consignment and for no other goods or services.[16] It is only by agreement or trade custom (the proof of which calls for strong evidence) that a carrier can, under the common law, acquire an active lien to sell the goods after a reasonable time and to hold them against freight due for other goods carried. However, neither any common law lien nor an express contractual lien will be good against the true owner of the merchandise if that owner is not a party to the contract of carriage.

4.251 Merchandise delivered to the Carrier will be received and held by it subject (a) to a lien for moneys due to it for the carriage of and other proper charges or expenses upon or in connection with such merchandise and (b) to a general lien for any moneys or charges due to it from the owners of such merchandise for any services rendered or accommodation provided in relation to the carriage or custody of merchandise, and in any case any lien is not satisfied within a reasonable time from the date upon which the Carrier first gave notice of the exercise of its lien to the owners of the merchandise, the merchandise may be sold and the proceeds of sale applied in or towards the satisfaction of every such lien and all proper charges and expenses in relation thereto, and the Carrier shall account to the owners of the merchandise for any surplus.

The general lien conferred by this Condition shall not prejudice an unpaid vendor's right of stoppage *in transitu*.

4.252 The lien does not come into existence until the goods have been carried to the place of destination. Transit must be over under the clause discussed earlier[17] before the carrier may exercise its lien. It is not justified in detaining the goods at the beginning of the transit and refusing to part with them until the general amount is satisfied.[18] Further, a carrier cannot investigate the consignee's title and therefore the word "owner" in the above lien clause must be interpreted as referring not to the

12. See *The Dominique* (above), *per* Lord Brandon at p. 442, citing *Stumore* v. *Campbell & Co.* [1892] 1 Q.B. 314.

13. *Ibid.*

14. See *Lakeport Navigation Co.* v. *Anonima Petroli Italiana (The Olympic Brilliance)* [1982] 2 Lloyd's Rep. 205.

15. See Palmer, *Bailment* (2nd ed., Sweet & Maxwell, 1991), p. 1014, note 55; cf. lien rights of a common carrier: *Skinner* v. *Upshaw* (1702) 2 Ld. Raym. 752. This right is not available to a private carrier: *Electric Supply Stores* v. *Gaywood* (1909) 100 L.T. 855 and a carrier by inland water transport is not a common carrier.

16. *Prenty* v. *Midland & Great Western Ry.* (1866) 14 W.R. 314.

17. Para. 4.221, above.

18. *Wiltshire Iron Co.* v. *Great Western Ry.* (1871) L.R. 6 Q.B. 776.

persons who in law are the owners at the time but to those who are entitled to demand delivery of the goods from the carrier, whether they are owners or not.[19] As has already been observed, the carrier has no right to sell the merchandise under the common law lien. However, it does have the same common law right to sell perishable goods, and the same duty of care with regard to them, as the carrier by sea, i.e. it can sell if there is a "real business necessity" to do so and if it is "practically impossible to get the owner's instructions in time to do what shall be done".[20] Although the authorities on this point are all railway cases, there is little doubt that they have equal application to carriage by inland water.[21]

The provisions to be found in the standard form terms of business of carriers by inland water are somewhat ambiguous in that it is unclear whether "all proper charges and expenses in relation thereto" include charges and expenses incurred in exercising the lien or merely those arising on the contract of carriage itself and draftsmen would, in future editions of their terms, be well advised to clarify this ambiguity. Certainly at common law the carrier, in exercise of its lien, is entitled to recover expenses incurred in preserving the goods (e.g. special refrigeration of "perishables" if they are not properly and legally sold) but it has no right to charge for warehousing while it detains them in exercise of its lien because such detention is not for the owner's benefit but for the carrier's own interest and benefit.[22] The carrier is bound to take proper care of the goods under its general lien and, unless they are perishable, should keep them for a reasonable time at a place reasonably convenient for the trader or the consignee, as the case may be, to obtain possession of them if it is prepared to pay the debts for which the lien is exercised. There is nothing to prevent the carrier from exercising its lien and simultaneously suing for the money due. If it gets judgment for the amount due it must hand over the goods when that judgment is satisfied but there is no obligation to do so earlier than this. 4.253

The carrier's duty is to deliver at the place to which the goods are consigned but, if the owner changes the carrier's instructions while the goods are in transit, the carrier must comply with this order, provided that it has satisfied itself that the person designating a new place of delivery is, in fact, the owner of the goods at the moment when the new delivery instruction is given.[23] There is, however, one case in which a person other than the owner can change the original place of destination of the goods before they reach that destination or are handed to the consignee and that is where an unpaid seller exercises its right of stoppage *in transitu* under the Sale of Goods Act 1979, ss. 44–46. This is a right given to an unpaid seller who has already transferred the property in the goods to the buyer by handing them over to the carrier. If the buyer becomes insolvent, the unpaid seller need not sit still while the goods are carried onward to their destination to be disposed of as part of the 4.254

19. *US Steel Products* v. *Great Western Ry.* [1916] A.C. 189.

20. *Per* Scrutton L.J. in *Sims & Co.* v. *Midland Ry. Co.* [1913] 1 K.B. 103 at p. 112; see also *Springer* v. *Great Western Ry. Co.* [1921] 1 K.B. 257.

21. Cf. the condition dealing with perishable merchandise other than under the general lien, para. 4.253, below.

22. See e.g. *Great Northern Ry.* v. *Swaffield* (1874) L.R. 9 Ex. 132; *Soames* v. *British Empire Shipping Co.* (1860) 8 H.L. Cas. 338.

23. *Scothorn* v. *South Staffordshire Ry.* (1853) 8 Ex. 341.

liquidation (when the seller will probably, at most, receive only a dividend). Instead the seller can stop the goods while still in transit and request that the carrier redeliver them back to the seller.[24]

4.255 In so far as a lien at common law is particular, it is stronger than the seller's right of stoppage *in transitu* but in so far as it is general, as under this clause, it is postponed to the right of the seller. This is of importance, because the cases in which the carrier exercises its lien are usually those in which the consignee buyer of goods is unable to meet its debts. A conflict of interest may thus arise between a consignor seller and the carrier, each of them wishing to get hold of the goods in order to satisfy claims against the consignee though, of course, if the carrier uses a clause in its contract in terms similar to those given above, it can seek payment of its charges directly from the trader/consignor. However, since the contract provides here that the seller's right of stoppage *in transitu* shall not be prejudiced by the carrier's general lien, it would appear that the carrier must, for the purposes of the rights under the Sale of Goods Act 1979, be regarded as having its general lien rights postponed once the right of stoppage has been exercised. Under a "particular" common law lien, on the other hand, the carrier need not actually redeliver the goods stopped in transit to the consignor before it has paid all the charges incurred in connection with those particular goods. Once the charges have been paid, however, the goods can no longer be retained, though money may be owing to the carrier by the consignee for other goods carried or stored.

4.256 A carrier may, at common law, sell perishable goods and pay over the proceeds of sale to the owner after deducting its own charges and expenses under the "agency of necessity" doctrine. The carrier must not, however, exercise this power unless there is a real business necessity to do so.[25] Accordingly almost all standard conditions of carriage by inland water contain, of necessity, a much enlarged right to sell or dispose of perishable merchandise.[26]

> Where perishable merchandise:
> (a) is refused by the consignee; or
> (b) is consigned to wharf or depot and is not taken away within a reasonable time after arrival; or
> (c) is not delivered in consequence of riots, civil commotions, strikes, lockouts, stoppage or restraint of labour from whatever cause, whether partial or general; or
> (d) is not delivered in consequence of damage or obstruction caused by flood, landslip, weather or otherwise where no reasonable alternative route is available,
>
> the merchandise may be sold by the Carrier and payment or tender of the proceeds of any such sale after deduction of all proper charges due on the merchandise and expenses in relation to the sale thereof shall (without prejudice to any claim or right which the sender or consignee may have against the Carrier otherwise arising under these Conditions) discharge the Carrier from all liability in respect of such merchandise or the carriage or delivery thereof.
>
> Provided that:

24. For a detailed analysis of the rules for stoppage *in transitu* see *Benjamin's Sale of Goods* (6th ed., 2002), Chap. 15, paras. 061–091.

25. *Sims & Co.* v. *Midland Ry. Co.* [1913] 1 K.B. 103; *Springer* v. *Great Western Ry. Co.* [1921] 1 K.B. 257; *Sachs* v. *Micklos* [1948] 2 K.B. 23. It must also be impossible to secure the owner's instructions: *China Pacific* v. *Food Corp. of India* [1982] A.C. 939.

26. For a discussion of the statutory right of sale under the Torts (Interference with Goods) Act 1977 see para. 4.259, below.

(i) The Carrier shall do what is reasonable to obtain the value of the merchandise.
(ii) Where the merchandise is not carried through to the destination to which it was consigned by the Trader, the charges payable to the Carrier shall be those in operation for the journey actually completed, but shall not exceed the charges for the full transit.
(iii) Where electronic (email) or telephonic communication is reasonable and practicable the power of sale shall not be exercised unless notice has been given to the consignee in cases under (b), (c) and (d) and to the Trader in cases under (a), and the consignee or Trader has failed to give immediate instructions for disposal by email, telephone, or otherwise to the Carrier at the wharf or depot from which the notice was sent.

The right created by this clause applies to perishable merchandise which is clearly in danger of deterioration if retained by the carrier and is exercisable: (a) if the consignee has refused to take delivery; or (b) if the merchandise is consigned to a wharf or depot and is not collected within a reasonable time; or (c) if the merchandise cannot be delivered because of riots, civil commotion or labour disputes[27] or (d) if the merchandise cannot be delivered because access routes are unusable because of flooding, landslip or other adverse weather conditions.[28] At common law, in order to exercise the right to sell, the carrier must, if it knows the name and address of the owner, or of the consignor, do what is reasonable in the circumstances to give notice that the goods will be sold within the time specified in the notice. This time must be reasonable. The only exception arises where, within the time limit, the merchandise is collected or instructions are given for its disposal. It is only when the address of neither the owner nor the consignor is known that the goods may be disposed of without notice. *4.257*

Under the clause quoted above the obligation on the carrier to give notice is more limited than under the common law. It only applies where e-mail or telephone communication is reasonable and practicable and there does not seem to be any obligation on the carrier to allow a reasonable time within which the goods will be sold. The party upon whom notice is served can only halt the sale by giving immediate instructions, on receiving the notice, as to what the carrier is to do with the goods. *4.258*

Having done "what is reasonable to obtain the value of the merchandise", the carrier must pay or tender the proceeds of the sale to the consignee (if known) or if not presumably to the trader (though most standard clauses are curiously silent as to whom, and in what order, payment or tender must be made) after having deducted all proper charges and expenses incurred in connection with the merchandise. This includes all unpaid charges and expenses relating to its carriage and warehousing but, if it was not carried through to its destination, the "deductibles" *4.259*

27. The meaning of these words has been discussed earlier in this Part: see paras. 4.95–4.96, above. This is not *force majeure per se* but is limited to the specific causes of riot or civil commotion. The rest of the sub-clause is confined to various kinds of labour disputes causing an impediment to delivery. This needs to be expressly stated since labour disputes would not necessarily be regarded as *force majeure*: *B. & S. Contracts and Designs* v. *Victor Green Publications* [1984] I.C.R. 128.

28. The clause also lists certain natural catastrophes, such as floods and landslips, which impede delivery. Again this is not a comprehensive *force majeure* clause. However, the words "or otherwise" may be taken to broaden the "natural catastrophe" list to include other disasters not specifically covered, since the *ejusdem generis* rule does not apply to the construction of *force majeure* clauses: *Chandris* v. *Isbrandtsen-Moller & Co. Inc.* [1951] 1 K.B. 240; *P.J. Vander Zijden Wildhandel N.V.* v. *Tucker & Cross Ltd.* [1975] 2 Lloyd's Rep. 240; *Navrom* v. *Callistis Ship Management S.A.* [1988] 2 Lloyd's Rep. 416.

cover only those charges incurred for the journey actually completed provided they do not exceed those which would have been payable for the full transit.

4.260 The clause contains the phrase "without prejudice to any claim or rights which the sender or consignee may have against the Carrier otherwise arising under these Conditions". The meaning of this element of the clause is somewhat obscure. It may mean that the carrier is free from liabilities for the act of selling the merchandise which, but for the condition, would have been an act of conversion, i.e. the carrier will not be liable for the difference between the proceeds of sale of the merchandise and its market value. Alternatively, it may mean that the carrier is free from liability for the event which gave rise to the need to sell the merchandise in the first place, even if this event was an act committed by the carrier's own employees, such as a refusal by the workforce to handle the goods in circumstances which, taken by themselves, would have rendered the carrier liable.

4.261 In *W. Young & Son (Wholesale Fish Merchants) Ltd.* v. *British Transport Commission*[29] McNair J. adopted the second of these two interpretations. He took the view that the carrier could only be made liable "where the claim of right arose before the happening of the events which gave rise to the right of sale" as, for example, "if goods in transit are damaged or pilfered in such circumstances as to impose liability . . . before the events occurred which made delivery impossible".[30] The result of this construction is that the right to sell can be exercised even if the carrier's inability to deliver was caused by its own employees and even if the goods were held up by acts which amounted to wilful misconduct on the part of the employees. Although McNair J. appeared far from confident that his construction of the clause was correct, some confirmation of his interpretation, or at least confirmation that such is what the draftsman intended, can be gleaned from the words providing that the carrier is discharged from all liability not only in respect of delivery (i.e. non-delivery) of the merchandise, but also of its "carriage"—words which would be meaningless if the correct construction placed upon the words was the former one advanced earlier in this paragraph rather than the latter settled upon McNair J. as the correct one.

4.262 Where merchandise (other than perishable merchandise):

(a) is held "to wait order" or "To be kept until called for" and such order is not given, or such merchandise is not removed within a reasonable time; or
(b) is of a description for which the Carrier has not or does not provide accommodation at the place of destination; or
(c) is unclaimed and the names and addresses of the Trader and consignee are not known and cannot be ascertained; or
(d) is refused by the consignee, or not delivered because the consignee is not known, and in either case the Trader fails to take delivery, or to give instructions for disposal;

the Carrier may sell, either separately or by inclusion in a sale of unclaimed goods, and payment or tender of the proceeds of such sale after deduction of all proper charges due on the merchandise and expenses in relation to the sale thereof shall (without prejudice to any claim or right which the Trader or consignee may have against the Carrier otherwise arising under these Conditions) discharge the Carrier from all liability in respect of such merchandise or the carriage or delivery thereof.

Provided that:

29. [1955] Q.B. 177.
30. *Ibid.* at p. 193.

(i) The Carrier shall do what is reasonable to obtain the value of the merchandise.
(ii) Where the merchandise is not carried through to the destination to which it was consigned by the Trader, the charges payable to the Carrier shall be those in operation for the journey actually completed, but shall not exceed the charges for the full transit.
(iii) The power of sale shall not be exercised (a) where the name and address of the Trader of the consignee is known unless the Carrier shall have sent notice in writing by post or otherwise to the Trader or consignee that the merchandise will be sold if not taken away within 14 days or (b) where the names and addresses of the Trader and consignee are not known unless the Carrier shall have retained the merchandise in its possession for not less than three months.

This clause empowers the carrier to sell merchandise (other than perishable goods) where it is held "to wait order" or "to be kept until called for" and such order is not given or the merchandise is not removed within a reasonable time. The power of sale further arises where the merchandise is of a description in respect of which the carrier has no accommodation at the consignment destination or where it is unclaimed and the names *and* the addresses (this might well be construed disjunctively to the extent that, if there is a name only, the carrier might be required to take reasonable steps to ascertain the address) of both consignee and trader are unknown. Finally, the power of sale is also available to the carrier where the goods are refused by the consignee or not delivered because the consignee is unknown and the trader fails to take delivery or to give instructions for disposal. The merchandise may, however, only be sold 14 days after the carrier has given notice of its intention to sell them. This notice must be given to the consignor or to the consignee. If the names and addresses of both are unknown, then no sale may take place until three months have elapsed from the end of transit. The carrier may deduct all proper charges in respect of the carriage and warehousing of the goods and other expenses incurred in relation to the goods. In addition to this contractual right to sell, the carrier may also have a statutory right to sell the merchandise where "the bailor is in breach of his obligation to take delivery of the goods" and in other circumstances defined by the Torts (Interference with Goods) Act 1977. The rights of sale granted by the Act only come into effect once the transit has ceased.[31] Notice must be given to the owner where possible[32] and the rights granted by the Act do not prevail over the rights of sale given by the contractual terms.[33] 4.263

31. S. 12.
32. Sched. 1, pt. 1, para. 1.
33. S. 12(8).

INDEX

All references are to paragraph numbers